CYPRUS
THE ROUGH GUIDE

THE ROUGH GUIDES

OTHER AVAILABLE ROUGH GUIDES
AMSTERDAM • BARCELONA • BERLIN • BRAZIL
BRITTANY & NORMANDY • BULGARIA • CALIFORNIA & WEST COAST USA
CANADA • CRETE • CZECH & SLOVAK REPUBLICS • EGYPT • EUROPE
FLORIDA • FRANCE • GERMANY • GREECE • GUATEMALA & BELIZE
HOLLAND, BELGIUM & LUXEMBOURG • HONG KONG • HUNGARY • IRELAND
ISRAEL • ITALY • KENYA • MEDITERRANEAN WILDLIFE • MEXICO • MOROCCO
NEPAL • NEW YORK • NOTHING VENTURED • PARIS • PERU • POLAND
PORTUGAL • PRAGUE • PROVENCE • PYRENEES • SAN FRANCISCO
SCANDINAVIA • SICILY • SPAIN • THAILAND • TUNISIA • TURKEY
TUSCANY & UMBRIA • USA • VENICE • WEST AFRICA • WOMEN TRAVEL
ZIMBABWE & BOTSWANA

FORTHCOMING
AUSTRALIA • ST PETERSBURG

Rough Guide Cyprus Credits

Text Editor:	Jack Holland
Series Editor:	Mark Ellingham
Editorial:	Martin Dunford, John Fisher, Jonathan Buckley, Greg Ward, Richard Trillo, Jules Brown
Production:	Susanne Hillen, Gail Jammy, Andy Hilliard, Vivien Antwi, Melissa Flack
Financial:	Celia Crowley
Proofreading:	Ellen Sarewitz

ACKNOWLEDGMENTS

At Rough Guides, editor **Jack Holland** generously put me up in addition to putting up with me, and matched my neurotic perfectionism with his own. For particular help in the South, thanks are due to Dimitris Theofylaktos and Marla for a good night out; Chrystofis Kykkas for illuminating conversations; Andrew and Monica at *The Hellenic Bookservice* for patiently entertaining all bibliographic queries; and the management at *Zeno's* for more of the same. In the North, Küfi Birinci provided travel arrangements and private tours after dark, as well as a humane and incisive analysis of the current situation; Brigitte and Tony in Karaman freely shared their time and knowledge about the area; and Adrian Higgs offered a lucid and hard-to-come-by summary of recent elections. I am also indebted to certain residents of the Koruçam and Karpaza peninsulas, who told me of their lives since 1974 and therefore must remain anonymous.

Published April 1993 by Rough Guides Ltd, 1 Mercer Street, London WC2H 9QJ.
Distributed by Penguin Books, 27 Wrights Lane, London W8 5TZ.

Typeset in Linotron Univers and Century Old Style to an original design by Andrew Oliver.
Printed in the UK by Cox & Wyman Ltd, Reading, Berks.
Maps by Judit Ladik.

Illustrations on p.xiii and p.257 by Henry Iles.

352pp. includes index

British Library Cataloguing in Publication Data
A catalogue record for this book is available from the British Library.

ISBN 1-85828-032-X

CYPRUS
THE ROUGH GUIDE

researched and written by

MARC DUBIN

THE ROUGH GUIDES

CONTENTS

Introduction viii

| PART ONE | BASICS | 1 |

Getting There from the UK 1
Getting There from North America and
  Australasia 7
Red Tape and Visas 9
Health and Insurance 9
Information and Maps 11
Costs 13
Money and Banks 14
Getting Around 15
Accommodation 19

Eating and Drinking 21
Communications: Post and Phones 27
The Media 29
Opening Hours, Holidays and Festivals 30
Sites, Churches, Museums, Mosques 32
Police, Trouble and Harassment 34
Sports and Outdoor Activities 35
Shopping 35
Directory 38

| PART TWO | THE SOUTH | 39 |

■ 1   Larnaca and Around 44
■ 2   Limassol and Around 66
■ 3   Páfos and the West 89
■ 4   The High Troödhos 125
■ 5   South Nicosia and Around 153

| PART THREE | THE NORTH | 179 |

■ 6   North Nicosia and Around 184
■ 7   Kyrenia and the North Coast 203
■ 8   Famagusta and the Kárpas Peninsula 228

| PART FOUR | CONTEXTS | 257 |

The Historical Framework 259
Wildlife 284
Books 303

Language 306
Glossary 314

Index 317

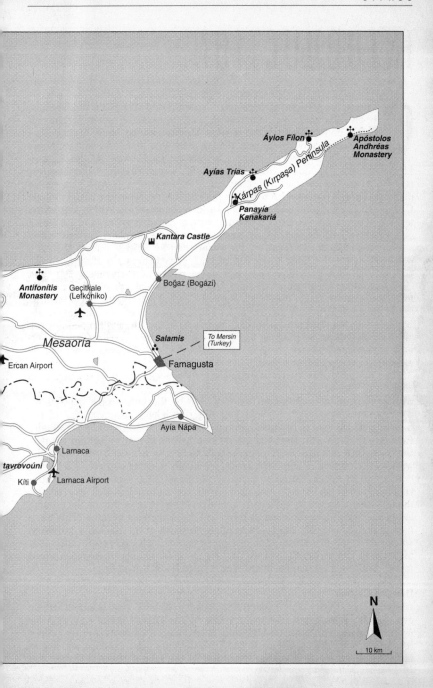

Áyios Fílon

Apóstolos
Andhréas
Monastery

Ayías Trías

Kárpas (Kırpaşa) Peninsula

Panayía
Kanakariá

Kantara Castle

*Antifonítis
Monastery*

Geçitkale
(Lefkóniko)

Boğaz (Bogázi)

Mesaoría

Salamis

To Mersin
(Turkey)

Ercan Airport

Famagusta

Ayía Nápa

Larnaca

tavrovoúni

Kíti

Larnaca Airport

N

10 km

INTRODUCTION

Cyprus, the Mediterraneans's third largest island after Sicily and Sardinia, is also the sole one, nominally at least, to exercise full sovereignty. It defers only to Malta as the **newest Mediterranean state**, having come into existence on 16 August, 1960. For the first time, following centuries of domination by whatever empire or nation held sway in the eastern Mediterranean – including, from 1878 to 1960, **Great Britain** – the islanders seemed to control their own destiny. Such empowerment proved illusory: no distinctly Cypriot **national identity** was permitted to evolve by the island's ethnic Orthodox Christian Greek and Muslim Turkish communities. Within four years, tension between the two groups rent the society asunder, followed in 1974 by a political and ethnic division of the island imposed by the mainland Turkish army.

However, **calm** now reigns on the island, and for British visitors there's a persistent sense of déjà vu to Cyprus, perhaps more than in any other ex-Crown Colony. Wall's ice-cream-type vans jingle along; pillar boxes still display "GR" and "ER" monograms near zebra crossings; grandiose colonial public buildings jostle for space with vernacular mud-brick and Neoclassical houses; and of course driving is on the left. Before the recent founding of universities South and North, higher education was pursued abroad, preferably in the UK, and **English** – virtually a second official language in the South – is widely spoken. Despite the bitterness of the independence struggle against the UK, all is forgiven (if not exactly forgotten) a generation or so later.

Even the most ardent Cyprus enthusiast will concede that it can't compete in allure with more exotic, airline-poster destinations, yet the place grows on you with **prolonged acquaintance** (as evidenced by the huge ex-pat population). There's certainly enough to hold your interest inland once you tire of the **beaches**, which tend to be small, scattered coves in the South, or longer, dunier expanses in the North. Horizons are defined by one of **two mountain ranges**: the convoluted massif of the Troödhos, with numerous spurs and valleys, and the wall-like escarpment of the Kyrenia hills, seemingly sculpted of papier-mâché.

In terms of **special-interest** visits, archaeology buffs, wine-drinkers, flower-sniffers, bird-watchers and mountain-bikers are particularly well catered for, though state-of-the-art nightlife and cultural diversions can be thin on the ground, in keeping with the predominantly forty- and fifty-something clientele. This has a natural consequence in the overwhelming presence of the **package industry**, supported by law in the South and placing several of the bigger resorts effectively off-limits to independent travellers. But for an undemanding, reasonably priced **family holiday** most months of the year, Cyprus is still a good bet.

Divided Cyprus

Long-dormant rivalry and resentment between Cyprus' two principal ethnic groups was re-awakened late in the 1950s by the Greek-Cypriot campaign for *énosis* or **union with Greece.** Following independence, disputes over the proper respective civic roles of the Greek- and Turkish-Cypriot communities, and lingering advocacy of *énosis*, or *taksim* (**partition of the island** between Greece and

Turkey) by extremists in each camp, provoked widespread, ongoing communal violence.

Abetted by interested outsiders, these incidents – and a CIA-backed coup against the elected government – culminated in the 1974 mainland-Turkish military operation which effectively **partitioned** the island, with both Greek and Turkish Cypriots on the "wrong" side of the cease-fire line fleeing their homes. Nicosia, the capital, approximately at the centre of Cyprus, was divided like Berlin, and remains so at present; much of Famagusta, formerly home to about eight percent of the island's population, lies abandoned. If this all sounds familiar in the wake of events in former Yugoslavia and the CIS, there was, in the 1960s and 1970s, a relative novelty to the crises that repeatedly convulsed Cyprus.

In the **aftermath** of 1974, the two zones of Cyprus nurse grievances against each other that are difficult for many outsiders to fathom, and North and South are **mutually isolated**, having developed over time into parallel societies, destined, perhaps, never to converge again. The island's division is comparable to that of Germany, though as Cyprus is a far more intimate place the scale of human tragedy has been more visible. **Re-unification**, if and when it comes, is bound to be hedged about with conditions, and fraught with pitfalls similar to the German experience: while South and North are both avowedly capitalist, the linguistic and religious gulf separating the two communities, compounded by nearly three decades of enforced segregation, may prove impossible to bridge.

Where to go

Because of the mutual hostility of South and North, you'll have to **choose** which side of Cyprus to visit on any given trip – you are not allowed to move from one side of the island to the other. If you go to the South after having been to the North, keep evidence of such a journey out of your passport (see "Visas and Red Tape" in *Basics* for a full explanation).

Yet either portion of the island has plenty to keep you busy for the typical **one-to-three-week** duration of package deals. When the **South's** busiest beaches east of **Larnaca** pall, there's the popular hill village of **Páno Léfkara**, unique sacred art at Byzantine **Angelóktisti church** and nearby Lusignan **"Chapelle Royale"** or the atmospheric Muslim shrine of **Hala Sultan** to the west. Beyond functional **Limassol**, the Crusader tower of **Kolossi** guards vineyards as it always has, while extensive ancient **Kourion** stands nearby atop seaside cliffs.

Of the three main south-coast resorts, **Páfos** has most recently awoken to tourism, but with its spectacular Roman mosaics and early Christian relics has perhaps the most to offer. The hinterland of Páfos district (a county, in Cyprus) belies its initial bleak appearance to reveal fertile valleys furrowing ridges sprinkled with brown-stone villages and, to either side of the **Akámas Peninsula**, the last unspoiled stretches of coast in the South. If you don't require lively nightlife, then **Pólis** or **Látchi** make good, comfortable overnight bases in this area, serving too as springboards into the foothills of the Troödhos mountains.

Inland from Páfos or Limassol, the **mountains** themselves beckon, covered in well-groomed forest, lovingly resuscitated from a nadir last century. **Plátres**, the original Cypriot "hill station", makes a logical base on the south side of the range; to the north, more authentic village character asserts itself at **Pedhoulás** or **Kakopetriá**. Scattered across several valleys, a dozen or so magnificently **frescoed, late-Byzantine chapels** provide an additional focus to itineraries here if the scenery and walking opportunities aren't enough.

Southern **Nicosia** – the Greek-Cypriot portion of the divided capital – while not immediately appealing, can boast an idiosyncratic old town in the throes of revitalisation, and, in the Cyprus museum, one of the finest archaeological collections in the Middle East. North Nicosia, on the other side of the nearly impervious 1974 cease-fire line, is graced with most of the island's Ottoman monuments – and also introduces the Frenchified ecclesiastical architecture bequeathed by the Lusignan dynasty.

For the majority of tourists in the **North**, however, **Kyrenia** is very much the main event, its old harbour the most sheltered and charming on Cyprus. Some resort development straggles to either side of town, but this coast is still light-years behind the South in that respect. The shaggy hills looming above support three medieval **castles** – **Saint Hilarion, Buffavento** and **Kantara** – whose views and architecture rarely disappoint. Add villages in picturesque settings below the ridgeline, and it's little wonder that outsiders have been coming here longer than anywhere else on the island.

The **beaches** north of Famagusta are Kyrenia's only serious rival for tourist custom, and hard to resist in tandem with **Salamis**, the largest ancient site on Cyprus. **Famagusta** itself is remarkable, another Lusignan church-fantasy wrapped in some of the most imposing Venetian walls in the world – though there's little else to see or do, the town having lain devastated since the Ottoman conquest. North of the beach strip, the **Kırpaşa (Kárpas) Peninsula** points finger-like towards Syria, its fine beaches and generous complement of early churches – most notably at **Áyios Fílon** and **Ayía Triás** – little-frequented.

When to go

Because of a situation as much **Middle Eastern** as Mediterranean, Cyprus repays a visit in almost any month; the overall mildness of the **climate** allows citrus to grow at altitudes of 450 metres, grape-vines to flourish up to 1000 metres and frost-tender cedars to sprout at 1500-metre elevations in the Troödhos. Such plant-zone limits would be unthinkable even on Crete, despite an identical latitude of 34 degrees north.

If you're coming for the **flora and birdlife** – as more and more people do – then **winter and spring**, beginning early December and late February respectively, are for you. Rain falls in sporadic bursts throughout this period and into March, leaving the rare spectacle of a green, prairie-like Mesaoría, the central plain which most tourists only know as a parched, stubbly dustbowl. You'll also **cut costs** significantly by showing up in the off-season.

As the months progress and the mercury climbs, you can either brave the multitudes at the seashore – considerable in the South – or follow the wildflowers inland and up the slopes of the Troödhos mountains, veritable havens of **coolness** and relative solitude. **Mid-summer** is a bit too hot for comfort in the coastal South, which rates **high season** as June or September; during July or August you're probably better off in the **North**, where the seaward, damper slope of the Kyrenia hills especially offers a refuge both from crowds and extreme temperatures.

Autumn is delightful, with the sea at its warmest, forays into the hills benefiting from **stable weather**, and the air (around Limassol or Páfos especially) heavy with the fumes of fermenting grapes. And if it's **resort life** you're after, the coastal strips don't completely wind down until after New Year.

AVERAGE TEMPERATURES AND RAINFALL						
	Jan	**March**	**May**	**July**	**Sept**	**Nov**
Nicosia						
Max °F	59	66	85	98	92	72
Min °F	42	44	58	70	65	51
Days of rain	14	8	3	0	1	6
Kyrenia						
Max °F	62	65	78	91	87	73
Min °F	48	49	60	72	69	58
Days of rain	13	7	2	0	1	7

[The Cypriot] is entering in thousands that trough – of how many generations? – between peasant honesty and urban refinement. "To be civilised," a Nicosia friend told me, "our people must first be vulgar. It is the bridge between simplicity and culture."

Colin Thubron

THE
BASICS

GETTING THERE FROM BRITAIN

The majority of visitors arrive in Cyprus, South or North, by air as part of an all inclusive package; from the UK there are frequent scheduled or chartered year-round flights from London, Manchester and Birmingham. The South is also easy to reach from most neighbouring countries except Turkey, from where you can only fly to the North.

Coming to the island-nation by boat, you can choose from among several embarkation points in Greece, Israel, Egypt and Italy (for the South) and Turkey (for the North).

BY PLANE TO THE SOUTH

Scheduled flights to either part of Cyprus are somewhat overpriced for the number of air-miles involved; except in winter you'll usually get better value from a charter, though see the warning under "Packages" in this section.

SCHEDULED FLIGHTS

Larnaca and **Páfos** on the coast are the southern Republic's two international airports. *Cyprus Airways*, the national carrier, offers summer service to Larnaca from **London Heathrow** (3 daily), **Birmingham** (2 weekly) and **Manchester** (4 or 5 weekly). Winter schedules shrink to daily from Heathrow, twice weekly from Manchester and once weekly from **Gatwick** and Birmingham. Frequencies to Páfos are somewhat less: 2 to 3 weekly from London Heathrow; 2

weekly from Gatwick; and 1 weekly each from Manchester and Birmingham. In winter departures decrease to just once weekly from London Heathrow and once from Gatwick. Sample winter **fares** from Heathrow to either Cypriot airport range from £205 to £272 for a 7–35-day APEX return, depending on whether or not you fly on holidays or at weekends. Summertime (1 July–31 Oct) APEX tickets with identical conditions will set you back £293–324, depending on the day of travel.

British Airways offers five weekly flights from **Heathrow to Larnaca** in winter, though except on weekends these tend to arrive in the small hours; fares are the same as *Cyprus Airways*, with whom the route is shared. Summer frequencies expand to complement *Cyprus Airways*, though for some reason high-season fares are marginally less (£273–293).

BUDGET FARES

Student/youth or **budget** fares to the South are limited, though among the specialist discount flight agencies, *STA Travel* is worth ringing. It offers deals on two Central European airlines, *Malev* and *TAROM*, not available directly through the carriers. These indirect flights stop in Budapest and Bucharest respectively, but both companies allow stopovers and both tickets are valid for one year from date of purchase. The *Malev* ticket, at £276, is available to anyone but no changes of travel date are allowed; the *TAROM* fare of £216 is for under-26s only but travel dates are flexible. Given that these prices are comparable to direct scheduled flights, they're options most worth considering if you'll be in Cyprus a long time or wish to visit Hungary or Romania as well.

CHARTER FLIGHTS

Charter companies such as *Eurocypria*, *Monarch*, *Caledonian*, *Air 2000* and *Excalibur* also provide air links from Britain, but owing to Cypriot law (see "Packages") seats are difficult to get on a flight-only basis. *STA* has a limited number of **seat-only charters** to Páfos, but these are available only on a one- or two-week basis. **High-street travel agents** also occasionally have seat-only deals.

FLIGHTS FROM NEIGHBOURING COUNTRIES

Larnaca can also be easily reached from most **neighbouring countries** by plane, with April–October flights on *Cyprus Airways* from Athens (3 to 4 daily), Cairo (3 weekly), Heraklion (1 weekly, 2 in summer), Rhodes (2 weekly, summer only) and Tel Aviv (4 weekly). *Olympic Airways*, and *Air Zimbabwe* on its way to Harare, also call in from Athens. Páfos is served only from Athens (1 weekly, 2 in summer). It's worth asking for student discounts if eligible; otherwise, you'll pay about £180 equivalent return from Athens, the longest haul in.

BY PLANE TO THE NORTH

Because of the IATA boycott of north Nicosia's "black" airport at **Ercan**, North Cyprus has **direct air links** only with Turkey, where all planes from northern Europe must first touch down. Despite this obstacle reasonably frequent scheduled flights start from several UK airports, and even a number of charter lines extend from Turkey into the North. With few exceptions they tend to arrive between 10pm and 2am.

SCHEDULED AND CHARTER FLIGHTS

Istanbul Airlines (İstanbul Hava Yolları) flies into Ercan twice a week from **London Heathrow**, once from **Stansted** and **Gatwick**, and alternate weeks from **Manchester** and **Glasgow** during summer; a charter subsidiary, *Pegasus*, often is substituted, especially for Gatwick and Manchester departures. In winter frequency drops to twice weekly from Heathrow, once from Gatwick. *Onur Air* offers three weekly flights, one apiece from **Stansted**, **Heathrow** and **Gatwick**. *Cyprus Turkish Airways*, a subsidiary of state-run *Turkish Airways*, offers one flight weekly from Heathrow to Ercan via İzmir, using Turkish Airways aircraft to get around the boycott. **Flight-only** arrangements, when available (often through *Onur Air*), tend to start at just under £200 return, roughly half that amount single, during winter, with substantial hikes in summer.

DISCOUNT OPERATORS

Among **discount flight agencies**, *Campus Travel* is able to provide seat-only deals on *Onur Air* at advantageous prices; *STA Travel* has an arrangement with *Cyprus Turkish Airlines*, though this tends to work out somewhat more expensive.

OTHER FLIGHTS FROM TURKEY

From Turkey itself, you can choose from a number of scheduled airlines. *Cyprus Turkish Airways (Kıbrıs Türk Hava Yolları* in Turkish) flies in from Adana (2 weekly), Ankara (5 weekly), İstanbul (daily), and İzmir (3 weekly). Private-sector airline *İstanbul Hava Yolları* offers two or three daily services from Istanbul, plus less frequent flights from İzmir and Antalya, for the lowish price of £25 return – if you don't have a car, a far better option than the ferry from southern Turkey (see next section).

PACKAGES

Cyprus South or North ranks as the most packaged destination in the Mediterranean after Malta, a status mandated by law in the **South**: only fifteen percent of charter seat capacity is allowed to be sold on a seat-only basis, and offending airlines are heavily fined. The message is clear – budget travellers need not apply – and has been reiterated by stiff hikes in package prices as from 1993. Expect to pay £400 to £500,

---

PACKAGE HOLIDAY OPERATORS

GENERAL OPERATORS TO THE SOUTH

Amathus Holidays 51 Tottenham Court Rd, London W1P 0HS (☎071/631 0483). Middle-of-the-road Greece and Cyprus specialist.

Cyprair Holidays 23 Hampstead Rd, London NW1 3JA (☎071/388 7515). Subsidiary of *Cyprus Airways*, concentrating on hotels and the fancier apartments.

Cypriana Holidays 31 Topsfield Parade, Crouch End, London N8 8PT (☎081/444 3333). Unusually wide selections of hotels, villas and restored houses across the island.

Cyprosun Holidays 163 Sutton Rd, Wylde Green, Birmingham B23 5TN (☎021/382 6611). Good for flight-only and fly-drive holidays, or flexible-duration packages.

Delta Holidays University Precinct, Oxford Rd, Manchester M13 9RN (☎061/274 4444). Cyprus

specialists with good balance of facilities across the South.

Libra Holidays 343 Ballards Lane, London N12 8LJ (☎081/446 8231). One of the few operators featuring the Troödhos Mountains.

Manos Holidays Yeoman House, 168–172 Old St, London EC1V 9BP (☎071/608 1161). Emphasis on three- and four-star hotels and villas in most major resorts.

Olympic Holidays 30 Cross St, London N1 2BG (☎071/359 3500). Another sizeable general tour operator, offering a range of self-catering villas in Ómodhos.

Sands Holidays Sands House, 436 Essex Rd, London N1 3QP (☎071/704 2244). Distinguished mainly by offerings of direct flights to Cyprus from most regional UK airports.

SPECIALISED OPERATORS TO THE SOUTH

Anthology Travel & Tours Stassándhrou 7, Suite 101, Nicosia, Cyprus (☎02/467763). Bird-watching, botany, cycling and hiking.

Exalt c/o David Pearlmann, PO Box 337, Páfos, Cyprus (☎06/143803). Specialises in jeep and walking safaris in remoter parts of Páfos district.

Ornitholidays (☎0243/821230). Bird-watching tour specialist.

Ramblers Box 43, Welwyn Garden City, Hertfordshire AL8 6PQ (☎0707/333276). Botany and hill-walking tours.

Sunvil Travel Sunvil House, 7/8 Upper Square, Old Isleworth, Middlesex TW7 7BJ. Quality villas and village houses throughout in Páfos district, as well as outdoor-activity packages in conjunction with *Exalt*..

GENERAL OPERATORS TO THE NORTH

Anatolian Sky Holidays Imex House, 52 Blucher St, Birmingham B1 1QU (☎021/633 4018). An operator with an emphasis on mid-range, self-catering facilities.

Celebrity Holidays 18 Frith St, London W1V 5TS (☎071/734 4386). The main emphasis is on packages in its wholly owned Celebrity complex of hotels and self-catering units to the west of Kyrenia.

Mosaic Holidays 45 South Audley St, Mayfair, London W1Y 5DG (☎071/355 3464), or in Manchester (☎061/236 2353). Specialises in the high end of the market, with stress on properties owned and managed by itself.

President Holidays 542 Kingsland Rd, London E8 4AH (☎071/249 4002). Represents virtually all package facilities in North Cyprus.

Regent Holidays Regent House, 31A High St, Shanklin, Isle of Wight PO37 6JW (☎0983/864212). Better than many for self-catering villas and flight-only deals.

Sunquest Holidays 9 Grand Parade, Green Lanes, London N4 1JX (☎081/800 8030). Turkey specialist, recently expanded into the North Cyprus market, focusing on mid-range self-catering villas.

T.K. Air Travel 46 Newington Green, London N16 9PX (☎071/359 9214). Relatively small programmes by the operators of Onur Air.

flight inclusive, for a two-week high-season package in a three-star hotel or detached villa, £350 for a two-star hotel or more modest house, and a minimum of £300 for a self-catering tower-block flat; peak season is May, September and October, as mid-summer is reckoned too hot to be fully attractive.

Prices in the **North** are if anything dearer for equivalent facilities, with little provision for the budget end of the market. However, unlike in the South high season is rated as mid-summer, making spring or fall visits a smart strategy. **Two-centre holidays** – a week in Turkey plus a week on Cyprus – are popular and make a virtue of the necessity of stopping over in Turkey.

BY BOAT

Despite the fact that Cyprus is an island, sailing there is not a conspicuously popular option except for ex-kibbutz volunteers taking it in as a stopover on the way back from Israel. Much of the fleet operating out of the South is devoted to (not particularly recommendable) 48-hour cruises taking in Egypt and the "Holy Land", pitched at package customers with a spare weekend.

TO THE SOUTH

You can reach Limassol, the South's main port, from Ancona (Italy), several mainland and island ports in Greece, Haifa or Ashdod (Israel), and Port Said (Egypt). Each company's frequency of departure tends to be once a week in season, and service never completely stops in winter with certain shipping lines. The Jounieh (Lebanon)–Larnaca line can not presently be used by casual travellers, as no tourist visas are given for Lebanon. Summarised following are the current offerings of various shipping companies. Student/youth, railpass and return-ticket discounts are usually available, as are stopovers.

All **fares** should be taken merely as guideline estimates only. In any case, sailing isn't a conspicuously economical way to reach the island unless you happen to already be in Israel, Rhodes or Crete and decide to tack Cyprus on to your travel plans. A cabin from Rhodes or Heraklion to Limassol, for instance, costs a significant fraction of a student/youth flight from either place to Larnaca; Haifa–Limassol is comparatively a better deal. Bringing a vehicle is such an expensive proposition that it usually works out cheaper to leave your car behind and hire one in Cyprus (see p.17).

SHIPPING LINE DIRECTORY

From	Shipping line
Ancona	only *Marlines*
Piraeus	all except *Marlines*
Heraklion	all except *Poseidon* and *Louis*
Rhodes	all companies
Haifa	all except *Marlines*
Port Said	only *Stability/Vergina*

For companies operating from Limassol (Cyprus), see the "Listings" under the Limassol city account, p.74.

Poseidon Lines runs all year between Piraeus–Rhodes–Limassol–Haifa and back via the same ports; Piraeus departure is early Monday evening, with arrival in Limassol Wednesday morning. Return from Haifa is Thursday evening, with arrival in Limassol the next morning. During July and August an extra stop is made in Heraklion, Crete, going both directions. Sample deck class fares are £46 Rhodes–Limassol low season, £53 high season; £38 Haifa–Limassol low season, £42 high season. Sample two-bunk cabin fares for the same itineraries and seasons are £65/75 and £45/52 respectively. £11 port tax per passenger is not included in these rates.

Stability/Vergina Lines runs the *Vergina* and *Queen Vergina* from the beginning of April to the end of October between Piraeus–Rhodes–Limassol–Haifa and back via the same ports; Piraeus departure is early Thursday evening, with arrival in Limassol Saturday morning. Return from Haifa is on Sunday evening, arriving in Limassol next morning. From mid-June onwards an extra stop is made in Heraklion (Crete) going in each direction, and during the same period a separate Monday evening sailing from Piraeus takes in Rhodes, Limassol (Wed morning), Haifa (Thurs morning), Port Said (Fri morning) and back through the outbound ports. This route is used extensively as a cruise option by Cypriot travel agents, but sample deck fares Rhodes–Limassol range £55/64 low/high season; Haifa or Port Said–Limassol a whopping £66. Sample cabin fares for the same routes and seasons are £81/100 and £96 respectively. A small car brought from Rhodes will cost £100/118. Port taxes in Greece are £11 per person and £28 per vehicle extra.

Afroessa Lines runs the *Panayia* from late May to late October between Piraeus–Heraklion–Rhodes–Limassol–Haifa and back via the same ports; Piraeus departure is Saturday evening, with arrival in Limassol Monday noon. Departure from Haifa is Tuesday evening, with arrival in Limassol the next morning. Sample deck fares Rhodes–Limassol are £36/48 low/high season, Haifa–Limassol £33/44 low/high season. A mid-range double cabin for the same sectors and seasons will set you back £73/81 and £48/62 respectively. A small car brought from Greece will cost you £60; again port taxes, currently £10 per passenger and £24 per vehicle, are not included.

Marlines runs the *Crown M* from early July to early September between Ancona–Igoumenitsa–Patras–Heraklion–Rhodes–Limassol and back via all these ports except Patras; Ancona departure is Friday evening, reaching Limassol Tuesday morning. Sample deck fare between Ancona and Limassol is £111; a simple double-occupancy cabin will set you back £199, and a small car £189. Port fees per person run £14, per vehicle £31. There are no student/youth reductions.

Arkadia Lines runs the *Silver Paloma* all year round between Piraeus–Rhodes–Limassol–Haifa and back via the same ports. Departure from

Piraeus is on Thursday evening, with arrival in Limassol Saturday morning; return from Haifa takes place Sunday evening, with the call in Limassol the next morning. Sample deck fare, high season, Rhodes–Limassol is £57, with a cabin on the same stretch costing £107. A small car is carried at the same season for £110. Port fees of £11 per passenger and £25 per car are additional.

Louis Lines handles three ships, the *Princessa Marissa*, the *Princessa Amorosa* and the *Princessa Cypria* but only the last of these is intended as a conventional ferry, with fares sold as such, the other two being reserved for the lucrative trade in weekend Israel/Egypt cruises out of Limassol. The *Princessa Cypria* operates in July and August only between Piraeus–Heraklion–Limassol–Haifa, with an odd return route (intended for cruise-hoppers) of Limassol–Rhodes–Tinos–Piraeus. The ship starts its outbound route in Piraeus on Tuesday night, reaching Limassol Thursday afternoon; return from Haifa is Friday evening, with docking at Limassol the next morning. For current fares, consult the agencies below.

SHIPPING LINE AGENTS FOR THE SOUTH

Afroessa Lines port agents
Piraeus Hariláou Trikoúpi 1 (☎01/42 82 920)
Heraklion *Arabatzoglou Travel*, Ikosipémptis Avgoústou 54 (☎081/226 697)
Rhodes *Anka Travel*, Gallías 13 (☎0241/26 835)
Haifa *Mano Seaways*, 39/41 HaMeginnim Ave (☎04/514233)

Arkadia Lines port agents
Piraeus *Hermes Intertraffic*, Kolokotróni 145 (☎01/41 81 097)
Heraklion *Pancreta Holidays*, Ikosipémptis Avgoústou 27 (☎081/223 753)
Rhodes *Red Sea Travel and Shipping*, Amerikís 11 (☎0241/22 460)
Haifa *Mano Seaways*, 39/41 HaMeginnim Ave (☎04/531631)

Louis Lines port agents
Piraeus *Louis Travel Agency*, Mavrokordhátou 11 (☎01/45 36 590)
Rhodes *Al Hambra Travel*, Alexándhrou Papágou 23 (☎0241/36 189)
Haifa *Dolphin Shipping Agency*, 104 HaAtzma'ut St (☎04/523953)

Marlines port agents
Ancona Via XXIX Settembre, 8A (☎071/202.566)
Heraklion *Arabatzoglou Travel*, Ikosipémptis Avgoústou 54 (☎081/226 697)
Rhodes *Kydon Tours*, Ethelondón Dhodhekanisíon 14 (☎0241/23 000)

Poseidon Lines port agents
Piraeus Aktí Miaoúli 35/39 (☎01/42 92 046)
Rhodes *Kouros Travel*, Karpáthou 34 (☎0241/22 400)
Haifa, *Jacob Caspi*, 76 HaAtzma'ut Rd, corner Natan St (☎04/674444).

Stability/Vergina Lines port agents
Piraeus *Stability Line*, Aktí Sakhtoúri 11 (☎01/41 32 392)
Heraklion *Arabatzoglou Travel*, Ikosipémptis Avgoústou 54 (☎081/226 697)
Rhodes *Kouros Travel*, Karpáthou 34 (☎0241/22 400)
Haifa *Jacob Caspi*, 76 HaAtzma'ut Rd (☎04/674444)
Port Said *Mena Tours*, El Gomhoria St (☎66/225742)

TO THE NORTH

Since only Turkey recognises the Turkish Republic of Northern Cyprus, the only way to reach the North of Cyprus by boat is to leave from one of two Turkish ports, Taşucu or Mersin. **Fares**, currently subsidised by the Turkish government, are relatively reasonable, and bringing your own vehicle into the North is marginally more tempting than into Limassol. This may change, of course, in the wake of any peace settlement, with free movement to the South for foreigners and a sharp hike in ferry tariffs equally likely possibilities. Again, sample figures are converted from Turkish lira and are intended only as guidelines. Note that in all cases service in either direction on **weekends** is extremely limited, so don't race through Turkey hoping to catch non-existent Friday or Saturday boats.

Mersin–Famagusta is the most reliable, weather-proof crossing owing to the large size of the ships, and is favoured by locals despite its relatively long duration. The only company on this route is the Turkish-state-run *TML*; for some years now its sailing pattern has featured Mersin departures at 10pm on Monday, Wednesday and Friday, with arrival the next day in Famagusta at 8am. Tuesday and Thursday the boat returns from Famagusta at 10pm, docking at Mersin at 8am the next day. Most of the weekend there is no movement, with the boat returning from Famagusta on Sunday night, not Saturday.

Sample deck-class fare, one way, is £10; a second-class shared cabin will run £13. Transporting a car costs £19; count also on £4 or so in taxes. It may be worth asking for a ten percent student discount or return-passage discount.

Taşucu–Kyrenia is near the closest point of contact between Anatolia and Cyprus. This crossing looks tempting on a map, but the standard of craft in service can be pretty poor, and a nominal four-hour trip easily becomes an eight-hour ordeal in case of storms in the straits, or malfunctioning engines. No cabins are available on the overnight crossings, another reason to recommend the afternoon hydrofoil services.

There are currently five **companies** – *TML* plus four private outfits – serving this route; only two of the boats carry vehicles. In theory departures happen all year, weather permitting, except for the *TML* ship which only works March–September. **Prices** are similar for all of them, but standards of service vary. Single fares range from £6.50 to £8.50, less any applicable discounts such as return passage or student status. A medium-sized car costs £12.50 to ferry, campers £20. There are in addition assorted annoying taxes and chits of formalised *baksheesh* totalling about £4.

Fergün and its broken-down tub the *Fatih* (cars carried) are worth avoiding if you have the choice. They leave Taşucu Sunday through Thursday at midnight (that is, 11.59pm of the days in question), arriving in Kyrenia the next morning. *Ertürk*, with its namesake boat (cars carried) is smaller and faster, keeping the same schedule, and is slightly cheaper than the others. *TML* runs its small passenger-only ferry the *Ayvalık* at midnight (ie 11.59pm) Monday through Friday, arriving in Kyrenia at dawn. At least one of two **hydrofoils**, the *Kıbrıs Ekspresi* and the ex-Soviet *İpek Yolu*, makes the trip over Monday to Saturday at noon; fares for this three-hour hop are about the same as for the conventional boats.

Alanya–Kyrenia crossing once a week, currently Sunday midnight from June to September only, the *Ayvalık* varies its schedule with a seven-hour trip from the popular Turkish resort of Alanya. To do this it has returned from Kyrenia at midday on Saturday. Passenger fare on this route, taxes excluded, is £16.

SHIPPING AGENTS TO THE NORTH

TML Port Agent
Mersin *Kuzeymanlar Gemi Acenteliği*, Büyükada Kadıyoran Cad 19 (☎74/116377)

Taşucu Port Agencies
Fergün ☎ (7593) 1782
Ertürk ☎ (7593) 1033
Kıbrıs Ekspresi ☎(7593) 1334

GETTING THERE FROM NORTH AMERICA & AUSTRALASIA

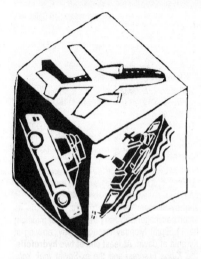

There are no direct air links between North America and Cyprus South or North, nor are there any organised package tours. Thus getting to Cyprus is an expensive proposition, which is probably best considered as an adjunct to a wider European or Mediterranean tour.

FLIGHTS TO THE SOUTH

The best strategy for reaching **the South**, then, is to choose an inexpensive gateway into Europe which also has reasonable connections onward to Cyprus. *American Airlines* pitches advertising in Cyprus to the expatriate community, offering advantageous add-on tickets into and out of Frankfurt, which is served by *Cyprus Airways* and *Lufthansa* from Larnaca. If cost is your primary consideration, then get yourself to London and shop around there for an attractive package – though be aware that on-the-ground costs in England could well eat up any savings. It may also be worth considering a flight to Athens from either Canada or the USA: though this is not always conspicuously cheap, you will have the advantage of guaranteed same-day connection on to Larnaca, with up to four or five departures daily on a combination of *Olympic Airways* and *Cyprus Airways*.

USEFUL AIRLINES IN NORTH AMERICA

FOR THE SOUTH:

American Airlines, PO Box 619616, Dallas/Fort Worth International Airport, Dallas, TX 75261 (☎817/267-1151 or 1-800/433-7300).

British Airways, 530 Fifth Ave, New York, NY 10017 (☎1-800/2479297); 1001 bd de Maisonneuve Ouest, Montréal, PQ H3A 3C8 (☎1-800/668-1059); 112 Kent St, Ottawa, ON K1P 5P2 (☎613/236-0881); 1 Dundas St West, Toronto, ON M5G 2B2 (☎416/250-0880).

Delta Airlines, Hartsfield Atlanta International Airport, Atlanta, GA 30320 (☎404/765-5000 or 1-800/241-4141).

KLM, 565 Taxter Rd, Elmsford, NY 10523 (☎212/759-3600 or 1-800/777-5553); 225 N Michigan Ave, Chicago, IL 60601 (☎212/861-9292); 1255 Green Ave, West Mount, Montréal PQ H3Z 2A4 (☎514/933-1314 or 1-800/361-5073).

Olympic Airways, 647 Fifth Ave, New York, NY 10022 (☎212/838-3600 or 1-800/223-1226); 168 N Michigan Ave, Chicago, IL 60601 (☎312/329-0400 or 1-800/223-1226); 500 South Grand St, Suite 1500, Los Angeles, CA 90014 (☎212/624-6441); 80 Bloor St West, Suite 502, Toronto, ON M5S 2V1 (☎416/920-2452).

Lufthansa, 1640 Hempstead Turnpike, East Meadow, NY 11554 (☎718/895-1277 or 1-800/645-3880); 875 N Michigan Ave, Chicago, IL 60611 (☎312/751-0111); 55 Yonge St, Toronto, ON M5E 1J4 (☎416/368-4777); 2020 University St, Montréal, PQ H3A 2A5 (☎514/288-2227).

FOR THE NORTH:

KLM, Addresses as above.

Lufthansa, Addresses as above.

Swissair, 608 Fifth Ave, New York, NY 10020 (☎718/995-8400 or 1-800/221-7370); 2 Bloor St West, Suite 502, Toronto, ON M5S 2V1 (☎416/960-4270).

THY Turkish Airlines, 821 United Nations Plaza, 4th floor, New York, NY10017 (☎212/986-5050).

FLIGHT AGENTS IN NORTH AMERICA

The **agents, travel clubs and consolidators** listed below are included because they offer good-value access to Europe (usually London, Greece or Turkey). Most should be able to sell you an add-on flight to Cyprus from the European point of entry they favour.

USA

Access International, 101 West 31st St, Suite 104, New York, NY 10001 (☎1-800/TAKE-OFF). Good East Coast/central US consolidator.

Airkit, 1125 W 6th St, Los Angeles, CA 90017 (☎213/957-9304). West Coast consolidator with seats from San Francisco and LA.

Discount Travel International, Ives Bldg, 114 Forrest Ave, Suite 205, Narbeth, PA 19072 (☎215/668-2182 or 1-800/221-8139).

Stand Buys, 311 W Superior St, Chicago, IL 60610 (☎1-800/331-0257). Good travel club.

STA Travel, 48 E 11th St, Suite 805, New York, NY 10003 (☎212/986-9470); 166 Geary St, Suite 702, San Francisco, CA 94108 (☎415/391-8407). Main US branches of the worldwide specialist in independent and student travel. Other offices in LA, Berkeley, Boston and Honolulu.

Travelers Advantage, 49 Music Square, Nashville, TN 37203 (☎1-800/548-1116). Reliable travel club.

Travac, 1177 N Warson Rd, St Louis, MO 63132 (☎1-800/872-8800). Useful consolidator.

CANADA

Travel Cuts, 187 College St, Toronto, ON M5T 1P7 (☎416/979-2406). Main office of the Canadian student travel organisation. Many other offices nationwide.

FLIGHTS TO THE NORTH

Because of the international air boycott of **the North**, getting there from North America means just one route: a flight to Istanbul, with onward connection to Ercan (North Nicosia) airport. *THY*, the Turkish state carrier, has four weekly services from New York to Istanbul, from where its subsidiary *Cyprus Turkish Airways* flies daily to Ercan in North Cyprus. From Canada there is currently no direct service even to Turkey – reaching North Cyprus from there involves a grueling relay via one of a number of European hub-cities, such as Zurich, Frankfurt or Amsterdam. In any case, count on a minimum of US$800 – more realistically US$1000 – round-trip from the East Coast to any point in Cyprus.

GETTING THERE FROM AUSTRALASIA

As with North America, there are no direct air links between Australia or New Zealand and any part of Cyprus, despite the sizeable expatriate Cypriot community in Australia. The most cost-effective strategy will be to get a good deal on a ticket to Athens, Istanbul or London, and have an "add-on" fare written from there.

BEST ROUTES

There are almost daily flights to Athens on one of a number of airlines – *Qantas, Olympic, Singapore* and *Thai International*. All involve a stop in either Singapore or Bangkok, and there's usually not a great deal of difference in fares: reckon on Aus$1500 return to Athens, with another Aus$350 add-on fare to **southern Cyprus**.

Options to Istanbul, for access to **the North**, are limited to the twice-weekly Singapore to Istanbul service on *THY* – which means first getting an advantageous ticket from Australasia to Singapore. Total costs to Istanbul are if anything even higher than getting to Athens, with the additional (if minimal) expense of continuing to Cyprus.

A somewhat cheaper, though more time-consuming, route would involve flying to London and then proceeding from there with the benefit of the well-developed package industry. For what is admittedly a difficult and expensive itinerary however you do it, you're well advised to contact one of the specialist agencies below, who can be of assistance no matter what your age or student status.

AUSTRALIA

STA 1a Lee St, Railway Square, Sydney 2000 (☎02/519 9866); 224 Faraday St, Carlton, Victoria, 3053 (☎03/347 4711).

NEW ZEALAND

STS Head office: 10 High St, Auckland (☎09/309 9723).

RED TAPE AND VISAS

British, EC and US nationals require only a valid passport for entry into either the south or the north sectors of Cyprus, and both sets of authorities routinely stamp you with a three-month tourist visa on arrival. However, you must choose which portion you will visit on any given trip – until and unless any peace settlement takes effect, there is no possibility of foreign tourists moving from the North to the South, and severely limited provision in the opposite direction.

Furthermore, the southern Republic has declared all seaports and airports in the North "prohibited ports of entry and exit"; this means that if there's any evidence in your passport of such a visit to North Cyprus, you will be subsequently denied entry to the South – and quite possibly Greece as well. So upon arrival in the North, be sure to ask for the visa to be stamped on a separate, loose slip of paper; vehicles can also be entered on the same detachable visa. Most Turkish Cypriot customs officials speak good English, but if in doubt the Turkish for "On a loose sheet, please" is *Lütfen gevşek kağıtda*. Staff at Ercan airport are fairly used to such requests and keep a stack of loose visa slips handy.

The other potential sticking point on entry to the South is the ban on any imported **perishables**; eat those apples on the boat or plane in, or the customs officers will eat them for you.

HEALTH AND INSURANCE

In general, Cyprus is a healthy place, and you're unlikely to experience any problems other than a spell of constipation brought on by initial contact with the rather heavy food. Water is fit to drink almost everywhere except Famagusta (where the sea has invaded well bore-holes), though not always so tasty; bottle water is widely available. No inoculations are required for any part of Cyprus, though as ever it's wise to keep your tetanus booster up to date.

HEALTH HAZARDS

Most routine threats to your health have to do with overexposure, the sea and flying insects. Wear a hat and drink plenty of fluids during the hot months to avoid the danger of **sunstroke**. **Jellyfish** are rare, **sea urchins** more common; their presence on rocky coasts indicates a mild pollution problem as well. If you are unlucky enough to tread on, or graze, one, a sterilised sewing needle, scalpel and olive oil are effective aids to removing spines. And they should be extracted, or they will fester. A pair of swim goggles and footwear for walking over tidal rocks should help you avoid both.

The worst maritime danger – fortunately quite rare – is the **weever fish**, which buries itself in tidal sand with just its poisonous dorsal and gill spines protruding. If you step on one the sudden pain is unmistakeably excruciating and the venom exceptionally potent. Consequences range up to permanent paralysis of the affected area, so the imperative first aid before rushing to a doctor is to immerse your foot in water as hot as you can stand. This degrades the toxin as well as relieving the swelling of the joints and attendant pain.

In terms of dry-land beasties, there are **scorpions** about – tap out your shoes in the morning before donning them – and one stubby, mottled species of **viper**, called *kufi* locally; antivenins for it are available. Those enormous, two-metre-long black **whip** or **montpellier snakes** which you'll see on the road are **harmless** to humans, and in fact were imported to hunt both rodents and venomous serpents. **Mosquitos** (*kounoúpia* in Greek, *sivrisinek* in Turkish) can be troublesome in summer, especially between Famagusta and the Kırpaşa (Kárpas) peninsula; solutions offered by hotels include pyrethrum incense coils, electrified vapour pads, or air-conditioned rooms with closed windows.

There are few stray animals on Cyprus and thus (uniquely for this part of the world) **rabies** is not much of a danger. Indeed one of the few things the Greek and Turkish Cypriot communities agreed on before 1974 was to round up and put down most stray dogs, since many carried **echinococcosis**, a debilitating liver fluke which could spread to humans. Adherence to the practice is laxer now in the North, but overall the canine population is still not up to previous levels.

MEDICAL ATTENTION

The standard of health care is relatively high in Cyprus, with many English-speaking and -trained doctors. The fancier hotels can generally make recommendations of local practitioners, and may even post lists of them. General **hospitals** in both sectors of the island have walk-in casualty wards where foreigners can have cuts sewn up and broken bones set at little or no cost, but any other treatment is expensive (see below).

Minor ailments can be dealt with at **chemists** (*farmakío* in Greek, *eczane* in Turkish); pharmacists are well trained and can often dispense medicines which in Britain would only be available on prescription. In the South, you can dial the operator on ☎192 to ask for the rota of night-duty chemists.

INSURANCE

In neither South nor North Cyprus does the social insurance system extend to foreigners, and fees for non-urgent medical procedures range from £30 for a surgery visit to £400 for a simple appendicectomy, making it *essential* to take out some form of **travel insurance** policy. Just about any travel agent, bank or insurance broker will sell you comprehensive cover which includes not only medical expenses but also loss or theft of belongings. In Britain, policies issued by branches of *Endsleigh Insurance* (in London at 97 Southampton Row, WC1; ☎071/436 4451) are among the least expensive, from about £22 per month.

If you intend to hire an off-road vehicle or motorbike, or engage in **special activities** such as para-sailing, horse-riding or scuba-diving, you may need a more specialised policy: be sure to check with your insurers when getting cover.

To make a **claim**, you'll need documentation of all expenses, including pharmacy receipts. If you have anything stolen, go to the nearest police station, report the theft and get a copy of the report or the identification number under which it has been filed: you will need this when making a claim back home. In the South, the Cyprus Tourism Organisation has a special corps of "Tourist Assistants" to act as trouble-shooters in the event of mishaps.

INFORMATION AND MAPS

Before leaving home it's worth stopping in at the tourist office of whichever part of Cyprus you intend to visit, since their stock of brochures and maps is invariably better than what's to be found once you're on the island. The Cyprus Tourism Organisation (CTO) of the internationally recognised Republic of Cyprus, with longer experience of such things, not surprisingly showers you with an avalanche of professionally presented and often useful material on every conceivable topic; the North Cyprus Tourist Office's offerings, while both less slick and less substantial, are suggested reading mainly because they include the only existing town plans with current Turkified street names.

USEFUL FREE PUBLICATIONS: SOUTH

Among the **CTO titles** to look out for include the *Guide to Hotels, Travel Agencies and other Tourist Services*, a massive but elusive compendium of virtually every licensed lodging in the South, plus car-hire firms, supposedly published each May but always delayed; *Cyprus, 9000 Years of History and Civilisation*, summarising points of interest and with (fairly up-to-date) site and museum opening hours; *Cyprus Travellers Handbook*, containing nuts-and-bolts facts, rules and handy addresses; a *Diary of Events*, a yearly calendar which should be supplemented by a more current and detailed monthly cyclostyle available in Cyprus; *Cyprus Domestic Transportation Services, Itineraries and Tariffs*, a complete tally of bus and taxi schedules and fares between the major towns and resorts; the cryptically-named *Info Paper, Unit 2*, which details schedules and agents for all international ferries calling in the South; and *Urban Bus Routes*, foldout maps/schedules for Limassol and Nicosia.

The CTO has **offices** in the Republic of Cyprus at Nicosia, Limassol, Larnaca, Páfos, Ayía Nápa, and (April–Oct) Plátres. Hours are typically Monday to Saturday 8.15am–1.45pm, plus late Monday and Thursday afternoon hours (4–6.15pm summer, 3–5.30pm winter), with small local variations and addresses given in the text of the *Guide*.

USEFUL FREE PUBLICATIONS: NORTH

Essential **North Cyprus publications** are the *North Cyprus Tourist Map*, which in addition to being virtually the only printed source of villages

---

CYPRUS TOURISM OFFICES ABROAD

THE REPUBLIC OF CYPRUS
UK CTO, 213 Regent St, London W1R 8DA (☎071/734 9822)
USA CTO, 13 East 40th St, New York NY 10016 (☎212/683-5280)
NETHERLANDS Cyprus Verkeersbureau, Prinsengracht 600, 1017 KS Amsterdam (☎020/62 44 358)
SWEDEN Cypriotiska Statens Turistbyra, Vasagatan 11, S-111-20 Stockholm (☎08/115578)

GREECE CTO, Voukourestíou 36, Athens (☎01/36 10 178)

NORTH CYPRUS
UK North Cyprus Tourist Office, 28 Cockspur St, London SW1Y 5BN (☎071/930 4853)
CANADA 300 John St, Suite 330, Thornhill, Ont L3T 5W4 (☎416/731-4000)
USA 821 United Nations Plaza, 6th Floor, New York, NY 10017 (☎212/687-2350)

as renamed in North Cyprus, also shows most of the southern villages from which the refugee Turkish Cypriots came; the *City Plans* for Girne, Lefkoşa and Gazimağusa, as Kyrenia, Nicosia and Famagusta are called in Turkish; and a glossy pamphlet entitled *Hotels*, with photos and descriptions of amenities, which could be useful if found in the UK.

North Cypriot **tourist offices** are found only in Kyrenia, Famagusta and Nicosia; hours are typically Monday to Friday 7.30am–2pm, Monday 3.30–6pm in summer, Monday to Friday 8am–1pm and 2–5pm in winter.

MAPS – AND PLACE NAME PROBLEMS

There are numbers of complimentary and commercial maps available for Cyprus, but no single one of them is entirely satisfactory, and most handle the fact of the island's division awkwardly .

SUGGESTED ROAD MAPS

It's wisest to get an overall touring map of the island, as well as any topographical maps, before leaving home. The best **small-scale road maps** are the *Freytag Berndt* 1:250,000 folding map (£5.50), the *Bartholomew Clyde Leisure Map* at 1:300,000 (£3.50), or the *AA-Macmillan* 1:300,000 (£3.95). The *FB* has place names with Greek lettering and accentuation, and its depiction of minor roads is much better; *BC* has better town plans included on the back, with accented Roman-alphabet renditions of villages on the main map; while the *AA* map's main strength lies in its being the only commercial map showing the new Turkish village names in the North, though its road network is often wildly inaccurate.

The CTO gives out a number of **free maps**: "A Visitor's Map of Cyprus", the entire island at 1:400,000; Nicosia city centre; Limassol town and environs; Larnaca town and environs; Ayía Nápa and environs; Páfos and environs; and the Troödhos. These are all reasonably accurate, but as some – particularly the Troödhos and Ayía Nápa maps – are just under, or over, ten years old, errors and obsolescences have inevitably crept in.

TOPOGRAPHICAL MAPS

Topographical maps are prepared by the Department of Lands and Surveys in Nicosia. They are easiest available through specialist map shops abroad, such as *Stanfords*, 12–14 Long Acre, London WC2E 9LP (☎071/836 1321) and *Map Link*, 25 E. Mason St, Santa Barbara, CA

93101 (☎805/965-4402). The 1:50,000 series is out of print, and only certain sheets of the 1:25,000 series, mostly of the southwest and southeast corners of the island, are still available at a cost of £4.95 apiece.

Fortunately the popular Troödhos area is still covered, but maps date from 1960 and are lettered in English only. Not surprisingly the Turkish military occupying the North do not make available to the public anything they have prepared. Unless you plan to do some hard-core, cross-country exploration, the walking maps in this book are adequate to take you around safely.

PROBLEMS WITH BOUNDARIES AND PLACE NAMES

All existing island-wide maps, however, have **limitations** to usefulness owing to international non-recognition of the **Turkish Republic of Northern Cyprus** (TRNC) – and poor documentation of the **Attila/Green Line**, the cease-fire line marking the Turkish Army's furthest advance in August 1974, and the attendant **buffer zone** to either side of it. This zone, also called the "dead zone" or No-Man's Land, is off-limits to everyone except UN personnel or local farmers, and varies in width from a few paces in Nicosia to a few kilometres at the old Nicosia airport and the Nicosia–Larnaca expressway. Greek Cypriot depictions of the Line tend to be optimistic, placing it at the limit of the Turkish advance rather than at the southern Republic's edge of the buffer zone; maps in this guide correct that boundary where necessary.

A bigger problem is that all maps except the TRNC's tourist handout, and the *AA-Macmillan* product, continue to show **only Greek place names** in the North as it existed pre-1974, despite the fact that all Greek signposts and place names have long since vanished there. The southern Republic considers this Turkification just one aspect of the "cultural vandalism and falsification of history", as they put it, which has taken place in the North since 1974. Even the Turkish Cypriots in the North, whether native or resettled refugees, are often nonplussed by the official village names imposed on them, since virtually every place had a Turkish Cypriot form – often phonetically related to the Greek rendition – which is still used in conversation in preference to the often clumsy official name. Only certain villages and towns which had always had Turkish names were exempted from the Turkification campaign.

In chapters Six, Seven and Eight of **this guide**, first the "new" name as it appears on road signs is cited, followed by the local Greek and (if known) Turkish Cypriot names **in brackets**. Maps also show first the post-1974 name, and then the internationally recognised name in brackets.

Throughout the book the **international forms** for the five largest towns – Nicosia, Limassol, Larnaca, Famagusta and Kyrenia – are used in preference to the vernacular renditions, which are given just once for reference at the beginning of accounts.

COSTS

The main Cyprus travel season begins early in spring and extends well into autumn, with July/August visits fairly unappealing for a number of reasons. Obviously you'll save a lot on accommodation tariffs in either part of Cyprus if you're willing to go outside of mid-summer, a sensible strategy whatever your budget. Some form of student identification is useful for discounted admission to archaeological sites and museums, whose fees in any case are modest throughout the island.

THE SOUTH

The southern **Republic of Cyprus** has a somewhat unfair reputation for being nightmarishly expensive. This is a leftover from the days when it *was* pricier than almost any other nearby country, but with rampant inflation prevalent in both Greece and Turkey, costs in the South's well-regulated economy are beginning to seem relatively reasonable.

As an approximation, costs are between 15 and 20 percent higher than in Greece or Spain, but that much less so than in France. In the wake of Britain's departure from the ERM, however, southern Cyprus will seem rather closer to French levels of expense until the pound recovers some of its

value. For North Americans, Cyprus is not a conspicuously cheap country – the French comparison will seem valid for the forseeable future.

Travelling independently in the South, you should budget a **minimum** of around c£14 per person a day (see below for a discussion of Cyprus pounds). This assumes, however, exclusive reliance on **public transport** at c£1–2 a go, staying in one of the limited number of basic village **rooms** or pensions at c£5–9 single a night, and only one modest **meal** out for about c£5.

To travel in some degree of **comfort** and style, though, you'll want at least c£30 disposable per person, which should let you book a modest but acceptable **hotel** on double occupancy basis and share the cost of a **hire car** (and petrol – slightly less than in Britain), as well as two full main meals. **Beer and wine** are good, and cheapish at c£0.65 and c£2 per large bottle respectively.

THE NORTH

The economy of **Northern Cyprus**, both before and since it adopted the Turkish lira as official currency in 1983, has lagged behind that of the South and consequently it is significantly cheaper – except in the confines of a three- or four-star resort. You'll even find certain items less expensive than in Turkey, owing to a combination of subsidies, local production and judicious direct imports from Britain.

For various reasons it's paradoxically much harder to travel independently in the North despite its lower costs at street level; you're at a considerable disadvantage at the limited number of **hotels**, where over-the-counter prices for the theoretical walk-in trade are considerably higher than those granted to advance bookings and agencies. Owing to the unstable nature of the Turkish lira (see below), accommodation rates are invariably quoted in hard currency, usually pounds sterling, and the *Guide* follows this example. It is possible to find small **pensions** in Girne, for example, poised between Turkish mainland clientele on a shopping spree and the bottom end of the package trade, for £6–10/$10–16 per person a night; elsewhere in the North you can count the number of such places on one hand.

Eating out can often be cheaper than in Turkey, for example; outside of the Girne area or the major hotels it's difficult to spend more than £4/$7 a person on a meal, plus a pound or less for imported Turkish booze. **Car hire** is inexpensive, starting at about £11/$18 a day all-in, and petrol is also astonishingly cheap at 27p/$0.43 a litre. **Overall**, budget about **£24/$38** a day per person to live moderately well.

MONEY AND BANKS

Unusually among travel destinations, Cyprus's low crime rate – South or North – and British affiliations make pounds sterling notes, plastic and sometimes even an ordinary bank chequebook preferable to travellers' cheques as a way of carrying your money. In general the Southern banking system is more efficient, but by way of compensation you can pay for many things in the North directly with foreign cash.

THE SOUTH

The currency of the southern Republic of Cyprus is the **Cyprus pound** (c£) and though not traded internationally is a strong, stable currency with a current unit value equal to roughly £1.40 sterling or $2.10. You may import travellers' cheques without **restriction**, but cash amounts in excess of £500/$800 should be declared if you intend to re-export a significant portion of it. You are officially allowed to import or export only c£50, but checks on this are rare. If heading for Greece, for instance, you can easily exchange any excess Cypriot pounds for Greek drachmas at a good rate.

CURRENCY

The Cyprus pound is divided into 100 cents (*sent* in Greek): there are coins of 1, 2, 5, 10, 20 and 50 cents, and paper notes of 50 cents, plus 1, 5, 10 and (recently introduced) 20 pounds. Before 1983 the pound was divided into 20 shillings; it was also divided into 1000 mils. You still hear people referring habitually to a sum of 50 *sents* as *dhéka shillingia* (ten shillings) or *pendakósia mil* (500 mils), so be prepared.

BANKS AND EXCHANGE FACILITIES

Southern **banks** are open 8.15am–12.30pm, Mon–Fri, with many branches in well-touristed areas offering a supplemental afternoon service from 3–5.30pm. Banking and exchange facilities in the two airport arrival lounges are open for all flights. Almost any **monetary device** is easily exchanged: cash (with no commission), travellers' cheques and Eurocheques (subject to standard fees). If you have an account with *Barclay's* you can withdraw cash using a personal cheque (supported by a guarantee card), at *Barclay's* branches in the South only. **Plastic** is also useful: the cashpoint machines of *Barclay's* and the *Popular Bank* (*Laïki Trapeza*) will accept overseas *Visa* cards, provided you know your PIN number. *Access/Mastercard* holders must obtain their cash advances from (human) tellers at the *Bank of Cyprus* or the *National Bank of Greece*. *American Express* has offices offering the usual facilities to its card holders in Limassol, Larnaca and Nicosia; addresses are in the *Guide*.

THE NORTH

Since 1983, legal tender in the Turkish Republic of Northern Cyprus is the **Turkish lira** (TL) – a decision taken more for ideological posture than sound economic reasons, and one with which few inhabitants are happy, given its current devaluation/inflation rate of close to 70 percent yearly. As a result prices quoted in TL are fairly meaningless, and in the *Guide* all northern rates are given in pounds sterling. You can in fact still use the c£ in many hotels, but it's treated like any other foreign note and change given in TL. Rumour has it that, with any durable settlement, the Cypriot pound will be re-introduced as the uniform currency throughout the island, regardless of what the details of territorial jurisdiction are.

CURRENCY

The Turkish lira comes in coins of 500, 1000 and 2500 denomination, and paper notes of 1000, 5000, 10,000, 20,000, 50,000 and 100,000. Coins of less than 500TL still exist, but are inadequate even to pay for a pee in a public convenience.

At present there are no strict **controls** on the amount of cash or travellers' cheques imported into the North, but you should leave with as few TL as possible – for the simple reason that they're worthless outside of Turkey or Northern Cyprus.

BANKS AND EXCHANGE FACILITIES

The several **banks** operating in North Cyprus are fairly inconvenient as tourist facilities for two reasons: the red tape involved in exchange is fairly off-putting, and most foreign tills keep inconveniently short working hours (8.30am–noon Mon–Fri), the single exception being the *Türk Banaksı*, which stays open until 1 or 2pm and also has a 3.30–6pm shift on Monday. With typical late-evening arrival times at the North's two airports, the banks there – which keep no special after-hours – are similarly useless. A much better bet are the **money exchange houses**, at least one of which functions in each of the major towns. Open from 8am to 6pm Monday to Friday

except for a possible lunch break, plus Saturday morning, they give speedy service and top rates for foreign cash and travellers' cheques without taking commission.

Foreign-currency **notes** are in many ways the best form in which to bring funds, the chance of theft being very slim. You can often pay directly for hotel bills and souvenir purchases, though not many restaurant meals, with overseas cash – and you may well *have* to pay the airport cabbie in sterling. At least one of the exchange houses (in northern Nicosia; see p.197) accepts **personal cheques** drawn on a British bank and supported by a guarantee card – though you should certainly not rely on this as a sole method of getting cash. Finally, **plastic** is very handy, both for large transactions such as car hire, and for use in the handful of cashpoint machines scattered across the North – they accept both *Visa* and (with some coaxing) *Access/Mastercard*, upon entry of the proper PIN number. Locations are detailed in the *Guide*.

GETTING AROUND

Cyprus has decent bus services throughout the island, and in the South the useful institution of the service (shared) taxi makes getting around straightforward and cheap. Private taxis are relatively expensive; there has been no train service since the early 1950s. Car hire is reasonable by European standards, making it a hugely popular option for visitors to either side of the island – and something you should seriously consider.

LOCAL BUSES IN THE SOUTH

The most important **inter-urban routes** in the **South** are served by a number of private companies, whose terminals tend to be clustered at various points in the main towns: there's never really anything that could be singled out as a central bus station. Except on Sundays, when services can be skeletal, departures are fairly frequent during daylight hours – up to six times a day between Nicosia and Limassol, or eight times from Larnaca to Ayía Nápa. **Fares**, sold at kerbside offices or on board, are reasonable; crossing the island from Nicosia to Páfos, for example, won't set you back much over c£2. If you make forays into the Troödhos, however, you'll find frequencies dropping sharply, with the need to plan an overnight in the hills; to explore up there it's far simpler to have a car, using the coastal towns as bases.

Worth just a mention are the villagers' **market** buses – essentially Bedford truck chassis with a sort of multi-coloured charabanc mounted on top. These mostly southern institutions are marvellously photogenic, but with their typical once-daily, 6am-out-2pm-back schedules – plus school-bus seating – they're unlikely to be of much use.

LOCAL BUSES IN THE NORTH

In the **North**, local buses are more consciously modelled on the Turkish system, with coaches gathered at a single vehicle park and a ticket-sales/waiting building adjacent. With fewer cars in the poorer economy, locals are more dependent on buses and accordingly departures are more frequent – as much as quarter-hourly between north Nicosia and Kyrenia. **Fares** are also lower than in the South, but once again you'll find public buses inconvenient to do much adventuring. Often your fellow passengers will not be native Cypriots, but Anatolian settlers and soldiers returning to postings.

On both sides of the island, coaches – even aside from the rainbow-scheme market buses – come in a variety of colours and styles, with destinations not always conspicuously marked, so ask around at terminals.

URBAN BUSES

Of all the island cities, only Nicosia and Limassol are really big enough to make **urban buses** an absolute necessity. With very few exceptions, however, these run only from about 5.30am to 7pm (8pm in summer in Nicosia). Fares cost between c£0.25 and c£0.35, and route maps – worth snagging if you're staying long – are available from the pertinent tourist office. In and around Larnaca and Páfos, a few routes are of interest to visitors, and are detailed in the town accounts.

SERVICE TAXIS AND DOLMUŞES

One of Cyprus's more useful ways of gettting about is the shared taxi or minibus, called a **service taxi** in the South or a **dolmuş** in the North. Service taxis carry four to seven passengers, can be booked by phone, and will pick up and drop off at any reasonable point (eg a hotel or private house). Price-wise they are extremely reasonable – not more than double the bus fare for the same route – and journey times are quick, though sometimes drivers' style may have you fearing for your life.

In the South, some of the so-called scheduled **minibus services** up to the Troödhos resorts or out to the lonely northern beaches near Pólis seem to straddle categories a bit; they may offer pick-up service and/or refuse to depart at all without a certain quota of passengers. Strictly speaking, there are no shared saloon cars in the North, but rather minibuses which dawdle in bus parks until they are full or nearly so, thus meeting the definition of *dolmuş* – "stuffed".

TAXIS

Privately hired **taxis** within urban areas in the **South** have rigidly controlled fares, not exorbitant by British standards. The meter starts at c£0.35, with a minimum charge of c£0.60. The meter ticks over at the rate of c£0.17 per kilometre on a single trip, c£0.13 per kilometre on an out-and-back journey. Between 11pm and 6am a night supplement of fifteen percent on the taximeter amount is applicable, with a minimum charge of c£1. The first thirteen kilos of luggage are carried free, with each successive thirteen-kilo increment accruing a twenty-cent charge.

There also exist numbers of **rural taxis** providing service between Troödhos resorts or foothill villages and nearby towns; for these trips you should know the going rate as meters will not be used. As guidelines, Nicosia to Pródhromos will cost about c£18 per carful; from Limassol to the same place slightly less; from Larnaca to Páno Léfkara about c£9.

In the relatively small towns of the **North**, there's less need for urban taxis; moving between population centres, fares are about the same as in the South, say £10 from Ercan airport outside Nicosia to Kyrenia.

HITCHING

With public transport costs reasonable, **hitch-hiking** is not conspicuously popular in the Republic of Cyprus, among either locals or tourists, and would not be pleasant in the blisteringly hot months of summer. But there are no laws against it, the CTO even recognises it as an option in their pamphlets, and in the rural areas it's an excellent way to meet people. It's probably best to reserve hitching as a strategy for getting between isolated villages in the Troödhos. In the North it would be slow work indeed, given the limited number of private cars.

DRIVING

Well on three-quarters of visitors to either part of Cyprus end up driving themselves around at some time during their stay, and this is really the best way to see the country. Either a licence from your home country or an International Driving Permit is acceptable throughout the island.

ROAD RULES AND CONDITIONS

Traffic moves **on the left** as in the UK and most Commonwealth nations. **Front-seatbelt** use is mandatory on the open road but discretionary in towns; children under five year of age many not occupy the front seats, and kids five to twelve only if wearing seatbelts. **Drunk-driving** laws are nearly as strict as in the UK or North America: 39mg of alcohol allowed per 100ml of breath, 90mg alcohol per 100 ml of blood.

Speed limits in the South are 100km/hr on dual carriageways, 80km/hr on other rural roads, and 50km/hr in towns. Entry into urban zones is announced by big signs reading "*Katikómeni Periokhí*" (Built-up Area). In the North, limits are roughly the same but posted in miles per hour: 60mph on the Kyrenia–Nicosia–Famagusta highway, 40mph on smaller backroads, and 30mph in built-up areas. These aren't signposted but there are remarkable numbers of khaki-drill-clad policemen maintaining speed traps with hand-held radar devices at town outskirts.

In the larger Southern towns, use the designated lots for **parking**; they're not expensive – c£0.30 or c£0.40 for half-day use is the norm – and often the attendants can't be bothered to collect the fees. Meters on some commercial streets take ten-cent coins, and yellow lines at kerbsides mean the same thing as in Britain: single, no parking during business hours; double, no parking *or* stopping. No-parking zones are poorly indicated in the North, though a policeman may appear and politely tell you if you're being blatantly illegal.

Roads themselves range from the excellent dual carriageways linking Nicosia with Kyrenia, Limassol and Larnaca to unspeakable hill tracks fit only for jeep or mountain bike. The Limassol–Páfos road in particular, not yet replaced by an expressway, is inadequate for the traffic load it has to carry and easily rates as the most dangerous road in Cyprus. Many secondary roads throughout the island, while usually paved, are **single-lane** colonial relics with merely a thin layer of asphalt strewn over cobbles. This makes them extremely bumpy, with very sharp edges over which you're forced to put two wheels by oncoming traffic.

Signposting varies, too; village exits are usually not obvious, so you'll get acquainted with the boys in the central café asking directions; otherwise you may well end up caught in a steep cul-de-sac with reversing the only way out. By contrast, the Troödhos and Kyrenia range forestry roads, despite their often horrific condition, are almost always admirably marked. However, in North Cyprus, many rural signs are badly faded, not having been maintained since 1974.

All **road distances** are marked in kilometres in the South, but appear – if at all – in miles in the North. Yet all hire car speedometers indicate kilometres, as do internationally sold maps. If you're obsessive on the subject, you might try watching for old colonial milestones in the North.

PETROL

In the **South**, four-star **petrol** costs about c£0.32 a litre, or slightly less than in the UK (though a good deal more than in North America); unleaded fuel was recently made available. Stations are normally open Monday to Friday 6am to 6pm (sometimes 7pm), with Saturday and Sunday closure at 4pm. On Sundays and holidays only about ten percent of the South's stations are open, on a rota basis; it's remarkably easy to run out of petrol if you're not careful, so plan ahead. A few automatic, 24-hour stations have begun operation in Limassol and Nicosia; at these you feed c£1, c£5 or c£10 notes into a machine which then shunts that amount's worth of fuel to your pump.

Owing to various subsidies which may not survive a peace settlement, petrol in **North Cyprus** is remarkably cheap at present, about 27p/$0.43 per litre; unleaded fuel is not yet available. Stations, especially in the Kyrenia area, tend to be open until 8pm, with near-normal service on Sunday.

CAR HIRE

It's worth stressing that the **condition** of hire cars on either side of the Line can be appalling, with bad brakes the most common fault; if at all possible, take the candidate car for a spin around the block before accepting it. Reputable chains in the South will furnish you with a list of their branches Republic-wide, which should be contacted in event of a breakdown. Hire cars in both South and North have distinctive red **number plates** beginning with "Z", and their drivers are usually accorded every consideration by police – for example, a warning instead of a ticket for not buckling up. However, visitors may not cross the Green/Attila Line in either direction with hire (or indeed their own) cars.

In the **South**, numerous agencies, including all international and several local chains, offer primarily A- and B-group compacts both at airports and in towns. Rates start at c£11 a day, unlimited mileage and most insurance included, VAT exclusive, a figure which should be kept in mind as a yardstick when pre-booking an "A" group vehicle from overseas. In or near high-season you will have to reserve in advance, not difficult since so many fly-drive packages are offered. You are virtually obligated to accept the additional daily fee of c£3 for Collision Damage Waiver (CDW); remember also that venturing onto dirt tracks with a non-4WD vehicle will usually void your insurance coverage if you damage the undercarriage.

Minimum hiring age is generally 21; credit cards are the preferred method of payment. An unusual quirk of Southern rentals is that you will be asked to deposit a sum (eg c£12 for a 40-litre tank), in cash or with credit card, covering the cost of a **full tank** of petrol; the idea is to return the car as empty as possible, rather than full as in other countries.

Because the **North** is unrecognised internationally, none of the overseas chains are represented there, leaving the field clear for local entrepreneurs. More hiring seems to be done in towns and at resorts because the rental booths at the **airports** are shut at (typically late) flight arrival times. For a genuine fly-drive package, contact agencies noted in Chapters Six, Seven and Eight from overseas to ensure that a vehicle and staff are awaiting you. **Left-hand-drive** cars made in Turkey are invariably cheaper to rent than rarer right-hand-drive vehicles; **rates** for a bottom-end Renault 12 start at about £10.50 per day plus £2 CDW in high summer; expect to pay 25 percent less out of season. Credit cards or foreign cash are preferred payment methods.

BRINGING YOUR OWN CAR

Like their owners, cars brought over on boats to either side of Cyprus are allowed to stay for three months, and may not move over the Attila/Green Line. In the event of any formal settlement between the Greek and Turkish zones, this will probably change, with all sorts of new regulations pertaining. In neither the southern Republic nor in the North are **Green Cards** of foreign insurance valid; you will be insured on the spot as you roll off the boat, for a fee roughly proportional to your intended length of stay; as an example, £7/$11 will get you two weeks of third-party cover in the North.

Mechanics in the South are largely geared to the Japanese models which have virtually captured the market there, but other European makes are represented. Try very hard not to have a breakdown in the North; owing to the small internal market and international boycott, it can take days if not weeks to find parts, either new or scoured from the limited number of junkyards.

CYCLES

In the coastal resorts of the South, you can hire small **mopeds** for about c£3 a day; few people will want to take them further than the beach, as you will get scant respect from four-wheeled motorists on curvy mountain roads. Rental motorbikes have yet to appear in the North.

By contrast, the uplands of either South or North are ideal for **mountain biking**. Both the Troödhos range and the Kyrenia hills are laced with a network of dirt forest tracks which would be extremely tedious for hiking but constitute a mountain-biker's dream. With planning or guidance (group bike tours are beginning to be advertised) you could cover either range from end to end in a matter of a few days. Mountain bikes are for sale in south Nicosia (see "Listings" for that city), and for hire in the main Troödhos resort of Plátres.

ACCOMMODATION

The majority of visitors to Cyprus arrive on some sort of package that includes accommodation. That's not to say that independent travel is impossible: most of the southern hotel listings in the Guide are for establishments which are more geared for walk-in trade, and not block-booked by foreign operators.

Despite the literally hundreds of thousands of beds, overbooking in the South has been a serious problem in recent summers. The limited number of pensions and rooms in private houses are mostly in the South, in the Troödhos or Páfos district, and often occupied by Cypriot holiday-makers.

Northern Cyprus, on the other hand, has scarcely fifty resort-standard hotels or self-catering places, rarely if ever full. Much of the tourist industry there is carried on in hotels abandoned by Greek Cypriots and let out on a concession basis by the government, and such establishments are often inefficiently run. Only recently have numbers of privately funded, purpose-built and professionally managed resorts sprung up. Our accommodations listings show a preference for these, and it is worth making an effort to book into them.

HOTELS, GUEST HOUSES AND PRIVATE ROOMS IN THE SOUTH

The CTO grades and oversees most accommodation outfits in the South, be they hotels of zero to five stars, guest houses or self-catering units. Their names, locations and current prices are shown in the *Guide to Hotels* issued yearly, but this can be hard to find, and does not distinguish between the relatively few establishments which welcome independent travellers and the vast majority of which are pitched at package bookings. Neither does it distinguish between those among the bottom-end listings which are geared for conventional tourist trade, and some which are a bit insalubrious.

HOTELS

All **hotels** of one star or over, and many of the unstarred ones, have en suite baths. Hotel rooms are most frequently offered on a bed-and-(continental) breakfast basis; charged separately, breakfast rarely exceeds c£1.50, but frankly if you're having to pay it's better to go out and find a full English breakfast somewhere for c£2–3.

Single occupancy **prices** tend to be well over half the double rate, and maximum rates must be posted either in the room itself or over the reception desk on a CTO-validated placard. Generally there won't be any fiddling in this regard, and except between June and August you may have some scope for bargaining, again stipulated by CTO rules. Travelling **independently** outside peak season, it's usually possible to find comfortable if modest hotel rooms vacant for less than c£19 double; if you insist on arriving in summer, then you're probably wisest to book in advance from Britain on a package basis.

GUEST HOUSES AND PRIVATE ROOMS

Guest houses, charging c£4–9 per person, are a feature of life in the centres of the larger Southern towns and certain Troödhos resorts. Some, as in Nicosia and Larnaca, are reasonably reputable; others (in Limassol especially) are pretty grim or dodgy in some respect. We've made distinctions clear in the town accounts.

The CTO disavows all knowledge of, or responsibility for, **rooms** in private rural houses, but they do exist in some numbers, particularly in the villages of Páfos district and the Troödhos foothills, both north and south slopes. The going rate currently is about c£5 per person, and this often includes some sort of breakfast. They can offer quite a good look at country domestic life, and are recommended at least once – particularly welcoming families may lay on an evening meal at little or no extra cost, feeding you far better than at the nearest tourist grill. If there are no advertising signs out, the best strategy is to contact the *múkhtar* (village headman) and have him arrange something.

THE NORTH: A NOTE

Choice is more limited in **Northern Cyprus**: the broad middle ground between luxury compounds and soldiers' dosshouses is thinly inhabited, making just showing up on the off-chance a risky endeavour. The North's tourism authority nominally exercises some control over hotel standards and prices, though in practice things tend to be a bit more free-wheeling – often to the advantage of the customer in the chronically undersubscribed establishments.

"APART-HOTELS", VILLAS AND LONGER STAYS

An increasing percentage of Cypriot accommodation, in both the South and the North, is **self-catering** in so-called tourist apartments or **"apart-hotels"**, or the more appealing semi-detached **villas**. In the Republic the best of these tends to be concentrated in Páfos district, with more scattered around Larnaca and Ayía Nápa; in Northern Cyprus it is almost exclusively in and around Kyrenia. The majority of villas have good amenities and are well maintained by Mediterranean standards, the odd water shortage or power cut aside. See *Packages* in "Getting There" for specialists offering something out of the ordinary.

If you intend to **stay longer** in the South it's worth scanning adverts in travel or estate agency windows and in the back pages of the *Cyprus Weekly*. Rents for one-bedroom furnished flats start at about c£150 a month; two-bedrooms fall in the c£200–250 range. In Northern Cyprus such lettings are done almost exclusively through agencies, with rents beginning to climb lately to near-South levels.

BUDGET OPTIONS: HOSTELS, MONASTERIES AND CAMPSITES

Neither the South or the North is on the backpackers' trail, and what few independent travellers they get tend to be impecunious former or future kibbutz workers awaiting the next boat to or from Israel. Yet a number of official YHA and private hostels are worth mentioning, plus (in the South) some attractive campsites.

HOSTELS

In the **South**, there are simple but clean **hostels** in Nicosia, Larnaca, Limassol, Páfos and on Mount Olympus in the Troödhos; a YHA card is generally not required, and bunk charges won't exceed c£3, plus another pound for sheets if needed. There is also the extremely popular forestry lodge at Stavrós tis Psókhas in the Tillyrian hills. Full details for all of these are given in the *Guide*.

In the **North**, just two privately run establishments, at Güzelyalı and Yeniboğaziçi, offer rooms on a dormitory basis for £5 a head. You'll also find a number of workmen's and soldiers' dosshouses in Kyrenia, Famagusta and (especially) Nicosia, but these are in general pretty unsavoury and only for desperate males. The Alevkaya (Halévga) forestry refuge in the Kyrenia hills, still shown on many maps, closed some years ago and is now a botanical museum and herbarium.

MONASTERIES

Because hospitality at the various **monasteries** of the South has been so abused in recent years, and the hotels which claimed to lose business so vociferous in their complaints, several large monasteries in the South are now extremely reluctant to give overnight shelter to the non-Orthodox. In any case they are prevented by law from doing so in summer; virtually the only exception is Stavrovoúni near Larnaca, but you had better display a sincere interest in Orthodox Christianity.

CAMPSITES

The South of the country has six official **campsites**, at Ayía Nápa, Larnaca, Troödhos, Governor's Beach (near Limassol), Yeroskípou (near Páfos) and Pólis; most of them open from March to October inclusive, with fees ranging from c£0.75 to c£1.50 daily per tent or caravan. In addition, the forestry department runs a score or so of more or less amenitied **picnic sites**, mostly in the Troödhos, where you could probably get away with a discrete overnight in a caravan – any more than that and the rangers would move you on.

The North can muster just two established campsites – one west of Kyrenia, the other near Salamis – and a bare handful of picnic areas, for example at ancient Salamis and in the Kyrenia hills.

EATING AND DRINKING

Food throughout Cyprus is generally hearty rather than refined, and on the tourist circuit at least can seem monotonous after a few days. In many respects resort food is the unfortunate offspring of generic Middle Eastern, and British, cooking at its least imaginative; the fried potato is the tyrant of the kitchen, resulting in a "chips with everything" style of cuisine. If all else fails you can seek solace in the excellent beer and wine of the South. Restaurant fare in the North is a bit lighter and more open to outside influences, especially mainland Turkish, but still heavily Anglicised.

All this is unfortunate, since once off the beaten track, or in a private home, meals are interesting and appetising, even if they'll never get three stars from Michelin. Less obvious, vegetable-based delights based on such home cooking are featured in the following food lists.

BREAKFAST

In the **South, breakfasts** offered through hotels tend to be minimum-effort continental, with tea/coffee and orange juice accompanying some miniature slices of white toast with pats of foil-wrapped butter, jam and (if you're lucky) a slice of processed cheese. If you crave more, you'll have to pay extra for bacon-and-eggs-type English breakfasts, either at the hotels or at special breakfast bars in town.

Northern Cyprus has embraced the mainland Turkish breakfast, which means untoasted bread,

beyaz peynir or white cheese, *kaşar* (kasseri) cheese, olives and either tea or coffee. In the better hotels, these will be presented as a buffet with cold meats and fresh fruit as well.

SNACKS

Cypriots are not as prone to eating on the hoof as Greeks or Turks. On both sides of the Line small British-style caffs sell sandwiches and drinks, but local solutions are less numerous.

Stuffed baked goods in the **South** include *eliópitta*, olive-turnover; *takhinópitta*, a pastry with sesame paste, or *kolokótes*, a triangular pastry stuffed with pumpkin, cracked wheat and raisins. *Aïráni* (*ayran* on the Turkish side) is a refreshing street-cart drink made of diluted yoghurt flavoured with dried mint or oregano and salt. *Soudzoúkou*, a confection of almonds strung together and then dipped like candle wicks in a vat of grape molasses and rosewater, are sold everywhere in the South for about c£4 a kilo and make an excellent food for the trail; so does *pastelláki*, a seasame, peanut and syrup bar costing about the same. Other less elaborate dried seeds and nuts are easily available in markets.

In the **North**, street stalls also offer *börek*, a rich, flaky layered pastry containing bits of round meat or cheese. You'll have to sit down in a *pideci* or "pizza parlour" for a *pide* or Turkish pizza; usual toppings are *peynirli* (with cheese), *yumurtalı* (with egg), *kıymalı* (with mince) or combinations of the above. Usually a small bowl of *çorba* (soup) is ordered with a *pide*.

FRUIT

In the South especially, Cypriot **fruit** has a well-deserved reputation. Because of the long growing season, varieties tend to appear well before their counterparts in Europe – for example strawberries in April, watermelons in June – and provide a refreshing snack in hot weather. Everything is grown locally in the South, since the government bans imported products – ostensibly to keep the island pest-free but also to protect the local farmers and specifically exclude sales from the North.

Froutaría is Greek for a roadside fruit-and-vegetable stall, *manav* the Turkish word. The central covered bazaars of all the major towns also usually have a good selection, though in the

North much comes from Turkey, since the orchard potential of the Kyrenia hills is limited.

Strawberries are seen principally in the South for a brief season. Medlars and loquats ripen in mid-spring; their large pips and papery husks may have you wondering why people bother until you taste them. Apricots are next up, followed by peaches, imported from Turkey into the North. Watermelons grown in Páfos district and around Nicosia are everywhere from June on, followed by dessert melons. Plums are also excellent in early summer; cherries, solely from the Troödhos villages of the South, are delicious in their several varieties.

Towards autumn prickly pear fruit constitutes an exotic challenge, tasting like watermelon once you penetrate its defences. Table grapes of marketable quality are confined to the South, an adjunct of the wine industry. Citrus, specifically oranges, mandarins and grapefruit, is ready in winter. Recently exotics such as bananas, guavas, kiwis and starfruit have also been introduced in the warmer corners of Páfos district, and avocados and mangos will probably soon follow.

FOOD SHOPPING

Shopping for yourself in the South, supermarkets and corner stores are laid out in the British fashion and easy to find your way around. Labelling is always in English as well as Greek. Local dairy products in all flavours and sizes are conspicuous, as are smoked breakfast and picnic meats; the best are listed overleaf. In the North things aren't so self-explanatory, nor abundant, but you certainly won't starve.

RESTAURANTS

It takes some diligence to avoid the bland, over-fried stodge dished out to undiscriminating tourists at most restaurants. Generally this means going upmarket, to (often) expat-run restaurants with more imaginative menus; to a remote village setting (in the South), especially to the *exokhiká kéndra* or country tavernas which cater to locals but only serve lunch except in summer; or to mid-town *ouzerís* (Gr) or *meyhanes* (Trk), where local delicacies are served to accompany drink. A watered-down, taverna version of this is the *mezé*, a succession of up to twenty small plates served in succession until you're sated. This is usually very good value, though in the South there is a minimum party of two, often four, persons.

As a rule main-dish portions are generous (if a bit too heavy on the chips), somewhat offsetting the apparent highness of the **prices**. Entrees cost between c£3 and c£5, with prices usually not including a ten-percent service charge and a three-percent levy which helps fund the activities of the CTO.

MEAT AND FISH

Meat dishes tend to predominate, both on and off resort menus. *Kleftikó* (Gr) or *küp kebap* (Trk) is arguably the national dish, a slab of lamb roasted with vegetables until tender in an outside oven – you see them next to virtually every farmhouse. Lamb chops – *païdhákia* (Gr) or *pırzola* (Trk) – are small by English or North American standards but tasty; *souvláki* or *şiş* is the generic term for any flesh arrayed in chunks on a skewer and grilled. The Venetians introduced pigeons to the island and they're much tastier than you'd imagine; quail is the gamier alternative, and both seem much more common than chicken. *Afélia* means pork chunks in coriander-seeded sauce and not surprisingly is found only in the non-Muslim Greek community; *sheftália/şeftalya* are small rissoles of mince, onion and spices wrapped in gut, found all over the island. *Moussakás/musaka*, aubergine and potato slabs overlaid with mince and white sauce in its truest form, is better on the Greek side; *karnıyarık* is a meatier Turkish eggplant dish without the potato or sauce.

Fish is not as plentiful as you'd think around the island, and not as cheap; the best places to get it are around Pólis in the South and on the Kırpaşa (Kárpas) peninsula in the North. *Marídhes*, the least expensive fish in the South, are traditionally sprinkled with lemon slices, rolled in salt and then eaten whole, head and all. Barracuda and *sokan* are best grilled, and either grouper or *lágos*, usually batter-fried, must be well done to be appetising. In North Cyprus, *sokan* and *barbun* are the two best-value species. Throughout the island squid and octopus are also standard budget seafood options.

VEGETARIAN FOOD

Vegetarians may have more limited options at times, especially in the South. *Meze*, fortunately, is largely meat-free, consisting principally of *húmmos/humus* (chickpea paté), *takhíni/tahın* (sesame puree) olives, fried *halloúmi/helim* cheese and other titbits. Salads are offered with all entrees, usually a seasonal medley of whatever's to hand: lettuce, tomatoes, parsley, cucumbers, cheese and onions (the latter served on a separate plate). Chefs who try harder may treat you with *rokka* greens (like baby mustard sprigs), coriander sprigs or purslane weed – this last much tastier than it sounds. Caper plants are served pickled whole, thorns and all. In the South, fava beans are pureed into *louvána* soup, not to be confused with *louviá* (black-eyed peas); *óspria* is the general term for any pulse dish. In winter especially *trakhanás/tarhana*, a soup of grain soaked in yoghurt, is prepared, though it is sometimes made with chicken stock. Healthier starch sources than the potato include *kolokássia* (Jeruslaem artichoke tubers) and *pourgoúri* (cracked or bulgur wheat).

DESSERTS AND SWEETS

Ice cream is everywhere, made by small local dairies, and far more prominent than the traditional Levantine sweets; Turkish- or Italian-style bulk-pack is invariably better than the pathetic imitation-British, Walls-truck packaging. Creme caramel and European-style pastries are also well represented. Among oriental **sticky cakes**, you'll most often find *baklavás* (Gr)/*baklava* (Trk), phyllo pastry layers alternating with honey and nuts; *galaktopoúreko/su böreği*, phyllo pastry filled with custard; and *kataïfi/kadayıf*, similar to *baklava* but in a "shredded wheat"-type winding. There are in addition a number of pancake-and-filled-crepe sweets which you are unlikely to encounter except in a village-festival setting. *Gliká*, preserved candied fruit (and vegetables) of assorted types, is another village specialty but one occasionally sold to outsiders.

DRINKING

Traditionally Cypriots drink only as accompaniment to food, and prefer nothing stronger than brandy or *raki*; inebriated north European louts staggering down the streets are apt to offend local sensibilities in either community.

WINE

Owing to near-ideal climate and soils, Cypriot experience in wine-making stretches far back in antiquity, and the tradition has been carried on with excellence – indeed **wine-drinking** is one of the highlights of a vacation here. The industry is based almost entirely in the South, and largely dominated by four vintner-owned co-operatives, KEO, ETKO, LOEL and SODAP, though there are a number of smaller enterprises.

A Cyprus Trade Centre booklet lists close on forty labels of wine, sherry and brandy, quite a total for a medium-sized island, with more being added slowly as the result of research and new varietal planting. You would have to be a pretty dedicated toper to get through all of them during a short stay, so the evaluations below should give you a head start.

Arsinoe is a very dry **white** offering from SODAP, while LOEL's *Palomino* is a dry white, smoky in colour and taste; both are available in small, tenth-of-a-gallon bottles. ETKO's *White Lady* is its contender in the dry-white market. *Bellapais* (KEO), a medium dry sparkling wine a bit like Portuguese *vinho verde*, comes in white and **rosé** versions. *Afrodhite* (KEO), an acceptable medium dry cheap white, or LOEL's *Saint Hilarion*, are about as sweet as you'd want to drink with food; *Saint Panteleimon* (KEO), essentially a dessert or mixer white, is too sugary for most tastes. *Soda* is the lingua franca for plain soda water – useful for making wine spritzers of those sweeter varieties.

KEO's *Rosella* is a very dry, dark **rosé**; the same company makes *Othello*, a full-bodied **red** not unlike a Cabernet Savignon. *Hermes* is for those liking a a rough, dry red. Every major vintner has a version of *Commandaria*, a red dessert wine related to Madeira, with an interesting pedigree going back at least ten centuries. After ageing in barrels, some residue is left in before filling the next batch, so theoretically every bottle contains a trace of that long-ago original vintage.

In the Troödhos foothill villages, it's worth asking for the local **bulk wine**, cheaper, often very good and sold in half- or full-litre measures. The Khrysorroyiatissa monastery bottles a reputedly excellent dry white, *Ayios Andronicos*, and a pale red, *Ayios Elias*. Each major vintner produces dry, medium and sweet cream **sherries**, most famous of these ETKO's *Emva* line.

BEER

KEO **beer** is a pleasant pilsener, in deceptively large 645-ml bottles; you'll drink it all easily, as it's a bit watery. *Carlsberg* is the "other" beer. In North Cyprus, your choices are the Turkish mainland *Efes* label or *Gold Fassl*, an Austrian lager made locally under licence.

A GLOSSARY OF FOOD TERMS

In the following lists, the Greek term precedes the Turkish, finally the English. If there is no Greek or Turkish equivalent, a dash is shown.

Basics

neró/su	water	piláfi /pilav	cooked rice	méli /bal	honey
eliés/zeytin	olives	pourgoúri /bulgur	cracked wheat	voútiro/	butter
pítta/pita	flat Arab bread	yiaoúrti /yoğurt	yogurt	tereyağ	
psomí/ekmek	bread	gála/süt	milk		

Appetisers (Mezé) and Picnic Items

talatoúra/cacık	yogurt, cucumber and herb dip	halloúmi /hellim	minty ewe's cheese, often fried
taramás /tarama	pink fish roe paté	anári/lor	soft, crumbly sweet cheese, byproduct of above
húmmos/humus	chickpea mash		
takhíni /tahın	sesame seed paste		
loúntza/–	smoked pork loin slabs	fétta/beyaz peynir	white goat's- or ewe's-cheese
hirómeri/–	cured local ham	kasséri/kaşar	kasseri cheese
tsamerélla/–	goat-based salami		

Meat and Game Entrees

kleftikó/küp kebap	lamb baked in an outdoor oven	glikádhia/–	sweetbreads
		zalatína/–	brawn
souvláki/şişkebap	meat chunks grilled on a skewer	kotópoulo/piliç	chicken
		peristéri/güverçin	pigeon
rífi/–	whole lamb on a spit	kounélli/tavşan	rabbit
sheftália/şeftalya	grilled mince-and-onion pellets in gut casings	ortíkia/bıldıırçìn	quail
		ambellopoúlia/–	pickled songbirds trapped in snares
keftédhes/köfte	meatballs		
pastirmás /pastırma	greasy sausage or cured dry meat	karakóles/salyangoz	snails

Typical Dishes

távas/tava	sweetish stew with onions	–/karnıyarık	similar to above but no sauce or potato
moussakás/musaka	aubergine and potato slabs overlaid with mince and white sauce	koupépia/yaprak dolmasıı	vine leaves filled with rice
		bourékia/börek	turnovers filled with meat or cream cheese

Preparation Terms

tis óras, sta kárvouna/komurde, ızgarada	grilled
tiganit(ó)(á)(és)/yağda	fried
stifádho/yahni	stewed in a sweet onion sauce
parayemist(á)(és)/dolması	stuffed
plakí /pılakı	vinaigrette, marinated

Fish and Seafood

péstrofa/–	trout (farmed)	fangrí/mercan	common bream
parpoúni/tekir	big red mullet	spáros/karagöz	two-banded or ringed bream
koutsomoúra /barbun	small red mullet		
sorkós/sargoz	bream	skathári/sarıgöz	black bream
marídhes/–	whitebait	tsípoura /çipura	gilt-head bream
gópes/kupes	bogue	sinagrídha/sinagrit	dentex
parakoúdha/–	barracuda	hános/asil hanı	comber
lagós/lagos	a rich cod-like fish	smérna/merina	moray eel
rófos/orfoz	grouper, rather boney	garídhes/karides	small prawns
–/sokan	cheapish medium size fish	khtapódhi /ahtapod	octopus
		kalamarákia/kalamar	small squid

Vegetables

saláta/salata	any salad	kapária/gebre	pickled caper plants
maroúli/marul	lettuce	angináres/enginar	artichokes
rókka/rokka	salad greens	spanáki/ispanak	spinach
koliándhros/–	coriander	patátes/patates	potatoes
maídhanós/maydanos	parsley	kolokássia/yer elması	Jerusalem artichokes
glistirídha/semiz otu	purslane	kolokithákia/kabak	courgettes
lákhano/lahana	cabbage	bámies/bamya	okra
domátes/domates	tomatoes	bezélia/bezelye	peas
kremídhi/soğan	onion	fasólia/fasulye	beans
skórdho/sarmısak	garlic	koukiá/bakla	broad beans
repánia/turp	radish	kounoupídhi/karnabahar	cauliflower
(kafteró) pipéri/ (acı) biber	(hot) pepper	louviá/burulce	black-eyed peas
manitária/mantar	mushrooms	óspria/–	generic for any pulse

Soups

avgolémono/düğün	egg-lemon	patsás/iskembe	tripe
trakhanás/tarhana	grain, yogurt, spices		

Nutty Snacks

soudzoúkou/–	almond string dipped in rosewater and grape molasses	pastelláki/–	sesame, peanut and syrup bar
		halepianá/şam fıstığı	pistachios
fistíkia /fıstık	peanuts	amígdhala/badem	almonds

Fruit

fráoules /çilek	strawberries	síka/incir	figs
moúsmoule/muşmula	medlars	stafília/üzüm	grapes
méspila/yeni dunya	loquats	míla/elma	apples
kaïsha, khrisómila/kayısı	apricots	akhládhia/armut	pears
rodhákina/şeftali	peaches	portokália/portakal	oranges
karpoúzi/karpuz	watermelon	lemónia/limon	lemons
pepóni /kavun	dessert melon	mandarínia/mandalin	mandarins
paraméles/erik	plums	gréypfrout/grepfrut	grapefruit
kerásia/kiraz	cherries	banánes/muz	banana
papoutsósiko/frenk inciri	prickly pear		

Desserts and Sweets

pagotó/dondurma	ice cream	*muhallebí /mahallebi*	rice-flour and rosewater pudding
baklavás/baklava	phyllo pastry layers with nut-honey filling	*gliká/reçel*	preserved candied fruit
kataïfi/kadayı\f	same as above but with "shredded wheat" instead of pastry sheets	Types of *gliká* in the South include:	
		víssino	sour morello cherry
loukoumádhes/lokma	deep-fried batter rings	*kerási*	Queen Anne-type cherry
halvás/helva	grainy paste of semolina or tahini	*petrokéraso*	dark red cherry
		kitrómilo	Seville orange
krem karamel/krem karamel	creme caramel	*vazanáki*	baby aubergines
		síko	fig

Drinks

aïráni/ayran	diluted yoghurt with herbs	*glikós/şekerli*	cloying
		tsaï/çay	tea
himós/meyva suyu	fruit juice	*bíra/bira*	beer
kafés/kahve	Oriental coffee, served:	*krasí/şarap*	wine
		áspro/beyaz	white
pikrós/sade	unsweetened	*mávro/kırmızı*	red
métrios/orta	medium sweet	*kokkinélli/roze*	rosé

SPIRITS

Stronger local **firewater** includes *zivánia*, nearly pure grape alcohol produced greatly in excess of local requirements. Some is flavoured with botanical agents for home use; the rest is sold to the southern government or exported to fortify weak drink as far away as Russia. KEO also makes a range of **hard liquor**, though imported booze is easily available. As for **brandy**, KEO *Five Kings* is fine, though locals prefer both sides of the Line to tipple the *Hadjipavlu Anglias*, smuggled into the North. "Brandy sour", brandy spiked with lime or lemon juice and bitters, is effectively the national aperitif and beloved of holiday-makers.

WINES AND SPIRITS IN THE NORTH

In **North Cyprus**, one lonely distillery near Famagusta makes *raki* – an aperitif similar to *ouzo* – and a decent brandy, but *Aphrodite*, the single red/white wine from straggly grapes in the Kyrenia hills and the Karpas, is laughable. Most wine at restaurants in North Cyprus is imported from Turkey; *Kavaklıdere* and *Doluca* are two names worth ordering.

TEA, COFFEE AND JUICES

Tea in both communities comes in somewhat expensive packs of bags, though in the North Anatolian settlers have introduced, in the villages at least, the practice of brewing loose tea in a double-boiler apparatus known as a *çaydanlık*. *Rombouts* instant **coffee** may be preferable to *Nescafé*. Traditional Middle Eastern coffee, fine-ground, boiled without filtration and served in demitasses, comes in three grades: plain, medium sweet, and cloying. **Juices** throughout the island come in a rainbow of flavours and are excellent, available at markets in either litre cartons or bottles. Fresh citrus juice goes briskly at most resort bars.

COMMUNICATIONS: POST AND PHONES

Both the postal and phone systems of post-independence Cyprus were modelled on those of Britain, but since the events of 1974 these facilities have diverged somewhat in North and South. Both offer fairly reliable services, though outgoing mail is invariably quicker than incoming.

POST

Post offices in the **South** are generally open Monday to Friday 7.30am to 1pm (1.30pm in the cooler months), with a limited number of branches in the four largest towns keeping additional afternoon hours (4–6pm summer, 3.30–5.30pm winter). **Outgoing mail** is reliable though not especially cheap at c£0.31 for a 20-gramme letter to the UK, c£0.21 for a postcard, c£0.36 and c£0.26 respectively to North America. Stamps can also be purchased from newsagents, but they may not know the exact rates for your destination. Numbers of quaint colonial **pillar-boxes** survive, the royal monograms "GR" and "ER" still visible

SENDING MAIL TO NORTH CYPRUS

Because of the international postal union boycott of North Cyprus, both incoming and outgoing mail is initially routed through Turkey. When writing to anyone in North Cyprus, you must add a special code – **Mersin 10, Turkey** – to the last line of the address. If you fail to do so, the letter may be misdirected to the South or more likely to the "addressee unknown" bin.

through coats of fresh yellow paint. The same central post offices which have afternoon services also have **poste restante** and **parcel** facilities; these city-centre branches are listed in the *Guide*.

In **Northern Cyprus**, post offices are open 7.30am to 2pm and 4pm to 6pm Monday to Friday, 9am to noon Saturday. **Outgoing mail** is tolerably quick, considering that it has to be shuffled through Turkey to get around the international postal union boycott; despite this North Cyprus issues its own stamps, with a postcard rate to the UK of about 15p, 20p for a letter. As in the South, look for kerbside pillar-boxes, now a distinctly faded yellow. Parcels are best sent from Nicosia. **Poste restante** service is theoretically available in the three or four largest towns.

PHONES

Cyprus has fair-to-good phone service, though call boxes are fewer than in the UK or North America throughout the island, verging to nonexistentence in the North. Southern services are modelled on UK prototypes; that in the North (not surprisingly) is an extension of the mainland Turkish system.

THE SOUTH

Phones in the **Republic of Cyprus** are administered by the Cyprus Telecommunications Authority, CYTA for short. Town- and village-centre **call boxes**, while not as common as they should be, usually work, and take either coins or telecards (see below). The **coin-operated** variety accepts 2-cent coins as a minimum, but these won't get you far (and you rarely receive them as change), so in effect 5-, 10- and 20-cent coins are the norm for local and trunk calls respectively.

For **overseas calls**, a better bet are **telecard-phones**; you can purchase c£2-, c£5- and c£10-value telecards from CYTA offices, certain banks, post offices, corner kiosks and wherever you see the telecard logo displayed. The c£10 cards permit about twenty minutes of chat to the UK, less than half that to North America. All call booths should have detailed calling instructions in English, but if not, to phone overseas from Cyprus, dial 00 – waiting for changes in tone – and then the country code (posted in all booths), national code and subscriber number. The quality of connections is usually very good. There are automatic direct-dial connections with virtually everywhere except North Cyprus and Turkey – with whom the Republic is still technically in a state of belligerence and mutual non-recognition (though curiously you *can* phone the South automatically *from* Turkey).

All phones have six-digit numbers and two-digit area codes, the first digit of which is always zero. Dialing the Republic of Cyprus from overseas, the country **code** is 357, followed by the area code minus its initial zero.

Cheaper than hotel phones and quieter than call boxes for international calls are the limited number of **CYTA walk-in stations**; these are found only in Nicosia, Larnaca, Limassol, Páfos and Pedhoulás (Troödhos) and open up to twelve hours a day. Here you pay after completing your call from special booths, without the threat of cut-off from exhaustion of coins or card.

THE NORTH

Phones in the **Turkish Republic of Northern Cyprus** are handled by the *Telekomünikasyon Dairesi* or Telecom Division. The pre-1974 network (though not numbers) has been completely replaced by an imported Turkish system, which features orange **call boxes** that use tokens or **jetons**. These come in three sizes – small, medium and large – and you need stacks of the largest ones to make an international call. In any case, call boxes are exceedingly rare and seem to be following their 1960s predecessors into dereliction and disconnection; when you do find a working one it invariably has a long queue.

Nor will you get much joy from the bare handful of **Telekomünikasyon offices** themselves, whose booths and tills work much shorter hours than their counterparts in the South. When they are shut you can sometimes buy *jetons* from the post office; there are no cardphones in the North, despite the theoretical acceptability of mainland Turkish telecards.

All in all, it's best to place any calls from your **hotel room**; the modest surcharge is more than worth the extra convenience and privacy, and frequently the front desk forgets to charge you in the end. Once clear of the hotel circuitry, dial 00 to get an international line, followed by the usual repertoire of country and area codes. Overseas connections are satisfactory, though parties in North Cyprus often sound like they're talking underwater. Contrary to prevailing propaganda, it is possible – just – to make operator-assisted calls to the South, though this will involve at least three operators (including UN personnel), takes nearly an hour, and hence requires a very good reason for doing so.

Northern Cyprus has retained the pre-1974 **number scheme** of three-digit area codes and five-digit subscriber numbers. Calling in from overseas, you must make a special manoeuvre which reflects the fact that, as with the post, Turkey "fronts" for the phone system here. The access **code** for the North is 905, the "90" being Turkey and the "5" analogous to the "Mersin 10" postal dodge. That "5" replaces the initial zero of the area code used when phoning within North Cyprus: thus to reach Girne (whose local code is ☎081) from London, dial ☎905 81 instead. Ringing from Turkey, simply dial ☎581, and then the subscriber number.

THE MEDIA

For a modest-sized island, Cyprus is served by a disproportionately large number of printed publications and TV or radio channels. Part of this is a result of non-market factors, such as sponsorship of print media by political groups on both sides of the Line, and also to its critical position in the east Mediterranean, enabling the island to both tap and beam to neighbouring countries.

NEWSPAPERS AND MAGAZINES

While the vernacular-language print media will be inaccessible to most visitors, there are a number of worthwhile and informative, locally produced English-language publications aimed primarily at ex-pats. A very few foreign newspapers are available – at a price.

THE SOUTH

Nearly a dozen Greek-language newspapers, many toeing a particular party line, cater to native readers in the **South**. Among English-language papers, the *Cyprus Weekly* (c£0.30, Fridays) is a bit more professionally put together than the daily *Cyprus Mail* (also c£0.30). Besides news, both have analysis, extensive small ads and daily/weekly programmes for most radio and TV stations. The *Mail* features brief "what's on" sections for movies and exhibits, and chemist rotas; chemist and Sunday petrol station schedules also appear in the *Weekly*, along with a more extensive, pull-out what's-on section called "Leisure". **Foreign newspapers** are pricey: c£1 for the *International Herald Tribune* and c£0.90 for *The Independent.* In 1991 a glossy, full-page-format, English-language **magazine**, *Cyprus View*, began appearing bi-monthly for c£1.50, worth a glance for its features if it's still around.

THE NORTH

You'll see only the very occasional *Financial Times* in the **North**, plus the weekly *Cyprus Today* (Saturday, 33p) in English; this has radio and TV listings, plus the rota of late night chemists and complete Ercan airport flight info. There are also a half-dozen Turkish-language papers, nearly all affiliated with a political party, and

several, like *Cyprus Today*, owned by the embattled Asil Nadir.

RADIO, TV AND CINEMA

The advantages of having your own electronic media for propaganda purposes are not lost on either of Cyprus's two main communities, so that there's an ongoing "battle of the transmitters" . However, TV is only broadcast for a few hours per day – the result of meagre advertising revenues and a limited audience.

RADIO

On the **radio**, the *Cyprus Broadcasting Corporation's* (*CyBC*) strictly Greek Programme I can be found at 96.4 FM, 6am to midnight. *CyBC's* Programme II, at 91.1 FM and 92.4 FM during the same time slot, has a more cosmopolitan lineup with programmes in Turkish, English (including news at 10am, 2pm and 8pm), Arabic and Armenian. The *BBC World Service* broadcasts at 1320 AM from 6am to 2.30am except from 10.30 to noon when it goes to 639 AM; reception is very strong, since the transmitter for the whole Middle East sits on the coast between Larnaca and Limassol. The British Sovereign Bases operate the *British Forces Broadcasting Service* (*BFBS*), in English with western programming, on Programme 1 (24hrs) at 92.1 and 99.6 FM and Programme 2 (6am to 1am) at 89.9 and 95.3 FM. Skipping along the dial you'll also find several private, local stations.

TV

CyBC 1 and 2 beam **TV** from the South daily only from about 5pm to midnight, owing to the small internal market; the programming is a lively mix of soaps, films, music, talk-shows and documentaries. There's a lot of foreign material in the original soundtrack, and even the Greek transmissions have English and Turkish subtitles. Otherwise people tune in to the Greek *ET1* from Rhodes, or independent stations *Logos* (7pm to midnight, less on weekends), *Star Plus* or the mildly evangelical *Middle East Television* from southern Lebanon.

In the **North**, the official *Bayrak Radyo* functions most of the afternoon and early evening; *Bayrak Televizyon* broadcasts Monday to Friday from 6.30pm to about 10.30pm, with English news at opening time. Otherwise people make do with *TRT* from Turkey.

CINEMA

In terms of **cinema**, there are just three regularly functioning movie-houses in south Nicosia, two in Limassol, and one in Larnaca; the British, French and Russian cultural centres in south Nicosia (see p.173) also screen their share of films. Fare at the commercial cinemas tends to be first-run but somewhat gormless caper/action

releases, while the cultural centres predictably feature more art films and retrospective series. Prints are generally in the original language, with Greek subtitles. Screening times are not shown in the foreign-language press, so you must phone or walk by the cinema for details.

At the moment no international-standard cinemas operate in the **North** – only impromptu affairs screening imported Turkish-language films, largely for the benefit of Anatolian conscripts.

OPENING HOURS, HOLIDAYS AND FESTIVALS

Business hours throughout the island are scheduled around the typical Mediterranean mid-day siesta. Generally the South's public holidays have a religious focus, reflecting the Greek Orthodox Church's pre-eminent position in the culture, while the North – technically a secular society – has more commemorations of salient events in Turkish communal history. In recent years many special events have been developed by the southern tourism authorities, with a view to a foreign audience, to supplement the bedrock of traditional religious festivals.

OPENING HOURS

Town shops in the **South** are meant to be open daily in summer 8am to 1pm and again from 4 to 7pm, except for Wednesday and Saturday when there are no afternoon hours. Summer is

construed as 1 May to 30 September. Winter hours are 8am to 1pm and again from 2.30 to 5.30pm, with the same Wednesday and Saturday afternoon closures. Both mountain village stores and establishments in tourist resorts are likely to keep longer hours.

In the **North**, summer hours are supposedly 7.30am to 1.30pm and 4 to 6pm Monday to Friday, with a morning session only on Saturday. In winter shops are meant to be open 8am to 5.30pm Monday to Saturday. Observance of schedules may be haphazard, with 2 to 3.30pm apparently a common period of summer closure.

PUBLIC HOLIDAYS IN THE SOUTH

In the South, there is near-complete overlap between religious and bank **holidays**, so of the following dates official business is only conducted (after a fashion) on *Kataklismós*. Whenever most of these dates fall on a Sunday, the subsequent Monday is also a public holiday.

RELIGIOUS HOLIDAYS IN THE SOUTH

New Year's Day in Cyprus is the feast day of **Áyios Vasílios** (Saint Basil), and the evening before, most homes bake a *vasilópitta* or cake containing a coin bringing good luck to the one finding it in their slice. The saint is also the Cypriot equivalent of Santa Claus, and gifts are exchanged today, not at Christmas.

Epiphany marks the baptism of Christ in the Jordan, and the conjunction of the Holy Trinity; the Greek name *Fóta* or "Lights" refers to the resulting inner illumination. Holy water founts in churches are blessed to banish the *kalikándzari*

UPCOMING HOLIDAYS IN SOUTH CYPRUS

1993	1994	1995	
1 January	same	same	Áyios Vasílios (New Year's Day)
6 January	same	same	*Fóta* (Epiphany)
1 March	14 March	6 March	Green (Lent) Monday
25 March	same	same	Annunciation of the Virgin
1 April	same	same	Southern Republic Day
16 April	29 April	21 April	Orthodox Good Friday
18 April	1 May	23 April	Orthodox Easter Sunday
1 May	same	same	Labour Day
7 June	20 June	12 June	*Kataklismós* (Flood Feast)
15 August	same	same	Dormition of the Virgin
1 October	same	same	Cyprus Independence Day
28 October	same	same	Greek National Day
25–26 December	same	same	Christmas/Boxing Day

demons said to run amok on earth since Christmas. As a finale at seaside locations, a local bishop hurls a crucifix out over the water, and young men swim for the honour of recovering it.

Green Monday comes at the end of the ten days of **Carnival**, the occasion for fancy-dress balls and parades, most notably at Limassol. In rural areas the day also signals the beginning of a strict meatless fast of seven weeks for the devout. March 25 is usually billed as "Greek National Day", but is more properly the feast of *Evangelismós* or the **Annunciation**.

Observance of **Easter** starts early in **Holy Week**, and the island's small Catholic community celebrates in tandem with the Orthodox majority. The most conspicuous customs are the dyeing red of hard-boiled eggs on Maundy Thursday, the baking of special holiday cakes such as *flaoúnes*, and on Good Friday the solemn procession of the *Epitáfios* or Christ's funeral bier in each parish, whose women provide its elaborate floral decoration. On Saturday afternoon Judas Iscariot is often bonfire-burned in effigy, before the moving and spectacular midnight *Anástasi* or Resurrection mass.

At the crucial moment the officiating priest appears from behind the altar screen bearing a lighted candle and the news of eternal life for believers, and soon church interiors and courtyards are ablaze with the flame passed from worshipper to worshipper. It is considered good luck to get your candle home still alight, to trace a soot-cross over the door lintel; then the Lenten fast is broken with a special soup, and family members crack their dyed eggs against each other (owner of the last unbroken egg "wins").

Kataklismós or the **Festival of the Flood**, seven weeks after Easter, is unique to Cyprus; elswhere in the Orthodox world it is merely Pentecost or the Feast of the Holy Spirit, but here it's a pretext for a week or so of popular events. At all coastal towns people crowd into the sea and sprinkle each other with water; the festival ostensibly commemorates the salvation of Noah and his family from the Flood, but it's likely a vestige of a much older pagan rite in honour of Aphrodite's birth, or perhaps her purification after lying with Adonis.

Christmas (*Khristoúyenna*) is relatively subdued in Cyprus, though inevitably European-style commercialisation has made inroads. The most durable old custom is that of the *kálanda* or carols, sung by children going door-to-door accompanying themselves on a triangle.

OTHER EVENTS

In addition to the strictly ecclesiastical holidays, municipalities and tourist boards lay on a number of other events, with a steady eye on the foreign audience. The most reliable of these include the May *Anthistíria* or **Flower Festivals**, best in mid-May at Páfos; the Limassol and Larnaca municipal festivals in July; the **Limassol Wine Festival,** with free tasting sessions in the central park, in September; the **Páfos festival** during the same month; and a **handicraft festival** in Nicosia the latter half of September. If you're determined to coincide with any or all of these, get a copy of the CTO's annual "Diary of Events" or the monthly cyclostyled update produced at each local tourist office.

1993	1994	1995	
1 January	same	same	New Years Day (*Yilbaşı*)
24–26 March	13–15 March	2–4 March	Şeker Bayramı
23 April	same	same	Turkish National Sovereignty and Children's Day
1 May	same	same	Labour Day
19 May	19 May	19 May	Youth and Sports Day
1–4 June	21–24 May	10–13 May	*Kurban Bayramı*
20 July	same	same	Peace Operation Day
1 August	same	same	TMT Day
30 August	same	same	*Zafer Bayramı* (Victory Day)
8 September	28 August	17 August	Mevlûd (Muhammad's Birthday)
29 October	same	same	Turkish Republic Day
15 November	same	same	TRNC Foundation Day

PUBLIC HOLIDAYS IN THE NORTH

In the **North**, the holiday calendar is again a mix of religious holidays – all receding eleven days yearly because of the lunar Muslim calendar – and official commemorations, many imported from Turkey. Unlike in the South, there's just not the budget or inclination for laying on big theme bashes. The most extravagant are occasional folk-loric performances at the castles of Famagusta and Kyrenia, and unpredictably dated harvest festivals on the Mesarya (Mesaoría) for the cherished orange, strawberry and watermelon crops.

The official holidays of the North are fairly self-explanatory, though a word on the moveable religious feasts is in order. *Şeker Bayramı* marks the end of the fasting month of Ramazan, and is celebrated with family get-togethers and the distribution of presents and sweets to children. *Kurban* commemorates the thwarted sacrifice of Ishmael by Abraham – a Koranic version of the Abraham-Isaac story – and used to be distinguished by the dispatch and roasting of vast numbers of sheep; the custom is now on the wane in Cyprus.

SITES, MUSEUMS, CHURCHES, MOSQUES

Archaeological sites and museums throughout the island have user-friendly opening times, though you may find many Northern museums and monuments shut for restoration. Admission fees are modest, especially compared to neighbouring countries, and in the South at least polite signs instructing you to "Please ask for your ticket" are a far cry from the growling human Cerberus blocking the way in Greece or Egypt. Churches and mosques of interest to visitors have less established visiting hours and operate on a "donation" basis.

OPENING TIMES AND ADMISSION FEES

The more popular ancient sites in the **South** are fenced but accessible from roughly 7.30am to near sunset all year, though even at the longest

days they're rarely open past 7.30pm. Most museums shut for lunch between 1 and 3 or 4pm, with finally evening closure usually at 6pm, never later than 7pm. On public holidays (see previous section) most outdoor sites are unaffected, but many museums keep short – or no – hours, and everything shuts on Easter Sunday. Exact details for each establishment are given in the text of the Guide. No entrance fee exceeds c£1, and most are currently c£0.50.

Operating hours at the limited number of museums and sites in **Northern Cyprus** are vaguely similar; admission fees cost 40p–£1, depending on the attraction.

CHURCHES

Most of the famous **frescoed churches** of the South are still used in some sacred capacity, and

CHURCHES IN THE NORTH

Since the events of 1974 only a bare handful of **churches in the North** (detailed in the *Guide*) continue to function as houses of Christian worship. The rest have been either converted into mosques or museums, or desecrated in various ways, mostly by the Turkish army but occasionally by Anatolian settlers or Turkish Cypriots.

This behaviour is naturally seized on by the outraged Greek Cypriots as further proof of (mainland) Turkish barbarism, and used to good effect in their sophisticated "public relations" efforts – one particularly graphic publication is entitled *Flagellum Dei* (The Scourge of God), referring to Attila the Hun, lately re-incarnated in the Greeks' view. The Southern government pointedly contrasts the treatment of these buildings with the relative consideration accorded to mosques in the South, which are held in trust by

a Religious Affairs Department, provided with a tiny budget to maintain the buildings.

For their part, the Northerners either tend not even to acknowledge that an injury has been done, or justify it as the understandable venting of frustrations and aggressions on the most tangible, helpless reminders of the atrocities perpetrated on the Turkish Cypriots by EOKA. What this means to a visitor is the Northerners are touchy about requests to visit churches not specifically prepared for public use. You will often find abandoned churches off-limits as military depots, and/or appallingly vandalised, sometimes with their entrances bricked up to prevent further damage. In any case it's a depressing exercise visiting these battered buildings, empty of the devotion which the Greek Cypriots lavished on them, and something most people will only do once or twice.

kept locked to protect them from thieves and the elements; accordingly they often don't have set visiting hours. Part of the experience is locating the key-keeper, not always a priest, who may live or work some distance away. A donation to the collection box, if not the person himself, is required; complete instructions are given for each monument described in Chapter Four, *The Troödhos*. Since all but a few churches are still consecrated, men may not usually enter in shorts, nor women in pants of any sort, and neither sex in sleeveless tops – wraps are not provided, so bring suitable garb. Photos, especially with flash, are simply not allowed.

MOSQUES

Most **mosques** in the South are now kept locked, presumably awaiting the hypothetical return of their Turkish-Cypriot users; one apiece

still functions in south Nicosia, Limassol and Larnaca, meeting the needs of the Republic's sizeable population of Arabs and Iranians. The *tekke* of Hala Sultan near Larnaca is also still an active place of pilgrimage as well as a tourist attraction.

Some rules of **etiquette** apply to any mosque throughout the island. Contrary to what you may read in other sources, shoes must be removed at the entrance, and one does not enter scantily clad – this in effect means the same guidelines as for churches, above. Native Cypriot Muslims are remarkably easy-going (eg their tolerant attitudes towards drinking and dogs) and flattered at any attention to their places of worship, so you would have to do something fairly insensitive to irk them. As a minimum, don't enter mosques when a service is in progress, and try not to walk in front of a praying person.

POLICE, TROUBLE AND HARASSMENT

In general, Cyprus has to be one of the safest Mediterranean travel destinations: assault and burglary are almost unknown, and what little crime there is tends to be overwhelmingly of the fraud-and-smuggling variety. The atmosphere is so unthreatening, in fact, that you catch yourself feeling silly for locking a hire car.

Authorities and police in both communities go out of their way to make tourists, so vital to the island economy, feel welcome, and the most likely occasion for misunderstandings will be the various military zones – far more numerous in the North than in the South.

Do heed the **"no photography"** signs near military bases throughout the island, as well as along the Attila Line (the Green Line in Nicosia). If you are caught photographing, even inadvertently, a military installation anywhere in Cyprus, your film will probably be confiscated – politely, and possibly returned after processing and screening, in the South; more brusquely by the Turkish Army in the North. In the southern Republic some or all of certain monasteries are

off-limits to cameras, since the monks grew tired of being zoo-animal-type attractions. Similarly, don't sneak snaps of the interiors of the South's frescoed churches – caretakers accompany you inside to prevent this, among other reasons.

Casual visitors are unlikely to see much evidence of the more unsavoury types of smuggling; a certain amount of **drugs** passes through both sides of the island, brought on by plane or ship and apparently in transit for elsewhere. It makes an unwise souvenir purchase, to put it mildly.

If you have anything **stolen**, go to the nearest police station, report the theft and get a copy of the report or the identification number under which your report is filed: you will need this if you intend to make an insurance claim once you get back home (see "Health and Insurance").

SEXUAL HARASSMENT

Both Greek and Turkish Cypriot men are more reserved than their mainland counterparts, though as throughout the Mediterranean, resort areas support numbers of underemployed Romeos. Limited instances of north European women arriving specifically to look for adventure fuel the myth of the "easy", available blond Nordic type and do not make life simpler for foreign women uninterested in such attention. Told to desist in no uncertain terms, the lechers usually will. In the more traditional inland areas, unescorted women will generally be accorded village courtesy.

Foreign men who stumble on the **red-light districts** of Limassol and Nicosia in the South will probably find the invitations from open doorways and bar-fronts more ridiculous than threatening; unaccompanied foreign women should avoid these areas.

SPORTS AND OUTDOOR ACTIVITIES

Because of its mild climate, Cyprus is a good place to indulge in assorted open-air athletic activities. The CTO even devotes an entire six-page, large-format leaflet to the subject, detailing indoor facilities as well sport. In terms of spectating, football and tennis – for which the South hosts several major international tournaments yearly – are the big events.

WATER SPORTS

Virtually all resorts in the South cater well to any water sport you could mention, from kayaking to para-sailing by way of water-skiing. **Windsurfers** are available everywhere, but you only get strong breezes around the island's capes: in the far southeast, between Ayía Nápa and Protarás; around Páfos; and occasionally on the exposed coast west of Pólis. Small sailcraft can be hired from the marinas at Larnaca, Limassol and Páfos; at Kyrenia in the North thus far there are just small motor boats for hire.

Perhaps the biggest attraction is underwater; unusually for the east Mediterranean where submerged antiquities are theft-prone, **scuba** is actively promoted by numerous dive operators, and it's worth taking advantage.

In **North Cyprus** windsurfing and sailing facilities concentrate west of Kyrenia, and at the luxury hotels near ancient Salamis.

ON LAND

Cypriots are big **tennis** buffs, participatory as well as watching, and most hotels over three stars in either the North or the South will have their own courts. Otherwise, courts are open to the public in all the big southern towns. When not being used by local teams, it may be possible to practise or have friendly matches at town running **tracks and stadiums**.

Mountain-biking has already been noted as a possibility in "Getting Around", but there are some bona fide marked trails – as opposed to tracks – in the southern hills, prepared expressly for **hiking** by the CTO in conjunction with the forestry division. The *Guide* covers all of them, though the longest itinerary will fill just a single day; there are as yet no long-distance routes the length of the Troödhos. It's more difficult, but still possible, to walk in the steeper Kyrenia hills as long as you steer clear of military areas.

Southern Cyprus can boast the exotic attraction, for the Middle East, of a **ski** resort. There's a single complex of three lifts on the northeast face of Mount Olympus, the island's summit. The season lasts approximately from January to early April; don't come specially.

For some arcane reason the Turkish Cypriots are very keen on **tae kwan do**, and despite the North's recognition problems, international competitions have been held there.

SHOPPING

Cyprus, North or South, is not a souvenir hunter's paradise, but while you're travelling around there are certain items worth looking out for. See also the note on Bargaining in the "Directory", following.

THE SOUTH

The South is most famous for **lacework**, produced principally at Páno Léfkara, equidistant from the three largest towns, and at Fíti in Páfos district, where coloured, **loom-woven** items are also available. Reed **basketry** is another distinctive product, especially in Páfos district; of particular interest are the almost Amerindian-looking, bi- or tri-colour circular **mats** (called *tsétsos* in Greek); they adorn the walls of many tavernas and could make excellent trivets. You can find them at the central covered markets of Páfos, Limassol and Larnaca, among other spots.

Another taverna-decor staple which can still be purchased are *kolókia* or **etched gourds**, embossed with designs either painted or burned on.

More urban specialties include **shoes**, **silver jewellery** and **optical goods**. High-quality sunglasses at the numerous opticians cost about the same (less VAT) as in North America, owing to direct importation, and thus much less than in Britain. The much-vaunted stock of contact lenses seems limited to Bausch and Lomb products.

THE NORTH

There is rather less on offer in the **North**, though the basketry products seem more refined, and comparatively expensive; you can find very strong, large **baskets** suitable for clothes hampers in north Nicosia, especially inside the covered market. Junk and antique dealers in Nicosia and Famagusta have a limited and expensive stock of **old copper** and **household implements**.

Otherwise you are faced with the task of sifting through a fair amount of second-rate kitsch (garish backgammon sets, thin-gauge copper lanterns, onyx eggs, ceramic ashtrays), offloaded from Syria and Turkey, lying in wait for someone insisting on something "Oriental".

DIRECTORY

ADDRESSES In the Greek Cypriot sector, addresses are written either in Greek or in English. When in Greek, the number follows the street name, for example Leofóros Faneroménis 27. The same place in English would be cited in the British or American manner as 27, Faneromenis Avenue. Post codes exist but are not yet used much; more often a district within the municipality is cited.

In Northern Cyprus, addresses can be somewhat vaguer. They are generally given bilingually (Turkish/English) on visiting cards and bumph, but if not, *Caddesi*, abbreviated Cad, means avenue;

Bulvarı (Bul) is boulevard; *Meydan(ı)* (Meyd) is plaza; *Sokak/Sokağı* (Sok) means street; and *Çıkmazı* (Çık) is a dead-end alley. *Karşısı* means "opposite from", as in "PTT karşısı", opposite the post office. Writing from outside Cyprus, you must add a special code – Mersin 10, Turkey – since the international postal union does not recognise Northern Cyprus, and all incoming and outgoing mail must be funnelled through the Mersin post office.

BARGAINING Not a regular feature of Cypriot life, except in the case of any souvenir purchase where price is not marked. Don't expect the vendor to come down more than twenty percent, however. Hotels and pensions in the South have prices prominently displayed, and there is generally no upward fiddling in this respect – at slow times you can get rooms for twenty percent less than posted rates: the same applies to car hire. In the North things are more flexible; written rates and prices are not so conspicuous, but again expect only small discounts.

BRING... a water container for hot-weather ruin-tramping; a torch for dark corners of same, and for outlasting power cuts in Northern Cyprus; bath/sink plugs (rarely supplied) for washing clothes, 37mm and 44mm best; a line and clips for hanging said clothes; a small alarm clock;

some form of flying bug repellant (sold in the South, though) or netting; and sunscreen cream with a protection factor of over 15. In the North you'll additionally want slide photo film and contact lens solutions from home; in the South these can be found with some diligence.

CAMPING GAS In the South, 190-ml cannisters for Bluet stoves are commonly available from scuba and sports shops, plus selected appliance shops; in the North they are harder to find, but begin by asking at hardware stores and service stations. If you're showing up with a big stove in a yacht or a camper van, be aware that the nipple fittings at the crown of the standard ten-kilo tank are peculiar to the island, in both zones, and are not compatible with European ones, so come with a full spare! 250-gramme cylinders are also available throughout Cyprus.

CHILDREN AND BABIES They are sacred in both communities, and should present few problems travelling; in most resorts geared for the package trade on either side of the island, family-sized suites are easy to come by. Baby formulas and nappies are available in pharmacies or supermarkets everywhere.

CIGARETTES AND SMOKING In the South there is a small homegrown tobacco industry, plus hoardings and ashtrays everywhere, but despite this locals are relatively light puffers – certainly compared to all the surrounding countries and Britain – and non-smoking areas and campaigns are gaining ground. Nicotine habits are a bit more pronounced in Northern Cyprus, based almost entirely on rough Anatolian brands, but again you won't die of asphyxiation if you're a non-smoker.

CONTRACEPTIVES Throughout the island condoms are sold in pharmacies; the Greek for them is *profilaktiká*, the Turkish is *preservatif*. Users of other methods should come prepared from home.

DEPARTURE TAX Included in the price of air and ferry tickets in the southern Republic; in the North, various annoying chits are dispensed upon check-in at either ferry harbour and either airport, whose total value (payable in Turkish lira) equals £2–5.

ELECTRIC CURRENT Throughout the island, this is 220–240 volts AC, with triple, rectangular -pin plugs as in Britain: hence you don't need any sort of adaptor to run electrical appliances. In very old buildings you may still encounter double, round-pin sockets. Two-to-three pin adaptors are often

furnished in better hotels and villas for use by continental customers; if not, they are easily purchased.

Visitors from mainland Europe or North America may well want to come equipped with a two-to-three adaptor suitable for hair dryers, as they are expensive and not as easily found. You can easily and cheaply prepare one by replacing the 1-amp fuse in a unit marked "for shaver only" with a 5-amp fuse.

EMERGENCIES In the South, dial ☎199 for Police/Fire/Ambulance; ☎192 for information on night-duty chemists. In the North, emergency numbers are peculiar to each of the largest towns, but good luck finding a working public phone – better to flag down a taxi and take victim(s) to the hospital.

GAY LIFE This is virtually non-existent, at least above ground, in the tight-knit, family-orientated Cypriot society – in either community. In the South all homosexual acts between men are illegal, with offenders liable to five years in gaol; even "attempts to commit" homosexual acts (that is, propositioning somebody) face a sentence of three years. The North, while having no specific legislation, shares the same attitude, and both communities will be hostile to any open display of gay affection between foreigners. Contact is thus subtle: the few bars that have reputations as gay meeting places (chiefly in Limassol and Nicosia) are mentioned in the text.

LAUNDRY Most major towns in the South have at least one laundrette; otherwise it's DIY.

NATURISM Unisex topless is the rule in the busier resorts of the South, and with some discretion in Northern Cyprus. And that's about as far as you'll wisely go.

TIME Two hours ahead of GMT, and seven hours ahead of EST. Clocks go forward for summer time the last weekend in March and back again the last Sunday morning in September, so for most of October the whole island is only one hour ahead of Britain, and in April, eight hours ahead of New York. A recorded time message can be heard by dialling ☎195 in the South.

TIPPING Since a ten-percent charge is included on virtually all restaurant bills in the South, no extra amount need be left; in the North, where only the fancier places will tack on an identical fee, use your discretion. Taxi drivers, especially in the South, expect a gratuity.

TOILETS In the South, these tend to be found in parks, on coastal esplanades, etc; sometimes there's a five- or ten-cent fee. In the North, they are well signed in strategic crannies of Kyrenia harbour, Famagusta old town and Nicosia, but while passably clean (if malodorous) you're more likely to be using restaurant and hotel loos. When present, bowl-side baskets are for collecting paper which would block temperamental drains.

VAT Since 1 July 1992, a five-percent VAT (Value Added Tax) has been instituted in the southern Republic; it will supplement, and not replace, the ten-percent service charge and three-percent CTO levy added to all bills. There is as yet no VAT in the North.

WEIGHTS AND MEASURES The southern Republic went completely metric in 1987, while North Cyprus clings stubbornly to many Imperial units, most obviously the mile. There are two Ottoman holdovers on both sides of the Line: the *dönüm*, a measure of land equal to about a third of an acre, and the *oka*, equal to 2.8 pounds and still occasionally met with in food markets.

WORK Despite a growing labour shortage in the tourism and agricultural sectors of the **southern Republic**, a job there is only strictly legal if arranged before you leave home. Your prospec-tive employer will apply on your behalf for either a three- or six-month permit, though positions in hotels sometimes merit a two-year permit.

Of late many of these jobs tend to be taken by hungry Bulgarians, Romanians, Egyptians and Lebanese. Most other foreigners you see at work in resorts are invariably tour group couriers recruited, and paid from, abroad. Native teachers of English are of a sufficiently high standard that you are unlikely to land an ESL/TEFL-type job. Unions are well organised and aggressive in look-ing after their own; employers can only hire foreigners after having satisfied the authorities that the help cannot be recruited locally. So it's best, showing up on spec straight off the boat from Israel or Egypt, not to bank on anything other than an informal spell of picking grapes for a rural family.

Opportunities for work in **Northern Cyprus** are even more limited; your only chance is to start a business with imported capital, such as a wind-surfing school, which stakes out a patch in which locals can't or won't compete. Economic stagna-tion is a big issue here, and a likely consequence of any peace settlement is the repatriation of as many Anatolian settlers as possible and general consolidation by the North Cypriot authorities to protect the locals in their jobs.

PART TWO

THE SOUTH

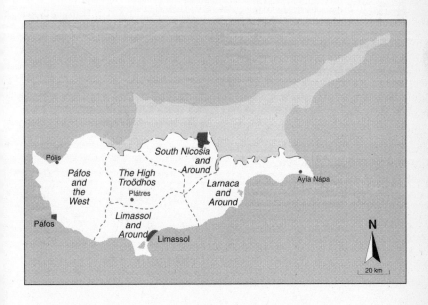

INTRODUCTION

F oundation of the island-wide **Republic of Cyprus** in 1960 was a compromise solution to a Gordian knot of imperial, regional and ethnic problems. Independence was the middle way between remaining a British colony, union (*énosis*) with Greece or a double partition between Greece and Turkey reflecting the **mixed Greek and Turkish population.** Like most compromises it left few happy, in particular the Turkish-Cypriot minority community – and the more intransigent enosist guerrillas in **EOKA** (*Ethnikí Orgánosis Kypríon Agonistón* or National Organisation of Cypriot Fighters). Tragedy was almost inevitable, and by 1974 control of the northern 38 percent of the island had passed to the Turkish Cypriots and the Turkish Army. Yet for most of the world, Cyprus still means the Greek-Cypriot-inhabited, southern Republic of Cyprus.

If you're used to Greece, you'll find the South more **civilised**: things work better; there's less wasted motion; drivers are more courteous to pedestrians and each other. People in general – often educated abroad and multi-lingual – seem relatively cosmopolitan, a useful trait when hosting thousands of tourists.

Scratch this veneer, though, and island society proves paradoxically more **traditional** than Greece: the social scale is cozy, with much of the population acquainted on sight if not exactly on first-name basis. Until recently the village was the core social unit; women – despite public presence – are still expected to "know their place"; and the Orthodox Church remains enormously influential, tapping a vein of uncomplicated, fervent faith co-existing with the worldliness.

Parochialism and internationalism were exhibited to destructive effect over the **fourteen turbulent years** between independence in 1960 and the catastrophe of 1974. Power-sharing between the two communities, regulated by a meticulously detailed constitution, had by 1964 collapsed in an orgy of recriminations and violence orchestrated by EOKA and its Turkish counterpart **TMT** (*Türk Müdafaa Teskilati* or Turkish Defence Organisation). The island was further destabilised through meddling by "mother" countries Greece and Turkey; soon the superpowers and the UN were inextricably involved.

Cyprus limped along as a unitary state for ten more years, albeit with a thoroughly poisoned civic life: Turkish Cypriots withdrew from the mainstream into a series of TMT-defended **enclaves**, while the Greeks retaliated by severely restricting traffic in goods or persons across their boundaries. Feeble intercommunal overtures alternated with fresh incidents, but Cypriot society was already split, with Turkish Cypriots relegated to second-class citizenship in their laagers.

When all-out war erupted in July 1974, only the exact timing and details came as a surprise. EOKA–B, successor to EOKA, staged a **coup** aimed at effecting *énosis*; in response the Turkish army, technically acting as guarantor of the island's independence, **landed** on the north coast and instead presided over de facto partition. The Greek Cypriots fled, or were expelled from, the North, the population of the scattered Turkish-Cypriot enclaves soon replacing them.

In the immediate **aftermath** of the war, all Cyprus was prostrate, with both ethnic communities demoralised and fearful, the economy in tatters. The South was particularly hard hit: 165,000 Greek Cypriots had immediately fled the North, to be followed within a few years by 15,000 more. The Turkish Army held the most productive portions of the island, assiduously developed since independence: the Greek Cypriots lost the fertile citrus groves around Mórfou, the busy port of Famagusta with its bulging warehouses, and the tourist facilities in Kyrenia and Varósha. Southern unemployment stood at forty percent until 1976, with the added burden of providing emergency shelter for the refugees.

South Cyprus today

Since 1974, the South has wrought an **economic miracle** – but at a price. Developing the untouched southern coast for tourism, with few zoning restraints and maximum financial incentives, was seen as the quickest fix for a dire predicament. Twenty years on, with **tourism** the country's biggest foreign-currency earner, the results are all too plain: the coast around Larnaca, Limassol, Ayía Nápa and Páfos forms a hideous strip of uninterrupted tower blocks.

Inland, crash programmes re-housed the refugees in often shoddily built **housing estate**s, whose grimness never diminished the appeal of a return to the North. The relocation of nearly a third of Cyprus's population has meant overcrowding (artificial, given the relative emptiness of North Cyprus) and inflated real estate prices. Private, speculative development has taken too much precedence over delayed and underfunded public works.

All this threatened not only the visual **environment** but the ecological one, too: on an island permanently short of water, with most of it trapped in the North, supplies barely suffice for the hotels which continued to sprout uncontrollably. Lately there are signs of a rethink, as conservationists organise to protect remaining unspoiled landscapes, and to promote human-scale tourism. The government provides muddled direction: while one agency designates national parks, the tourism authority adheres to a policy of encouraging five-star, high-impact tourist installations. Cut-rate package tourism is now seen as damaging to the social and environmental fabric, but mid-recession there are few customers at the undersubscribed luxury facilities. The compromise – Green **"agro-tourism"** in Páfos district – is still in its infancy, so gauging effectiveness seems premature.

By way of balance to this dependency on volatile tourism patterns, the demise of nearby Beirut as a business centre came as a welcome windfall for Cyprus. The South is now established as a popular venue for **international conferences**, and – thanks to its taxation policies and reliable infrastructure – as a base for **offshore companies**. Liaisons begun in the heyday of the non-aligned movement, and the traditional importance of the local Communist Party, continue to pay dividends in trade relations with East-central Europe, Africa and the Middle East.

Light industrialisation resumed after 1976, with export quality in various goods made necessary by the South's tiny internal market. Labour-intensive handicraft co-operatives set up in 1975 preserve skills particular to the lost northern homelands. Spurred by well-trained and -paid workers, **economic growth** since 1977 is impressive, with lately an unskilled labour shortage arising.

While all credit is due the Greek Cypriots for reviving their part of the island, there's no denying that much of the recovery was subsidised by **foreign aid**. Only the southern Republic has membership of such international bodies as UNESCO and the World Bank, and so is eligible for assistance.

Despite retaining its original name, the contemporary Republic of Cyprus is a fundamentally **different country**: mono-ethnic, yet with *énosis* buried as a realistic option; its 1960 constitution a dead letter; and public life pre-occupied with *Toh Kypriakó* (**National Question**) – the imposed partition of the island.

Everywhere posters and graffiti refer to the events of 1974, as do periodic heartfelt demonstrations, with little need of stage-managing. The right of Greek Cypriots to **return** to their homes in the North is the most emotion-charged issue: nostalgically-named refugee clubs attempt to link the generation born in exile with ancestral towns, and maintain community solidarity for a possible day of repatriation.

Strategies for reconciliation

Without the military means to expel the Turkish Army, the South has instead exploited its monopoly of world forums to mount a relentless propaganda campaign against, and **boycott** of, the Turkish Republic of Northern Cyprus (TRNC) in an attempt to bring it to heel. Ire is directed at Turkey too, in overseas court cases demanding an accounting of vanished property or persons. When advised that this is unlikely to create a favourable climate for reconciliation, the South retorts that giving North Cyprus more breathing space would remove any incentive for it to come to a federal agreement.

With the benefit of **hindsight**, some Greek Cypriots have assimilated bitter political lessons, and recognise the wisdom of contrite gestures towards the Turkish Cypriots, initiatives unthinkable before 1974. Despite the official campaign against the TRNC, many willingly admit past errors – in particular there's widespread revulsion at the activities of EOKA-B, who during the short-lived 1974 coup killed more Greek Cypriots than Turkish Cypriots. A retrospectively rosy view of intercommunal relations before 1960 prevails in the South – whether genuine or promulgated to counter Northern pessimism is debatable.

Officially the southern Republic is still **bi-communal**, though just a few hundred island Turks continue to live there. Banknotes and many public signs remain trilingual in Greek, Turkish and English; radio and TV broadcast Turkish-language programmes; the 80-seat parliament functions with only 56 deputies, the balance reserved for hypothetical Turkish representatives. In its propaganda and negotiating position the government woos the North, offering generous constitutional concessions if Turkish Cypriots would abandon their insistence on separate states – and if the demographic outcome were more favourable than at present.

The Southern government tried to prevent the 45,000 **Turkish Cypriots in the South** from fleeing to the North in 1975, correctly fearing that the Turkish side would label this a quid pro quo for the involuntary expulsion of northern Greeks. Prodigal-son-type publicity greets the rare Turkish Cypriot returning to the South, as they represent a tiny reversal of the island's apartheid and thus justification of partition. All property of southern Turkish Cypriots is held in trust by the government, current Greek-Cypriot occupiers having only rental agreements with their departing true owners.

After repeatedly failed UN-sponsored inter-communal negotiating sessions, the Southern government is determined to carry on as the sole "legitimate representative of Cyprus", with or without the consent of the Turkish Cypriots. When the Republic of Cyprus filed an application for associate EC membership in 1990, the North objected that the South had again presumed to speak for the whole island – a fairly typical example of the long-running **gap in understanding** as to what the appropriate roles of communities and central government are on Cyprus.

CHAPTER ONE

LARNACA AND AROUND

The southeast flank of Cyprus, centred around **Larnaca**, is the most touristed portion of the island – a consequence of the 1974 Turkish invasion, and the subsequent conversion of hitherto sleepy Larnaca airfield into the southern republic's main international airport. Except for its hilly western part, the district can't be reckoned very alluring scenically: not that this is likely to bother many of the patrons of the burgeoning resorts, who seldom venture far from a clear, warm sea and their self-contained hotels.

Despite being a moderate distance from the mega-resorts at the tip of the island, historic **Larnaca** is still a popular base for the area, and just large enough to retain – for the moment – some character independent of tourism. Southwest of the town are two of the most appealing, and most easily accessible, monuments in the area, the Muslim shrine of **Hala Sultan** by Larnaca's salt lake, and the mosaic-graced

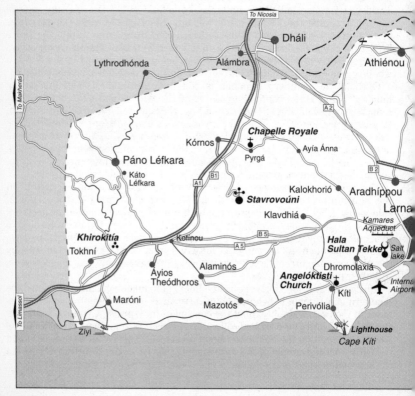

Byzantine church of **Angelóktisti** at Kíti. The Kíti cape, with **Perivólia** village, is perhaps the last human-scale resort in this part of the island, but the coast beyond will reward only the most determined explorers, preferably kitted out with a jeep.

Inland, a number of attractions are scattered to either side of the Nicosia–Limassol expressway. Neolithic **Khirokitía** is the oldest known habitation on the island, and a visit easily twinned with one to **Páno Léfkara**, a picturesque village in the Troödhos foothills renowned for its handicrafts. More directly approached from Larnaca along a secondary road, the **"Chapelle Royale"** at Pyrgá is a rare example of Lusignan sacred mural art, and the nearby **monastery of Stavrovoúni** an equally unusual instance of a strictly penitential Cypriot Orthodox monastery. Between the two, **Kórnos** village has a reputation as a pottery centre, as does **Kofínou**, next settlement down the highway, though the latter is more famous for a particularly ugly intercommunal incident during the days of the unitary republic.

East of Larnaca, there is little to specifically recommend: the sandy crescent of Larnaca Bay, the British Sovereign Base Area of Dhekélia and the slender beaches to either side of Cape Gréko are each blighted in their own way. **Ayía Nápa**, though by no means the largest permanent community, mushrooms in season to become the busiest downmarket resort in the area, while the strip at **Protarás** on the northeast coast is newer and more exclusive.

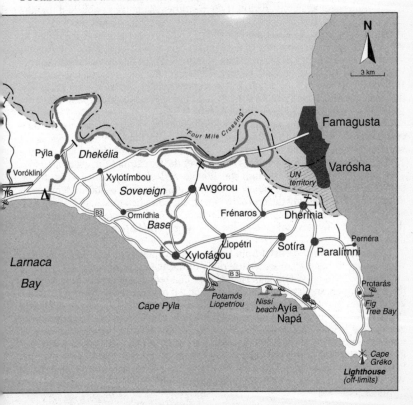

LARNACA (LÁRNAKA)

LARNACA has little tangible evidence of its eventful history, and is today a tourist centre and minor port forgetful of its past; yachts in its marina far outnumber freighters in the adjacent commercial harbour. Gone is the romantic town of eighteenth-century engravings, with only horrific summer heat, an adjacent salt lake and palm trees to impart a nostalgic Levantine touch. With a permanent population struggling to crest 100,000, Larnaca is barely half the size of Limassol, and more encroached upon by (mostly Scandinavian) tourism: the shore esplanade is touted as an echo of the French Riviera, and the hotel "ghetto" to the north of town is proportionately less important. Amidst the holiday-making it's sobering to consider that much of the recent growth is due to regional catastrophe. Numbers were first swelled by Greek refugees from Famagusta in 1974, and a year or two later by Christians from Lebanon – for whose benefit the occasional passenger ferry to and from Jounieh principally operates.

Some history

The site of Larnaca was originally colonised by Mycenaeans in the thirteenth century BC but had declined, like many other Mediterranean towns, by about 1000 BC. It emerged again as **Kition** two centuries later, re-established by the Phoenicians, and resumed its role as the port exporting copper from the rich mines of Tamassos. A subsequent period of great prosperity was complicated by the city's staunch championing of the Persian cause on Cyprus: Kimon of Athens, heading a fleet sent in 450 BC to reduce Kition, died outside the wall in the hour of what proved to be a fleeting victory. Persian influence only ended with the Hellenistic takeover of the whole island a century later, a period which also saw the birth of Zeno, Kition's most famous son (and a Phoenician), expounder of the Stoic philosophy in his adopted hometown of Athens.

Christianity came early to Kition, traditionally in the person of Lazarus, the man resurrected by Christ at Bethany. Cast adrift in a leaky boat by irate Pharisees not wanting evidence of miracles, Lazarus supposedly landed here to become the city's first bishop and, following his (definitive) death, patron saint. After an otherwise uneventful passage through the Roman and early Byzantine eras, Kition suffered the same seventh-century Arab raids as all Cypriot coastal settlements. It didn't really recover until the end of the Lusignan era, when the Genoese appropriation of nearby Famagusta prompted merchants to move here to take advantage of the small port; by now the anchorage was called *Salina*, after the salt lake just inland.

The name *Larnaca*, derived from *larnax* (a sarcophagus or urn, of which there were plenty to hand from various periods of the town's past), only gained wide currency at the start of Ottoman rule. By the eighteenth century its new status as the premier port and trade centre of the island – it briefly eclipsed Nicosia in population – saw numerous foreign consuls take up residence at Larnaca. That of Britain often simultaneously administered the English Levant Company, (analagous to the British East India Company. Around the consuls gathered the largest foreign community on the island, leading lives of elegant and eccentric provinciality, the inspiration for reams of travel accounts of the time. In 1878 the British landed here to take over administration of Cyprus, and it was not until after World War II that Larnaca again fell behind Famagusta and Limassol in importance.

Arrival, orientation and information

Landing at Larnaca **airport**, you'll find a **CTO** office open for all arrivals – which means pretty much around the clock – and ample exchange facilities, including two *Visa*-accepting **cashpoint machines**. Quite likely you'll have a hire car awaiting you as part of a fly-drive arrangement; if not, there are a half-dozen rental booths in the arrivals area. Otherwise, the **municipal bus** #19 goes into town up to 17 times daily between 6.30am and 7pm in season, dropping you at Ayíou Lazárou Square. Alternatively, a taxi into town won't cost much more than C£2.

Larnaca's street plan, with its numerous jinks and name-changes, is confusing, made only slightly less so by the sea, with two north–south boulevards paralleling it, being due east. The *Finikoúdhes* or palm-tree esplanade, officially **Leofóros Athinón**, constitutes the heart of the tourist industry and, at its north end, hosts several important **bus terminals**. Also there is the large **Platía Dhimokratías** (still Vasiléos Pávlou on most maps), home to the **CTO office** (Mon–Sat 8.15am–1.45pm; Mon & Thurs 3.45–6.15pm), which in addition to the usual bumph has a noticeboard worth checking for coming events. From here, **Leofóros Grigóri Afxendíou** is the main bypass avenue out to the Nicosia and Limassol roads, while the inland parallel of the sea front, **Zínonos Kitiéos**, leads back south to the covered central market and, via the alleyways of the bazaar, to **Platía Ayíou Lazárou**, home to its ornate namesake church and more bus stops. **Odhós Ayíou Lazárou**, later **Stadhíou**, reaches the roundabout giving onto the Nicosia road and also **Leofóros Artemídhos** to the airport and beyond along the coast.

Finding a place to stay

The **hotel and pension** situation for those showing up on spec is not good, though much better than in Páfos, owing to Larnaca's size. For budget rates you can pretty much forget about a room with a seaview, let alone on the Finikoúdhes.

Youth hostel, Nikoláou Róssou 27 (no phone). Housed partly in the disused Zuhuri Mosque; passably clean, with kitchen facilities. C£2.50 per person, plus C£0.50 sheet fee.

Rainbow Inn, Zínonos Kitiéos 102 (☎655874). Old standby dosshouse at the edge of the bazaar; singles C£6, doubles C£10.

Harry's Inn, Thermopýlon 2 (☎654453). Very central, not a brothel despite its ramshackle appearance, sympathetic management, small garden. C£7–8 single, C£12–13 double.

La Maison Belge, Stadhíou 103 (☎654655). Not as conveniently located as the preceding but across from a park on the main roads out of town (and also opposite its apparently closed-down competitor *Zenon O Kitefs*). Slightly less expensive than the *Pavion*.

Pavion Hotel, Platía Ayíou Lazárou 11, overlooking church (☎656688). Well-located one-star standby; breakfast rather perfunctory. Bathed rooms C£9–10 single, C£13–14.50 double.

Rebioz, Arkhiepiskópou Makaríou 98, well north of downtown (☎635300). Well-priced two-star at C£12 single, C£17 double.

Atalanti, Umm Haram street, old Turkish quarter (☎656800). Secluded one-star, close to some good restaurants. Singles C£10.50, doubles C£16.

Larco, Umm Haram street, alley off of; near preceding (☎657006). Technically a large hotel-apartment, and as such good value at C£15.50 single, C£20 double.

The Larnaca area phone code is ☎04

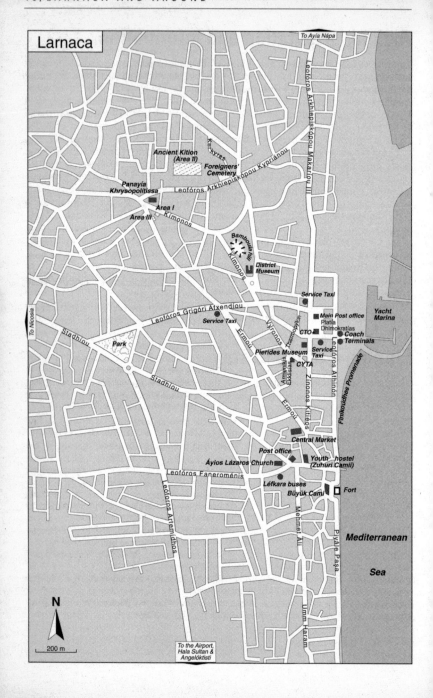

Larnaca

To Ayía Nápa

Leofóros Arkhiepiskópou Makaríou III

Kartyras

Ancient Kition (Area II)

Foreigners' Cemetery

Leofóros Arkhiepiskópou Kyprianoú

Panayía Khrysopolítissa

Area I

Area III

Kímonos

Kímonos

Bamboula hill

District Museum

Service Taxi

Yacht Marina

To Nicosia

Stadhíou

Leofóros Grigóri Afxendíou

Service Taxi

Park

Stadhíou

Thermopylón

Main Post office

Platía Dhimokratías

CTO

Coach Terminals

Vyronos

Pierídes Museum

Service Taxi

Ermoú

Armenias Ekklisías

CYTA

Zínonos Kitíeos

Leofóros Athinón

Ermoú

Central Market

Finikoúdhes Promenade

Post office

Áyios Lázaros Church

Youth hostel (Zuhúri Camii)

Leofóros Faneroménis

Léfkara buses

Büyük Cami

Fort

Leofóros Artémidhos

Mehmet Ali

Mediterranean

Sea

Piyále Pașa

N

Umm Haram

200 m

To the Airport, Hala Sultan & Angelóktisti

The city

The sights (and sites) of Larnaca can be seen in a leisurely day, preferably a cool one, as points of interest are scattered in such a way as to make use of the minimal city bus service difficult and a walking tour appealing.

Áyios Lázaros church

A most obvious place to start a tour of the city is the landmark church of **Áyios Lázaros** (daily 8am–12.30pm, 3.30–6.30pm summer, 2.30–5pm winter). Poised between the old Turkish and bazaar quarters, it was first erected late in the ninth century to house the remains of Lazaros, fortuitously discovered here. The church is distinguished by a graceful Latinate belfry, part of a thorough seventeenth-century overhaul and a miraculous survival of Turkish rule; the Ottomans usually forbade the raising of such structures, considering their height a challenging insult to the minarets of Islam, and (more realistically) fearing they would be used to proclaim insurrection. Indeed the place had to be ransomed from the conquerors in 1589, and was used for joint worship of Latins and Orthodox for two centuries after – as evidenced by Greek, Latin and French inscriptions in the Gothic-influenced portico, and Byzantine and Lusignan coats-of-arms near the main south door.

Inside, the spare stone interior (consequence of a fire in 1970) is a relief after the busy decoration of many Cypriot churches. Three small domes (currently blocked off with planks) are supported on four pillars slit into doublets with narrow arches springing from wedged-in Corinthian capitals. The wooden *yinaikonítis* (women's gallery) seems similarly recent, though a Rococo pulpit on one pillar (for Latin use) and the celebrated carved *témblon* (altar screen) are some 300 years old. On another pillar hangs a filigreed icon of Lazaros emerging from his tomb, an image paraded reverently in the presence of the Bishop of Kition every Easter Saturday eve.

In the musty-smelling crypt under the altar, the Lazaros relics supposedly lay very briefly until being taken to Constantinople by Leo in 901, whence they were stolen only to turn up later in Marseilles. But the tomb billed as his eventually formed part of a catacomb of general use, as witness several sarcophagi lying about here. In the northeast corner of the outside compound are more graves in a locked enclosure – this time of British consuls, merchants and family members who died in Larnaca's unhealthy climate during the sixteenth to nineteenth centuries.

The former Turkish quarter

The extensive Turkish quarter has retained its old street names, but is now home to Greek refugees from Famagusta and the Kárpas villages. Judging from some impressive houses and bungalows, the Turks here seemed wealthier than in Pàfos – but there are "chicken shacks" as well. Originally the late medieval church of the Holy Cross, the porticoed, flying-buttressed **Büyük Cami** (Cami Kebir), at the north end of quarter, now sees use by the local Egyptian/Lebanese/Iranian population; they allow visits, subject to the usual guidelines, but only just after prayer hours (posted on a chalkboard by imam's office at base of stairs). The nearby **fort** (daily 8am–6pm, c£0.50), a 1625 Turkish refurbishment of a Lusignan castle, stands mostly empty at the south end of the Finikoúdhes, but its upper storey hosts a small museum of oddments from Hala Sultan Tekke and Kition. The place is also the occasional venue for evening functions, when you can inspect the courtyard, and reflect on the fact that before World War II the British used this as a prison.

The beach and bazaar area

Immediately north of the fort stretches the **Finikoúdhes** promenade, which is fronted in turn by the town beach – some 800 mediocre metres of gritty hard-packed sand, well patronised despite its condition, and the fact that its rear half seems in the process of being torn up for a car park. If it's not to your taste, there are somewhat better beaches to either side of town (see p.55 & 60).

The bulk of the bazaar sprawls north of Áyios Lázaros; at its heart stands a covered French-type *halle*, a good place for fruit and veg or reed-woven souvenirs. Even if you're not staying at the youth hostel, stop in a moment to examine the unusual nineteenth-century **Zuhuri Cami** (literally, "Clown Mosque") housing it, with a double dome.

The Pierides Museum

Conveniently on the way to various tourist facilities on Platía Dhimokratías, the **Pierides Museum** (9am–1pm Mon–Sat, c£0.75) shares an old wooden house at Zínonos Kitiéos 4 with the Swedish consulate, though there has been talk of a move – don't be surprised to see a sign on the door referring you elsewhere. The building was the home of Dhimitrios Pierides, who began his conservation efforts in 1839, using his wealth to discretely salvage what archaeological treasures he could from tomb-plunderers, including Palma di Cesnola, first US consul at Larnaca. Unlike state-run district museums, the collection (expanded by his descendants) ranges across the whole island and is strongest on Archaic terracottas, plus other unusual small objects escaping the attention of official museums.

The collection

Among the oldest items in the four small exhibit rooms are some greenish picrolite idols from the Chalkolithic period, and the contemporary, famous **"Howling Man"** from Souskiou, featured on the museum poster. He could be filled with liquid through his hollow head, to "pee" out of a prominent member as he sits on a stool; the mechanics give little clue as to whether he had a religious or secular function. Numerous examples of painted **Archaic ware** are notable, especially one decorated by a so-called "astronaut" figure (beloved of Erich von Daniken and other extraterrestial-visitation nutters), bouncing on what appear to be springs or other mechanical devices. Among the imported Attic painted pottery, Theseus is about to run the Minotaur through with his sword, while on another pot two centaurs, presumably emblems of lust, flank a courting couple.

Many relatively rare Classical and Hellenistic **terracottas** include a funerary reclining man from Marion, in perfect condition down to the fingers, and a model sarcophagus with three pull-out drawers. More expected Archaic female statuettes brandish drums and other votive offerings; they were left in shrines as "permanent" worshippers, since the god was believed to reside at least part-time in the place. Other oddities include a surprisingly delicate spoon among a trove of early Bronze-Age black incised ware; a Classical baby's bottle, plus a glass fish, a glass pig, and a variegated bird from the Roman era.

The district museum

Larnaca's other archaeological collection, the **district museum** (Mon–Fri 7.30am–2.30pm, Thurs 3–6pm except July/Aug; c£.050) stands a ten-minute walk away north of Grigóri Afxendíou. It's purpose-built and so better laid out and lit than the Pierides, with excellent labelling and explanatory panels, but there's a feel of pickings and leavings compared to Nicosia's Cyprus Museum or the Pierides itself. The management has been reduced to displaying, in the entry hall, copies of a famous Artemis statue and funerary stele (the originals in Vienna and Berlin respectively). But it still rates as a worthwhile destination.

The collection

There's a reconstruction of a **Neolithic tomb** from Khirokhitía, complete with a stone atop the corpse's chest indicating a fear of it returning from the dead. The late Bronze-Age pottery, especially the so-called "white slip ware", prefigures the decorated dishes of the Geometric era. The fact that the latter were painted only on the outside (discounting the possibility that any inside designs were worn off by use) suggests that they were meant to be hung up by their handles as decoration, like the woven trivets of today.

Vast amounts of **Mycenaean pottery** in the so-called "Rude" (ie Rustic) Style, dug up at adjacent Kition, demonstrates Argolid settlement around 1200 BC; the prize exhibit is a fish *kratir* from Kalavassos. Yet Cypriot literacy dates to at least two centuries earlier, as evidenced by a display of Cypro-Minoan inscriptions, and a case of items imported towards the end of the Bronze Age demonstrates trade links at same time; notice an ivory lamp in the shape of a fish. Back among indigenous ware, there's an unusual clay torch from Pyla, and a clay brazier-pan from Athienou – perhaps meant to heat bedclothes or a small room. Terracotta highlights in the Archaic section include a horse-and-rider with emphasised eyes, plus a couple – possibly royal or divine – in a horse-drawn chariot.

Ancient Kition

Most of ancient Kition lies under modern Larnaca, and thus cannot be excavated, though the Swedes under Einar Gjerstad began to make attempts during the 1920s. The British made matters worse in 1879 by carting off much of what had survived above ground to fill malarial marshes with "rubble". Their depredations were severest at the ancient acropolis on Bamboúla hill, directly behind the museum in a fenced-off parkland; consequently there's little to see except for a nearby dig site – possibly the Phoenician port, far inland from today's shoreline – next to the municipal tennis courts on Kilkís Street. So-called Areas I and III, further down Kímonos, are Mycenaean holes-in-the-ground of essentially specialist interest now that they have disgorged their treasures; across the street from them, the belfry of **Panayía Khrysopolítissa** church is a weird, top-heavy, Siena-type article.

Area II

The one exception to this inaccessibility is the so-called **Area II**, beyond Arkhiepiskópou Kypriánou, from which you turn up Kérkyras to reach the gate at the northwest corner of the site (daily 7.30am–2.30pm; c£0.50). A wooden catwalk is provided for an overview of ongoing excavations, though until these are completed, not as well-labelled or as edifying as they might be. The remains are of three eras, the Phoenecian resettlement atop Bronze Age and Mycenaean foundations, and abut the mixed mud-brick and masonry wall which bounded Kition to the north. The main structures are a large ashlar-foundationed shrine, reconsecrated in Phoenician times to Astarte, and four smaller earlier temples, one of them linked to the smelting workshops found here, suggesting if not worship of a copper deity then a priestly interest in its production. In another of the shrines, thought to be that of a masculine seafaring god, a pipe for the ritual smoking of opium was discovered. Few Hellenistic or Roman artefacts were found here, making the site unusual and archaeologically important – as well as politically touchy, as the Greek Cypriots are often less than enthusiastic about remains indicating Asiatic cultural origins.

Still on the subject of foreign settlement, the nearby **English/Protestant cemetery** is in fact multi-ethnic and multi-denominational, with numerous Swiss and German Catholics here of late, plus a mass grave for victims of a 1973 air disaster.

Eating and drinking

It doesn't take much nous to work out that you're going to get ripped off at the glittery, "international cuisine" restaurants along the Finikoúdhes. But despite their discouraging presence, it is possible – just – to eat well for a reasonable amount a ways out of the hotel strip.

Things improve heading south from the fort along Piyale Paşa, as the shore-front road is called in the former Turkish district. At the southern tip of the urban grid, near the fishing harbour, a pair of **tavernas** – *Koullis* and *Vassos Varoshiotis* – cater to a local clientele with traditional home cooking. Continuing out of town in the same direction, *Flamingoes Restaurant Café* at the Hala Sultan Tekke has a wonderfully atmospheric setting, marred only by nocturnal mosquitoes, and does original food for no more than the stodge at Finikoúdhes would cost.

For a slice of vanishing Cyprus, look no further than *I Mavri Helona*, around the corner from *Hotel Pavion* at Mehmet Ali 9. This is an authentic *ouzeri*, faintly disreputable but popular with slumming locals (and tourists), featuring live, inebriated guitar/accordion music on Fridays and Saturdays. The *meze*-plates are good, abundant and unusual – baby crabs, octopus, snails, beets, mushrooms – and won't make you much poorer than c£6 for two, with liquid refreshment.

If not as fantastic as the name implies, the *Yummy-Yummy* snack bar at Víronos 60 is one of several on the same street, well poised for lunch after museum visits; for every kind of ice cream, iced cake and pastry, *Panetone* at Faneroménis 27B, across from Áyios Lázaros church, serves until 10pm.

Nightlife venues are not consistent; watch the hoardings of the Larnaca municipality for events, especially during the June *Kataklismós* fair. There is one cinema, the *Attikon* (☎652873), usually offering grade-B fare.

Listings

American Express c/o A.L. Mantovani & Sons, Platía Dhimokratías (across from tourist office), (☎465 2024).

Bookstore *Academic & General*, Ermóu 41.

Car hire Most firms are along Leofóros Arkhiepiskópou Makaríou, north of the CTO, so comparison shopping is often just a matter of a short stroll. Only the big international chains, plus *Thames*, maintain booths at the airport. *Andy Spirou*, JGL Building, Dhekélia Road (☎656590); *Budget/Petsas*, Karydes Court, Leofóros Afxendíou (☎623033); *Astra*, Artemídhos 9 (☎624422); *Champion*, Arkhiepiskópou Makaríou 62 (☎621644); *Europcar*, 7/8 Joanna Court, Leofóros Artemídhos (☎657442); *Eurodollar/Glamico*, Arkhiepiskópou Makaríou 50 (☎654091); *Hertz/Melissas*, Karouana Court 1, Arkhiepiskópou Markaríou 38 (☎655145); *Panipsos*, Galiléou 25 (☎656014); *Phoenix*, Arkhiepiskópou Makaríou 65 (☎623407); *Thames*, Makaríou 34 (☎656333); *Theodoulou Self Drive*, Stadhíou 117 (☎627411); *Thrifty*, Aradhippióti 8B (☎625177).

Coach companies Principal outfits include *Kallenos*, to Nicosia, Limassol, Ayía Nápa and Protarás, from the terminal between the *Sun Hall* Hotel and the yacht marina; *EMAN*, to Ayía Nápa and Limassol, from a terminal adjacent to the preceding; and *Lefkara*, to that village from Platía Ayíou Lazárou.

Exchange Most convenient bank branches are immediately around the CTO office (*Visa*-accepting cashpoint machines, too), with a few more on Ayíou Lazárou.

Laundrette *Artemis*, Armenikís Ekklisías 12; Mon–Fri 8am–6pm, 8pm in summer; Sat 8am–3pm. Service wash at C£3.50, including drying.

Post offices Main branch, next to the CTO on Platía Ayíou Pávlou, keeps short afternoon and Saturday morning hours; a small branch opposite Áyios Lazáros church is open Monday to Friday mornings only.

Service taxis *Acropolis* (☎655555), corner Grigóri Afxendíou and Arkhiepiskópou Makaríou, to Limassol and Nicosia; *Makris* (☎652929), on Platía Dhimokratías, same destinations; *Kyriakos* (☎655100), Ermóu 2C corner Afxendíou, Nicosia only.

Telephones CYTA is on the corner of Armenikís Eklisías and Víronos.

AROUND LARNACA

Larnaca is conveniently situated at the centre of its administrative district, with a number of archaeological sites, handicraft villages and rather less traditional resorts scattered in a broad arc all around.

With Larnaca as a base, it's easy to make three full- or half-day trips to surrounding attractions; to do this with any degree of flexibility, you'll need a car, since while public transport links the town with the majority of the sites detailed, there are few connections between them. Outside of Larnaca itself, accommodation can be found only at Perivólia and the overgrown resorts around Ayía Nápa.

Southwest from Larnaca: the coast route

The main expressways to Limassol and Nicosia take off well inland west of the city, leaving the coastal plain to the southwest relatively untravelled except for local village traffic. This is one patch of Cyprus, though, where the best bits are the easiest of access.

Hala Sultan (Umm Haram) Tekke

The mosque or **Tekke of Hala Sultan (Umm Haram)**, 5km southwest of Larnaca just past the airport, is quite possibly the first thing you'll see in Cyprus, since it's clearly visible from jets coming in to land on the nearby runway. According to the foundation legend, Muhammad's maternal aunt, accompanying her husband on an Arab raid of Cyprus in 649, was attacked by Genoese forces here, fell from her mule, broke her neck and was buried on the spot. A shrine grew up around the grave on the west shore of the salt lake, surrounded today by an odd mix of date palms, cypress and olives. Rain permitting, a tank and a series of channels waters the grove, adding to the oasis feeling of this peaceful, bird-filled place.

Tekke literally means a dervish convent, but this was always merely a *marabout* or saint's tomb. Despite the events of 1974, it's still a popular excursion target for Greek Cypriots and **place of pilgrimage** for Larnacan and foreign Muslims, for Hala Sultan ranks as one of the holiest spots of Islam, after Mecca, Medina, Kairouan and Jeruslaem. The twin name is Turkish/Arabic: *Hala Sultan* means the "the Ruler's paternal aunt", while *Umm Haram* or "Sacred Mother" seems an echo of the old Aphrodite worship.

The site and environs

Having left your shoes at the door, you're ushered inside (daily, nominally 7.30–sunset; donation) the present eighteenth-century mosque to the **tomb recess** at the rear, on one side of the mihrab. Beside the presumed catafalque of the Prophet's aunt, there's a recent tomb of the Turkish wife of King Hussein of the Hejaz. Above the graves you see the three slabs of rock forming the dolmen which probably marked the grave until the mosque was built. The horizontal slab is said to have been suspended miraculously in mid-air for centuries, before being forcibly lowered into its present position to avoid frightening the faithful who prayed underneath.

The original dolmen and the later mosque were by no means the first permanent structures here; remains of a **late Bronze-Age town** were recently excavated west of the access road and car park, yielding various treasures (many, appropriately enough, from present-day Egypt).

Flamingoes and other migratory birds stop over at the **lake** during winter and early spring (see "Wildlife" in *Contexts*), hence *Flamingoes*, the excellent adjacent taverna. Salt is still mined commercially here in late summer, the season of the lake's greatest shrinkage, though the turnover doesn't remotely approach the export trade that thrived here until Ottoman times. Like the *tekke*, the lake has a foundation legend, too: lately resuscitated Bishop Lazaros, passing by, asked a woman carrying some grapes for a bunch; upon her rude refusal, he retaliated by turning her vineyard into the salty lagoon, now three metres below sea level.

The *tekke* can almost be reached by **public transport** on the #6 municipal bus from Platía Ayíou Lazárou in Larnaca; have the driver set you down at the sign-posted one-kilometre side road, just the far side of the causeway over the salt lake.

Another rural Turkish monument in the area, on the north shore of the lake near the Limassol-bound road, is the so-called **Kamares aqueduct**, built in 1747 at his own expense by Abu Bekir, the only popular Ottoman governor of the island. The 75 surviving arches were in use as recently as 1939.

Angelóktisti church

That same #6 bus continues, a dozen times daily during daylight hours, to **KÍTI** village, 11km from Larnaca. At a prominent three-way junction there, where roads head shoreward for Perivólia, back to Larnaca or on to Mazotós, stands the Byzantine **church of Angelóktisti** (Mon–Fri 8am–4pm; Sat 10am–4pm; Sun 6am–noon and 2–4pm; donation). If necessary the key can be fetched from the nearby snack bar, and smocks are provided for the scandalously dressed, since this is still Kíti's main church, making visits during Sunday morning liturgy in fact problematic. The exterior, with its many curved surfaces, is pleasing; most of the church dates from the eleventh and twelfth centuries, having replaced an original fifth-century sanctuary destroyed by the Arabs. What today serves as a narthex and old-icon display area (signs in Greek warn the faithful not to kiss them if wearing lipstick) began life as an apsed and groin-vaulted Latin chapel in the thirteenth or fourteenth century. The main nave has three aisles, a single apse and no true narthex, though there's a large *yinaikonítis*, and all-seeing eyes to either side of the *témblon*.

The mosaic
But the highlight of Angelóktisti is the **mosaic** (illuminated on request) in the conch of the apse, probably the last surviving section of the original building. Inside a floral/vegetal border, the *Virgin*, labelled unusually "Holy Mary" in Greek, lightly balances a doll-like infant on Her left arm as She gazes sternly and unwaveringly at a point just left of the viewer. The pair is attended by two dissimilar *Archangels* with fish-scale wings – Gabriel on the right is fleshier, more masculine – proffering celestial orbs and sceptres in the direction of the Infant. The age of the mosaic is controversial, but the Ravenna-esque artistic conventions, especially Mary's stance on a jewelled pedestal and inclination to left, would suggest the sixth century. Yet it is far more refined than the purportedly contemporaneous mosaic in North Cyprus's church of Kanakaria, which was the only other one in Cyprus until its desecration (see Chapter 8, p.252).

Perivólia, Cape Kíti and beyond

Just 2km southeast of Kíti, **PERIVÓLIA** is developing as a resort for the sake of Cape Kíti's **beaches**. To either side of the lighthouse, these are mostly scrappy, narrow and sharply shelving, with large pebbles on a sand base. Nonetheless, self-catering apart-hotels are springing up on the outskirts and "Flats to Let" signs abound in the village, an indication of just how desperate for fresh shorefront resorts the South is. Numerous **tavernas** in the village centre make this a good destination for a night out from Larnaca, and if you've a hire car, Perivólia could be a good, relatively quiet base as it's not too tatty yet.

A restored sixteenth-century **Venetian watchtower** looms conspicuously on its knoll just over a kilometre north of the modern lighthouse. Dirt tracks converge there from all directions, and it's always in sight – though not especially compelling when you get there.

Returning to Kíti, it's possible to continue on pavement towards MAZOTÓS, adopting a badly signposted dirt track 2km before the latter to follow the coast. The track is fairly rough, more so if you make a wrong turn, when it would be easy for a saloon car to founder in a deep rut or sand pit. The shore here is little developed except for farms and Cypriots' weekend villas, and frankly there's not much to justify any exploitation; the few beaches are rocky and difficult to reach, though once in the water the seabed is sandy enough.

Zíyi and Maróni

You finally return to civilisation at either **ZÍYI** or **MARÓNI**, the former a small fishing anchorage with a rocky beach, most notable for the nearby BBC World Service transmitter. Maróni, a blend of old and new houses, spreading appealingly over several hills, is home to numerous expats, and also a major hothouse-vegetable centre. Between Zíyi and the turnoff up to Maróni a small sandy bay, **Limanáki**, has a single café and sees heavy use in season.

Western Larnaca district

Compared to the parched, apparent wastelands around Nicosia or Larnaca and the bungaloid excesses of outer Limassol, the gently rolling country at the western end of Larnaca district presents a welcome change: there are trees, streams, and the hint of the Troödhos foothills still further west. Several points of interest flank the Limassol–Nicosia expressway, suitably provided with exit roads across and onto the old highway, which in many respects is better for short distances here.

Khirokhitía

Virtually the earliest traces of human settlement in Cyprus, around 6800 BC, are found at Neolithic **KHIROKITÍA**, roughly halfway between Larnaca and Limassol on the modern expressway. The name is that of the modern village to the northwest, since as with all prehistoric sites the original name is unknown.

The excavated area forms a long ribbon on a southeast-facing slope dominating a pass in the age-old highway from the coast to Nicosia. It's supposedly open daily from 7.30am to sunset for c£0.50 (c£0.35 extra for an explanatory pamphlet at the ticket booth), but at weekends at least it's unwise to show up after 1pm. The site is not well fenced, however, and can be easily entered along the well-trodden path beginning behind the booth. Despite noisey distraction from the new motorway, Khirokitía ranks among the most rewarding of minor Cypriot ruins. The only nearby amenity is a taverna across the bridge over the Maróni creek on the access road, closer to the main highway.

The site

The combination of arable land below, plus an easily defensible position, was irresistable for the settlement's founders, thought to have come from the Near East or Anatolia. Archaeological investigations are continuing the earliest inhabited sector, a saddle between the two knolls at the top of the grade; despite the limited area uncovered to date, it seems certain that most of the hillside was inhabited.

What's visible thus far are housing foundations – most substantial and recent at the bottom of the slope and a maze of lanes, dictated more by the placement of dwellings than any deliberate planning. What you walk up on, and which appears to be the main street, is in fact a defensive **perimeter wall**, something which becomes more obvious at the top of the hill; very few houses were built outside it, and a secondary wall was later added to enclose them also.

The sixty-odd, circular or nearly so **dwellings** exposed to date, all of the **tholos** or beehive-type are single-storeyed structures with vaulted or flat roofs. The largest dwelling, an egg-shaped chieftain's **"mansion"** with an inner diameter of just under 6 metres, had two rectangular piers supporting an attic. Interior walls were lined by stone benches doubling as sleeping platforms, with scanty illumination provided through slit windows.

As the huts deteriorated, they were flattened into rubble and built atop by the next generation, a practice which prompted the now-discarded theory that the perimeter wall was in fact the main street, whose elevation was tentatively explained by its having been constantly raised to keep pace with the level of the new houses. This "urban-renewal" method also greatly complicated modern excavations which began in 1936, two years after the site's discovery; these have yielded vast troves of small Neolithic objects, undisturbed by vandals and now to be seen at the Cyprus Museum in Nicosia (see p.169).

Estimates for the maximum population of Khirokitía run as high as 2000, an astounding figure for the time; the **local culture** was unusual in other ways. Though wheel-less pottery techniques were known, the inhabitants preferred to work in stone, turning out, for example, relief-patterned grey andesite bowls and rather schematic idols. Flint sickle blades and grinders hollowed out of river boulders, along with preserved cereal grains, provided proof of a largely agricultural basis of the community, though hunting was important, too.

The Khirokitians **buried their dead** in the fetal position under the earth floor, or just outside the entrance, of each round-house – a rather convenient form of ancestor reverence; beneath one dwelling, 26 graves on eight superimposed levels were discovered. The deceased were surrounded by offerings and personal belongings, exquisite stone-and-shell necklaces being found in female graves; more ominously, the corpses usually had their chests crushed with a grinding quern to prevent the dead returning. Infant mortality was high, and adult skulls show evidence of ritual deformation by tightly binding surviving infants on a cradle-board to flatten the back of the head.

Páno Léfkara

The very next junction on the highway, 3km north of Khirokitía, is the turning for **PÁNO LÉFKARA**, 700 metres above sea level at the fringes of the Troödhos and reached along an easy climb on the well-made E105 road into the hills northwest. Approaching, it's best not to take the first signed turnoff into the village – there's no parking and you've a bit of a hike into town.

In Lusignan times a retreat of the Orthodox clergy, Páno Léfkara is almost a small town, a very handsome one to boot, and should be visited for that reason alone: arches make veritable tunnels in the streets, and fine door frames and balconies complete the picture. Many of the old houses are being restored by Cypriots and foreigners, though prices are high owing to equidistance from the South's three largest towns. There was a small Turkish quarter here, too, down at the low end of the village by the mosque.

But the usual reason for coming is to sample the **lace and silver** for which the place is famous; it is claimed, somewhat apocryphally, that Leonardo da Vinci purchased a needlepoint altarcloth for Milan cathedral when he came to Cyprus in 1481. The silver jewellery and ware, men's work, seems more reasonably priced than the women's lace, and both are sold in a half-dozen-plus shops, mostly along the main commercial street – though the villagers all have an eye for the main chance, and everyone from petrol pump attendant to café owner will happily trot out the work of relatives at the first opportunity. The **Patsalos Folklore Museum** (Mon–Sat 10am–4pm), devoted largely to the two crafts, might be a useful first stop before going on a shopping spree. Páno Léfkara is also noted for its Turkish delight (*loukoúmia*), and if you're lucky you can catch a demonstration of its manufacture.

On the practical side, an excellent small **hotel**, *Lefkarama* (☎04/342000), has singles starting at c£10, doubles c£15, but with really advantageous half- and full-board rates. In any case the restaurant, good value even à la carte, has the most complete menu in town; of the other cafés and **eateries** on the main street, courtyarded *Lemonies*, across from the traditional *Kafenio Hambis*, has good kebabs but isn't especially cheap.

Páno's lower neighbour, **KÁTO LÉFKARA**, is much less frequented, but also architecturally of a piece, and can boast the twelfth-century church of the Archangel Michael, with contemporary frescoes.

Pottery villages: Kofínou and Kórnos

Back on the route towards Nicosia, you'd detour almost immediately for **KOFÍNOU**, which has just a single pottery workshop, the *Skutari Craft Pottery*, to delay you. The villagers are all Greeks from the North; this was once one of the largest, nearly all-Turkish communities in the South, attacked on scanty pretext by EOKA on 15 November 1967. Before a truce was arranged two days later, 25 villagers had died, and the incident nearly precipitated a Greek-Turkish war. Scars of the battle are still evident, as the old quarter was never really rebuilt, before or after 1974.

KÓRNOS, 11km north on the other side of the highway, is a more cheerful place, set in a tree-lined stream valley, and also occupies itself with pottery. Signs point you to the main works (shut Sunday) at the northeast edge of town, where you'll see large piles of unsifted, coarse clay, mixing pits and a pair of kilns. If you want large *kioupiá* or plant-pots for a villa terrace, this is the place, though transporting them overseas would be another matter.

Stavrovoúni monastery

Proportionate to its population, Cyprus contributes more monks to the monastic enclave of Mount Áthos in northern Greece than any other Orthodox country. You can get a glimpse of why at the **monastery of Stavrovoúni**, perched atop an isolated, 689-metre crag dominating this corner of island.

Its foundation legend places it as the oldest religious community on the island: Saint Helena, mother of Roman Emperor Constantine, supposedly came through here in 327 on her way back from Jerusalem, leaving a fragment of the True Cross (plus the entire one of the Penitent Thief). From this peak, previously home to a temple of Aphrodite, took its modern name (*Stavrovoúni* = Cross Mountain), and a religious community quickly sprang up around the holy relics.

In Lusignan times Benedictine monks displaced Orthodox ones, but despite an imposing fortified design, both monastery and revered objects were destroyed after the 1426 rout of King Janus nearby (see below). Today's silver reliquary crucifix, if not the venerated sliver of the True Cross supposedly encased within, dates only from the late fifteenth century; perhaps the contents are identical with the purported Cross of the Penitent Thief which a wandering Dominican friar claimed to have seen here, still intact, by the altar in 1486.

After the Turkish conquest the monastery was burned again, and only in the last century was Stavrovoúni rebuilt, on the old foundations, and repopulated – by both monks and dozens of cats, the latter a scourge of snakes here as at the Cape Gáta nunnery at Akrotíri. But by the late 1970s the place was in decline once more, with just two elderly monks besides the abbot (still here, in his fiftieth year of residence). Stavrovoúni had given up its once-extensive holdings to surrounding villages, a process doubtless completed by the pressure of refugees from the 1974 invasion, though it retained the nunnery of Ayía Varvára at the base of the hill as a dependency.

Monastery life

Today about twenty very committed, mostly young monks perform a rota: six or seven up in the citadel, the rest down at Ayía Varvára at any given time. They are on an **Athos-type regimen,** strictest on the island, which entails a day divided into roughly equal thirds of prayer and study, physical labour and rest. "Rest" means only two frugal, meat-less meals just before midday and an hour or so before sunset, taken together in the tiny refectory, plus sleep interspersed between the nocturnal devotional periods. As a minimum there are four communal liturgies in the courtyard church: matins before dawn, the main liturgy after sunrise, vespers before the evening meal and compline afterwards.

Life has been eased somewhat by the recent paving of the steep, twisty road up and provision of mains water and electricity, but winters on top are severe, and the brothers still do a full day's work on the surrounding agricultural terraces in addition to their devotions. Honey and sultanas, the latter legendarily having their first Cypriot cultivation here, are said to make up some of the harvest.

Visits

Equally strict conditions apply for **visiting**. In accordance with Athonite rules, no women are currently admitted at all – even female infants; no entry is allowed from noon to 3pm (11am–2pm in summer – the monks don't keep summer time), and no photos: cameras must be left at the guard house at the foot of the long stairway up from the car park. In sum, you don't come here to gawp – except maybe at the amazing views, since there's little remaining of artistic or architectural merit after the pillaging and fires – but on pilgrimage, possibly to stay the night on invitation.

A Greek sign in the entry hall sums up the monastic creed: "If you die before you die, then when you die you won't die." In other words, he who has renounced the world gains eternal life. When a monk *does* die bodily, he is interred for the prescribed three years of Orthodoxy and then exhumed for display in the charnel house, his religious name emblazoned across the forehead of his skull.

Pýrga: the "Chapelle Royale"

Near the centre of **PÝRGA** village, just 3km from Kórnos east of the expressway, stands the **"Chapelle Royale"**, a small Lusignan church (Mon–Fri 8am–4pm, Sat 8am–1.30pm, Sun closed; c£0.50) actually dedicated to Saint Catherine. It owes its alias to the fine wall painting of King Janus, who built this in 1421, together with his queen Charlotte of Bourbon. They appear as tiny figures at the foot of a Crucifixion on the east wall. "Good King Janus" was among the last of Cyprus's Crusader monarchs, as respected as he was ineffective; just a few kilometres south, near Khirokitía, runs the Maróni stream where his armies were defeated by the Mamelukes in 1426. Janus was held prisoner for two years in Cairo before being ransomed, and the little church is his only surviving monument. The build-ing itself is quite simple, merely a single-vaulted structure with three doorways. Besides the royal portraits you can make out the *Raising of Lazarus* and a *Last Supper*, restored in 1977 and – unusually for Cyprus – identified in French.

North and east from Larnaca: the resort coast

As you head out of town, the bight of Larnaca Bay bends initially north. It takes nearly 5km to outrun the oil refineries and tankers at anchor; paragliders and clusters of hotels, neither yet so densely packed as at Limassol or Káto Páfos, indicate that you have done so. The **beach** here is acceptable for a dip, but noth-ing to scream about: the tidal zone is reefy, the water interrupted by rock jetties and breakwaters. Beyond "Hotel Row", there's even less to stop for as the route curls east, and halting is awkward once inside the Dhekélia Sovereign Base – home to an enormous and ugly power station, between the highway and the sea, in addition to British Forces.

Once outside the Sovereign Base (see box on p.80, Chapter Two), your first detour might be to **Potamós Liopetríou**, a long, narrow creek/inlet that's a genu-ine, rare fishing anchorage. The only facilities are two tavernas, though the fish in particular is not cheap, and the northerly one is quite unwelcoming. This is a shame, as the place is attractive – if beachless, though some sand has been hope-fully strewn at a suitable bathing spot near the mouth of the inlet. It appears that the French poet Rimbaud stopped in, too, working as a quarry foreman in 1879 before supervising the construction of the governor's residence in the Troödhos.

Ayía Nápa

In his book *Journey into Cyprus*, Colin Thubron describes cooking a fish, in the summer of 1972, on the empty beach below the then-fishing village of **AYÍA NÁPA**, and later being awoken by sandflies. Were he today to find an unpoliced stretch of sand, he would be lucky to sleep at all over the din of nearby clubs and discos. Any local identity has been utterly swept aside since Thubron's visit, with Ayía Nápa press-ganged into service as one of the South's largest package resorts, replacing the lost paradises around Famagusta. You don't really need a guidebook to find your way about here – all is pretty self-explanatory – but rather a fat wallet, and a large liver capacity.

The beach is still obvious enough, but packed out, a cresent swathe extending east hundreds of metres from the fishing harbour whose tavernas are among the most expensive on the island. Ayía Nápa also has a reputation for (by Cypriot standards) hard nocturnal living, with a baker's dozen-plus of bars and discos, thronged to by a rowdy, largely working-class clientele from various points in northern Europe. Above Platía Seféri, nominal centre of the old village, anything not a pub is likely to be a clothes shop or an overpriced restaurant: striking out in virtually any direction, you can pick up your copy of the *Express* or the *Daily Mail* (incidentally far outnumbered by Swedish tabloids), or tank up on Woodpecker cider and beans on toast.

The monastery of Ayía Nápa

Amidst all this, the Venetian-style **monastery of Ayía Nápa** comes as a beautiful, peaceful shock with its arched cloister enclosing an irregularly shaped, flower-decked courtyard. In the middle spurts an octagonal **fountain**, its sides decorated with reliefs and the whole surmounted by a dome on four pillars. Across the way burbles a boar's-head spout, the terminus of a Roman **aqueduct** whose spring-fed waters were the original impetus for sporadic settlement here since Hellenistic times – and the focus of the monastery's foundation legend.

During the sixteenth-century Venetian heyday in Cyprus, some hunters had a mangy dog whose coat improved markedly after visits to a hidden spring. Curious, the hunters followed the wet dog, finding not only the source of the abandoned aqueduct but also an icon of the Virgin hidden here for 700 years since the Iconoclast crisis, when Byzantine zealots briefly outlawed the adoration of such images. News of the healing waters spread, with humans availing themselves, and soon a monastery was founded around the lower end of the refurbished aqueduct. Work was completed just in time for the Turkish conquest, after which the Catholics were expelled from the complex and replaced with more tractable Greek Orthodox monks; they too soon departed but the forerunner of the ex-village sprang up around the abandoned monastery, attracted by the flow of water.

SPECIAL USES FOR BRITISH SOVEREIGN BASES

The existence of the Dhekélia Sovereign Base (see box on p.80), and its inviolability even in the wake of the 1974 invasion, has given rise to some anomalies in the supposedly hermetic separation of Cyprus North and South. Both Turkish and Greek Cypriots continue to hold jobs on the base; access from the South is unrestricted, and with the right paperwork Northerners can enter along the so-called "Four Mile Crossing" from Famagusta, plus at two or three other points. Turkish Cypriots wishing to make clandestine visits to the South, especially for night-life, need only leave their Northern number-plate cars in the base, and have Greek friends with suitable cars waiting for them.

PÝLA, in the buffer zone near a point where the borders of the North, the South and the Dhekélia base meet, has further notoriety as one of only two remaining mixed Greek/Turkish communities in the southern Republic (the other is Potamiá, near Nicosia). To be sure, relations are not always cordial – café society is separate, and disputes over Turkish-Cypriot-owned property boundaries often require UN mediation – but tacit co-operation is agreed on in the matter of the smuggling of vast amounts of agricultural produce from the North, just 5km away across base territory at Beyarmudu (Pérgamos).

This loophole makes a mockery of the Republic of Cyprus's imposed quarantine of "foreign" produce, with even fruit from Turkey (of all places) entering via this corridor. Certain Pýla shops selling designer clothes duty-free also add to the illicit traffic – Greek-Cypriot authorities set up sporadic roadblocks in the area to search for such contraband, so beware, espcially if receipts show you've purchased from a Turkish-Cypriot-owned shop.

The **church**, off to the right (west) of the sloping courtyard, is partly subterranean and has a magnificent fanlight-cum-rose window over the door. In the gloom at the base of the stairs down, you find a supplementary Latin chapel, from the time of its original, dual dedication, though the miraculous icon has long since vanished. Back outside you can clamber up onto part of the perimeter wall, looking towards the sea over a cistern and two giant sycamore figs, said to be six centuries old.

The Venetian designers enclosed the monastery with that high, blind **perimeter wall**, originally intended to keep pirates at bay but now with the unforeseen but happy effect of cordoning off the place from the new Viking barbarians. Immediately around it, a half-dozen of the louder pubs must test the resolve of the ecclesiastical conference delegates who are the only people allowed to stay as guests in the nominally still-functioning monastery, restored during the early 1970s and made available to the World Council of Churches.

Practical details

Orientation is straightforward: **Nissí** is the initial name of main road west to Nissí and Larnaca, 39km distant; **Arkhiepiskópou Makaríou** descends from the central square to the harbour; and **Krýou Neroú** heads out east towards Cape Gréko. Above **Platía Seféri**, the trunk routes dissolve into a welter of narrower streets on the hillside. *EMAN* **buses** will drop you either down at the main ticket office near the base of Makaríou, or up at stops near the none-too-enthusiastic **CTO** (Mon–Sat 8.30am–1.45pm, Mon & Thurs only 4–6.15pm) at the corner of Krýou Nérou and Makaríou, next to the *Cyprus Airways* office.

If you're **staying** here, it's 98 percent certain that you've come on a package; even the most rock-bottom hotel, the one-star *Napa Sol*, Nissí 79 (☎03/722044), is firmly on the tour-operator's lists, though with nominal walk-in rates of c£11.75 single, c£17.50 double. The only other comparable hotel option is the somewhat better-positioned *Leros* (☎03/721126) across from *EMAN*, a bit pricier at c£14 single, c£25 double. Most other affordable accommodation in Ayía Nápa is self-catering, with studios suitable for two starting at about c£14, two-bedroom units at roughly double that figure. Don't expect much Cypriot character when **eating out**, though *Markos* near the monastery is acceptable. Aside from the manifold bars, more "wholesome" **entertainment** is laid on the last week of September as part of the Ayia Napa **festival**: several days of folkloric displays, music dance, theatre and other events in and around Platía Seféri, by the monastery.

Rounding out amenities, the **post office** keeps limited afternoon and Saturday-morning hours. The numerous **banks**, if shut, are liberally sown with *Visa*-accepting cashpoint machines. All international **car hire** franchises, plus the local chains *Spirou*, *Petsas* and *Panipsos*, are conspicuously represented, mostly at the start of Krýou Nérou, Nissí or Arkhiepiskópou Makaríou avenues.

West of Ayía Nápa

Some 2km west of central Ayía Nápa on its namesake avenue, **Nissí beach** is for once as attractive as touted – but in high season it will be hopelessly crowded as the four or five hotels here, a discrete distance back, disgorge their occupants onto the mere few hundred metres of sand, or into the handful of snack kiosks above the tidemark. At such times especially you can retreat by wading out to the islet which lends the beach definition, and its name (*nissí* = island).

The local **campsite** is nearby, between Nissí and the turnoff for **Astéria beach** on the Makrónissos peninsula; it's open March to October, charging C£1.50 a day per tent or caravan plus C£1 per person.

Also on the peninsula, in the grounds of the Voula Beach Hotel, is the recently established **Marine Life museum** (Tues–Sun 11am–1pm & 5–8pm; C£0.50), funded by the Pierides Foundation and consisting mostly of the sea-shell collection of a certain Mr Tornaritis, but also boasting an aquarium full of sea-turtles rescued by the Lára hatchery project.

Inland: the Kokkinokhoriá

Away from the south coast, the gently undulating terrain is dotted with the *Kokkinokhoriá* or "Red Villages", so called after the local soil, tinged red by large amounts of iron and other metallic oxides. This is the island's main potato-growing region, the little spuds irrigated by water drawn up by the dozens of windmills, and harvested in May to appear subsequently in British corner shops. (Lately the overdrawn aquifer has been invaded by the sea, and fresh water must be brought in from the Troödhos). Less salutary is the area's reputation for the trapping of songbirds for food (see "Wildlife of Cyprus" in *Contexts*), particularly at Paralímni; the *ambelopoúlia* (Gr) or *beccafico* (It) are small fig-eating blackcaps, pickled whole and exported to the Middle East.

Other than this, there is little to be said of the hinterland, and even the CTO admits as much in its earnest, rather reaching promotion of the handful of unheralded medieval churches scattered in and around the various relentlessly modern villages. Despite their inland location, however, they are too close to the seashore fleshpots to have escaped notice from tourists and expatriates, so at Dherínia and Paralímni in particular there are various facilities.

Dherínia

In **DHERÍNIA**, expensive but tasty *Taylor's* on the Sotíra road is just one of several tavernas – the others are on the FRÉNAROS road – which attract foreigners. Dherínia is most visited, however, for its hilltop setting virtually on the Attila Line and resulting overlook of the "dead zone" towards Famagusta and and its modern suburb Varósha. Disconnected windmills spin aimlessly, or stand devaned and idle in the abandoned fields to the north. Two view-cafés charge C£0.50 for the privilege of using their binoculars to take in the sad tableau of Varósha crumbling away, its rusty construction cranes frozen in their positions of August 1974. The buffer zone is quite wide here, because although the Greek Cypriots abandoned Varósha on 15 August 1974, the Turkish army was unable to completely occupy it before the UN-brokered cease-fire went into effect the next day, and since then the chief human presence in the ghost city has been that of UN patrols.

Paralímni

In the wake of the invasion, **PARALÍMNI**, a few kilometres south of Dherínia, became the administrative capital of "Free Famagusta" district, and as such has a concentration of banks, petrol pumps, shops and venues for cultural events – as well as the most northerly access to the strip of Greek-Cypriot-controlled coast below Famagusta. Beachfront development extends to just a bit north of Ayía Triás cove; working your way south on the still-narrow road to the miniscule beach at **PERNÉRA**, you can eat at *Taverna Onasis*, which is where the numerous building-site crews in the area go for a no-nonsense feed; until the next tower block rears up, it even has a sea view of sorts. If you fancy staying, there are numbers of self-catering **apartments** that could be had early or late in the year on a walk-in basis, both along the Paralímni–Ayía Triás road and immediately around Pernéra.

Protarás and Cape Gréko

Pernéra merges southwest into the formerly pristine stretches of **PROTARÁS**, aka "Fig Tree Bay", a developmental disaster of some twenty wall-to-wall hotels, packed out from mid-May onwards with relatively well-behaved Scandinavian families. The famous but rather narrow sandy beach itself, equally crowded, is not even indicated from the inland bypass road with its dozen restaurants – only the hotels themselves are signposted. Thus if you don't know that the *Sunrise Beach Hotel* marks the north end of the bay, and the *Nausicaa Beach Hotel Apartments* the southern extreme, it's quite easy to drive right past Protarás resort without ever seeing the sea. Once you do figure it out, big shoreline lawns and swimming pools supplement the lack of sands substantial enough to accommodate the crowds – and convey a clear message that, unless you're actually staying at one of behemoths or using their manifold shoreline recreational facilities (water-skiing, paragliding, etc), you're not welcome here. It's difficult to imagine a setting less appropriate for non-packaged visitors. If you do manage to reach it, the ocean at least is as clear and warm as you'd hope for.

Chances for a quiet swim are slightly better south of Protarás, where the coast road passes through a brief patch of forest tufting mostly rocky shore en route to **Cape Gréko**, Land's End for this corner of the island and recently declared a national park. The tippy-tip, however, remains off-limits owing to a radar station; reefy coves to either side of the final isthmus see some yacht traffic, and landlubbing sightseers, though swimming is dicey if the wind is up, as it frequently is. All told, the region's intrinsic merits are sufficiently limited to make you suspect that it would have scarcely been developed for tourism, had the much better beaches from Famagusta northwards remained under Greek-Cypriot administration.

travel details

Buses

From Larnaca to Nicosia 10 or 11 daily Mon–Sat on *Kallenos*; 1hr: to Limassol 6 or 7 daily Mon–Sat on *Kallenos*; 1hr 15min: to Páno Léfkara 1 daily, at 1pm, on the village bus; 45min: to Ayía Nápa 10 daily Mon–Sat, 4 daily Sun in season; 5 daily out of season, on *EMAN*; 6 to 8 daily Mon–Sat on *Kallenos*; 45min: to Paralímni via Protarás on *Kallenos*, 8 daily Mon-Sat, 1hr; via the Kokkinohoriá on *Paralímni Bus*, 6 or 7 daily Mon-Sat; 45min.

From Ayía Nápa to Paralímni via Protarás local service plying 9 times daily Mon–Sat, 5 daily Sun in season, falling to 3 or 4 weekday services out; 20min: to Nicosia 1 daily in early morning on *EMAN*; 1hr 30min.

Planes

Besides innumerable charters to Britain and the rest of northern Europe, scheduled services from Larnaca include at least 4 daily to Athens (1hr 40min); 1 weekly to Harare, Zimbabwe (8hr 30min); 2 weekly to Birmingham (5 hr); 2 weekly to Heraklion, Crete (1 hr 40min); 3 daily to London Heathrow (4hr 30min); 4 or 5 weekly to Manchester (5hr); 2 weekly to Rhodes (1hr

20min); 4 weekly to Tel Aviv (1hr); and 3 weekly to Thessaloniki (2hr 15min).

Except for the Harare link on *Air Zimbabwe*, all of these flights are on *Cyprus Airways*, *Olympic Airways* or *British Airways*, and consequently pricey. Budget-minded island residents make use of the less expensive *Malev* or *ČSA* indirect flights to northern Europe.

CHAPTER TWO

LIMASSOL AND AROUND

Limassol (*Lemesós* in Greek), the South's second largest town, will be your introduction to the Republic of Cyprus if you arrive by sea. It's a brash, functional place, with little to recommend it even as a base for touring other than gritty authenticity. More than anywhere else in the South, the city has acted as a magnet for extensive and debilitating urban drift from the poor, low-altitude hill villages just north, leaving just the elderly behind.

In those foothills, whose nearer settlements are now little better than commuter bedrooms for the big city, the most interesting spots, such as **Potamioú, Ómodhos** and **Vouní**, might not rate a special detour, but are easily visited en route to the high Troödhos (see Chapter Three). Other half-inhabited hill hamlets, such as Akapnoú and Odhoú, see few outsiders despite tourist board promotion, and require considerable energy to reach.

Moving along the coast east of Limassol, you must outrun thirteen kilometres of fairly horrific hotel development, some of the worst in the Mediterranean, before the tower blocks halt near ancient **Amathus**, a small but evocative site. Just before the coast road veers inland towards Nicosia there's access to **Governor's Beach**, virtually the last relatively unspoiled stretch of sand in the district.

Heading out of Limassol in the opposite direction holds more promise; a long if unscenic beach fringing the **Akrotíri cape**, home to one of the island's two

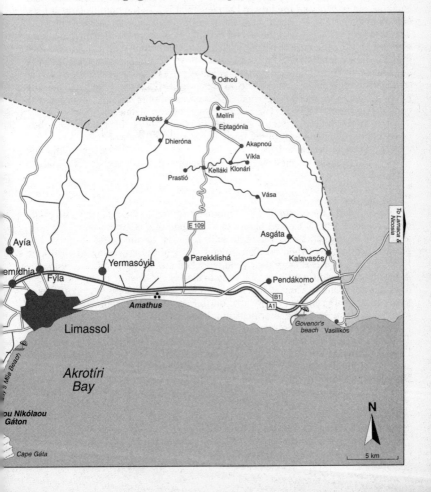

British bases plus a salt lake, ends near the legend-hung convent of **Ayíou Nikoláou ton Gáton**. On the far side of the lagoon, orange and eucalyptus groves soften the landscape en route to the atmospheric crusader castle of **Kolossi** and the clifftop ruins of **Kourion**, together with its associated **Sanctuary of Apollo**, one of the most impressive ancient sites in the South. You can swim at the beach below the palisades, but it's probably better to wait until reaching the more secluded bays near **Pissoúri**, a favourite hideout of British ex-pats.

Limassol (Lemesós)

Although not without charm in its old centre of Levantine stone buildings and alleyways, **LIMASSOL (LEMESÓS)** is primarily the industrial and commercial capital of the southern coast, specialising in wine-making, carob-milling and canning. Since 1974 and the loss of Famagusta, it is also the South's largest port, with container ships at anchor near the seafront esplanade throughout the year. The transient presence of sailors, and off-duty Brits from the nearby base, may also account for the largest red-light district in the island. With close to 200,000 more ordinary inhabitants, Limassol basks in its reputation as a mini-Texas of conspicuously consuming, gregarious *nouveaux riches*. Money is frittered away at "exclusive" nightclubs, just off the expressway to Larnaca, which supposedly never close; even receipts in modest town restaurants are apt to be A5-size computer printouts more appropriate to a warehousing business.

Most of the tourist industry hereabouts is ghettoised in a long, unsightly ribbon of development east of the town, leaving the workaday atmosphere of the centre relatively unscathed. But after looking in at the several museums and winery, and perhaps taking a stroll around the bazaar, you'll probably be ready to move on.

Some history

A near-complete lack of significant monuments attests to the relative youth of the town. Limassol hardly existed before the Christian era, being for centuries over-shadowed by Amathus to the east and Kourion to the west; it burst into prominence in 1191, when the fiancée and sister of the crusading English king Richard the Lion-Heart were nearly shipwrecked just offshore, and subsequently ill treated by Isaac Comnenus, self-styled ruler of the island. Upon appearing a few days later, and hearing of this insult to his women, Richard landed nearby in force, married Berengaria of Navarre on the site of the present-day castle, and went on to claim the island after defeating Isaac in battle.

There followed two centuries of prosperity, with both the Hospitallers and Templars having extensive holdings around Limassol after the loss of the Holy Land. But then an earthquake and devastating raids by the Genoese, Mamelukes and finally the Turks, combined to level the settlement by the beginning of the Ottoman era. It's only since the end of the last century that the town has grown again, and squalidly at that.

The Limassol area phone code is ☎05. All subscriber numbers now begin with 3, which should prefix any five-digit numbers on older literature.

Arrival, orientation and information

All passenger **ferries** dock at the new port, about 4km southwest of the town centre: bus no. 1 runs into town every 15–20 minutes, but only during daylight hours, after which the half-hourly no. 30 takes over; its route extends along the coast boulevard down to the hotel strip. If you're in a hurry to be elsewhere, phone service taxis (see "Listings") to be picked up at the port gate.

Arriving by **long-distance bus**, you'll be dropped at one of the terminals shown on the map; those driving their own vehicles should make for the **car-parks** on the sea-front promenade, conveniently across from two of the less expensive hotels.

The coastal boulevard, whose name changes first from **Spýrou Araoúzou** to **Hristodhoúlou Hadjipávlou**, then to Ikosiogdhóis Oktovríou as you move north-east, is a fair fraction of what you need to know to get around in Limassol; just inland, the main shopping street, **Ayíou Andhréou**, roughly parallels it out to the municipal gardens and archaeological museum, while Anexartisías, threading the central downtown area, is the most important perpendicular of the two. The main **tourist information** office (Mon–Sat 8.15am–1.45pm, Mon–Thurs 3–5.30pm in summer) sits also at the west end of Spýrou Araoúzou (bus #15), but their stock of leaflets is not the greatest – owing to the British presence, material in English can disappear quickly. There's also a branch in the port terminal, open for boat arrivals.

Finding a place to stay

Low-cost accommodation in Limassol is scarce, with little in between the funky guest houses of the bazaar, catering to refugees and those awaiting ferries to Israel or Greece, and the pricey digs of the resort strip. Certain no- or one-star hotels, like the *Metropole* in the bazaar, or the *Panorama* in the red-light district, are worth avoiding.

Hostels and guest houses

Youth Hostel, Angíra 120 (☎363749). Closed for renovation in 1992, but should have re-opened. Has mostly its location, near the castle, to recommend it. C£2.50 a person.

Hellas Guest House, Zik Zak 9, just off Angíra behind the Jami Kebir (☎363841). Sparse but clean enough in an old stone building; the least weird of the ultra-budget guest houses. Get a bathless room with a balcony overlooking the tradesmen's alley and the minaret. C£3 single, C£6 double.

Excelsior Guest House, Anexartisías 35 (☎353351). A slight improvement on the preceding, as it attempts to pitch itself to foreigners. C£3.50 single, £6 double.

Luxor Guest House, 101 Ayíou Andhréou (☎362265). On the pedestrianised portion of the shopping street, which is barred to traffic at night, and so quiet and clean – but the single rooms are dingy. C£5.50 single, C£10 double.

Inexpensive hotels

Limassol Palace, Spýrou Araoúzou 97–99 (☎352131). Good-value one-star place on seafront; decent rooms with fan and attached facilities, helpful management, reasonable restaurant. C£9.50 single, C£16 double.

Continental, Spýrou Araoúzou 137 (☎362530). Atmospheric 1920s two-star relic that's deservedly popular, particularly (but not exclusively) with gay clientele. C£12 single, C£20 double.

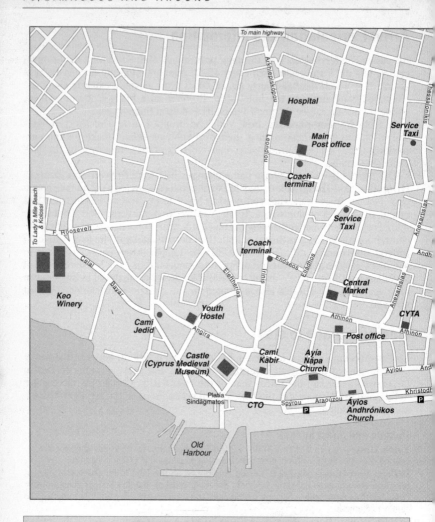

Limassol Castle p.72.

Cyprus Medieval museum p.72
(Winter/summer Mon–Fri 7.30am–
5pm/6pm, Sat 9am–5pm/6pm).

KEO Winery Tour p.73.

Folk Art museum p.73 Mon–Fri
8.30am–1.30pm & 3–5.30pm, closed
Tues afternoon).

Archeological museum p.72 (Winter/
summer Mon–Fri 7.30am–5pm/6pm,
Sat 9am–5pm/6pm, Sun 10am–1pm).

Zoo/aviary p.73 (Daily 9am–noon &
2.30–6.30pm).

Tourist information Spýrou Araoúzou
(Mon–Sat 8.15am–1.45pm, Mon–Thurs
3–5.30pm).

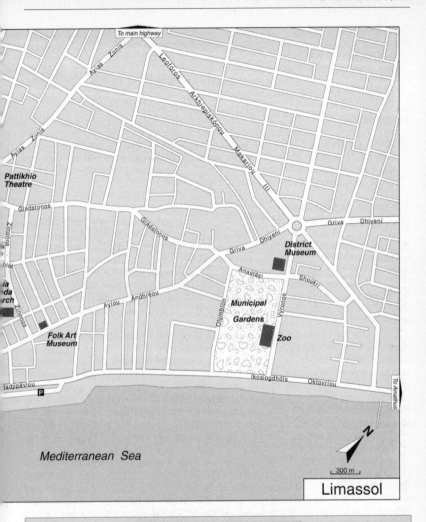

Limassol

To main highway

ACCOMMODATION

Youth Hostel, Angíra 120 (☎363749).

BUDGET
Hellas Guest House, Zik Zak 9 (☎363841).
Excelsior Guest House, Anexartisías 35 (☎353351).
Luxor Guest House, 101 Ayíou Andhréou (☎362265).

MODERATE
Limassol Palace Hotel, Spýrou Araoúzou 97–99 (☎352131).
Continental Hotel, Spýrou Araoúzou 137 (☎362530).
Eastland Hotel, Andhréa Dhroushióti 23 (☎377000).
Sunny Beach Hotel, Ikosiogdhóïs Oktovríou (☎364626).

Eastland, Andhréa Dhroushióti 23, Platía Iróon (☎377000). Comparable in category to the former, but probably worked by prostitutes, as the *Panorama* across the square definitely is. C£10.50 single, C£19 double.

Sunny Beach, Ikosiogdhóïs Oktovríou, corner Gríva Dhíyení (☎364626). One of the cheaper waterfront two-stars, near the east edge of the town's built-up area. C£12.50 single, C£22.50 double.

The city

Limassol presents a number of isolated points of interest rather than a town personality to savour: believe it or not, since 1974 this has been the number-one tourist base in the South, but it won't take more than a full day, sandwiched between two overnights, to take in all there is to see.

The castle and the bazaar

Unassuming from the outside, **Limassol castle** stands in a pleasant garden immediately north of the old port. What you see today is a careful restoration of Byzantine foundations, Venetian vandalism, Turkish adaptation for military purposes and British justice (it was a jail during the colonial period). Tradition places, on 12 May 1191, the marriage of Richard the Lion-Heart and Berengaria in the long-vanished Byzantine chapel of Saint George, somewhere under the existing walls; anticipating his rout of Isaac, Richard also had himself crowned King of Cyprus and his bride Queen of England, in the presence of assorted Latin clerics and nobility.

Currently the castle houses the **Cyprus Medieval Museum** (winter/summer Mon–Fri 7.30am–5pm/6pm, Sat 9am–5pm/6pm, closed Sun; C£0.50), though the building, with its musty, echoing vaults, air shafts and masonry groins, is as interesting as any of the exhibits, most of which are on the upper floor. The stress is on metalware, heraldry and sacred art, including bas reliefs and pottery with Christian designs; the best bits are silver Byzantine plates showing events in the life of David, part of the Lambousa Treasure (see p.213 in Chapter Seven) and two sets of armour from the Lusignan period (twelfth to fifteenth century). You can climb to the roof terrace, and then up the secondary tower, for excellent views over the town.

The surrounding neighbourhood was once the Turkish commercial district, as street names will tell you, and its lanes are still worth a brief wander. The **Cami** (pronounced "Jami") **Kabir**, its minaret visible from the castle roof, is still used by Limassol's Arab population, though the **Cami Jedid** (also known as the Köprülü Hacı İbrahim Ağa mosque), at the far end of Angíra nearer the former Turkish residential quarter, is firmly locked. Also on Angíra, identifiable by a huge, fragrant eucalyptus in the yard, is a café that's much more genuine than the fast-food joints immediately around the castle. These alternate with tacky souvenir stalls; the **covered market halls** indicated on the map may appeal more. A few minutes' walk past the Cami Kabir, past the hideous turn-of-the-century cathedral of Ayía Nápa, the old *mitrópolis* of **Áyios Andhrónikos**, built in mock-Byzantine style during the 1870s, hides in a cul-de-sac accessible only by a single alley from the waterfront.

Winery tours

The city's four distilleries are strung in a row along Franklin Roosevelt, southwest of the old harbour; most offer morning tours, though the one laid on by KEO, the largest booze outfit on the island, is the most famous. Some parking in front of the plants is available, but it's a brief walk from the castle area, or a #19 or #22 bus ride along Roosevelt – either perhaps better options after the final tasting session.

To join the daily 10am tour at KEO, just show up at 9.50 (except in summer when you should book on ☎362053) in the reception area of the administration building, just behind the parking lot. In the space of about half an hour you're rather perfunctorily shown the Commandaria cellars, where a third of each barrelful is retained as the *mána* or "mother" fermentor for the next cycle; the distillery for *eau de vie* (aka *zivánia*), used to fortify KEO's line of hard liquor; the 40,000-litre oak ageing barrels for brandy; and barrels of sweet and cream sherry ageing out in the sun (the dry stuff stays in a dark cellar). The primarily middle-aged, British patrons barely supress their eagerness for the tour to end at the tasting session, a wonderful excuse to get as pissed as you like for free, and before noon to boot (though you're encouraged to buy bottles from a sale counter). It is, in fact, a good opportunity to familiarise yourself with Cypriot wine types so that you don't get stuck with an unlovely vintage in a taverna.

The Folk Art Museum

At the opposite end of Ayíou Andhréou, near the corner of Óthonos keh Amalías at no. 253, the **Folk Art Museum** (Mon–Fri 8.30am–1.30pm & 3–5.30pm, closed Tues afternoon; c£0.30) has filled a grand old mansion with rural and domestic knick-knacks, woodwork, traditional dresses and jewellery. But the lighting and labelling aren't good, and you're virtually obliged to buy the guide booklet to make much sense of the exhibits.

A short stroll northwest along Xínonos from Ayíou Andhréou will bring you to Platía Iróön, the heart of Limassol's **red-light district**, populated in large part by Thai and Filipino bar girls who haunt the dozen or so cabarets and Asian restaurants around the square. If you found find anyone seriously interested in cooking at midday, and had a taste for slumming, the restaurants could provide an unusual lunch.

The municipal gardens and the Archaeological Museum

Beyond the Folk Art Museum sprawl the **municipal gardens**, a couple of acres of well-tended greenery fronting the sea on one side. It's the venue for the **September Wine Festival** (first half of the month), and at other times is an excellent place to wait for a ferry boat. There's also a **mini-zoo** (daily 9am–noon & 2.30–6.30pm; c£0.20), really mostly an aviary.

The district **archaeological museum** (winter/summer Mon–Fri 7.30am–5pm/6pm; Sat 9am–5pm/6pm, Sun 10am–1pm; c£0.50) is strongest on Archaic, Geometric and Bronze-Age artefacts. The left-hand gallery is ninety percent pottery, best of which are the Geometric-era dishes – an obvious inspiration for those modern woven circular wall hangings you see everywhere. Archaic terracotta figurines also abound, with possibly some toys in amongst the animal-drawn chariots and other votive offerings. Highlights include a *rhyton* in the form of a bull, and a headless torso with unusually detailed hands holding a bird to its chest. Female figures, possibly offerings for fertility, clasp their breasts or a mirror (a symbol of Aphrodite/Astarte), and one plays a frame-drum. A column capital in the guise of Hathor demonstrates the introduction of Egyptian gods to the island, and bird-necked zoomorphic Bronze-Age pots with vestigial noses and ears round out the hall's exhibits.

The smaller, central Classical room is sparsely stocked except for some gold and precious-stone jewellery; there's also a curious anthropomorphic lamp-stand, with ears for an oil wick and the head hollowed to accommodate a candle or incense. The Roman section on the right contains the usual painted and multi-coloured glass; incidentally, ancient glass was little different from modern products – the rainbow/oil-slick effect is the result of sodium and potassium ions leaching into the alkaline soils in which the objects were embedded before discovery.

Eating, drinking and nightlife

The plastic-fantastic "international cuisine" **eateries** along the waterfront are all pretty dismissable, with the exception of the *Limassol Palace*'s pink-tablecloth diner, which has a good and not exorbitant local menu (c£4 or under per person for lunch). At the entrance to the old harbour, now the fishing port, are two good adjacent choices: *Ladas*, one of the oldest fish tavernas in town, with biggish portions and local clientele, and the new *Nitayia Far East Restaurant*, where the wrap-around aquarium decor will distract you from authentic Chinese, Japanese and Thai dishes. The bill for two at either place shouldn't top c£13. Inland, the one place worth mentioning is *O Vasilikós* at Ayíou Andhréou 252, quite posh and favoured by locals for supper. There's no menu – just several entrees per evening, plus *meze*.

That end of Ayíou Andhréou is also something of a nucleus for a modest **nightlife**; diagonally across from *O Vasilikos*, at the base of Elénis Paleoloyínas, *Jazzy Bar* has live music most nights, not always jazz. *Irodhio*, nearby at Ayíou Andhréou 238, is a more sedate wine bar in an old mansion; *Cuckoo's Nest*, at no. 228, has a more idiosyncratic clientele and also does food. *Alaloum*, a disco-bar at Ayíou Andhréou 216 with some gay patronage, also comes recommended. Name music acts perform at the *Pattikhio Theatre* on Ayías Zonís, or at the *Disco Malibu* out in the hotel strip; watch hoardings for details. The town's main **cinemas** are *Othello*, Thessaloníkis 19 (☎352232), and *Oscar* (☎374306).

Listings

American Express c/o *A.L. Mantovani & Sons*, Spírou Araoúzou 130 (☎362045).

Bookstore *Book World*, Ayíou Andhréou 158; *Kyriakou*, Gríva Dhiyení 3.

Car hire *Andy Spyrou* Omonías 38–40 (☎371441); *Astra*, Yioryíou tou Prótou, Sea-Gate Court (☎323365); *Budget/Petsas*, Limassol–Nicosia highway (☎323672); *Eurodollar*, Arkhiepiskópou Makaríou 24 (☎346020); *Europcar*, Ikosioghóis Oktovríou, 4B Blue Sea House (☎324025); *Louis Self Drive*, Gládstonos 64B (☎363161); *St George's Car Hire*, Arkhiepiskópou Markaríou 62 (☎336077).

Coach companies Biggest or most useful outfits include *EMAN*, to Larnaka, on recently renamed Rikárdhou keh Verangéras (Richard & Berengaria) by the castle; *KEMEK*, to Nicosia, Páfos and select Troödhos villages, corner Irínis and Enóseos, about 300m north (☎363241); *Costas Bus*, Thessaloníkis 9B, to Nicosia and Páfos (☎354394); *Platres*, Eleftherías 50 (☎362907); and *Agros Bus*, on Gládstonos opposite the post office.

Exchange Plenty of banks in the bazaar; the *Barclays* on Spírou Araoúzou, near the tourist office, has the most convenient of several ATMs from which to withdraw cash.

Ferry agents *Amathus*, Sindágmatos 2, entrance to old harbour (☎346033), for *Poseidon Lines* (*Sea Wave, Sea Serenade, Sea Harmony*); *Louis Cruise Lines*, Franklin Roosevelt 158, out towards the wineries (☎358660), for *Princessa Cypria*; *Salamis Tours*, Hristodhoúlou

Hadjipávlou 179, corner Katsounótou on shore esplanade (☎355555), for *Marlines* (*Crown M*) and *Arkadia Lines* (*Silver Paloma*); *GAP Navigation*, Éyinis 2 (☎375630), for *Afroessa Lines* (*Panayía*); and *Vergina Lines*, Olimbíon 3B, Honey Court, near beach and central gardens (☎343978), for *Vergina* and *Queen Vergina*. For a description of routes and prices, see "By Boat to the South" under "Getting There".

Laundrette Anastási Shoúkri (formerly Kánningos), near the archaeological museum. Mon–Fri only during normal shopping hours.

Post offices Main branch, with late-afternoon hours and parcel/poste restante service, somewhat inconveniently located on Gládstonos; more central station for outbound letters just off Athinón in the bazaar.

Service taxis Principal operators are *Karydas/Kyriakos*, Thessaloníkis 21 (☎364114), to Nicosia and Páfos; *Kypros*, Spírou Araoúzou 49 (☎363979), same destinations; and *Makris*, Elládhos 166 (☎365550), to Larnaca.

Shopping Aside from the usual bazaar fare, *Skaraveos*, Ayíou Andhréou 236, features out-of-the-ordinary souvenirs and objets d'art – but not cheap. The Cyprus Handicraft Service outlet is at Thermídhos 25, off Anexartissías in the bazaar. Mountain bikes are available at *Micromania*, Kránou 15, Yermasóyia suburb.

Telephones CYTA is at the corner of Athinón and Márkou Bótsari (daily 7am–7pm).

The Limassol foothills

The foothills of the Troödhos range, inland from Limassol, are home to the bulk of Cyprus's vineyards; at vintage time in autumn, huge lorries groaning with grapes lumber along the narrow roads, and signs warn of grape-juice slicks on the pavement. Otherwise there's little other significant economic activity as far as the outside world is concerned. Many of the villages, on poor land covered in maquis vegetation, are dying, with futures only as weekend retreats for city-dwellers, or holiday homes for foreigners.

The rise to the highest peaks of the Troödhos is not a straightforward one: roads going inland roller-coaster past the first set of barrier ridges into hollows and hidden valleys that contain most of the places below.

The eastern villages

Perhaps the most isolated and forlorn of these villages are a cluster near the border of Larnaca district, described in a deceptively well-written CTO pamphlet entitled "Remote Villages of Cyprus". While the text doesn't quite make the area out to be some miniature version of Tuscany, you do need to take the descriptions with a grain of salt.

Easiest access to this area is via either the Yermasóyia or Pareklishá exits of the Limassol–Nicosia expressway. The former side road is a bit better, running 22km out of Yermasóyia to DHIERÓNA and **ARAKAPÁS**, with its much-restored Latin church of **Panayía Iamatikí** on the outskirts as the road turns east towards EPTAGÓNIA. The two latter villages are the closest things to going concerns hereabouts, with olive and mandarin orchards providing a precarious living.

The twistier road in from Pareklishá emerges after 16km on a knoll at **KELLÁKI**, with a grand view of the ridges of Pitsilliá on the far side of the valley. But otherwise neither Kelláki nor its neighbour Prastío, downhill to the west, are up to much, despite a hopeful sign "Area Tourist Information Here" at the Kelláki *kafenío*. The problem, from a tourist-development point of view, is that just

enough money has trickled in to finance a certain amount of unsightly improvements and ruin the architectural homogeneity of the places.

You may get a better idea of local vernacular architecture by following the tourist board's suggested detour east of Kelláki. **KLONÁRI** hamlet, some 6km east,
has a fine church of Áyios Nikólaos, bare inside though built in the standard
Troödhos style (see Chapter Three), but the tenants of the smelly dovecotes far
outnumber the remaining humans. The dozen houses of **VÍKLA**, a couple of dirt-
road kilometres further, are completely abandoned despite a fine setting, and the
best road on to Akapnoú takes off from Klonári, not from here as most maps
indicate. **AKAPNOÚ**, to the north on a hillock surrounded by relatively fertile
and well-watered land, has retained about thirty inhabitants and some attractive
houses; though the people are friendly enough, the place is visibly poor, with
next to nothing on offer at the *kafenío* by the square with its recent but appealing
church of Áyios Yióryios. West of the village, in the fields, the small chapel of
Panayía tou Kámbou boasts some sixteenth- and seventeenth-century frescoes.

You return to the main road at **EPTAGÓNIA**, like Arakapás a relatively busy
place; west, on the road between the two, a new purpose-built primary school
serves the region's children, the individual village schools long since having
closed down. **MELÍNI**, 4km north, has another standard-issue gabled church and
marks the start of the impressive climb up to **ODHOÚ**, at the edge of the high
Troödhos. Marvellously set amidst 850-metre crags overlooking the canyon up
which you've come, the village itself is again an unhappy architectural hotchpotch, modest prosperity having prompted some cheap and easy renovations; it
enjoys some summer trade owing to its cool climate.

Beyond Odhoú an extremely steep dirt road climbs to an 1100-metre pass in the
Pitsillian ridges; once over the watershed, paved road appears simultaneously with
a view down onto handsomely spread-out FARMAKÁS and KÁMBI (see Chapter
Four), your reward for getting a car this far.

Villages en route to the Troödhos

Rather than venture through the eastern villages of Limassol district, outsiders
are more likely to pass through the various settlements just off the two main high-
ways up to the Troödhos, which begin at Polemídhia and Episkopí on the
Limassol coastal plain. At one time or another most of these places were fiefs of
the Hospitallers or other Lusignan nobility; they are all about 800 metres above
sea level, which makes them pleasant even in high summer.

The first possible detour is just past ÁYIOS AMVRÓSIOS, a two-kilometre drive
towards mostly abandoned but highly picturesque VOUNÍ, where the remaining
elders sit at a few *kafenía* on the *Paliostráta*, the old high street. The village has
recently been listed as a protected architectural showcase, and the few ongoing
renovations are to be carried out with traditional materials and methods. But so
far there's little other evidence of gentrification, and no real tourist facilities yet,
though a cultural centre in the old school is planned.

KILÁNI, 5km north along a much better road than maps imply, is architecturally less of a piece but more lively; there's an artist's studio here and a pedestrianised area with several *kafenía*, one of which serves *muhalebí* (a rose-water
flavoured jelly) as a sweet. Behind the ugly modern church of Panayía Eleoússa,
the Limassol Archbishopric has set up an **Ecclesiastical Museum** of items
scoured from crumbling churches roundabout. It's a better-than-average collec-

tion, with a stress on intricately crafted sacred objects as well as icons. Hang purposefully about the church square and a rather demented old man will accost you, admit you to the two-room exhibit and thrust an informative leaflet in your hands. Evidently Kiláni was chosen as the venue for its past importance in church affairs; nearly a half-dozen bishops of the sixteenth through the eighteenth centuries hailed from here, and indeed the archbishopric of Limassol itself was based here for some years during the seventeenth century, when Limassol was at its nadir.

Continuing a kilometre up the valley of the Krýos stream, you can't possibly miss the twelfth-century chapel of **Ayía Mávra**, set in the river gorge by some trees and a handful of *exokhiká kéndra* or rural weekenders' tavernas. The little church is all that remains of a much large monastery, and a spring still burbles from the apse; according to legend the water flows from a cleft in the rock created when Mávra, pursued against her will by her father and proposed fiancé, appealed to the Virgin to preserve her vow of chastity – and was promptly swallowed by the low cliff. Inside are some smudged fifteenth-century frescoes, but *Áyios Timothéos* (Saint Timothy) and *Mavra* herself have been cleaned, and face you as you enter (key is always in the door); a rendition of the *Virgin Enthroned* graces the conch of the apse.

The westernmost cluster of settlements astride the route up to the Troödhos are called the "Krassokhoriá" (Wine Villages) in CTO promotion, and whether or not anyone else does, they are indeed renowned for their dry wine. At KISSOÚSA a turning leads up to **POTAMIOÚ**, arguably more beautiful than Vouní and graced by the sixteenth-century Ayía Marína church, plus the ruins of Byzantine Áyios Mnáson outside the village.

Ómodhos

Three kilometres further and you reach the more heavily promoted **ÓMODHOS**, unusually laid out around its **monastery of Timíou Stavroú** (the Holy Cross), with a vast cobbled square leading up to it – probably an instance of Lusignan town planning, since rarely in the Greek world is a monastery the core of a settlement. Although of Byzantine foundation, what you see now dates entirely from the early and mid-nineteenth century. Dositheos and Khryssanthos, sponsors and abbots of the monastery during its late medieval revival, were hanged by the Ottoman authorities with various others in 1821 when news of the mainland Greek rebellion reached the island. The last monk departed in 1917, and the money changers have in fact stormed the temple, with two stalls'-worth of tourist schlock on sale right by the very doors of the old church (usually locked). The most interesting bits of the building are the cane-ceiling and window lattices on the upper storey of the cloister; a **folk/national struggle museum** inside is only accessible by hunting down the guardian somewhere in town, and isn't worth the effort.

The village itself is pleasant enough, despite written and verbal blandishments to visit rather bogus traditional houses and an alarming concentration of *Visa* and *Access* signs. Best souvenir buys might be bottles of the red and white local wine, or *loukoúmia* (Turkish delight); only some of the basketry and lace displayed here are locally crafted. A number of simple restaurants and cafés alternate with the souvenir displays on the field-stoned plaza. The liveliest time to visit would probably be 14 September, when the monastery church functions as the focus of the festival of the Holy Cross, which spills out onto the square outside.

East from Limassol

The town beach at Limassol, stony and flanked by intermittent breakwaters, is pretty forgettable; recognising this, the CTO has improved a beach at **Dhassoúdhi**, about 4km east of town near the edge of Hotel Row. But you really need to travel further towards Larnaca before reaching any monuments of interest, or patches of fairly natural coastline.

Amathus (Amathoúnda)

Some 13km east of Limassol town centre, just past the end of the resort strip, **ancient Amathus** (fenced but gate unlocked, no fee) is signed just inland from the coast road. Limassol city bus #25 passes within a kilometre or two of the site, but you really need your own transport to reach it.

Some history

Amathus is among the oldest of Cyprus' city-kingdoms, with a purported foundation by a son of Hercules, who was revered as a god here. The legend seems to indicate settlement by the original island colonists, with a later Phoenecian religious and racial overlay. In some versions of the myth Ariadne, fleeing from the labyrinth on Crete, was abandoned here and not on Aegean Naxos by Theseus; she died here in childbirth, and was buried in a sacred grove, where her cult melded easily with that of Aphrodite. Lightly Hellenised, and prone to worship Egyptian gods as well as Asiatic ones, Amathus sided with Persia against Salamis and the other Cypriot kingdoms during the fifth- and fourth-century BC revolts, though it later declared for Alexander the Great.

The Romans made it capital of one of the four administrative districts of the island; this anticipated a bishopric in Byzantine times, when it was the birthplace of St John the Almoner, founder of the Order of the Knights Hospitaller. But decline and destruction ensued after the seventh century, and the city was largely forgotten until the nineteenth century, when its tombs to the west were looted and much dressed stone taken to Egypt to line the locks of the new Suez canal.

The site

Of the place itself, you see mostly a vast paved **agora**, studded with a dozen restored and re-erected columns, including three spiral-fluted and two square ones. In the middle of the area, a square foundation filled with rubble and masonry fragments is of uncertain function – either an altar base, or the centre of an atrium-centred stoa. Under a corrugated-roof shelter are more column chunks and pediments which await final disposition, all found since excavations resumed in 1975.

Backed into the bluff at the northwest end of the marketplace is what appears to be an elaborate **waterworks system**: the flow of a niche-spring was diverted through tunnels to sluices feeding a small basin at the head of more channels running to a pair of large cisterns. Some water appears to have run through open gutters, but you can still see a conspicuous large water-main which, exposed, leads some way out into the marketpalce. A stair-street leads up the partly excavated slope past rows of Hellenistic-era **houses**.

At the seaward end of the agora, the symbolism in some pebbled floor mosaics suggests that a round precinct containing them may be the foundations of a

Christian basilica. The site is still unlabelled and thus less rewarding than it might be; a raised viewing dais near the presumed basilica will hopefully get a site plan installed on it soon.

Up on the bluff is the ancient acropolis, with stretches of defensive **walls** and the remains of a **temple** jointly dedicated to Aphrodite and Hercules. Across the road, towards the sea, are more sections of wall and traces of the ancient port, submerged to a distance of several hundred yards from the present shoreline; earthquake and subsidence have laid them low. It is claimed that Richard the Lion-Heart landed at this particular bay in May 1191, to begin his march on Limassol.

Governor's Beach (Aktí Kivernítou)

Something resembling undeveloped beaches can be found 29km east of Limassol, right on the district border and just a few kilometres off the expressway at Exit 16. Despite the singular name, this is not one but several coves at the base of the low chalk cliffs here, endowed with fine, contrasting dark sand that fills quickly on warm weekends. Each cove is lorded over by rustic tavernas, each of these claiming to be at the "real" beach.

The road forks almost immediately, and the left-hand turning splits again, each junction festooned with contradictory signs. The right-hand option leads to *Adamos*, overlooking the broadest stretch of sand and sunbeds, with *Sofroniou* nearby; *Faros*, as the name (Lighthouse) implies, is out on a rocky cape beyond, looking towards the ugly cement plant at VASILIKÓS which mars the area. The coves on the far left are narrower and cliff-girt, served by cheap and cheerful *Panayiotis* and the adjacent new **campsite**; this is rather bleak and shadeless, popular with caravans but not really suitable for tents until the trees have grown up a bit.

Southwest from Limassol: Akrotíri

At the southwest end of Limassol, near the entrance to the new port, you're presented with a choice of means for leaving the city: along the minor, eventually unpaved road paralleling the Akrotíri peninsula's east shore, or roughly west across the base of the cape to the Fassoúri plantations.

Lady's Mile Beach

The east shore, known for obscure reasons as **Lady's Mile Beach**, is closer to four miles of grey, hardpacked sand, largely undeveloped because, foremost, it's the property of the British Ministry of Defence and also since, with a mosquito-ey salt lake behind, it's not very good as a beach (though the bird life in the lake is rewarding; see "Wildlife" in *Contexts*). The almost unsloping tidal flats are better for jogging (and dune-buggying, as dozens of locals do) than sunbathing; every few hundred metres there's an impermanent-looking café or taverna catering for the weekend crowds of city people, so you won't starve. There's no camping allowed as, surprisingly, parts of the beach are supposedly a turtle-nesting area; in any case occasional summer buses venture beyond the #1 and #30 terminus at the new harbour.

The convent of Ayíou Nikoláou ton Gáton

At the south end of Lady's Mile, the dirt track takes a bend inland to follow the south shore of the salt lagoon; after less than a kilometre an unsigned driveway on the left wiggles through a gap in the fence and past hedgerows to the grounds of the convent of **Ayíou Nikoláou ton Gáton** (Saint Nicholas of the Cats).

The peculiar name springs from a wonderful Byzantine **legend**, according to which Saint Helen imported hundreds of cats from Egypt or Palestine, at the time of Saint Nicholas' fourth-century foundation, to control the population of poisonous snakes which infested the place. The monks at what was originally a monastery would summon their moggies to meals by the tolling of a bell, and another bell would send them out into the surrounding fields to battle the serpents, so that "nearly all were maimed [in the words of a visiting Venetian monk of 1484]: one has lost a nose, another an ear; the skin of one is torn, another is lame; one is blind of one eye, another of both."

The habit of keeping cats to battle the island's numerous snakes spread quickly to most of the other Cypriot monasteries, and also to Rhodes; when the Knights Hospitaller of Saint John moved there, they are said to have taken a whole shipload of cats with them. More recently, the Greek Nobel laureate George Seferis used the inter-species struggle as a metaphor for opposition to the dictatorship then in power in Greece, in virtually his last published poem "The Cats of Saint Nicholas":

> *Wildly obstinate, always wounded,*
> *They annihilated the snakes, but in the end they were lost,*
> *They just couldn't endure so much poison . . .*

The contemporary reality of Ayíou Nikoláou is not so lofty: a working cloister, in the throes of renovation and of little architectural interest other than a fine

---

THE BRITISH SOVEREIGN BASES

One of the conditions of Cypriot independence in 1960 was the setting aside of a certain percentage of the island's area as British military bases, known as the **Sovereign Base Areas** or SBAs for short. In fact, the date of nationhood was delayed by disputes over the exact size of the SBAs, which eventually resulted in a figure of about 99 square miles. Most of this area consists of the Episkopí Base, around the village of that name; the adjoining Akrotíri Air Field; and the Dhekélia Base between Larnaca and Ayía Nápa. The borders of the bases were drawn in such a way as to exclude almost all private land and villages – the only exception being Akrotíri village. In addition to these main bases, fifteen so-called "retained sites" or annexes are scattered across the South; the most conspicuous of these include the RAF radar domes on Mount Olympus, the BBC transmitters at Zíyi, and the posted artillery range on the Akámas Peninsula.

Technically the bases form British Dependent Territories administered by a military governor, though the population of about 9000 (roughly half servicemen, the rest their dependents and other civilians) is subject to a civil legal system based closely on Cypriot law. Justice is dispensed at a courthouse and jail, which recently held two British airmen accused of espionage; after considerable expenditure of taxpayers' money, the prosecutor's case collapsed in an ignominy of poor documen-

coat-of-arms over the door of the thirteenth-century church. Today the convent is home to a handful of aged nuns and – still – dozens of cats, many as ragged-looking as those seen by the Venetian. They stalk about like the denizens of a temple to the Egyptian cat-god which may once have stood here, and Cape Gáta (She-Cat), out past the runway of the Akrotíri airfield, is named for them, too.

Akrotíri

The main dirt access road heads west back to asphalt at the village of AKROTÍRI, distinguished mainly by the privilege of dual nationality for its inhabitants – it is the only Cypriot village not excluded from Sovereign Base territory (see "The British Sovereign Bases", below) – and the improbable number of tavernas, aimed at the dependents of Her Majesty's Finest. They are stationed beyond the check-point to the south, in a no-go area; you have to turn northwest towards Fassoúri and Kolossi, passing close by a forest of listening and transmitting devices.

West to Kolossi and Kourion

The good road west from near the Limassol new harbour, signed towards ASÓMATOS and FASSOÚRI, is the most scenic route to Kolossi and Kourion, far less dangerous and no longer than the main inland highway. Giant junipers, planted long ago as windbreaks, have grown up to form lofty tunnels over the road; eucalyptus clumps drained the swamps here and allowed extensive orange groves to flourish. At roadside stalls near the *Red Seal Plantation*, you can buy giant sacks of the fruit, the cheapest in the South.

tation. Despite the presence of a separate SBA police force, there is no border control: the only way you know that you've entered a base is a sudden outbreak of UK-style street signs with names like Pembridge Housing Estate or Yorkshire Road. South Cypriots as well as foreigners circulate freely across SBA boundaries, and some 2300 Greek Cypriots have jobs on the two largest bases.

Strangely, about 300 Turkish Cypriots also continue to work at the Dhekélia base; they enter via the "Four Mile Crossing", a thin sliver of British territory abutting the outskirts of Famagusta, and the Attila Line. With the proper identification, British forces and their families can also cross in the other direction. After August 1974, almost 10,000 Turkish Cypriots from the Limassol area, escaping reprisal attacks by EOKA-B, sought shelter for six months in the Episkopí base, until they were airlifted out to Turkey – and from there to the North.

The official rationale for the bases' 1960 establishment and continued existence asserts their vital importance to British strategic interests as listening posts, east Mediterranean airfields, and warm-winter training areas. Indeed Britain's 1878 acquisition of Cyprus as a complement to Malta and Gibralter, and stubborn retention of the island in the face of nationalist agitation, was premised on such logic. But it is more an irony of history than a demonstration of accidental foresight that only since the late 1950s, with the winding up of empire and successive Middle Eastern crises, have the SBAs come to play the role originally envisioned for the whole island.

Kolossi

Long before citrus, sugar cane and grapes were cultivated in this area; the **castle of Kolossi** (daily 7.30am–sunset/7pm winter/summer; c£0.50; frequent #16 or #17 **bus** from Limassol, Mon–Fri only), just south of the village of that name, still stands evocatively amid the vineyards that helped make it famous. Its story is also linked inextricably with the Hospitallers, whose *commanderie* it was, the name later bestowed on the rich dessert wine.

The Knights were first granted land here in 1210 by the Lusignans, and the castle that grew up subsequently became their headquarters after the Crusaders' final loss of the Holy Land. Even after the Order shifted to Rhodes exactly a century later, the Knights kept Kolossi as the headquarters of their local fiefs, which included dozens of foothill villages. Mameluke raids of the fifteenth century virtually levelled the original castle, later rebuilt on a smaller scale; in 1488 the Venetians appropriated it, along with the Order's other holdings. The Ottomans allowed the place to slowly fall into disrepair until the British restoration of 1933.

Today's three-storey, keep-style structure stands among the ruins of a much larger castle; from the **coat-of-arms** of the Grand Master Louis de Magnac, set into the east wall, a restoration date of approximately 1450 has been deduced. Modern stairs have replaced a defensive retractable ramp up to the first-floor door; the ground floor with its critical well, in effect a three-chambered storage basement, originally had no entrance from outside. In the left-hand, vaulted room of the middle storey, probably the kitchen, you'll see the first of several huge **fireplaces**, more appropriate to north European chateaux and not equalled on the island since. By the spiral stairway in the other room, a glass plate protects a damaged **fresco** of the *Crucifixion*. The upper storey has thinner walls, and two grand halls perpendicular to those below – presumably the quarters of de Magnac, as his heraldry again appears on one of the two back-to-back fireplaces. Benches flanking most of the window niches add a homely touch. Steps continue to the flat roof-terrace, where machicolations over the gate permitted the pouring of noxious substances onto uninvited guests.

The other roofed building in the precinct is the **sugar factory**, a barn-like vaulted structure also buttressed externally; first the Knights, and later the Venetians produced sugar locally, though the establishment of slave-worked plantations in the Caribbean put paid to the Cypriot industry early in the Ottoman occupation. The still-visible cane-crushing millstone outside was watered by sluices fed in turn by a huge aqueduct, now shaded by a giant pepper tree, at the northeast corner of the grounds. Evidently the springs still ran until recently, as modern, metal sheathed extensions of the spillways snake through burgeoning flower gardens. Within sight of the castle, to the northeast, the usually locked twelfth-century church of **Áyios Evstáthios** was the Knights' place of worship.

Kourion (Curium)

Perched dramatically on a sheer bluff overlooking the sea, **Kourion** is easily the most spectacular of the South's archaeological sites – even though close up some of its individual attractions may be out of bounds or incoherent while excavations continue. Curiously, they are a bit of the ancient world that is forever (?) England, since the ruins are entirely contained within the Episkopí Sovereign Base. Kourion consists of two sites: the ancient city, closer to Kolossi, and the sanctuary of Apollo Hylates, a few kilometres west – you'll want half a day to see them both. The ruins lie about 5km west of Kolossi, and benefit from the same bus service.

Some history

Despite discouraging water-supply problems, this easily defensible clifftop may have been first settled in Neolithic times, but a recognisable city only got underway following Mycenaean colonisation between the fourteenth and twelfth centuries BC. Kourion played a leading – negative – role in the **Cypriot rebellion against Persia**; at a critical moment its king Stesenor defected to the enemy with a considerable body of troops, guaranteeing the island's re-subjugation. Like Amathus, however, it later championed Alexander against the Persians, and remained an important town throughout the Roman and early Byzantine periods; indeed, most of what can be seen today dates about evenly from those two eras. Following a cataclysmic earthquake in 365 AD, the city was utterly destroyed, and only tentatively re-built and resettled over the next few decades. After the seventh-century Arab raids, Kourion, like many other coastal settlements on Cyprus, was abandoned for good, and its bishop moved to nearby Episkopí.

The notorious American consul-turned-antiquarian **Palma Di Cesnola** began excavating (or rather plundering) in 1865, and eleven years later claimed to have chanced on several untouched hoards of gold, silver, bronze and precious-stone-inlaid objects, suggesting that Kourion had been far wealthier than anyone imagined. Even at the time many doubted his story, accusing him of doctoring the evidence and assembling the collection from his activities at various sites scattered across the island. Whatever, the troves were shortly sold en bloc to the New York Metropolitan Museum and came to be known as the **Curium Treasure**.

Between 1933 and 1954, George McFadden of the University of Pennsylvania carried out rather desultory **archaeological excavations** at both the ancient city and the nearby sanctuary of Apollo. But while popular locally he was not a particularly systematic or effective archaeologist, and after his untimely death by drowning just below the site, more important work was undertaken by a Cypriot team. In the early 1980s they were succeeded by the American David Soren and assistants, who soon dramatically established not only the exact date of the mid-fourth-century quake which had levelled Kourion, but also – from jewellery found on skeletal remains of several victims – that its population was already substantially Christian. Soren's account of these discoveries (see "Books") is invaluable for making sense of the ruins, and placing the city in some historical context.

The ancient city

More than usual, it's imperative to visit the site of the **ancient city** (7.30am–sunset/7pm winter/summer; c£0.50) early or late, since coach tours between 10am and 1pm utterly clog the walkways and make it physically impossible to see the place. If you're driving yourself, there are two separate entrances, with the more important, eastern one vaguely signed. "Curium Beach Road" goes *only* to the beach; you want the next turnoff west, "Curium Theatre Road East", which leads to most of the points of interest. Coming from Páfos, there is another, much less used, entrance, signed for its CTO kiosk. **Public bus** service, via Kolossi and Episkopí village, departs hourly 9am to noon from just outside Limassol castle; curiously, there are only two scheduled returns, at 11.50am and 2.50pm.

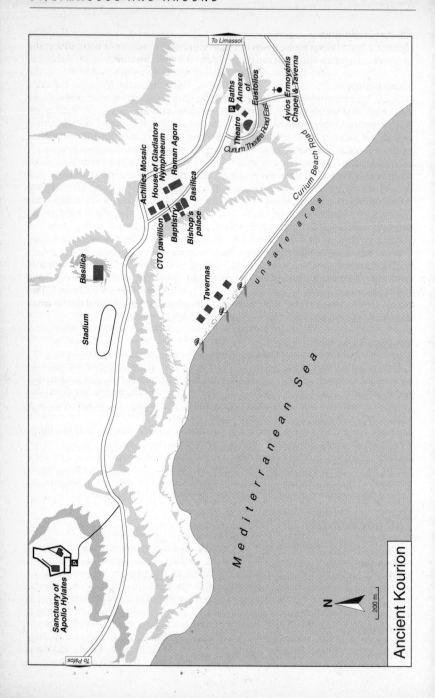

Ancient Kourion

Eastern highlights

Curium Theatre Road East passes traces of Kourion's ancient **necropolis** and the medieval chapel of **Áyios Ermoyénis**, built to house the relics of an Anatolian martyr whose coffin floated ashore here; a lively festival takes place in the surrounding eucalyptus grove each 5 October. Once inside the site gate, the main car-park and bus turn-around area is just behind the **theatre**, a second-century AD reworking of an earlier Hellenistic version. This has recently been again rather brashly restored, and is used for performances in high tourist season (watch for posters locally with acts and ticket venues); the most famous, held every year since 1961, are the mid-June and September Shakespeare plays.

Immediately northeast, under sheltering roofs, lie the foundations of **baths** and the so-called **annexe of Eustolios**, both built originally as a private villa in the late fourth century AD, and later donated for public use. Wooden catwalks take you around and above the intricate, sub-floor heating system of the baths, plus the celebrated **mosaics**. The baths have as their highlight, in the central room, mosaics of a partridge and of Ktisis, the spirit of Creation personified as a woman holding a rule measure. The annexe to the south features on its atrium pavement a beautiful panel showing fish and birds, commonly used decorative symbols during the early years of Christianity. A long inscription reflects the establishment of Christianity: "In place of rock and iron, or gleaming bronze and diamonds, this house is girt with the much-venerated signs of Christ." Two others, at the west vestibule, bid the vistor welcome and mention both the original owner Eustolios and the former patron god Apollo by name.

Western highlights

From the car-park the track continues hesitantly west some distance to a 70-metre-long fifth-century **basilica**, once supported by two sets of a dozen columns each but now quite ruinous. Working with straitened, post-'quake budgets, the bishops cut corners and recycled ancient masonry wherever they could. At the southwest, narthex end you can admire the view over the sea and also an unsual, deep hexagonal **fountain**.

Next door the smaller **baptistry**, of a slightly later date, is in better condition, with more complete geometric floor mosaics and the odd standing column. In the middle is another hexagonal pool for holy water, and on the south side of the nave a marble-lined, cruciform font which shows signs of having been modified for infant baptism once the entire adult population of Kourion had been converted. At the seaward end of the building, some surviving arches are thought to be part of a **bishop's palace**.

Between the basilica and the CTO restaurant there's a securely locked barrier, which stays closed unless you can find a keeper to open it; also currently shut for ongoing excavations are the nearby Roman **agora**, with its stretch of restored second-century colonnade, and what is labelled as a **nymphaeum** (fountain-house), once fed by an **aqueduct** which also must have supplied some conspicuous **baths**. You have to drive or walk all the way around the north face of the Kourion bluff to reach the other side of the locked gate, and will probably discover that both the late Roman "**House of Gladiators**" and the **Achilles Mosaic** are off-limits.

"Gladiators" takes its name from a floor mosaic of two gladiators in combat, attended by a referee; all the figures are named with inscriptions, and presumably were stalwarts of contests in the nearby theatre. The badly damaged Achilles Mosaic shows Odysseus detecting Achilles disguised as a maiden; the same building, possibly used for public functions, has a panel of Ganymede being kidnapped by an eagle. Again you'll have to find a guard to let you in to these areas – start at the barrier shelter, or ask at the CTO facility.

The museum and the beach

The **site museum** is some distance away from the old city, in the large village of EPISKOPÍ, and easier visited in tandem with Kolossi. Follow signs through Episkopí to the church of Ayía Paraskeví; the museum (Mon–Sat 7.30am–2pm/ 1.30pm winter/summer), in the old rambling house once lived in by archaeologist George McFadden, stands opposite. The collection, occupying two wings, consists largely of terracotta objects not only from Kourion but also the Sanctuary of Apollo (see below) and two minor sites nearby.

The **beach** southwest of the ruins, reachable by one of two roads past Áyios Ermoyénis and its attendant *exokhiko kéndro*, may be more compelling. Once you're clear of the prominently marked unsafe area, the water is cleaner and deeper (beyond the pink buoys) than the 800 metres of hard-packed sand suggests. The swimmable end of the beach is dotted with a number of impromptu tavernas, their minimal construction, like the ones at Lady's Mile, owed to short-term concessions from the British; the *Sunshine Tavern*, with such delicacies as grilled pigeon, is perhaps the best of the bunch.

Sanctuary of Apollo Hylates

At the large sacred complex surrounding the sanctuary of Apollo Hylates (7.30am–sunset/7pm winter/summer; c£0.50), about 2km west of Kourion proper, Apollo was worshipped as the god of the surrounding woodland and as protector of the pre-Christian city. Today a huge RAF antenna farm west of the sanctuary distracts somewhat from the atmosphere, but it is still an attractive archaeological site.

The sacred precinct was consecrated during the eighth century BC, but the present buildings are early Roman, flattened by the great earthquake of 365 AD. The two ancient **gates**, that of Paphos on the west and of Kourion on the east, are no longer intact, though the path from the ticket office passes the stumps of the former. On the right, before reaching the Kourion gate, you'll see the **palaestra** area, in one corner of which still stands a large water jug, used by athletes to cool off. Beyond, to the northeast, the **baths** sprawl under a tin shelter protecting piles of hypocaust stones.

The **processional way** starts at the extensive **xenon** or inn for pilgrims, with its restored Doric colonnade, and passes the presumed **priests' quarters** and precinct walls as it climbs a slight slope to the partly restored **temple of Apollo**. Two columns, a wall corner, and an angle of the pediment enclose the altar area, open to the sky even in its day, and most holy; unauthorised individuals profaning it even with an inadvertent touch were hurled off the Kourion cliffs to appease the god's wrath. On the west of the grounds, near the site of the Paphos gate, are the foundations of the **display hall** for votive offerings; between it and the processional way hides a curious round structure or **vothros**, not yet completely excavated, where it is surmised the priests discretely disposed of old and surplus gifts to the god.

A curious and ubiquitous feature of the sanctuary are series of broad **stone channels** hacked out of the strata: once thought to be aqueducts, current theory identifies them as planter boxes used by the priests of Apollo for landscaping the grounds in a manner fitting for a woodland god.

Not much is left of the imperial Roman **stadium** (access unrestricted), 500m to the east; it once seated 6000, but now just a few rows of seats, and three gaps where the gates were, can be distinguished. On a knoll still further east, fenced but with its gate always open, a sixth-century **basilica** has a huge well in the floor, and traces of floor mosaic in the altar area. Much of the flooring, however, was found in 1974 to be marble plaques pilfered from the nymphaeum in the city, laid face-down so that bas reliefs of pagan mythological scenes would not offend Christian sensibilities.

West towards Páfos: beaches

The limits of the Episkopí Sovereign Base extend almost to the boundary of Páfos district, again having the happy side effect (whatever you think of its political wisdom) of protecting the local coast from gross despoliation. Some 27km west of Limassol, watch for a sign to seaward pointing to **"Evdhímou jetty"**, not to be confused with the inland village of Evdhímou (Avdhímou), which like its three western neighbours was Turkish-inhabited before 1974. What's actually indicated is a decent shingle-and-coarse-sand beach alongside the mooring facility. A single restaurant serves fish on occasion.

Pissoúri

The only really sizeable coastal settlement between Episkopí village and the Páfos border is **PISSOÚRI**, draped appealingly over a ridge a bit south of the highway, though disfigured with too many new buildings to be really attractive close up. Owing to a relative calm and proximity to the Episkopí Sovereign Base, it's a favourite of service families, with a half-dozen places to **stay** and **eat**. Most famous of these is the *Bunch of Grapes Inn* (☎05/221275), a restored, hundred-year-old farmhouse with singles at C£13.50 and doubles for C£19.50; meals are dear and it's a bit snooty, however, and this is by no means the only establishment in town.

Pissoúri's **beach**, 3km below the village along a good but twisty road, is a lot longer (nearly a kilometre) than it appears from above, well protected and sandy. You could do worse than base yourself here, with thus far just a handful of tavernas, villa developments and hotel-apartments. Of the latter, *Kotzias* (☎05/221014) is attractively set; the *Monte Beach* restaurant at the strand's west end, despite a mega-casino appearance, is not at all bad and reasonable at well under C£4 a head.

Pétra tou Romíou

Beyond Pissoúri the coast road is desolate until, just over the boundary in Páfos province, the imposing shoreline monolith of **Pétra tou Romíou** invariably prompts drivers to slam on their brakes at a strategic viewpoint and fish for the camera. (You can admire the view at more leisure from the CTO food/drink/souvenir pavillion here, just inland and up the hill.) In legend this was the spot where Aphrodite, ancient patron goddess of Cyprus, emerged from the sea foam, though the formation actually takes its name (Rock of Romios) from the Byzantine folk hero Dhiyenis Akritas, aka Romios, who used this and other boulders as missiles against pirates.

A longish pebble-and-coarse-sand beach extends mostly to the west of the largest rock and its satellites, though it must be said that its popularity is due mostly to its mythic associations and ease of access; the high-speed traffic whizzing by just overhead makes it hardly alluring. The ocean here is also prone to murkiness at most seasons – were Aphrodite to repeat her performance today, she would most likely emerge draped in seaweed, not foam.

travel details

Buses

Limassol to **Nicosia** 6 daily Mon–Fri on *KEMEK*, 1 or 2 daily Mon–Sat with *Costas*; 1hr 15min: to **Lárnaca** 5 daily Mon–Sat on *EMAN*; 1hr: to **Páfos** 4 daily Mon–Fri on *KEMEK*, 1 or 2 daily Mon–Sat with *Costas*; 1hr 15min: to **Plátres** 1 daily Mon–Fri at about noon with *Karydas*, 3 a day in August; 1 daily at 2pm with *Platres Bus*; 1hr 30min: to **Ágros** 1 daily Mon–Fri at 11.45 am on *Agros Bus*; 1hr 30min.

International Ferries

Two to four weekly, depending on season, from Limassol to Haifa (Israel), Rhodes and Piraeus (Greece); 2 or 3 weekly to Heraklion (Greece), summer only; 1 weekly to Ancona (Italy) and Port Said (Egypt), summer only. See "By Boat to the South" in *Basics* for a detailed summary of ferry routes.

CHAPTER THREE

PÁFOS AND THE WEST

Since the final collapse of the Byzantine empire in the fifteenth century, the western end of Cyprus has always been its remotest and least-developed portion. Following the Ottoman conquest, the district of Páfos also became the most Turkified part of the island, with close to a third of the population being Turkish Cypriot before the events of 1974.

These changes inevitably had a profound effect on local customs and speech, with the accent and dialect of both communities strongly influencing each other – and virtually incomprehensible to outsiders. Another result of the area's relative isolation was the Greek community's retention of a large vocabulary of Homeric Greek, a heritage of the original Mycenaean colonisation which further complicated the linguistic profile. Other Cypriots labelled the Pafiots as mongrel bumpkins; the Pafiots retorted that this was simply jealousy at work, since they were more intelligent than the other islanders. Towards off-islanders, this takes the form of an extroverted bluntness which might cause offence if you didn't realise they generally mean well.

With the departure of the Turkish commmunity in 1975, and the opening of the the Páfos international airport in the early 1980s, local idiosyncracies have inevitably diminished, and the level of touristic development is rapidly coming to match that of the other coastal districts. But big chunks of Páfos are still exhilaratingly wild, villages characterful, and the beaches perhaps the best in the South.

Páfos town is showing signs of too-rapid growth, but it still makes for a comfortable overnight stay and has much to offer in the way of antiquities; more of these, from several eras, dot the coastal plain towards the district border, at **Yeroskípou** and **Koúklia**. Middle and late Byzantine monuments await you in the opposite direction, at **Émba** and the **monastery of Áyios Neófitos**, and further afield near handsome villages – such as **Péyia** and **Dhroúsha** – on the base of the Akámas peninsula. The coast itself improves as you head north from Páfos, with the beaches around **Lára** in particular still the focus of battles between developers and conservationists, the latter for the moment at least prevailing.

Pólis, on the north shore of the island, provides a blissfully peaceful retreat, with uncluttered beaches stretching in either direction. The small town and a limited number of surrounding resorts form bases for jeep, boat or foot explorations along the rugged tip of the **Akámas peninsula** to the west – thinly vegetated, slashed by ravines, and containing the South's only national park. East of the road linking Páfos and Pólis, the landscape becomes gentler and life in the villages around the showcase monastery of **Khrysorroyiátissa** is easier, but there's still scope for adventure (and good hiking) in the uninhabited forests of **Tillyría**.

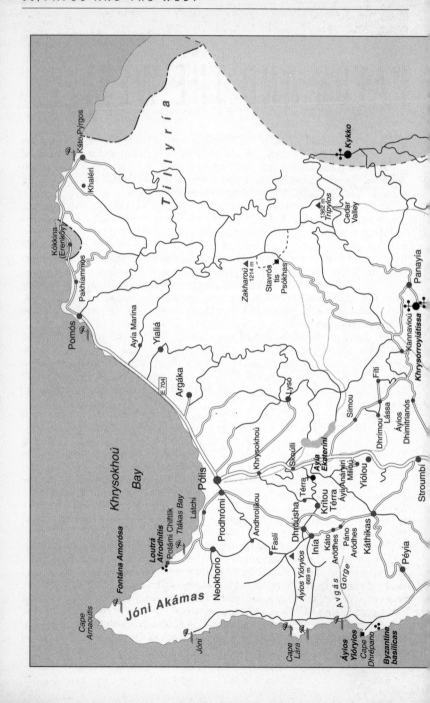

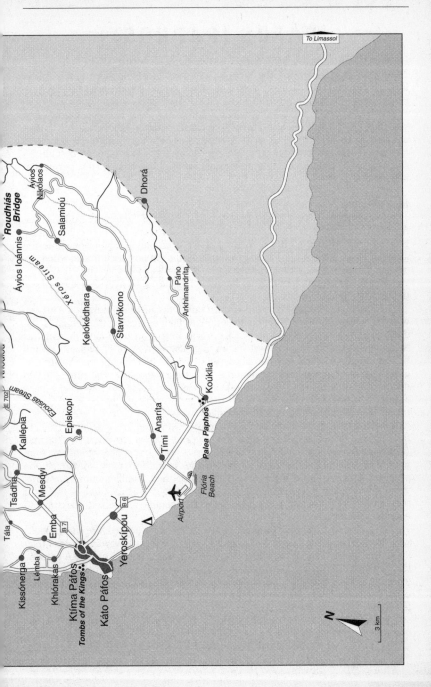

PÁFOS (PAPHOS)

Perhaps the most noteworthy feature of the district capital PÁFOS is its layout. Two distinct settlements – the harbour, archaeological zone and hotel strip at Káto Páfos, and the true town centre of Ktíma three kilometres up the hill – are jointly and confusingly referred to as Néa (New) Páfos to distinguish it from Paleá (Old) Páfos, now called Koúklia, 16km to the east. The upper town, first settled by the Byzantines as a haven from coastal attacks, seems in some danger of losing its separate identity, as the blank spaces between it and the lower resort area are slowly but surely filled in by tower blocks. For the moment, though, it's still a pleasant if unremarkable provincial capital of less than 30,000 permanent inhabitants.

Some history

The foundations of "new" Páfos are obscure; in legend Agapenor, leader of the Arcadian contingent to Troy, was shipwrecked near here in the twelfth century BC and decided to stay. But it seems to have been only a minor annexe to the sanctuary and town at old Páphos (see p.103) until Hellenistic times, when the last independent Pafiot king, Nikoklis, actually laid out a proper city. Its perimeter walls enclosed much of the headland behind the harbour, which shipped out timber from the hill forests.

The Ptolemies made Páfos the island's rather decadent administrative centre, which it remained during the Roman period, when it rejoiced in the pompous title of Augusta Claudia Flavia Paphos. Cicero was proconsul here for two years, as was one Sergius Paulus, the first recorded official convert to Christianity, at the behest of apostles Paul and Barnabas. Acts 13: 6–12 records the event, with (for good measure) the incidental blinding of a pagan sorcerer who attempted to distract the new believer. Despite this success Paul seems to have had a hard time combatting Aphrodite's love-cult here, and was reputedly scourged for his troubles on the site of the Byzantine basilica.

Repeated earthquakes, including two in the fourth century, relegated Páfos to the status of a backwater, and the Cypriot capital reverted to Salamis (Constantia), though Páfos was designated – and has since remained – an important bishopric. The Arab raids of the seventh century completed the process of desolation, however, and for more than a millennium afterwards visitors were unanimous in characterising the shabby port as a hole – that is, if they were lucky enough to survive to write about it and didn't succumb to endemic diseases.

Under British administration the town's fortunes perked up: the harbour was dredged and the population began to climb from a low point of less than 2000. During the late 1950s, when Páfos district was a hotbed of EOKA activity, the British had a major interrogation and confinement centre in the town. But when in 1974 Archbishop Makarios took refuge here following the EOKA-B coup, it was the British who saved his bacon by airlifting him out by helicopter to the Akrotíri air base (see p.121).

The telephone code for the entire Páfos district is ☎06.

Arriving

Taxis from the 15-kilometre-distant airport (there is no bus service) shouldn't set you back more than c£3 to Ktíma, c£4 to Káto Páfos – if you haven't arranged a fly-drive you'll be using them, as there are only a pair of car-hire booths, and a part-time tourist info booth, at the arrival lounge.

Driving into Káto Páfos from elsewhere, if you're not booked into accommodation with parking space, you'll probably end up in the enormous, apparently free dirt lot behind the waterfront – in high season the narrow streets will be out of the question. Up in Ktíma you're best off using the enormous public car park at the foot of the bluff on which the bazaar and old Turkish quarter is built.

Bus services

The car-park is also near the central stop for the ALEPA municipal bus service, with several useful lines along the main drags: Káto Páfos and Ktíma are linked every 15 minutes during daylight hours Monday to Saturday (half-hourly on holidays) by bus #11, which plies Leofóros Apostólou Pávlou, connecting the two districts, and Posidhónos, the easterly shorefront road of Káto's southerly "Hotel Row". The #15 bus goes further afield, diverging from Apostólou Pávlou at Táfon ton Vasiléon and heading out past the northwesterly resort strip en route to Coral Bay.

Orientation and information

Other main streets in Ktíma, splitting off from the central Platía Kennedy, include Gríva Dhiyení, the road towards Limassol; Evágora Pallikarídhi, which becomes Elládhos and then the Pólis-bound road; short but busy Arkhiepiskópou Makaríou, the main commercial street leading to the older bazaar and ex-Turkish quarter; and Pávlou Melá, still cited as Gladstone on many maps, home to most tourist services, including the tourist information office (Mon–Sat 8.15am–1.45pm, Mon and Thurs 3.45–6.15pm), which has an unusually complete stock of maps and handouts.

Finding a place to stay

Since the recent wave of gentrification, little decent accommodation remains that is not part of the pre-booked package scene. Most of the places below are no exception, but at least can be approached individually.

Youth Hostel, Eleftheríou Venizélou 37, Ktíma (☎232588). A fifteen-minute walk northeast of the town centre, but clean and quiet enough. c£2.50 per person in one of three six-bed rooms.

Lazaros Omírou, Ayíou Kendhéa 25, Ktíma (☎232909). A pension run out of an old house; you can't get much more central. c£5 per person.

Ambassador Hotel Apartments, Malióti 1, a stair-street off Apostólou Pávlou, Ktíma (☎235440). Furnished studios that are good value at c£15.50 double.

Kiniras Hotel, Arkhiepiskópou Makaríou 91, Ktíma (☎241604). Small hotel in a restored 1920s building, with its own bar and garden-restaurant. Singles c£14.50; doubles c£26.

The Park Mansion, Pávlou Mélá (ex-Gladstone), below tourist office (☎245645). Rambling old renovated building overlooking a park. Seems to get a retired-colonial-civil-service clientele straight out of a Graham Greene novel. Singles c£17, doubles c£26; c£21/c£34 on a half-board basis.

The Pelican Inn, Apostólou Pávlou 102, Káto Páfos yacht harbour (☎235538). Fairly spartan rooms in a concrete building – basically you're paying for the location. Singles C£14, doubles C£27.

Pyramos Hotel, Ayíou Anastasíou 4, Káto Páfos (☎235161). Surrounded by medieval monuments, and worth trying to squeeze in between the tour groups. C£14 single, C£20 double.

Káto Páfos

The main resort "strip" in Káto Páfos, east of Apostólou Pávlou and the harbour, constitutes a repertory of opticians, estate agents, glitzy restaurants, clothes shops, souvenir kiosks, banks and travel agencies with little character, the pattern repeating itself every couple of hundred metres. It's a fairly lacklustre sequence, and to begin a tour of the lower town you're better off heading straight for the yacht harbour, roughly equidistant from most points of interest.

The yacht harbour

Big doings are afoot in the yacht harbour, as the pavement around the anchorage is being torn up and replaced, and the old customs house on the quay has been gutted in anticipation of who knows what. The foundations of the Byzantine church Panayía Limeniótissa, destroyed like so much else in the seventh century, can be seen behind the Pelican Inn; the Danish crusader Eric the Good, one of many who died here, was supposedly buried inside the ruins. On the waterfront, Kokos the tame pelican struts, and glass-bottom-boat cruises are on offer: C£5 for a short hop to a wreck, C£8 up to Lara Bay, or C£15 all the way around Akamas point.

The castle

The diminutive castle (Mon–Fri 7.30am–2pm, Sat 7.30am–1pm; C£0.50) guarding the harbour entrance is reached by a small stone bridge across a narrow moat. Currently empty, the building's main attraction is the chance to climb up to the roof for unrivalled views over the port and town. In fact the fort is merely the reworked western tower of a much larger Lusignan castle dating from 1391, which the Venetians demolished nearly a century later. The stump of the easterly tower is still visible about seventy metres along the modern mole, itself pointing towards the ancient breakwater, half awash. The Ottomans repaired what was of use to them in 1592, and seemed to have spent most of their time on the roof terrace, where eight canon slots are angled in odd directions; the ground floor served as their dungeons, which the British used as a salt warehouse till 1935.

The Paphos mosaics

Whatever else happens in Páfos, the entire headland between the harbour and the lighthouse will remain open space, as it's suspected that as much archaeological wealth lies buried as has so far come to light. The most spectacular find unearthed to date are the Roman mosaics (daily 8am–5.30/7pm winter/summer; C£1), discovered accidentally by a ploughing farmer in 1962. Subsequent excavations revealed an extensive complex of Roman buildings, fitted

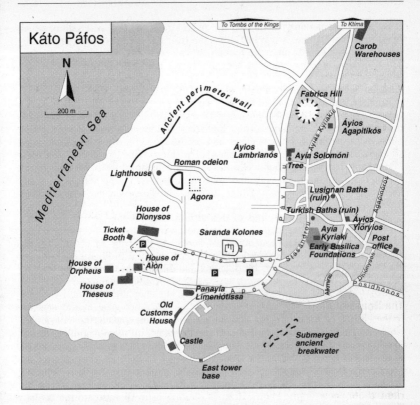

Káto Páfos

N

200 m

Mediterranean Sea

To Tombs of the Kings

To Ktima

Carob Warehouses

Fabrica Hill

Ancient perimeter wall

Áyios Agapitikós

Áyios Lambrianós

Ayía Solomóni

Roman odeion

Tree

Lighthouse

Agora

Lusignan Baths (ruin)

House of Dionysos

Turkish Baths (ruin)

Áyios Ylóryios

Ticket Booth

Saranda Kolones

Ayía Kyriakí

Post office

House of Orpheus

House of Aíon

Sofías Vémbo

Early Basilica Foundations

House of Theseus

Panayía Liméniótissa

Old Customs House

Castle

Submerged ancient breakwater

East tower base

with exquisite floor mosaics showing episodes from ancient mythology and considered perhaps the best in the eastern Mediterranean. Nowhere is the wealth and opulence of imperial Roman Paphos better suggested than in these vivid floorings, new stretches of which seem to be discovered every few years. Mosaics have always been an expensive medium, far more so than frescoes, requiring not just the retainer of master craftsmen and several assistants, but often the application of gold leaf as well as paint to the tiny glass cubes or tesseraewhich made up the images. Other, less costly, tesseraewere chipped from stones of the appropriate colour. Modern shelters protecting the mosaics are naturally lit and provided with ample catwalks for viewing – though often the colours are not dazzling since the tesserae are not kept polished as they were in their day.

The House of Dionysos

The largest building, next to the ticket booth, is the House of Dionysos, so called because of repeated representations of the god, and probably the late second/early third-century villa of a wealthy merchant. However a much earlier Hellenistic pebble-mosaic, showing the monster Scylla, has been relocated to a previously undecorated floor, and is the first thing you see on entering. Towards the rear of the building Zeus as an eagle abducts Ganymede, while Dionysos frolics with Ariadne, attended by Cupid and a hunting dog.

But the most famous panels ring the main atrium, on the west side of which Apollo pursues Daphne, while her father the river-god reclines below; in a nearby panel Poseidon chases after the nymph Amymone with similar lack of success. The *Triumph of Dionysos*, with the god riding a chariot pulled by two she-leopards, apparently pointing at his brow in self-congratulation and flanked by dissolute followers, reflects the decadence of the Roman town.

Another long panel, familiar to every London underground rider who's read a Cyprus Wine Board advert, shows first Dionysos proffering a bunch of grapes to the nymph Akme; next King Ikarios, legendary first manufacturer of wine, with a bullock-drawn cart of the new elixir; and on the far right, two lolling, inebriated shepherds rather redundantly labelled "The First Wine-Drinkers". The First Piss-up apparently ended badly – in the curiously unshown sequel, friends of the shepherds, thinking them poisoned, murdered Ikarios. To the left of this group the tragedy of *Pyramus and Thisbe* unfolds, the lion escaping with Thisbe's mantle.

Around the other three sides of this atrium, there is fine animal detail in a series of hunting scenes, and elsewhere a peacock dominates the central square in one of several excellent geometrical floors. At the edge of several panels, visitors are exhorted to "Rejoice" (*Hairei*), presumably with liberal quantities of wine – from these inscriptions it's deduced that this was the floor of a banqueting hall.

The House of Aion
In the **House of Aion**, a recent Polish discovery and excavation, the mosaics are later (mid-fourth-century), and more sophisticated in theme and execution. Apollo judges the satyr Marsyas, who dared challenge him to a musical contest, to his fate of being flayed in the lower right panel. In the next scene above, the results of a beauty contest between Cassiopeia and several nereids is depicted; the latter, losers, ride sulkily away on an assortment of sea monsters. Still on the right, the topmost frame shows Hermes offering baby Dionysos to the centaur Trofeus for rearing, surrounded by nymphs preparing a bath. The left-hand scenes are less intact; of the god Aion, from whom the building takes its name, only the head is visible, and a version of Leda preparing to meet the Swan is somewhat damaged. Except for the statue niche in the west wall, the building itself is a purpose-built reconstruction, though of old masonry.

The House of Theseus
The next precinct, the **"House of Theseus"**, also a Polish dig, takes its name from a round mosaic of coarse tesserae portraying Theseus brandishing a club against a (vanished) Minotaur while Ariadne and personifications of Crete and the Labyrinth look on. Under the same sheltering roof, in the next room, the *Birth of Achilles* is shown: a nursemaid carries him firmly in the presence of the Three Fates and Peleus the river god. It is speculated that this building, or a vanished adjacent one, was the location of Sergius Paulus' interviews with the apostles.

The House of Orpheus and House of the Four Seasons
At present the **House of Orpheus** is closed to the public, but should it have opened by the time you read this you'll be treated to the sight of Orpheus charming a naturalistic bestiary with his lyre, in an exceptionally large floor panel.

The **House of the Four Seasons**, a new area discovered early in 1992 and still under investigation, was provisionally named for personifications of the seasons, though only autumn has survived. Most of the images in what was evidently another sumptuous mansion are engagingly realistic hunting scenes: a tiger claws the haunches of a wild ass, and a hunter faces off with a marauding lion, while a deer runs away from the melee. On the floor of what was possibly the banqueting hall are more animal portraits, including a dog chasing a hare and a goat unusually shown full-face – in both pagan and Christian mosaic or fresco imagery, only humans and (later) Christians are depicted that way, but animals, pagans and the wicked only in profile.

Other Roman and Byzantine sites

From the northerly mosaic access road, a short lane leads up to the **Roman odeion** (gate open dawn to dusk, free), a workman-like restoration of the 1970s and not very compelling unless there's an event on. Of the contemporary agora, beyond the stage to the east, there's virtually nothing to see at the moment except weeds. From the odeion parking lot a passable dirt track leads northwest to the picturesque **lighthouse**, beyond which are the most intact stretches of the city's **perimeter wall**.

Saranda Kolones

Right beside the mosaic road (officially re-named Sofías Vémbou in honour of a patriotic 1940s Greek torch singer), the fortress of **Saranda Kolones** (unrestricted access) signposted as Byzantine, is actually a Lusignan structure built atop its predecessor. It was destroyed almost as soon as it was completed by an earth tremor in 1222, and before excavations undertaken between 1957 and 1983, the only objects visible above ground were numerous tumbled columns – hence the name which means "Forty Columns".

It is still a confusing jumble of moat-ringed masonry; some well-worn latrines, near the remaining arches, are the only obvious items – they were fitted with doors, in deference to Christian modesty. The pavement is riddled with sewer tunnels, vaults and stables, some interconnecting and offering rather claustrophobic touring. For a supposed stronghold, an improbable number of sally ports fitted with stairs breach the roughly square walls; the ramparts were originally entered by a gateway on the east, and sported eight mismatched towers.

Ayía Kiriakí (Khrysopolítissa)

Crossing busy Apostólou Pávlou, you can find the hotel-obscured start of pedestrianised Stassándhrou, which leads directly to **Ayía Kiriakí (Khrysopolítissa)**. This late (eleventh- or twelfth-century) Byzantine *naos*, with a later belfry, is dwarfed by the vast foundations of an earlier, seven-aisled basilica and an archiepiscopal palace, both destroyed by the all-scouring Arab raids. What's left are extensive fourth-century floor mosaics and a scattering of probably contemporary columns, including one dubbed "Saint Paul's Pillar" after the obviously apocryphal tradition that the apostle was tied to it and scourged. Since it's still being excavated, the zone, considerably below modern ground level, is currently off-limits; access to the small existing church is via a catwalk.

Ayía Kiriakí is bare of any decoration inside, and has recently been ceded by the orthodox bishop of Páfos to the Catholic and Anglican expatriate communities – perhaps the first time heterodox rites have been celebrated here since the Lusignans displaced the Orthodox with a Catholic diocese here in 1220. To the north of the excavations are scattered the domes of the Lusignan baths, a Byzantine church converted to a mosque, and a tiny, cottage-like modern mosque used by local Turks until 1975.

The catacombs of Ayía Solomóni and Fabrica hill

Ayía Kiriakí lies near the easternmost circuit of ancient walls, and other points of historical interest lie up Apostólou Pávlou. The **catacombs of Ayía Solomóni**, just east of the pavement, are overshadowed by a huge terebinth tree festooned with knotted-together kerchiefs and (at a last look) a complete lady's nightie, either votive offerings or sacrifices to placate the guardian spirits. Steps lead down to a multi-chambered, sunken sanctuary honouring one of those obscure, weirdly-named saints in which Cyprus seems to specialise – in this case a Jewish woman whose seven children were martyred by one of the Seleucid kings of Palestine. It's thought that the subterranean complex was once the synagogue of Roman Paphos, and doubtless a pagan shrine before that. The frescos in the small chapel are a mess, first vandalised by the Crusaders; more curious is a sacred well, accessed by a separate flight of stairs, with water so clear that you'll step into it unintentionally even though you've been warned. Directly across Apostólou Pávlou is the similar catacomb-shrine of Áyios Lambrianós.

The rock outcrop just north, known as **Fabrica hill**, contains more tunnelled-out tombs and churches, including those of Áyios Agapitikós and Áyios Misitikós. The latter two honour saints even more shadowy than usual, and pointedly unrecognised by the Orthodox Church. According to legend, dust gathered from the floor of the former can be used as a love-charm (*agápi* = "love" in Greek), while the same stuff from the latter has the opposite effect (*misós* = "hate"): useful magic that presumably ensures the saints' long-running veneration.

The Tombs of the Kings

From the vicinity of Fabrica hill, a major, well-signed, road leads 2km northwest to more rock-cuttings, the so-called **Tombs of the Kings** (daily 7.30am–5.45/7.30pm winter/summer. Rock outcrops near the shore – called *Paleokástra* (Old Citadels) for their similarity to castles – conceal dozens of tombs hacked out of the soft strata, since this was a permissable distance outside the city walls. There's no evidence of royal use, merely that of the local privileged classes, starting in the third century BC. Their design, curiously, is not strictly indigenous but heavily indebted to Macedonian prototypes, passed on from Alexander's legions to the Ptolemies who ruled Cyprus.

Eight complexes of tombs are singled out for you by number, and include several reached by stairs down to sunken courts, ringed by peristyles of rough square – or fluted round – Doric columns carved from the living rock. Beyond the colonnades, passages lead to rooms with alcoves or niches provided for each corpse. At death anniversaries of the deceased, relatives would troop out to the tomb for a *nekródhipno* or ceremonial meal, with the leftovers deposited near the actual sepulchre; variants of this custom still prevail in Greek Orthodox observance. Carved crosses and traces of fresco pigment in a few suggest their use as catacombs in early Christian times. Later they were systematically looted (have no fear of encountering skeletons, or hopes of artefacts) and scholarly excavations only began in 1977. Today it's still an eerie place, the drumming of the distant sea and chirps of nesting birds the only sounds.

Ktíma

Looking down from the edge of the escarpment on which **Ktíma** is built, you can appreciate the Byzantines' defensive reasoning: it's a 175-metre elevation drop to the coastal plain, with the harbour fort assuming toy-like dimensions at this distance. The main thoroughfares of Pávlou Melá and Pallikarídhi subdivide the upper town yet again: to the east a dull cantonment of broader avenues lined by the courts, police station, archbishops house, the park, tourist facilities and museums, while on the west the more vernacular neighbourhood forms a warren of narrower, denser-gridded streets encompassing the bazaar and the old Turkish quarter.

The market and old Turkish quarter

Heading west on Agorás, the continuation of Makaríou, you quickly reach a relatively ornate, turn-of-the-century building, the **covered market**, which has a good selection of local souvenirs as well as fresh produce. South of this, over the edge of the palisade, you'll spy a medieval **Turkish hamam** down by the car park, being restored for an as yet-unknown purpose.

Continuing northwest, the alleys of the former **Turkish quarter of Mutalloú** narrow in, and you can reflect on the fact that before 1974 this was a guarded enclave, with many refugees from outlying Pafiot villages. The sole architectural monument here is the **Cami Kebir** or Great Mosque, once the Byzantine church of Ayía Sofía and still a handsome building.

Finally, near the end of the clifftop neighbourhood, there's a plaza dotted with kebab houses and clubs used by the locals, all Greek refugees from the North. Overhead a metal archway reads *Ne Mutlu Türküm Diyene* ("How Fortunate for Him Saying 'I am a Turk' "). The Greek Cypriots have not defaced or changed this or any of the numerous Turkish street signs, but merely edited it with an addition of their own. Dangling below, it says: "We do not forget the enslaved territories" (ie the North). After the often conspicuous wealth of urban Greek Cyprus, the meanness of the bungalows here may come as a shock – you are not merely looking back twenty years in time, but also at the consequences of government measures against the enclaves, whereby a long list of materials deemed "militarily strategic" were forbidden to be brought in.

The museums

First stop in the "cantonment" might be the privately run **Ethnographical Museum** at Éxo Vrýsis 1, south of the park (Mon–Sat 9am–1pm, Mon–Fri 2–5pm winter, 3–6pm summer, Sun 10am–1pm; c£0.50). Put together by one George Eliades, the collection actually has a stronger archaeological bent, including coins, Stone-Age axe-heads, amphorae and two tombs in the garden of this private residence, plus the expected domestic implements and wardrobes of traditional dress. A **Byzantine museum** (Mon–Sat 9am–12.30pm), mostly medieval

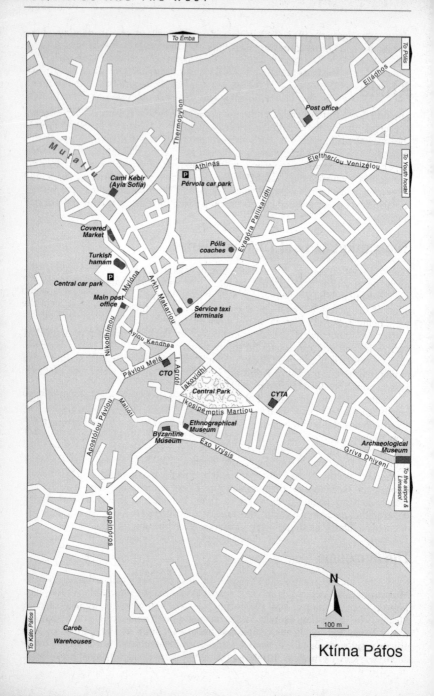

To Émba

To Pólis

Eliághos

Post office

To Youth hostel

Muralju

Thermopylon

Athinás

Cami Kebir
(Ayía Sofía)

Pérvola car park

Eleftheríou Venizélou

Evagóra Pallikarídhi

Covered
Market

Pólis
coaches

Turkish
hamám

Central car park

Mylóna

Árkh Makaríou

Main post
office

Sérvice taxi
terminals

Nikodhímou

Ayíou Kendhéa

Pávlou Melá

Ioakovídhi

CTO

I. Agrótí

Central Park

CYTA

Apostólou Pávlou

Mailótí

Byzantine
Múseum

Ikosipémptis Martíou

Ethnographical
Museum

Exo Vrýsis

Archaeological
Museum

Gríva Dhiyení

To the airport & Limassol

To Káto Páfos

Agapínoros

Carob
Warehouses

N

100 m

Ktíma Páfos

ikons from country chapels of the district, is housed nearby in the archbishop's house, near the church of Áyios Theódhoros; whatever you may read elsewhere, there is no longer any such collection on Ikosipémptis Martíou, by the park.

Ktíma's **archaeological museum** (Mon–Fri 7.30am–2.30pm, Thur 3–5pm, Sat–Sun 10am–1pm; c£0.50) is well east out of town, off most maps. It requires a special detour, and sufficient time for the extensive, interesting exhibits. The chronological displays begin with Chalkolithic figurines and rather wild abstract pottery which has become recognisably zoomorphic by the time the Bronze Age is reached. The exotic trend continues, in a more refined manner, in the Archaic display case, and the Geometric-era artefacts outshine the imported Attic ware. The Hellenistic-Roman room as usual features myriad glass objects, and more figurative representation, though pottery does not appear again until the the Byzantine and Lusignan section, much of it from the Saranda Kolones fort. Perhaps the strangest later items are Hellenistic clay hot-water bottles, moulded to fit various afflicted body parts, and a finely wrought crouching lion of the same age.

Eating and drinking

In the wake of the tourist invasion, characterful, good-value **restaurants** are few and far between in either upper or lower Páfos, so most recommendations would be futile; Ktíma is a somewhat better bet if only because it has to perform the functions of a real market centre. In the bazaar itself, *Sovos,* at Petrákis Miltiádhous 15, is a tradesmen's lunch-only *sheftália* and kebab joint, with soups and vegetables, too, and a view out the back that's the envy of posher places. Otherwise, the *Trianon,* across Arkhiepiskópou Makaríou from the *Kinyras Hotel,* is reasonably authentic and tasty, as is *Fettas Corner* at Ioánni Agróti 33, supper only but with limited outdoor seating by the park.

Down in Káto, the one place worth singling out is *Hondhros,* Apostólou Pávlou 96, at the edge of the archaeological zone and run by and for ex-patriates. The menu's not astoundingly cheap but at least it's different from the norm. The clientele here, largely students from the Lemba art school, tends to be found **drinking** between or after meals at Andreas Haralambidhis' pub *La Boite 67,* virtually the last – and the least expensive – establishment on the yacht harbour; it also attracts a low-key gay contingent.

Listings

Bookstores *Bookworld,* corner Apostólou Pávlou and Pávlou Melá, Ktíma; *Axel,* Arkhiepiskópou Makaríou 66, Ktíma.

Car hire *Andy Spyrou,* corner Posidhónos and Natalías (☎236944); *Astra,* Apostólou Pávlou, Marina Court (☎242252); *Budget/Petsas,* Apostólou Pávlou 86 (☎235522); *Eurodollar,* Agapinóros 2 (☎236488); *Europcar,* Posidhónos 77, Constandinos Court (☎234149); *Geko,* Dhionýsou 8 (☎232848); and *Thames,* Apostólou Pávlou 62 (☎244569).

Coach companies Most useful companies include *KEMEK,* on Leondíou, just off Thermopýlon, opposite the Pérvola car-park (☎234255), whose coaches run to Limassol; *Costas,* at Nikodhímou Milóna 2B, near the central post office (☎241717), has coaches to Limassol and Nicosia; and *Nea Amoroza,* Evagóra Pallikarídhi 79 (☎236740), to Pólis, sometimes beyond with prior arrangement.

Exchange Most banks are up around Kennedy Square in Ktíma, including *Barclays* – and *Bank of Cyprus* in the bazaar – with cashpoint machines.

Laundrette Near corner of Posidhónos, the shore road past Hotel Row, and Alkmínis in Káto Páfos.

Post offices The main branch on Nikodhímou Mylóna, in an old colonial building, has a late-afternoon shift and is the place for parcels and poste restante; other branches include one on Elládhos, near the youth hostel, and the Káto Páfos branch on Ayíou Andoníou, also with afternoon service.

Service taxis All companies have offices and terminals on Evagóra Pallikarídhi in the very centre of town, and all offer direct service to Limasassol only; service to anywhere else is via Limassol. *Karydas* (☎232459), *Kyriakos* (☎233181), *Kypros* (☎232376) and *Nea Páfos* (☎332132) are the four operators.

Telephones CYTA is on Gríva Dhiyení, just past the park (daily 7.30am–7pm).

Travel agency *Exalt*, PO Box 337, or Ayías Kiriakís 24, Káto Páfos (☎143803). Where you go for something out of the ordinary: organises trekking or jeep safaris throughout the Akámas.

BEYOND PÁFOS

Leaving Páfos behind in almost any direction, rolling, well-tended hills and the deep river valleys that characterise rural Páfos provide relief from the occasional tattiness of the town. The sudden, recent growth of tourism on the coast halted the continual depopulation of the closer hill villages, but chances of traditional livelihoods surviving in the remoter settlements are pretty slim; accordingly the rural areas are a favourite target for foreign second-home hunters.

To the southeast, there is little beyond what meets the eye from the Páfos–Limassol highway; northwest of town, the coast is surprisingly deserted once past the last gasp of resort development. Head north by a choice of routes towards Pólis, second town of the district, and you're seemingly on a different island, while east of the main Pólis-bound road lies some of the emptiest country on Cyprus, essentially abandoned after 1975 or relegated to backwater status by the proximity of the Attila Line.

Southeast from Páfos

The hopelessly overcrowded main road southeast from Páfos passes over a trio of rivers, the lower reaches of streams beginning far up in the Pafiot corner of the Troödhos range. A resulting fertility, especially in melons, softens the usual mineral, parched yellowness of the south Cypriot coast. This relative lushness is age-old, as if in sympathy with the worship of the island's patron goddess, Aphrodite, at Yeroskípou and Palea Paphos. Little tangible remains of her shrines, but her worship continues in faintly Christianised forms.

Eastern beaches

The Páfos town beach, specifically that fringing the eastern hotels, aren't up to much; to reach anything moderately attractive you have to get some ways out of town. The first substantial strip is the maintained and improved **CTO beach** along the shore below Yeroskípou, near the Zenon Gardens Campsite (c£1.50 per site, plus c£1 per person). The other is **Flória beach**, seaward of TÍMI village, about halfway along the airport spur road – follow signs pointing to the dirt drive leading to some ramshackle tavernas and the first hints of development. There's also an official picnic ground in a eucalyptus grove nearby.

Yeroskípou (Yeroskípos)

Yeroskípou village has lately become virtually a suburb of Páfos, beginning just a kilometre or so beyond the district archaeological museum. The name is a modern rendition of the ancient "Hieros Kipos" or Sacred Garden and Grove, consecrated to Aphrodite, which grew in the fertile plain below, towards the sea.

These days Yeroskípou has some reputation as a crafts centre, as reflected by numerous stalls on the main road peddling basketry and Turkish delight, and by the Yeroskípou **Folk Art museum** (Mon & Wed–Fri 7.30am–2.30pm; also Thurs 3–6pm in winter; c£0.50). This is lodged in the former house of a certain Andreas Zoumboulaki, British vice-consul here in the early nineteenth century, and better known as Hadji Smith, having adopted his sponsor's surname. The museum, on two storeys, is better than most of the genre, emphasising domestic implements on the ground floor, local costumes upstairs, plus decorated gourds, including one fashioned into a stringed instrument.

Ayía Paraskeví church

Nothwithstanding the name, the village proper is probably of Byzantine origin, and the best demonstration of this is the renowned church of **Ayía Paraskeví** (key at house opposite if locked) bang in the middle. Its frescos date construction to the ninth century, and the church is unique on the island in having six domes. Up in the cupola hides the oldest fresco in the building, a primitive but engaging *Virgin Enthroned*. Other surviving frescoes, recently cleaned, date from the fourteenth or fifteenth century; opposite the south door are the *Last Supper*, the *Washing of the Feet*, the *Betrayal* – where figures in Crusader armour date the images – and *Pilate Washing his Hands*. Across from these you see the *Birth and Presentation of the Virgin*. Further up towards the altar screen, there's an unusual representation of *Simon carrying the Cross for Christ*, with a *Nativity* and *Baptism* opposite. The church itself was originally cruciform with a single nave, but had an ungainly narthex added to the south side last century, and also at some point a *yinaikonítis* or women's gallery in the rear. July 25–26 marks the **feast** of the patron saint.

Palea Paphos (Koúklia)

Approaching the boundary of Limassol district, some 11km east of Yeroskípou, you can't help noticing a large, solidly built structure surveying the landscape from a prominent rise. This is **La Cavocle**, a medieval manor that's the inevitable marker-cairn and introduction to both the ancient city of **Palea Paphos**, and the large village of Koúklia just to the north. Once a mixed Turkish-Greek community, **Koúklia** remains a pleasant if unremarkable place of low houses whose meandering lanes converge on a small *platía* with a church and some coffeeshops. Indifferent to the trickle of tourists visiting the nearby ruins, it has changed little – except for the departure of its Turks – since independence.

THE PAPHIOT CULT OF APHRODITE

The cult of the ancient Cypriot patron goddess Aphrodite is of considerable antiquity; it was already established in a hilltop temple at Palea Paphos in about 1500 BC, and a town sprang up around it, capital of one of the original island kingdoms. Foundation legends credit the hero Kinyras with being first king and consort of Aphrodite, who supposedly emerged from the sea nearby at Pétra tou Romíou. Their daughter Myrrha was turned into a fragrant bush by the jealous goddess, and Adonis, born of its wood, completed the cycle by also becoming lover of the goddess.

All this reflects historical facts about the Kinyrid dynasty, who not only "wedded" the goddess through the temple prostitutes, but married their own daughters upon the death of their wives – royal descent was reckoned through the women of the line. Despite the incest it was a relatively civilised observance, considering that the Asiatic love goddesses, to whom Aphrodite owed much in pedigree and ritual, used to sacrifice their consorts after the rite of lovemaking.

The sacred prostitutes were apparently island matrons and damsels obliged by custom to give themselves at least once to strangers in the temple precincts. The business of prostitution was invariably brisker at the spring festivals for Aphrodite and Adonis, when separate processions of garlanded men and women made their way from Nea Paphos to the shrine via Yeroskípou. The ritual survives in the *Anthistíria* or modern spring flower festival, with special enthusiasm in Ktíma, and in *Kataklismós* (where the obligatory sea-plunge seems to commemorate Aphrodite's emergence from same). Worship here continued until the fourth-century edict of Theodosius banning paganism, nearly 800 years after the foundation of Nea Paphos.

The Site

The ancient temple stood on a knoll about 2km inland, overlooking the sea but probably not the orchards and gently sloping fields which have appeared since. Despite the hoariness of the cult here, there's little above-ground evidence of it or of the city which grew up around, and the archaeological site itself is really of specialist interest. The courtyard-type **sanctuary of Aphrodite** (daily 7.30–sunset/7pm winter/summer; c£0.50), with rustic, relatively impermanent buildings, was common in the pre-Hellenic Middle East; thus little has survived other than low foundations to the north as you enter. Matters were made worse for posterity when a wealthy Roman chose to build a private villa, bits of its mosaic floor still visible, next to the archaic shrine in its last years, and the medieval placement of sugar milling machinery atop the convenient stone foundations was extremely destructive to anything remaining above knee level. Finally, the nearby villagers, from Byzantine times onwards, treated the ruins as a quarry – virtually every old building in Koúklia incorporates a cut stone or two from the shrine area.

In one corner of the precinct a sign points along the short path to the **"Leda Mosaic House"**, but fails to mention that the central figure, Leda baring her behind to the lustful Zeus-swan, is a copy. The replica was installed after the original was stolen by art thieves, then luckily recovered, to be lodged in the relative safety of Nicosia's Cyprus Museum.

Outside the sacred precinct, there's even less to see until the Swiss-sponsored excavations are completed. To the northeast, off the road towards ARKHIMANDHRÍTA, are the remains of a **city gate**, and a **siege ramp** built by the Persians in 498 BC to breach the city walls, under which the defenders then tunnelled in a vain attempt to collapse the ramp and Persian war-engines atop it.

The **necropolis** (still under investigation) lies to the southeast of the hill, and appears to have escaped the notice of tomb robbers.

Just east of the precinct stands the usually locked twelfth-century church of **Panayía Katholikí**, new goddess of the local cult. Until recently Koúklia village women used to light candles nearby in honour of the Panayía Galatariótissa – the Virgin-Who-Gives-Milk-to-Mothers.

La Cavocle and the local museum

The most obvious and worthwhile item in the main archaeological zone is the four-square Lusignan manor of **La Cavocle**, whose name is a rendering of (take your pick) the Greek *kouvoúkli*, "canopy"; *kovoukuleris*, the royal bodyguard; or more likely the Latin *cubiculum*, "pavillion" – corrupted in whichever case to Koúklia, the name of the modern village. La Cavocle was headquarters of the Crusaders' surrounding sugar plantations, and continued to serve as the "big house" of a large farm in Ottoman times. Only the east wing survived the Mameluke raid of 1426; the rest, including a fine gate tower, is a Turkish reconstruction. Because the courtyard level has risen over the centuries, you descend slightly to the ground floor of the east wing, where a purported thirteenth-century banquet room has a groin-vaulted ceiling.

This fine specimen of domestic Crusader architecture is being prepared for use as part of an expanded **local museum**, presently housed entirely upstairs. Among the few existing exhibits in Gallery I is one of several existing *betyls* or phallic cult monoliths (the biggest one is in Nicosia) which used to be anointed with olive oil by local women, not unlike a Hindu Shiva *lingam*, well into modern times. Gallery II contains finds of all eras from the site, in chronological order. Best is the huge chalk bathtub of the eleventh century BC, complete with a soap dish. Most of the other items are painted pottery, with some bronze work, much of which was found in the rubble piled up by the Persians to support their attack ramp.

North from Páfos

North of Páfos the landscape is initially flat and uninspiring, dotted with large villages that are essentially dormitories for the district capital, and increasingly for long-term foreign residents. Only as the terrain begins tilting gently up at the first outriders of the Troödhos mountains does development diminish and the mystique of the country reassert itself.

Most of the inland settlements immediately **north from Páfos** town can boast some late Byzantine church or remains, but with the exception of the following two monuments, all have had their appeal compromised by ill-advised additions or renovation.

Émba and Panayía Khryseléousa

In the middle of **Émba village**, 3km north of Páfos, the eleventh-century church of **Panayía Khryseléousa** sits in exalted isolation, though the parkland all around it burns to a crisp by June. A dome perches at each end of the double-cruciform ground plan, and the narthex with stairs up to the mortared roof is an eighteenth-century addition. Loiter about purposefully and a guardian with the key will appear, but only if you're suitably dressed.

Inside, sixteenth-century frescos were recently cleaned, but they'd been badly retouched during the late nineteenth century, and some were damaged by the 'quake of 1953. However, anything that remained out of reach of the "restorer" is still worth scrutiny. A good example is the *Apocalypse* and *Second Coming* on the right of the main nave's vault, which is very fine high up but mauled below. The *témblon* (altar screen) dates from the early fifteenth century, and just as the guard says, the eyes of Saint John the Divine (on the panel left of the main icon) seem to follow you around the room. The revered icon of the Virgin is unique in that both She and Child are crowned; there is also a sixteenth-century icon of the apostles.

If you're without a car, the *ALEPA* #4 or #5 urban bus passes through Émba ten times daily.

The monastery of Áyios Neófitos

Nine kilometres from Páfos and 5km from Émba, at the head of a wooded canyon, the **monastery of Áyios Neófitos** (Ayíou Neofítou) appears suddenly as you round a curve, the indirect result of the piety of the hermit Neophytos. Born in 1134, he moved here from the monastery of Khrysostómos near Nicosia at the age of 25, seeking solitude in this then-desolate region. His plan backfired badly; such was Neophytos' reputation that he became a guru of sorts to numerous disciples who gathered around his simple cave-hermitage, founding the monastery shortly before his death in 1220. Unusually for one of the desert saints, Neophytos was a scholar of some note, and a few of his manuscripts have survived. Among these are the *Ritual Ordnance*, a handbook for monastic life, and a historical essay on the acquisition of Cyprus by the Crusaders in 1191, deeply disparaging of the two protagonists Isaac Comnenus and Richard the Lion-Heart. That he could write this with impunity is perhaps a measure of the respect in which he was held during his lifetime.

The katholikón and hermitage of Neophytos

The enormous monastery compound, home now to just seven monks, consists of a square perimeter cloister enclosing a garden-with-aviary, with the **katholikón** or central church on its own terrace. In the vault over the northernmost of three aisles, rather Italianate fifteenth-century frescos of events from the life of Christ face others portraying mystical aspects of Christ and the Virgin. A window in the apse splits the *Communion of the Disciples* into unusual halves: Jesus appears in each, bestowing the Eucharist on six disciples. But pleasant as they are, the *katholikón* and the monastery grounds are not the main reason visitors come up here.

On the far side of the car park with its café (lively during the feasts of 24 January and 27 September), at the very head of the ravine, cave-niches form the **énkleistra** or **hermitage of Neophytos**. This has parallels most obviously with the roughly contemporary man-made cave-shrines of Cappadocia; here, too, Neophytos supposedly dug many of the cavities himself, and it is conceivable that the oldest frescos are by the saint, or at least done under his supervision.

Visits begin with stairs mounting to a pair of chambers on the left comprising a chapel, dedicated to the Holy Cross by an inscription dated 1196. Their frescos, of a "primitive" Syrian/Cappadocian style, were restored in 1992, and it's easy to make out scenes such as the *Last Supper* (complete with Judas reaching over the carrots and radishes of the Hebrew Passover to snatch, by iconographic tradition, the Fish of the Believer), the *Washing of the Feet*, and Roman soldiers portrayed as

Crusaders, all culminating with the *Ascension* on the dome hacked from the soft rock. In the central chamber, two archangels seem like celestial policemen (as they indeed are in Orthodox belief), escorting Neophytos to Paradise in a ceiling-painting of the more fashionable Constantinopolitan school. The chamber furthest right was Neofiytos' private quarters, with benches, niches and a desk carved for his use, as well as his sarcophagus – appropriately presided over by an image of the *Resurrection*, but prematurely emptied in 1750 so that Neophytos' bones might serve as relics. Today pilgrims to the *katholikón* kiss his skull in its silver reliquary.

The upper caves of the cliff-face are undecorated and currently inaccessible. Neophytos retreated there after the lower levels became unbearably busy with his unintended followers; he is said to have insured his privacy with a retractable ladder.

Northwest along the coast

Leaving Páfos towards the northwest, the road past the Tombs of the Kings continues as a broad avenue for some kilometres, passing phalanxes of new hotels and self-catering apartments sprouting at an alarming rate regardless of the nature of the (often rocky) shore below. It's strange to reflect that in the 1950s this shore was so deserted that EOKA chose it as a landfall when smuggling in arms and men from Greece. Today, signs for Chinese and Indian restaurants lend the only exotic touches, along with the banana plantations inland that testify to the mildness of the climate. Overall, it is not a prospect that holds much promise for seclusion and beauty, but surprisingly you are headed towards one of the most unspoiled stretches of coast in the South.

Coral Bay and Áyios Yióryios

With the coast hitherto inaccessible or claimed by hotels, the first place to stop is **"Coral Bay"** (officially Máa), 10km out of Páfos and blessed with a public access beach: hotels do not quite monopolise it, and this is the end of the *ALEPA* #15 line from town. A sandy, 600-metre crescent is hemmed in by a pair of headlands, with two snack bars and sun-bed rental places behind. Atop the promontories and up on the access road, however, are plenty of hotels and a burgeoning village; if it weren't for the signs you probably wouldn't find the beach. Fenced off on the southern headland are traces of **Paleókastro**, a Bronze-Age settlement in the process of excavation.

Just past Coral Bay, developments cease fairly abruptly amid vineyards and grain fields; the road, while still asphalted, dwindles, too. The Roman town at **ÁYIOS YIÓRYIOS**, 8km beyond, has shrunk to a modern Christian church on Cape Dhrépano, with a nearby wish-tree like that at Ayía Solomóni in Káto Páfos, and the substantial remains of **Byzantine basilicas** from two different eras, one atop the other. Patches of mosaic flooring feature a bestiary panel, including at centre a rampaging octopus – common enough in ancient pottery, but rare in Christian art. This, plus an unidentified nearby building, are still under excavation. Four **hotel/pension/eateries** are scattered about the cape within walking distance of each other: of these the unclassified *Saint George* (☎621075) is the rather overpriced (c£17 double) sea-view establishment, while *Yeronisos*

(☎621078), slightly inland by the access road, is a cheaper one-star with singles for c£8, doubles for c£13. All in all the place is overrated except for its spectacular sunsets, and possibilities as a base for exploring the Akámas peninsula. Don't bother following signs down to Moudhális harbour/beach – the anchorage is fine for the local fisherpeople, but the sand is artificially strewn and badly littered, the water hardly better.

The Avgás gorge, Cape Lára and beyond

Inland from Áyios Yióryios, at the junction, the right-hand dirt track signposted for "Lara" and "Joni" is perhaps more rewarding, taking you to the finest canyons and beaches on this coast. The road, badly chewed up by British military vehicles, is passable with caution in a saloon car as far as Cape Lára, but for any forays beyond you really need a four-wheel drive vehicle to handle the sand bogs and ditch-sized ruts.

The Avgás gorge

The first attractive sandy bay lies some 2.5km north, at the mouth of the **Avgás gorge** system. With your own vehicle (the only way to Áyios Yióryios or beyond, bar hitching), bear right, then immediately left and up onto the driveway towards an odd hilltop compound ringed by palms; this is, in season, a café/tavern run by a friendly fellow named Savvas. An ordinary car can continue down past it to the point where the valley, initially given over to grapefruit and banana plantations, splits into the two notable ravines.

Park near the more spectacular left-hand (northerly) one and start off on the trail which quickly appears. The canyon walls soar ever higher, and before June at least there's plenty of water, duly tapped by irrigation piping for the thirsty orchards downstream. Some fifteen minutes along, the gorge narrows into a spectacular gallery where the sun rarely penetrates, before opening again at the foot of a rather steep, scrambly pitch that becomes nearly impassable at the half-hour mark. Yet *Exalt* (see Páfos "Listings") leads trek groups through here, admittedly downhill, and you would, after two hours of uphill trekking through scrub forest, eventually end up in KÁTO ARÓDHES village, the more usual starting point.

Cape Lára

The symmetrical cape at **Lára**, just over 6km **north of** Avgás and nearly 28km from Páfos, shelters large sandy beaches on either side, which you choose from according to how the wind is blowing – and the whims of green and loggerhead sea turtles. A slightly overpriced but beautifully set **café/snack bar** overlooking the kilometre-long southerly beach is so far the only facility; the slightly smaller northerly bay is a nesting ground for the turtles, and is even more scenic, backed by low cliffs and buffeted by the surf from Africa which wafts the turtles in on moonlit nights to lay their eggs in the tidal zone. Accordingly the whole area is fenced, with a gate which may be locked at nesting times.

It's hard to be sure about the lock-out schedule, since an explanatory sign has been defaced, possibly a symptom of the battles raging over this deceptively peaceful place. The archdiocese of Páfos intends to put up a five-star hotel within sight of the sand, and the Carlsberg brewery's holding company plans to build a bungalow complex as well. Virtually the only group consistently opposing such schemes is the Laona Project (see below).

The road, jeeps-only now, continues past more tiny coves on its way to JÓNI and the haphazardly controlled British Army firing range (see p.116). The only **way out** of the Lára area, except for a complete retracing of your steps, is the signed dirt track from near the snack bar up to ÍNIA village. In dry weather you can just make the 500-metre climb, past the southerly outcrops of Áyios Yióryios peak, in the lowest gear of an ordinary auto.

Villages of the Akámas heights

North of an imaginary line joining Coral Bay and Áyios Neófitos, the **Akámas peninsula** begins. Named after a legendary lover of Aphrodite, this is the most desolate, and nearly the most thinly populated, portion of Cyprus. An inclined plane of sparsely vegetated chalk and limestone, it drops off sharply to the east but falls more gradually west towards the sea, furrowed by ravines that hide precious water. At its centre the land climbs to a spine of hills nearly 700 metres high, supporting the only permanent habitation in the area, though in ancient times the coastline was more important.

Several of the villages here were partly or wholly Turkish Cypriot before 1974, and the subsequent exodus left them almost empty: their lands, however extensive, were generally too poor to attract Greek refugees from the North. Other, wholly Greek Orthodox, communities have shrunk as well – the usual emigration overseas or to Cypriot towns, sometimes no further than the service jobs of the Páfos resorts. Mostly the old remain, some wondering why the "miracle" of Ayía Nápa (see Chapter One) shouldn't be repeated here.

Virtually the only organisation to suggest otherwise is the **Laona Project**, a venture of the Cypriot chapter of Friends of the Earth, supported by the European Commission and the philanthropic Leventis Foundation. Theirs is a two-pronged programme: to secure protection for the natural environment of the wildest parts of the Akámas, already nominally a national park, and to revive the dying villages by introducing "sustainable tourism" – specifically the restoration of controlled numbers of old properties for use as visitor accommodation, and the involvement of tourists in the day-to-day activities of the villages. So far *Sunvil Travel*, a responsible British tour operator, has been the main taker, offering a variety of accommodation between Páfos and Pólis. For more information on the aims of the Laona Project, they can be contacted at PO Box 257, Limassol (☎05/358632; fax 352657).

Péyia and Káthikas . . .

Some 4km above Coral Bay, along good roads shown incorrectly on most maps, the large village of **PÉYIA** tumbles down a hillside overlooking the sea. After the excesses of Káto Páfos, the place's very ordinariness counts as an asset, but already identity is shifting uneasily as it becomes a dormitory community for vast numbers of ex-pats buying purpose-built villas or renovating old houses. You can **stay** short term at the *Christina* villas (☎233742) for c£12 double occupancy, or at a handful of other less formal establishments. It's worth coming up here just to **eat** at some of the half-dozen carniverous tavernas grouped around the fountain-square; the *Kyrenia* and the adjacent *Peyia* are perhaps the most no-nonsense and generous-portioned for the money. Péyia is important enough to rate its own *ALEPA* bus conection (lines #3 or 6).

The initially westerly road uphill then curls east as it climbs scenically through dense pine forest on its way to **KÁTHIKAS**, up on the Akámas watershed at the very edge of the commercial grape-growing zone. Here again there are a couple of tavernas and the possibility of staying, though most accommodation is controlled by *Sunvil*.

... and the ridge route to Pólis

At Káthikas the best road turns north to follow the spine of Akámas; it's a drive worth doing at least once for its own sake, as opposed to the quicker, main valley route.

All the villages along here require slight detours – bearing left initially towards PÁNO and KÁTO ARÓDHES. Páno is still mostly inhabited, but there are no amenities for outsiders, and Káto is a sad casualty of 1974, many houses emblazoned with the Turkish star-and-crescent standing empty, the fields around largely abandoned. Humbler ÍNIA, in the shadow of craggy Áyios Yióryios peak, roof of the Akámas, can offer the *Panorama Taverna*, but most of the tourist activity hereabouts takes place in neighbouring, handsome DHROÚSHA.

Dhroúsha

Despite incipient gentrification, courtesy of magnificent views and a growing community of foreigners, **DHROÚSHA**, with its fine stone dwellings and winding streets, is still perhaps the best single target along this ridge. There are just 400 current inhabitants, but it's claimed that fifty times that many loyal emigrants and descendants live abroad, whose simultaneous appearance at holiday times put such a strain on resources that the locally funded and staffed *Dhrousha Heights* hotel (☎332351) was the result. At c£19 single, c£23 double it's not especially cheap, and you can rustle up less expensive private **rooms** by asking around at the several **tavernas** – of which the *Foinitzia* is the poshest, and *Bwana Yiangos* more down-to-earth, run by a returned East African Cypriot.

The Térra villages and Ayía Ekateríni

From Dhroúsha, the route descends east towards the main ridge road to Pólis; cross it at the four-way junction, and the drive on the opposite sidewinds 2km down to Krítou Térra and its neighbour TÉRRA, a kilometre north down the same valley. **KRÍTOU**, with its old houses lining the lush, upper banks of the ravine, supposedly dates from Roman times, and was the birthplace of Hadjiyiorgakis Kornesios (see Chapter Five). It also marks the start of one approach to the late Byzantine church of Ayía Ekateríni, the best preserved in the Akámas.

To get there, pass the single *kafenío* and exit Krítou on the cement drive descending south into another canyon on the far side of the village, then follow this track as it bends north-northeast until after 4km you reach the lonely church, in the middle of some vineyards. **Ayía Ekateríni** is unusual for its southwest-to-northeast orientation, its lofty single dome and its arcaded narthex betraying Lusignan influence. Any frescos are long gone but the masonry is largely intact, and the setting, looking across the Stávros tis Psókhas stream valley to the Tillyrian Troödhos, is enchanting – try to be here towards the end of the day, as the sun sets on the hills opposite.

In theory Ayía Ekateríni should be much easier to reach from the main Páfos to Pólis asphalt road, from which it's a mere 1.5km distant – except that there's no sign for the turning, and nobody around to help you find it. The junction of the steep drive lies almost exactly a kilometre south of SKOÚLLI village, directly opposite a peculiar stone barn with niches about three-quarters of the way up the wall.

The main asphalt north from the four-way junction between Dhroúsha and Krítou ends at PRODHRÓMI, just outside Pólis, without any complications.

The way to Pólis

The busiest route north out of Páfos, officially the B7, climbs to a saddle near TSÁDHA and then roller-coasters through the gentle hills around STROMBÍ and YIÓLOU, two of several local villages devoted to wine-grapes. The hummocky terrain is softened, too, by fruit trees and the occasional hedge of artichokes, budding until May. Beginning the gradual descent to Pólis, you might detour 2km west to the calcium-sulphate spa of ÁYII ANÁRYIRI MILIOÚ, with its modest one-star **hotel** (☎632318; singles c£9, doubles c£18) and mineral-water pool in a secluded, citrus-planted valley.

At SKOÚLLI there is a roadside reptile exhibit (c£0.50) in the spring, though not much else to prompt a stop. Approaching Polis, you can't help but notice the forlorn mosque, once a Byzantine chapel, of KHRYSOKHOÚ village, abandoned like many other Turkish settlements to the south and east of Pólis in 1975.

Pólis

Set back slightly from the Stavrós tis Psókhas stream as it enters Khrysókhou bay, **PÓLIS** is the most easy-going of the island's coastal resorts, and the only one that makes much provision for independent travellers. The small, linear town straggles along a ridge, and the road down to the shore, with hotels only slowly displacing citrus on the the surrounding coastal plain. The scenery, whether looking west towards the tip of Akámas, or out to sea, is magnificent, the local restaurant fare still reasonably priced, and nearby beaches, if not always brilliant, more than serviceable.

Pólis Khrysokhoú – to give the full formal title – occupies the sites of ancient Marion and Arsinoë, the former a seventh-century BC foundation which grew wealthy from the nearby copper mines until being destroyed by Ptolemy I, leaving little evidence of its existence other than thousands of tombs. A later member of the dynasty founded the replacement town of Arsinoë slightly to the west, and it came to be called Pólis in Byzantine times. Recent years have not been as peaceful as present appearances suggest; Turkish villages on the coast and in the valleys to the east got on poorly with the pro-*enósis* Greeks of the town, with a UN post required to keep order until the evacuations of 1975.

There are few specific sights in Pólis other than its old downtown stone buildings, with their ornate doorways and interior arches; the outstanding exception is the late Byzantine church of **Áyios Andhrónikos**, northwest of the pedestrian zone by a car park. Long the central mosque for the Turkish community, since their departure it has been examined by archaeologists, and the cleaning of extensive sixteenth-century frescos is nearly complete – watch for its opening as a tourist attraction in the near future. (The small chapel of Áyios Andhréas, on the way to the campsite, is bare inside.)

Practical details

Outside July and August, this is one place in the South where you could get away with driving up and finding a **hotel or room** on the spot. Rock-bottom hotel option, clean but not particularly quiet on the main street, is the no-star *Akamas* (☎321330), with singles at C£3, doubles for C£6. Pensions and hotel-apartments are better value here: choices range from the modest *Lemon Garden* (☎321443), inland on the road to Pýrgos, for about C£6 per person, to the fancy sea-view *Vougenvilea* (☎321684), C£15 single, C£18 double, part way along the pension-lined access road to the campsite.

The **campsite** itself (March–Oct) is magically set in a jungle of eucalyptus and calamus 1.5km north of town, at the east end of the long beach stretching all the way to Látchi (see below). At C£1.50 per tent/carvanan, and C£1 per person, it can't be faulted except for its relative remoteness, though the road back up to Pólis is lined with a few snack bars, groceries, the hospital and an excavated patch of ancient Arsinoë.

Other amenities include a **post office**, four **banks**, a rash of **moped hire** agencies, the *Nea Amoroza* **minibus** booking office (☎321114) and the municipal **market hall** that's the best place to buy fruit and meat for miles around.

Eating and drinking are easily seen to in the compact town centre. *Arsinoe* specialises in fish, not cheap but good, and homemade wine, and is always mobbed. Across the street and a bit south, *Charles Mikis* has a wider-ranging menu; in the opposite direction, *Kebab House* is ideal for just that.

Most **nightlife** seems to revolve around a recently pedestrianised three-way junction, now the triangular central plaza, where a half-dozen self-styled "café-bar-snacks" vie for your attention. Elsewhere, several more alcoholic pubs occupy old buildings, strangest of them perhaps being the *Brunnen* in one of the many abandoned Turkish houses tucked below the summit ridge.

Northeast to Káto Pýrgos: remote beach resorts

There's relatively little traffic up the coast towards Káto Pýrgos, partly because its backwater status was reinforced in 1974 by the cease-fire line just beyond – the former direct route to Mórfou and Nicosia can no longer be used. The area only comes alive in summer, when it's a retreat of some importance for Cypriots who haven't the appetite or the wallet for the purpose-built hotel strips elsewhere in the South. Public transport is rare along this stretch – at most two buses daily to Káto Pýrgos, the end of the line – so you really need your own wheels.

Pómos and Pakhíamos

The first twenty-odd kilometres towards PÓMOS parallel the little-developed but exposed shoreline, though cement villas are already going up, perhaps to handle the overflow from Páfos in the future. **PÓMOS** itself has a few self-catering apartments and modest tavernas, but the village is quite featureless, and the beach still not much to scream about. Things improve scenically as you round the prominent cape and bounce along the deteriorating road into aptly named **PAKHÍAMOS** (Broad Sand); here the settlement tilts downhill towards the beautiful beach, though organised amenities seem limited to a taverna at the local Áyios Rafaélos, and a mini-market.

Kókkina

Beyond Pakhíamos the narrow road, barely maintained since 1974, climbs sharply inland through forested hills, by way of avoiding the problematic enclave of **KÓKKINA** (Erenköy), off-limits to Greek Cypriots years before the Turkish Army made it a beach-head in 1974. Turkish-Cypriot extremists had long used it as an off-loading port for supplies from Turkey, just as their EOKA counterparts used the empty westerly Páfos coast. Matters came to a head on 3 August 1964 when 3000 National Guard troops under the command of General George Grivas (see p.166) attempted to put a stop to this activity by attacking Kókkina and several surrounding Turkish hamlets. The outnumbered defenders were forced to fall back into Kókkina itself, at which point Turkish jets appeared from the mainland, bombing and strafing nearby Greek villages (including Pólis), with heavy casualties. Outright war between Greece and Turkey was only narrowly avoided through UN intervention, and the irreparable estrangement of the two island communities, which had begun the previous year, was now virtually complete. Until 1974, Turkish Cypriots from the hills around continued to enter the fortified enclave; after the invasion, all civilians were relocated to the Kárpas peninsula, and Kókkina became strictly a Turkish army base, which it remains. Hence the tedious, 24-kilometre detour.

Káto Pýrgos

When you reach the sea again, having passed numerous vigilant National Guard posts, you're almost to **KÁTO PÝRGOS**, end of the line to non-UN vehicles. There's a good beach here, too, and the place is more equipped than any preceding for guests, boasting no less than three starred hotels, mostly at the west end of the beachfront: the *Ioannou* (☎522001), with singles c£10, doubles c£15; the *Pyrgiana Beach* (☎522322), at c£7/c£13; and the *Tylo Beach* (☎522348), with rates in between the two. Other than going swimming and watching Greek-Cypriot or UN troops, there's little to do here except perhaps visit the Byzantine church of **Panayía Galoktistí**, twenty minutes' walk up a valley towards KHALÉRI village.

West of Pólis: Látchi and Neokhorío

Once clear of the "suburb" of PRODHRÓMI, with more villa-type accommodation, the road west from Pólis hugs the so-far-undeveloped but often windswept beach on its way to **Látchi**, often confusingly spelled "Latsi" in both Greek and English lettering.

Látchi

The one more or less genuine fishing village of Páfos district consists of a line of shops, two banks, a few small hotels and apartments, with a half-dozen fish tavernas jostling to be close to the picturesque anchorage inside the rubble breakwater. Cheapest **accommodation** is the one-star *Souli* (☎321088, single/double c£9/14), by itself well west of town, or the *Latsi* (☎321411, same rates), close to the harbour but again hardly state-of-the-art lodging. For a well-executed luxury complex, available through *Sunvil Travel* in advance, try the *Elia Latchi Village* (☎321011); Sunvil also controls some excellent villas a few kilometres inland.

Among the hotly competing **restaurants**, *Porto Latsi* is the poshest, while the *Latchi Village Taverna* stakes out the opposite end of the market with rather plain food for locals. The *Periyiali*, out towards the *Souli*, is okay for a decent mid-range meal, but lately the best value seems to be had at the waterfront *Sea Fare*, partly because they're new and so try harder.

Látchi has a good pebble **beach**, with low-key water sports like windsurfing or canoeing on offer; but the beach improves as you head east towards the Pólis campground, or west towards the Baths of Aphrodite. A real recreational find in town is *Atlantis Diving*, which offers a variety of **scuba outings** to underwater highlights along the northeast Akámas shore. Certification courses start at c£135, or you can dive twice daily over five days for c£110. One-week packages, booked into *Atlantis*' own harbourside apartment complex, start at c£230 per person. Contact them directly on ☎06/322096, fax 05/221503.

Neokhorío and around

Beyond Látchi, there's an important junction. The inland turning leads to **NEOKHORÍO**, with a dramatic hillside setting for its stone houses, one kebab *taverna*, plus a few apart-hotels to get booked into. Barring that, you can ask the *múkhtar* (village headman) Sotiris to fix you up with a room in a family's house.

Once clear of the village, bear left and down at the first junction (right goes to Smiyiés picnic spot, see next section). The scenic lefthand dirt track goes to the former Turkish villages of ANDHROLÍKOU and FASLÍ, deserted except for one goatherd family in the former; despite a reasonable amount of water by Akámas standards, the soil was too poor to attract fleeing northerners. A saloon car can just get through, but as always in the Akámas you'll feel more confident with a four-wheel drive as you wind past the ghost hamlets and under the antenna-crowned crenellations of **Áyios Yióryios**, summit of the Akámas, en route to Ínia.

Staying with the coastal route below Neokhorío, you'll pass the turnoff for the friendly and reasonable *Ttakkas Bay Restaurant* , with a loyal return clientele. The bay in question, just out front, has a good pebble **beach** with showers and rental sunbeds; carry on east around some rocks and you'll find about a kilometre more of the same, undisturbed except for one motel-restaurant on a low bluff.

The Akámas wilderness

Neokhorío is the last bona fide village before the final, tapering tip of the roughly triangular Akámas peninsula, whose base can be reckoned somewhere down near Áyios Neófitos. Except for dense pine groves along the summit ridge, the region is quite deforested – though despite such appearances, springs and tiny streams are tucked into relatively lush hollows and gorges. The coast drops off fairly sharply, especially on the northeast shore, and there's very little sand anywhere. It's a severely impressive rather than a calendar-page beautiful land-scape, much of its appeal residing in the near-absence of human activity.

Yet un-Green as this may sound, it's territory often best explored in a four-wheel drive or on some sort of two-wheeler. The few marked trails are summar-ised following, but an infinity of unmarked jeep tracks go virtually everywhere, and the often shadeless terrain will not appeal to aimless wanderings on foot, especially between June and September.

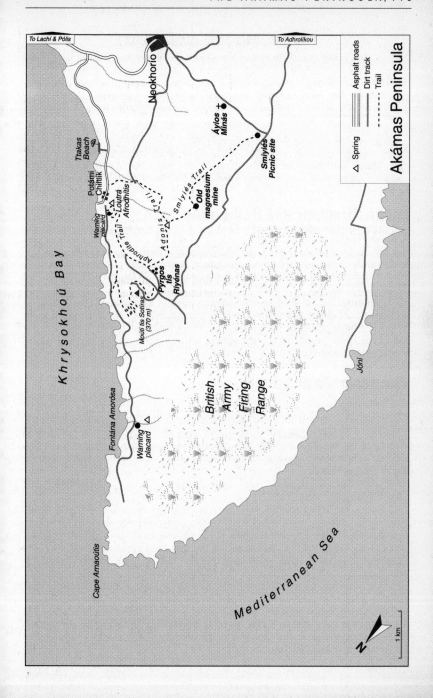

Akámas Peninsula

THE AKÁMAS FIRING RANGE

One of the conditions of Cypriot independence was the reservation by the UK of various "retained sites" on the island other than the Sovereign Bases, and an extensive **artillery firing range** west of the Akámas watershed is one of them. Periodically the range is closed to the public for military exercises; *Yangos and Peters'* taverna in Látchi maintains a notice board with the current month's schedule for the Akámas firing range.

Ironically, the British military has helped keep the area in a relatively pristine state; now that much of the peninsula is officially a national park, it remains to be seen what the extent of protection for one of the island's last wilderness areas will be. Those responsible for the dreariness of the major Miami-style strips on the southern coast will doubtless attempt to do the same here, if they're allowed to.

Loutrá Afrodhítis (the Baths of Aphrodite)

The road in from Pólis and Látchi ends at a car park and CTO pavilion just past the few houses of POTÁMI CHIFTLIK hamlet. Here, the named "Aphrodite" nature trail, diverging from a rough coastal jeep track at a distinctive wooden canopy and archway, begins with a five-minute walk to **Loutrá Afrodhítis** (the Baths of Aphrodite). In legend the goddess retired here to bathe before (and after) entertaining assorted lovers; today's reality is a flagstoned area beside an attractive pool about four metres across, the headspring of the irrigated oasis below, fed by drips off the rock face of a grotto smothered in wild fig trees. Signs forbid you to succumb to the temptation of bathing in the shallow water, drinking it or climbing the trees.

Akámas trails and tracks

From the pool, you proceed downstream on a narrower path to rejoin the coastal track, inland of which is a warning placard with this cheery notice from the Ministry of Defence: "Keep out when red flags are flying as (artillery) firing is then in progress. Do not touch any object on the ground as it may explode and kill you". (It is wise to consult the notice board at Látchi harbour before bothering to venture this far.)

The "Aphrodite" nature trail

Just before that MOD placard, you head up the continuation of the **"Aphrodite"** nature trail, climbing from carob, mastic and eucalyptus near sea level up to juniper, pine and other species labelled in Greek and Latin; in May, white *Cistus* (rock rose) is everywhere. At the top of the first hard climb you've good views east over the Pólis coastal plain and nearby offshore islets, before a straight-marching trail heads west through an old firebreak. There are some waymarks, plus lots of shotgun shell-casings: birds, especially quail, love the *frígana* (scrub biome), and Cypriots are keen (and in this case illegal) hunters. Somewhat under an hour above Aphrodite's baths you'll arrive at a picnic area in a hollow shaded by a gigantic oak tree; a spring here is unreliable. Adjacent, the Pýrgos tis Riyénas archaeological site – apparently the remains of a Byzantine monastery or Lusignan fort – is self-explanatory.

Track-walk about five or ten minutes west-northwest from the ruins and oak tree, before bearing right onto the trail's continuation (marked by a cairn), and again right when you shortly encounter the track system again. The path is finally subsumed into the narrow, sharply climbing track, which ends some twenty minutes above the oak with an opportunity to detour left on a path to the viewpoint atop the 370-metre summit known as Moúti tis Sotíras. There's a suicide leap out towards Cape Arnaoútis, the very end of Akámas, so you retrace your steps – all of a ten-minute detour – down to the signed junction for the descending, onward footpath to the coast.

Ingeniously engineered into the seaward-facing slopes of the mountain, this offers one more bush-shaded viewpoint before meeting up with the coastal track within around half an hour. You can avoid a fair amount of track-walking on the way back to the car park by keeping to the slightly higher path system until it ends a few minutes before some smelly goatpens to seaward. You'll need to budget approximately two and a half hours for the entire loop out of the CTO pavillion.

The "Adonis" and "Smiyiés" nature trails

From the oak-shaded picnic area, another as yet partly marked nature trail, the **"Adonis"**, heads off south on a most interesting course. The path initially climbs for fifteen minutes over a saddle, then becomes a wider track heading southeast. After ten minutes on this, you bear left (east) again onto the resurgent trail, which in five more minutes reaches a reliable spring in a forested dell at the head of a canyon.

There's also another important marked junction here: northeast down the canyon back to Loutrá Afrodhítis along the Adonis trail, or south onto the **"Smiyiés"** path. Follow this for just over five minutes to the kiln stack and tunnels of a derelict magnesium mine, which is also accessible by jeep track along the ridge to the west. The path continues briefly east, then heads south again on a fairly level course before reaching the Smiyiés picnic site within another hour.

From the dell-spring, the continuation of the "Adonis" trail back towards the CTO pavillion descends northeast along the ravine, following a water pipe at first, before curling east. Next you bear north, away from the pipe, then east again across what is now a plateau along the much-widened track through the scrub. Rather suddenly there's a zig-zag plunge down towards the coastal road, the route debouching under a now-familiar standard-issue nature trail canopy, about a kilometre southeast of the CTO parking lot. From the spring-junction down to the coast road, count on a good hour.

Logistics

Some combination of these three named trails would give you the best possible transect of the Akámas watershed, but you've a small problem when you reach the Smiyiés picnic grounds – getting out to Neokhorío, the closest habitation. The road there, via the chapel of ÁYIOS MINÁS, is quite rough – an ordinary car could just make it, but a taxi driver would probably refuse the trip or charge you dearly. So whether starting or ending a trek here, you'd likely have to either shuttle between in a jeep, or count on walking the four extra kilometres to/from the village.

The Fontána Amorósa coastal track

The most straightforward – and arguably the least exciting – Akámas walk is the one leading to **Fontána Amorósa**, a popular excursion destination almost at Cape Arnaoútis. It's perhaps best done in conjunction with one of the inland nature trails, and is frankly more enjoyable on a motorcycle or mountain bike. If you intend to walk much of it, you'd do well to arrange a boat ride from Látchi to drop you off at Fontána Amorósa, and walk back along the route of your choice – it's very tedious both ways. A simple tramp back to the CTO pavillion takes about 90 minutes; just keep to seaward at every option. Some path shortcuts are possible, especially those mentioned above at the base of Moúti tis Sotíras. Vegetation en route is mostly juniper and mastic bush, with scattered pines. The coast itself, disappointingly, is not very usable; the sea is quite clear, but a northern exposure means lots of debris in the mixed sand-and-pebble coves. If it's beaches you're after, they're better, if less private, at Ttákkas and east of Látchi.

Despite the mythological hype, often confused with that of Loutrá Afrodhítis, the celebrated **spring** at Fontána Amorósa is a crashing non-event – diligent combing of the bushes turns up nothing more substantial than a tiny, murky well on the cliff overlooking the protected bay. Those drinking the water were legendarily supposed to become randy forthwith, though today you're more likely to just throw up. On the bright side, the best swimming along the route is just below, where a small sand-and-gravel beach at the base of the cliff lies out of the wind.

More marvellous than the *fontana* perhaps is the canyon track up behind the second artillery-range warning sign to the east; about 400 metres along this, in a stream gully, **drinkable water** trickles amid the greenery.

Alternatively, it's possible to continue two-plus kilometres northwest along the track towards Cape Arnaoútis after your boat has dropped you off, lengthening any hiking by about an hour. There's not much out here except for the wreck of a freighter which foundered some years ago.

Eastern Páfos district: hill villages and monasteries

East of the main Páfos–Pólis road, the severity of the Akámas yields to more forgiving, stereotypically beautiful countryside, largely given over to vineyards and almond groves; the sea is more distant here, and you begin to feel that you're really in the hills. The goal of most trippers here is the large village of Panayía, and two historic monasteries just south.

You've a choice of approach roads. Coming from Páfos, the quickest route – on a recently improved highway – passes through POLÉMI and descends to KANNAVIOÚ, negligible except for the chance to eat at tree-shaded tavernas, before the final climb to Panayía. Starting at Pólis, the best road threads the villages of SÍMOU, DHRÍMOU, LÁSA and DHRINIÁ, all scattered on the south-bank ridge of the Stavrós tis Psókhas stream canyon, before linking up with the Polémi–Kannavíou road.

At Lása it's worth making a brief detour up to **FÍTI,** the most architecturally distinguished of this group, where locally woven lacework is sold both out of the old houses and at the restaurant on the main square.

Panayía

Though shown on most maps as "Pano (Upper) Panayía", no Káto (Lower) is visible and the town limits sign merely announces **PANAYÍA**, the largest of several settlements near the headwaters of the Ezoúsas stream. Here, 750 metres up, you're at the fringes of the Troödhos mountains, with walnut trees and tufts of forest visible on the ridge behind. The village is famous as the birthplace of the late Archbishop and President Makarios III, honoured by two small museums and an enormous statue in the main square. At the rear of the plaza sits the **"Makarios Cultural Centre"** (Tues–Sun 9am–1pm & 2–5pm; free), devoted to photos and paraphernelia of the great man's activities. While the mock-up of the radio set over which Makarios broadcast his defiance of the 15 July 1974 coup is of some interest, the displays are in general pretty feeble, padded out with such vaguely pertinent items as the slippers and alarm clock of a cousin, and rosters of the 1974 war dead from the village.

More atmospheric, perhaps, is **Makarios' Childhood House**, well signed south of and below the central *kafenío* crossroads. If the gate's locked (nominally open daily 10am–1pm & 2–6pm; donation) hang about purposefully and an old crone in black will appear with the key. With its pleasant garden and two interior rooms, it seems surprisingly large for a peasant house of the early twentieth century – until you realise that the livestock occupied the back room, with two adults and four children up front. Photos of crucial moments in Makarios' life – some duplicates of those in the Cultural Centre – and assorted household knick-knacks make up the exhibits.

In terms of **practicalities**, there's a line of tavernas across the road from the statue *platía*, including one offering beds for c£4 a person, c£1 extra for breakfast. Several buses daily call in from the Pérvola car park terminal in Páfos.

Khrysorroyiátissa monastery

Just 3km south of, and slightly higher, than Panayía, the **monastery of Khrysorroyiátissa** (Khrysorroyiatíssis) stands at a shady bend in the road, gazing out over terraced valleys to the west. Revisionist derivation of the unusual name, "Our Lady of the Golden Pomegranate", from an epithet of the Virgin as Golden-Breasted, seems to point suspiciously back in time to Aphrodite's similar attribute. A twelfth-century foundation legend centres on the hermit Ignatius, who retrieved a glowing icon of the Virgin from the Pafiot shore but, as so often when miraculous images make their wishes known, heard a celestial voice advising him to build a home for Her here. Over the years this particular manifestation of the Virgin became the patronness of criminals, who prayed to avoid arrest or for a light sentence – probably a holdover of the safe haven granted to fugitives in certain pagan temples. Dating like the rest of the structure from 1775, the *katholikón* is plunked down in the middle of the triangular cloister dictated by the site. Its most interesting (indeed unique) feature is the carved and painted wood-panel *yinaikonítis* in the rear of the nave, rather than the *témblon* or the (hidden) icon.

Khrysorroyiátissa is ostensibly a working monastery – the reasonably priced products of the basement winery are on sale in the shop, and the current abbot, a refugee from the North, is involved with manuscript restoration. But the few monks are shy of the tourist hordes, and the guest quarters are shut for repairs until early 1995.

ARCHBISHOP MAKARIOS III (1913–77)

Makarios III, President-Archbishop of Cyprus and the dominant personality in post-independence Cyprus until 1974, was a contradictory figure. Both a secular and a religious leader, his undeniable charisma and authority were often diminished by alternating spells of arrogance and naivete, coupled with a debilitating tendency to surround himself with pliant yes-men. Many observers, not least Turks and Turkish Cypriots, found it difficult to understand the fusion of his two roles as spiritual and political leader of the Greek Cypriots, in what was nominally a secular republic; they failed to take into account the fact that such a strategy was institutionalised in Greek communal history since the fall of Byzantium. Cyprus is still ambivalent about him: officially revered in the South, detested in the North, a balanced, homegrown appraisal of his life – including his alleged numerous relationships with women – seems unlikely in the near future.

One among four children of Christodhoulos and Eleni Mouskos, he was born Michael Mouskos in Panayía on 13 August 1913. Mouskos herded sheep in the forest above the village before spending his adolescence as a novice at Kýkko Monastery in the nearby mountains – where he made friendships and contacts later to be invaluable. The monks paid his matriculation fees at the prestigious Pancyprian Gymnasium in Nicosia; after graduating in 1936, Mouskos proceeded to Greece, where he attended university and managed to survive World War II. Postgraduate work in Boston was interrupted in April 1948 by the news that he had been chosen Bishop of Kition (Larnaca).

Adopting the religious name Makarios (Blessed), he also turned his attention to politics in his homeland. Soon after co-ordinating a plebiscite in early 1950 showing 96 percent support among the Greek Orthodox population for *énosis* or union with Greece, he was elected Archbishop of all Cyprus, which made him the chief Greek-Cypriot spokesman in future negotiations with the British colonial masters. With George Grivas, in 1952 he co-founded EOKA (Greek Organisation of Cypriot Fighters) to struggle for *énosis*. But Makarios initially baulked at the violent methods proposed by Grivas, and for various reasons the rebellion did not begin until April 1955. Makarios' connections at Kýkko proved essential, as both he and Grivas used the monastery as a hideout, recruiting centre and bank.

It didn't take the British long to determine who was behind the revolt, and Makarios plus three other clerics were deported to the Seychelles, but released after a year of house arrest on condition they not return to Cyprus. So Makarios was able to continue his tactic, evolved since 1948, of travelling round world power centres watching the strategies of others and drumming up support for his cause – particularly among newly independent portions of colonial empires. Among tactics to be emulated were accepting help from whatever quarter offered – including AKEL (the Cypriot Communist Party) and the Soviet Union. In the short run this went some way towards uniting polarised Greek-Cypriot society and much of world opinion behind *énosis*, but in the more distant future would generate accusations of unscrupulousness – and earn him the undying, and ultimately destructive, enmity of the overwhelmingly right-wing membership of EOKA.

The last straw, as far as most of EOKA was concerned, was his reluctant acceptance in 1959 of the British offer of independence for the island, rather than *énosis*. Grivas returned to Greece, soon to plot more mischief, while Makarios was elected first president of the new republic. He faced an unenviable task, not least convincing suspicious Turkish Cypriots that his departure from the cause of *énosis* was genuine. In this he failed, most signally in 1963 and 1964, by first showing considerable lack of tact in proposing crucial constitutional changes to the Turkish Vice-Presidency, then by failing to decisively restrain EOKA appointees in his cabinet and EOKA gunmen in the streets, and finally by outright threats of violence against the Turkish-Cypriot community during the Kókkina incident (see p.113).

It's conceivable that, during the early years of the Republic, Makarios was backpeddling towards *énosis*, but following the colonels' coup in Greece of April 1967, Makarios again saw the advantages of non-aligned independence, especially if the alternative were union with a regime he openly detested – and his own relegation in status to that of a backwater bishop. By early 1968 he had publically proclaimed the undesirability of *énosis* and began looking for ways out of the impasse, specifically by re-opening negotiations with the Turkish Cypriots. But these talks, which continued intermittently until 1974, were never marked by any sufficiently conciliatory gestures – though admittedly such an action would have exposed him to danger from unreconstructed EOKA extremists, which shortly materialised anyway.

To these vacillations on the relative merits of *énosis* and independence, and Makarios' continued espousal of the non-aligned movement (not to mention his relations with communists at home and abroad) can be traced the roots of the USA's growing opposition to the archbishop. President Nixon vilified him as "Castro in a cassock", while Secretary of State Kissinger openly sought a way to remove this obstacle to more malleable client-states in the Mediterranean. The Greek junta's views on Makarios matched his opinion of them, so they needed little encouragement to begin conspiring, through cadres planted in the National Guard and EOKA-B (a Grivas revival) for his overthrow. Despite repeated unsuccessful, junta- and CIA-instigated plots to assassinate him between 1970 and 1974 – including the shooting down of his helicopter – Makarios unwisely vacillated on how to handle their proxies, EOKA-B; by the time the archbishop and his supporters decided on firm suppression, in April 1974, it was too late.

On 15 July 1974, the EOKA-B-infiltrated National Guard and Greek junta officers stormed the archiepiscopal palace in Nicosia, Makarios' residence, inflicting such comprehensive damage that a clear intent to kill him was evident. Makarios miraculously escaped, however, being spirited by loyalists first to his old refuge at Kýkko and later to the archiepiscopal palace in Páfos, where he broadcast a message disproving announcements of his death. From there his old adversaries the British airlifted him onto the Akrotíri airfield and thence to London and exile. Neither the British nor the Americans initially bestirred themselves much to re-instate a leader whom they felt had received his just desserts for years of intriguing.

Yet Markarios' long practice as emissary to and of the Third World paid off, particularly at the UN, and late in 1974 he was able to return to Cyprus, addressing a huge rally in Nicosia with the consummate showmanship which came so naturally to him. He resumed office as president, but the multiple attempts on his life and the depressing fact of the island's continuing division must have weighed on him. On 3 August 1977 Makarios suffered a fatal heart attack, and five days later was buried in a cave on Throní hill, near Kýkko.

Controversy surrounded even the unseasonable downpour at the time of his funeral: the Greek-Cypriot eulogists characterised the rain as the tears of God weeping for His Servant, while the Turkish Cypriots – watching the proceedings on television to make sure their bogeyman was really dead – retorted with their folk belief that the sins of the wicked deceased were washed away by the rains before burial.

The courtyard seems open for visits all day, but the shop and *katholikón* close from noon to 2pm. Outside the walls a panoramic snack/drink bar is not grossly overpriced, and presumably comes alive at the local 1–2 February and 14–15 August **festivals**.

Ayía Moní monastery

In comparison, the small monastery of **Ayía Moní**, 1.5km beyond Khrysorroyiátissa and abandoned in 1571, has little to offer. Restoration – the latest of several – is nearly complete, but has been done in such a way that the church, originally built atop a temple of Hera and thus one of the oldest (sixth century) in Cyprus, now appears to belong to no particular era. Judging from the beds and en suite facilities being installed in the "cells", an educated guess might be that Ayía Moní will be serving as a pilgrims' hostel during its neighbour's closure.

If you've come this far, better to keep going 8km via KILÍNIA to the end of the asphalt at abandoned, ex-Turkish VRÉCHA, from where a rough track descends to the more compelling medieval **Roudhiás bridge**, a restored double-decker span over the Xéros creek valley.

The Tillyrian wilderness

North of Panayía extends a vast, empty, wooded tract of hills, historically known as **Tillyría**, though strictly speaking the label doesn't apply until you're past the Stavrós tis Psókhas forestry station. Unlike the highest stretches of the Troödhos, the region is not and never has been appreciably settled, frequented in the past mainly for the sake of its rich copper mines (now worked out). If you're staying anywhere on the Pólis coast, a drive through here satisfactorily completes a day begun in the Páfos hills.

The "Cedar Valley"

Leaving Panayía on the road signposted for Kýkko monastery, follow the paved road until it gives out after 6km. Next you have 14km of good dirt road, again always veering towards Kýkko at the well-marked junctions, until reaching the **Cedar Valley**. This is no more or less than that, a hidden gulch with thousands of specimens of *Cedrus brevifolia*: a type of aromatic cedar indigenous to Cyprus, first cousin to the more famous Lebanese variety and now principally found here. At a hairpin bend in the track, there's a picnic area and a spring, while a sign points to the wide but no-vehicles track leading 2.5km up to 1362-metre Trípylos peak. Strangely, the hike passes few of the handsome trees; they're mostly well downstream, and (perhaps intentionally) inaccessible.

Kýkko itself, some 20km further on, is much more easily approached from Pedhoulás in the Troödhos. If you've come from the south you'll prefer to back-track 4km from the picnic site to the junction marked "Stavros". Heading there, you'll pass (after 6km) the labelled jeep track coming down from Trípylos summit.

Stavrós tis Psókhas and beyond

Some 7km further, there's another, important junction: right goes down and north to the coast, left and south descends 3km more to the colonial-era forestry station and rest house at **Stavrós tis Psókhas**. The name is that of a monastery, abandoned last century, which once stood here, and is usually politely translated as "Cross of Measles"; it actually means "Cross of the Mange", and in the days before pesticide lotions a spontaneous cure of scabies must have seemed well-nigh miraculous.

Facilities at Stavrós tis Psókhas

The attractive **facilities** at Stavrós include a small café with snacks, the forestry headquarters for Páfos district, a petrol pump intended for staff, a **campsite**, and the extremely popular **hostel**, whose bunks must be reserved in advance from June to August (☎06/332144 or 722338): c£5 for a bunk in simple rooms with en suite bath. The rangers will proudly assure you that this is the coolest spot in the district (850 metres up in deep shade, it's not hard to believe); most visitors drive up the easy way, on the road taking off between Kannavioú and Panayía.

The nature trails

Forestry staff can point you in the direction, near the campsite, of an enclosure for Cyprus **mouflon**, only just saved from extinction – they're now the logo of *Cyprus Airways*. Wild members of the small herd also roam the surrounding ridges, but you're exceedingly unlikely to see one running free while hiking one of the two surveyed **nature trails**. It's unhappily difficult to hike these as a loop, though you can nearly do them back-to-back, making the most of a day sandwiched in between two nights here. The first, heralded by the same distinctive archway and canopy as used on the Akámas peninsula, begins about halfway along the seven-kilometre stretch of forestry track east of Stavrós, and plunges off the ridge to end near the final side-turning into the station. The second one begins downstream from the campsite and climbs up the ridge towards Zakhárou peak (1212 metres), ending prominently in another archway up at the three-way saddle-junction where auto tracks go to Trípylos, the coast or back down to the station.

Out to the coast

The route **to the coast** is, as ever, well signed but it's slow going and requires stamina which may not be available at the end of a long day. Occasionally rally-style driving in an ordinary car will end you up in Pómos (29km from the junction) in about an hour, Káto Pýrgos (37km) or the inland salient of the Kókkina detour (25km) in just over an hour. En route you'll notice how the careful husbandry of the British and Republican forestry services was set back considerably by the Turkish Air Force, which set the trees alight with napalm in 1974; patterns of long reafforestation terraces are still some years from fully reversing this act of economic sabotage.

travel details

Buses

From Páfos to **Limassol** 4 daily Mon–Fri on *KEMEK*, 1 or 2 daily Mon–Sat with *Costas*; 1hr 15min: to **Nicosia** (via Limassol) 1 or 2 daily, Mon–Sat, on *Costas*; 2hr 45min: to **Pýrgos** (via Pólis) 2 daily Mon–Fri, 1 on Sat, with *Pyrgos*; 1hr 45min: to **Pólis** 12–13 daily Mon–Fri, 8 Sat, with *Nea Amoroza*; 45min.

Flights

Aside from numerous charters to the UK, scheduled services from Páfos include 1–2 weekly to Athens (1hr 40min); 1 weekly to Birmingham (4hr 45min); 2–3 weekly to London Heathrow (4hr 45min); 2 weekly to London Gatwick (4hr 45min); and 1 weekly to Manchester (5 hr). However these direct hops to Britain, on *British* or *Cyprus Airways*, are extremely expensive, and savvy expats who need long-term open tickets, or to get home on short notice, typically use the indirect *Malev* or B*SA* flights from Larnaca.

CHAPTER FOUR

THE HIGH TROÖDHOS

Rising to nearly 2000 metres, the Troödhos mountains ("Troh-dhos" rather than "True-dhos") form the backbone of the southern Republic's territory. Geologically they are a volcanic mass, long extinct and well worn down, but with rich mineral or metallic deposits formerly (in some cases still) mined. Too low and hummocky to be stereotypically alpine, the Troödhos still acquit themselves as a mountain resort area, and in their western part supports what is boasted, with some justification, as the best managed island forest in the Mediterranean.

In every era the range has been both a barrier and a resource, and later a refuge for Hellenic culture. Ancient miners clear-felled its trees to feed smelting furnaces, the forests growing conveniently close to the copper works of Tillyría. The devastating coastal raids of middle Byzantine times left the hills untouched, and during nearly four centuries of Lusignan rule, when the Orthodox church was humiliatingly subordinated elsewhere, the Troödhos provided a safe haven for a minor renaissance in its fortunes – most strikingly evidenced in the famous collection of frescoed rural churches here. The Ottomans didn't bother to settle the region, and when the mainland Turks returned in 1974 the obstacle the mountains represented, as much as any cease-fire agreement, may have deterred them from overrunning the entire island. Among foreign occupiers, only the British, homesick and sweltering down in the flatlands, realised the recreational potential of the mountains, with a lacework of roads and assorted architectural follies.

Uniquely in Cyprus, South or North, the independent traveller has a slight edge (or at least not a strong disadvantage) in the Troödhos. While there certainly are package groups in the fancier hotels, more modest establishments – of which there are numbers – welcome walk-in business, geared as they are to a local clientele. The only catch is that much of the cheaper accommodation only opens during the height of summer, so outside that you may find yourself with a limited choice. Despite nominally short distances between points, touring here is time-consuming, and you'll be more comfortable changing base of operations on occasion, moving on once the potential of a valley is exhausted, rather than pitting yourself and car against a hundred-odd kilometres of serpentine road on a daily basis. Reckon on a leisurely week to see all the Troödhos have to offer, and don't expect much help from very infrequent bus connections to Limassol or Nicosia.

The functional, though beautifully set, resort of **Plátres** is the usual gateway to the region from the south, with the largest concentration of hotels on that side of the watershed. Its higher neighbour **Troödhos** has no village character to speak of but is the jump-off point for a day's walking around the highest summit, **Mount Olympus**. Good roads lead from either to **Pedhoulás**, chief village and resort of the Marathássa valley – and also your introduction to the painted churches of the Troödhos, both here and downstream at **Moutoullás** and **Kalopanayiótis**. Pedhoulás also offers the easiest access to **Kýkko monastery**, out by itself at the edge of the Tillyrian wilderness.

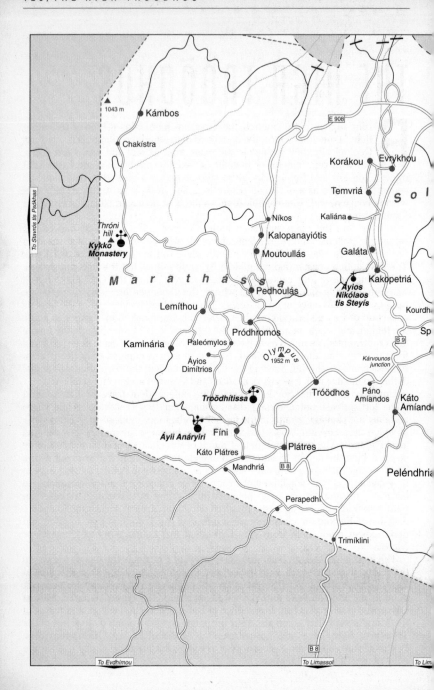

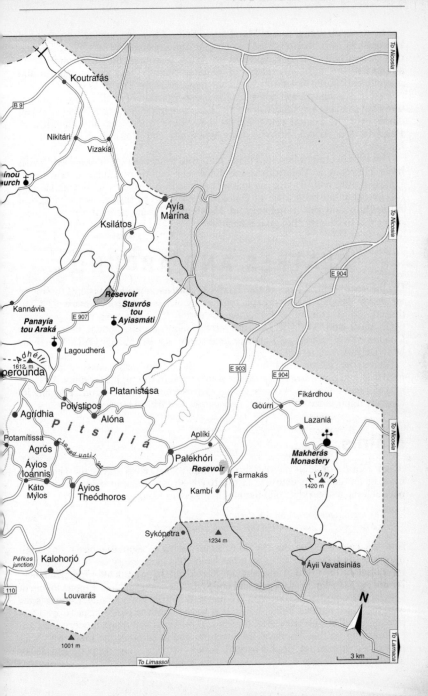

The next sub-region east of Marathássa, Soléa, has as its "capital" the resort of **Kakopetriá**, with its preserved old quarter and unusually accessible concentration of frescoed churches, up-valley at **Áyios Nikólaos tis Steyís** and downstream at the adjacent village of **Galáta**. Slightly less convenient is the magnificent church of **Asínou**, arguably the finest in the Troödhos.

East of Marathássa and Soléa lies the harsher terrain of Pitsiliá, largely bare of trees but in many ways more dramatic than its neighbours. From Kakopetriá you climb over the central ridge and to the valleys where the fine churches of **Panayía tou Araká**, **Stavrós tou Ayiasmáti** and **Panayía Kourdhalí** are hidden.

The best overnight base in Pitsiliá is **Agrós**, from where you're poised to visit more churches at **Peléndhria** and **Louvarás** before beginning a descent to Limassol. Alternatively you can follow the Troödhos peak line to its end, passing the lively, untouristed town of **Palekhóri** en route to the showcase village of **Fikárdhou** and the **monastery of Makherás**. From there, the most logical descent is to Nicosia, though it is fairly easy to reach Larnaca.

PLÁTRES AND AROUND

On the south-central flank of the Trödhos, **Plátres** is the first taste of the range for many people, and (perhaps too) easily accessible from Limassol, 37km distant, by a pair of well-engineered roads. The quickest route goes via MONÁGRI and TRIMÍKLINI; the other, more scenic option, described in Chapter Two, starts at Episkopí and ends up at either PARAPEDHÍ or MANDHRÍA.

Above the lateral road linking these three, vineyards cease and cherry orchards and pines begin, signalling your arrival in the high Troödhos. A tangle of major and minor roads converges on Plátres from every direction, reflecting its touristic importance – though not necessarily its intrinsic interest.

Plátres

At an altitude of 1150 metres, forest-swathed **PLÁTRES** stays cool and green most of the summer, courtesy of the Krýos stream rushing below. The Greek poet Seferis described its nightingales in his poem *Eleni*:

> *"The nightingales won't let you sleep in Platres."*
> *And just what is Platres? And this island, who knows it?*

And it's true that, during the May/June mating season the birds sing until midnight. As for what Plátres is, it has been characterised as the "Cypriot Simla" for its role as the premier "hill station" in colonial days. Long after independence, it remains a big haunt of ex-pats and enlisted men – you can watch footie in one of several pubs, and many tavernas are tuned to British Forces radio. Comparisons with the more famous Indian hill station were doubtless partly inspired by a few remaining villas with whimsical turrets and rooflines, but many modern piles are encroaching on the "Raj days" architecture, and in summer the main drag is an unenticing uproar of double-parked buses, strolling day trippers and tacky souvenirs.

Practical details

The extent of the "village" is a single high street, with a combination **post/ telephone office**, and adjacent **tourist information branch** (April–Oct Mon, Wed–Fri 9am–4.30pm, Tues and Sat 9am–1pm) behind the large central car park. From this same square daily market charabancs run to Nicosia and Limassol, while *Karydas* runs a **minibus** to Limassol on a service basis. You can also hire **mountain bikes** (look for the sign) to explore the myriad wide dirt tracks in the surrounding hills, and a **supermarket** (the *"New"*) at the lower junction sells food for hikes.

Accommodation
Many of the dozen **hotels** are scattered away from the high street, their locations shown on a helpful placard. The cheapest, a little out of town on the way to Psilódhendhro, is the *Spring* (☎05/421330), open May to December, with singles c£8.50, doubles c£17, perched at tree-top level on the very edge of the stream canyon. Other budget options are the *Pafsilipon* (☎05/421738), south of the central car park, open all year with similar rates, and the *Kallithea* (☎05/421746), on the upper road with slightly higher rates but a better location. The next notch up is occupied by *Lanterns* (☎05/421434), across from the *Pafsilipon*, at c£10.50 single/c£18 double, and the *Vienna* (☎05/421718; c£8/16), near the *Kallithea*. Among starred hotels the *Minerva* (☎05/421731), catering to British Forces families, is the least expensive at c£15/22, but if you're going to splurge the place to do so would be at the two-star *New Helvetia* (☎05/421348; c£16/26), a magnificent period piece just above the *Spring*, though not as intimate with the river.

Eating
Restaurant prices are nearly identical, and inflated – it's hard to get out the door for less than c£6. Currently the best food is at the *Riverdale*, or (lunchtime only) the Psilódhendhro **trout farm**. In addition to the rash of pubs, a single **disco** operates in high season about halfway along the high street.

Around Plátres

Two popular excursions – one riding, the other mostly walking – start from Psilódhendhro. The remote **monastery of MESOPÓTAMOS** lies 7km east along a dirt track pelted hazardously by rock falls. Having been abandoned for some time, it is now derelict and of little interest except as something to point your mountain bike towards; church-sponsored youth groups apparently unlock the courtyard gate for weekend outings. The streamside Arkolakhaniá picnic site about 1km before might be more compelling as a goal.

The Caledonian falls
More absorbing is the drive-walk up to **Caledonian falls**, dubbed "Nature Trail number 3" by the CTO, also beginning (or ending) at Psilódhendhro. The first 45 minutes of climbing are along a car track, with one right fork, after which the route dwindles to a marked trail. The impressive, eleven-metre cascade, highest on the island, beckons a few minutes later, in a pleasantly wooded ravine. Lots of water crossings are involved in continuing upstream along the path; you'll get your feet wet in the springtime. Some 45 minutes beyond the falls you emerge at

the opposite trailhead, marked by the familiar canopied notice board, about one kilometre from Troödhos resort (see next heading). If you do this walk in the opposite direction, the access slip road off the Troödhos-bound highway is unmarked; going down also takes about 45 minutes, owing to the roughness of the trail at some points – those with trainers beware.

The walk is short enough that retracing your steps is not so arduous; if you're vehicle-less and intent on leaving Plátres, it's worth noting that this trail, despite its steep-steepiness, is much the quickest way of getting up to the Troödhos resort on foot.

Before British administration began in 1878, the area was little visited except for gatherers of snow (used for refrigeration), but soon thereafter a military training camp was established near the site of present-day Troödhos, and a **summer residence** built for the British High Commissioner. Now the retreat of the president of the southern Republic, this stands just above the high end of the Caledonian falls trail. Signs discourage entry at the start of the driveway, but you may want to stop in to read the rather startling plaque to one side of the door of what looks like an ordinary Highland shooting lodge. Written in French, it declares: "Arthur Rimbaud, French poet and genius, despite his fame contributed with his own hands to the construction of this house, 1881." Rimbaud's two visits to Cyprus were sandwiched between time with the Dutch colonial army in Java, recuperation from typhoid in France, and a stint in the Horn of Africa; he in fact merely supervised a work party here and did no actual manual labour – nor was he yet famous.

Mount Olympus: resorts and hiking

At 1952m (6404ft), the Khionístra peak of **MOUNT OLYMPUS** is the highest point on Cyprus. It does not rise particularly dramatically from the surrounding uplands, which are cloaked in typically dense and pampered forest of hardy black and Calabrian pine, with a smattering of Cypriot cedar and junipers. The trees keep things cool except perhaps in August, and provide much of the justification for three marked nature trails. In winter, the northeast-facing slopes are host to the island's only ski resort. The area is worth a visit at any time of year; however the altitude and terrain can act as traps for sudden storms in most months, so don't step off unprepared onto the paths. When you do, you'll find them refreshingly empty.

The Troödhos resort

The only thing resembling permanent habitation in the peak zone is a strip of development, called **Troödhos**, flanking the main road junction about 1700 metres above sea level. By no stretch of the imagination is this a village, merely a resort complex with a petrol pump and the opportunity for some very tame horseriding. All day long through much of the year it's beset by tour coaches whose clients barely venture off the single parade with its handful of undistinguished kebab houses. There seems little to recommend an overnight here other than the piney air, with a limited choice of **hotels**: the one-star *Troöhdos* (☎05/421635) at c£9.50 single, c£15 double, and the pricier *Jubilee* (☎05/421647) at c£16/24 single/double. Just north of the major T-junction, the **youth hostel** asks a bit more than usual at c£3 per person, plus a c£1 sheet fee, and at last look the plumbing was out of order; alternatively, the **campsite**, 2km northeast of the intersection on the road to Nicosia, charges c£1.50 per tent and c£1 per person. The only public **bus** up here operates from the Costanza bastion in Nicosia at noon from Monday to Saturday, returning the next day at dawn.

A summit loop-hike

Perhaps the **best high Troödhos hike** is the circuit made possible by combining nature trails #1 and #4. It can be done in half a day – slightly more if you make the detour to the actual summit – and in clear weather offers simply the best views of the island, as well as an attractive plant (and bird) community en route. The walk is most enjoyable in the springtime, when numerous streams (and the one improved spring) are still flowing.

Itineraries **begin** at the archwayed trailhead for nature route #1, at the north end of the resort parade, opposite the phone station. A signpost reading "Chromio 8km" is somewhat misleading, since while the labelled path is approximately that distance, you never actually end up at the abandoned chromium mine in question. Your first fork is some twelve minutes out; go left for now, following red-dot waymarks. The proper trail skims the 1750-metre contour with little significant height change. Some forty minutes along, there's a three-way junction; ignore a wide track up the ridge to the right but not the onward trail taking off behind a wooden bench. Within ten more minutes there's a masonry fountain, running much of the year. An abandoned chromium mine shaft 1 hour 25 minutes out is often flooded and probably dangerous to explore; again shun wider tracks in favour of the narrower path hairpinning back left along the far side of the creek valley here. Just under two hours along, you've a first view of Pródhromos village far to the west, and its giant, empty Hotel Berengaria. Soon a

---

TROÖDHOS RANGE NATURE TRAILS

Since 1981 the CTO, in conjunction with the forestry department, has undertaken to lay out and mark a growing number of **nature trails** in the high Troödhos. In truth, many of the rights of way existed long before then, usually colonial projects of the 1930s, and were merely refurbished where necessary, signposted and fitted with numbered wooden markers calling walkers' attention to selected natural features. The labelling, however, is pretty perfunctory, with only Latin species names given – if at all – and many specimens embarrassingly dead or missing. To enjoy the trails as they were intended, it's essential to get the new 28-page CTO publication "Nature Trails of the Troödhos" containing the number keys for three of the more popular trails. There's little hope of snagging one in Plátres, and even in distant Limassol or Páfos you may only find a French or German version.

At present there are four trails in the Troödhos/Plátres area: **number 1**, nicknamed "Atalanta", nearly completes a circuit of Mount Olympus; **number 2**, "Persephone" in CTO parlance, is an out-and-back to a viewpoint known as Makriá Kondárka; **number 3**, logically enough named "Kaledonia", links the presidential forest lodge with Caledonian falls; and **number 4**, called "Artemis" but as yet unlabelled, executes a complete loop of Khionístra summit at a higher contour than number 1. There is also a new trail, to date unnumbered and sparsely labelled, along the Madhári ridge above Kyperoúnda, some kilometres east of Troödhos.

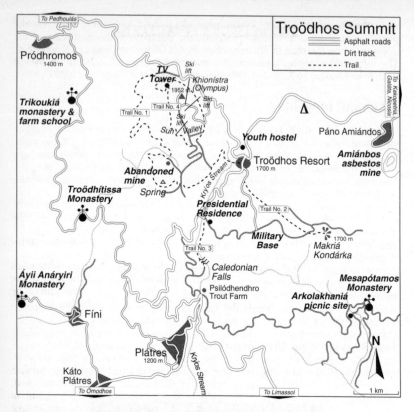

TV tower looms overhead, then the trail becomes a track through mossy pines about ten minutes before ending, two-and-a-half hours into the hike, on the Troödhos–Pródhromos road.

Rather than emerging onto the road, bear up and right along a **link trail** for just three minutes – worn yellow plastic discs on some trees serve as waymarks – to the intersection with Trail #4, a true loop closer to the summit. It's possible to follow it right (anti-clockwise), but for the quickest way back to the original trailhead, take a left, crossing the runs of two T-bar ski lifts. Once past the second lift, there's a fine view northeast over northern Cyprus, as you progress roughly parallel to the road back to Troödhos. You soon meet the tarmaced side road up to Khionístra peak with its RAF radar domes – another retained site – and TV tower, and winter-only café; cross to the nature-trail canopy opposite to stay with the path. At the next track junction bear left, keeping to path surface; three minutes along this bear left again at trees tacked with a yellow arrow and a red dot, forsaking both a track ahead down the ridge and the onward nature trail in favour of an older track dropping down into the valley on your left.

Rocks here are splashed with a few **blue dots**; followed in reverse up the hill, this blue-marked route passes a giant, labelled black pine and the top of the "Sun

---

SKIING MOUNT OLYMPUS

No one comes specially to Cyprus **to ski**, but if you're here between New Year's and the end of March, you just might consider the slopes for their novelty value. Each T-bar serves perhaps twice as many runs of 200 to 600 metres in length, none rated as difficult. Snow surface, alas, tends to be slushy or icy rather than powder, owing to warmish, sunny days alternating with freezing nights, even in the pit of winter. The shorter Sun Valley runs are considered beginners' areas, and this is where equipment is rented and lessons given; the more advanced northern runs are often given over to competitions. Lift tickets cost about c£9 a day, ski rental about the same, with half off for Cyprus Ski Federation members – temporary membership available but only worth it if you'll be here a few days. For current information, ring the Ski Federation in Nicosia (☎02/365340).

Valley" lift on its route to the summit area. This is a better detour than following the previously encountered paved drive; in addition to the electronic installations, there is sparse evidence up top of a Venetian watchtower and an ancient temple of Aphrodite.

Resuming the descent, you drop through a defile, and then the narrowing track curls back to join Trail #1 just below the *Jubilee Hotel*. You should be back at the starting point roughly an hour and fifteen minutes from the "Chromio" end of the same path (not counting any detours to the peak), for a total walking time of 3 hours 45 minutes.

The Makriá Kondárka trail

This additional short walk is just the thing if you haven't had enough for the day. The path begins inconspicuously at the southeast end of the Troödhos resort, beyond the police station; miss the trailhead and go too far, and you'll end up in an off-limits British base. At a moderate pace, the out-and-back route should take just over 90 minutes; the destination is the viewpoint of **Makriá Kondárka** at 1700 metres, allowing unobstructed views southeast over the Limassol foothills and coastal plain. On the way back you get to look at the incongruous radar "golf balls" and telecom tower on Khionístra, as well as the huge scar of the AMIÁNDOS open-pit asbestos mine, largest in the world, to the northeast.

West of Plátres and Troödhos: the way to Marathássa

Rather than proceeding directly from Plátres or Troödhos to the Marathássa valley (see next section), it's worth backtracking slightly to take a more interesting, roundabout **western route**. Closest to Plátres lies workaday FÍNI village, with a crafts tradition and inexpensive meals; north of here and above, Troödhítissa monastery is easiest reached on a direct secondary road from Plátres. Beyond the monastery, travelling further north via the alpine settlement of Pródhromos is straightforward.

Fíni and beyond

Descending from Plátres towards Mandhría junction, you'll reach KÁTO PLÁTRES, where there's a signed right up a couple of kilometres to **FÍNI**. Unlike its resort neighbours this is a working village with an attended primary school, failing to attract many visitors with its scenery (average) or architecture (less than). It does have a few potteries, turning out an assortment of primitive/kitsch wares, an old-fashioned chairmaker, and the privately run **Pivlakíon museum** (daily, reasonable daylight hours; donation). This is lodged in the exceptionally traditional house of Theofanis Pivlakis, who personally escorts visitors through his collection of rural oddments. A few **tavernas** – which may not be open for lunch outside summer – are far cheaper than anything in Plátres, and include a trout farm.

The tertiary road shown on maps, from Fíni up towards Troödhitissa monastery (see below), is passable only with a jeep; otherwise you must return to the edge of upper Plátres for the eight-kilometre paved way up to the monastery. The usual onward journey from Fíni involves following the paved road east out of the village, passing the medieval monastery of **Áyii Anáryiri** 2km along before turning north to thread the pleasant but nondescript hamlets of ÁYIOS DHIMÍTRIOS, PALEÓMYLOS and LEMÍTHOU, finally ending up in Pródhromos.

Troödhítissa monastery

Nestled in orchards and pines 8km northwest of Plátres at about 1200m elevation, the **monastery of TROÖDHÍTISSA** (daily 6am–noon, 2–8pm) is the highest working monastery in the land. It owes its thirteenth-century foundation to a wonder-working icon which, as ever, floated mysteriously over from Asia Minor at the height of the eighth-century iconclast controversy. Two hermits guarded it in a nearby cave for some years; after they had died and the memory of the relic faded, an unearthly glow alerted a succeeding generation to its presence, and a suitable home was built for the image.

The present buildings date mostly from 1730, supplemented by a modern **hostelry**, off-limits from 15 June to 15 September. Eight monks still live here, and the same austere regimen as at Stavrovoúni (see Chapter One) prevails, so frivolous requests to stay the night are not appreciated. In the **katholikón** it's traditional for monks to encircle young women with a medallion-studded girdle, said to induce fertility – in the old days any resulting boy-child had to be dedicated to the church as a monk, or "ransomed" with a generous donation. A marvellous icon, a silver-sheathed Virgin Enthroned, is displayed to the left of the Holy Door in the fine *témblon*; except for an extravagant crystal chandelier, fairly restrained for a Cypriot church. Outside, you can climb a signed path to the cave where the icon lay hidden; adjacent to the monastery is a *exokhikó kéndro* for refreshments, at its busiest on the 14–15 August and 20–21 November festivals of the Virgin.

Pródhromos

The onward highway north from Troödhítissa skirts Mount Olympus higher up on its west flank than the villages north of Fíni; just past two shady picnic sites sprawls the eighteenth-century Trikoukiá convent, now deconsecrated and the core of an agricultural academy. It marks the outskirts of **PRÓDHROMOS**, along with Páno Amíandos the highest true village in the country at 1400m. Pródhromos is also famous for its apples, but unless it's the season the most interesting item here is the rambling, hilltop chateau of the Hotel Berengaria, abandoned in 1980 – it couldn't compete with the luxury *Churchill Pinewood Valley*, just downhill to the north. Rumour suggests that a foreign consortium has purchased it for refurbishing, but its dereliction is rapidly approaching write-off status. The vandalised interior makes for oddly absorbing rumaging, scattered correspondence files providing a thumbnail social history of the British empire.

Practically, Pródhromos could be a fallback base with its unstarred *Alps Hotel* (☎02/952553) at c£6 single, c£11 double. In addition to a combo **bank/post office**, there's one of the few bona fide **CYTA** stations in the Cypriot hill country (Mon–Sat 9am–1pm and 4–6pm).

MARATHÁSSA

Directly north over the ridge from Pródhromos yawns the valley of **Marathássa**, an introspective, deep canyon of Asiatic grandeur. Like most watercourses on the north side of the Troödhos, the Setrákhos stream draining it runs at present into North Cyprus, and a dam has been built to rescue the water that would otherwise go unharnessed into "enemy" territory. Marathássa is famous for its cherry orchards, from which it partially lives; tourism, while catered to, is not the be-all and end-all that it is at Plátres. The valley can boast a respectable concentration of frescoed churches (see overleaf), and while not actually in Marathássa, the prestigious monastery of Kýkko is easiest reached from here.

Pedhoulás

At the top of the Marathássa valley, 1100 metres up, **PEDHOULÁS** has a much different feel from Pródhromos: more compact and amphitheatrically laid out in tiers, though close up most of the buildings are not so attractive. As a base it's preferable, both for convenience to Marathassan sights and for the range of choice in eating and sleeping.

Arkhángelos church

The main sight, and very likely your first frescoed church of the Troödhos, is **ARKHÁNGELOS**, in the lower quarter of the village. The warden, Panayiótis, lives in a house with pale green shutters and doors, fifty metres uphill on the same side of street; otherwise he can often be found at the junction of the Moutoullás road, 300 metres uphill, near a café and two stores.

The core of the church dates from 1474, so the style of its recently cleaned images is humanised and unaustere as befits the post-Byzantine revival. The archangel Michael himself looms left (north) of the minimalist *témblon*; beside him is shown the Sacrifice of Abraham, the usual signature-mark of Goul or an apprentice, with the principals of the potentially gruesome drama radiating a hieratic serenity

Starting on the south wall, there's a clockwise life cycle of the Virgin and Christ: in *The Betrayal* a miniature Peter lops off the ear of a centurion, while two disciples cense the Virgin's bier in the *Assumption*. Over the north door, donor

Basil Khamadhes and his family, in noble costume of the period, hands a model of the church to the Archangel, who emerges from a curtain-like fold of cloud. Above the *Virgin Enthroned* in the apse, in lieu of the usual *Pandokrator*, looms a smudged *Ascension*.

Practical details

Best among inexpensive **hotels** is the year-round *Christy's Palace* (☎02/952655), on the main commercial road with singles at c£7.50, doubles c£15; the adjacent *Central* hotel and *Kallithea* guest house, further east near the CYTA office, are not as good value for roughly the same rates, and open high summer only. The haphazardly maintained *Elyssia*, next to Christy's, is probably best avoided. Best all-round spot, when it's open (July–Aug only), is the two-star *Marangos* (☎02/952657), c£8.50/17, an old stone structure panoramically sited at the northwest edge of town, on the road to Kýkko.

Eating, most authentic is the sixty-year-old *To Vrysi* (aka *Harry's*), a shady *exokhikó kéndro* on a minor road up to the main highway. This features good local red wine, home-style entrees and candied fruit – a good consolation prize if you miss the local cherry season. If they're shut, often the case at night, the alternative

---

FRESCOED CHURCHES OF THE TROÖDHOS

Indisputably the most remarkable monuments in the Troödhos, if not the whole island, are a group of lavishly **frescoed Byzantine churches**, mostly on the north slopes of the range. The earliest of these date from the eleventh century, with construction continuing until the early 1500s; frescos were applied sporadically over the whole period, so that they serve as a chronicle of changing styles and tastes, often juxtaposed in the same building. The oldest frescos were executed in what is termed the **hieratic or monastic style**, with roots in Syria and Cappadocia; later Byzantine work reflected the arrival of artisans from Constantinople in the twelfth and thirteenth centuries. As Lusignan rule advanced, the building and decorating of these chapels became of necessity a provincial, rear-guard action, since the Orthodox were effectively banished from the larger towns. The so-called **post-Byzantine revival style** of the fifteenth and sixteenth centuries is at once more naive and naturalistic, with fascinating period details, humanistic liberties taken with Orthodox iconographic conventions, and in general echoes the art of the Renaissance.

Architecturally, most of these country churches were originally simple rectangular structures about the size of a small barn; later they often grew domes, less frequently narthexes. If it didn't originally exist, an all-encompassing, drastically pitched roof would be added at some point to shed dangerously heavy snow, with ample provision for domes if necessary. Most importantly, by extending down to the ground on one or both side, they enclosed L- or U-shaped spaces which *de facto* served as narthexes, so that many frescoed exterior walls were now afforded some protection. It's worth saying that almost every Troödhos village has such a pitched-roof church – but only a very few are still painted inside.

Certain departures from the usual **iconography** were caused by the many pitched, domeless roofs; there were often no cupola, squinches or vaults for the usual hierarchical placement of the *Pandokrátor* (Christ in Majesty), cherubim, evangelists and so on. However the cartoon-strip story-telling format, chosen to teach the Gospel to largely illiterate parishioners, was enhanced in small rectangular churches. The usual arrangement is a fairly complete life cycle of the Virgin and Jesus, with emphasis on the crucial dedications to God of both and various miracles

is the more central, posher *Mountain Rose*, with trout prominent on a wide-ranging menu; the upper storey looks set to become accommodation soon. Rounding out the list of amenities are **banks**, the **CYTA** station and a miniscule **post office**. The once-daily market **bus** on the Nicosia–Plátres line passes through here.

Moutoullás: Panayía Moutoullá

The earliest surviving example of the Troödhan pitched-roof church, **PANAYÍA MOUTOULLÁ** (1279), stands next to the cemetery at the highest point of **MOUTOULLÁS** village, 3km below Pedhoúlas. A set of steps leads up from the road, just above the sharp turn in the ravine, to a somewhat crotchety caretaker's house just below the church.

You enter via two sets of doors, the outer pair piercing the protective structure grown up around the original church, the inner ones (and the altar screen) very fine, carved antique pieces. The village is still renowned for its carved feed-troughs and other utilitarian objects, as well as its spring water, bottled way down in the canyon.

and events of His ministry. Over the door, the donor/builder usually appears in a portrait, presenting the church in miniature to Christ or the Virgin, below an inscribed request for mercy at the Last Judgment.

Variations from the pattern – details such as shepherds playing rustic instruments of the time, period costumes and humorous touches – are what make each church interesting. Selected Old Testament personalities or episodes, rarely seen outside the Troödhos, such as the *Sacrific of Abraham*, recur particularly in late fifteenth-century churches, and act as the signature of a certain **Philip Goul**, presumably a Latinised Greek, or one of his apprentices.

Most of the churches are proudly proclaimed on their identifying plaques as being listed on the UNESCO World Cultural Heritage roster, and kept firmly **locked**, with no set opening hours. Thus hunting down the key is an integral part of your visit; instructions on how to find it are given in the account of each church. Sometimes the **caretaker** is a layman who lives nearby, otherwise a peripatetic priest who might not show up until the next day, as he could be responsible for conducting liturgies at several neighbourhood churches. Wardens vary in terms of knowledgeability (none are trained guides, though some have a basic grasp of the images if you understand Greek) and cordiality, the latter not surprisingly often a function of how many importunate foreigners they have to escort. While there is no set admission fee, a **donation** is expected, especially in cases where you've taken the key-keeper miles out of his daily routine. Usually a box is provided in the church; otherwise you should tip the responsible person at the conclusion of your visit. Fifty cents is sufficient for a small church where the guard lives next door; a pound for a large monument off in the woods.

Binding **recommendations** would be subjective; if you're keen, you can see all of the churches in a few days. If your interest is more casual, three or four will be enough – the most important are reckoned to be Asínou, Áyios Ioánnis Lambadhistís, Áyios Nikólaos tis Steyís, Panayía tou Araká and Stavrós tou Ayiasmáti. If you develop a compulsive interest in the subject, a recommended specialist guide is *The Painted Churches of Cyprus*, by Andreas and Judith Stylianou (originally The Research Centre, Nicosia, 1964; revised edition Trigraph, London, 1985).

On the original exterior wall of the church, now within the L-shaped "narthex", Christ is enthroned over the inner doors, flanked by *Adam and Eve*, *Hell and Paradise* (with the saints marching in). Inside, the cycle of events is similar to that of Arkhángelos in Pedhoúlas, but less complete, and stopping with the *Assumption* rather than the *Ascension*; the caretakers claim that the British, while engaged in an anti-EOKA raid, damaged many scenes. An unusual *Nativity* shows the Virgin rocking the Christ Child in his cradle (She's usually still reclining after having given birth) an equally rare martial *Áyios Khristóforos* (Saint Christopher) stands opposite *Áyios Yióryios* (Saint George). On the rear (west) wall, *The Raising of Lazarus* includes the obligatory spectator holding his nose against the reek of the tomb; on the north wall, there's a portrait of donor Ioannis Moutoullas and wife. Overall, the images don't rank among the best in the Troödhos, but are the earliest, unretouched frescos among the churches.

Kalopanayiótis

Just over a kilometre further down the Setrákhos valley from Moutoullás, **KALOPANAYIÓTIS** seems a bit less concrete than Pedhoulás, more geared to tourists than facility-less Moutoullás, and the most compact of the three villages – though it has a pair of rhyming satellite hamlets, NÍKOS and ÍKOS, downstream across the river. Many old handsome houses have retained their tiled roofs; there are fine views up-valley to Pedhoulás (and vice versa of course). The village is thought to be the descendant of ancient Lampadhou, which produced the saints Iraklidhios and Ioannis.

Various unstarred **hotels**, which seem geared to the local spa trade, include the *Kastallia* (☎02/952455) at C£8 single, C£16 double and the slightly fancier *Loutraki* (☎02/952356) at C£7.50/15 single/double; the rock-bottom *Synnos* (☎02/952653), at C£5/9 in a rickety, vine-covered premises, operates only in high season. **Eating** out, you're restricted to your hotel's diner or two kebab stands.

Monastery of Áyios Ioánnis Lambadhistís

Plainly visible from Kalopanayiótis across the river, and accessible by a one-kilometre track, the rambling **monastery of ÁYIOS IOÁNNIS LAMBADHISTÍS** (daily 8am–noon, 1.30–6pm) is probably the successor to a pagan shrine, owing its foundation to some cold sulphur springs just upstream. This is one of the few early Troödhan monasteries to have survived relatively intact from foundation days – many of the painted churches are lonely *katholiká* of long-vanished cloisters, and those monasteries that still exist have been renovated beyond recognition over the centuries. If the courtyard and church doors are not open during the posted hours, enquire at the café adjacent for the (none too friendly or patient) caretaker-priest. The local **festival** takes place on 3–4 October.

Huddled together under a single, huge pitched roof, are three **Siamese-triplet churches**, the whole wider from south to north than long, and built to an odd plan. The double main nave, one part dedicated to Iraklidhios during the eleventh century, the other to Ioannis a hundred years later (though redone in the mid-1700s), is entered from the south side; other doors lead to a later narthex and a Latin chapel added towards the end of the fifteenth century.

The frescos

By virtue of the building's sheer size, there is room for nearly complete coverage of the synoptic gospels, and a number of duplications, stemming from the **frescos** having been added in stages between the thirteenth and fifteenth centuries. The *Pandokrator* in the dome, and panels over the side entrance, are the oldest frescos.

The subjects are the usual locally favoured ones, with slight variations: in the *Resurrection*, Christ only lifts Adam, and not Eve, from Hell; the *Sacrifice of Abraham* is idiosyncratic also. There are several versions of *Christ before Pilate*, and two *Raisings of Lazarus* from obviously different eras, both on the south side of the nave. As so frequently in Troödhos frescos, children shimmy up a palm tree for a better view of the *Vaïofóros* or *Entry into Jerusalem*. Later frescos in the far (north) chapel include the *Hospitality of Abraham* to three rather Florentine angels at his table. The attempt at incorporation of western styles is unique, and intriguing: by the small apse, a naturalised *Arrival of the Magi* shows the backs of all three galloping off, on horses turned to face you, as if part of the background to a Renaissance canvas, not the main subject. In a further dating and typing of influences, the Roman soldiery in several panels are not only in Crusader dress, but fly pennants with the Islamic red crescent.

Kýkko monastery and around

Nineteen paved but twisty kilometres west of Pedhoulás sits the enormous, fabulously wealthy **monastery of KÝKKO** (Kýkkou), one of the most celebrated in the Orthodox world. Here Michael Mouskos, better known as Makarios III, began his secondary education, and later served as a novice monk, prior to using the monastery as a hideout during his EOKA days (when Grivas' headquarters were nearby); thus Kýkko is inextricably linked with the Cypriot nationalist struggle.

Despite these hallowed associations, the place is of negligible artistic or architectural interest; the mosaics and frescos lining the corridors and the *katholikón*, however well intentioned, are workman-like and of recent vintage – some as new as 1987. Repeated fires since Kýkko's twelfth-century foundation by the hermit Isaiah have left nothing older than 1831. Isaiah had been given an **icon** of the Panayía Eleoúsa, the Most Merciful Virgin, by the Byzantine Emperor Alexios Komnenos in gratitude for curing the latter's daughter. The monastery grew up around this relic, claimed to be painted by Luke the Evangelist, and now has pride of place in a rather gaudy shrine in front of the *témblon* or altar screen. Considered too holy for the casual glances of the possibly impious and unworthy, who would run the risk of a most unmerciful instantaneous blinding, the original image has been encased in silver for almost four centuries now. Nearby in the *katholikón* is a brass arm, said to be that of a blasphemous Turk who had it so rendered by the icon's power when sacrilegiously attempting to light his cigarette from a lamp in the sanctuary.

On weekends Kýkko is to be avoided (or gravitated towards, according to your temperament), when thousands of Cypriots descend upon the place. A ban on photos in the church is cheerfully ignored by proud relatives video-ing and snapping the relay baptisms which take place there; lottery ticket-sellers circulate out in the courtyard as howling babies are plunged one after another, accompanied by a barrage of flashbulbs, into the steaming fount. Monks at more austere monasteries ridicule the practice – what's the matter with one's local parish church for christening your child, they say – but this ignores the tremendous prestige of Kýkko, and the ease of access from Nicosia along recently improved roads in a Japanese compact.

Other than the pilgrimage activities, there's a **museum** of ecclesiastical treasures (open reasonable hours, like the monastery; c£0.30) adjoining the inner courtyard. At Room 13, to the right of the main gate of the outer courtyard, you can request a room in the enormous *ksenónas* or guest quarters, though if non-Orthodox you will certainly be quizzed as to why you wish to stay overnight.

Throní

The longish, scenic trip in from Pedhoúlas is much of the attraction; it can be prolonged by another two kilometres to a final car park below **Throní**, the hill atop which is built the **tomb of Makarios**. This is a bunker-like capsule, with the main opening to the west and a National Guardsman keeping a permanent vigil. A modern shrine just south adorns the true summit, which allows comprehensive views of the empty Tillyrian hills to the west, and Mount Olympus to the east; in many ways it's a better vantage point than the latter. Here on the 7–8 September yearly festival the numinous icon is paraded amid prayers for a rainy winter. The stark concrete design of the chapel is further offset by a wish-tree (more accurately, wish-bush) on which old ladies have tied votive hankies, tissues and streamers as petitions for more personal favours from the goddess of the place.

Kámbos

Just before Kýkko, signs beg you to head north 8km to visit **KÁMBOS**, the only substantial habitation in Tillyría, poised in isolation about halfway down the slope towards the Attila Line. There seems little reason to go, other than the appeal of a quite untouristed place; you may even stay at the unstarred hotel *Kambos* (☎02/942320), with modest rates of c£6 for single, c£12 for doubles.

SOLÉA

The region of Soléa, centred on the Karyótis stream valley, was the most important late Byzantine stronghold in the Troödhos, as witnessed by its large concentration of churches. The terrain is much less precipitous than adjacent Marathássa on the west, from which Soléa is accessible by a steep but passable dirt road taking off from just above the *Churchill Pinewood Valley* resort. Kakopetriá is Soléa's chief village and showcase, conveniently close to several frescoed churches, but nearly half a dozen other small hamlets are scattered downstream, in varying states of preservation, and worth (ideally) a bicycle visit.

Kakopetriá

KAKOPETRIÁ, "Wicked Rock-Fall", takes its name from a rash of boulders which originally studded the ridge on which the village was first built. Most were removed, but some had to stay, including **Pétra tou Andhroyínou** (Couple's Rock), a particular outcrop on which newlyweds used to clamber for good luck – until one day the monolith heaved itself up and crushed an unlucky pair to death.

Low enough at 660m elevation to be very warm in the summer, Kakopetriá was formerly a wine and silk-weaving centre, but is now a busy, trendy resort, the closest Troödhos watering-hole to Nicosia. The village straddles the river, which lends some character, along with the officially protected (and not yet too twee) old quarter. This was built on a long ridge splitting the stream in two; a preservation order was slapped on it in 1976, but a few new buildings apparently got in after it went into effect. Derelict traditional dwellings are being bought up at premium prices and being redone tastefully, mostly by Nicosians.

Down in the western stream, across an old bridge, hides an old water-powered grain mill, also refurbished, and bird houses for the ducks and pigeons that frequent the place. An adjacent drink stall has seats at the base of the towering *Maryland at the Mill* restaurant, a creation (in vernacular style) of John Aristidhes, one of the conservation advocates. It's expensive, but not as much as you might imagine, with seating on two levels to accommodate regular tour groups.

Practical details

Many **hotels** are grouped around the telecommunications tower on the east bank of the river, on Gríva Dhiyení, but they're relatively expensive and have little character compared to establishments lining the river, with the chance of a balcony overlooking it. Cheap options there include the pensions *Romios* (☎02/922456) and adjacent *Zoumos* (☎02/922154), plus the recently renovated one-star hotel *Kifissia* (☎02/922421) with singles at c£7.50/14, all on the way to Áyios Nikólaos tis Steyís church (see next section). Down past the bridge on the old road to Galáta – in fact near the edge of the latter – are two places renting **rooms**: *Kendro Dhilinia* (☎02/922455), nice with bath at c£5 per person, and next door at the restaurant *Kouspes*. There's nothing in the old quarter except the *Olga* pension (☎02/922615), open high summer only.

Other than *Maryland at the Mill*, **eating** options are not brilliant. You won't save much money or do your stomach any favours by dining in the noisy, car-plagued high street on the east bank, so you may as well enjoy the atmosphere in the old district for the same price. *Kendro Meteora* (food in summer only) perches above Pétra tou Andhroyínou, *The Village Pub* – with food as well as drink – just below. Kakopetriá has all the **bank/post/phone**-type amenities you'd expect for a medium-sized resort, and frequent **buses** to and from the Costanza bastion terminal in Nicosia.

Áyios Nikólaos tis Steyís

The engaging church of **ÁYIOS NIKÓLAOS TIS STEYÍS** stands about 4km above Kakopetriá, to the west (river) side of the dirt road over to Marathássa; if you pass an *exokhikó kéndro* you've gone too far. Once part of a long-gone monastery, it is now isolated at the edge of the archdiocese's YMCA-type camp and recreation centre, signposted better than the church itself. You cannot drive up to it, but must walk through a gate/turnstile and along a path skirting the playing pitch. Áyios Nikólaos is open during reasonable daylight hours (nominally daily 9am–4pm), when an attendant can point out the salient features in English.

The core of the church, with some of the oldest frescos in the Troödhos, dates from the eleventh century: a dome and narthex were added a hundred years later, and during the fifteenth century an unusually extravagant protective roof (hence the name, *tis Steyís* meaning "of the Roof") was superposed on the earlier domed cross plan. As so often, the frescos are attributable to a sequence of periods, from the eleventh century to (in the south transept) fourteenth and fifteenth, thereby spanning all schools from the traditional to post-Byzantine revival.

The most unusual, later images are found in the transept: the north side has a *Crucifixion* with a personified sun and moon weeping, and an unusual *Myrrofori* (*Spice-Bearers at the Sepulchre*), with the angel sitting atop Christ's empty tomb, proclaiming Christ's resurrection to the two Marys (Magdalene and the mother of James) and Martha.

The *Nativity* in the south transept vault shows the Virgin breast-feeding the Child with a symbolic, anatomically incorrect teat – icons of the subject abound but it's claimed that this fresco is unique in world; around her goats gambol and shepherds plays bagpipe and flute, while a precociously wizened duplicate infant Jesus is given a bath by two serving-maids.

Similarly unusual is the *Archangel Holding the Child* in the same corner. Opposite the Nativity unfolds the also infrequently seen ordeal of the *Forty Holy Martyrs*, including one shedding his tunic to join his fellows, condemned to death by immersion in a freezing lake at Anatolian Sebastaea. The warrior saints *Yióryios and Theódhoros* (George and Theodhore), in Crusader dress, brandish their panoply of arms on one column of the nave.

The churches of Galáta

Though its centre is almost within walking distance of Kakopetria, the notable churches of **GALÁTA** – next village down-valley – are numerous and scattered. You'll need a vehicle, and some patience in tracking down the busy guardian/priest: he lives in a one-storey brick farmhouse at the end of the lane leading east from the school; a small sign on a power pole reads "*Ikía Iereá*/Priest's House". The school road in turn is narrow and unmarked, taking off inconspicuously northeast, parallel to a cement retaining wall shoring up the main Galáta–Nicosia slip road.

Arkhángelos and Panayía Podíthou

This same street also leads north a few hundred metres to the adjacent sixteenth-century churches of Panayía Podíthou and Arkhángelos, the most notable of several in and around Galáta. The former was once part of a monastery, but today both stand alone, awash in springtime beanfields.

ARKHÁNGELOS (1514), the first and smaller church, is also known as Panayía Theotókou but described as such to avoid confusion with a nearby church of same name (see below). The interior adheres to local conventions as to style and choice of episodes, featuring an unusually complete Life, with such scenes as the *Prayer in Gethsemene*, the *Washing of the Feet* and *Peter's Denial*, complete with crowing cock; fish peer out of the river Jordan in the *Baptism*. The chronological sequence begins with the *Prayer of Joachim* (the Virgin's father) near the door, finishing with the *Redemption of Adam*. Most unusually there's the signature of the painter, Simeon Axentiou, in the panel depicting the donor Zacharia family.

Further west, the unusual shape of **PANAYÍA PODÍTHOU**, built in 1502, dictates an equally unconventional arrangement of the cartoons. Abbreviated lives of the Virgin and Christ are relegated to the *ierón* (the area beyond the altar screen). In the apse, Solomon and David stand to either side of the *Communion of the Disciples*; at the top of the pediment formed by the roofline, the Burning Bush is revealed to Moses. The walnut *témblon* itself, complete with gargoyles from which lamps are hung, is magnificent despite its icons having been stolen or taken to Nicosia for restoration.

Above the west entry door, its favoured position, there's a very detailed *Crucifixion*, complete with the two thieves and the soldier about to pierce Christ's side with the lance. Out in the U-shaped "narthex" – created as ever by the later addition of the peaked roof – the donor Dhimitrios and his wife appear on the left of the *Redemption*; above this the *Virgin Enthroned* appears in the company of various Old Testament prophets, rather than with the usual *Fathers of the Church* as at neighbouring Arkhángelos.

In the village: Áyios Sozómenos and others

If you wish, the same genial priest will accompany you to **ÁYIOS SOZÓMENOS**, fifty metres behind and uphill from Galáta's big modern church. Its iconography is very similar to that of Arkhángelos – hardly surprising since the artist (Axentiou) and construction date are identical. The frescos are numerous but relatively crude, and can't compare to those at Podíthou or Arkhángelos.

However there are some wonderful touches: in the lower echelons of saints on the north wall, the dragon coils his tail around the hind legs of Saint George's charger as he's dispatched; a maiden chained at the lower right demonstrates how the tale is a reworking of the Perseus-and-Andromeda myth. On the south wall, *Áyios Mámas* holds his lamb as he rides an anthropomorphised lion (see p.149 for an explanation). Overhead, the original painted wooden struts are still intact (they've rotted away in most other churches); behind the *témblon*, the *Pentecost* takes place on the left, in addition to the typical episodes of Abraham's life to either side of the apse. Out in the U-shaped narthex, there's a damaged *Apocalypse* left of the door, while various ecumenical councils (complete with banished heretics) meet on the other side.

Two more churches, one of essentially specialist interest, flank the road up to Kakopetriá. The sixteenth-century **PANAYÍA THEOTÓKOU** is next to the *BP* petrol station, where the key is kept; the interior preserves an unusually large panel of the *Assumption*, with Christ holding Her infant soul, plus the *Pentecost* and a fine *Angel at the Sepulchre*. Behind the handsome *témblon*, the *Hospitality of Abraham* is offered on the right, with his vivid attempted *Sacrifice* opposite. In the apse conch, the *Virgin Enthroned* reigns over the six *Ierárkhi* (*Fathers of the Church*) below, while over the entrance, the donors huddle with a half-dozen others.

Ayía Paraskeví, contemporary with Áyios Sozómenos and Arkhángelos, is a bit downhill on the opposite side of the pavement, next to a playground, but it's not worth the bother to fetch the key opposite as there's nothing inside but some fresco fragments in the apse and a faded painted *témblon*.

Asínou (Panayía Forviótissa)

Arguably the finest of the Troödhan churches, **ASÍNOU (Panayía Forviótissa)** lies out in the middle of nowhere, but emphatically worth the detour off the B9 Kakopetria–Nicosia road. The key-priest, rather formal but civil, lives in **Nikitári village**, reached via Koutrafás or Vizakiá; you ask after him in the café across from the modern church. Asínou gets some coach-tour attention, so he may already be up there, 4km above village, or at home for an undisturbable afternoon nap.

The popular, less formal name of the church stems from the ancient town of Asinou, founded by Argolid Greeks but long since vanished; the same fate has befallen any monastery which was once here, leaving only an *exokhikó kéndro* across the road, with the beautiful countryside an ideal place for a Sunday outing. *Panayía Forviótissa* means "Our Lady of the Pastures", though only the church-crowned hilltop is treeless, with forested river valley all around. A barrel-vaulted nave, remodelled during the fourteenth century, dates originally from 1105; an unusual narthex with dome and two bays was added a century later, giving the church a "backwards" orientation from the norm. Panayía Forviótissa's frescos span several centuries from the construction date to the early 1500s, and were cleaned in the 1960s.

The interior

Many of the myriad **panels** in the nave were skilfully redone in the fourteenth or fifteenth century. The vaulted **ceiling** of the nave is segmented into recesses by two arches: one at the apse, the other about two-thirds of the way west towards the narthex door. In the westernmost recess, the *Forty Martyrs of Sebastaea* on the north curve seem more natural than those at Áyios Nikólaos tis Steyís; the Holy Spirit descends at *Pentecost* overhead, and Lazarus is raised on the south of the same curve. In the middle recess, the Life of Christ from *Nativity* to *Resurrection* is related; unlike in higher, barn-like churches where it often dominates the triangular pediment over the door, the *Crucifixion* is treated equally as just one panel of many. Generally, the fresco style is highly sophisticated and vivid: *Saint Trifon* on one arch could be a portrait from life of a local shepherd; the three *Myrrofóri* (spice-bearing women at the sepulchre) recoil in visible alarm from the admonishing angel. In the **apse**, an almost imploring twelfth-century *Virgin* raises her hands in benediction, flanked by the two archangels, while to either side Christ offers the wine in the *Communion with the Disciples* (save for Judas, who slinks away). Over the south door, the builder Nikiforos Mayistros presents a model of the church to Christ in a panel dated 1105 by its dedicatory inscription, while a fine *Dormition of the Virgin* hovers over the west door of the nave.

The **narthex frescos** are of the fourteenth century, with wonderful whimsical touches. On the arch of the door to the nave, a pair each of hunting hounds and sheep make an appearance, heralds of the Renaissance. In the shell of the north bay, *Earth* (riding a lion) and *Sea* (upon a water monster) are personified; in the opposite bay, the donors appear again, praying in period dress before a naturalistic *Virgin and Child*, above an equestrian *Saint George* and the lion-mounted *Áyios Mámas*. Below the Earth and the Sea, Saint Peter advances to open the *Gates of Paradise*, while the patriarchs Abraham, Isaac and Jacob wait to one side. In the cupola the *Pandokrátor* presides over the *Twelve Evangelists*, with *The Blessed and the Damned* depicted on arches to either side.

PITSILIÁ

Moving southeast and uphill from the Soléa valleys, the region of **Pitsiliá** is a jumble of bare ridges and precipitous valleys forming the east end of the Troödhos range. Instead of forests, groves of hazelnut and almonds grow, though there are pines on the north slopes. Grapevines flourish, too, but for local use, not the vintners' co-ops; in some villages they're guided on elaborate trellises over streets and houses.

Pitsiliá is noticeably less prosperous and less frequented than Marathássa or Soléa, though surprisingly three large villages – almost small towns – are strung along near the ridgeline: Kyperoúnda, Agrós and Palekhóri. Roads, though in the process of regrading, are still challenging and slow-going to say the least; virtually the entire ridge route between Kyperoúnda and Palekhóri will be a torn-up mess, closed in parts or one lane at best, until 1994.

Approaches from the west and north

The easiest roads into Pitsiliá head east from Troödhos resort or southeast from Kakopetriá, converging at the junction known as the Kárvounos crossroads 1200 metres above sea level. From there you are within easy reach of Kyperoúnda and the ridge walk above it, or the historic church at Kourdhalí, actually a short way off the road up from Kakopetriá.

From Asínou, you're best off returning to Nikitári (you will have to chauffeur the priest back anyway), then heading east to VIZAKIÁ to adopt the road signed up to KANNÁVIA – which eventually also ends up at Kárvounos, via Kourdhalí. Alternatively, about 3km above Vizakiá, a passable dirt road veers east towards AYÍA MARÍNA (with an extremely rough option to KSILIÁTOS part way). You are now well placed to visit the two finest churches in Pitsiliá; the paved main road, signposted to Lagoudherá, climbs through a forested canyon, passing a dam that makes a tempting picnic spot.

Panayía tou Araká

The large, single-aisled church of **PANAYÍA TOU ARAKÁ** (Our Lady of the Pea) enjoys a wonderful setting amid trees – and the wild peas of the name – on a terrace 500 metres northwest of **Lagoudherá village**, about halfway to SARANDÍ village (where a taverna operates seasonally). Unusually, the caretaker priest lives in the large adjacent building, possibly a surviving portion of the monastery which was once attached. The local **festival** on 7–8 September celebrates the Birth of the Virgin.

The **interior frescos** of 1192 are not as numerous as they might be, since the original west wall was removed when the existing narthex was built. They are exceptionally clear, however, having been cleaned between 1968 and 1973, and include, unique in the Troödhos, a rare undamaged *Pandokrátor* in the dome (which protrudes partially through the pitched roof). Below Christ, Old Testament prophets, rather than the usual apostles, alternate with the twelve dome windows, and edging further down, the Archangel Gabriel approaches the Virgin opposite for the *Annunciation*.

Above the *Virgin Enthroned* in the apse, strangely averting her eyes to the right, Christ ascends to heaven in a bull's-eye mandorla (an almond-shaped aura often used by painters to enliven the risen Lord), attended by four acrobatic angels. The *témblon* is intact, its Holy Gates (for the mysterious entries and exits of the priest during the liturgy) still in place. Instead of a true transept, there are two pairs of painted recesses on each of the side walls. Flanking the south door, *Zozimadhon Spoon-feeds Osia Maria (Mary the Beatified) of Egypt*; Maria was an Alexandrine courtesan who, repenting of her ways, retired to the desert to perform austere penances for forty years and was found, a withered crone on the point of death, by Zozimadhon, abbot of Saint Paul's monastery near the Red Sea. Above them there's a fine *Nativity*, with, as ever, a preternaturally aged Infant being bathed, while on the right the angel gives the good news to the shepherds, one of whom plays a pipe. In the north recess nearest the apse, Simeon (see Luke 2:25 for the full story) holds Christ for his *Presentation in the Temple*.

Stavrós tou Ayiasmáti

In the next valley east of Lagoudherá, **STAVRÓS TOU AYIASMÁTI** is an attractive basilica-church, again once part of a long-disappeared monastery. You need to stop first in **Platanistása village**, where the key-keeper Mikhalis Passoulis lives – he is most easily found by enquiring at Makis' café, or rung in advance (if your Greek is up to it) on ☎02/642618. The church itself is located 7km to the north: 3km down-valley on tarmac, the balance on a good dirt road. The setting is even better than Panayía tou Araká, in an almond grove at the margin of the forest, with a patch of the Mesaoría visible to the northeast. Nearby benches and a *kleftikó* oven doubtless see use on the 13–14 September **festival**.

The church

The church is filled with recently cleaned, late fifteenth-century **frescos** by Philip Goul; an inscription over the south door records both his artistry and the patronage of the priest Petros Peratis. As per the name (*Stavrós* = Holy Cross), the highlight is a **painted cross** in a niche on the north wall, surrounded by small panels of episodes relating (however tenuously) to its power, sancification and rediscovery, such as the Hebrews petitioning Pharaoh (top), or the vision of Áyios Konstandínos (left).

Behind the *témblon*, and above an interesting Holy Table (for celebrating the Orthodox liturgy), the *Virgin and Child* both raise hands in blessing in the apse, flanked by Old Testament prophets David, Daniel, Solomon and Isaiah; nearby *Christ Offers the Eucharist to the Twelve Apostles* with his right hand, and the Communion wine with his left. The *Four Evangelists* are arranged in pairs to either side of the altar screen; the *Archangel Michael*, in the arched recess to the right of *témblon*, holds not the usual opaque orb but a transparent "crystal ball" containing the Christ Child.

Elsewhere along the vaults and walls of the nave there's a complete gospel cycle, including such details as *Pilate Washing his Hands*, trumpeters in the panel of the *Mocking*, and *Doubting Thomas* probing Christ's lance wound. In the otherwise serene *Assumption of the Virgin*, a miniature angel strikes off the hands of an infidel with a sword. On the pediment of the west wall, the *Ancient of Days* presides over the *Descent of the Holy Spirit*, above the *Crucifixion*. Christ's blood drips down into Adam's skull below, the key-warden will tell you, to revivify it for the *Redemption*, shown outside in a niche of the uncleaned narthex.

This and other exterior frescos are thought not to be by Goul, and were repainted last century to detrimental effect. Right of the Redemption the *Last Judgment* unfolds, while on the left stand the three *Patriarchs Abraham, Isaac and Jacob*. The U-shaped narthex, extending around the north and south sides of the church, was used by local shepherds as a sheep pen before the monument's importance was recognised.

The Madhári ridge walk

From either Lagoudherá or Platanistása paved roads complete the climb to the Tro̎odhos summit ridge, where the vine-draped villages of ÁLONA and POLÝSTIPOS huddle just under 1100 metres. The watershed is crossed a little higher, with a side track signposted to the CYTA transmission station on the sides of 1612-metre Mount Adhélfi.

If you're interested in walking the half-finished **nature trail on Madhári ridge**, this is one possible starting point. The other is some kilometres away, via KHANDHRIÁ and **KYPEROÚNDA** (one unstarred hotel, *Livadhia* (☎05/521311) with singles at c£5, doubles at c£8, but no compelling reason to stay). At the western edge of Kyperoúnda, just beyond the Mitsubishi representative and the *Amazel Restaurant* on the bypass road, an unmarked dirt track heads north for 1.8km to the saddle at about 1400m elevation. Just to one side stands the familiar wooden paraphernalia marking the start of such trails, with a sign proclaiming "Glory to You, Oh God" in New Testament Greek – plus the precise distance to be covered (3750m).

After some initial tangling with a more recently cleared firebreak track, the path settles into a rhythm of wobbling either side of the watershed (also the boundary between Limassol and Nicosia districts) as it meanders through scrub and thin forest. Some 45 minutes along, you reach the 1500-metre saddle between Madhári ridge and Adhélfi peak, with another half-hour's hiking bringing you to the fire lookout hut atop Point 1612 – a bit more if you detour to the modestly described "Excellent Viewpoint" part way. The service road from the pass above Álona and Polýstipos to the CYTA station continues to the very base of Adhélfi, where a group could perhaps be picked up by a non-walker's car without having to retrace their steps.

Except for some clumps of man-high golden oak (*Quercus alnifolia*), there's little but low, thin scrub en route, so the exposed ridge is best traversed early or late in the day during summer. Views of virtually half the island, from the Kyrenia hills to the Akrotíri salt lake, are the thing: you gaze over nearer valleys and villages both north and south of the ridge, with the sea on three sides of Cyprus visible in favourable conditions.

Kourdhalí: Panayía

If you continue along the dirt track from the western trailhead of the Madhári nature path, you end up just outside SPÍLIA village (usually approached from the Kakopetriá–Tro̎odhos road), near the junction for **KOURDHALÍ**, 2km beyond. Here the sixteenth-century church of **Panayía**, next to a hump-backed bridge, preserves post-Byzantine frescos of the same period.

Agrós

The best – indeed, except for the lone inn at Kyperoúnda, the only – overnight option in Pitsiliá is **AGRÓS**, a surprisingly large village more or less at the top (1000 metres) of Limassol district's commercial wine-grape district. Supposedly known also for its sausage and ham, it won't win many beauty contests but is ideally placed for a couple of days' forays to surrounding attractions. One of the best **hotel** deals in the Troödhos, despite an indifferent position on the high street, has to be the one-star *Vlachos* (☎05/521330), with rooms at c£11 per person half-board; supper is a groaning *table d'hôte*, and anyway there's just one other restaurant in Agrós (next door). Your only other options are the luxury *Rodon* (☎05/521201), well out of town (if you need to ask how much, you can't afford it), or the guest house *Meteora* (☎05/521331), 200m up the street and very basic at c£5 per double. If you get a room there overlooking the canyon you've the best view in town, but the single shared bath is roach infested. Agrós also has two **banks** fairly well used to tourists, and a **post office**.

Around Agrós: churches and villages

Agrós lies roughly equidistant from a handful of post-Byzantine frescoed churches, which can all be visited on a single day with an early start. Being less frequented than the monuments of Marathássa and Soléa, there's more of a sense of personal discovery, and the villages in which they stand deserve a brief stroll as well.

Peléndhria: Stavrós
PELÉNDRHIA is currently the easiest village to reach from Agrós, the road in through ÁYIOS IOÁNNIS, KÁTO MÝLOS and POTAMÍTISSA completely paved and better than map appearances suggest. The main attraction here is the four-teenth-century painted **church of STAVRÓS**, isolated at the south edge of Peléndhria, overlooking a reservoir; the friendly key-keeping priest lives 200 metres up the road towards Káto Amíandos. A square ground plan divided into three aisles, unique in Cyprus, is capped by a very narrow, high dome supported by four columns; for once there is no narthex.

On your right as you enter, there's a *Tree of Jesse* (showing the genealogy of Jesus). Straight ahead on a column, the two donors of the church are shown below a *Doubting Thomas*; just to the left is a Lusignan coat-of-arms. At the rear of the central aisle, above the wooden lattice of the deacon's pulpit, are scenes from the life of the Virgin, the best preserved (or at least the cleanest) frescos in the entire building. Opposite this, a *Nativity* tells much about Lusignan domestic life, and in the *Last Supper* a strange, homunculus-like Virgin replaces several missing disciples. A multi-coloured *témblon* is in good condition, and to its left the enshrined cross for which the church is named stands encased in silver near a representation of the *Epitáfios* or the Dead Christ, next to a fresco of the three *Ierárkhi* (Church Fathers) in the left-most apse.

Peléndhria's other church, that of **Panayía**, is visible across a ravine from Stavrós, close to the centre of the village in a clearing of its own. It's a more typical peak-roofed "barn", with sixteenth-century frescos, but the key-keeper is a different individual and you'll very likely have to make repeated visits to track him down.

SAINT MAMAS AND HIS LION

Prominent on the north wall is a panel of the church's dedicatory saint, **Mamas**, cradling a lamb as he rides a rather bemused, anthropomorphised lion. The legend behind this peculiar iconography, found in many Cypriot churches, runs as follows: Mamas was a devout Byzantine hermit who refused to pay income tax since, as he logically pointed out, he had no income other than alms. The local governor ordered him arrested, but as he was being escorted into custody a lion – unknown on Cyprus – leapt from a roadside bush onto a lamb grazing peacefully nearby. The saint commanded the lion to stop his attack, picked up the lamb, and completed his journey into the capital riding on the chastened lion. Sufficiently impressed, the governor exempted Mamas from taxes thereafter, and ever since the saint has enjoyed fervent worship as the patron of tax-evaders (a highly developed cult in the Hellenic world).

Louvarás: Áyios Mámas

The main Limassól-bound E110 road from Káto Mýlos descends to the Péfkos junction above **KALOKHORIÓ**, where there's the only food and petrol for quite some distance around. Meals are had up at the café on the south side of the crossroads, and the fuel is sold from jerry cans at the postal agency across from the irrigation pool in the village centre.

A four-kilometre side road takes off southwest from the crossroads, ending at **LOUVARÁS**, whose dishearteningly modern outskirts give no hint of the traditional village core to the east, nor of the tiny but exquisitely painted **chapel of ÁYIOS MÁMAS**, hidden on the edge of the old quarter, at the very end of the paved road in. Don't confuse it with the bigger, newer, church of Pródhromos nearby, across from which lives Grigoris the key-keeper, in the house with a front garden. He speaks some English, learned (he claims) during five years as an aide to General Montgomery.

The little chapel, dating from 1454, features Philip Goul at perhaps his most idiosyncratic. On the south wall, *Christ Heals the Paralytic and the Blind Man*, teaches, and meets the Samaritan at the well; the three sleeping guards at the *Resurrection* wear Lusignan armour. Beside the west door, the *Gadarene Swine* leap over the brink – you can see the demons entering them; above the door appear the donors of the church. In the *Last Supper* on the same surface, Christ does not attempt to prevent Judas from reaching for the Fish, as in other local murals. At the very top of the apsidal pediment on the east side, the *Ancient of Days* hovers over the *Annunciation* – these images may be of a different hand than Goul's, since the *Annunciation* is repeated on the south wall.

Palekhóri: Metamórfosi tou Sotírou

From Agrós, Louvarás or Peléndhria the best road to Palekhóri detours through ÁYIOS THEÓDHOROS. The direct ridge route from Agrós is currently shut, and don't be tempted to curl around from Kalokhorío via Arakapás and Sykópetra – the mountain road beyond the latter is horrendous.

However you arrive, **PALEKHÓRI** proves to be a sprawling, friendly worka-day place hidden in a gulch at the headwaters of the Peristeróna River – there are a few *kafenía* down by the stream, but no other concessions to tourism. The small fifteenth-to-sixteenth-century chapel of **Metamórfosi tou Sotírou**, signposted from the main by-pass road, perches at the east edge of the old quarter, atop the grade up from the river. The very engaging key-keeping priest lives in the apartment building two doors north, beside which you should park, but in the evening (a likely arrival time if you've been touring all day) he may be conducting the liturgy down at Panayía Khrysopantánassa, which though contemporaneous has few surviving frescos.

Sotírou is another legacy of Philip Goul, and rivals Áyios Mámas at Louvarás for whimsy. Lions and rivers seem to be the main themes here: *Saint Mamas* appears again, riding a particularly vivid feline; another lion approaches, as per tradition, to bury Osía María (Mary the Beatified of Egypt) with his paws on the south wall, and opposite her *Daniel Braves the Lions* in their den. To his left is portrayed a miracle, whereby the angelic diversion of a river saves a monastery; in *Christ's Baptism*, a crowned-and-sceptred water sprite rides a fish in the Jordan. As befitting a chapel dedicated to the Transfiguration (*Metamórfosi* in Greek), the panel of the same on the south wall is particularly vivid, and there are no scenes whatsoever from the Virgin's life. Goul has left his "signature" as usual with a *Hospitable Abraham* in the apse, with the warrior saints Yióryios and Dhimítrios to the north of the altar screen.

The other two churches visible in the western part of Palekhóri contain nothing especially compelling inside; the priest may, however, volunteer to escort you to another pair of local monuments east of the village in an orchard-cloaked valley, including the frescoed sixteenth-century church of **Áyii Anáryiri**, signposted off the road to APLÍKI.

The road towards Makherás: mountain villages

At APLÍKI junction, you can turn up towards Farmakás onto a narrow but paved road around a huge reservoir. **FARMAKÁS** and its neighbour **KAMBÍ** are both spectacularly set like Spanish or Tuscan villages overlooking the top of the valley draining to the dam, but as with so many communities in rural Cyprus where inhabitants have made good, the visual appeal diminishes on close examination. The two local showcase villages lie a few kilometres northeast along an improved road, better than maps imply, beyond GOÚRRI.

At **FIKÁRDHOU** the vernacular architecture of stone, mud-straw bricks and tiled roofs is preserved – or rather pickled – in the forty or so houses of this museum-village; the permanent population has dwindled to seven. Two of the dwellings constitute an exhibit (daily 9.30am–1pm, Tues, Sat–Sun 3–6pm winter, 3–7pm summer; c£0.50), with plans, photos and text in the ticket office giving a full explanation of the project's aims. The **house of Akhilléas Dhimítri**, as ethnographic collections go, is not too cluttered other than with a loom and period furnishings, since it's the occasional residence of the project's supervising archaeologist. The **Katsinióros house** has an olive press, *zivánia* stills and storage urns in its basement, and traditional women's implements (spinning wheel, loom, etc) on the peaked-roof upper storey.

All in all it's a conscientious restoration job, but ultimately with an obscure purpose – the effect seems a bit lifeless without even the animation of a weekend population (though some of the buildings are reportedly for sale). The only other tourist amenity thus far is the surprisingly authentic *Yiannakos Kafenio*, serving drinks and light meals (mostly to workmen on the project except in high season).

LAZANIÁ, 5km south on the way to Makherás monastery, is more of a going concern, still unlisted, and therefore less twee and perhaps more representative of such hill villages.

Makherás monastery

The **monastery of Makherás** just east of Lazaniá is distinguished by its setting on the north slope of Mount Kiónia, near the headwaters of the Pedhiéos River, and its associations with Grigorios Afxentiou, second in command of EOKA after George "Dhiyenis" Grivas, and by all accounts a more humane, sympathetic figure.

It was established by two hermits in 1148, who arrived from Palestine and, guided by the usual preternatural glow, found yet another icon of the Virgin attributed to the hand of Luke the Evangelist. Makherás ("The Cutler") is taken variously to mean the sharp-edged, thousand-metre ridge overhead, the biting wind swooping down from it in winter, or the point in the foundation legend when a knife materialised and a "voice not of earth" instructed the hermits to use it to free the icon from the underbrush. Soon the community had the support of the Byzantine Emperor Manuel Comnenus, and even enjoyed the subsequent patronage of Lusignan rulers – one of whom, Queen Alix d'Ibelin, was rendered mute for three years after sacrilegiously insisting on entering the *ierón* or priestly chambers behind the altar screen. Makherás claims five martyrs (six, counting Afxentiou), commemorated on plaques in the courtyard.

It has also suffered two comprehensive fires (in 1530 and 1892), the latter one explaining the rather bleak, echoing stone compound of minimal architectural interest, though the icon miraculously escaped and is the glory of the *katholikón*. There is a one-room, Greek-labelling-only museum featuring photos of EOKA hero Grigoris Afxentiou disguised as a monk. The monastery is open reasonable hours without midday closure, and there may be a chance of (men only) being put up for the night, except around the 20–21 November and 14–15 August **festivals**. A small restaurant by the car park fortifies you against the road above or below.

Krysfíyeto tou Afxentíou

When he was not in mufti, the brothers of Makherás continued to feed Afxentiou in his hideout, the **KRYSFÍYETO TOU AFXENTÍOU**, 1km below the monastery; a Greek flag, sign and memorial plaque point you down to the (much repaired) bunker in which he met his end in March 1957. Tipped off by a shepherd, British forces surrounded the dugout and called on the occupants to surrender – EOKA members were usually happy to comply in hopeless situations. All of them did except Afxentiou, who despite being wounded held off a platoon of sixty for ten hours before being dispatched with a petrol bomb and high explosives.

Approaching down stone steps, glints of what you first take for shiny rubbish are in fact the ribbons and labels on dozens of laurel wreaths left around the entry of the *krysfíyeto* (hideout); inside it's completely bare, without so much as a candle or photo. The wreaths are perhaps left over from the early 1992 dedication of the huge **statue**, erected just below the monastery at the expense of the diocese, showing a more-than-life-size Afxentiou standing arms akimbo, guarded by an eagle.

Onward routes from Makherás

From Makherás your most obvious course is down **to Nicosia**, 43km distant via the inviting, piney picnic grounds of Mándhra tou Kambioú and the adjacent sites of ancient Tamassos and Áyios Iraklídhios monastery (see Chapter Five). **Towards Larnaca**, a dirt road heads due south through forest and past another picnic grounds beside 1423-metre Kiónia peak, last outrider of the Troödhos range. ÁYII VAVATSINIÁS marks the start of the improved pavement down to PÁNO LÉFKARA, 38km away.

travel details

Buses

From Plátres to **Limassol**, by both *Platres* market bus and *Karydas* service minibus (daily at about 7am, 1hr 15min); to Nicosia via Pedhoulás and Kalopanayiótis with *Zingas* (1 daily at 6am; 3hr).

From Troödhos to **Nicosia** on *Solea Bus* (1 daily except Sun at dawn; 2hr).

From Kalopanayiótis to **Limassol** via Pedhoulás and Pródhromos on *Yero Dhimos* (1 daily at dawn; 3hr 30min for full distance); to Nicosia on *Zingas* (1 daily early morning; 2hr).

From Kakopetriá to **Nicosia** with *Solea Bus* (7 daily except 2 on Sun; 1 hr 20 min).

From Agrós to **Limassol** on *Agros Bus* (1 daily except Sun at about 7am; 1 hr 30 min).

CHAPTER FIVE

SOUTH NICOSIA AND AROUND

T he southern sector of divided **Nicosia** (*Lefkosía* in Greek) is the capital and largest town of the internationally recognised Cypriot Republic. Somewhat gritty and prosaically set, it's not on the usual package-tourist circuit – except perhaps for the occasional coached-in tour of the Cyprus museum, simply one of the best archaeological collections in the Middle East, and essential viewing. A relative lack of the rampant commercialism found on the coast is also refreshing, as is the surviving Gothic and Ottoman domestic and religious architecture of the medieval town. And if you're not averse to mixing politics with your holiday, and interested in getting to grips with what contemporary Cyprus is about, an evening or two in pubs and eateries near the Green Line is well spent.

By comparison, there is little of note in the surrounding countryside under Greek-Cypriot control, part of the vast **Mesaoría** ("Between the Mountains"). This is not so much a plain between the Troödhos range and Kyrenia hills as undulating country, with green or yellow grain according to season and dotted with large villages, lately become dormitory communities preferred to Nicosia itself. Here, more than anywhere else on Cyprus except within Nicosia, you are aware of the island's division: roads close to the boundary are diverted or barred suddenly, and watchtowers of one side or the other dot the horizon. Amidst this bleakness, only a few isolated spots really appeal, and then only with time on your hands: the adjacent ruins of **Tamassos** and nunnery of **Áyios Iraklídhios**, a fine church-and-mosque duo at **Peristeróna**, and another minor church at **Perakhorío**, paired with the scanty nearby remains of **Idalion**.

SOUTH NICOSIA

Great is the contrast between the town and its surroundings, and greater still between the objects within the city. There are Venetian fortifications by the side of Gothic edifices surmounted by the Crescent, on antique Classic soil. Turks, Greeks, and Armenians, dwell intermingled, bitter enemies at heart, and united solely by their love for the land of their birth.

Louis Salvator, Archduke of Austria, 1873

South Nicosia, depending on whom you ask and how many incorporated suburbs you count, today has between 170,000 and 250,000 inhabitants. Despite the small population, it's a sprawling, amorphous, modern city that makes a poor first impression. The heat and dust, beginning in April and lasting until October, are

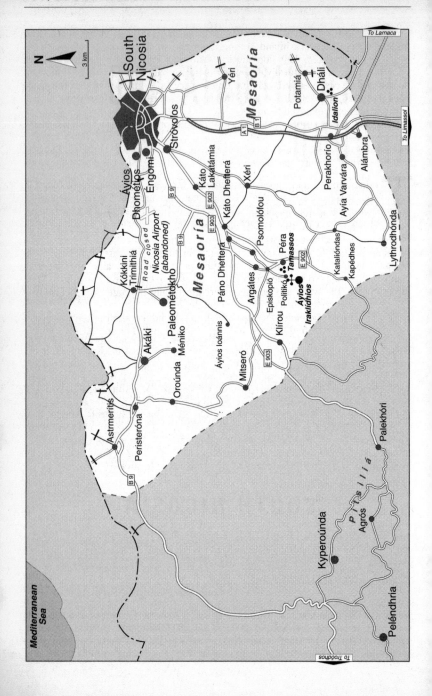

prostrating, grit coming in equal measure from the prevailing winds and nearby building sites. Nicosia's inland setting, near the west end of the Mesaoría, is prone to earthquakes, flash-flooding from the river Pedhiéos, and otherwise not particularly favoured naturally except in its near-equidistance from the important coastal towns. Since early Byzantine times every ruler has designated the place capital virtually by default, because the island's shore defences were (and are) poor, its harbours exposed to attack.

Medieval Nicosia's profile is owed in varying proportions to the Lusignans, Ottomans and Venetians; the latter endowed the old town with a five-kilometre circuit of walls which largely survives. The map outline of the medieval quarter, still the core of the city, has been compared to a star, a snowflake or a sectioned orange, but in the present, troubled circumstances a better analogy might be a floating mine, the knobbly silhouettes of its eleven bastions the detonators.

Old Nicosia began to outgrow its confines during the 1930s, with the post-war British cantonment-style development just outside the walls giving way in its turn, post-independence, to the Los-Angeles-style high-rise suburbs beyond. The British, as well as the Cypriots, are to blame for the neglect and even desecration of much in the old city; many monuments, including a Lusignan palace, were senselessly pulled down around the turn of the century, and the Venetian ramparts first pierced by viaducts and later allowed to crumble at the edges. Most streets inside the walls are no longer architecturally homogenous, defaced by thoughtless concrete construction of recent decades.

So the romantic orientalist's town which the Archduke admired on the eve of British rule has vanished forever. Indeed, Nicosia is not an immediately likeable city: especially around the Páfos gate, the old town can be depressing and claustrophobic, qualities made worse by the presence of the Green Line (see below), tensely palpable even when out of sight. Profuse wall graffiti in Hellenic blue concerns itself exclusively with what is delicately termed the National Question, the search for a solution to the island's de facto partition: "Attilas Out", "Federation = Sellout", "The Struggle Continues", or – simply and succinctly – "No". Absent is the Levantine ease of the coastal towns: clusters of men stand or sit about Platía Eleftherías expectantly, and unusually in Cyprus there is some hustle from shop and hotel proprietors. An entire neighbourhood is given over to obvious girlie bars and more discrete, dispersed prostitution; the only other significant industries inside the Venetian fortifications appear to be cabinet-making and offset printing.

Lawrence Durrell bemoaned Nicosia's lack of sophistication and infrastructure in the mid-1950s; it's no longer quite so dire, and a small capital that might be expected to be provincial supports a cosmopolitan leavening of Lebanese, Iranians and East Europeans, studying or surviving as refugees. Among the Europeans can also currently be numbered ex-Yugoslav draft-dodgers, or Serbian businessmen laundering money to evade sanctions – and even less savourily, Romanian women in particular swelling the ranks of the prostitutes, raising the cash to buy their homes under their government's recently implemented privatisation plans. Taken together, these are hardly foreseen legacies of non-aligned, 1960s Cyprus' diligent cultivation of ties all round. You will also come across journalists monitoring the Middle East from a relatively safe haven, and delegates to the numerous conferences which are a feature of Nicosia's winter calendar.

The **Green Line**, as the cease-fire line is known within the city limits, has existed in some form since the communal troubles of winter 1963–64: first as impromptu barricades of bedframes, upturned cars and other domestic debris, later more sturdily fashioned of oil drums, barbed wire, sandbags and sheet metal. Nicosia is, as the authorities repeatedly remind you on wall signs and in tourist literature, the last hermetically divided city, now that arrangements have been reached one way or another in Berlin, Jerusalem and Beirut.

As such, the barrier exercises a morbid fascination on visitors as well as locals. You find yourself drifting towards it again and again, trying to follow its length, peering through chinks when out of sight of the Greek, Turkish or UN checkpoints. Beyond the boundary stretches the "dead zone", here just a twenty-to-fifty-metre-wide stretch of derelict, rat- and snake-infested houses. Its very existence constitutes a provocation, to which a steady trickle of Greek Cypriots, not all of them certifiably unbalanced, have responded since 1974. Periodically refugee groups stage protest marches towards their home villages in the North, putting their own National Guard in the embarrassing role of trying to prevent them crossing the Attila Line (once they got several kilometres inside northern Cyprus); lone males crash the barriers on foot or in vehicles, only to be imprisoned by the Turks, with attempts every several months on average. A slogan overhead at one Greek checkpoint ("Our frontiers are not these, but the shores of Kyrenia") hardly argues for self-restraint.

Finally, then, the rift is the essence of Nicosia and, by extension, of the island: the Greek area of the city is mostly Greek from a monumental standpoint, the Turkish zone largely Turkish and Gothic, but in the midst of each are marooned traces of the other element: mosques and houses emblazoned with a star and crescent in the south, belfried churches and dwellings with Greek Ottoman inscriptions in the north, reminders of the pre-1974 heterogeneity of Cyprus.

Some history

Most authorities believe that present-day Nicosia lies on or next to the site of a Neolithic settlement, subsequently the Archaic town of Ledra. But the city only became prominent in Byzantine times, eclipsing Constantia (Salamis) after the disastrous seventh century, and embarking on a golden age with the arrival of the **Lusginan kings**. Particularly during the fourteenth century, they endowed the place with seven miles of fortifications, palaces, churches and monasteries appropriate to a court of chivalry. Their surviving monuments constitute much of Nicosia's appeal; nowhere else on Cyprus, except at Famagusta, can you take in the spectacle of Latin-Gothic architecture transplanted to the Levant. The underpinnings of such a hothouse fantasy were by their very nature transient: the Genoese raided Nicosia in 1373, and the Mamelukes sacked the city again in 1426. Following **Venetian assumption** of direct rule in 1489, Nicosia became even more of a stronghold. With an eye to the growing Ottoman threat, the Lusignan circuit of walls shrank between 1567 and 1570 to a more compact, anti-ballistic rampart system designed by the best engineers of the age. Monuments falling outside the new walls were demolished in the interest of a free field of fire. But it was all unavailing, as the Turks took the city on 9 September 1570 after a seven-week siege, swarming over the Podocataro and Costanza bastions. In a paroxysm of rape, plunder and slaughter graphically described by survivors, the victors dispatched nearly half the 50,000 inhabitants and defenders.

Under **Ottoman rule** the city stagnated, if picturesquely, not to regain such a population level until the 1940s. The three centuries passed quietly, except for riots in 1764, in which a particularly unpleasant governor was killed, and mass executions of prominent Greek Cypriots (including the island's four bishops) in 1821, to preclude an echo of the peninsular uprising. The British raised the Union Jack over the town in 1878, but saw their wooden Government House burnt down in the pro-*énosis* riots of 1931.

Colonial authorities moved the administrative apparatus outside the walls in 1946, paralleling the growth of the city. But during the 1950s and 1960s the capital was wracked, first by the EOKA struggle and later by violence between the Christian and Muslim communities. After the events of December 1963 (see "History" in *Contexts*), factional polarisation proceeded apace: Greeks and Armenians were expelled or fled from mixed neighbourhoods in the north of the city, and any remaining Turks deserted the south, so that Nicosia was already all but partitioned when the Turkish Army reached the northwestern suburbs, and then penetrated the Turkish quarter of the old town, on 22 July 1974.

Since then the runaway growth of the new southern boroughs has been spurred by the necessity of quickly providing housing for tens of thousands of Greek refugees from North Cyprus. By contrast old Nicosia has suffered even where not explicitly damaged by warfare, as shopkeepers and residents close to the Line deserted their premises, leaving often exquisite buildings to decay. Only recently has the trend of neglect been reversed, under the aegis of the **Nicosia Master Plan**, funded by the United Nations Development Programme and the EC. Tentative co-operation between urban planners in the Greek and Turkish sectors, based on the assumption of a re-united city in the future, has resulted in co-ordinated restoration and pedestrianisation of the most attractive and vital neighbourhoods on both sides of the Green Line, and even (in 1979) the mundane but necessary completion of a joint sewage plant, left stranded in the Turkish zone after 1974. The population of "Nicosia within the walls" seems to have stabilised, and it may have some future other than as a depressed, traumatised backwater.

Arrival, orientation and information

Whether approached from the south along the expressway from Larnaca or Limassol, or in a more leisurely fashion from the Troödhos foothills, **land arrival** in Nicosia is not an enticing prospect (the international **airport** has languished in the dead zone, used as UNFICYP headquarters, since 1974, its fate uncertain in the event of a peace settlement). You wind through seemingly interminable suburbs indistinguishable from those of any other Mediterranean or Middle Eastern city, until suddenly thrust into the ring system of streets paralleling the Venetian bulwarks. Most of the **coach terminals** are a short distance from the ramparts, or even on them; see "Listings" and our map for precise locations.

One of the various uses to which the municipality has put the Venetian walls and moat is that of several **car parks**; coming in your own or a hire vehicle, the best areas are the moat between the D'Avila and Costanza bastions, with the top of the Tripoli bastion a runner-up. Windscreen display tickets cost c£0.35 for either one morning or one evening period, and in theory you'll need coins to work the dispensing machines, but in practice the lots are still staffed by (usually absent) attendants.

Orientation

Most of what a visitor will want to see lies within the labyrinth of the **old quarter**, "Nicosia within the Walls" as some term it. Citing main streets there is made futile by the fact that the longest one, the ring boulevard looping between the bastions, changes names no less than four times. The busiest entrance to the old town is at **Platía Eleftherías**, giving onto pedestrianised and commercialised **Lídhras**, while in the opposite direction **Evagórou** leads out to "Nicosia outside the walls", as the **new town** is often called. This is somewhat more orderly but by no means grid-regular; **Leofóros Arkhiepiskópou Makaríou**, perpendicular to Evagórou, is the longest and glitziest boulevard, headed out towards the Limassol – Larnaca highway, and the ring road just outside the moat changes identity just as often as its counterpart inside the walls. A reliable map – either this book's (over the page) or one begged from the CTO – is therefore essential for navigating.

Getting around the city – and information

Nicosia has an **urban bus network** of about twenty lines, straggling off through the new town into further-flung suburbs at half-hourly intervals between 5.30am and 7 or 8 pm, twice as often at peak periods. They're cheap enough at about c£0.30, but you probably won't be using them much unless you want to visit a distant embassy or cultural centre. The **central terminal** is on Platía Solomoú, beside the Tripoli bastion. Full information is available there, or route and city maps are sporadically to be had from the **CTO** at Aristokýprou 35 (Mon–Fri 9am–2.30pm, Sat 9am–1.30pm, Mon & Thurs 4.30–6.30pm). This is the general enquiries office; for more unusual requests try the world headquarters of the CTO at Theofánous Theodhótou 18, some 600 metres outside the walls in the new town.

Finding a place to stay

Unless some international conference is being held – most of these between September and April – finding a free bed of some sort in Nicosia shouldn't be too difficult; hotels welcome walk-in trade, as there's not much of a package industry inland.

Appetising, good-value accommodation, however, presents a bit of a challenge, since many establishments which seem promisingly located at the edge of the medieval town fall inside the **red-light district**, a roughly triangular area bounded by Riyénis, Lídhras and Arsinöis streets. According to locals, the sleazy pubs and their regulars predate the heavy presence of UN forces, but the latter certainly helped it along. Even here, though, some hotels are acceptable for a mainstream clientele, and indicated in the listings below.

Just east of Lídhras, the **Laïkí Yitoniá** is a tourist-orientated area rehabilitated from its former status as an annexe of the disreputable zone: particularly on or near Sólonos street, there are several passable guest houses or small hotels, if universally mosquito- and noise-plagued, the commotion starting at about 6.30am

The south Nicosia phone code is ☎02

and not letting up until midnight. Budget or mid-range hotels in the new "cantonment" are almost non-existent, though again a couple of exceptions are given.

Unless otherwise noted, all rooms are with en suite facilities, and breakfast is included in the rates. However, summer water shortages can mean that bathing is a non-starter much of the day in the less expensive hotels.

Hostels and guest houses

Youth hostel Ioánni Hadjidháki 5, near Themistoklí Dherví, 700m from Platía Eleftherías, and recently moved from the suburb of Áyios Dhométios – beware of old address in IYHA guides (☎444808) C£2.50 per person, plus C£0.50 sheet fee.

Peter's Sólonos 5 (☎463153). Common areas are a bit dingy, and most rooms without bath, but the most savoury cheapo option. C£5.25 single, C£8 double.

Tony's Sólonos 13, corner Ippokrátous (☎466752). Rooms in shockingly authentic London B&B style – but safe, friendly, and an unbeatable roof terrace for English breakfasts. C£6.50–£9 single, C£11–15 double, without/with bath. Tony also has longer-term flats for rent in the new city.

Inexpensive and mid-range hotels

Regina Palace Riyénis 42/44, but entrance on Fokiónos (☎463051). Despite a dubious location, actually okay, at C£6–7.50 single, C£10–12 double, depending on bathroom options.

Sans Rival Sólonos 7G (☎474383). Currently closed for remodelling but when it re-opens should present another mid-range option in Laïkí Yitoniá; expect old rates of C£5 single, C£8.50 double to climb considerably.

Capital, Riyénis 94 (☎462465). Strange atmosphere, but not necessarily from the *artístes* (local euphemism for bar girls); clean and safe enough at C£8 single, C£12 double.

Carlton Pringipíssis de Týras 13 (☎442001). Old one-star in the new town but within a five-minute walk of the D'Avila bastion and various bus terminals. C£8 single, C£12 double.

City Lídhras 215 (☎463113) Recently renovated and perhaps the best value in the old town, though rooms don't quite fulfill the promise of the lobby: you've a choice of airy, noisy rooms up front or quiet gloomy ones out back. Singles C£8–9, doubles C£14–16, depending on whether you take breakfast or not.

Lido Corner of Filokýprou and Pasikrátous (☎474351). Well-priced two-star in the heart of Laïkí Yitoniá, popular with UN dependents. C£12.50 single, C£18.50 double.

Averoff Avéroff 19, 15-minute walk west of the walled quarter towards the Green Line (☎463447). Old-fashioned two-star standby near a public pool. Singles C£15, doubles C£20.

Venetian Walls Ouzoúnian 36 (☎450805). Again quite alright considering the location – though somewhat overpriced as a one-star at C£15 single, C£20 double.

Five divey hotels or pensions at which you'd get little sleep for one reason or another, and are thus worth avoiding, are the *Royal*, the *Delphi*, the *Gardenia*, the *Alasia* and the *Femina*.

The city

The preponderance of interest for a visitor to south Nicosia lies within, on or right outside the Venetian walls, and since their circuit is just less than 2km in diameter, highlights can be toured on foot in a fairly leisurely two full days. After dark the old town (except for the Famagusta Gate area) is essentially deserted, even eerie, and most life shifts outside the walls.

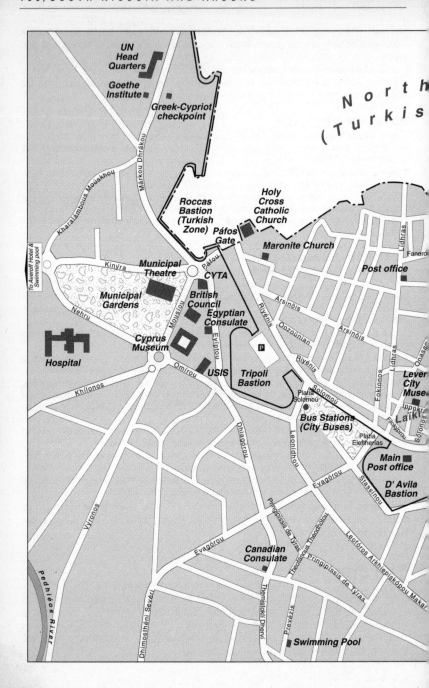

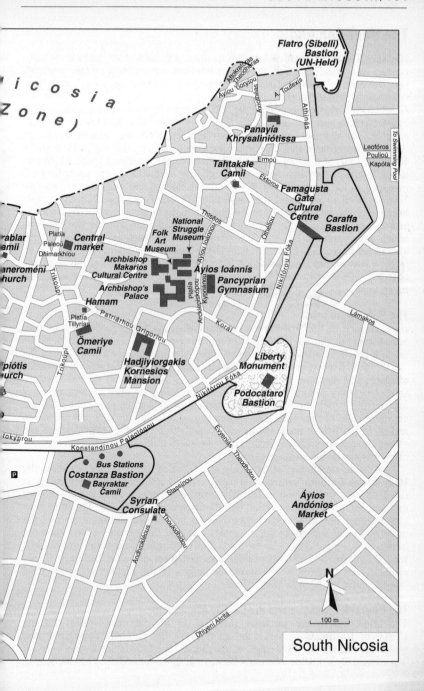

South Nicosia

The Venetian walls

Nicosia's **Venetian fortifications** are its most obvious feature, and a good place to start your wanderings. Of the eleven bastions, named for Venetian personalities, five each fall into the Greek/Turkish zones (the latter as usual having been confusingly renamed). The Flatro bastion, in the no-man's land between the Greek and Turkish zones, is under UN control. Three surviving gates, called Páfos, Kyrenia and Famagusta after the towns which they face, breach the walls roughly 120 degrees apart. The Venetians engaged the military engineers Ascanio Savorgnano and Francesco Barbaro to design the ramparts between 1565 and 1567: at the foot of the fortifications they appended a moat, which was never intended to carry water – though the Pedhiéos River, later diverted, managed to fill it sporadically. It was not the fault of the walls themselves that Nicosia failed to withstand the siege of 1570; the Turks took the city mainly because of the incompetence of the pusillanimous commander Nicolo Dandolo, and the exhaustion of the defenders. The Ottomans maintained the ramparts which were captured more or less intact; it is only since 1878 that substantial alterations have been made. Most of the following monuments are atop, or an integral part of, the bastions which form the most obvious bits of the ramparts; otherwise it's easy to tread the course of the walls without realising it, a testimony to how domesticated they've become.

The Páfos gate area

If you come from the Troödhos by car, the **Páfos gate** will probably be your grim introduction to the city: poised between the Greek and Turkish zones of the town, it has been a trouble spot since 1963. Now the flags of the South and the North, plus Greece and Turkey, oppose each other here across a ten-metre airspace, and signs on the Turkish-held Roccas bastion warn against "trespassers". Originally this gate was called Porta San Domenico, after a Lusignan abbey just outside, which the Venetians demolished in 1567 when they contracted the circumference of the walls. The Ottomans had a large barracks and arsenal in and on it; the British made the internal chambers their police headquarters and closed the gate to vehicles, though it re-opened to traffic after independence, and there was always a pedestrian tunnel.

Just inside stands one of the many anomalies of the post-1974 situation: the **Holy Cross Catholic church** and papal nuncio's residence, though squarely in the dead zone with its rear in Turkish-occupied territory, was allowed to re-open and function in 1976 on condition that the back door was sealed. The Maronites (see Chapter Seven) also have their church, school and clubhouse around the corner. Moving anti-clockwise, the moats and next three bastions have been put to use as dusty parkland, playing fields, bus terminals or car parks respectively, with D'Avila bastion also supporting a small cluster of public buildings. Three viaducts now compromise the walls, the largest (Platía Eleftherías) slated for a face-lift under the Nicosia Master Plan.

The Bayraktar mosque and the Liberty Monument

The small **Bayraktar mosque** (Mosque of the Standard-Bearer) on the **Costanza fortification** marks the spot where the Ottoman flag-carrier first scaled the walls in the 1570 siege; vulnerable as such individuals always were – it was essentially a suicide mission – he was cut down immediately by the defenders, and buried on the subsequently revered site. EOKA activists bombed the mosque and tomb twice in 1962 and 1963, toppling the minaret the second time, but the damage was repaired and the mosque grounds are now kept locked to prevent recurrences. The area is still as well landscaped as when Louis Salvator described it in 1873.

A haven of parkland also surrounds the **Liberty Monument** sculpture, on the **Podocataro bastion**, consisting of fourteen Greek-Cypriot figures in bronze being released from a white marble jail by two soldiers and being blessed by a cleric. Commissioned and opened to great hoo-hah some years back, the monument is now presumably such an embarrassing obstacle to communal reconciliation that it is absent even from most official tourist literature and maps.

The Famagusta gate

Tucked into an angle of the Caraffa bastion, the **Famagusta gate**, is the most elaborate and best preserved of the two on the Greek side. Designed by Giulio Savorgnano (brother of Ascanio) as a copy of another such Venetian structure in Iraklion, Crete, the gate is essentially a tunnel through the walls, the inner facade with its six coats-of-arms and original wooden doors far more aesthetic than the mean outer portal. After more than a century of neglect, the interior was refurbished in 1981 as an **exhibition and concert venue**; the heart of the latter is the acoustically marvellous, gently inclined tunnel surmounted by a dome like a miniature Parisian Pantheon. A side chamber, once either the Ottoman powder magazine or guard house, is now the exhibit hall. Beyond the outer portal stretches a small open-air amphitheatre used during the Nicosia September festival.

The traditional commercial centre

Using Platía Eleftherías as a gateway, you're set at the Y-junction of **Lídhras and Onasagórou** streets to explore the time-honoured city centre of Nicosia. A graceless architectural mix of British Raj, Greek neo-Classical and 1950s- and-60s Ugly lines these two main shopping streets were recently pedestrianised as part of the Master Plan. The Greek-Cypriot barricade at the north end of Lídhras, with its little shrine to the lost homelands and a "public relations" booth to one side, is the only point on the Green Line you may photograph; you're supposed to stay a healthy ten metres away from other checkpoints. Businesses, in any case, peter out upon reaching the last three or four premises away from the Line – the uncertainty (and in former years, proclamation battles by the opposing sides using loudhailers) was too nerve-wracking. It is not the first time the street has been embattled; during the late 1950s Lídhras was dubbed "Murder Mile" after EOKA's habit of gunning down its adversaries here.

Platía Faneroménis

The north end of Onasagórou gives onto **Platía Faneroménis**, slated to replace Eleftherías as the official city centre and named after the huge church dominating it. A hotchpotch of neo-Classical, Byzantine and Latin styles, it was erected during the final Ottoman years to replace an apparently more interesting but derelict medieval basilica. Inside the present structure are the remains of the four clerics murdered by the Ottoman governor in 1821. Behind the apse stands the neo-Classical Girls' Gymnasium, counterpart to the Pancyprian Gymnasium (see below).

More compelling than either, and virtually filling the adjacent tiny Platía Ikosiogdhóis Oktovríou, is the **Arablar Mosque**, originally the sixteenth-century church of Stavrós tou Missirikoú, a good example of the mixed Byzantine-Gothic style particular to Lusignan times. You're unlikely to gain admission, but if you do the octagonal-drummed dome is supported on magnificent columned arches. Taking advantage of the setting with outdoor sitting is the recommended *Matheos* taverna (see "Eating and Drinking").

Laïkí Yitoniá and around

Just east of the Lídhras pedestrianisation, and predating it as the first part of the Master Plan to be carried out, the so-called **Laïkí Yitoniá** or "Popular Neighbourhood" forms a showcase district reclaimed from the sin merchants in the late 1980s, with restored premises made available to half-a-dozen indifferent restaurants and numbers of souvenir shops. Unique and outstanding among the touristy schlock is *Gallery Dhiakhroniki*, Aristokýprou 2B, with antiquarian and facsimile engravings from Cyprus, the Middle East and Europe, as well as original art by locally resident painters, both Cypriot and foreign. The stock is reasonably priced and the engravings partly mounted – you can bargain for a slight discount on multiple purchases.

The south Nicosia municipality is also extremely proud of the nearby **Leventis City Museum** at Ippokrátous 17 (Tues–Sun 10am–4.50pm; admission free, but donation requested), which won the European Museum of the Year award in 1991. This folk-cum-historical collection occupies two floors of a restored mansion, and the collection is arranged in reverse chronological order: ideally you start at the rear of the first floor and work your way forward and down. Unfortunately labelling tends to be in Greek, with occasionally some in English and French. Exhibits include traditional dress, household implements, rare books and prints, with scattered precious metalware or archaeological treasures. The best sections are those devoted to the Venetian and Ottoman periods, with the ground floor exhibits dwindling to a disappointment of unlabelled, uncontexted archival photos as the present is reached. There's little on the history of individual monuments, and nothing yet on how the two zones of the city function together now, nor any background on the Laïkí Yitoniá or Khrysaliniótissa renewal projects.

Around the corner on Sólonos, the **Tripiótis church**, dedicated to the Archangel Michael, is the most beautiful of the old town's surviving medieval churches. On the south side, a glassed porch protects a pair of Gothic-arched windows. Over the door between, a fourteenth-century relief shows two lions being subdued by a being sprouting from leafy tracery, clutching hoops; to either side, mermaids and sea monsters gambol. Inside, the brown sandstone masonry has been left unpainted, as has the fine wood *yinaikonítis* – indeed the whole interior is relatively restrained for a Cypriot church.

The Ömeriye mosque and Hadjiyiorgákis Kornésios mansion

Variously spelled Omerieh, Omerye, or Omeriyeh, the **Ömeriye mosque** on Platía Tillyrías is the only converted Gothic house of worship in the Greek zone of Nicosia. Originally it was a church of Saint Mary, part of a fourteenth-century Augustinian monastery largely destroyed by the Ottoman bombardment in 1570. Many Lusignan nobles were buried here, but as in the case of the Ayía Sofía cathedral (see Chapter Six) the victors sacrilegiously "recycled" their tombstones to re-floor the mosque during reconstruction. The Ottoman conqueror of Cyprus, Lala Mustafa Paşa, got it into his head that the caliph Omar had rested here during the seventh-century Arab raids on Cyprus – hence the name. Today it serves the needs of the city's Arab and Persian population; you are welcome to shed your shoes and visit the simple, barn-like interior with its shallow pitched roof and series of (post-siege) arches.

The namesake **baths**, across the square, also still function, worth knowing about in winter or if you're stuck in a bottom-end pension. It's open 8am to 2.30pm, for c£1; women only Wednesday and Thursday. Platía Tillyrías itself is now a rather busy street and car park, but there are a few snack and drink cafés to one side where you can rest and admire the mosque.

The Hadjiyorgakis Kornesios mansion

A few steps down Patriárkhou Grigoríou from the Ómeriye mosque, the delightful fifteenth-to-eighteenth-century **Hadjiyorgakis Kornesios mansion** (daily 8am–1.45pm; c£0.50) is a hybrid of Venetian and Ottoman forms – a wooden Turkish lattice balcony perches over a relief coat of arms at the front door – that easily overshadows any of its contents. Supposedly home to the Cyprus Ethnographic Museum, only a single room in the back is a period recreation; most of the rest serve, as a contemporary antique gallery rather than featuring nineteenth-century furnishings, though several rooms do exhibit assorted metal, glass and ceramic items from various eras.

The house takes its name from one **Hadjiyorgakis Kornesios**, a native of Térra in Páfos district, who served as the dragoman (multi-lingual liaison between the Ottoman authorities and the Orthodox Christians) of Cyprus from 1779 until 1809. With a fortune accumulated from his vast estates and tax exemption, he was the most wealthy and powerful man on the island, but he met the usual end of Ottoman officials who became too prominent. A peasant revolt of 1804 was aimed at him and the Greek clerics as much as at the Muslim ruling class; fleeing to Istanbul, he managed to stay alive and nominally kept office by seeking asylum in sympathetic foreign embassies – until beheaded in 1809 as part of the intrigues surrounding the consecutive depositions of the sultans Selim III and Mustafa IV.

The ethnic centre: the archbishop's palace and museums

An alarming concentration of coffin-makers lines the street leading from the Hadjiyorgakis Kornesios mansion to Platía Arkhiepiskópou Kypriánou, flanked by a cluster of buildings including the archbishop's palace, the city's diminutive cathedral and three museums.

Around the archbishop's palace

The **archbishop's palace** is the most immediately obvious monument, a grandiose pastiche that has recently replaced its 1950s predecessor, shelled and gutted by EOKA-B in their 15 July 1974 attempt to kill Archbishop Makarios as well as depose him. Except for the museum wing described below, it is not open to the public. At the southeast corner of the palace precinct, a controversial, not to say downright hideous, statue of Makarios looks (below the waist especially) more like Lot's wife than a cleric, as he stares down Koráï street towards the Liberty Monument.

Across the way sprawls the imposing neo-Classical facade of the **Pancyprian Gymnasium**, one of the more prestigious secondary academies for Greek Cypriots this century and last. In *Bitter Lemons* Durrell described his experiences teaching here in the mid-1950s, when it became a hotbed of enosist sentiment.

Between the gymnasium and the palace sits the seventeenth-century **church of Áyios Ioánnis** (Mon–Fri 9am–noon, 2–4pm, Sat 9am–noon), which gets prizes for the quantity (if not always the quality) of its recently cleaned eighteenth-century interior **frescos**. Among recognisable scenes are the *Last Judgement* and the *Creation* over the south and north doors respectively, and on the south wall a sequence on the rediscovery of the apostle Barnabas' relics. Despite its small size (compared to Faneroméni, for instance), Áyios Ioánnis is the official cathedral of the city; here the archbisops of Nicosia are still consecrated, standing on the floor medallion featuring a Byzantine double-headed eagle.

GEORGE "DHIYENIS" GRIVAS (1898–1974) AND EOKA

Travelling about in the South, you can't help noticing that practically every town has a "Gríva Dhiyení" avenue – sometimes even two. They honour a man as controversial as Makarios – and who, particularly since independence, brought considerable misery, directly or indirectly, to both Greek and Turkish Cypriots.

Born on 23 May 1898, a native of Tríkomo (today İskele) in the North, **George Grivas** attended Nicosia's Pan-Cyprian Gymnasium before enrolling in the officers' academy in Athens. He graduated just in time to see several years' service in Greece's disastrous Asia Minor campaign – which doubtless fuelled his subsequent aversion to Turkey and Turks.

Grivas remained in Greece after the loss of Asia Minor, taking part under General Papagos in the repulsion of the Italians on the Epirot front during the winter of 1940–41. Having idly sat out most of the German occupation of his adopted homeland, in 1944 he formed a far-right-wing guerrilla band of royalist officers known as **Khi** – the letter "X" in the Greek alphabet– which by all accounts was collaborationist, devoting most of its time to exterminating left-wing bands and leaving the departing Germans alone. When full-scale civil war broke out 1946, he emerged from retirement as a lieutenant-colonel to help crush the communist-inspired rebellion, again with Papagos as his superior.

A semblance of normal life and elections returned to Greece in 1951; Grivas ran under the banner of Papagos' party but was defeated – his forbidding, abstemious personality, appropriate to the battlefield, did not strike a chord in the Greek electorate. Disgusted, Grivas swore off politics for good, and returned to Cyprus the same year to test the possibility of an uprising there to throw off British rule. It was then that he met Makarios, whom he tried to convince of the necessity of some sort of rebellion. Neither Makarios nor Grivas' Greek sponsors were persuaded until an Athens meeting in early 1953, when Makarios, Grivas and ten others resolved to fight for *énosis* or union with Greece, founding **EOKA**, the *Ethnikí Orgánosis Kypríon Agonistón* or "National Organisation of Cypriot Fighters".

At this point Makarios would only assent to violence against property, but during 1954 two clandestine caique-loads of explosives and weapons made their way from Rhodes to Cyprus. Most of the year was taken up with the establishment of EOKA in Cyprus, with recruits taking oaths of secrecy, obedience and endurance till victory, similar to that of the IRA.

Makarios gave the final go-ahead for the insurrection in March 1955; EOKA made its spectacular public debut on 1 April with bomb explosions across the

The Folk Art museum

Just north, the **Folk Art Museum** (nominally Mon–Fri 8.30am–1pm & 2–4pm, Sat 8.30am–1pm, admission c£0.50) occupies the surviving wing of a fourteenth-century Benedictine monastery, handed over to the Orthodox and done up as the old archbishop's residence after Latin rule ended. The building is currently shut, presumably for renovation; when the collection reshuffling is complete you should still be able to see chunks of wooden water-wheel in the exterior portico, and the typical assortment of textiles, woodcarving and household implements inside.

The Archbishop Makarios Cultural Centre

Within sight of both Áyios Ioánnis and the Folk Art Museum is the entrance to the **Archbishop Makarios Cultural Centre** (Mon–Fri 9am–1pm and 2–5pm, Sat 9am–1pm; 1 May–30 Sept 9.15am–1pm and 2–5.15pm; c£0.50), which

island. Self-introductory leaflets were signed **"Dhiyenis"**, after Dhiyenis Akritas, hero of a tenth-century Byzantine epic and Grivas' chosen *nom de guerre*.

The revolt gathered momentum throughout 1955 and early 1956, when Grivas halted a promising round of negotiations between Makarios and Governor Harding with timely explosions which also forced Makarios' deportation. Thereafter Grivas and EOKA included murder in the scope of their operations, targeting British servicemen, leftist or loyalist Greeks and occasionally Turkish Cypriots as victims. From his moveable headquarters in the Troödhos – at or near Kýkko monastery – Grivas mocked the British with a steady barrage of communiqués and ultimata. To the British, at their wit's end, he was not "Dhiyenis" but "Egregious" Grivas.

When Makarios returned to Cyprus in 1959, he found himself estranged from Grivas who, furious at the archbishop's acceptance of independence rather than *énosis*, stalked off to self-exile in Greece and a hero's welcome, including promotion to the rank of lieutenant-general. This all apparently went to Grivas' head, and his subsequent paranoid public utterances were deeply embarrassing to all concerned, earning him denunciation by the Greek government.

By 1964, however, Greece, Makarios and Grivas had patched things up to the extent that the Athens government sent Grivas back to Cyprus, ostensibly to impose discipline on irregulars of Greek nationality who had smuggled themselves onto the island. This he did, but he also assumed command of Makarios' new **National Guard** and led several attacks on Turkish enclaves: most notably at Kókkina in 1964 and Kofínou in 1967, pushing Greece, Turkey and Cyprus to the brink of war each time. After the 1967 episode, American diplomacy secured what was hoped would be his permanent removal from the island.

But the 1967–74 Greek junta, in its obsessive machinations to oust Makarios from office, found Grivas useful once again: in 1971 he secretly entered Cyprus disguised as a priest to organise **EOKA-B**, literally "EOKA the Second", whose express intent was the elimination of all enemies of Hellenism – and of the colonels – on the island. This came to include virtually anyone who stood in the junta's way: communists, socialists, centrists, Turkish Cypriots, and eventually Makarios himself. Whether Grivas subscribed to all of this as the junta's willing patsy, or as a royalist shared some of Makarios' disdain for the colonels and remained opposed to any "*énosis*" that would invite the Turks in for a chunk of the island, will never be known; he died in January 1974, still in hiding. Yet had he not left the scene when he did, it is possible to imagine Grivas persuaded to lead the 15 July 1974 coup against his erstwhile comrade-in-arms. With hindsight, it is possible to respect Grivas for his obvious dedication and skill as a guerrilla – but for little else.

comprises several research libraries, a Byzantine museum, Makarios' private art gallery and a collection of prints and engravings. The Byzantine wing, on the ground floor, displays nearly 150 icons from the ninth century onwards, rescued from various churches in Nicosia and elsewhere.

Makarios deputed a French Cypriot, Nikolaos Dikeos, to assemble the oil paintings on the next floor up, but somebody's taste was lacking as many of the attributions are doubtful and the works in any case of limited interest.

The top floor is devoted to more worthy antiquarian prints and maps of Greece, particularly since independence. Recently it has been necessary to add three more halls, one of which will soon house the famous Kanakariá mosaics, stolen from a church in North Cyprus in 1979 but returned to Nicosia in 1991 from the US after a lengthy court battle (see "The Theft of the Kanakariá mosaics", p.252).

The National Struggle Museum

Beyond all of this, and signed under a small arched alleyway, is tucked the **National Struggle Museum** (no set hours, admission free), an overwhelming accumulation of memorabilia, mostly photo-archival, on EOKA's 1950s anti-colonial campaign of demonstrations, sabotage and murder. The British reprisals, searches, tortures and detention camps are also documented in cartoons and press comment of the time. Also on display are fighters' personal belongings, plus arrays of weapons and gruesomely ingenious bombs. In the middle of the complex a shrine to EOKA's martyrs has been prepared: a memorial to those killed in engagements, plus a mock-up gallows commemorating the nine hanged at the city's Central Prison by the British in 1956. Labelling is minimal, which doesn't help non-readers of Greek; the propaganda impact is visual, and primarily intended for Cypriot schoolchildren. Interestingly, the main emphasis is on opposition to (and from) the British, with little on adverse Turkish-Cypriot action – and even some photos of Turkish Cypriots celebrating independence with their fellow islanders.

Oldest Nicosia: Tahtakale and Khrysaliniótissa districts

Heading north from Platía Kypriánou on pedestrianised Ayíou Ioánnou, you shortly reach the small **Tahtakale (Taht-el-Kala) mosque**, the homely focus of the eponymous neighbourhood. Here the Master Plan is in full swing, as dozens of old houses are being renovated for occupation by young families in an effort to revitalise the area. But for a taste of the exotic Ottoman town of the last century, accented with palm trees, arched mud-brick houses and domes, you really need to continue across Ermoú into the Khrysaliniótissa district, strolling along Axiothéas, Ayíou Yioryíou and Avtokratóras Theodhóras streets in particular.

Monumentally, this area is anchored by the namesake church of **Panayía Khrysaliniótissa**, a rambling L-shaped building with fine relief carving on its exterior, arches under the two domes, and an overwhelming collection of icons inside. Construction was begun in 1450 by Helena Paleologina, the Greek wife of Lusignan King John II; the name, "Our Lady of the Golden Linen", is supposed to derive from its vanished original icon having been found in a flax field.

Perhaps on the heels of the rehabilitation efforts, businesses and residences are used right up to the barriers here, in contrast to elsewhere in town; the dead zone also seems narrower, with North Cypriot/Turkish flags plainly visible over the housetops. This defiant stance gives an extra edge to many of the good ouzeris and tavernas (see "Eating and drinking") which have congregated here since the Famagusta Gate was restored. But of the 23 types of exotic bazaars catalogued by Louis Salvator, effectively bisecting the town between the Famagusta and Páfos gates, only traces of the cabinet-making, tin-smithing and candledipping industries remain in the Greek zone, mostly on the few commercial streets between Tahtakale and Khrysaliniótissa.

The Cyprus museum

Founded early in the British tenure, the **Cyprus museum** (Mon–Sat 9am–6pm, Sun/hols 10am–1pm; c£1) is easily the best assemblage of archaeological artefacts on the island. It stands between the Tripoli bastion and the pleasant **municipal gardens**, Nicosia's largest green space and a worthwhile adjunct to any visit. You should tour the galleries anti-clockwise from the ticket booth for chronological order, but the museum is organised thematically as well. Typically for Cyprus, the pre-Classical displays are the most compelling, though every period from Stone Age to early Byzantine is represented. All told it's an absorbing, medium-sized collection that requires at least two hours for a once-over. Individual labelling is often mercifully replaced with hall-by-hall or glass-case explanatory plaques placing the objects in context.

Highlights of the collection

Room 1 is devoted to Neolithic items, in particular andesite ware and shell jewellery from Khirokitia, and a case of Chalkolithic fertility idols. **Room 2,** the Early Bronze Age gallery, features fantastically zoomorphic or beak-spouted composite red-clay pottery from the Kyrenia coast. The central exhibits illustrate aspects of a pervasive early Cypriot cult: two pairs of ploughing bulls, a rite conducted by priests (wearing bull masks) in a sacred enclosure, and a model sanctuary crowned with bulls heads.

The pottery of **Room 3** presents the best pictorial evidence of Mycenaean influence in Late Bronze Age Cyprus. A gold inlaid bowl from Enkomi and a faience rhyton from Kition are the richest specimens here, though decorated *kratirs* (goblets) are more revealing in their portrayal of stylised humans in chariots being drawn by equally fantastic horses. Recurrent left- and right-handed swastikas predate any Nazi associations, and merely indicate Asian contacts.

Room 4 is dominated by its startling corner display, the panoply of seventh- and sixth-century votive figurines from a **sanctuary at Ayía Iríni** near Cape Kormakíti, excavated in 1929. The shrine was active since 1200 BC as the focus of a fertility cult, yet few of the two thousand figurines discovered were female. Most of the terracotta men, of various sizes, are helmeted, prompting speculation that the deity was also one of war.

A limestone **Zeus Keraunios** ("Thunderer") from Kition, familiar from the c£10 note, hurls a missing lightning-bolt in **Room 5**. This and other Greek/ Hellenistic statues are interpreted with marked Assyrian influence in beard, hairdo and dress; an oriental voluptuousness in male or female facial expression decreases as the Hellenistic period is reached, but never entirely vanishes. Among several renderings of the goddess is the first-century AD Roman statuette of **Aphrodite of Soli** – an image reproduced ad infinitum across Cyprus in tourist literature proclaiming it "her" island.

A cast-bronze, large-than-life-size nude of the second-century emperor **Septimius Severus**, unearthed at Kythrea in 1928, forms the centrepiece of **Room 6**. **Room 7A** showcases an intricate **wheeled stand** for a bowl, ranks of animal figures rampant on its four sides, with an account of its rescue by the Cyprus government from Turkish thieves (pre-1974) and German art dealers. Ancient Énkomi, near Famagusta, yielded this and other twelfth-century finds like the famous bronze **"Horned God"**, one hand downturned in benediction.

Subterranean **Room 8** demonstrates the progression from simple pit-tombs under dwellings, as at Khirokitia, to rock-cut chamber-tombs, accessed by a *dhromos* or passage. Other steps lead to **Room 11**, the royal Salamis tomb room. Trappings from a hearse, and chariot traces for the horses sacrificed in the *dhromos* (see Salamis, Chapter Eight) are overshadowed by the famous **bronze cauldron** on a tripod, with griffon and sphinx heads welded onto its edge. A metal throne was found together with an Egyptian-influenced, finely crafted bed and a throne or chair of wood and ivory.

Room 7B offers a miscellany of objects from around the island, including the famous original mosaic of *Leda and the Swan* from Palea Paphos. Gold specimens include that portion of the Byzantine Lambousa Treasure which escaped the attentions of plunderers and smugglers in the last century (most of the hoard went to US museums, particularly the Metropolitan museum in New York).

The exhibits are rounded off with **Room 14's** terracotta figurines from all eras. Among the more whimsical are three humans and a dog in a boat, and a thirteenth-century sidesaddle rider, recently recovered from thieves. Ex votos of expectant mothers depict midwives delivering babies, and strange bird-headed and earring-ed women fondling their own breasts. From the Meniko sanctuary dedicated to the Phoenician god Baal Hamman, an outsize, unsettling figure of a bull being led to sacrifice completes a spectrum of taurean worship begun in Room 2.

Further afield: Kaïmákli

Nearly 2km northeast of the UN-controlled Flatro bastion, the suburb of **Kaimakli** – until 1968 a separate village – boasts the finest domestic architecture outside the city walls. Local Greek Orthodox architects and stonemasons first came to prominence during the Lusignan period, when the Latin rulers trained and used this workforce in the construction of the massive Gothic monuments of the city centre; their ability persisted through later changes of regime, and during the late Ottoman years the master masons would often travel abroad for commissions.

With the coming of the British, there was no longer a need to conceal wealth from the powers that were, and the former simple but functional mud-brick houses, with perhaps just a pair of sandstone arches or a lintel, were joined by grandiose stone churches and dwellings sporting pillars, balcony grillework, and other architectural follies.

More recent Kaïmákli history has not been happy: as a mixed district, it was the scene of bitter fighting and EOKA atrocities during December 1963, particularly in the Omórfita neighbourhood (Küçük Kaymaklı to the Turkish Cypriots); this, like much of Kaïmákli proper, now lies in the Turkish zone.

Every Monday the south Nicosia municipality lays on a bus and walking tour of Kaïmákli; just show up at 10am at the Laïkí Yitoniá CTO office. The two-hour outing, which involves a coach transfer along the Green Line in addition to the foot itinerary, is free but patrons are "encouraged" to buy things when stopped at points of interest along the way. If you'd rather go by yourself, bus lines #46 and #48 serve Kaïmákli.

The Ledra Palace checkpoint: daytrips to the North

From the Páfos gate area, Márkou Dhrákou winds north towards the Green Line and the Canadian–UN contingent quarters in the former Ledra Palace hotel. As you approach, a bizarre sort of parasitic life makes itself felt: a shop in the "dead zone" prints commemorative T-shirts for UN forces, who hang the shirts out to dry from balconies of the Ledra Palace; a Karpasian Refugee Association Restaurant dishes up ethnic politics with meals near the checkpoint; and estate-agent signs pitch abandoned properties in the area, presumably at knock-down prices.

If you want to actually pass to **the other side of the Green Line**, this is currently the single legal crossing from Southern to Northern Cyprus, for day visits only. You cannot stay overnight and then expect to return to the South, since the Greek-Cypriot rationale is that all pre-1974 hotels in the North were expropriated illegally from their rightful owners, and by staying in them you would be using stolen property. The guidelines given below for passage are highly changeable, as the checkpoint is prone to closure without warning when things are going badly.

CROSSING THE GREEN LINE

There are actually three separate halts at the Ledra Palace crossing, at the Greek Cypriot, UN and Turkish-Cypriot posts respectively. The Greek booth, across from the Ledra Palace, is open daily from 8am to 1pm, 3 to 6pm. You fill in a form (among other things acknowledging the illegality of the Turkish occupation and absolving the South of any responsibility should anything go wrong on your visit) under the baleful shadow of a government placard: "Beyond this checkpoint is an area of Cyprus still occupied by Turkish troops since their invasion of 1974. Turkey expelled 180,000 Cypriots of Greek origin, and brought over colonists from mainland Turkey to replace them. Enjoy yourself in this land of racial purity and apartheid; enjoy the sight of our desecrated churches..." and so on in a similar vein. Those with Greek or Armenian surnames, holding any passport, shouldn't bother trying to cross as they won't be let in by the Turks. The Greek Cypriots don't allow overnight luggage or cars (your own or hired) headed north, or any shopping sprees while there; only force-majeure-type excuses for lateness in coming back are accepted.

Once vetted at the UN barrier and through to the Turkish side, you pay c£1 for a **day pass**, but make sure *not* to have your passport itself stamped as you'll be banned from re-entering south Nicosia – the pass should always be issued as a separate, detachable sheet. Money-changers and taxi-drivers cluster beyond the Turkish checkpoint, the latter flogging lightning day-trips to a big attraction in the North (usually you choose between Kyrenia or Famagusta), but some of them are unscrupulous fare-fiddlers and you really can't do the North justice in an eight-hour tour. On balance, the Ledra Palace crossing is not recommended except as a way to see north Nicosia (Lefkoşa) – see Chapter Six for complete coverage.

Eating and drinking

Old Nicosia has numbers of decent, authentic places at which **to eat**, but they are fairly well hidden – and most emphatically not to be found in the much-touted Laïkí Yitoniá, a twee tourist trap whose nature will be familiar to anyone who's visited Athens' Plaka or Paris' Quartier Latin. Many, though not all, of the better full-on tavernas and less pretentious *ouzeris* are scattered to either side of the Famagusta Gate, lodestar of the city's "alternative" set.

Restaurants

Except for listings in the new town, the establishments below are within walking distance of each other. An **ouzerí** is an imported Anatolian/Greek mainland concept: an establishment serving *meze*-type food and drink on equal footing, in sociable, intimate surroundings.

The commercial centre

Matheos Platía Ikosioghóis Oktovríou, behind Faneroméni cathedral and beside the tiny Araplar mosque. Similar idea to *Zanettos* (see below) but nicer setting (outdoor seats by the mosque) and wider menu, featuring quails, rabbit, *ospria*, puddings, etc. Open until 3am for the benefit of the local market sellers and cabaret staff.

Zanettos Trikoúpi 65, on the way to the central covered market. Features small *meze* plates and alcohol, but pitches itself as a "family" establishment.

Iraklis Lídhras 110. *The* spot for locally produced quality ice cream; always has customers out front, whatever the hour.

Between Flatro Bastion and Famagusta Gate

No-name grill Axiothéas, near junction Ayíou Kassianoú, around the corner from *Thermopiles*. From an old house emerges some of the best kebabs to be found in the city, at suppertime only; outdoor seating in this dead-end street smack up against a minor checkpoint.

Thermopiles Anastasías Toufexís 19, 200m from Flatro. Don't be put off by the dilapidated premises, unmaintained because of its proximity to the dead zone. This is a find, emphasising cooked vegetable entrees for lunch, leftovers and *meze* at night, when it's open till after midnight. The clientele is a motley assortment of locals, tourist, expats and UN forces, with intimacy foisted on patrons by the forty-square-metre layout. Hard to pigeonhole, but recommended.

To Steki tis Khrysaliniotissas Athinás 19, within sight of Flatro. More of a formal, sit-down taverna with both indoor and outdoor tables. Well-prepared food and not too expensive.

Enotiko Kafenio Egeon Éktoros 40. An oddball multi-purpose centre, comprising a record/book shop-cum-culture-club/taverna. Run by a one-time anarchist, now fanatically (and belatedly) converted to the cause of *énosis*; his souvlaki is more digestible than his politics. Evenings only; garden seating out back.

Ithaki A small *ouzerí* at the corner of Nikifórou Fóka and Thiséos; shut in summer.

The New Town

Tsolias, Theofánous Theodhótou 44, not far from the cinemas. Another *ouzerí* specialising in *meze*.

Fytro Khítri 11. Vegetarian and health fare, in premises next to L & M Health Food Stores. Lunch daily Mon–Fri, suppers Tues and Fri only.

Nightlife and events

There's actually a bit more going on after dark than the naff or dubious pubs in and around Laïkí Yitoniá would suggest, but most of this is out in the new suburbs, and you'll need both a car and local contacts to find it. It's as well to remember also that the concept of a bar or pub is a recent import, and traditionally Cypriots of all ages spent (and still spend) most of the evening lingering over a mix of food and drink in the same establishment.

An outstanding exception (on the Venetian ramparts, near Podocataro bastion) is the oddly named *Epea Pteroenda* at Nikifórou Fóka 30, a **musical bar** featuring live Greek *rembétika* (an underground urban music prevalent the first half of this century) and popular songs from the 1940s and 1950s, performed by young local talent. There are no performances Sunday or Monday, or between 1 June and 30 September, when tables move outside to function as a garden *ouzeri*. C£2 cover charge per person, drinks c£0.70–1.75.

Closer to Famagusta Gate, *Bastione* on Athinás is a trendy bôite with a smattering of gay customers; *Enallax* nearby on the same street is another option; while out in the new city, the English-style pub *Mythos* on Theofánous Theodhótou, near the two commercial cinemas, is a possibility for a drink before or after a film.

Theatre, music and film

For **theatre and musical events**, south Nicosia has four medium-sized indoor venues: the *Famagusta Gate Centre*, with good acoustics for chamber concerts in its small hall; the 1200-seat *Municipal Theatre* across from the British Council and Cyprus Museum at the edge of the Municipal Gardens; *ENA* at Athinás 4 (though most performances are in Greek); and the *PA.SY.DY Theatre*, for orchestral works, at Dhimosthéni Severí 3, the continuation of Leofóros Evagórou.

Film hounds are catered to by two commercial cinemas – the *Zena Palace* on Pringipíssis de Týras (☎444128) and the *Metropol* around the corner on Theofánous Theodhótou 3 (☎444840). The *Friends of the Film Society* screens weekly movies (usually Monday night) at the Russian Cultural Centre, and the British Council and French Cultural Centre also host films once or twice a month. For these addresses, see the "Listings" below, and for **current schedules** of all events consult the (fairly) useful pamphlet *Nicosia This Month*, published by the municipality and available at CTO, or the "Lifestyle" pullout section of the *Cyprus Weekly*.

Listings

Airlines Most air companies do not have actual terminals but rely on representative agencies. *Amathus Navigation*, Omírou 17, for *Olympic*, *SAS* and *Air France*; *Gateway Travel*, Mykínis 10C, for *Air UK* and *American Airlines*; *Alasia Cyprus Cruises*, Gríva Dhiyení 40, for all East European national carriers; *Mantovani & Sons*, Evagórou 35/37, for *Egyptair* and *PIA*; *Loizides Bros*, Evagórou 51, for *Air India* and *Canadian Pacific*; and *Aeolos Cyprus Travel*, Pringipíssis de Týras 6, for most north European charter companies. Actual offices include: *Aeroflot (Groutas)*, Omírou 31 (☎473172); *British Airways*, Arkhiepiskópou Makaríou 52A (☎442188); *Cyprus Airways*, Arkhiepiskópou Makaríou 50 (☎441996); and *KLM (Hollandia)*, Theofánous Theodhótou 24 (☎443144).

American Express c/o A.L. Mantovani & Sons, Agapinóros 2D–2E (☎443777).

Bicycles If you're suddenly seized with the urge to go mountain-biking in the Troödhos, try *Dikran Ouzounian & Co* on Gríva Dhiyení for a selection of Raleigh products, or *Micromania* at Ikosiogdhóis 72, Makedhonítissa suburb. Prices from c£100.

Bookstores *MAM*, Aristokýprou 3, Laïkí Yitoniá, specialising in books on Cyprus; *Moufflon*, Sofoúli 4, off Dhiagórou near Platía Solomoú; *Bridgehouse*, corner Víronou and Gríva Dhiyení, on the #10 or #15 bus line.

Car hire *Avis*, Víronos 2 (☎472062); *Airtour*, Náxou 4 (☎450403); *Andy Spyrou*, Midhías 2, Akrópolis district (☎494701); *Astra*, Haralámbous Móskhou 3, north of the museum park (☎475800); *Budget/Petsas*, Pídhou 2 (☎462042); *Eurodollar/Glamico*, Dhiágorou 6A (☎462014); *Europcar*, Santaróza 7 (☎445201); *Hertz*, Platía Eleftherías, Tryfon Building Suite 4 (☎477783).

Coach terminals *Costas*, on the Tripoli bastion, near Platía Solomoú, to Páfos and Limassol; *Kallenos*, at Leonídhou 34, to Larnaca; *EMAN*, on Konstandínou Paleológou east of the main post office, to Ayía Nápa; *Kemek*, on Leonídhou next to Kallenos, to Limassol; *Zingas*, also on Leonídhiou by Kemek and Kallenos, to Plátres via the Marathássa valley; *Solea Bus*, on the Costanza bastion, to Kakopetriá and Troödhos summit. Country market-buses for small villages also congregate at Costanza.

Cultural centres *British Council*, Mousíou 3 (☎442152); *French Cultural Centre*, Jean Moreas 3/5 (☎443071); *Russian Cultural Centre*, Alassías 16, Áyii Omoloyíti (bus #13 or #57 – ☎453876); *Goethe Institute*, on Márkou Dhrákou across from the Greek Cypriot checkpoint; *USIS*, Omírou 33B (☎473143). Most have morning and late-afternoon split shifts, with special events in the evening.

Embassies/high commissions/consulates *UK*, Alexander Pallis, northwest of the old town by the Green Line (☎473131); *Australia*, Ánnis Komnínis 4, corner Stassínou (☎473001); *USA*, corner Dossithéou and Theríssou, Likavitós district – buses #16, #50, #55 and #58 pass nearby (☎465151); *Canada*, Themistoklí Dherví 15, Julia House (☎451630). Other consulates important for procuring visas include *Egypt*, Eyíptou 3 (near CYTA), and *Syria*, corner Thoukidhídhou and Andhrokléous (across from the Costanza bastion).

Exchange Most banks cluster around Platía Eleftherías, including two with Visa-accepting cashpoint machines and three branches with afternoon tourist hours; more are not far away at the start of Arkhiepiskópou Markaríou.

Fruit and veg markets The old central market, best on Friday and Saturday, is up on Platía Paleoú Dhimarkhíou, at the end of Trikoúpi by the Green Line; two others are the Wednesdays-only street bazaar on Konstandínou Paleológou, by the Costanza bastion, and the daily Áyios Andónios market at the corner of Dhiyení Akritá and Evyenías Theodhótou.

Post offices Main branch, with late afternoon and Saturday morning hours plus poste restante service, sits atop the D'Avila bastion, entrance from Konstandínou Paleológou; a secondary branch, with early closure, at Lídhras 65A.

Service taxis Companies are all on the outer ring road, in its incarnations of either Omírou or Stassínou. *Acropolis*, Stassínou 9 (☎472525), to Larnaca; *Karydas*, Omírou 9 (☎462269), to Limassol; *Kyriakos*, Stassínou 27 (☎444114), to Larnaca and Limassol; *Kypros*, Stassínou 9A (☎464811), to Limassol; and *Makris*, Stassínou 11 (☎466201), to Larnaca.

Shopping In general, shopping opportunities in Nicosia are overrated; only optical goods are very cheap compared to northern Europe, but savings will have been eroded by the introduction of VAT in mid-1992. Shoes are good quality and reasonably priced, clothes rather less so; the focus for all three is pedestrianised Lídhras, and to a lesser extent its parallel Onasagórou. In the new town, most department stores are found along, or just off of, Arkhiepiskópou Markaríou. The *Cyprus Handicraft Service* has outlets at Aritokýprou 6 in Laïkí Yitoniá, and also out in the new town at Athalássas 186.

Swimming pools Largest is on Loúki Akritá, just off our map across the Pedhiéos river bed; others include one on Prevézis, off Dherví, and another down Leofóros Poulioú Kapóta (also off map).

Telephones CYTA, alarmingly sandbagged against the "Turkish threat", just outside the Páfos Gate on Leofóros Eyíptou, open 7.30am–7.15pm daily.

OUT FROM NICOSIA

The undulating expanses around the capital hold little of compelling interest for a traveller, and access to many sites is complicated by the presence of the Attila Line. Still, certain highlights can be easily taken in while in transit between Nicosia and either the Troödhos or the coast, and as such make worthwhile stops.

West of Nicosia: Peristeróna

Heading west from Nicosía towards the Soléa or Marathássa districts of the Troödhos, you've a long diversion round the disused airport in UNFICYP territory; 34km along, the village of **PERISTERÓNA** straddles a usually dry stream.

The church of Áyii Varnávas and Hilárion

The five-domed, tenth-century church of **Áyii Varnávas and Hilárion** on the riverbank is very handsome even just from the outside, but hang about purposefully and the café proprietor next door will appear with the key. The interior architecture is imposing, with its pair of apsed aisles separated from the nave by arches, but there's not much else to see: a surviving sixteenth-century wall painting of King David, the huge contemporary *témblon*, and an antique chest of uncertain date in the narthex depicting the siege of a castle.

The mosque

The CTO makes much of the church's juxtaposition with a **mosque** a couple of hundred metres southwest, one of Cyprus' oldest and finest, as a token of the supposedly long, peaceful co-existence of the two main island communities. Perhaps ironically, then, the Turkish Cypriots accused vengeful Greek Cypriots of setting fire to it in April 1976, though any arson seems to have been since patched up. The square groundplan with its high superstructure and arched, tracery-laden windows is decidedly Lusignan – prompting suspicions that this is in fact a converted church.

The grounds are locked and fenced to prevent vandalism, but the fence is holed, the minaret infested with pigeons, and the front door usually ajar for peeks into the vaulted interior.

Southwest of Nicosia

These two attractions, some 22km **southeast of Nicosia**, can easily be combined with a day visit to the monastery of Makherás, or longer forays into Pitsiliá (see Chapter Four). From central Nicosia, the route out passes through the suburb of STRÓVOLOS, and then the village of DHEFTERÁ.

Ancient Tamassos

One of the oldest Cypriot settlements, **ancient Tamassos** owed its existence to extensive local deposits of copper, first exploited in around 2500 BC. In Homer's *Odyssey*, Athena went to "Temese" to trade iron for copper; later the revenues from the local mines accrued to the Phoenicians, the kings of Salamis and the biblical Herod, though these beneficiaries fail to give a clear idea of who was actually living, working or ruling at Tamassos itself.

Excavations since 1975 have revealed the foundations of a Classical temple of Aphrodite/Astarte with traces of copper on the floor, implying, as at Kition, that metallurgy was considered sacred and that the priests controlled the deposits. Continuing the metallic and mercenary theme, local farmers dug up a life-size bronze statue of Apollo in 1836 – and hacked it apart, selling the bits to a scrap dealer. The head was salvaged and eventually found its way into the British Museum, though again it tells us little about Tamassan culture since it was made in Athens during the fifth century.

The **site** exposed to date (Tues–Fri 9am–3pm, Sat–Sun 10am-3pm, Mon shut; c£0.50) consists of about half an acre of jumbled foundations, on a slight slope overlooking grain fields at the northeast edge of the modern village of POLITIKÓ. The most interesting items are two sixth-century BC **subterranean tombs**, excavated in the 1890s though partially looted before then – in the pitched roof of the larger, double-chambered tomb, you can still see a hole made by the thieves. The sandstone masonry has been cleverly carved in places to imitate wood and bolts appropriate to wooden doors, a style reminiscent of the "house tombs" of Anatolian Lycia.

THE UN FORCES IN CYPRUS (UNFICYP)

In the wake of the communal disturbances of December 1963, the British announced themselves unable to single-handedly maintain civil peace on Cyprus, and the crisis was referred to the United Nations. A Security Council resolution of March 1964 mandated the dispatch of a 6000-strong UN peacekeeping force, henceforth known as UNFICYP. This originally drew its blue-bereted ranks from the armies of the UK, Canada, Austria, Finland, Sweden, Denmark, Australia and Ireland, though by late 1993 numbers will have dwindled to about 1000. The initially authorised period was three months, but this has been renewed more or less automatically ever since. What was intended initially as a stopgap measure pending a durable solution to Cyprus' ethnic problems showed signs over the years of becoming an apparently permanent island institution.

UNFICYP's brief has always been narrowly defined: to keep physically separate hostile communal factions; to discourage atrocities by their mere presence; and, in their capacity as potential witnesses, to verify the facts of such incidents. However, UN troops have limited means of imposing calm; they cannot launch a pre-emptive strike to nip factional violence in the bud, but are only allowed to return fire if attacked. Nonetheless, UNFICYP was fairly successful in preventing more casualties than actually did occur from 1964 to 1974.

Since the events of summer 1974 the deployment (if not the role) of UNFICYP has changed radically. Instead of policing the boundaries of a number of scattered Turkish-Cypriot enclaves, troops now patrol the single, 180-kilometre-long ceasefire line and the buffer zone of varying width straddling it, where 150 watchtowers constitute landmarks. Duties include maintaining utility lines crossing the zone, and ensuring the safety of farmers wishing to cultivate their fields right up to the boundary. UNFICYP has been instrumental in defusing sensitive spots – especially in and around Nicosia where opposing Greek and Turkish troops are close enough to verbally abuse each other. They also provide humanitarian aid to the remaining

Áyios Iraklídhios convent

The **convent of Áyios Iraklídhios**, near Tamassos, honours Cyprus' first bishop-saint, a native of the region, who guided the apostles Paul and Barnabas from Larnaca to Tamassos during their missionary journey across Cyprus. They subsequently ordained Iraklidhios (Heracleidius) first Bishop of Tamassus, and legend has it he was martyred on this spot at the age of 60. By 400 AD a commemorative monastery of some sort had been established here, to be destroyed and rebuilt a number of times (last in 1773), though the present *katholikón* is dated 300 years earlier. After twice being a brotherhood, an order of nuns took it over as a ruin in 1963, and transformed it as you see today.

To find the convent, drive through Politikó village until you see the obvious compound on a slight rise to the south. Inside (closed noon–3pm mid-May–mid-Sept), it's a peaceful, domestic, ship-shape world, alive with bird song: a dozen or so sisters read missals, water the well-tended flowerbeds or doze near sheets of newspaper laid down to catch droppings from the nesting swallows. The nuns sell pickled capers, as well as canaries from an aviary, and one of them may approach you to offer a whirlwind guided tour. In the *katholikón*, you'll be shown a smudged fresco of the two apostles baptising Iraklidhios; **reliquaries** containing his purported forearm and skull; some icons; and the sole exposed portion of an old **mosaic floor** regrettably covered over by modern tiling. From the side chapel to

---

Greek Cypriots and Maronites in the North, as well as helping to settle disputes between Greek- and Turkish-Cypriots in the two remaining mixed villages of the South.

Amazingly the cease-fire of August 1974 has substantially held since then, with only the odd (sometimes fatal) potshot in the buffer zone. UNFICYP troops are fairly popular among the populace, though one graffito in the North – "UN YOBOS SHIT" – suggests that opinion is not unanimous. Northern officialdom and the Turkish army have occasionally accused UN personnel of leaking strategic information to the Greek Cypriots: hence restrictions on UNFICYP movements in North Cyprus and signs forbidding passage of UN vehicles near sensitive military sites. But however tolerated UN personnel may be individually, many feel that their continued presence merely delays the day of reckoning – non-violent or otherwise – between the two Cypriot communities, and that the islanders should sooner rather than later be left to their own devices.

Such sentiments are increasingly endorsed at the UN Command, no doubt enhanced by the perceived hopelessness of UNFICYP's mission – and the $180 million arrears in maintenance payments by the UN. Until now the troop-contributing countries themselves have been footing most of the bill, which runs to $25 million yearly. The Swedes left Cyprus in 1988, saying they would not serve indefinitely without tangible progress towards a settlement. Denmark withdrew its troops in December 1992, and the Canadian contingent will follow suit by September 1993, leaving the UK with the main burden of peacekeeping – essentially a reversion to pre-1964 conditions.

These departures make it less probable that a fair system of assessing contributions from UN member states will be devised, an increasingly pressing need in light of the multiplying number of UN expeditions elsewhere since 1992. Yet UNFICYP may continue to be a Cyprus player, perhaps as guarantors of any federal settlement reached by the Cypriots which envisage an otherwise demilitarised island.

the south, a narrow stairway descends to a small **catacomb** where it is said the saint lived his last years and was later buried.

South of Nicosia: Perakhorío and Dháli

Heading **south of the capital** towards either Larnaca or Limassol, monuments near the two adjacent villages of Perakhorío and Dháli are worth a short halt if you've time. You wouldn't, however, make a special trip, and both places lie out of reach of the Nicosia urban bus system.

Perakhorío

PERAKHORÍO village is visited mainly for the sake of the twelfth-century church of **Áyii Apóstoli**, perched evocatively on a hill to the west, surrounded by Perakhorío's churchyard. Inside, the contemporaneous **frescos** are disappointing – surviving fragments appear to be of the same style as the work at Asínou, and if you've toured the Troödhos you needn't feel guilty about missing them. Highlight is the troupe of angels lining the drumless dome, just below a badly damaged *Pandokrátor*. The woman keeping the key lives in a house some 300m east, on the north side of the main residential street leading into the heart of Perakhorío. If you need a meal, the *Peristeri* taverna comes recommended.

Dháli and ancient Idalion

Four kilometres east, **DHÁLI** is an altogether busier place, a formerly mixed village perilously close to the Attila Line. (Potamía, 3km down the valley beside the buffer zone, remains bi-communal.) For a night out from Nicosia, the *Romantika* taverna here gets good marks, but again the main interest is not in the village, but a few hundred metres outside, to the south. Here the fortified hillside site of **ancient Idalion** is fairly obvious, though the place is still under sporadic excavation and there is little yet to interest the non-specialist, other than deep pits and courses of masoned wall in various states of exposure. The small city here dated from the Bronze Age and survived almost until the Roman era. American consul-turned-antiquarian Palma di Cesnola (see pp.50 & 83) spent several summers here, plundering (according to his boast) 10,000 tombs; yet such was the archaeological richness of the area that local farmers subsequently ploughed up many painted votive figurines of Aphrodite, the most important local deity, and an American team continues digging. Legend places the murder of Aphrodite's lover Adonis by a wild boar in the area, and in early spring you can still see red anemones, which supposedly sprang from his blood, poking out among the rocks here.

travel details

Buses

From Nicosia to Larnaca 11 daily Mon–Sat on *Kallenos*; 1 hr; to Limassol 9 daily Mon–Sat on *Kemek*, 1 or 2 daily on *Costas*; 1hr 30min; to Páfos 1 or 2 daily Mon–Sat, via Limassol, on *Costas*; 3hr; to Kakopetriá 11 or 12 daily Mon–Sat, 2 on Sun in summer, on *Solea*; 1hr 20min; to Troödhos 1 daily except Sun at midday; 2hr; to Plátres 1 daily except Sun at midday, via the Marathássa valley, with *Zingas*; 3hr.

PART THREE

THE NORTH

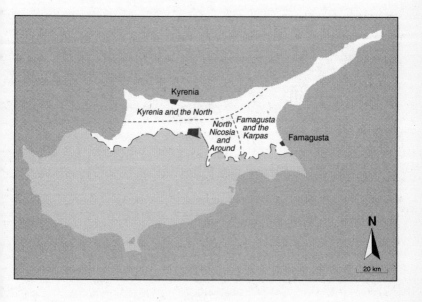

Kyrenia

Kyrenia and the North

North
Nicosia
and
Around

Famagusta
and the
Karpas

Famagusta

N

20 km

INTRODUCTION

he **Turkish Republic of Northern Cyprus** (TRNC) came violently into existence in August 1974 as a **refuge** for beleaguered Turkish Cypriots: first as the zone occupied by the Turkish Army, later as the interim Turkish Federated State of Cyprus, and finally, by a Unilateral Declaration of Independence of 1983, as the TRNC. Recognised diplomatically by no nation except Turkey, its creator and main sponsor, North Cyprus possesses at first glance a Ruritanian charm: antique Hillmans and Vauxhalls tooling about, policemen in grey Imperial summer twill, traffic lights that still have a colonial "STOP" stencilled over the red light. Travelling around, however, you'll find a number of conditions contributing to the North's image as a pariah state, and some obvious results of that status.

Public relations problems

The ubiquitousness of the **Turkish army** is most immediately off-putting: while there are fewer no-go areas than before, barbed-wire-fenced camps and unaesthetic military memorials abound, and an estimated 25,000 mainland conscripts, on- or off-duty, lend a barracks air to Kyrenia and north Nicosia in particular.

Although nearly 20,000 Greek Cypriots chose to stay in the Kırpaşa (Kárpas) peninsula and around Kyrenia 1974, and approximately 1000 Maronites on the Koruçam (Kormakíti) peninsula, **systematic harassment** by the army and the civil authorities has reduced those numbers to roughly 600 and 200 respectively.

The much-publicised **desecration** of Greek (and British) churches and graveyards is largely true, though Southern Cypriot public relations artists occasionally overstate their case: the Byzantine monastery of Akhiropiítos near Kyrenia and the monastery of Khrisostómos near Nicosia, both now occupied by the Turkish army, had already been partly de-consecrated and used by the Cypriot National Guard before 1974. According to the whim of the army and Turkish-Cypriot refugees, luckier churches were not battered but converted to mosques. Greek Cypriots are in the main careful to attribute the blame for this where it usually belongs – on the invading mainland army – since for many of the Turkish Cypriots, Orthodox shrines, monasteries and catacombs had also been sacred.

Arrested development

Overall there's a feeling of grass growing between the cracks, often literally – this atmosphere of **dereliction** can be attributed partly to the fact that the Turkish army in 1974 bit off rather more than the 120,000 Turkish Cypriots themselves could chew. Much of the North is under-utilised, its rural villages half empty: citrus orchards a couple of kilometres from Kyrenia die of neglect despite abundant water to irrigate them. Things four years old seem double that age, and anything left over from the unitary-republic era seems phenomenally ancient, obscured by multiple political posters, wrecked autos and tethered livestock.

The public **infrastructure**, too, is starved of improvement funds, one result of keeping the civil service rolls artificially swollen to stem a brain drain. Facilities appear to be kept ticking over, but no more; exceptions are the new Ercan airport and Kyrenia seaport, while improved, enlarged roads are limited to a single strip west of Kyrenia, and the vital Nicosia–Famagusta–Kyrenia highway. Except for some Saudi investment, most post-1974 international aid is shunted to the South, with increasingly less support from Turkey, which lately targets other priorities.

It's widely felt that sufficient aid would materialise, and the place would really take off, following **international recognition**, thus far withheld. At various times since 1974 certain pro-Turkish and/or Muslim nations like South Korea, Bangladesh and Pakistan, with turbulent origins similar to North Cyprus, have considered extending recognition – but backed down in the face of Greek or Greek-Cypriot threats in the international arena.

Native islanders vs Anatolians

The best lands and houses were **allotted** in 1975 to refugees from the South according to a point system; people were credited points for both commercial and residential property according to the value of such assets left behind. This government scheme was, not surprisingly, prone to abuse – extra points could easily be bought, sold or bartered – and inequities in the distribution of real estate were widespread. Many buildings still bear the single-letter, double-digit "inventory control" code assigned them at the time.

Poorer, isolated spots – fit mainly for goat-grazing – were assigned to **settlers** from Anatolia. Turkey long treated the North as a transportation colony, off-loading families of 1974 campaign veterans, surplus urban underclass, landless peasants, and even low-grade criminals and psychiatric cases, until the islanders had had enough, began to actively oppose the process, and sent the worst elements packing. As no accurate census has been conducted on Cyprus since 1973, estimating current immigrant numbers is an inexact science, with guesses ranging from 30,000 to 80,000. Their fate is a big sticking point in any potential peace agreement, and their presence has crystallised the chronic tension between native Turkish Cypriots and Turks, with the former (usually correctly) considering themselves to have a higher standard of living and education.

Since 1974 the Turkish army and nationalist idealogues in the local government have acted to **dilute** the British-ness and Cyprus-ness of the North, not only with settlement programmes but also by erecting stark monuments commemorating the events of July and August 1974, and by planting a bust of Atatürk in every village square. But the public has resisted giving up left-hand driving and roadside milestones, visible tokens of their separate identity. In Turkey a long-standing, patronising quip characterises Anatolia as *anavatan* (mother home-land) and North Cyprus as *yavru vatan* (baby homeland); the islanders return the compliment by dubbing mainlanders *karasakal* – "black beard": perhaps after the facial hair of the more religious settlers, or a corruption of *karasal*, "continental".

Tourism

Owing to the Greek-orchestrated embargo of the stigmatised North – for example, all inbound flights must touch down first in Turkey owing to the IATA boycott of Ercan airport – **tourism** is hardly more developed than in 1974, and this constitutes one of the North's attractions. Unless the situation changes you will enjoy the TRNC's sandy beaches, Crusader monuments and seafood in relative solitude, at a leisurely pace so opposite to that of the busy South. Especially off the beaten track, people's helpfulness and hospitality can be overwhelming.

Obstacles to reconciliation

Currently, the position of more accommodating Turkish Cypriots is that the South must decisively **renounce** the ideal of *énosis* and make the most of an independent, federal republic. But many adults in the North, not having spoken to a Greek Cypriot in two decades, find it hard to believe that *énosis* has almost no support in the South now. Those born since 1974, who have never met a Greek, are indoctrinated in school to believe that EOKA activists will make kebab out of them should the existing barriers fall. As a gesture of earnest and good will prior to establishment of a federal state, progressive Turkish Cypriots would like to see remaining crypto-EOKA-ists **purged** from from the Southern government. What they got instead in 1992 was the early release by the South of jailed 1963 Turk-assaulter and 1974 coup protagonist Nikos Sampson, which caused enormous offence and cut the ground from under more conciliatory northerners.

Such examples of continuing EOKA influence are seen in the North as further evidence of an underlying unreconstructed Greek-Cypriot attitude, perceived as "You (Turkish Cypriots) are just 400-year guests. Now go". At one point the Makarios government was offering money and a one-way plane ticket to any Turkish Cypriot willing to re-settle overseas, while the Orthodox church encouraged the Greek-Cypriot purchase of Turkish property at double its value, if need be (a carrot-not-stick version of "ethnic cleansing"), before the violent **coercion** of EOKA spawned open hatred and the physical basis of partition.

Both practices swelled the size of the large **exile** community; while about 100,000 Turkish Cypriots still reside on the island, almost three times that figure live abroad, mostly in Turkey, Britain, Australia and North America. (Proportionately, there is not nearly such a diaspora from the Greek side.) Since 1974, not enough Turkish Cypriots abroad have responded to their government's pleas to return and "rebuild the homeland"; instead there's a slow leak outwards of those fed up with the settlers and the political/economic stagnation. Whether the recent establishment of three universities will help change this is debatable.

Huge flocks of sheep, far outnumbering tourists and residents, graze the grain-stubble of the Mesarya or central plain; a steady trickle of these, along with market-garden produce and water from underground reservoirs near Güzelyurt, heads clandestinely south **across** the officially impervious Attila Line. The South reciprocates by providing the North with electricity from its plant at Dhekélia, as a "humanitarian" gesture. About 1500 Turkish-Cypriot workers also shuffle daily through the Dhekélia Sovereign Base, for jobs there or even in the South itself, especially in the construction trades. Cyprus is too small to ever be hermetically divided: its regional economies, if not always its peoples, were too **interknit** under past unitary administrations. And until the 1950s, intermarriage between the two communities was more common than generally admitted.

Despite their overwhelming economic and diplomatic advantage, it is the Greek Cypriots who are pressing for a **resolution** of the island's division. The northerners, even in the face of global ostracism (travel with a North-Cypriot passport is extremely difficult) feel that they have more to gain than to lose from persistence of the status quo; their present "enclave" is more comfortable than the besieged ones of 1963–74, with more ways out. On a human level, many Turkish Cypriots feel sorry for the northern Greeks who were forced from their homes, but consider the Attila Line, guarded by mainland Turks, as the best guarantee of continuing to wake up with a whole skin.

CHAPTER SIX

NORTH NICOSIA AND AROUND

Although most visitors to North Cyprus, as with the South, will be interested in reaching their coastal resort of choice as quickly as possible,
it's worth remembering that **north Nicosia** *is* to a great extent North
Cyprus, with easily a third of its population. The events of 1974 and
North Cyprus' UDI of 1983 resulted in the city becoming the capital of the as yet
unrecognised and perhaps provisional state. What the relatively few day visitors
to north Nicosia are after, though, is a concentration of Gothic and Ottoman
monuments: there's little else available for the casual tourist.

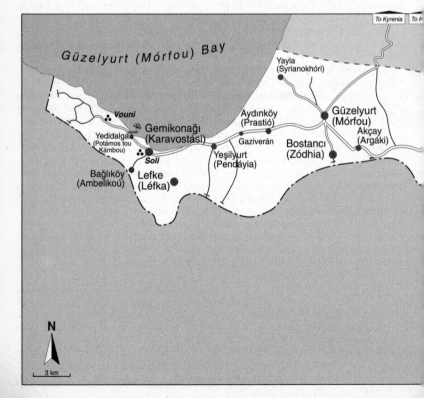

Excursions elsewhere in North Cyprus' patch of Nicosia district head exclusively west past the agricultural centre of **Güzelyurt**, with a museum and former monastery, to the intriguing ancient sites of **Soli** and **Vouni** on the coast. Inland from these, the oasis of **Lefke** makes a relaxing destination, though again with few specific attractions.

NORTH NICOSIA

Compared to the southern portion of the city, **north Nicosia** is a sleepy town of 60,000, one-fourth the size. Obviously the history of the two sectors, enclosed at their core by the same Venetian wall, was largely shared until 1974; the approaching Turkish Army was quite deliberate in ensuring that all traditionally Turkish districts in the northwest of the city fell under their control.

The justification for north Nicosia's emergence as capital of the North, and indefinite continuance in that role, is epitomised by the story behind the huge Turkish-Cypriot flag picked out in white rocks on the foothills of the Kyrenia range, just north of town, placed for maximum provocative effect on south Nicosia. The inhabitants of the nearest village, Taşkent (Sykhári), all came from Tókhni (near Khirokitia) in the South; on 15 August 1974 most of the village's

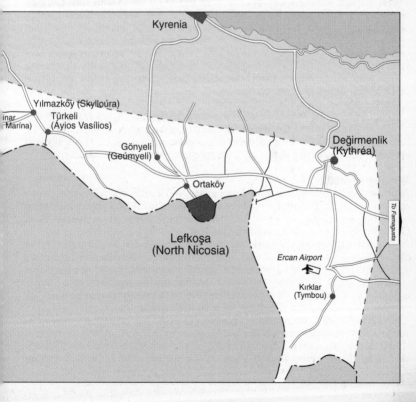

Turkish men of military age were massacred there by an EOKA-B contingent. For the survivors, the continued existence of North Cyprus is insurance against a recurrence of such nightmares.

Much more than in south Nicosia, the reality of the old town is desolation: dust-devils eddy on the battered streets, windows are broken even on used buildings, and fine domestic and monumental architecture seems preserved more through inertia than any conscious effort. Outside the walls there is little of interest, with colonial-era brownstones being outstripped by the tatty modern construction that increasingly disfigures the whole island.

Arrival and orientation

Arriving in Lefkoşa is relatively painless, owing to its small size; junctions are fairly well signed, though if driving yourself it's easy to get caught up in one-way systems. Like most other aspects of tourist service in town, provision of tourist **information** tends to be haphazard – attractions are not well marked, for one thing.

Arriving by air
Ercan airport lies 17km east of town, well signed off the initially dual carriageway towards Famagusta. It's a modern terminal, too large for North Cyprus' needs at the moment, but there's no public bus service at the airport; you either take a taxi into Lefkoşa, or if arriving as part of a package, meet a courier who bundles you into a tour-agency minibus for transfer to your resort, or hands over your pre-reserved car. There are a number of car-hire booths at the airport, but unless prior arrangements have been made, these shut long before the typical flight arrival times of 10pm to 2am, as do the money-exchange booths – have some sterling notes handy for taxi drivers.

About once a year Ercan is closed for maintenance and flights are diverted to an airport 3km south of **Geçitkale** (Lefkóniko, Lefkonuk). This is nearer to the Famagusta resort area, but as it's normally a military base, car hire probably isn't available, and you'll have to taxi out if an agency minibus doesn't collect you.

Arriving by land
Approaching Nicosia by car **from Famagusta**, you'll make the acquaintance of a roundabout north of town, currently at the edge of the built-up area, which gives buses the opportunity to barrel south to the **bus terminal** on **Kemal Aşık Caddesi**, near the corner of **Atatürk Caddesi**.

If you're **outbound**, the buses are grouped, west to east as you move across the terminal, by towns and villages falling into Kyrenia, Nicosia and Famagusta districts respectively; hunt down your destination accordingly, it's not a big place.

Coming **from Kyrenia**, you'll be caught up in another, even larger roundabout-with-monument at the northwest edge of the city, poised between the suburbs of Ortaköy (Orta Keuy) and Gönyeli (Geunyeli).

Given the small town population, **parking** presents few problems – as long as you you don't do anything rash like leaving your car in the congested commercial streets of the old quarter. There are no fee car-parks, but spaces are usually available along **İkinci Selim Caddesi**, just outside the old walls and within walking distance of most attractions.

The north Nicosia phone code is ☎020

Orientation and information

This northwestern roundabout shunts traffic in every direction, including southeast along the road which eventually splits into **Mehmet Akif Caddesi** and **Bedreddin Demirel Caddesi**. Both Bedreddin Demirel and Kemal Aşık come very close to meeting at the **Kyrenia Gate**, the most historic entrance to north Nicosia's bit of the old town; just inside it, **İnönü Meydanı** marks the north end of **Girne Caddesi**, the main thoroughfare and continuation of Lídhras on the Greek side. Partway along its length is the swelling known as **Atatürk Meydanı**, effectively the city centre.

Any year now the **tourist information office** is supposed to open a branch in the upper guard room of the Kyrenia Gate, but until then you'll have to trudge a considerable distance northwest along Mehmet Akif to the ministry headquarters themselves at no. 95 (summer Mon–Fri 8am–2pm; winter Mon–Fri 8am–1pm and 2.30–5pm).

The city

North Nicosia's sights can be seen in a single longish day; as on the other side of the Line, you won't need to learn bus routes but should rely on good shoes. Wander the backstreets the least bit away from the standard tourist circuit and you're an instant celebrity; stray too far off the main thoroughfares or get too close to the Green Line, though, and members of the Turkish armed forces may shadow you, particularly if there's any indication that you have a camera.

Urban renewal, in accordance with the Master Plan, has so far been limited to the partial pedestrianisation of the bazaar and gradual re-occupation (though not necessarily maintenance) of some stately houses in the Arabahmet district, near the Green Line; you're made painfully aware of what a judicious influx of funding could accomplish.

The ramparts

The five bastions lying wholly within the Turkish zone are not put to as much use as on the Greek side, though the moats are often nominally parkland. What used to be the vice-presidential residence in unitary republican days, on the Cephane (Quirini) bastion, is now the North Cypriot presidential palace; on the Musalla (Barbaro) bastion the army has erected a National Struggle Museum (free admission when sentry on duty) in response to the one in south Nicosia.

Between these two ramparts stands the **Kyrenia Gate**, the classic entry into the Turkish quarter but looking very useless plopped in the middle of İnönü Meydanı. In 1931, broad swathes were cut through the walls to either side of the gate to allow the passage of motor traffic, isolating it into a sort of pillbox-cum-guardhouse. The Venetians knew it as the Porta de la Proveditore, or Gate of the Military Governor, and fitted it with a portcullis and still-visible lion; after their victory, the Ottomans added an inscription lauding Allah as the "Opener of Gates".

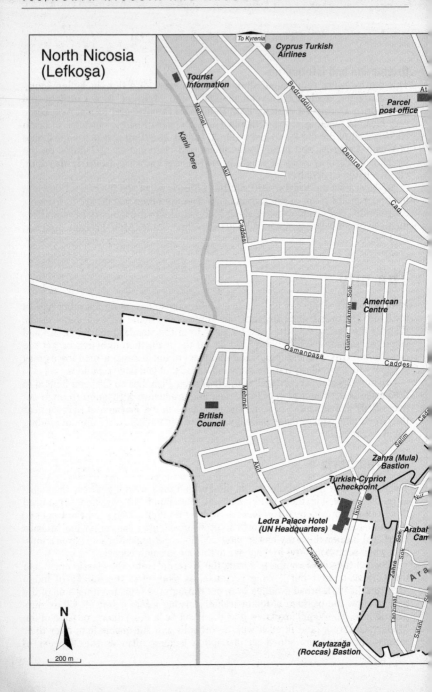

North Nicosia (Lefkoşa)

To Kyrenia

Cyprus Turkish Airlines

Tourist Information

Parcel post office

A1

Bedreddin

Demirel

Cad.

Mehmet

Kanlı Dere

Akıl

Caddesi

American Centre

Güner Türkmen Sok

Osmanpaşa

Caddesi

Mehmet

Cad

British Council

Selim

Akıl

Zahra (Mula) Bastion

Turkish-Cypriot checkpoint

Nur

İkinci

Arabah Cam

Ledra Palace Hotel (UN Headquarters)

Caddesi

Zahra Sok

Tanzimat

Arab

Selâhi Sok

N

200 m

Kaytazağa (Roccas) Bastion

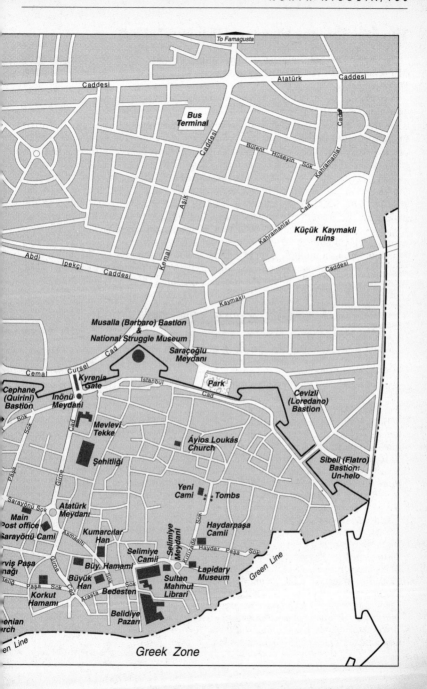

The Ethnography Museum (Mevlevî Tekke)

Once inside the gate, almost the first thing on your left is the **Ethnography Museum** (Mon–Fri 7.30am–2pm, 3.30–6pm; 40p), housed in the former Mevlevı dervish *tekke* of Nicosia.

The museum collection

The Mevlevı order survived here as a vital *tarikat* until 1954, long after their proscription in Republican Turkey. As so often in Cyprus, the early seventeenth-century building overshadows most of the exhibits. Centrally there's the fine pine-wood turning floor, just big enough for perhaps ten devotees; the musicians' gallery was perched overhead. The best souvenir on sale here is an archival photo-postcard showing one of the last ceremonies: the *şeyh* or head of the order watches over six dervishes turning in the confined space, while above in the gallery sit the players of *ney*, *oud* (Levantine lute) and *kudum* (paired drums). Display cases offer a motley collection of traditional clothing, musical instruments, archival photos, as well as more arcane items like Mrs Denktaş' Victrola gramophone. In a multiply-domed side hall, whose outline is so distinctive seen from the street, are serried tombs of the sixteen *şeyhs* associated with the *tekke*, including founder Arab Ahmet and the last *şeyh* Selim Dede, who died in 1953.

RAUF DENKTAŞ (1924–)

President of the Turkish Republic of Northern Cyprus (and its predecessor the Turkish Federated State of Cyprus), **Rauf Denktaş** is a classic example of a big fish in a small pond, simultaneously managing to enjoy a position in the world spotlight far out of proportion to the size of his realm. His non-recognition as a head of state – Denktaş' official title at UN-sponsored negotiations since 1974 is "representative of the Turkish-Cypriot community" – has never prevented him from acting like one.

Born in the Soléa valley village of Áyios Epifánios, Denktaş studied in London before serving as a protege of Dr Fazil Küçük, later first Vice-President of the unitary republic. Probably with the latter's knowledge, Denktaş in 1957 founded Volkan, the right-wing Turkish nationalist organisation modelled on the lines of Sinn Fein to counter the Greek Cypriots' EOKA. This was succeeded by the even more militant and reactionary **TMT** (*Türk Müdafaa Teskilati* or "Turkish Defence Organisation"), analogous to the IRA provos, banned (like EOKA) by the British but revived soon after independence.

Officially, Denktas had no connection with TMT after 1960, having accepted instead the more respectable chairmanship of the Turkish Communal Chamber. But he was expelled from Cyprus in 1964 for indirect involvement in the December 1963 disturbances, and sought refuge in Turkey. Denktaş was again sent to Anatolia upon being caught trying to land on the Kırpaşa (Kárpas) Peninsula in 1966, but returned under amnesty in 1968 to resume his leadership of the Communal Chamber. As the dominant personality in the Turkish community, overshadowing even his mentor Dr Küçük, he acted as the regular negotiator in the sporadic intercommunal negotiations which took place until the summer of 1974 – a strange role given his life-long conviction that living side by side with Greek Cypriots was undesirable if not impossible.

Girne Caddesi to Atatürk Meydanı

Tucked into a side street south of the *tekke* are more graves – this time arranged as a Şehitliği or Martyrs' Memorial created in 1963, and representative of many such in the North. A trilingual sign extolling the hundred-plus "unarmed and defence-less victims of Greek thugs" is somewhat undercut by the burial here of dozens of mainland Turkish soldiers who fell in the attack on the city 21–22 July 1974.

The commercial aspect of Girne Caddesi and the streets immediately around Atatürk Meydanı seems a faint echo of southern Nicosia, pitched primarily at soldiers and others from Turkey taking advantage of cheaper North Cyprus cloth-ing prices. In certain photo shops you see a popular ready-frame – intended for mainland conscripts writing home – in which airplanes, paratroopers and artillery pieces swirl around a blank spot for sticking one's mug shot, with overhead the motto *Barış için Savaş* ("War for Peace"). The 1974 Turkish intervention is universally proclaimed the "Peace Action" in North Cyprus, an Orwellian concept if there ever was one.

Atatürk Meydanı itself has been the hub of Turkish life in Nicosia since the Ottoman conquest, and is still surrounded by the British-built post office, law courts and a disproportionate number of banks. In Ottoman days it was known as Konak Meydanı, after the governor's mansion (*konak*) or more popularly *Saray*

Even before the establishment of a mono-ethnic North Cyprus in 1974–75, Denktaş was never squeamish about rough-and-tumble politics and (when neces-sary) resorting to pressure tactics. In 1963 he managed to get the Turkish Ambassador to Cyprus recalled for condemning the TMT murder of two leftist barristers who favoured greater intercommunal co-operation. Between 1970 and 1988, outspoken domestic opponents, such as Özker Özgür and Ahmet Berberoğlu, were intimidated or placed under house arrest. Lately, however, the North has acquired more earmarks of a democracy, including multi-party elections.

His own party, the **UBP** (*Ulusal Birlik Partisi* or "National Union Party"), has held power uninterruptedly in North Cyprus since 1975, and while as president Denktaş is officially non-sectarian, the UBP is still very much his creature: little tolerance is exhibited within the party apparatus towards those who disagree with him, government jobs are much easier to get with UBP membership, and once employed, civil servants are "encouraged" to vote for the party in various ways. He recently announced his intention to resign from all public offices in 1995, news greeted by relief in those domestic quarters fed up with his overbearing and auto-cratic manner. Despite (or because of) the UDI of 1983, more left-wing or commu-nally conciliatory elements in North-Cypriot life regard him as a mere cat's-paw of mainland Turkish policy, not acting in the long-term interest of the Turkish-Cypriot community.

Denktaş may attract some grudging admiration for a lifetime as a wily and tenacious negotiator, but as the years pass most observers are coming to realise that his consistent strategy of teasing the Greek Cypriots with proposals not really made in earnest, together with a moving of the goal posts when matters look hopeful, is merely a cover for incorrigible intransigence. Thus Denktaş can be currently reckoned the chief obstacle to any federal settlement of the Cyprus issue – sentiments officially reflected in a UN Security Council resolution of November 1992.

(palace) which stood to the southwest, in part the remains of a Lusignan/Venetian palace. Its gatehouse was the remnant of the palace destroyed by the British (see p.155); the name only lives on in the shape of the modern Saray hotel, and the mock-Moorish, *Belle Époque* Saray Önü Cami. In the centre of the roundabout, a grey **granite column** from Salamis, stuck here by the Venetians after 1489 and so erroneously called after them, was once surmounted by a Lion of Saint Mark; the Turks did away with the lion and toppled the column in 1570, which remained prone until 1915 when the British re-erected it, capping it with a neutral globe.

Baths and inns

From Atatürk Meydanı, Asmaaltı Sokağı leads southeast towards the bazaar and the main monumental zone. The **Büyük Hamam**, on a short street of the same name bearing off Asmaaltı, was once part of a fourteenth-century church, of which only the portal remains, slightly below ground level. In its current guise as north Nicosia's largest **public bath**, it's open from 7.30am to 10pm daily. Part of the existing complex is taken up by a souvenir shop specialising in good-quality basketry, but they're expensive – upwards of £20 for something suitable as a laundry hamper – and the proprietor is not much inclined to bargain. Another steambath, the **Korkut Hamamı** (daily 8am–10pm), is nearby on Beliğ Paşa Sokağı.

The Kumarcılar hanı and Büyük han

Within sight of the Büyük Hamam is the seventeenth-century **Kumarcılar hanı** or "Gamblers' Inn", well restored with shops occupying its outer perimeter, though the interior seems permanently shut. Once slated as the tourist office, it now houses the Antiquities Department of North Cyprus: if by chance you can get in, it's worth a stroll round the grassy courtyard through one of two arcade levels.

At the corner of Asmaaltı and Kurtbaba looms the **Büyük han**, one of the first Ottoman public works following the conquest; a *han* in medieval Turkey was an inn for both travelling merchants and their horses to spend the night. This one became the first city prison under British administration, but reverted in 1893 to a hostel for destitute families, something more like its original role. Finally realising plans on the drawing boards since before independence, the Büyük Han is now being restored for use as a museum. Accordingly there's only sporadic admission at present, at the whim of the construction crew: try to get in though, as it's a fine building, each of the guest rooms in the upper arcade originally heated by fireplaces. A little *mescit* (Islamic equivalent of a chapel), balances on six columns over its own *şadırvan* or ablutions fountain, a design seen elsewhere only at the Koza Hanı in Bursa, Turkey.

The bazaars

If you instead follow Girne Caddesi towards the Green Line, you intersect pedestrianised Arasta Sokağı, heart of North Nicosia's **main shopping district**. Clothing (especially cheap jeans) and yardage predominates, with machinists and junk metal depots in surrounding streets, but again it's a far cry from the twenty-six different bazaars of a century ago. A section of Girne Caddesi is still called the *Eski Kadınlar Pazarı* or "Former Women's Bazaar": not a female slave market, but rather where female vendors hawked a variety of textiles and household items of interest to other women. *Arasta* means a bazaar either physically built into the ground floor of a mosque, or if separate, one whose revenues go to the upkeep of a religious foundation. In this case the foundation concerned was probably the Selimiye Camii, reached by following Arasta Sokağı east until emerging in front of the covered bazaar and Bedesten (see below). The **Belediye Pazarı**, or covered municipal market (Mon–Fri 6am–1pm, Sat 6am–noon), shelters some worthwhile craft stalls in addition to the expected foodstuffs.

The Bedesten

The **Bedesten**, squatting between the Selimiye Camii and the covered market hall, was originally a sixth-century Byzantine church which 800 years later had the Roman Catholic Saint Nicholas church of the English grafted onto it, the whole being made the Greek Orthodox cathedral during the Venetian period. Under the Ottomans it served for a while as a grain store and cloth market (*bedesten* means a covered drapery or yardage bazaar), but was later allowed to deteriorate so that only the north vaulting remains intact. Today the building is kept locked to protect the collection of medieval tombstones stored here; even from outside the ground plans of two separate churches are apparent. The magnificent north portal, with six coats of arms above, is a lesser version of the fine Gothic arches of the Selimiye Camii's narthex.

The Selimiye Camii (Ayía Sofía)

The **Selimiye Camii**, originally the Roman Catholic cathedral of Ayía Sofía, is the oldest and one of the finest examples of Gothic art in Cyprus, the work of French masons who accompanied the Crusades. Construction began in 1209 during the reign of Lusignan King Henry I and lasted 150 years; it was consecrated in 1326 while still incomplete, and the blunt-roofed bell towers were never finished. The intricate west facade with its triple, sculpted portal and giant window above, seem transplanted directly from the Île de France. Within, Lusignan princes were crowned kings of Cyprus before proceeding to Famagusta for a second, essentially honorary coronation as king of Jerusalem.

When the Ottomans took the city in 1570, they reserved special hatred for the cathedral, chopping up the pulpit and pews for firewood and opening the tombs, scattering the bones within and using the tombstones as flooring; just a few escaped such treatment, and can be seen stacked in a former side chapel. The pair of incongruous, fifty-metre-high **minarets**, which constitute an unmissable landmark almost at the exact centre of the old city, were added immediately, but the building was only was officially renamed the Selimiye Camii in 1954.

As a still-active house of worship, there are no set visiting hours; try to visit during the five prayer times, when you are allowed in shoeless, modestly covered and silent. The sense of internal space is as as expected from such a soaring Gothic structure; abominating as good Muslims did all figurative representation, the Turks whitewashed the entire interior as part of their conversion process, so that the Selimiye presents a good example of clutter-free Gothic. But unhappily most of the original window tracery has disappeared over the centuries, replaced by tasteless modern concrete grilles. Other significant adaptations for Muslim worship include a *mihrab* (niche indicating the direction of Mecca) and *mimber* (pulpit from where the congregation leader may speak) set into the south transept, plus a women's gallery in the north transept.

Outside along the south wall, there's a rustic **café** patronised mostly by soldiers at the moment, but poised admirably for a future role as tourists' simultaneous vantage point for both the Selimiye and the Bedesten.

Other monuments

Behind the apse of the Selimiye, the diminutive **Sultan Mahumut Library** (Mon–Fri 7.30–2pm, 3.30–6pm; 40p admission) was founded by the Ottoman Governor Ali Ruhi in 1829 on behalf of the reforming Sultan Mahmut II. The appealing octagonal, domed building, which doubled as a *medrese* or religious academy, houses an impressive array of precious manuscripts.

Across the roundabout here (the Selimiye Meydanı) sits the **Lapidary Museum** (same hours and fee), an old Venetian house formerly known as the Jeffery Museum after the colonial official in charge of antiquities early this century. More compelling than any of the contents (bas reliefs from various other monuments) is the ornate Gothic window fitted into the north wall, all that was rescued from the Lusignan gatehouse which stood west of Atatürk Meydanı until being demolished under British rule.

Walking up Kırlızade Sokağı from the roundabout, you can't miss the **Haydarpaşa Camii**. Once the Lusignan church of Saint Catherine, and recently restored as an art gallery with restricted admission, it is the most substantial Gothic monument in Nicosia after the Selimiye Camii. This strange, assymmetrical building has buttresses and windows only on its curved south side. Over the south door sprouts an ornamental poppy or acanthus bud; the west facade decoration is similar, minus decoration but adorned with (appropriately) a Catherine window, shaped like the wheel of the saint's martyrdom. The minaret was tacked awkwardly onto the southwest corner of the structure; as at the Selimiye Camii, the original window tracery is long vanished.

Around the corner on Haydarpaşa Sokağı, Captain Horatio Herbert Kitchener – later the hero of Khartoum – lived from 1880 to 1883 while engaged in the first trigonometric survey and mapping of Cyprus. Unfortunately the house in question is too close to the Green Line to be visited without undue attention from the sentries.

Continuing north along Kırlızade Sokağı, you soon reach the **Yeni Cami** or "New Mosque", the eighteenth-century replacement for a previous one destroyed by a rapacious pasha in his dream-inspired conviction that treasure was concealed underneath. The townspeople complained to the sultan, who executed the impious malefactor, presumably confiscating his assets to build the new mosque. Just the minaret and a Gothic arch of the original building, which must have once been a church, remain marooned in what is now a schoolyard; the successor stands to one side, next to the tomb of the disgraced one. There are two more domed **tombs** across the narrow street.

A final item of interest east of Girne Caddesi is the former eighteenth-century church of **Áyios Loukás** near Alsancak Sokağı; Greeks hailing from this formerly mixed district claim it was completely wrecked during the disturbances of 1963–64, but be that as it may the church has been meticulously restored to house the municipality's Popular Art Association, with occasional exhibits.

The Arabahmet district

West of Girne Caddesi, the **Arabahmet district** is the counterpart to south Nicosia's Khrysaliniótissa neighbourhood, as you'll see strolling past imposing Ottoman houses on Zahra, Tanzimat and Salahi Şevket streets. But Master Plan or no, there's little sign yet of massive rehabilitation, given scarcer funds for this and lower population pressure than in the South; the Green Line is less obtrusive here, so many houses are still inhabited despite semi-dereliction.

The Arabahmet Cami

The unremarkable nineteenth-century **Arabahmet Camii**, named after the founder of the Mevlevi *tekke*, serves as the fulcrum and namesake of the district. A hair of the Prophet's beard is said to be kept therein, and shown to the faithful once a year; Archduke Salvator saw instead an ostrich egg suspended before the *mihrab*. As at the Selimiye Camii, the courtyard is paved partly with Lusignan tombstones taken from a church formerly on this site, and also shelters the more venerated tomb of Kâmil Paşa, briefly Grand Vezir of the Ottoman Empire around the turn of the century and the only Cypriot ever to have that honour.

Arabahmet was, until the troubles, a mixed neighbourhood, as witnessed by scattered houses with Greek or Armenian inscriptions. The spire of the Roman Catholic church, straddling the Line between North and South, punctuates the south end of Salahi Şevket Sokağı; east of it, inaccessible in the dead zone, stands the fourteenth-century Armenian church of the Virgin. The Armenian community was expelled from this area at the end of 1963 by TMT, on the grounds that they had allied themselves with the Greek Cypriots.

The first street north of the Line on which you can head east without obstruction is Beliğ Paşa Sokağı (the Turkish spelling of Bligh), with its **Derviş Paşa Konağı** (daily 7.30am–2pm & 4–5pm; 40p), an ethnographic collection that's the North's version of the Hadjiyiorgakis Kornesios house. And once again, the well-restored building being at least as interesting as the embroidery, copperware and basketry adorning the room mock-ups. Original builder and owner Derviş Paşa was the publisher of Cyprus' first Turkish **newspaper**, archival copies of which are also displayed. In the courtyard a **bar** sporadically functions, and behind it certainly the cleanest **loos** in the city.

Sleeping and eating

North Nicosia has almost no international-standard tourist facilities since few foreigners stay the night. There are just three **hotels**: the expensive *Saray* on Atatürk Meydanı (☎83115), tallest building in the old quarter; the *Orient*, way out near the junction of Akif and Demirel (☎72162); and the mid-range, recently built *Demerka* (☎83406), very near the bus terminal with rates starting at £10 single bed and breakfast. Considering the location it's reasonably comfortable and quiet, as long as you're at least two floors below the roof bar/restaurant – or don't expect any early nights.

For the sake of completeness, it's worth mentioning the dozen or so dilapidated **pensions** tucked in various corners of the old city. But these, with nostalgic Anatolian names like *Antalya* and *Bursa Uludağ* are intended for off-duty soldiers and shoppers from the mainland, and signs like "Monthly rate 150,000TL" (about £12 sterling at contemporary rates), plus the pong of bad drains, do not bespeak Sheraton comfort. Of interest only to compulsive slummers.

Restaurants

The range of choice in **restaurants** is slightly better. The best cheap lunchtime kebab in town, costing not more than £2.50, is widely acknowledged to be had at *Sabır*, near the entrance of the Büyük Han car park. The name, appropriately, means "patient" in Turkish, since on busy days it can take 45 minutes for your order to appear – and you won't get served at all if the eccentric proprietor doesn't like your looks.

For those not so fanatical about their kebab, *Anibal*, on the Saraçoğlu Meydanı off İstanbul Caddesi, is a good alternative. Other choices include *Zir*, on İstanbul Caddesi across from the National Struggle Museum, and the *Sahara Et Lokantası* on Yirmidokuz Ekim Sokağı, behind the Mevlevi Tekke, clean and cheerful on the ground floor of an old house. For sweet teeth, the *Londra Pastanesi* at İnönü Meydanı dishes up Turkish ice cream.

If you've a car, *Ballı* in Gönyeli, on the old road to Kyrenia, is worth the trip for more elegant grills at supper time. But the most famous "suburban" nocturnal eatery is *Bizim Ahır*, on Kahramanlar Sokağı near the corner of Bülent Hüseyin Sokak, in Küçük Kaymaklı. The name, meaning "Our Barn", stems from the fact that the premises were once an abandoned house used as a sheep pen; it's popular with the power elite, including on occasion North Cypriot leader Rauf Denktaş himself. The *meze* plates – everything from mushrooms to *kağıt kebab* (paper-roasted meat) – are excellent, and the colourful proprietor – a former smuggler into the enclaves, jailed by the Greeks – can sometimes be persuaded to converse in English.

Bizim Ahır lies at the edge of a vast area of desolate houses. You are still more than 200m from the Green Line; this devastation was perpetrated between 22 and 25 December 1963 by Nikos Sampson and his EOKA-B irregulars (see p.274), who shot up the Turkish streets of what was then the mixed district of Omórfita. Except for a 1978-erected cenotaph honouring the many casualties, the ruins have never been repaired or re-occupied, but left as a memorial, and shown to schoolchildren to keep fear and hatred of the Greeks alive, part of an ongoing process that ensures the island's division.

Listings

Airlines *Cyprus Turkish Airlines*, main terminal at corner Bedreddin Demirel Cad and Hüseyin Boru Sok, branch office on Atatürk Meydanı (☎83820); *Onur Air*, Kemal Aşık Cad, opposite bus terminal (☎85827); *Pegasus Air*, c/o President Travel, Mecidiye Sok 7 (☎82711); *Istanbul Airlines*, Mirata Apt 3–4, Osman Paşa Cad (☎83140).

Bookstores *Kemal Rüstem*, Girne Cad 26, is a bit dusty but has a limited stock of English books on the island, including some co-published here. *Hazım Remzi*, ground floor of the Saray Hotel, is a newsagent with a selection of foreign newpapers and magazines, usually fairly recent.

Car hire Try *Capital*, in the Firko Building on Uluçamgil Sok, behind the Orient hotel (☎78172); *Elite*, Girne Cad 103; *Elmaslar*, Girne Cad 89; *Sun*, Abdi İpekçi Cad (☎78787); and *Travelöz*, Muzaffer Paşa Cad, Hacı Ali Apt 50 (☎77147).

Cultural centres/interest offices Because of North Cyprus' international non-recognition, none of the foreign institutions here can officially have consular or ambassadorial status, despite depiction as such on tourist maps. They exist primarily for cultural outreach to the Turkish Cypriots, provision of libraries and events for expatriates, and assistance in dire emergencies for travellers. They are: the *American Centre* on Güner Türkmen Sok, in Köşklu Çiftlik district northeast of the walled precinct; the *British Council* (☎71938), housed in the former embassy chancellery of the old unified republic, near the Green Line off Mehmet Akif Cad 23 (summer hours Mon–Fri 7.30am–1.30pm; Tues & Thurs 3.30–6pm; no afternoon hours in Aug; earlier afternoon hours in winter); an *Australian representation division* (☎77332) in the Saray hotel; and the *German Cultural Centre*, at Yirmisekiz Kasım Sokak (☎75161). Each publishes lists of forthcoming events.

Exchange The *Kıbrıs Kooperatif Merkez Bankası* on the corner of Nuri Efendi and Mahmut Paşa in the old town has a *Visa/Access*-accepting cashpoint machine. Otherwise, *Sun* car hire on Abdi İpekçi, also a currency exchange house which claims to accept personal cheques; *Ertuğrul Akbel*, Hacı Ali Apt, Osman Paşa Cad; *Merimann Currency Exchange*, İkinci Selim Cad 49E.

Post offices Central branch on Sarayönü Sok, just off Atatürk Meydanı (Mon–Fri 7.30am–2pm and 4–6pm; Sat 8.30am–12.30pm); parcels at the Yenişehir branch, Atatürk Cad 6–9, corner Ecvet Yusuf Caddesi.

Public toilets Near the Büyük Hamam, and on the ramparts east of the Kyrenia Gate.

Shopping Try antique shops by the Selimiye Camii, or the mentioned basket shop in the Büyük Hamam.

Travel agency A very helpful one with fluent English-speaking management is *Birinci Turizm*, at Girne Cad 158A (☎83200), which can arrange hotel bookings and car hire in particular at competitive prices.

AROUND NORTH NICOSIA

It is actually easier to approach the western salient of North Cyprus from Kyrenia, but since the end of Ottoman rule the attractions in this section have always been part of Nicosia district. With an early start, all the following sites can be toured in a single day – as you're advised to do, as there's just a single, modest hotel along the way (*Güzelyurt*, ☎071/43412).

Given the orientation of the Attila Line, use of the direct main road from Nicosia to the west is not possible; from the northwestern roundabout between Ortaköy and Gönyeli, traffic heads first to YILMAZKÖY (Skylloúra) and then via paved but secondary roads to Güzelyurt.

Güzelyurt (Mórfou)

Mention **GÜZELYURT** (Mórfou, Omorfo) to even the more moderate among the Greek- and Turkish-Cypriot communities and you'll quickly learn just how far apart are their negotiating positions on acceptable minimums. Besides the loss of the tourist infrastructure and the port of Famagusta, the abandonment of the Mórfou plain with its burgeoning citrus orchards, melon patches and strawberry fields irrigated by vast underground water reserves was a crushing blow to Greek-Cypriot enterprise. Not surprisingly, the South insists on the return of some, preferably all, of the basin as part of any settlement; North Cyprus, with more than ten percent of its population now settled here, and the *Sunzest* citrus export co-op based here being one of its few dependable hard-currency earners, demurs. Moreover, the Turkish side claims that before 1974 the Greek Cypriots overdrew the local water table, causing the nearby sea to contaminate it; with Turkish aid the Northern administration improved existing reservoirs east of the town to recharge aquifers.

Today, as in the past, Güzelyurt serves as a busy market town for the fertile plain around, with little to detain casual tourists. Approaching from Kyrenia – a more likely prospect – railway buffs should keep an eye peeled for an isolated section of track east of the road supporting a **Baldwin locomotive** made in Philadelphia in 1924. This is one of two surviving relics (the other is in Famagusta) of the vanished railway across the Mesaoría, which ceased operating in 1951. Bear right at the edge of town, following signposts towards Lefke. Soon you should see a nineteenth-century church with its belfry-top shot off, then the double minarets of a new Saudi-financed mosque, and finally the dome of Áyios Mámas church.

The museum and monastery

You can park nearby in front of the local **archaeological and natural history museum** (vague hours; 50p admission). Specimens of the stuffed-animal collection, including two-headed and eight-legged lambs, are a bit bedraggled, but the bird section is a good way to learn their Turkish names. Upstairs, several galleries contain clay objects from all periods, including one wing devoted to the nearby Bronze-Age site of Toúmba tou Skoúrou, but it can't compare to any collection in the South.

The museum warden will admit you to the adjacent church of **Áyios Mámas**, long the focus of the cult of Cyprus' most beloved saint. Originally built in Byzantine times on the site of a pagan temple, it acquired Gothic embellishments in the fifteenth century, and had a dome added 300 years later. The interior is in reasonable condition, if dusty, and currently functions as a warehouse for icons rescued from around the district. A magnificent *témblon*, where lamps dangle from gargoyles, is the equal of massive columns and imposing masonry; you have to stoop under arches to reach the seats of the upstairs *yinaikonítis*, evidence that it was added long after the original construction.

The tomb of Mamas

But you have come, as did the faithful pre-1974, mainly to admire the purported **tomb of Mamas**, on the left as you enter the north door; above the marble sarcophagus, undeniably ancient, a dangling curtain is festooned with votive offerings in the shape of ears – a strange image in view of the fact that the saint principally warded off tax collectors. But the story runs that early during Ottoman rule, Turks, convinced that there was treasure hidden in the coffin, bored holes in its side, at which a sort of nectar oozed out, terrifying the desecrators into desisting. The stuff, which appeared thereafter at unpredictable intervals, was claimed sovereign against earache, and additionally had the property of calming a stormy sea if poured on the waves. On the exterior west wall, there's a naive relief of Mamas on his lion; the legend behind this iconography is given on p.149.

On the roundabout behind the museum, a larger-than-usual **monument** honours Turkish Cypriots killed by EOKA in the South between 1950 and 1974 – plus a recent casualty in 1980.

Lefke and its coast

Soon after Güzelyurt you emerge on the great bight forming the namesake bay, but initially it's a shingly, windswept coast not tempting for a swim. At **GEMİKONAĞI** (Karavostási), 17km along, is an old ore-loading pier wrecked by bombs in August 1974, although the mines inland were nearly played out by then anyway. It's been replaced by a new conveyor-belted jetty for other cargoes besides ore, but Gemikonağı will always lag far behind Famagusta and Kyrenia as a commercial port.

You'll probably be needing to **eat** by this point: between Yeşilyurt (Pendáyia) and Gemikonağı, *Nüvid'in Yeri* is an unpretentious but good-value fish-and-meat grill overlooking the sea, while *Mardin Plajı*, between the two jetties, is not so cheap, but the food is okay and they've strewn sand for a small beach at the edge of the premises. Beyond the westerly jetty and ancient Soli (for which see below), at **YEDİDALGA** (Potamós tou Kámbou), acceptable **beaches** finally appear; the shore is pebbly but the warm sea shelves gently over a sand bottom, fine for pre- or post-ruin dips.

Lefke (Léfka)

To reach Lefke, turn inland at Gemikonağı, passing a former Danish UN post labelled "Viking Camp" before bumping over the level crossing of a rare surviving section of the Cyprus railway. **LEFKE** (Léfka) itself is an old Turkish-Cypriot stronghold at the base of the Troödhos foothills; abundant water audible in runnels everywhere has fostered lush orchards forming a stark contrast to the naked hills. *Léfka* means "poplar" in Greek but it's predominantly a date-palm and citrus oasis, claiming to have the best oranges on Cyprus, with apricots and plums thrown in for good measure. A single open-cast copper mine still supposedly works nearby in northern territory, but after the erection of the Attila Line and severance of any connection with the main mines further inland at Skouriótissa, the population fell from over 5000 to under 3000.

Drive through the town – which has no conventional tourist facilities – to catch a glimpse of the unremarkable but pleasing **Piri Osman Paşa** mosque at the edge of the oasis, flanked by palm trees and with the sere mountains as a backdrop. In the courtyard of the little mosque (usually locked) stands the ornate marble tomb of Vezir Osman Paşa, an Ottoman worthy supposedly poisoned as part of a political intrigue and buried here in 1820. Back in Lefke proper, rambling old houses are scattered among the aqueduct-webbed greenery; up on the main road you'll see

KIBRISLI ŞEYH NAZİM & CO

Lefke has of late earned some notoriety as the power base of Naqshbandi Sufi leader **Kıbrıslı Şeyh Nazim**. The Naqshbandi order of Sufism, currently also active in Bulgaria and what was formerly Yugoslavia, emphasises the importance and personal authority of the *murshid* or spiritual leader – a doctrine eminently suitable for demagogues or people with political ambitions. The teachings of the order tend towards the reactionary, often attracting a similar brand of follower. A trained engineer speaking a half-dozen languages fluently, Şeyh Nazim is said to be dangerously persuasive; Dr Küçük, vice president under the old republic, saw fit to jail, then exile him to Lebanon. In 1974 he returned, and reportedly both Turkish President Özal and North-Cypriot leader Denktaş number among his adherents – as well as numbers of locally resident Westerners, including (briefly in 1988) pop singer Cat Stevens, or Yusuf Islam as he is now known. Recently a major scandal erupted here, with several of the Europeans busted for cannabis use; the *şeyh* disavowed all responsibility.

some British Imperial architecture, a small university campus, and a trilingual plaque marking the graves of the **Gaziveran incident** victims.

In 1964 hundreds of EOKA activists had attacked the enclaved village of Gaziveran, near Yeşilyurt, whose inhabitants held them off with a dozen hunting rifles, at the cost of these casualties, until Turkey threatened action and a ceasefire was negotiated. On the roundabout just below is a more-extreme-than- usual equestrian statue of Atatürk on a prancing stallion.

Ancient sites: Soli and Vouni

Less than a kilometre after the *Mardin* restaurant, the ruins of ancient Soli (daily during daylight hours; admission 50p) is signposted inconspicuously on the inland side of the road – stay alert, as it's easy to miss.

Soli

Soli was one of the ten ancient city-kingdoms of Cyprus, legendarily founded early in the sixth century BC when the Athenian law-giver Solon, who supposedly lived here for a while, persuaded King Philocyprus to move the city down from a bluff overhead to its present site. But like Leonardo Da Vinci's purported visit to Léfkara, this probably never happened, and there appears to have been a town at this location since the late Bronze Age, its name more likely a corruption of the Hittite word Sillu. Whatever its origins, it became a hotbed of pro-Hellenic sentiment, and was the last holdout against the Persians in 498 BC. The name in turn engendered that of Soléa, the Troödhos foothill region inland, whose copper mines near present-day Skouriótissa spurred the growth of Soli, especially during Roman times, from which period most of the surviving ruins date. A Swedish expedition, funded by the archaeology-loving Crown Prince of Sweden, excavated the theatre between 1928 and 1930, while the post-independence government restored it badly with modern materials in 1963 (the original masonry now lines the Suez canal and the quays of Port Said). A Canadian team uncovered the basilica and part of the agora after 1964.

The site

The over-restored-in-concrete **theatre** from the second century AD looks out over the narrow but lush coastal plain, courtesy of the streams draining from Lefka, towards the new conveyor-jetty. Judging from the plywood stage and electrical fittings, the theatre is still a venue for occasional summer performances.

Lower down by the car park are foundations of a large fifth-century **basilica**, whose floor boasts fine **mosaics**, both abstract and animal. As at Nea Paphos in the South, it's evident that the mosaic floor belonged to a huge basilica destroyed in the seventh century; some of the mosaics were built over during construction of a smaller, later church closer to the apse where a mosaic inscription has been partly obliterated. During the Lusignan period, Soli was apparently the see of the banished Orthodox bishop of Nicosia, who would have mulled over the vagaries of fate amid little but rubble.

Excavations in the **agora**, west of the custodian's hut and below the amphitheatre, were suspended after 1974 (as was all work in the North) and it is now fenced off, but before then a colonnaded paved street leading through the market to a nymphaeum (fountain shrine) had already been uncovered, as had the famous Aphrodite statuette and the bronze boy's head, both now in the Cyprus Museum.

The palace of Vouni

At the mysterious hilltop **palace of Vouni**, five twisty kilometres west towards the nearby Atilla Line, there's less to see, but a most spectacular setting with views both over the sea and inland to the Tillyrian ridges. Watch for a "Vouni Sarayi" sign pointing right a few hundred metres after the coast road's pavement ends. Along the side road, you'll notice charcoal burners' pyramids, more vital than ever since wood-burning bread ovens were banned recently in the interest of air quality and tree preservation.

A little history

Vouni's history is controversial and obscure; even the original name is unknown, the modern one merely meaning "mountain" in Greek. It seems probable that the palace was first built around 480 BC by a pro-Persian king of Marion as an outpost to intimidate pro-Athenian Soli in the wake of a failed revolt; a few decades later another insurrection established a pro-Hellenic dynasty, which redesigned the premises. All sources agree that some time after 400 BC the palace was destroyed by agents unknown upon re-establishment of Persian dominion. The Swedish Expedition dug here concurrently with their work at Soli.

The site

The site is partially enclosed, and the ticket booth only sporadically attended. Focus of the palace is a monumental **seven-stepped stairway** leading down into a couryard, where a guitar-shaped stele, slotted at the top for a windlass, is propped on end before a deep **cistern**. This is one of several collection basins on the bluff top, as the water supply was a problem – and a priority, as suggested by the sophisticated bathing and drainage facilities of the luxury-loving ruling caste in the northwest corner of the palace. At the centre of the **stele**, where you'd expect the "sounding hole" to be, is an unfinished carved face, thought to be a goddess.

The original **Persian entry** to the royal apartments, along a natural stone ramp at the southwest corner of the precinct, is marked by a rusty sign; it was later closed off after the change of rulers and the entry moved to the north side of the central court, the residential quarters subsequently arrayed around this in the Mycenaean style. In the wake of the remodelling, the palace is thought to have grown to 137 rooms on two floors, the upper storey of mud bricks and thus long vanished.

Between the palace and the access road on its north flank is what appears to be a temple with remains of an obvious **altar** at the centre; on the opposite side of the site, beyond the car park and just below the modern trigonometric point, are the scarcely more articulate traces of a late fifth-century BC **Athena temple**, all but merging into the exposed rock strata here. Yet it must have been popular and revered in its day, for a large cache of votive offerings (now in the Cyprus Museum) was found here.

travel details

Buses

From Nicosia to **Girne** Several hourly during daylight hours; 30min: to **Famagusta** every 20 min; 1hr: to **Güzelyurt** half-hourly; 45min: to **İskele** 5–6 daily; 50min.

From Güzelyurt to **Lefke** half-hourly; 30min.

Flights

From Ercan to **Gatwick** 4 weekly in season; to **Stansted** 2 weekly in season; to **Heathrow** 2 weekly in season; to **Manchester** 1 weekly in season.

Remember that all flights into and out of North Cyprus make a stop in Turkey to get around the international boycott. Thus total travel time can vary from seven to nine hours, rather than the five you'd expect.

CHAPTER SEVEN

KYRENIA AND THE NORTH COAST

Kyrenia and its environs have long been considered the most beautiful landscape on Cyprus, thanks to the imposing line of high hills to the south which temper the climate and separate the area from the rest of the island. More than one writer has characterised the Kyrenia mountains as the quintessential Gothic range; the limestone crags seem to mimic or suggest not only the handful of castles which stud them, but also the delicate tracery of the Lusignan cathedrals in Nicosia and Famagusta, towns clearly visible from the heights, and the pointed arches of the contemporary abbey at Bellapais, in the foothills.

These hills seem remarkably two-dimensional, rising to over a thousand metres from a very narrow coastal plain and running for some 70km roughly east to west, but plunging equally swiftly down to the Mesarya (Mesaoría) plain to form a veritable wall. In particular they act as an efficient barrier to moisture-laden cloud, with rainfall on the north flank a good fifty percent higher than on the inland side. Springs erupt suddenly partway down the grade on the the seaward slopes, keeping things relatively green and cool even in high summer and permitting the irrigation of various orchard and market-garden crops. Under exceptional conditions, Anatolia's Toros mountains are clearly visible across the Karamanian Straits.

Kyrenia, capital of the namesake district, is also lynchpin of tourism here with its compact old quarter arrayed around a harbour. When the distractions of the town pale – fairly quickly for most – **Karaman, Alsancak** and **Lapta**, spectacularly set foothill villages in the lushest part of the barrier range, beckon to the west. A mixture of Turkish military facilities and hotels co-exist uneasily along the shore below, with the fishing anchorage of **Güzelyalı** marking the end of the "strip". Beyond, the thinly populated **Koruçam (Kormakíti) peninsula** with its dwindling Maronite villages makes a good destination for a day's drive, returning via the southwestern slopes of the Kyrenia hills on scenic, if little-travelled, back roads.

Southeast of Kyrenia, the Lusignan abbey of **Bellapais** very much tops the list of things to see, despite its relative commercialisation; the surrounding village of **Beylerbeyi**, with its neighbours **Ozanköy** and **Çatalköy**, have always been relatively elegant bedroom annexes of Kyrenia. Down on the coast, a succession of excellent beaches – in particular **Lara, "Turtle Bay"** and **Onüçüncü Mil** – remain as yet almost undeveloped.

The **Kyrenia hills** themselves offer satisfying destinations for a few days' outings: the celebrated castles of **Saint Hilarion** and **Buffavento**, and the less-known attractions of the Alevkaya area, including the remote, abandoned **monastery of Antifonítis**.

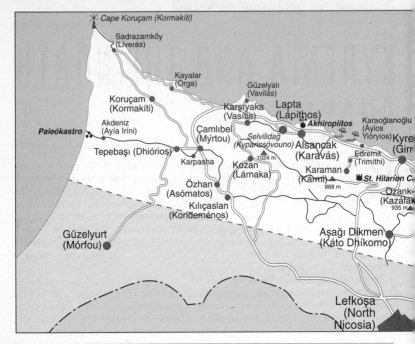

Kyrenia (Girne)

Despite unsightly expansion since 1974, **KYRENIA (GİRNE)** can still easily lay claim to being Cyprus' most attractive coastal town, and the one with the most resonant reputation in foreign circles – helped along by Lawrence Durrell, along with scores of other eulogising and expatriate Brits. It's certainly the only resort on the island that has anything of the feel of the central Mediterranean; down at the ruthlessly picturesque harbour the Turkish Cypriots have no qualms about playing "Zorba's Dance" on endless loop tapes to impart Aegean "atmosphere". Move away from the kernel of the old town, however, and you could be almost anywhere in coastal Turkey or Cyprus: new three-to-four-storey blocks redeemed only by the magnificent backdrop of the Kyrenia range. The highlights of Kyrenia can easily be seen on foot in a day, even if the two museums that are currently shut re-open; the harbour and its guardian castle are most of what's on offer.

Some history

Kyrenia was founded by Mycenaean settlers in the tenth century BC, and figured among the ten city-kingdoms of Classical Cyprus, but little was heard from it until the Byzantines built the castle in the wake of the seventh-century Arab raids which contemptuously swept through the town's rickety outer walls. Thereafter the history of the place more or less parallels its castle (for which see p.207). Like the other ports on the island, Kyrenia only began to grow after the start of British administration, following the construction of roads to the interior and improvements to the harbour.

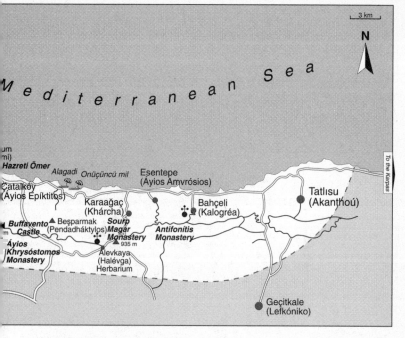

As the British Empire imploded after World War II, and redundant or retired colonial civil servants drifted homeward from less pleasant postings via Cyprus, many got no further than Kyrenia and its stage-set harbour. Especially those without family ties reckoned correctly that "home" had uncongenially changed beyond recognition, and even after Cypriot independence British ex-pats made up a substantial fraction of the town's population, with hundreds more in the surrounding villages. Foreign numbers plummeted after the events of 1974 in response to the rigours of early Turkish administration, and only recently have they again attained three figures, against the town's current population of over 7000.

Arrival, orientation and information

If you've **flown** in, taxis tend to take the wider road from Ercan airport to Kyrenia via Nicosia; this becomes Ecevit Caddesi as it enters city limits from the south, depositing you at the central roundabout, **Belediye Meydanı** Under your own steam it's also possible to use the narrower but quicker bypass road via DEĞERMENLİK (KYTHRÉA), which enters Kyrenia to the east.

Ferryboats from Turkey dock at the new commercial harbour, about 1km east of the town centre. The main east–west thoroughfare through town doubles as the coast road and changes names a few times: **Hürriyet Caddesi** west of Ecevit, **Cumhuriyet Caddesi** (but still shown as Mustafa Cağatay on many maps) on the east side of town, becoming **İskenderun Caddesi** between the turning for Bellapais and the access road to the port.

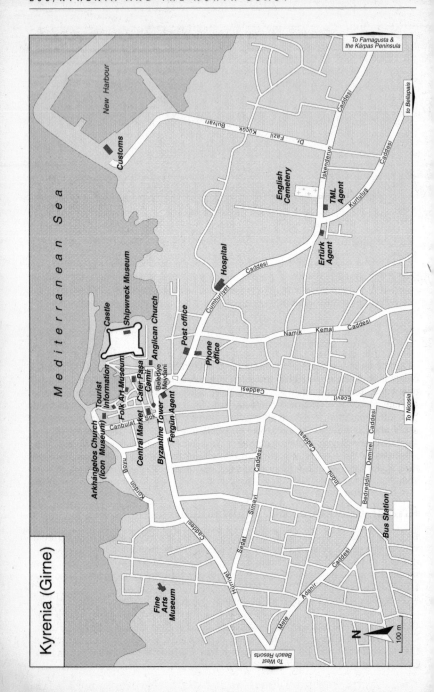

Kyrenia (Girne)

Mediterranean Sea

New Harbour

Customs

To Famagusta &
the Kárpas Peninsula

to Bellapais

Dr Fazıl Küçük Bulvarı

İskenderun Caddesi

Kurtuluş Caddesi

English
Cemetery

TML Agent

Ertürk
Agent

Hospital

Cumhuriyet Caddesi

Namık Kemal Caddesi

Ecevit Caddesi

Post office

Phone
office

Castle

Shipwreck Museum

Anglican Church

Cafer Paşa
Camii

Belediye
Meydani

Tourist
Information

Folk Art Museum

Central Market

Byzantine Tower

Fergün Agent

Sok

Canbulat

Arkhángelos Church
(Icon Museum)

Kozan Boyu

Bedreddin Demirel Caddesi

İnönü Caddesi

To Nicosia

Bus Station

Sinavi Caddesi

Sedat Caddesi

Hümüm Caddesi

Mete

Adanır

To West
Beach Resorts

Fine
Arts
Museum

N

100 m

Despite post-1974 sprawl, Kyrenia is not dauntingly large, though **parking** is a problem in high season; besides the central lot, a limited number of spaces lie along two dead-end streets down by the castle. Except for the old harbour itself, cars are allowed to circulate along **Kordon Boyu**, the shore road.

The **tourist information** office, set just back from the old harbour, stays open Monday to Friday 7.30am to 2pm, with an extra Monday afternoon shift of 3.30 to 6pm, but is fairly useless – leaflet stocks are low and English may not even be spoken. If you're staying any amount of time, the **expat notice board** in front of the post office, with info on outings, group meetings, real estate and services, is likely to give more joy.

Kyrenia castle

An amalgam of different periods and thus irregularly shaped, **Kyrenia castle** (daily 8am–1pm, 2–5pm; 75p) has only the citadel of Famagusta as a rival for interest on the island. The present Venetian structure represents an adaptation of previous Byzantine and Lusignan castles, as at Nicosia: much of the walls' present thickness was achieved by simply filling in with rubble the space between the compact Byzantine and overextended Lusignan fortifications, and you can still see a now-superfluous round tower stump up on Hürriyet Caddesi, near Belediye Meydanı, and another remnant – possibly the base of a medieval lighthouse – out in the middle of the old port.

Some history

The Byzantines probably built atop the site of a Roman fort; Guy de Lusignan seized the castle in 1191, finding the Armenian wife and daughter of Isaac Comnenus hiding inside. It subsequently served as an ultimate funk-hole during turbulent periods, as in 1426 when the Mamelukes overran the island, and again between 1460 and 1464 by Queen Charlotte, until her deposition by half-brother James. Rebels and disgraced personalities were also incarcerated here throughout the Lusignan period, including the rebellious Ibelin lords during Henry II's rule, and Peter I's mistress, shut up briefly by his wife.

The castle was never taken by force, repelling a fierce Genoese attack in 1374; its defenders always starved under siege or surrendered, as in 1570 when the Ottomans induced the defenders to capitulate by sending as a threat the severed heads of the Venetian commanders of fallen Nicosia. Thus the massive southeast, southwest and northwest towers – all raised to slightly different specifications by the Venetians according to their military application – were not put to the test as at Famagusta. As elsewhere in the Ottoman empire, non-Muslims were forbidden access to the citadel after dark, when the ruling caste would retire there for the night. The British used it as a prison early in their administration, and again between 1954 and 1960 for EOKA captives.

A tour of the walls and the Shipwreck Museum

Today you enter the castle from the northwest via a bridge over the former moat. The first passage on the left leads to the tiny but perfectly formed **Byzantine chapel**; it stood outside the perimeter walls until the Venetians incorporated it into their circuit. The next ramp left, originally used for wheeling cannon, heads up to the round **northwest tower**, and the start of a partial wall circuit (it's not possible to go all the way round owing to military use). The expected views of the harbour are at your feet, and you can make out Saint Hilarion castle up on its peak; along the original Byzantine **west wall**, the remains of Lusignan apartments and a chapel are also visible. The **northeast bastion** contains a large vaulted room, its coolness welcome in summer despite its use as a toilet by birds and humans; from here steps descend to a series of chambers and finally the courtyard.

This is used for occasional performances, and also gives access to the **Shipwreck Museum** (same hours; additional 75p admission). The displays concern a cargo boat which sank just off Kyrenia some 2300 years ago, discovered over a hundred feet down by a local diver in 1967. It is the oldest shipwreck known, and carbon-14 dating indicates it had been in service for nearly eighty years and much repaired when it foundered. The boat had just plied the coast of Anatolia, judging by freight from Samos, Kos and Rhodes – most of it stone grain-grinders which could double as ballast, and nearly 400 amphoræ of wine. A four- or five-man crew existed mainly on almonds, large quantities of which were found intact, and such fish as they managed to catch.

The upper levels of the exhibit halls show photos of the archaeological dive, and lead to the viewing platform over the **wreck** itself, soaked in preservative and kept in a cool, dry, dimly lit environment now that it's out of the protecting seabed mud. Curiously, the ship was built in the reverse of modern techniques: the lengthwise planks of Aleppo pine were laid down first, the cross-ribbing later.

Around the harbour

Although the British closed off its former north entrance and extended the breakwater east past the castle after World War II, Kyrenia's little **harbour** had ceased to be a working one even before 1974, despite being by far the safest anchorage on the north coast. It is now devoted entirely to pleasure craft touting all-day tours along the coast (for about £15, including a meal and drinks), the rental of speedboats, scuba-dive operations, and berths for several dozen yachts.

The former church of Arkhángelos (the Archangel Michael), whose belfry provides a prominent landmark on the rise west of the water, now houses the **Icon museum** (daily 9am–1pm and 3–5pm; 50p). The large collection offers an assortment of folky seventeenth- to nineteenth-century examples, rescued from unspecified churches in the district. Most interesting is a rare icon of the ecumenical council of 843 which restored icon worship after the Iconoclastic period.

By contrast the **Folklore museum** midway along the quay, said to contain traditional rural implements in a reconstructed-house format, is closed indefinitely for "repairs", as is the **Fine Arts museum,** the non-Cypriot knick-knack collection of a former ex-pat, out at the west edge of town. More specifically Ottoman and Cypriot, the chunky **Cafer Paşa Camii** stands one street back from the water; sometimes you can't get in because of a funeral, when the municipality lays on a hearse inscribed in Turkish "Only God is Immortal".

Inland from the icon museum, near the intersection of Canbulat Sokak and Hürriyet Caddesi, the covered **central market** stands very near the relict Byzantine castle tower.

The Kyrenia city phone code is ☎081

Finding a place to stay

If you want to savour the atmosphere of the old quarter and aren't sold on the idea of basing yourself in a remote, self-contained holiday complex, there are a number of modest but acceptable **hotels** within a short distance of the harbour, sometimes with a partial view of the water. All offer discounts for stays of a week or more, but if you can pay three-star rates, however, it probably is best to be out of town somewhere.

Hotel Bristol, Hürriyet Caddesi (☎52298). Colonial one-star relic with a courtyard garden, though some street noise; £6 single, £9 double.

Girne Pansiyon, Canbulat Sok 3 (☎53603). Used to backpacking or long-stay foreigners; coyly refuses to quote prices – you bargain. **Kanguru**, down the same street a bit towards the water (☎54587), is similar, cites a double price of £8.

Sidelya Hotel, Nası Güneş Sok 7, downhill from the Belediye Meydanı (☎53951). A newish, mid-range option that deserves a try; convenient and quiet except for occasional broadcasts from nearby minaret; £8 single, £12 double.

Hotel British (formerly the *Ergenekon*), right on the yacht harbour (☎52240, fax 52742). Despite the name, you have to squeeze in between mostly German and Austrian tour groups, and the location is determining the price at £15 single, £19 double.

Hotel Atlantis, one street back from the old harbour (☎52242). A Germanophone-group clientele here also; £13 single, £18 double.

The three-star *Grand Rock* and four-star *Dome* hotels on Kordon Boyu, despite their colonial-institution status and (in the latter case) Durrellian associations, figure prominently in tour brochures but seem over-priced for what they offer; the *Anadol* and *Dorana*, well inland on Hürriyet Caddesi, are pitched at a less well-heeled package market.

Eating, drinking and nightlife

It's difficult to resist eating or at least drinking in the old port at least once, where a half-dozen-plus restaurants and bars shamelessly exploit their position. Starting from the east end of the quay, the *Harbour Club Downstairs* (as opposed to the flashy *Upstairs*) is okay for quick snacks, though even these are pricey; the place is obviously banking on its reputation as a watering-hole of assorted nobs from the 1950s onwards. For a full meal, *Halil's* at the northwest end of the quay is longest established and marginally the least expensive of the bunch, offering roast chicken and full *meze* for just over £4, drinks extra; elsewhere you should count on £5 or more for a rather light, non-seafood meal. Away from the water prices don't drop much but quality improves, for instance at *Rahat Köşe* near the Cafer Paşa Camii or at the *Perge*, perched above some ancient rock-cut tombs opposite the Icon museum. Best of all is *Tepebaşı*, well inland on Nurettin Ersin Caddesi, behind the bus station, with view-terrace seating and a set meal of salads and meat plates aside from the usual kebab – go with an empty stomach.

Nightlife – or rather the lack of it – conforms very much to the tenor of fifty-something family tourism hereabouts. Certain hotels, such as the *Dome*, *Mare Monte* and the *Celebrity* (the latter two well west of town), have **discos** attached, open to non-guests; the only independent disco seems to be *Tunnel*, on Ecevit Caddesi, operating like the others from 10pm onwards. The *Dome* and *Celebrity* also have **casinos**, pitched mostly at visitors from Turkey – whose citizens, in particular the numerous public employees, are forbidden to patronise their own gambling dens.

Listings

Bookstore *Merdiven*, on Kurtuluş Caddesi (the road to Bellapais), has a very limited stock of English-language books.

Car hire *Canlı Balık*, on the old harbour (☎52182); *Atlantic*, in the Dome Hotel (☎53053, fax 52772); *Tri Sun*, on the Bellapais road (☎53076, fax 54850); *Oscar*, on Kordon Boyu opposite the Dome Hotel (☎52272, fax 53858); *Yeni Kartal*, out near the Deniz Kızı Hotel in Alsancak (☎082/18644).

Exchange *Sergeant Mustafa*, on Atatürk Caddesi, swaps foreign currency notes instantly, travellers' cheques with a bit more bother. The cashpoint machine of the *Kıbrıs Türk Kooperatif Merkez Bankası* on the central square will accept foreign plastic.

Ferry boat agents *Fergün*, on Belediye Meydanı opposite the town hall (☎52344); *Ertürk*, corner of Cumhuriyet Caddesi and the Bellapais road (☎52308); *TML*, on İskenderun Caddesi across from the English cemetery (☎53508).

Post office Just off Belediye Meydanı (Mon–Fri 7.30am–2pm, 4–6pm, Sat 9am–noon). Also sells phone *jetons* when the telephone office is shut.

Public toilets At the base of the north jetty, on the old harbour – clean enough if a bit pongy.

Telephones Across from the post office, but uselessly short hours – do your phoning from your accommodation.

West of Kyrenia

The stretch of coast **west of Kyrenia** is the district's "Hotel Row", with a good two-thirds of the North's tourism facilities either on the sea or just inland. Beaches are not brilliant, often merely functional, but the character of the foothill villages, with their eyrie-like situations and usually lush vegetation, redresses the balance.

Karaoğlanoğlu (Áyios Yióryios)

The first separate municipality west of Kyrenia on the coast, **KARAOĞLANOĞLU (ÁYIOS YIÓRYIOS)** is remarkable only as the site of the Turkish landing at dawn on 20 August 1974; the village has been renamed in honour of the Turkish commanding officer who was killed as he came ashore. A higher density than usual of grotesque monuments, including a cement abstract suggestive of an artillery piece, marks the spot some 8km west of Kyrenia; there's also a "Peace Action" museum consisting mostly of burnt-out military vehicles from both sides, a chronicle of EOKA atrocities against Turkish Cypriots, and general glorification of the Turkish intervention.

The **beach** itself, the first decent strand this side of Kyrenia and sheltered by a large offshore rock, was "Five-Mile Beach" in British times, but is now known as Yavuz Çıkarma ("Resolute Outbreak" in Turkish) – though **Beşinci Mil** (Fifth Mile) is still widely understood. *Topset Hotel Bungalows* here has its own small beach, and nearby also is one of the only official **campsites** in the North: the *Riviera Mocamp*, charging about £3 a day for caravans. Back in Karaoğlanoğlu, some humble kebab houses congregate around the turning up to Karaman, if you're curious as to how and what the North Cypriots eat out of view of tourists.

Karaman (Kármi)

With its whitewashed houses set among dense foliage and a webbing of arcaded, cobbled lanes, **KARAMAN** is arguably the most beautiful of the Kyrenia hill villages. Still referred to even by officialdom as **KÁRMI**, it has in recent years acquired a reputation as a bohemian outpost. After lying abandoned since 1974 (it was too marginal agriculturally to appeal to Turks, either Cypriot or Anatolian), the place was in 1982 designated a special category of the tourism development concessions. Only Europeans – except for two Turkish-Cypriot war heroes, one married to a foreigner – were allowed to renovate the hundred or so derelict properties on 25-year leases: tennants bore all costs of restoration and continue to pay a yearly ground rent.

As a social experiment and architectural showcase, it is more successful than many such, though inevitably twee, and a bit of an ingrown and bitchy scene, where recently there seemed little better to do than count heads to see whether English- or German-speakers predominated.

The ex-pats, who include such high-powered personalities as two present/former British MPs, are generally strong supporters of the North's position (the very act of settling here is a political statement), and consider that their predecessors got their just desserts. Greek-Cypriot Kármi was an EOKA-B stronghold, and for many years any heavy rain would leach the blue paint of ENOSIS slogans through the covering of new whitewash.

The foreign community here views the possibility of any peace settlement with almost as much ambivalence as the native islanders. Some ex-pats are elated at the possibility of longer-term leases and the opportunity to go for trips to the South; others are apprehensive about the steamroller of mass tourism – the backwater quality of the North was usually an important factor in their coming here – and the theoretical return, one fine morning, of irate Greek-Cypriot owners demanding their homes back.

Practical details

Whatever their attitudes towards each other, the Greek Cypriots or the Northern authorities, the "villagers" welcome visitors, who might make their first stop at the pair of **pubs** (especially the *Crow's Nest*) before moving on to **eat** at either the Dutch-run *Levant* (☎081/55431; tasty if a bit expensive) in the village centre, or the British-managed *Duckworth House* (☎081/52880; closed Thurs), at the edge of Kármi. If you fancy **staying** – though not between January and March, when the forested, north-facing setting is extremely dank and sunless – this needs to be arranged beforehand through *Sunquest Holidays* or *President Holidays,* which can book you into certain of the premises, whose leaseholders when absent make a little pocket money on the side in this fashion. Finally, if you're here on a Sunday between 11am and 1pm, it's worth stopping in at the old church to view the **icon collection** which the residents have assembled from other abandoned churches in the area. Near the Duckworth House restaurant, a small sign also points towards some early **Bronze-Age tombs**.

Going up to Kármi you'll pass through the much smaller village of **EDREMİT (TRIMÍTHI)**, where there is an ex-pat-run restaurant or two, some shops and a few foreigners putting down roots; the place was until this century notorious for slave-trading.

ASİL NADİR (1953–)

Travelling in North Cyprus, it's nearly impossible to avoid encountering traces of the business holdings of **Asil Nadir**. This secretive entrepreneur briefly made UK headlines in late 1990 when his vast financial empire spectacularly crashed, sending shock waves across both the City and North Cyprus; resulting court proceedings are unconcluded at present.

Born in 1953 in the traditional Turkish-Cypriot stronghold of Léfka (Lefke) and the son of a prominent businessman, Nadir studied briefly in İstanbul before moving to London during the early 1970s. Having made his first bundle in the East End clothing industry, he used it in 1980 to acquire a controlling interest in a small company called Polly Peck. It provided a handy umbrella when Nadir began diversifying into electronics (the Japanese brand *Sansui* and Turkish *Vestel*), fruit-packing (*Del Monte* of California and *Sunzest Citrus* in North Cyprus), plus an array of newspapers and magazines in Turkey and North Cyprus too numerous to list. Large numbers of hotels were also purchased or constructed in Turkey and North Cyprus. His sister, Nevzat Bilge, was placed in charge of *Noble Reardon*, a London outfit with two divisions devoted exclusively to tourism: *Mosaic Holidays* for packages to Turkey and North Cyprus, *Noble Air* to fly the customers there. You only saw the name "Polly Peck" on the large fleet of cargo ships plying between Famagusta and northern Europe, trading North Cyprus' agricultural produce for manufactured goods. The Nadir family empire, worth billions of pounds sterling on paper, became after the public sector the largest single employer in the North, keeping 9000 adults in work at its peak.

Despite occasional murmurs of discontent from lending agencies, everything went swimmingly until October 1990, when sudden, severe cash flow problems at Polly Peck triggered a sharp dive in its share value on the London stock market. Several subsidiaries were compelled to cease trading immediately, and by mid-1991 Nadir had been declared personally bankrupt, with debts of nearly £100 million.

Court-appointed administrators have since devoted much of their efforts to civil suits filed to retrieve funds improperly removed from Polly Peck and subsidiaries, on behalf of former shareholders. Unfortunately for them many of the more valuable assets such as hotels, warehouses and ships are out of reach in unrecognised North Cyprus, where court orders would have no effect; the selling off of other,

Alsancak (Karavás)

Some 6km west of Karaoğlanoğlu, the main district of **ALSANCAK (KARAVÁS, KARAVA)** lines a single ravine, with runnels everywhere irrigating the lemon orchards. Carob and olive groves are interspersed with abandoned houses higher up the slopes. Founded after the first Turkish conquest as an overflow of Lapta (see below), most of its present inhabitants are refugees from Páfos, who have converted the huge church into a mosque; its carved *témblon* is still there, though the icons have vanished.

Directly north of Alsancak, out on a promontory, stands the twelfth-century **monastery of Akhiropiítos**, which can only be glimpsed from a distance as it falls squarely within a Turkish army camp, the buildings being used as storage depots. The monastery takes its name (Made Without Hands) from a foundation legend asserting that the central church was teleported whole from Anatolia to save it from marauding infidels. Adjacent to seaward stands the emphatically made-with-hands **chapel of Áyios Evlálios**, supposedly carved from a single

more accessible, holdings – in particular the Turkish media titles – produced very little. Following lengthy Scotland Yard fraud-squad investigations, criminal proceedings against Nadır have only reached the stage of preparatory hearings; indictments for alleged false accounting and/or embezzlement have yet to be drawn up.

In retrospect it appears the root causes of the crash were fairly similar to the BCCI scandal: Nadir's pre-emptory and highly personalised management style relied heavily on largesse to friends and purchase of favours, preferably with other people's money. Recipients included the UK Conservative Party, as embarrassingly revealed by a letter, leaked in late 1990, of effusive gratitude for Nadir's generous contribution, signed by then-Prime Minister Thatcher. Many North Cypriots, aware of his dubious reputation all along, derived a grim sort of told-you-so satisfaction out of the whole affair, noting that Nadir's backers were exclusively foreign and that no Turkish Cypriot had been gullible enough to invest in his schemes.

As noted, a fair portion of the family fortune remains intact in North Cyprus, for the moment out of reach of investigators and administrators, and Nadir's influence in the North is still pervasive. Polly Peck freighters still lumber in and out of Famagusta; the Olive Tree and Jasmine Court resorts near Kyrenia, and the Palm Beach Hotel in Famagusta continue as affiliates of Noble Raredon; and the high-tech, four colour newspapers _Kıbrıs_ and _Yeni Gün_, essentially mouthpieces of the ruling UBP party, as well as the English-language _Cyprus Today_, have survived.

Perhaps the greatest lingering cause for concern is not Asil Nadir's long-running financial antics but the near-identity between Polly Peck and the UBP (National Unity Party), Rauf Denktaş's political machine which has ruled the North since 1975. The Nadir-controlled local media have always been completely at the disposal of the UBP regime, especially at polling time, and the numerous employees of Polly Peck and its subsidiaries were allegedly threatened with the sack during the hard-fought 1990 elections if they did not vote for UBP lists. In return Denktaş – a personal friend of the Nadir family – tries to ensure that no legal harm befalls them, at least within the confines of North Cyprus. In such a small society – perhaps 100,000 adults at present, including Anatolian settlers – it seems unlikely that more than one such prodigy as Asil Nadir would emerge in a generation, but at the same time it's an unhealthy sign that the most internationally famous Turkish Cypriot should have chosen to run the North as essentially his private fiefdom.

monolith. Both share the peninsula with the scant ruins of **ancient Lambousa**, of which the most famous evidence is the so-called "Lambousa treasure", quantities of sixth-century Byzantine silver and gold items dug up beside Áyios Evlálios in 1905 and presently distributed among the Cyprus museum, the Medieval museum in Limassol, the Metropolitan museum in New York, and the British museum.

Practical details

Most local tourist facilities are along or north of the coast road, around the Deniz Kızı Hotel. **Staying**, try and get booked into _The Riverside_, in Alsancak almost 3km inland but well designed, or _The Villa Club_ self-catering bungalows, east of Alsancak in Yeşiltepe district, which is small (34 beds) and attractively set in a citrus grove. On the inland side of the highway, the _Allah Kerim_ is a very simple family-run **restaurant** with _meze_ and fish on weekend nights, meat otherwise, and outdoor seating. Inconspicuous and small on the seaward side of the pavement, the _Bamboo_ – so named for its windbreak – comes highly recommended by the Kármi crowd for its excellent _mezes_ prepared by an Anatolian Turkish chef.

Lapta (Lápithos)

A sprawling community draped over several spurs separated by canyons, its houses scattered in spring-fed greenery or perched on bluffs, **LAPTA (LÁPITHOS)** seems a more elaborate, shaggy version of Alsancak. Its abundant water supply has attracted settlers since the twelfth century BC, who lived however mostly down at Lambousa until the turbulence of the seventh century AD compelled retreat inland. Lápithos was one of the original city-kingdoms of Cyprus, and during the Roman era served as a regional capital.

Three hundred metres up the steep grade and accessible by a network of paved but appallingly narrow, hairpin roads, the **Başpınar** or "Headspring" (*Kefalóvrisi* in Greek), haphazardly signposted and source of all this lushness, bursts into the village after a long journey down the mountain; the nearby taverna of Greek-Cypriot days is just barely ticking over as a café and nighttime neighbourhood grill – the view and setting are the thing.

Lapta was famous in former times for its silk, carved chests, potters and water-powered corn mills – and lately for a strange **snake-charmer** who lives in a houseful of serpents, some poisonous. He has not only tamed them, but is apparently able to neutralise their venomous bites, and once appeared on Turkish TV to demonstrate his talents to 1980–84 junta leader Kenan Evren.

Lapta was formerly a bicommunal village; the pair of mosques and seven churches or monasteries correspond to the nine separate historical districts, but the minaret of the seventeenth-century Mehmet Ağa Camii was vandalised during the 1963–64 troubles and the Turkish Cypriots "encouraged" to leave. It's still mixed after a fashion: Turkish Cypriots, Anatolians and a handful of foreigners occupying a few properties on 25-year leases from the tourism authorities.

You can **stay** short term at the *Lapta Gardens* self-catering apartments up in the village, arrangeable through *President Holidays*, or down at *Club Lapethos*, closer to the sea and featured in all the catalogues. There is at least one good, authentic **restaurant** below the town hall on the main shopping street: *Süleyman's*, featuring a special vegetarian buffet on Wednesday evenings. Still technically within Lapta, but actually out along the touristic coastal strip a kilometre west of the huge *Celebrity* complex, *Rita on the Rocks* (☎082/18922 for bookings) is a good, British co-run eatery with live music on Thursday nights.

Karşıyaka (Vasília) and Güzelyalı (Vavilás)

Some 18km west of Kyrenia, you reach an unmarked crossroads, though to the seaward side of the road there's an Atatürk statue and a plaza ringed with coffee houses. The inland turning leads shortly to **KARŞIYAKA (VASÍLIA, VASILYA)**, whose gushing fountain contrasts with a barren, sunbaked setting near the western end of the Kyrenia range. The abundant water allows for the irrigation of farmland in the plain below, but the village is about as far west as expats – and more casual tourists – are inclined to settle, and thus far there are few takers. Above Karşıyaka stand the shattered remains of the **monastery of Sinai**.

If you instead follow small signs to seaward from the statue roundabout, **GÜZELYALI (VAVILÁS, VAVILLA)** soon appears. Formerly a functional port for the shipping out of carob pods, beautiful (*güzel* in Turkish) it ain't – nor are there any beaches worth mentioning – but it is an authentic outpost of North Cypriot fishing culture.

Practical details

The *Şirinyalı* restaurant, run by the Üçok family, is an inexpensive seafood place with indoor and outdoor seating overlooking the water, and makes an excellent halt while touring. Even better, and unbelievably reasonable at about £3.50 a head for a fish-plus-*meze* meal, is the nearby *Birka Motel/Restaurant* (☎082/18950). Their self-catering flats, suitable for up to four, go for £10–12 per night, £60 per week, and provided you have your own transport Güzelyalı is not a bad base. Next door the *Sunkiss Hotel* (☎082/18588) constitutes the only alternative, a former carob warehouse run by a German couple as a youth hostel for eastern Germans with limited funds, and an assortment of overlanding backpackers. The resulting comraderie at the waterside bar goes some way towards offsetting the spartan rooms, £5 a head with or without en suite facilities.

The Kormakíti (Koruçam) peninsula

The western reaches of Kyrenia district terminate in the **Kormakíti Peninsula** (Koruçam Burnu to the Turks), a rolling expanse of farmland and sparsely vegetated hills. Like the other great promontories of Cyprus – the Akámas in Páfos district, and the Kárpas (see Chapter Eight, following) – it has a back-of-beyond feel and an interesting demographic history, in this case as the last stronghold of the island's thousand-year-old Maronite community.

Once past the turnings for Güzelyalı and Karşıyaka, and a vast new hotel complex shortly after, the previously generous road dwindles somewhat as it bears inland on its long, indirect way towards Nicosia; the entire route is heavily militarised from here on, as it's the easiest way round the Kyrenia hills.

Less than a kilometre inland, an unmarked but paved, narrow road heads west back towards the coast, and the half-empty village of **KAYALAR (ÓRGA)**, where a handful of foreigners' villas perch incongruously above crumbling dwellings occupied by settlers from Turkey. Just before reaching Kayalar, a few coves look appealing from afar, but up close prove to be rocky and filthy – barely fit as a platform for jumping in.

The next settlement, **SADRAZAMKÖY (LIVERÁS)**, is too poorly sited to have attracted more than a handful of Anatolian settlers, who have been recently forbidden to graze goats in the surrounding scrub – it's been declared a "forestry region" in a possible ploy to discourage their continued residence. You can bump further along dirt tracks to the unmanned beacon out on bleak **Cape Koruçam** (Kormakíti) itself; this is Cyprus' nearest point to Turkey, some forty nautical miles from the promontory to Cape Anamur in Anatolia.

Koruçam (Kormakíti) village

The road hairpins on itself from Sadrazamköy to head back southeast, passing the tiny medieval chapel of the Virgin just before arriving at the formerly prosperous Maronite "capital" of **KORUÇAM (KORMAKÍTI)**. Its permanent population has dwindled to 150 mostly elderly residents, and just seven children keep the primary school going, the latter run by two nuns from a small convent in the village centre. A priest is still resident, with mass celebrated daily in the enormous modern church of Áyios Yióryios, though you can visit the interior at other times by applying to the convent. There is no doctor and no means of summoning one since the authorities ripped out the pre-1974 telephone apparatus next to the municipal **coffee house**; inside this, Beirut football pennants hang next to portraits of various Maronite patriarchs.

Despite their obviously straitened circumstances, the people are overwhelmingly hospitable and cheerful, even by the standards of Cyprus. Wandering the streets between crumbling, unmaintained houses, you may be invited in if you speak any Greek, only to feel embarrassed at accepting generosity from those who have so little to spare. The watchword in conversation is *apó ekí* – "over there", that is, the South – where the only future is seen to lie.

Onward from Cape Kormakíti

ÇAMLIBEL (MÝRTOU), near the high point of the road, has become a major Turkish army depot and much of it has to be detoured round; in the same vein, the direct road from adjacent **TEPEBAŞI (DHIÓRIOS)** to Koruçam is often closed at the whim of the sentries, who may ask to see a special pass. It is best to make visits to Koruçam via Kayalar and Sadrazamköy, exiting through the tricky checkpoint; presented with an accomplished fact, the sentry may merely request a handful of imported cigarettes (*Rothmans* will do) as "toll".

Another road leads west from Tepebaısi towards **AKDENİZ (AYÍA IRÍNI)**, near the important namesake Bronze-Age site excavated in 1929; beyond beckons one of the best sand beaches in the North, but it's been strictly Turkish army

---

THE MARONITES OF KORMAKÍTI

The **Maronites** are an ancient Middle Eastern sect, whose identity arose out of a seventh-century theological dispute between the Monophysites, who postulated a single, divine nature for Christ, and the Orthodox, who believed Christ simultaneously God and Man. When asked their opinion by the Emperor Heraclius, the monks of the the Monastery of Saint Maron in Syria proposed that Christ had a dual nature but a single divine will. For a time this was championed as an ideal compromise, but later the doctrine was deemed heretical and its adherents had to seek safety in the mountains of the Lebanon.

Supposedly the Maronites first came to Cyprus in the twelfth century with the Crusaders, whom they had served in Palestine as archers and guides, settling primarily in the Kárpas and Kormakíti areas. A contending theory asserts that these merely supplemented an existing Maronite colony which had existed on the island since the seventh century.

Although Uniate Christians – they acknowledge the supremacy of the Pope, and still call themselves *Katholiki* (Catholics) – the Maronites have always been culturally similar to the Greek Orthodox majority, being bilingual in modern Greek as well as their own medieval Syriac, and using Greek personal names. The Kárpas community assimilated some time ago through intermarriage, and like the island's Latin Catholics, the Maronites have for some years celebrated Easter on the same date as the Orthodox, not least so that children at university can visit parents during a uniform week of holiday.

Despite all this, the Maronites attempted to remain neutral in the struggle between the Greek Orthodox and Turkish Muslim communities, taking no part in EOKA excesses either before or after independence. In their opinion the current situation in Cyprus is largely the result of pre-1974 government policy, and they

territory since 1974 and gifts of cigarettes are most unlikely to have a calming effect on patrols.

You can, however, proceed unhindered a couple of kilometres south from Çamlıbel to **KIRPAŞA (KARPÁSHA)**, where the Maronite church at the east edge of the village stands locked except for the once-weekly Friday mass, and only a dozen elderly Maronite couples soldier on. There is no longer a functioning Maronite primary school here; the teacher was tried on cooked-up espionage charges and then expelled a few years back. Some hay in spring, barley in summer and pasture for a few sheep are all that the land here affords to the inhabitants.

An alternate return to Kyrenia

Returning to the main road and heading towards the capital, you sense the beginnings of the Mesaoría corn fields become increasingly common, and all open water disappears. For an interesting **return route to the Kyrenia coast**, bear north at KILIÇASLAN (KONDEMÉNOS) towards **KOZAN (LÁRNAKA TIS LAPÍTHOU)**, beautifully set on the southern slopes of Selvilidağ (Kiparissóvouno), at 1024 metres the summit of the Kyrenia range. A few grapevines are coaxed from the sunny terraces here, but nothing like the profusion south of the Troödhos. The main church here is now a mosque, though the monastery of Panayía ton Katháron visible to the west was thoroughly sacked after 1974.

bear little animosity towards Turkish Cypriots, thinking it best that the two main Cypriot ethnic groups continue to live separated.

Accordingly the Maronites of Kormakíti were among the enclaved Christians theoretically allowed to remain in the North after 1974, though in practice Turkish military and civil administration has been every bit as hard on them as on the Greeks of the Kárpas. Houses, public buildings and farmland (including rich citrus groves and corn fields) have been expropriated without compensation, and secondary schools shut down, making the continued existence of a viable community virtually impossible. Almost everyone between the ages of 12 and 45 in the four traditional Maronite villages has elected to emigrate, either to the South or abroad: rarely to ancestral but troubled Lebanon, mostly to Italy and England, where intermarriage with other Catholics is common.

The remaining older Maronites are allowed to visit the South for five days at a time on a pass costing about £1 (though it is alleged that their economically more active children, making the reverse journey, are charged exorbitant fees). If they overstay their "visa", they can lose the right to return to the North. Their status as some of the few individuals allowed relatively free movement between the sides of the island makes them useful business intermediaries.

Most of what's left of the Kormakíti Maronite community now lives in the eponymous village, officially renamed Koruçam (see p.215). Of the other three settlements, Kırpaşa (Karpásha) can muster just a dozen households, Özhan (Asómatos) even fewer, and Gürpınar (Ayía Marína) has been completely deserted by the Maronites, despite the fact that their main monastery, Profítis Ilías, was nearby. For the ones choosing to stay behind, it's now mostly a matter of clinging grimly on, hoping to see an improvement in their lives if and when some sort of federal reunification settlement is reached.

The onward road over a 500-metre-high saddle in the ridge ahead is steep and single-lane, but also paved and scenic; near the top debouches a colonial-vintage dirt-track system, blazed in the early 1950s at a purported cost of £300 per mile. This can be followed, preferably with a four-wheel-drive or mountain bike, past the highest summits all the way to Saint Hilarion Castle. Once beyond this junction the tarmac route descends to Karşıyaka to pick up the coast highway.

Southeast of Kyrenia

Immediately **southeast of Kyrenia** cluster several inland villages which, perhaps even more than those to the west of town, have been particularly favoured by foreigners since the start of British administration. The coastal plain seems wider and more gently pitched; the hills are more in the backround, permitting more winter sun than at Kármi or Lapta. Even the laziest tourist manages to make it up here, if only to see the crown jewel of North-Cypriot tourism, the romantically half-ruined abbey of Bellapais.

Beylerbeyi (Béllapais): village and abbey

The village of **BEYLERBEYİ (Béllapais, Bellabayıs)** occupies a sloping natural terrace overlooking the sea, a ravine to the east providing some definition. **Lawrence Durrell's** sojourn here during the mid-1950s put it on the literary and touristic map, and his former house – more or less in the centre of the village – sports an ornamental ceramic plate over the door, reading: "Bitter Lemons: Lawrence Durrell lived here 1953–56". Here he finished the *Justine* volume of the *Alexandria Quartet*, and entertained a succession of British literati who before or subsequently made their mark as travel writers or chroniclers of the east Mediterranean. Since his time the large house has been somewhat tastelessly revamped, but out front the mains-water standpipe which figured so prominently in the drama of Durrell's purchase of the property still protrudes from the pavement.

Frankly there are more attractive villages in the Kyrenia hills than Beylerbeyi: there's little greenery and open space compared to Kármi or Lapta, and cobbles have long since vanished from the lanes. The glory of the place resides definitively in the Lusignan **abbey of Bellapais**, at the north edge of the village.

The history of the abbey

Bellepais abbey was originally founded as Saint Mary of the Mountain just after 1200 by Augustinian canons fleeing Palestine. Almost immediately the brethren changed their affiliation to the Premonstratensian order under Thierry, the man behind the construction of Ayía Sofía cathedral in Nicosia, and adopted the white habits which gave the place its nickname of the "White Abbey".

Lusignan King Hugh III richly endowed it later the same century: he also conferred on the abbot the right of wearing a mitre, sword and golden spurs, which only puffed up the abbey's pretensions in its frequent squabbles with the archbishopric of Nicosia – as did a gift of a supposed fragment of the True Cross in 1246.

Succeeding Lusignan kings were benefactors and even lived in the abbey, but it provided a tempting target for the Genoese plunderings of 1373, after which it spun into both moral and physical decline, when the friars' reputation became scandalous for their concubines and the fact that they would only accept their own children as novices; the Venetians also corrupted the long-standing name, *Abbaye de la Pais*, to *De la Pais*, from which it was an easy ellision to *Bellapais*.

The Turks dispersed the community in 1570 and handed the abbey over to the Orthodox church, while a village – apparently populated by descendants of the monks – grew up around the monastery. The site subsequently suffered from being used as a quarry by villagers and even the British, who despoiled the buildings in various ways before their embryonic antiquities department began repairs under George Jeffrey, he of the museum in north Nicosia, early this century.

Visits to the abbey

You approach through a promenade of palm trees lending an exotic fillip to the Gothic ambience, though the cloister's courtyard is still garnished with the robust cypresses planted by Durrell's Mr Kollis in the 1940s. Admission policies are somewhat flexible: there's a 75p charge when the warden is about, and the main gate shuts at 5pm in theory, but the *Kybele* restuarant operates inside after hours, so in practice you should be able to see much of the complex by patronising it.

Except for its western arcade, where the vaulting is gone, the graceful four-teenth-century **cloister** is intact and enlivened by carvings of human and monster heads on the corbels. Just south the thirteenth-century **church**, used by the Greek Orthodox community here until its last members were forced out in 1976, is locked but at least not vandalised, as can be seen by peeking in the upper windows from the walkway roof of the cloister. Several Lusignan kings are believed buried under the floor pavement. This parapet is also the best vantage point for the ruined **chapter house** to the east of the cloister, and leads also to a small treasury, atop the church's north aisle, and the upper-storey **dormitory**, of which only one wall survives.

On north side of the cloister, a Roman **sarcophagus** once served the monks as a wash basin before they trooped into the magnificent **refectory**. Six bay windows frame the sea, with a 30-metre drop below them along the edge of the escarpment on which Bellapais was built. A raised **pulpit** in the north wall, from where scriptural selections would be read during meals, is accessible by a narow spiral stairway; the hall itself is an occasional venue for performances. Late last century British forces used the refectory as a shooting range – hence the bullet holes in the east wall, where a higher **rose window** admits more light. A stairway leads from the ruins of the kitchen at the refectory's west end down to a pillared **undercroft** or storage basement.

Practical details

Lest he accomplish nothing all day, Durrell was warned away from the **"Tree of Idleness"** and its attendant café on the square south of the abbey. Today the distinctly decrepit mulberry tree is on its last roots, confined in a whitewashed cement well and not to be confused with a purple-flowered jacaranda adjacent. The coffee house, renamed *Huzur Agaç* ("Tree of Repose" in Turkish), is tackily souvenir-festooned and tour-orientated, part of a general local pattern – besides Kyrenia harbour, the abbey's surroundings are the only place in the North that could be deemed rampantly commercialised.

Of the half-dozen **eateries and cafés** arrayed in a half-circle around the abbey, the *Abbey Bell Tower* with its decor of hanging gourds is the simplest, the aforementioned *Kybele* inside the abbey grounds the best positioned, and the very posh *Abbey House* (supper only, reservations suggested on ☎53460, closed Sun) is considered one of the best restaurants in the Kyrenia area.

Should you want to **base yourself** here, the *Bellapais Gardens* and *Irini's Gardens*, in the ravine at the east edge of the village, are attractive self-catering bungalows bookable through *Sunquest* and *Mosaic Holidays* respectively.

Ozanköy (Kazáfani) and Çatalköy (Áyios Epíktitos)

Both of these attractive settlements are linked with Beylerbeyi by a secondary road. **OZANKÖY (KAZÁFANI)**, before 1974 a mixed village famous for its carob syrup and olive oil, can boast one of the less expensive and more characterful restaurants in the Kyrenia area: *The Old Mill*, formerly an olive press, open erratically and only for supper. Ozanköy can also boast the faded-frescoed medieval church of **Panayía Potamítissa**, where a fourteenth-century tomb in one corner sports a bas relief of the occupant in period dress.

Above **ÇATALKÖY (ÁYIOS EPÍKTITOS)** lies *The Olive Tree*, the most luxurious, privately run hotel-apartment complex in the North and represented by most package companies. The village itself, built atop a peculiar low escarpment riddled with **caves**, is attractive; in one of these lived the hermit Epiktitos during the twelfth century. At the outskirts of the village, on its westerly access drive, *Ziya's Fish Restaurant* offers a three-course seafood-based meal and a drink for a flat rate of about £5, but avoid late Friday or Saturday night if you don't want Turkish-style karaoke and dance-along with your supper.

East of Kyrenia: the coast

In contrast to the shoreline west of Kyrenia, the coast to the east is largely undeveloped and even deserted, any villages being built a ways inland, out of reach of pirates. Yet tucked between rocky headlands, however, are the best (if exposed) beaches in the district, lonely except on summer weekends.

Karakum (Karákoumi) and around

The first beach of any significance east of town is at **KARAKUM (KARÁKOUMI)**, accessible by a side road past a forgettable Chinese restaurant and then another right turn once the initially rocky shore is reached. Just inland from this junction, the *Courtyard Inn*, a pricey gourmet restaurant, is also a pension with five rooms (☎081/53343 to book either).

Below Çatalköy, the **tomb of Hazreti Ömer**, another Durrellian locale, is signed from the coast road. It has been renovated since the 1950s and despite posted 9am to 6pm visiting hours seems permanently locked. The tomb is reputed to be the final resting place of not one but seven warriors or holy men, and possibly dates from the Arab raids of the seventh century, though there was almost certainly a local pagan shrine before then. In the Cypriot fashion, the *tekke* or dervish convent which grew up around the tombs was venerated by both

Greek and Turkish communities (as "Áyii Fanóndes" in the former case) before 1974. Its setting on a sea-lashed rocky promontory is the thing, with views back towards the mountains.

One cove to the west, **Fortuna** – the house originally built by Durrell's friend Marie – still stands among greenery, but inaccessible today as it falls within a fenced-off military area.

The main eastern beaches

Unless you're staying there, it's best to skip **"Acapulco"** beach with its hotel resort complex, completely surrounded by a barbed-wire army camp and incorporating the Neolithic site of Vrysi. **Lara** beach, 3km east, is equally well maintained and with a single café-restaurant; startling rock formations at its west end, repeated in various forms throughout this coast, give you something to sunbathe on or snorkel round. Alternatively there is a small, little-known cove between "Acapulco" and Lara.

Beyond Lara the coast road, though paved, is far narrower and curvier than maps imply, and progress is quite slow. A new power plant, the subject of some controversy for its obsolete and polluting technology, has just been completed hereabouts in order to free the North from dependence on power from Dhekélia in the South.

Alagadi and "Turtle Bay"

Two **restaurants**, the popular *Hodja's* and the apparently less active *St Kathleen's,* along with a tiny villa complex, signal your arrival at sand-and-shingly **Alagadi (Alakáti) beach**. Better to continue a kilometre to a second "Halk Plajları" sign at a sharp curve which points to a 500-metre dirt sidetrack; this ends (careful you don't maroon your vehicle) at a vast sandy bay about a kilometre long, with no facilities at present. Unfortunately, because of the lack of development there is no clean-up of the enormous amount of rubbish – predominantly from Arab shipping, judging from product labels – that washes up here, but swimming is otherwise enjoyable.

THE PAY BEACH SCANDAL OF 1991

You may find, if you're not staying at shorefront hotels, that you will be charged a fee (£1–1.50 per person) for use of many beaches west of Kyrenia, artificially strewn or otherwise. This is a legacy of what has gone down in local history as the **Pay-Beach Scandal** of 1991, when the government, in an effort to keep "riff-raff" (meaning mainland Turkish conscripts and local picnickers) off beaches frequented by tourists, instituted the charges along with a ban on bringing one's own food and drink onto the sand. While the fees may not seem excessive to a foreigner, they are well beyond the means of the miserably paid soldiers, and represent a considerable hardship for a typically large Cypriot family, intent as well on doing its own barbecuing and not giving the beach-side snack bars much custom.

The local uproar was so great that the tourism ministry was forced to concede three sandy but virtually undeveloped bays east of Lara as *Halk Plajları* or "Public Beaches". They are accordingly very popular on weekends in season when large groups of Cypriots descend on them, though you should have the water almost to yourself as they're not keen swimmers.

The cove here is best known to expats as **"Turtle Bay"**, after its status as a loggerhead turtle egg-laying site, but between the rubbish, the new power plant whose stacks jab the horizon, the firepits of weekend barbecuers and the manoeuvring jeeps, the hatchlings' life expectancy must be rated low.

Onüçüncü Mil

The headland to the east is possibly the site of ancient Alakati; beyond this promontory is yet another bay, also accessible by a track signed "Halk Plajları", known as **Onüçüncü Mil** or "Thirteenth Mile" after its distance from Kyrenia. If anything it is even more attractive than "Turtle Bay", despite an abandoned, half-complete holiday village up in the trees, testimony to Asıl Nadır's financial troubles. Only the bravest of drivers make it down off the wooded bluff via the tracks that fizzle out in the dunes here, one turning leading back in fact to the east end of "Turtle Bay". To either end of Onüçüncü Mil's sandy crescent, eerie jumbles of eroded limestone rear up like ruined fortifications, making it difficult to distinguish between them and man-made ancient masonry.

Inland: castles and monasteries

Along the watershed of the Kyrenia hills are scattered a handful of **castles and monasteries**, evocatively set on rock spires or down in wooded valleys. They're justifiably some of the biggest tourist attractions in the North, and all are served by roads of passable standard taking off from the two main Kyrenia–Nicosia routes, or from villages at the east end of the Kyrenia coastal strip.

The castles in particular were built so as to be in visual communication with each other, Kyrenia and Nicosia – a Byzantine/Crusader early-warning system of pirate raids on the north coast. At the start of the Venetian era, all of them were partially dismantled, as warfare in general had changed and ballistics technology in particular had made them obsolete.

Saint Hilarion castle

Westernmost and best preserved of the three redoubts in these hills, **Saint Hilarion castle** (daily 8.30am–5pm; 75p) does justice to the much-quoted passage of Rose Macaulay's ("a picture-book castle for elf-kings"), and the rumour that Walt Disney used it as a model for the castle in *Snow White and the Seven Dwarfs*. Indeed it has a fairy-tale quality, walls and towers sprouting out of the rocks almost at random.

Local legend once credited Saint Hilarion with having 101 rooms, of which 100 could easily be found; the last, an enchanted garden, contained a fabulous treasure belonging to an elusive "Queen" of Cypriot folklore, probably a holdover of Aphrodite worship. Shepherds or hunters stumbling through the magic doorway of the treasury had a tendency to awaken years later, Rip Van Winkle-like, empty-handed among the bare rocks.

Some history

The castle's verifiable history is almost as intricate as its battlements, with occasional valiant or grisly episodes belying its ethereal appearance. The saint of the name was a little-known hermit who fled Palestine during the seventh century to live and die up here, purging the mountain of still-lurking pagan demons; a Byzantine monastery, and later a fort, sprang up around his tomb.

Owing to its near-impregnability, it was one of the last castles taken by the Lusignans in 1191, who improved its fortifications throughout the early thirteenth century and rendered *Didhimi*, the Greek name for the twin peaks overhead, as *Dieu d'Amour*. Saint Hilarion was the focus of a four-year struggle between Holy Roman Emperor Frederick II and regent John d'Ibelin for control of the island, won by John's forces at the battle of nearby Agírda (today Ağırdağ) in 1232. During the subsequent 140 years of peace, sumptuous royal apartments were added, so that the castle doubled as a summer palace and (during 1349–50) as a refuge from the plague.

In 1373, during the Genoese invasion, the castle again acquired military importance as the retreat of the under-age King Peter II. His uncle and regent John of Antioch, misled by his hostile sister-in-law Eleanor of Aragon into believing his bodyguard of Bulgarian mercenaries treasonous, had them defenestrated one at a time from the highest tower of the castle; miraculously somebody survived the several-hundred-foot drop to tell the tale. Without his loyal retinue, John – implicated in the murder of Eleanor's late husband, Peter I – was easy prey for the vengeful queen and her followers.

The Venetians rendered the castle useless, they thought, for modern warfare. But in 1964 the beleagured Turkish Cypriots found the castle not so militarily obsolete after all, using it as headquarters of their main enclave which included several Turkish communities on the main Kyrenia–Nicosia road. A small garrison of teenage TMT activists was able to fend off EOKA attacks on the castle, and the Turks remained in control of the place thereafter. With passage on the traditional main highway denied to Greek vehicles, or possible only in slow, UN-escorted convoy, the central government was forced to construct a bypass via Pendadháktylos (see below). In 1974 Saint Hilarion and its surrounding enclave was a primary goal of Turkish paratroop landings early on 20 July.

The site

Although Saint Hilarion is now very much open to visits, the twisty but well-signed approach road from the main highway still passes through a Turkish army base, with signs forbidding stopping or walking, let alone photography. Partway along, the restricted zone ends just past a clearing where the Crusaders held their jousting tournaments, and suddenly the castle appears, draped over the bristling pinnacles before you.

Once up in it, you'll spend a good hour scrambling over the juniper-tufted crags to see it all. It's hot work: come early or late in the day, hoping for longer hours at peak season, and bring stout shoes – beach- or pool-wear won't do on the often uneven ground.

First you cross the vast, grassy **lower ward** beyond the ticket booth, where medieval garrisons kept their horses; the wood-and-plaster work of the lower towers must have appeared during the period of the TMT occupation. Once through the hulking **gatehouse and tunnel** into the middle enceinte (the name given to the defended area enclosed by the castle walls), your first detour is to the half-intact **Byzantine chapel**, earliest structure in the castle. You continue through a myriad rooms on a variety of levels; these include the monastic **refectory**, later the royal banqueting hall, up some stairs north of the chapel, and the handsome vaulted **belvedere** just beyond it.

Occasional modern roofing dates from the colonial era, though the catwalks at the east end of the castle (comprising the kitchen and living quarters) have been allowed to decay since 1974, making thorough exploration rather dangerous. The best-preserved hall here has been pressed into service as a **bar**, featuring fresh squeezed oranged juice and unbeatable views over the Kyrenian coast.

An **arched gate** allows entry to the upper enceinte; you can scramble immediately up south to the **highest towers** (elevation 732m), the more outrageously placed called "Prince John's" and venue for the massacre of his Bulgarian auxiliaries – and not a spot for acrophobics to linger. Alternatively, climbing the stoney stair-paths towards the west end of the complex, you'll pass the **aqueduct** and **cistern** (the latter now just a dangerously deep mud puddle) supplying the otherwise waterless garrisons here. Excursions end at the **royal apartments**, whose windows afforded the TMT garrison a good view of their mortal enemies in Kármi before 1974.

The dirt ridge road to Selvilidağ is also plainly visible, and it's possible to proceed cross-country to the point where a proper trail down to Kármi kicks in – a wonderful outing of about an hour, starting from the west apartments.

Buffavento castle

Buffavento (unrestricted access), the least well preserved but most dramatically sited – and at 940m the highest – of the Kyrenian hill castles, requires considerable effort to reach, but will appeal to those who like their ruins wild and sinister.

Getting there

To **get there**, first take the inland turning, following the signs for Ercan airport and Famagusta, just past Çatalköy; the excellent surfacing is a legacy of the Greek Cypriots having bulldozed this route in 1969–70 to get around the Turkish-Cypriot enclave at Saint Hilarion.

The only local village, reached by a side drive partway along, is **ARAPKÖY (KLEPÍNI, KLEBİNİ)**. A curious legend once held that no more than forty families could reside in the place, or the Angel of Death would cull the surplus within the year; there are still only about 150 people here, a mix of native Turkish Cypriots, Anatolian settlers and foreigners attracted by the views. The countryside itself is a bit bleak, and east of here few outsiders wish to live, with most amenities lacking.

At the very top of the grade, when the Mesaoría comes into view, take the rough track heading west, opposite the signed Alevkaya (Halévga) forest road. The first 400m are fortunately the worst; thereafter the surface improves along the total 6km to a roundabout where non-four-wheel drive vehicles must park. A jeep track, indicated by a rusty sign apt to be uprooted, continues a few zig-zags further up to the true trailhead, where an olive tree grows in a stone planter ring next to a trilingual marble memorial to victims of a 1988 air crash: a small aircraft, approaching Ercan in misty conditions, failed to clear the ridge above and disintegrated nearby.

From the lower turning, it's a full 45-minute climb to the castle, which blends well into the rock on which it's built; while the path is in good condition, there's a consistent southern exposure, so you'll bake to death unless you go early or late.

The site

Buffavento probably dates from at least the eleventh century, since it was surrendered to Guy de Lusignan in 1191; the Lusignan kings used it as a political prison, in particular Peter I who, warned by his friend John Visconti of Queen Eleanor's infidelity, repaid the favour by locking Visconti up here to starve to death.

The buildings themselves, almost all fitted with cisterns, are in poor-to-fair condition since their decommissioning by the Venetians, and home now only to bats; they're a pretext, really, for a nice walk in the hills. You can follow the stair-path from the graffitied **gatehouse** up through the jumble of walls to the highest tower, where a natural terrace affords superb views, and would have been the site of signal fires to communicate with Saint Hilarion and Kantara (for which see Chapter Eight).

Up top here, you'll usually learn how the place got its name (*Buffavento* = Wind-Battered), and be treated to the best views on Cyprus: Kyrenia, Nicosia and Famagusta are all visible in the right conditions, as are the Troödhos mountains and indeed half the island. At dusk there's the added bonus of the spectacle of Nicosia's lights going on.

Incidentally, don't believe maps – either the internationally issued ones or that of the North Cypriot tourist office – which imply that the easiest way up to the castle is from the south, via GÜNGÖR (KOUTSOVÉNDIS) and the tempting-looking monastery of Áyios Ioánnis Khysóstomos. Beyond the village all tracks are unmarked, and a giant army camp blocks the way, placing the thoroughly desecrated monastery off-limits as well. (In all fairness, the Greek-Cypriot National Guard was using the grounds as a barracks before 1974, though you could still visit the main church).

Around Beşparmak (Pendadháktylos)

Coming up from the north coast, you can't have helped noticing the sculpted bulk of **Beşparmak (Pendadháktylos)**, the "Five-Finger Mountain", just to the east of the Kyrenia–Nicosia bypass road. Although of modest elevation at 740 metres, its suggestive shape has attracted legend: the Greeks say the Byzantine hero Dhiyenis Akritas left the imprint of his hand here after leaping across the sea from Anatolia, while the Turkish community doubtless has its own story – both the Greek and Turkish names have the same meaning.

There's a good view of the peak's south flank by turning left at the watershed (away from the unmarked Buffavento turning); downhill to the north after 7km, you'll also glimpse the roofless, thoroughly vandalised remains of the **Armenian monastery of Sourp Magar** or the Blessed Virgin. Originally founded by Copts in the eleventh century, it became the property of the island's Armenian community 400 years later, and the now-overgrown garden and orchard hosted an important festival every May until 1974.

Just east of the monastery the forestry track emerges onto a secondary paved road up from DEĞERMENLİK (KYTHRÉA); turn left to reach the vast picnic grounds around the ex-forestry station at **Alevkaya (Halévga).** In 1989 this was refurbished and opened as the **North Cyprus Herbarium** (daily 8am–4pm) under the direction of Dr Deryck Viney of Kármi; the exhibits consists of nearly a thousand preserved specimens of plants endemic to the island, with a small explanatory booklet available.

Antifonítis monastery

The twelfth-century **monastery church of Antifonítis**, tucked into a piney valley northeast of Alevkaya, was once the premier Byzantine monument of the Kyrenia hills. It takes its name – "(S)he Who Answers" – from the foundation legend, in which a rich man and a poor man met at the place. The pauper asked the grandee for a loan, who retorted, "Who will act as witness that I have loaned you the money?", to which the penniless one replied, "God". At once a celestial voice was heard sanctifying the transaction, and the monastery grew up around the miracle.

Getting there
There are two possible approaches. From the herbarium and recreation area, proceed northeast on the paved road, shunning the turn down to KARAAĞAÇ (KÁRCHA) and leaving the tarmac above Esentepe in favour of a dirt track contouring along just north of the watershed. Some 14km from Alevkaya, at an X-shaped junction, a sign points back against you, giving the distance to Alevkaya (9 miles), and another down and hairpin left to Esentepe (3.5 miles). Bear left ahead onto a steep, unmarked track – best to have a four-wheel drive vehicle – and at the foot of this valley look out for the dome of the monastery church peeking above dense foliage.

From the coast road east of Kyrenia, turn off at the large village of **ESENTEPE (ÁYIOS AMVRÓSIOS, AYKURUŞ)**, once known for its apricots and crafts, and now resettled partly by natives of Áyios Nikólaos village in the Páfos hills. Traverse to its high end, following signposting to Alevkaya and Lefkoıa, but at the next junction, marked by a derelict forestry placard, go straight onto the dirt surface, rather than right with the pavement. The tiny monastic **church of Apáti**, not to be confused with Antifonítis and not worth the trouble getting up to, is soon seen above and to the right among pines. Shortly you'll reach the crossroads described above.

The site
In any case the final couple hundred metres of approach must be made on foot. A neglected, overgrown courtyard surrounds the twelfth-century *katholikón* which, while appealing, wins no prizes for architectural purity: the Venetians added an arched loggia to the south during the fifteenth century, while the vaulted Lusignan narthex on the west side predates it by a hundred years.

Since 1974 the church's interior has been heartbreakingly vandalised, and is currently used as a goat pen. Of its once-vivid and notable **frescos**, only the magnificent *Pandokrator* survives undamaged in the huge irregularly shaped dome – supported by eight columns and covering the entire nave – plus the occasional saint or apostle on arches and columns out of reach. The tracery has been knocked out of the dome windows, allowing nesting swallows free passage.

Leaving, you can continue eastward on the forestry track system, though signposting has been allowed to deteriorate since 1974. Within a minute or two there's another major junction at a pass: down to the south leads towards GÖNENDERE (KNODHÁRA), straight keeps following the crest, and down and left goes to the rather poor village of BAHÇELİ (KALOGRÈA), just above the coast road.

travel details

Buses

From Kyrenia to Nicosia, every 15min; to Famagusta, hourly; to Güzelyurt, several daily via Tepebaza. Daily out-and-back services exist for most villages between Bahçeli in the east and Tepebaşı on the Kormakiti peninsula, but usefully frequent schedules only for Çatalköy, Ozanköy, Beylerbeyi and Lapta.

Ferries

From Kyrenia to Taşucu (Turkey), 2–4 daily except Sat/Sun, between 11am and 1.30pm (4–8hr); to Alanya (Turkey), 1 weekly at Sat noon (7hr). See *Basics* for a complete discussion of companies and fares.

CHAPTER EIGHT

FAMAGUSTA AND THE KÁRPAS PENINSULA

The Mesarya (Turkish for Mesaoría) plain, hummocky and relatively confined around Nicosia, opens out to steppe-like dimensions as it approaches the long, gradual arc of Famagusta Bay. This coast has been advancing slowly east over the centuries, courtesy of silt brought down by the Kanlıdere River (the Pedhiéos in Greek), in recent centuries flowing inter-mittently at best.

At the southeast corner of the Mesarya, just as the land begins to rise appreciably to bluffs beyond the Attila Line, the town of **Famagusta** rears up, a Turko-Gothic chimera with no equal on Cyprus. It's the successor to ancient **Salamis**, a few miles north on the far side of bird-haunted wetlands fed by the sluggish Kanlıdere and fringed by beaches. Salamis in turn replaced older **Enkomi-Alasia** as the main port of the region; the narrow strip of plain between the two is

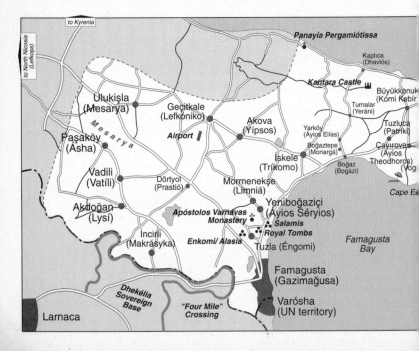

peppered with **tombs** of various eras, one – supposedly that of the Apostle Barnabas – Christianised and until recently venerated. A **monastery** which honoured him now serves as the North's newest archaeological museum.

The sandy shoreline here and at Varósha south of Famagusta saw the first mass tourism in Cyprus after independence, but now that Varósha is off-limits, the little fishing anchorage of Boğaz anchors the otherwise functional row of resorts extending north of Salamis. It's also the gateway to the long, narrow **Kırpaşa (Kárpas)** peninsula, the island's panhandle and likened by more than one demagogic Turkish politician to a "dagger aimed at the underbelly of Anatolia". Today it is in fact almost insignificant militarily – depopulated, remote, and sprinkled with traces of past importance, especially at the early Christian sites of **Ayía Triás**, **Áyios Fílon** and **Aféndrika**. The castle of Kantara effectively marks the base of the peninsula; the barely functioning **monastery of Apóstolos Andhréas** sits near the far end, between the finest beach on Cyprus and the desolate cape itself.

THE FAMAGUSTAN MESARYA

The de facto capital of Cyprus has always been in the immediate environs of Famagusta, with a combination of geology and military history determining its current location. Famagusta town presents a stark contrast to its featureless surroundings, which, particularly at twilight, take on a sinister aspect, perhaps from the numerous ancient dead in the graves of the Mycenaean and Roman cities.

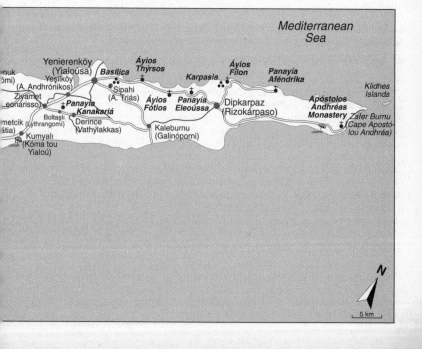

Famagusta (Gazimağusa)

Its Venetian walls now enclosing almost nothing, the tracery of its exotic Gothic churches colliding in your field of vision with palm trees and upturned fishing boats, **FAMAGUSTA** (GAZİMAĞUSA, MAĞOSA, AMMOKHOSTÓS) is the architectural equivalent of a well-behaved houseplant gone to seed in its native jungle. *Ammokhostos* means "sunken in sand" in Greek: the ramparts and deep harbour protect the old town from such a fate, but on the north sand piles up in dunes, while offshore Maymun Adası (Monkey Island) is essentially a shifting spit. The climate is nearly subtropical, the sea air eating away metal and stone alike; in the years before swamp drainage, the malarial mosquitoes had a similar effect on the people. All told, not much of a prospect for greatness.

Yet this was, briefly during the thirteenth century, the wealthiest city on earth, of sufficient romance for Shakespeare to make it the partial setting of *Othello*, a theory based on the brief stage instruction "a seaport in Cyprus".*

Today Famagusta is a double city: the compact, ghostly old walled town, a Lusignan-Venetian legacy, and the sprawling, amorphous new town, similarly derelict since 1974. If conditions do not change on Cyprus, it is easy to imagine both portions living up to the epithet of "sunken in sand" within decades.

Some history

By Cypriot standards Famagusta is a young settlement, though not quite so new as Limassol. Some historians derive the name from "Fama Augusta" after the Emperor Augustus, implying an imperial Roman foundation, but the place is really first heard from only after the seventh century, when the survivors of Arab-sacked Salamis drifted here; it pottered along as a Byzantine fishing port, taking advantage of the only natural deep-water harbour on the island.

Boom

All that changed suddenly in 1291, after Palestinian Acre fell to the Saracens; Christian merchants poured in as refugees from a dozen entrepots on the Middle Eastern mainland. The Pope forbade any trafficking with the infidel on pain of excommunication, guaranteeing Famagusta's monopoly – and spectacular growth. Every commodity of East and West, no matter how exotic, changed hands here; the city became a babel of creeds, tongues and nationalities, reducing the native islanders to a minority. Fortunes were literally made overnight, engendering spectacular exhibitionism and vulgarity: merchant's daughters wore more jewels at their wedding than certain European monarchs, and the prostitutes were as wealthy as the merchants, one of whom allegedly ground up a diamond to season a dish at table in full view of his guests.

Foreigners were fascinated and horrified in equal measure, reporting these anecdotes: Saint Bridget of Sweden, preaching in front of the cathedral (to a doubtless cynical audience), railed against the immorality of the city. The multiplicity of

---

*The character of **Othello** appears to be based on an historical Venetian soldier serving in Cyprus, most probably Francesco de Sessa, known as *Il Moro* for his dark complexion and banished in 1544 for an unspecified offence – along with two subordinates, possibly the models for Iago and Cassio.

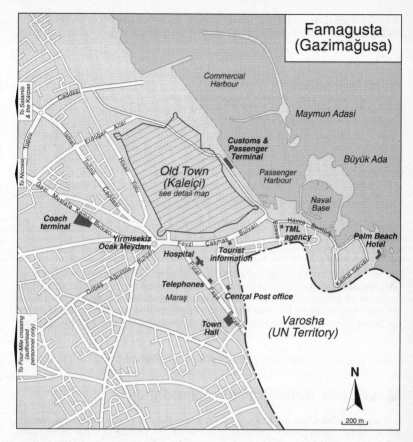

Famagusta (Gazimağusa)

Commercial Harbour

Maymun Adasi

Customs & Passenger Terminal

Büyük Ada

Old Town (Kaleiçi) see detail map

Passenger Harbour

Naval Base

Coach terminal

TML agency

Palm Beach Hotel

Yirmisekiz Ocak Meydanı

Hospital

Tourist information

Telephones

Maraş

Central Post office

Varosha (UN Territory)

Town Hall

To Salamis & the Kárpas

To Nicosia

To Four-Mile crossing (authorised personnel only)

N

200 m

sects and perhaps guilty consciences resulted in scores of churches being built, supposedly one for every day of the year – many of them still standing.

Decline

But Famagusta's heyday lasted less than a century, for in 1372 a diplomatic contretemps triggered its decline. At the coronation of the Lusignan boy-king Peter II, a tussle between the Genoese and Venetian envoys as to the protocol of leading the royal horse degenerated into a brawl with massive loss of Genoese life and property. In revenge a Genoese expedition ravaged Cyprus over the next year, occupying Famagusta and inducing its traders to leave for Nicosia. James II expelled the Genoese in 1464, but it was already too late, and his Venetian widow, Queen Caterina Cornaro, presided over a diminished town before abdicating at the behest of her Venetian handlers in 1489.

Anticipating the growing Ottoman threat, the Venetian military governors busied themselves improving Famagusta's fortifications just as they had at Nicosia and Kyrenia, thickening the Lusignan walls to make them withstand the most powerful ordnance of the day. So when the Turks appeared in October 1570, having taken the rest of the island, it required a ten-month siege to reduce the city, where the Venetian garrison put up a heroic defence, though outnumbered twenty to one.

Turkish Famagusta

Under Ottoman rule, walled Famagusta became an emblem of decay; the bombardment needed to subdue it levelled or severely damaged almost every building, and for centuries the space within the walls lay desolate and weed-choked, inhabited only by garrisons under the command of soldiers disgraced elsewhere, and political prisoners. Christians were forbidden entry, let alone residence, to *Kaleiçi* (the area within the ramparts), so that the predominantly Greek Orthodox town of Varósha (Maraş in Turkish) sprang up just south of Kaleiçi.

With independence and subsequent communal troubles, old Famagusta again acquired significance as a Turkish stronghold. Greek Cypriots who had early this century ventured into Kaleiçi to live were expelled in 1964, while Turkish-Cypriot refugees streamed into the town from vulnerable villages on the Mesarya. This trend accelerated during the tense weeks between 20 July and 15 August 1974, when the EOKA-B-dominated National Guard attacked any Turkish Cypriot they found outside the walls; the luckier ones entered Kaleiçi via a network of predug tunnels, joining both besieged civilians and the small TMT garrison holding down the port and walled town. Old Famagusta was relieved by the advancing Turkish Army on 15 August, after the Greek Cypriots abandoned Varósha in the face of intense Turkish air raids – but when the cease-fire went into effect the next day, the Turks had not yet occupied most of it, and it remains UN territory (see p.239).

> The Famagusta area telephone code is ☎036

Arrival, information and accommodation

Coming **by boat** from MERSİN, Turkey, you'll dock at the customs and passenger terminal, conveniently just east of the Sea Gate leading into the heart of the old town. Arrival **by land** is equally uncomplicated; both the road from Salamis (İsmet İnönü Bulvarı once within city limits) and the Nicosia highway (**Gazi Mustafa Kemal Bulvarı**) converge on **Yirmisekiz Ocak Meydanı**, the roundabout directly opposite the Land Gate of the old city. Generally, **parking** within the old town presents no problems; if necessary drive to the thinly populated areas around the Canbulat Gate or Othello's Tower.

The main **tourist information** bureau (Mon–Fri 7.30am–2pm, plus Mon 3.30–6pm) is on **Fevzi Çakmak Bulvarı**, east of the main roundabout, and a sporadically functioning booth is inside the branch post office at the Land Gate.

Places to stay

Since virtually all of the pre-1974 hotels were in now-inaccesible Varósha, there are few options for staying in or around Kaleiçi – most visitors stay out on the beaches near Salamis. The self-catering apartments *Kulup* (poorly placed inland) and *Laguna Beach* which appear in some literature are available only on long-term basis through tour operators.

Panorama, İlker Karter Caddesi, Maraş (☎65880). Overlooks the dead zone and apparently barely ticking over; £10 double.

Altun Tabya, Kızıl Küle 9, Kaleiçi (☎65363). Haunt of travelling salesmen, but the only vaguely modernised (one-star) facility in the old town. £10 double.

Palm Beach Hotel, at the southeast extreme of town, by the dead zone (☎62000). Well-run, newish five-star outfit with small private beach; bookable through all package operators and more cheerful than the location would suggest.

The city

Given its dearth of accommodation, Famagusta is usually visited as a full day trip or two shorter outings from a beachfront base further north. Interest is confined almost entirely to the Kaleiçi, but don't raise your expectations too high. This is not Dubrovnik, Jerusalem or Carcassone – what you get are the walls, built to last by the Venetians, and such churches as escaped Turkish shot and British vandalism. It's claimed that the Ottomans bombarded the town with more than 100,000 cannonballs during their siege, and many of these are still to be seen lying about. The devastated neighbourhoods were mostly never rebuilt, leaving vast expanses of desolate ground that can have changed little since the day the Ottomans entered the city.

The city walls

More complete than Istanbul or Antioch, stronger than Fez, Jerusalem and even Avila, [a] prince of walled cities . . .

So enthused Colin Thubron in 1972 – and well he might, given the **walls'** average height of 15 metres, thickness of 8 metres, 15 bastions and 5 gates. Yet they were ultimately an exercise in futility, considering the Ottoman victory, though structurally they mostly withstood the test of the siege. The Venetians had gradually raised them atop existing Lusignan fortifications between 1489 and 1540, according to the latest precepts of engineering and ballistics.

The ramparts are still dry-moated on their three landward sides, overgrown with prickle-bushes on top, and impossible to walk around owing to partial occupation by the Turkish Army. Content yourself instead with a stroll up the ramp near the southwestern **Land Gate** to the most spectacular bit, the **Ravelin** or **Rivettina Bastion**. This vast complex of guardhouses and galleries was protected by a double moat, the main one now crossed by an alarmingly rotten wooden bridge. The Ottomans knew it as the *Akkule* or White Tower, from the Venetians' waving of the white flag of surrender from this point.

At the southeast corner of the perimeter, the **Canbulat Bastion** (sometimes Canpolat or Cambulat) takes its name from a Turkish officer who, confronted by a spinning wheel studded with knives which the Venetians had mounted in the gate here, charged it with his horse. Both were cut to ribbons, but the infernal machine was also destroyed and for years Turkish women used to come to his tomb in the bastion to pray for sons as valiant as Canbulat.

Today the interior is home to a **small museum** (Mon–Fri 9am–1.30pm, 4.30–6.30pm; 50p), not money terribly well spent as it's merely an assemblage of mediocre pottery, trad dress, Ottoman weaponry, amphorae and Iznik tiles. On the wall, a famous engraving by Stephano Givellino of the siege, translated into English, somewhat redeems the collection .

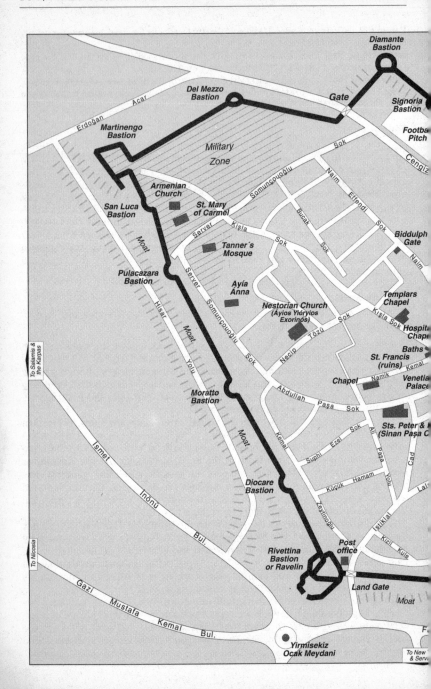

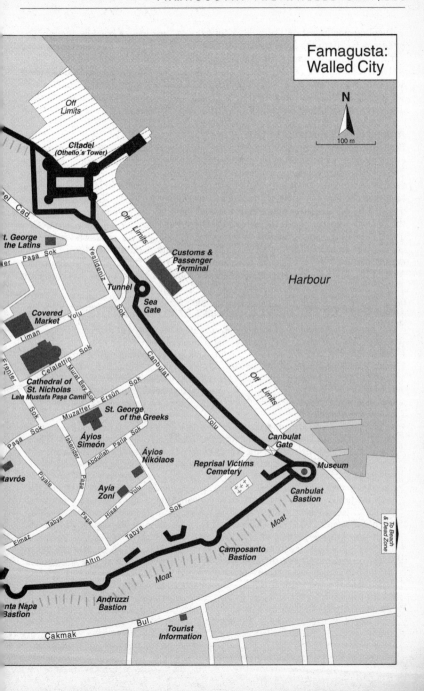

Famagusta: Walled City

N

100 m

Off Limits

Citadel (Othello´s Tower)

...nel Cad.

...t. George the Latins

...er Paşa Sok

Yeşildeniz Sok

Tunnel

Off Limits

Customs & Passenger Terminal

Harbour

Sea Gate

Covered Market

Liman Yolu

Fremel

Celalettin Sok

Muzaffer Bey Sok

Canbulat Yolu

Cathedral of St. Nicholas
Lala Mustafa Paşa Camii

Ersün Sok

Off Limits

Muzaffer Sok

St. George of the Greeks

Áyios Simeón

Abdullah Paşa Sok

Canbulat Gate

Áyios Nikólaos

Museum

...Paşa Sok

Iskender Sok

Reprisal Victims Cemetery

...avrós

Pıyale

Paşa Sok

Ayía Zoní
Yolu

Canbulat Bastion

Hisar

Tabya

Sok

Moat

Elmaz

Altın

Tabya

Paşa

Camposanto Bastion

Moat

...nta Napa ...Bastion

Andruzzi Bastion

Çakmak

Bul.

Tourist Information

To Beach & Dead Zone

Heading northwest on Canbulat Yolu from the namesake bastion, most of the buildings facing the wall are devoted to warehousing and customs brokerage – the harbour is just the other side of the ramparts, accessible by the Sea Gate, along with the Citadel (see below) one of the earliest Venetian improvements. Beside it squats a more naturalistic than usual **Venetian lion**: a legend says that once a year the mouth opens, and anyone lucky enough to be there at the unpredictable moment can stick their hand down its throat and extract a valuable object.

Around Namik Kemal Meydanı

Entering Kaleiçi through the Land Gate and along İstiklal Caddesi, you pass a concentration of tradesmen's restaurants and jewellery shops before seeing the fourteenth-century church of **Saints Peter and Paul** (later the Sinan Paşa Camii) on the left. Supposedly built by a merchant from the profits of a single business transaction, it's a rather inelegant, workaday building, its good condition assured by its former use as a mosque and current role as a venue for the state theatre. Just north across the street, the Venetian governor's palace is mostly a shell, most of the site ignominiously cleared for use as a car park. The remaining east facade is admittedly impressive, facing **Namik Kemal Meydanı**, the town centre named after a dissident Ottoman writer of the late nineteenth century; a bust of the man stands outside, near the Kaleiçi's main taxi ranks. His **dungeon**

THE SIEGE OF FAMAGUSTA AND BRAGADINO'S MARTYRDOM

The **siege of Famagusta** ranks as one of the great battles of medieval times: for ten months a force of 8000 Greeks and Venetians held off an Ottoman army of almost 200,000, and the outcome might have been different had promised relief from Venice and Crete ever arrived. The Venetian commander, **Marcantonio Bragadino**, was brilliant and as resourceful with the limited means at his disposal as could be expected; Lala (Teacher) Mustafa Paşa, his Ottoman counterpart, was a seasoned if unimaginative campaign veteran whose one weakness of character was an explosive temper.

The entrance of Famagusta harbour could be chained shut, starting from a salient of the Othello Tower; the opening at the south end of Maymun Adası (Monkey Island) didn't then exist. Thus the Turks concentrated on assaults of the south and west land walls, avoiding the north wall with its formidable Martinengo Bastion. Armenian sappers dug coils of trenches towards the ramparts so deep as to completely conceal the Turkish soldiery except for the tops of their turbans; the main evidence of their presence on the plain around the city was a forest of campaign tents, three miles wide. The sappers also burrowed under the walls, setting off mines, while the Ottoman artillery of 150 guns (as opposed to the 90 small-bore weapons of their adversaries) reduced the walls from afar.

Despite this pounding, little progress was made by the attackers over the initial winter of siege, with Bragadino organising bold sorties to create the impression that he had manpower to spare – and also to raid for necessary food. On 7 July the Turks gained a foothold on the Rivettina Bastion, and started to scale the walls. Seeing the structure was useless for its intended purpose, the Venetian command detonated a mine of their own prepared for such a moment, burying 1000 Turks (and 100 of their own men) in the resulting rubble, which partly blocked further enemy advance. The defenders fell back behind hastily improvised baricades of earth-filled carts and sandbags; with the relief fleet having failed to materialise, the situation inside the city became increasingly desperate, with plague spreading and

(closed for renovation), where he spent 38 months at the Sultan's pleasure for writing a seditious play, incorporates a surviving bit of palace, as does the lower storey of the (not otherwise recommended) Side Pansiyon, whose facilities are suitably medieval. North of the palace precinct, the equally ruined church of Saint Francis abut a set of **Turkish baths**, now home to a disco.

Lala Mustafa Paşa Camii (Saint Nicholas Cathedral)

Dominating the east side of the square, the **Lala Mustafa Paşa Camii** (10p donation suggested; headscarves and leg-coverings provided) is the most magnificent and best-preserved Lusignan monument in town. Completed between 1298 and 1326 to a design resembling the cathedral at Rheims, it outshines its sister church in Nicosia; here the Lusignan royalty received the honorary crown of lost Jerusalem after their coronation in the official capital, and Queen Caterina Cornaro formally abdicated in 1489.

Regrettably, the twin towers were decapitated during the bombardment of 1571; after seizing Famagusta the Ottomans perpetrated more deliberate alterations. As at Nicosia they emptied the floor-tombs, including presumably that of James II and his infant son, last of the Lusignan dynasty, destroyed all implements of Christian worship, and added the minaret which – lower than the pair of Nicosia's Selimiye Camii – happily detracts little from the building's appeal.

---

rats or cats figuring in the diet. On 1 August, having lost nearly three-quarters of his forces, Bragandino ran up the white flag, and negotiated a surrender whereby civilians were to be unmolested and he with his men were to be given safe conduct to Crete in Turkish ships.

When the remnant of the garrison emerged from the smoking ruins and staggered over to the Turkish lines, the besiegers were amazed that so few men had been able to mount such courageous resistance against hopeless odds, and were moved to pity by their woebegone appearance. At first the defeated were received with kindness and all courtesy, even by the volatile Lala Mustafa himself, but the flouting of Turkish might for so long – and his own casualties of over 50,000 – must have preyed on the general's mind, for Bragadino's audience with him suddenly turned sour.

Lala Mustafa abruptly demanded retention of the Venetian officer Quirini as security against the safe return of the Turkish fleet from Crete; when Bragadino protested that this hadn't been part of the agreed surrender, Lala Musta accused him of murdering fifty prisoners in the last weeks of the siege. Working himself up into one of the towering rages he was known for, the Turk summoned his executioner and before Bragadino's horrified eyes Quirini and two other assistant commanders were hacked to bits. Then came Bragadino's turn: his nose and ears were sliced off, and he was thrown into a dungeon for ten days before being retrieved, publically humiliated in various ways, and finally chained between two pillars in front of the cathedral and flayed alive. Witnesses agree that Bragadino bore all these torments in dignity and silence, and that even many Turks disapproved of these and other atrocities perpetrated by their frenzied leader.

But Lala Mustafa Paşa was not to be mollified: he gutted the body, stuffed Bragadino's skin with straw, and paraded it around the city on a cow, under the red parasol which the Venetian had jauntily used when marching out to give himself up. The stuffed skin was later ransomed from Istanbul at considerable cost by Bragadino's descendants, and it now rests in an urn at the Venetian Church of SS Giovanni e Paolo.

The church-mosque reveals itself to best advantage from the **west**, where the gables of three magnificent porticoes point still higher to the fine six-paned window with its circular rose. Two series of seven columns stalk the **interior** of the nave, supporting the superb vaulting; as at Nicosia, the austere, whitewashed decor allows an appreciation of the cathedral's elegance, undistracted by the late-medieval clutter which would have accumulated had the building remained a church. In the **courtyard** out front, a giant sycamore fig is rumoured to be as old as the building; opposite, in front of a small Venetian loggia converted to an Islamic ablutions fountain, stand a pair of granite columns from Salamis, between which the hapless Bragadino was flayed. Across Liman Yolu, unsung in most tourist literature, the **covered market** occupies a building at least partly Venetian.

The Citadel (Othello's Tower)

The treasure-lion on the Sea Gate, at the seaward end of Liman Yolu, is complemented by a larger relief Lion of Saint Mark above the entry to the **Citadel** (daily 8am–5pm; 75p), 100m north across the oval roundabout. Remodelled in 1492, this Venetian strongpoint is popularly known as **Othello's Tower**, after Famagusta's Shakespearean connections. On the far side of the courtyard, partly taken up by a stage used for folkloric performances, the **Great Hall**, 28m long, boast fine vaults whose limestone groin ribbing is, however, mostly eaten away by the all-corroding sea air.

From the **northeast tower**, you can peer over the industrial harbour; you'll get no closer, as the protruding citadel mole is as militarily important today as in medieval times. Up on the perimeter parapet, **ventilation shafts** or cistern mouths alternate with rooms whose roofs were stoved in by the bombardment. Some of these shafts lead down to Lusignan passages and chambers which the Venetians either filled up or simply sealed at one end, giving rise to the persistent theory that somewhere in this citadel is hidden the fortune of the Venetian merchants, who were only allowed to leave the city empty-handed by the victorious Ottomans. This legend has exercised the Turkish imagination every since, with investigations conducted periodically; similar hollows in the Martinengo bastion served as a bomb shelter for two thousand civilians during August 1974.

Minor churches: the north of town

Just southwest of Othello's Tower, **Saint George of the Latins** is one of the oldest Famagustan churches, originally part of a fortified monastery which may predate the Lusignan ramparts. Today it's merely a shell, but a romantic one; on the surviving apse and north wall, a group of carved bats peer out of a column capital. Nearby on Naim Effendi Sokağı, **Biddulph's Gate** is a remnant doorway of a vanished mansion and named in honour of an early High Commissioner who made it an exception to the pattern of British destructiveness.

Naim Effendi leads towards the northwest corner of Kaleiçi, a military zone since 1974; the Martinengo Bastion in the wall was never stormed by the Turks in their first campaign, and the returning modern Turkish army seems to have taken the hint of of impregnability. Therefore access to the churches of **Ayía Ánna**, **Saint Mary of Carmel** and the **Armenians**, or the (converted) Tanners Mosque, is restricted at present.

One church which you can at least approach is the fourteenth-century Nestorian church of **Áyios Yióryios Exorinós**, usually locked but used as an occasional cultural centre by the new Eastern Mediterranean University. Built by one of the fabulously wealthy Lakhas brothers, he of the jewel-sprinkling incident, it was before 1964 the parish church of the small Greek Orthodox community. The epithet *exorinós* means "the exiler", after a strange legend, reminiscent of the one pertaining to Áyios Misitikós in Páfos: dust gathered from the floor and tossed in an enemy's house would cause them to die or leave the island within a year.

Nearby on Kışla Sokağı, on the way back to Namik Kemal Meydanı, the adjacent, box-like churches of the **Knights Templar** and **Knights Hospitallar**, both fourteenth century, enjoy a proximity which those rival orders never had in their day. The chapel of the Templars is distinguished by a pretty rose window out front, and is now used as a private art gallery.

More churches: the south

The otherwise unremarkable Lusignan church of Stavrós, two blocks south of Namik Kemal Meydanı, marks a small concentration of **arched lanes and medieval houses** on Lala Mustafa Paşa Sokağı, all that survived the siege and later developers. A few steps east, half-demolished **Saint George of Greeks**, an uneasy Byzantine–Gothic hybrid whose three rounded apses clash with the two rows of column stumps, stands cheek-by-jowl with the purer Byzantine but equally ruinous **Áyios Simeón**, tacked onto its south wall.

Two more tiny but exquisite late Byzantine chapels stand to the south amid palm-tree greenery: battered **Áyios Nikólaos**, and intact **Ayía Zoní**, which make a satisfying duo when seen juxtaposed.

▮ VARÓSHA GHOST TOWN ▮

Only a small fraction of the new town, called Maraş by the Turks, is currently inhabited; the rest, by the terms of the 16 August 1974 cease-fire, is technically under Turkish control but effectively a **ghost town**, entered only occasionally by UNFICYP forces since that day. Their patrols, and specially escorted journalists, reported light bulbs burning for years, washing in tatters on the line, and uncleared breakfast dishes, so precipitous was the Greek Cypriots' departure.

Behind the barricade of wire and oil drums, weeds have attained tree-like dimensions on the streets and inside buildings, while cats, rats and snakes prowl as in Nicosia's dead zone. The fate of the Famagusta District Museum's contents is unknown, though the magnificent, private Hadjiprodhromou archaeological collection was **looted** and dispersed for sale quite openly on the international market.

The disposition of Varósha has figured high on the agenda of nearly every inter-communal negotiating session since 1974. Greek Cypriots see its return to use as an initial good-faith gesture for progress on any other issue: the town has practical as well as symbolic significance, since with 40,000 former Greek inhabitants its **resettlement** could solve a goodly fraction of the South's refugee problem.

With northern tourism at its current modest level, the Turkish Cypriots have little need for the row of 33 mouldering, not-quite-state-of-the-art **hotels** which line Varósha's long, narrow beach; but they have periodically proposed that a limited number of Greek Cypriots return to manage the 3000-bed resort. The South has refused, objecting that these offers are always couched in such a way as to make it clear that the hotels would be run largely for the financial benefit of the North.

Meanwhile, fully exposed to the elements, much of Varósha is approaching write-off condition, and it's hard to avoid the suspicion that the Turkish side is maintaining Varósha in its present status for use as a **bargaining chip** at some crucial stage of negotiations.

Maraş

Polat Pasa, the high street of inhabited **Maraş**, currently parades grandiosely to nowhere – behind the oil-drum-and-sand-bag barricades at its south end, where it detours abruptly, a rusty street sign in Greek and the dome of a church are visible. About halfway down, in front of the courthouse, a parked **locomotive**, built in 1904 by a Leeds company, seems far less derelict than anything in the dead zone. It plied the now-vanished Lefke–Famagusta railway from 1907 until 1951: the tracks were to have been extended to Larnaca, but the mayor vetoed the plan to protect local camel drivers from the competition. At the time he was roundly jeered for the decision, but in the event the camel caravans outlasted the trains by over a decade.

Out on the shore, the Palm Beach Hotel is virtually the last occupied building in North Cyprus; beyond sheet-metal baricades, emblazoned with no-photography signs, begins the long, Benidorm-like row of abandoned 1970s hotels, some showing signs of shelling and the northernmost one partly bulldozed to form a clear zone.

Eating, drinking and nightlife

Given the relative lack of accommodation within the actual city limits, eating and drinking options are similarly limited – you can count the **restaurants** of distinction on one hand, and simple affairs for local tradesmen on the other.

Just inside the Land Gate on Elmaz Tabya 17, *Agora* specialises in *küp kebab* (clay-oven-baked meat) and serves lunch and supper daily except Sunday; you can get more meat dishes at the *Viyana*, in a garden setting near the apse of Lala Mustafa Paşa Camii on Liman Yolu. For a more vegetarian slant, try *Hummus*, directly opposite the mosque on Erenler Sokak, while *Cansu Lahmacun Salonu* on İstiklal Caddesi is fine for a quick lunch. One to avoid is the *Damaş*, near the *Hummus*, whose obnoxious proprietor inveigles everyone within a hundred-metre radius into his premises with the blandishment of an ideal photo op of the Lala Mustafa facade – a rare instance of hustle in North Cyprus.

Opposite the telephone office on Polat Paşa Bulvarı in accessible Maraş, *Cyprus House* also serves daily except Sunday amidst an interesting antique decor, with a more varied menu and occasional evening floor shows.

There are even fewer **nightspots** in Famagusta than in Kyrenia; you're pretty much restricted to the nightclub and casino in the *Palm Beach Hotel*, or the rather amateurish disco occupying the baths adjacent to the Saint Francis chapel.

Listings

Car hire *Atlantic*, c/o *Adataş*, Sinan Paşa Sokağı (☎63277); *Deniz*, actually out by the beach hotels in Yeniboğaziçi (☎65510); *Sur*, İsmet İnönü Bulvarı (☎65600).

Exchange The *Kıbrıs Türk Kooperatif Merkez Bankas* has installed a free-standing cashpoint machine 1km out on Ismet Inönü Caddesi, on the way to Salamis; otherwise use *Batu*, across from Saints Peter and Paul in the old town.

Ferry agency *TML* has its poorly marked sales office on Ecevit Caddesi, southeast of the Venetian walls near the naval base; you might also try in the passenger terminal itself a few hours before sailing.

Post offices Main branch on İlker Karter Sokak, Maraş, with a more convenient branch in the Ravelin; hours at as Kyrenia.

Public toilets Easiest to find are those behind the Cansu Lahmacun Salonu on İstiklal Caddesi.

Telephones The *Telekomünikasyon Dairesi* boasts all of two rickety phones, and closes by 7pm; do it from your hotel.

Salamis

The most famous and important ancient city of Cyprus, **SALAMIS** remains the island's most prominent archaeological site, for once living up to the tourist-brochure hype. Even if your interest is casual, you'll need a few hours to see the best-preserved highlights; a full day can easily be spent on the site, especially if you allow periodic intermissions at the wonderful beach which fringes Salamis to the east. Various, mostly Roman and Byzantine, monuments are widely scattered – it's well over a kilometre from the entrance to the ancient harbour, for example – so if you have a vehicle, bring it along on the site, as well as stout footwear, sun protection and drinking water.

Some history

To Salamis are ascribed quasi-mythical foundations in the twelfth century BC by the Trojan war hero **Teucer** (Tefkros), exiled by his father King Telamon from the **Greek isle of Salamis**. The young city shared not only the name but the Mycenaean culture of its parent – borne out spectacularly by the finds in the nearby royal tombs (p.244) – and quickly replaced nearby Enkomi-Alasia as the chief settlement on the coastal bight here. By the eighth century it was already the greatest of the ten Cypriot city-kingdoms, and within two hundred years Salamis was the first place on the island to mint coinage.

The city was the leader in the first fifth-century revolt against the Persians; Onesilus temporarily deposed his brother King Gorgos, a Persian collaborator, and comanded a hastily thrown-together Hellenic confederacy at the Battle of Salamis – lost mostly because of treachery on the part of the Kourion faction. Later that same century, native son Evagoras – a remarkable man for whom every other street seems to be named in the South – more shrewdly united the Cypriot city-kingdoms in another, somewhat more durable, pro-Hellenic federation, with culture as well as politics orientated towards peninsular Greece. Despite his political and military ingenuity Evagoras could not actually prevail against Persia, but over a period of a decade fought the oriental empire to a stand-still, finally negotiating a vassalage relationship.

Salamis actively assisted **Alexander the Great** and was subsequently rewarded with the copper revenues of Tamassos. But under the Ptolemaic kings, the city briefly fell on evil times. Its last king, Nicocreon, rather than surrender to the besieging Ptolemy I, committed suicide in 295 BC, as did all his surviving relatives, who torched the royal palace before doing so.

During the **Roman** era, although Paphos was designated the official capital of Cyprus, Salamis remained the island's main commercial centre and figured prominently in early Christianity: another native son, the Apostle Barnabas, lived and died here (for the full story see "The monastery-museum of Apóstolos Varnávas", p.246). In the Jewish revolt of AD 116, it is thought that the city's entire gentile population was slaughtered; after the Romans had put down the rebellion, Jewish residence on the island was forbidden, an edict not effectively countermanded until a small colony of European Jews settled nearby at the Mesaorian village of Koúklia (today Köprülü) late in the nineteenth century.

The **Byzantines** renamed Salamis as Constantia and designated it an archbishopric and capital of the island again, but the earthquakes and tidal waves of the mid-fourth century badly hurt the city, and the Arab invasions of the seventh century, along with the silting up of its harbour, administered the final blow. From this time neighbouring Famagusta began its ascendancy. Bits of ancient Salamis, used as a convenient quarry throughout medieval times, are scattered throughout contemporary villages and towns of the Kanlıdere (Pedhiéos) River's flood plain which drains the region.

Salamis had only been partially **excavated** by a Franco-Cypriot team before 1974, and assuming a future political settlement which permits further research, more archaeological treasures can be anticipated under the dunes that have largely covered the city since its abandonment.

The main site

The ruins lie eight to nine kilometres north of Salamis between the main highway and the beach, served in theory by any bus heading for Boğaz or beyond. More effectively than the small signs, the monolith of the Salamis Bay Hotel marks the one-kilometre side turning off the coast road, passing a piney picnic area to the north (and currently only) **entrance** (daily 8am–8pm; £1), flanked by an attended beach and the *Bedi* restaurant.

The gymnasium and baths

A rusty arrow directs you towards the walkway of the **gymnasium's east portico**, probably once covered over and still mosaic-paved in variegated Byzantine-era marble, with two rectangular plunge-pools at either end. The northerly one is ringed by a gallery of headless statues, decapitated by Christian zealots in a fury against pagan idolatry; some are now in the Cyprus museum in south Nicosia, others have allegedly disappeared since 1974.

To the west, an impressive, photogenic **colonnade**, re-erected during the 1950s after being tumbled by earthquakes, stakes out the quad of the gymnasium's **palaestra**. The eastern series is taller, and the whole mismatched and hotch-potchy, because the Byzantines recycled Hellentistic and Roman columns from the theatre and another building without too much regard for symmetry or which capitals belonged where. The semicircular structure at the southwest corner of the palaestra is a **latrine**, capacity 44; the flush pipe and tank are still visible at the rear, as are armrests to one side – privacy was not a concern, elimination being considered by the Romans as another social event.

East of the palaestra and portico loom the **baths**, like the gymnasium a Byzantine reworking of Hellenistic and Roman predecessors. Just off the portico another set of cool-water pools – one nearly circular, one octagonal – sandwich the giant **west-central hall** (reckoned the *tepidarium* or mildly steamy anteroom) whose hypocaust cavity is well exposed. Over the south entry, a Christian **fresco fragment** shows two faces, one angelic, executed in a naturalistic, almost Buddhist style.

At the seaward end of the **east-central hall** (probably the *caldarium* or hot-plunge room) another, elevated, pool has been partially restored, and a dank,

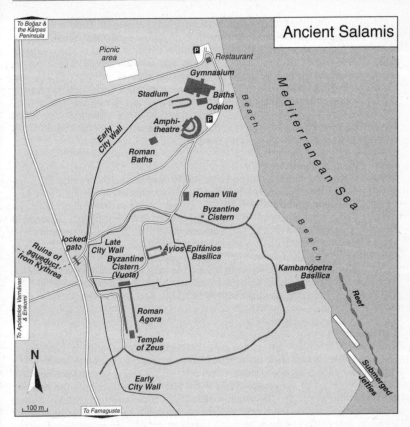

Ancient Salamis

To Boğaz &
the Kárpas
Peninsula

Picnic
area

Restaurant

Gymnasium

Stadium

Baths

Odeion

Amphi-
theatre

Early
City Wall

Roman
Baths

Roman Villa

Byzantine
Cistern

locked
gate

Ruins of
aqueduct
from Kythrea

Late
City Wall

Áyios Epifánios
Basilica

Byzantine
Cistern
(Vuota)

Kambanópetra
Basilica

To Apóstolos Varnávas
& Enkomi

Roman
Agora

Temple
of Zeus

Reef

N

Early
City Wall

Submerged
Jetties

100 m

To Famagusta

Mediterranean Sea

Beach

Beach

crypt-like cavity under its floor can be entered. There are more mosaics here: a patch of abstracts in a niche of the north wall, and another one of an orange on its tree in the northerly semi-dome of the **north hall**, probably a hot-steam "sauna" chamber.

The best, most complete **mosaics** in the entire complex, however, are found in the south bays of the south hall, possibly an alternate entry way to whole ensemble: the smaller one shows the river god Evrotas, the other the lyre and quiver of a fragmentary Apollo.

The stadium and Áyios Epifánios basilica

Another paved and partially colonnaded way leads south from the palaestra, between a vaulted structure with banks of seats against its south wall – probably an **odeion** – and an unexcavated area to the west, thought to be a small **stadium**. Both are overshadowed in all senses by the fine Roman **amphitheatre**, dating from the reign of Augustus and not overrestored as these things go. From the top eighteen surviving rows of seats you have excellent perspectives over the site. Occasional performances still take place during tourist season, though not attracting anything like the original capacity of 15,000.

Continuing southwest from the theatre along the paved drive, there seems little left at first glance of the six-aisled **basilica of Áyios Epifánios** other than the stumps of four rows of fourteen columns, but at the rear (east) of the southern-most naves, mosaic flooring covers a **crypt**, the presumed tomb of the patron saint, emptied by Byzantine Emperor Leo for the sake of its holy relics. In the manner of so many post-Arab-raid churches on Cyprus, this shrunken area around the crypt was refurbished for use after the rest of the basilica was destroyed.

Nearby, an aqueduct bringing water from Kythrea ended at the giant **Byzantine cistern** or *Vuota* beside the **Roman agora**, at the far end of which are the negligible remains of a **Zeus temple**.

Kambanópetra basilica

Most recently excavated, and perhaps more interesting, the romantically set fourth-century **Kambanópetra basilica** overlooks the sea from one curve of a dirt track leading towards the southwest corner of the archaeological zone. Its western forecourt, with small rooms giving onto it, may have been a colonnaded agora or an early monastic cloister. The central apse of the three-aisled nave was provided with a *synthronon* or seats for church dignitaries, while a fourth aisle to the south contains a half-dozen marble sarcophagi.

A handful of standing columns to the east belong to yet another set of **baths**, as suggested by some tumbled-over hypocaust bricks and a tank with a fill-hole. The highlight here is a magnificent **mosaic** of interlocking circles, the most elaborate at Salamis.

The beach

The **beach** fringing the entire site is particularly accessible just below Kambanópetra. A reef encloses a small lagoon, extending all the way south past a cape before subsiding; snorkelling in the metre-deep water, you see not only fish but long courses of man-made stone – the **jetty** or breakwater of the **ancient port** – on the sea floor. The wind is often brisk here, and the ancient harbour facilities were distributed to either side of the point, for use according to the weather. But there has been so much 'quake-generated subsidence, and silting-up courtesy of the river, that it's difficult to envisage the ancient shore profile.

The Royal Tombs

Just south of the disused Salamis south gate, a side road heads off west for less than a kilometre to yet a smaller turning, signed for the **Royal Tombs** (partially fenced; 50p fee when warden present). Two of the nearly 150 eighth- and seventh-century burial sites and graves here caused a sensation when discovered in 1957, because they confirmed Homer's descriptions of late Bronze-Age funerary rites, and their observance five centuries after the original Mycenaean homeland on the Greek Peloponnese had passed its zenith.

Most of the tombs had already been looted in antiquity, but others, in particular **tombs 47 and 79** east of the access drive, yielded the elaborate remains of several royal funerals. Hoards of precious metal or ivory objects, pottery, weapons and food containers were all intended to serve the dead in the underworld, and included the famous ivory inlaid throne and bed – showing profound Phoenician-Egyptian influence – now in the Cyprus museum.

All of the tombs save one opened to the east, and were approached by gently slanting *dhromi* or ramps – on which the most telling artefacts were unearthed. Over the years at least four ceremonial chariots bearing a king's bier had been drawn by pony-like horses to a certain point on the ramps, where the deceased was cremated after the horse (and frequently favourite human servants) were ritually sacrificed. East of three of the tombs the preserved, paired skeletons of the slaughtered horses have been left rather gruesomely in situ, protected by glass plates. Some of the terrified horses broke their own necks at the deadly moment by lunging in their tackle, and at least some of the attendants did not willingly follow their masters in death, as gathered by human remains in the *dhromi* bound hand and foot.

Officially **tomb 50**, the so-called "Saint Catherine's prison" became associated with the Alexandrian saint through a Cypriot legend proposing her as a native of Salamis, briefly imprisoned here by her father the Roman governor for refusing an arranged marriage. That this tomb didn't start life as a Christian place of worship is dramatically borne out by the well-preserved doublet of fossilised horses found adjacent; the T-shaped subterranean interior, with a vaulted antechamber and tiny tunnel-like room that was the tomb, still bears some ecclesiastical trappings. The upper courses of masonry date from the Roman/Byzantine era, when they were built atop the tomb itself, hidden from Christian worshippers until the excavations.

Three tombs to the west of the access drive include a prominent tumulus concealing a mudbrick **"beehive" chamber** nearly identical in design to those at Greek Mycenae. South of these, less exalted citizens were interred in the Kellarka complex, apparently used well into Christian times.

The small adjacent **museum** (daily 8am–sunset, same ticket) displays plans and photographs of the tombs and excavations, plus a reconstruction of one chariot used to transport the dead kings to the necropolis: the brass fittings and horse ornamentations are original, remounted on facsimiles of the long-rotted wooden structures.

Salamis area practicalities

In the immediate environs of Salamis various tourist amenities are worth considering. South of the ruins, once past a soldiers' beach, **Glapsides** and **"Silver" beaches** tout camping as well as swimming, though in this case "camping" seems merely to mean the pitching of sun-flaps for day use. The only nearby organised **campsite**, *Onur* (☎037/65314), with a good attached restaurant, lies a couple of kilometres north of the archaeological site; inland, at YENİ BOGAZIÇI (ÁYIOS SÉRYIOS), there's a basic bed and breakfast place (☎036/64301) charging about £5 per person.

Between Salamis and Boğaz, the shoreline features intermittent sandy patches, occasionally ballooning out into respectably wide beaches; eucalyptus, planted by the British to drain the local marshes, thrive just inland, though there are still plenty of mozzies about on summer nights. The self-contained luxury complex *Salamis Bay* is well placed and amenitied, but a bit of an overwhelming behemoth; adjacent there's the more intimate, though similarly priced, three-star *Mimoza*, which shares some of the *Salamis Bay* facilities. The expensive four-star *Park* (☎036/65511) stands slightly to the north, while the new, well-designed *Cyprus Gardens* (☎037/13722) and *Long Beach* (☎038/88282) apartments are more or less halfway between Salamis and Boğaz (see below).

Places not to be stuck at on this stretch include the *Rebecca* (which may have closed down) or the *Giranel*, both badly placed on the inland highway.

Monastery-museum of Apóstolos Varnávas

Continuing on the same minor road serving the Royal Tombs, you soon approach the former **monastery of Apóstolos Varnávas** (the Apostle Barnabas; daily 8am–6pm; 75p), recently refurbished as a museum. A monastic community first grew up here in the fifth century following the discovery of the purported tomb of the Apostle Barnabas, with funds provided for its construction by the Byzantine emperor himself. The Arab raiders destroyed this foundation during their seventh-century pillagings; the present church and cloister date from 1756, though some columns from Salamis are incorporated into the church.

Until 1974 Apóstolos Varnávas was a favoured goal of pilgrimage among Famagustans, with sequential baptisms being conducted by one of three look-alike, Santa-Claus-bearded monks: Barnabas, Stefanos and Khariton. Since 1917 these three (biological) brothers had presided over the monastery, supporting it through sales of honey and mass-produced icons popular with the nearby villagers, but of rather limited artistic merit. Somehow they contrived to stay after August 1974, but finally, too weak and old to combat Turkish harrassment, gave up and moved to the South in 1976, living out their days at Stavrovoúni monastery (see Chapter Four).

The museums

It's certainly not the **icon collection**, housed in the former *katholikón*, that justifies the entrance fee; of them, the oldest and most artistically worthy is an unusual *Herod's Banquet* (1858), with John the Baptist being beheaded in the lower frame. Most seem scrabbled-together replacements for 35 more valuable ones which went mysteriously missing from the lightly guarded premises in 1982.

The former cells around the appealingly landscaped court have been converted into what is at present the North's best **archaeological museum;** how much, if any of it, is based on the looted Hadjiprodhomou collection or the holdings of the inaccessible Famagusta District museum (see "Archaeology in Cyprus" in *Contexts*) is uncertain. Eras are presented slightly out of order, proceeding clockwise from the Bronze Age to the Venetian period, with a strangely mixed Ottoman/Classical Greek wing at the end. Labelling gives only dates, with few indications of provenance.

The Bronze Age room features incised red-polished and white-slip pottery, as well as bronze items. A model house and set of miniature plates appear in the Geometric room; Archaic jugs betray Mycenaean influcence in their depiction of an archer and birds. Among terracotta votive figurines and chariots stands an unusual wheel-footed horse – definitely not a chariot – on which a lyre player entertains two other riders.

Star of the Classical section is a woman in a head-dress – possibly the goddess Demeter – holding a poppy; Cyprus was one of the earliest centres of opium production. Two stone lions squat, haunch to haunch, with their tongues out, near a a perfectly formed sphinx; continuing the animal theme, some Hellenistic child's rattles have the shape of wild boars.

The tomb of Barnabas

To one side of the monastery car park stands a small, undesecrated little mausoleum-chapel, shaded by a carob tree and erected during the 1950s over a catacomb that is the presumed **tomb of Barnabas** (see below). A switch at the top illuminates stairs leading down to two rock-cut chambers with room for half-a-dozen dead, similar to the crypt of Saint Lazaros in Larnaca – and far older than Christianity. Occasional fresh candle drippings and flower offerings would suggest that the local Turks continue to revere the cave regardless of the departure of the Orthodox custodians. The stratum of simple, fervent belief runs deep in Cyprus, predating the monotheistic religions and not respecting their fine distinctions.

BARNABAS AND THE AUTOCEPHALOUS CHURCH OF CYPRUS

Barnabas (*Varnávas* in Greek), a native of Salamis, was the companion of the Apostle Paul on missionary voyages round Cyprus and Asia Minor before their falling-out over whether or not Barnabas' cousin Mark was to accompany them overseas. He is generally credited with being the apostle most influential in introducing Christianity to the island, and long after his demise with perpetuating its independent status through a miraculous intervention.

His activities having aroused the ire of the Salamis Jewish community into which he had been born, Barnabas was martyred by stoning in about 75 AD; thereafter matters become apocryphal, with most accounts having Mark interring the corpse at an undisclosed location. There things would have stood had it not been for an ecclesiastical squabble 400 years later.

Late in the fifth century the Church of Antioch, having been founded by Peter and thus an Apostolic See, claimed precedence over that of Cyprus, which retorted, initially unsuccessfully, that as a foundation of the Apostle Barnabas the island's Church was also apostolic and of equal rank. Subordination to the Syrian archbishopric was only avoided through the supernatural intervention of Barnabas himself, who appeared in a dream to Anthemios, Archbishop of Salamis, and bid him unearth the apostle's remains from a lonely spot on the Mesaoría marked by a carob tree. Following these instructions, the cleric indeed found a catacomb matching the description and containing what could well have been the bones of Barnabas, clasping a mildewed copy (in Hebrew) of the Gospel of Saint Matthew to his breast. Armed with these incontrovertible relics, the Cypriots went to Constantinople, where a synod convened by the Emperor Zeno was sufficiently impressed to grant special privileges to the island's church.

Foremost it was to remain autocephalous (autonomous), deferring only to the Sees of Constantinople, Alexandria, Antioch and Jerusalem in importance, and in later centuries pre-eminent over larger autocephalous churches, such as those in Russia. Cypriot bishops retained the right to elect their own archbishop, who was permitted to sign his name in red ink in imitation of the emperor's custom, wear imperial purple, and wield a sceptre instead of a pastoral staff.

When Cyprus fell to the Ottomans, these hitherto symbolic privileges acquired practical import inasmuch as the churchmen were charged with the civil as well as the spiritual administration of their Orthodox flock. Following independence, Archbishop Makarios revived the medieval term *ethnarch*, further blurring the lines between secular and ecclesiastical power, with ultimately catastrophic consequences for the island.

Enkomi-Alasia

From the monastery-museum it's a short drive southwest to a T-junction just beyond which, making a right turn, lies the poorly signed Bronze-Age town of **ENKOMI-ALASIA** (partially fenced; 50p admission when warden present), opposite a water tank. Founded in about 2000 BC, it first appeared historically 400 years later on some Pharaonic tablets, referred to as "Alashya" (Éngomi is the modern Greek name of the nearest village). Alasia figured on Egyptian trade documents because from the sixteenth century on it acted as a thriving copper-exporting harbour, in an age when the coast was much closer and the river Pedhiéos more navigable than it is today. Mycenaean immigration had swelled the population to 15,000 by the twelfth century, but fire and earthquake mortally weakened the city during the eleventh century, after which it was abandoned in favour of Salamis.

The site

British museum-sponsored excavations began in 1896, revealing the most complete Mycenaean city on Cyprus, and continued at intervals by French, Swedish and Cypriot missions until 1974. The town plan was a grid of narrow, perpendicular streets and low houses, surrounded by a wall; Alasia was initially thought to be a necropolis for Salamis, since human skeletons were discovered under each dwelling as at Khirokitia (see Chapter One, p.56).

Also found here was an as-yet undeciphered tablet in Cypro-Minoan script; the famous "Horned God", possibly an avatar of Apollo whose worship was imported from Arcadia in the Peloponnese; and an exquisite silver bowl inlaid with ox-head and floral designs, whose only known equal also came from the same region. These and other treasures are distributed between the British and Cyprus museums.

For all that, the site today is of essentially specialist interest, with little remaining above waist level; problems of interpretation are made more difficult by the fact that survivors of the eleventh-century earthquakes divided up damaged open-plan houses with crude rubble barriers. The walled precinct is entered via a north gate; west of the main longitudinal street, the **"Horned God"** was found in a namesake sanctuary, surrounded by the skulls of animals presumably worn as masques during the celebration of his cult. Beyond it, a baronial house is known prosaically as **Building 18**, while at the south edge of the exposed grid stands the so-called **House of Bronzes**, where many such objects were discovered in 1934.

The cenotaph of Nicocreon

If you turn left at the T-junction towards Famagusta, you'll pass through the modern village **TUZLA (ÉNGOMI)**, at the far side of which stands the cut-open tumulus known as the **cenotaph of Nicocreon**. Excavations revealed an elevated platform on which an ancient mock cremation had taken place; among the limited number of items recovered were various clay dummies, thought to represent the actual family of Nicocreon, who had killed themselves in their palace rather than surrender to Ptolemy I. Its burning, collapsing beams were their real pyre; another unsolved mystery here is who conducted the memorial ceremony honouring of the recently defeated dynasty.

Boğaz and around

BOĞAZ (BOGÁZI) makes a pleasant base with its fishing anchorage and small beach, though oil storage tanks and a cement plant across the bay, built virtually on the site of a vanished Templars' castle, is a bit disconcerting. Of the half-dozen seafood **restaurants** here, *George's* is about the simplest, *Kocatepe* the fanciest, with others like *Çarlı* and *Karsel* filling various niches in between – all are considerably cheaper than their equivalents in Kyrenia. Either of the two local three-star **hotels**, represented by *President* and *Celebrity Holidays*, are good choices: the sea-level *Boğaz* (☎037/12559), across the fairly quiet road from the beach, or the hilltop *Sea View* (☎037/12651), actually closer to the hilltop village of BOĞAZTEPE (MONAGRÁ), where most of the rooms live up to the name, and with tennis courts and a pool. Booked through an agency, rates at either run about £20 a day double occupancy, half board.

Approaching Boğaz from Nicosia or Kyrenia, you'll almost certainly pass through **İSKELE (TRÍKOMO)**, notable as the birthplace of EOKA leader George Grivas, and less controversially that of Vassos Karageorghis, Cyprus' foremost archaeologist. In the central square and roundabout, the diminutive fifteenth-century Dominican chapel of **Áyios Iákovos** seems plunked down like a jewel-box; supposedly Queen Marie of Romania was so taken with it that she had an exact replica built on the Black Sea coast as a royal chapel. To the west of the village, on the way to GEÇİTKALE (LEFKÓNIKO), you'll pass the larger, twelfth to fifteenth-century church of the **Panayía Theotókos**, preserving some frescoes and recently opened as an icon museum – though there are allegations that at least one of the exhibits has been spirited away from another, still-functioning church (see p.254).

THE KIRPAŞA (KÁRPAS) PENINSULA

The remote "panhandle" of Cyprus, known variously as the **Kırpaşa, Kárpas or Karpaz peninsula**, presents a landscape of rolling hills and grain fields, partly domesticated with vineyards, tobacco fields or olive and carob trees, and fringed by some of the loneliest beaches on the island. In ancient times it was much more densely inhabited, something attested to by a surprising concentration of small archaeological sites and early Christian churches, taken together considerably more interesting than the celebrated monastery of Apóstolos Andhréas near the far cape. The inhabitants were once noted for their craftwork, relict traditions which had died out elsewhere, and a smattering of blue or green eyes, and more finely chiselled features, that hinted at Frankish or Arab settlement. Until 1974 it was a communal mosaic, Turkish villages such as Áyios Simeón, Néta and Koróvia alternating with Greek ones like Rizokarpaso, Ayía Triás and Yialoússa. However only a few, like Áyios Andhrónikos, were actually mixed; Denktaş reportedly came there in 1964 to urge its Turks to segregate themselves. They refused then, though the small Turkish-Cypriot minority of Áyios Theódhoros moved to Galátia when the troubles started, and a fortified enclave eventually formed around the kernel of the three all-Turkish villages cited.

Today the crumbling villages seem at least fifty-percent resettled by mainland Turks. But the peninsula is no longer heavily garrisoned by the Turkish army, superfluous as it is to the argument of who controls the North.

Kantara castle

Poised at the spot where the Kyrenia range subsides into rolling hills, **Kantara castle**, the easternmost and lowest of the Byzantine/Crusader trio, is as good a spot as any to consider the base of the peninsula. Even here the Kárpas is so narrow that it simultaneously surveys impressive arcs of shoreline along both the north coast and the Bay of Famagusta. The name is thought to derive from the Arabic *qantara*, "arch" or "bridge", though it's difficult to pinpoint such a structure in surrounding landscape.

Traditionally the castle is reckoned to be where Isaac Comnenus surrendered to Richard the Lionheart in 1191. Like Saint Hilarion castle, it figured prominently in the 1229–30 war between the supporters of the Holy Roman Emperor Frederick II and the Lusignan-Ibelin cartel, and again during the Genoese invasion, when regent John of Antioch was smuggled out of gaol in Famagusta to this hideout disguised as a pot-tinner. Kantara shared the fate of the other castles at the hands of the Venetians early in the sixteenth century, but the castle is still the best preserved of the three.

Getting there

From Boğaz you'll need the better part of 45 minutes driving to get to the castle, climbing via dilapidated YARKÖY (ÁYIOS ELÍAS); TURNALAR (YERÁNI) with a conspicuous, desecrated church; and finally pine-swathed **Kantára** village, the closest thing to a hill station in the Kyrenia range.

Among the boarded-up Greek summer villas and dried-up fountains, there's a sporadically operating restaurant and an apparently abandoned hotel. Nobody has bothered to obliterate some of the more extreme EOKA-B graffiti near the church: "Greeks, listen to the voice of your hearts, *énosis* or death" and "Dhiyenis [ie Grivas] didn't die, he lives in our souls" – the latter precisely every Turkish Cypriot's misgiving about their erstwhile countrymen. Pray for no oncoming traffic on the one-lane surface between Turnalar and Kantára – it's a long way back to the next lay-by – and bear right once in the hill station, following signs for "*Piknik yeri*" (picnic grounds) once on the watershed. The tarmac gives out shortly before the castle's car park, 4km east of the village.

The site

Seven hundred metres above sea level, most of the complex faces east, the only direction from which it is easily accessible. You enter the outer enceinte through a **barbican** flanked by a pair of towers, then climb steps to the inner ward. First stop here will probably be the massive **southeast tower**, its lower part a cistern which occasionally doubled as a dungeon. Further along the southeast wall are the **barracks**, a trio of rooms fitted with loopholes; adjacent, an obvious latrine was flushed by the castle's sophisticated plumbing system. Thus far the buildings are in good condition, down to the woodwork and groin-vaulted ceilings, and could be used tomorrow. Beyond this point, however, Kantara is quite ruinous until the southwest corner of the battlements, where one chamber contains a hidden **postern gate** for surprising besiegers.

Crossing the rubble of the inner bailey, or returning to the southeast tower, you can attain the militarily remarkable **northern towers**, where two long galleries equipped with arrow slits are joined by a square chamber. Just one wall and a Gothic window survive of the highest watchtower, used for communicating with Buffavento to the west; the **northeast bastion**, by contrast, is impressively complete.

The coast below: Kaplıca (Dhavlós) and around

From either the castle or village of Kantára, you can plainly see **KAPLICA (DHAVLÓS)** and its bays just below on the north coast. To get there, return to the four-way junction in Kantára village for the sharp but brief descent. The village, re-settled by mainlanders, is actually 1km inland from the main, rather average beach and drinks stand, popular with islanders; just east there's an anchorage and a small fish-fry shack, plus another sandy patch about 3km west, but frankly neither would be worth the bother of travelling all the way from Kyrenia.

Ten kilometres west, near the boundary between Famagusta and Kyrenia districts, the lonely late Byzantine church of **Panayía Pergamiótissa** sits about 400m inland from the road. Once completely frescoed and the seat of a monastery, it's now thoroughly bricked up to prevent further vandalism, and more evocative seen from afar.

Beaches and churches: the route to the cape

The most obvious excursion from Boğaz is to the northeast, towards Zafer Burnu (Cape Áyios Andhréas). You can see the most interesting sights in a single, long day, but to really savour the area you'd want two.

For very private, sandy **beaches** relatively near Boğaz, two nameless strands to either side of Zeytin Burnu (Cape Eléa) fit the bill well. For the first one, head southeast out of the central crossroads in the village of ÇAYIROVA (ÁYIOS THEÓDHOROS) on the most prominent dirt track, always turning towards the sea when given the choice. Soon you emerge at an impromptu car park/turnaround area very near Zeytin Burnu; the shore below can be rubbishy and seaweed-strewn, but walk to the far end of the 400-metre beach and the litter thins out. Up on the headland closing off the cove are supposed to be the sparse remains of an ancient town.

For the other local beach, bypass Çayırova in favour of BAFRA (VOGOLÍDHA), from where another, briefer dirt road continues to a decent beach deposited by a rather stagnant stream. A holiday village under construction here seems to have run out of steam, testimony to the collapse of the Asil Nadir empire.

If you want facilities with your swim, your next opportunity will be the small, reefy **beach** below KUMYALI (KÓMA TOU YIALOU), encroached on somewhat by a "restaurant/camping" (really a day use area) and a fishing port.

Panayía Kanakariá church

The intriguing sixth-to-twelfth-century monastic church of Panayía Kanakariá stands at the very western edge of BOLTAŞLI **(LYTHRANGOMÍ)**, just east of ZÍYAMET (LEONÁRISSO) on the main Karpas trunk route. Today it is locked – rather a case of bolting the stable door after the horse has fled (see below) – but enough can be seen of the design from outside to convince you of the building's merit. Nave and aisles represent an eleventh-century revamping of the original sixth-century structure, of which only the apse (former home of the mosaics) remains. The domed narthex was added shortly afterwards, while the high, drummed central dome followed in the 1700s.

Beyond Boltaşlı

The narrow but paved side road beyond the village passes through the historically Turkish enclave before ending at **KALEBURNU (GALINÓPORNI)**, a remarkable semi-troglodytic village wedged in between two hills. Both the slopes and The surrounding areas are rife with rock-cut **tombs.** A seaward track just before reaching the village leads to **Üsküdar beach,** not utterly wonderful but acceptable for a dip. Dirt tracks shown to Yenierenköy and Dipkarpaz from here on virtually all maps are negotiable only with a 4WD or vehicle with high clearance.

THE THEFT OF THE KANAKARIÁ MOSAICS

The **mosaics** which formerly graced the apse of Panayía Kanakariá are contemporary with those at Ravenna; they consisted of a Virgin and precociously aged Child surrounded by unusual depictions of the Evangelist Matthew, Apostle Andrew, Saint Iakovos and an archangel, among other figures. Art historians disagree on their merit, but the expressiveness of the figures compensates somewhat for the crudeness of the *tesserae* (pigmented or gilded glass cubes used to compose the mosaic).

Even before independence, the mosaics had suffered at the hands of superstitious villagers who believed that the tesserae were efficacious against skin disease. Much worse was to follow, however, at some undetermined moment between 1974 and 1979, when thieves broke in through the windows of the drum, hacked four sections of mosaic off the wall, and spirited them off the island.

The whereabouts of the fragments were unknown until the late 1980s, when American art dealer Peg Goldberg purchased them for $1.8 million from a Swiss intermediary who claimed to have an export permit from the North Cyprus government. They were then offered for sale to the Getty museum for ten times that amount, but by now the Autocephalous Orthodox Church of Cyprus had got wind of the dealings.

Acting jointly with the church, the government of the South sued for the return of the mosaics in the US District Court of Indianapolis, finally winning their case in August 1989; the presiding judge essentially agreed with the Greek-Cypriot contention that an export licence granted by an internationally unrecognised state was similarly invalid, and that the artwork remained the property of the Orthodox church. Following a failed appeal by the dealers, the mosaics returned to the South in the summer of 1991, and are being readied for display in the new annexe of the Archbishop Makarios Cultural Centre (see Chapter Five, p.168). Whether this is a precedent that can be used in other instances of antiquities theft remains to be seen.

Yenierenköy and around

YENIERENKÖY (YIALOÚSA, YALUSA), the second largest village on the peninsula and centre of the local tobacco industry, has been resettled by the inhabitants of the Kókkina (Erenköy) enclave in Tillyría (see p.113) since 1975. Just northeast, the small **beaches** and boat jetties of "Yeni" and "Malibu" lie almost within sight of the main coast road, but except for one fish restuarant there seems no compelling reason to take advantage of them unless the south wind is up, when these coves will be more sheltered than usual.

More churches

The alternate, inland turning from Yenierenköy leads to **SİPAHİ (AYÍA TRIÁS)**, where the handsome **mosaic floor** of a sixth-century, three-aisled Christian basilica survives, as does the adjoining baptistry paving; in the church mosaic you can pick out the name of the artist, Heraclios. The site is just outside the village to the north, going downhill to sea, some 20m west of road.

This inland detour and the coast route re-join well before **Áyios Thýrsos**, a tiny resort grouped around two namesake churches: the desecrated modern one up on the road is of little interest, but the older one down at sea level contains a crypt at the rear in which a healing spring once trickled. One or the other is still actually used for the 23 July festival by the remaining local Greeks. Miniscule, tenth-century **Áyios Fótios**, the next church passed, is accessible by a non-motorable, 300-metre track some 5km past Áyios Thýrsos; after another 3km, another bumpy drive leads up through the pines to the medieval monastery church of **Panayía Eleoússa**, romantically overlooking the broad sweep of Ronnás Bay. Here dunes give way to a fine beach possibly favoured by egg-laying turtles, but the prevailing north wind brings a lot of garbage, and you've a bit of a hike in over the tyre-confounding sand.

Dipkarpaz – and more churches

From Ronnás the road turns inland to **DİPKARPAZ (RIZOKÁRPASO)**, the remotest and yet largest village on the peninsula, with a population of around three thousand. Here a huge new mosque overshadows the church of the remaining Greeks; there's a single *pansiyon*/restaurant, though you'd be hard pressed to find a reason to patronise it. Once a prosperous place, Dipkarpaz has been reduced to the status of an Anatolian village, with added poignancy in the use of once-imposing arcaded houses as poultry pens and hay barns.

North from Dipkarpaz: Áyios Fílon and Aféndrika

Both of these early Christian sites are well worth the slight detour north from Dipkarpaz; once up on the northerly of the two ridges enclosing the village ask for the road to the fisherman's anchorage, (*balıkçının barınağı* in Turkish, *psaradhikó limáni* in Greek).

The basilicas of **Áyios Fílon**, 3km along this, are the most obvious remains of ancient Karpasia – even from the ridge you can easily pick out the seven bedraggled washingtonia palms and ruined resort buildings surrounding them. Typically the half-ruined tenth-century chapel, of which only the apse and south wall are intact, sits amid foundations of a far larger, earlier basilica, perhaps the archiepiscopal seat of the saintly Fílon, first bishop of Christian Karpasia. Its extensive

THE GREEKS OF THE KÁRPAS

The 1974 war effectively bypassed the peninsula, so that there was no panicky exodus of civilians in the path of the oncoming army. Thus of the nearly 20,000 **Greeks** who chose to stay in the North, most of them lived on the Kárpas. But since 1975, systematic harassment by the Turkish army and the North Cypriot government has reduced this population to a handful of middle-aged and older individuals. There have been forcible expulsions to the South when property was coveted by settlers or Turkish-Cypriot refugees, and the remaining Greek Cypriots require permits to travel outside their home village. Secondary education is no longer allowed, with only two Greek primary schools still functioning, so that any children over the age of eleven must go to the South for continued education, without any right of return. Similarly, no Greek-Cypriot doctor practises anywhere in the North.

Not surprisingly, then, only about 570 stubborn Greeks continue to live on the peninsula: over 400 in Dipkarpaz (Rizokárpaso), 140 in Sipahi (Ayía Triás) and perhaps half-a-dozen in Yeşilköy (Áyios Andhrónikos). The UN post in Ziyamet (Leonárisso), staffed by Canadians, exists to protect their interests; primarily they bring food from the South at regular intervals, as lack of facility in Turkish and their restricted participation in the local economy mean the Greeks can't or won't shop locally. The Greeks are allowed to visit doctors and relatives the South on one-week, Friday-to-Friday visas, but again are shuttled to the Ledra Palace crossing in Nicosia by the UN, since they're not allowed to take their own vehicles.

Relations between the Greek Cypriots and goat-grazing Anatolian settlers are strained, somewhat better with Turkish Cypriots or Bulgarian-Turkish immigrants used to farming, though the coffee houses in Sipahi and Dipkarpaz are ethnically segregated. The conditions of the Greeks' continued residence here are undeniably humiliating: "We live like animals" can be an unsolicited comment on the state of affairs, voiced in tandem with the fatalistic, almost Byzantine belief that the invasion and its aftermath were God's punishment for their sins – sentiments expressed by Greeks at regular intervals since the Turks first appeared in Anatolia during the tenth century. Medieval harassment extends even to religious observance: the church bell in Dipkarpaz may not be rung lest it offend the Muslims, although the bells in Sipahi – with a proportionately higher Greek population – may be sounded. The icon of the Siphai village church went missing in December 1991, allegedly appearing subsequently among the exhibits of the museum in İskele (Tríkomo).

Despite their troubles, the Greek Cypriots of the Kárpas are a friendly, hospitable lot when approached, though some discretion is in order to avoid compromising them: their pleasure at having someone new to talk with is well dampened by awareness that being seen in unsupervised conversations with outsiders can later result in unpleasant interrogations by the police. One definitely does not go banging on doors or barging through coffee houses asking after Greeks; if someone gives you a knowing nod or searching look in the fields or on the street or addresses you in English, odds are they are Greek Cypriot. It's really best to have a name and address to call on in advance; at any rate, be judiciously discreet.

---

mosaic flooring includes an abstract ring design similar to that of Kambanópetra at Salamis. Just north of the two churches, you can find the ancient jetty sticking 100m out to sea, its masonry furrowed where long-vanished iron pins held the stones together. The balance of Hellenistic and Roman Karpasia, which supplied building stone for both churches, lies scattered to the west of the road in, but it's a long slog through thornbushes to never-excavated walls and a necropolis.

Beyond Áyios Fílon the paved but narrow road swings east to follow the coast 8km more to **Aféndrika**, another important ancient town on an even large scale than Karpasia, with three ruined churches: Panayía Khrysiótissa, a twelfth-century ruin inside which is a smaller chapel 200 years younger; domed Áyios Yióryios; and three-aisled Panayía Asómatos. West of the group of churches is a necropolis, while in the opposite direction rooms of the citadel are partly cut into the outcrop on which it is built.

The cape environs

The main road, bearing south from the central junction in Dipkarpaz, soon narrows permanently to one (paved) lane; pines of the Kárpas forest, centred round the village, subside to terebinth as you change sides of the narrowing peninsula and emerge on its south shore.

Some 5km east of Dipkarpaz, the road passes the *Blue Sea* **restaurant,** an ideal lunch stop if touring these parts, offering fresh fish from the adjacent fishing anchorage. The proprietors, refugees from the Páfos area, also let several **rooms** upstairs for £5.50 per person – tidy but rather basic, with no electricity and no phone to book on.

Continuing, the road bears inland again for a while, passing through fields and pastures surpisingly well tended for such a deserted region. Some 14km beyond the *Blue Sea* begins the **best beach** in the North, if not the entire island, initially hidden behind a straight line of scrub-covered knolls halting the advance of vast dunes. Westerly access is provided by a dirt lane starting by some old stone foundations at the roadside; this track threads through a conspicuous gap in the barrier hillocks, leaving you with a ten-minute walk across the sand to the water. Alternatively, you can proceed until the road skirts the edge of the hard-packed dunes themselves, and the beach extends obviously southwest, though the walk in from several lay-bys here is no shorter.

The five-plus kilometres of sand could easily accommodate most of the North's population on a summer weekend, and very likely does on occasion; there's some hope for its preservation, as the tip of the peninsula has recently been declared a protected area – good news for the quail and other birds living in the dunes, and the turtles who reportedly lay eggs on this wild, spectacular beach.

Apóstolos Andhréas monastery

The downed phone lines which have shadowed the road for miles end at the sprawling, barracks-like **monastery of Apóstolos Andhréas**, until 1974 a lodestar for Cypriot pilgrims. The spot has been revered since legend credited the Apostle Andrew with summoning forth a miraculous spring on the shore during a journey from Palestine, and using the water to effect cures. By Byzantine times there was a fortified abbey here, long since disappeared but a historical alternative to Kantara as the site of Isaac Comnenus' capture by Richard the Lionheart.

The tradition of mass pilgrimage and popularity, however, only dates from the well-documented experience of one **Maria Georgiou**, an Anatolian Greek whose small son was kidnapped by brigands in 1895; seventeen years later the apostle appeared in a dream and commanded her to pray for the boy's return at the monastery. Crossing the straits from Turkey in a crowded boat, Georgiou happened to tell the story to a young dervish among the passengers, who grew more and more agitated as the narrative progressed. He asked the woman if her lost son had any distinguishing signs, and upon hearing a pair of birthmarks described, cast off his robes to reveal them and embraced her. The son – for he it was – had been raised a Muslim in Istanbul, but upon docking on Cyprus was re-baptised, to the general acclaim of the population.

Subsequent **miracles** – mostly cures of epilepsy, paralysis and blindness – at the monastery further enhanced its prestige and rendered it enormously wealthy in votive donations. But the faithful never missed the opportunity for a fun day out as well, eventually scandalising the church into censuring the weekend carnival atmosphere.

All that came to an abrupt end **after 1974**, since when the pilgrims' hostel has been occupied by the army, and the monastery shrunk to a pathetic ghost of its former self. In a reversal of policy from the years when the place was off-limits to outsiders, it is now signposted by yellow-and-black placards (*'Manastır'*) as a tourist attraction, run like a sort of zoo by the authorities to prove North Cyprus' religious tolerance. "Zoo" is not such an arbitrary characterisation, with about fifty cats far outnumbering the human population, plus an enormous sow – presumably kept to wind up the majority Muslim population in the North. Amazingly, the major 30 November and 15 August festivals are still observed after a fashion, and the priest comes from Dipkarpaz to conduct liturgies at other times.

Visits begin with a check-in at a small police post, where your personal details (bring your passport) and time of arrival are logged in a giant notebook. Then one of five remaining Greek caretakers, too dispirited or intimidated to talk much, will show you the nineteenth-century **katholikón**, of little intrinsic interest except for the giant wax votive candles which keep coming from the South to judge by their wrapping; you might be generous at the donations box, as the monastery is plainly in reduced circumstances nowadays. Finally, an old woman will take you down to the fifteenth-century seaside **chapel**, now essentially a crypt below the main church, where the **holy well** of the apostle flows audibly below a heavy stone cover.

Zafer Burnu (Cape Apostólou Andhréa)

From the monastery, 7km of rough track brings you to **Zafer Burnu**, the definitive, if somewhat anti-climactic John O'Groats for Cyprus. A cave-riddled rock was the site of an ancient Aphrodite temple, of which nothing remains; the goddess was by most accounts in a savage aspect here, a siren-like devourer of men in the sea below. Beyond an abandoned guardhouse and around the offshore **Klidhés Islets** (the "Keys"), beloved of seabirds, many a ship has been wrecked. Even modern shipping, often evident on the horizon, gives the cape a wide berth as it plies the sea lanes between Syria, Lebanon, Turkey and Cyprus.

travel details

Buses

From Famagusta to Nicosia, half-hourly (1hr); to Kyrenia, half-hourly (1hr); to Yenierenköy, several daily (1hr 15min).

Ferryboats

From Famagusta 3 weekly (currently Tues, Thur, Sat evening) to Mersin, Turkey (10hr); details of fare structures in "Getting There" in *Basics*.

THE
HISTORICAL
FRAMEWORK

With its critical location on the way to the Middle East, the history of Cyprus can't help being long and chequered. The following summary is heavily biased towards antiquity and events of this century, enabling a reader to grasp what they are most likely to see in a museum – and on the street.

BEGINNINGS

Settlements of **round stone dwellings**, particularly along the north coast and at Khirokitía near Larnaca, indicate habitation in Cyprus as early as 7000 BC; the origins of these first **Neolithic** settlers is uncertain, but items in obsidian, a material unknown on the island, suggest the Middle Eastern mainland opposite. The first Cypriots engaged in hunting, farming and fishing, but were ignorant of pottery, fashioning instead rough vessels, idols and jewellery from stone. Religious observance seemed limited to **burial practices** – the dead were interred under or near dwellings in a fetal position, with their chests crushed by boulders to prevent them from haunting the living.

After this initial colonisation, a 1500-year-long hiatus in archaeological evidence, so far unexplained, ensued until the so-called **Neolithic II** culture appeared after 4500 BC. Sites near Áyios Epíktitos on the north coast and Sotíra in the south yielded quantities of so-called "red combed" and abstractly painted ware, the first indigenous **ceramics**.

The **Chalkolithic** period, whose cultures emerged after 4000 BC in a gradual transition from the late Neolithic, was distinguished by the settlement of the previously neglected western portion of Cyprus. The era takes its name from the discovery of copper (*chalkos* in Greek) implements, but more important, as indications of developing **fertility cults**, are the limestone female idols at Lémba and Kissónerga, and cruciform grey-green picrolite pendants at Yialiá, reminiscent of similar work in the west Aegean.

With the advent of the **Early Bronze Age** (reckoned 2500 BC and onwards), the focus of Cypriot life shifted to the Mesaoría and its perimeter, conveniently near the first **copper mines**, where the importation of tin permitted the smelting of bronze. Curiously no confirmed habitation has yet been excavated, but settlement has been inferred from the distribution of elaborate subterranean chamber **tombs or shrines** and their contents, especially at Vounous near Kyrenia. Ceramics executed in red clay seem to have spread across the island from north to south; deeply incised, whimsical zoomorphic or composite ware, imaginatively combining humorous aesthetics with function, appeared along with cruder models of schematic figures engaged in elaborate religious ceremonies pertaining to a bull-centred fertility cult. The **bull**, imported from Asia, permitted for the first time the ploughing of hitherto unusable land, and models show this also.

Well into the second millennium BC, during the so-called **Middle Bronze Age** period, settlements appear on the south and east coasts of Cyprus, facing probable **overseas trading** partners; commerce with immediate neighbours, fuelled by the copper deposits, would by now have been well developed. The most important eastern port was Enkomi-Alasia, the second name soon to be synonymous with the island. Rectangular or L-shaped **dwellings** with flat roofs completely supplanted round ones, and ominously **forts** – their inland positioning indicative of civil conflict over the copper trade, rather than threats from outside – sprang up at various sites around the Mesaoría. Both transport and warfare were facilitated by the recent importation of **horses**. In religious life, female **plank idols**, alone or nursing infants, and bird-headed, earringed figurines were important – the latter probably intended as symbolic companions for interred men, or manifestations of an earth goddess reclaiming one of her children.

THE LATE BRONZE AGE, AND ARRIVAL OF THE MYCENAEANS

As Cypriot political and commercial transactions became more complicated, a **writing script** became necessary: the earliest known Cypriot document, from the **late Bronze Age**, is an incised clay sixteenth-century tablet unearthed at Enkomi-Alasia. Called **Cypro-Minoan** after its supposed derivation from Cretan Linear A, the origins or language of the eighty still-undeciphered characters have not been proved, though pottery finds at Toúmba tou Skoúrou and Ayía Iríni on the Bay of Mórfou indicate the necessary contacts with Minoan culture. Fragmental passages were inscribed frequently on cups, cylinder seals and loom-weights, implying that the language was common throughout Cyprus, though the Enkomi-Alasia tablet remains the only known complete text. Variations of this script remained in use long after the arrival of the Mycenaeans, who did not impose the use of their own presumed form of Linear B.

Other people's records, especially those of the Egyptians, suggest that the island was consistently referred to as **Alashiya** (or Asy, or Alasia) by the fifteenth and fourteenth centuries BC and also imply that for the first time Cyprus formed a loosely united **confederation** of towns. Of these, **Kition** and **Enkomi-Alasia** came to the fore, their high standard of living reflected in elaborate **sanitary facilities**, including bathtubs and sewers. Two new ceramic styles emerged: so-called "Base Ring", shiny and thin-walled in imitation of metal, usually with a basal ring; and "White Slip" – provided with a primer coat of white slurry on which brown or black patterns were executed.

THE MYCENAEANS

But the most dramatic change in island culture was fostered by the first **arrival of the Mycenaeans** from the Greek Peloponnese, who replaced the Minoans as the main Hellenic influence in the east Mediterranean after 1400 BC. Their immediate influence was most obvious in **pottery** of that era – "rude style" pictorial *kratirs*, showing mythological scenes and bestiaries (including the octopus, a Minoan favourite) – though it's still uncertain whether such items were brought by the Mycenaeans to trade for copper, or their production techniques taught to local potters using wheels for the first time. From the same period date the notable enamelled *rhyton* (a horn-shaped drinking vessel – see p.169 and 315) from Kition, with three series of hunters and animals, and the famous silver bowl of Enkomi-Alasia, inlaid with a floral and bull's-head design.

Around 1200 BC, Mycenaean civilization in its **Peloponnesian homeland collapsed** when confronted with invasion by the Dorian peoples, events which had a profound knock-on effect on Cyprus. Rogue Mycenaean survivors fled Greece via Anatolia, where others joined them to become the raiding "sea peoples" mentioned in Egyptian chronicles of the time. They established an initial Cypriot foothold at **Maa** in the west of the island, choosing a headland easily defensible from both land and sea, and proceeded to destroy Enkomi-Alasia and Kition. Both were soon rebuilt with fortification walls reminiscent of the Mycenaean Argolid, with ashlar blocks used for these and individual buildings.

Religious shrines were closely associated with the **copper industry**; in separate temple niches at Enkomi-Alasia the famous "Horned God" was discovered, possibly a version of Apollo melded with aspects of the indigenous bull cult, and the so-called "Ingot God", a spear-wielding figure poised atop an ingot shaped like an oxhide, then the standard form of copper export. While Kition was not so spectacularly rewarding in artefacts, the sanctuaries here formed a huge complex of multiple temples with more Middle Eastern characteristics, though again in intimate association with copper forges. Large numbers of **bull skulls** have been found on the floors of all these shrines, implying their use as ceremonial masks – and the retention of bull worship and sacrifice.

At this time the **Aphrodite** shrine at Palea Paphos first attained prominence. Her cult and that of the smithing deity were not so disparate as might seem at first: in mainstream Greek culture, Aphrodite was the consort of Hephaestos, the god of fire and metal-working. A voluptuous female statuette in bronze found at Enkomi-Alasia is thought to be the consort of the martial ingot deity, and terracotta figurines of the Great Goddess with uplifted arms were among archaeological finds at the Kition temples.

In general, Mycenaean influence was in ascendance on Cyprus even as the same culture died out in its Aegean birthplace. But the immigrants introduced few of their religious practices and conventions wholesale, instead adapting their beliefs to local usage. Mycenaean technology did, however, invigorate local **metallurgy**, permitting the fashioning of such exquisite objects as the square, often wheeled stands for libation bowls found at Enkomi and Kourion, their sides intricately decorated in relief figures. The concept of kingship and **city-states**, along with Hellenic foundation-legends, became institutionalised after another wave of Mycenaean-Anatolian settlement around 1200 BC, at the seven "capitals" of Salamis, Lapithos, Marion, Soli, Palea Paphos, Kourion, and Tamassos; pure or "Eteo"- Cypriot culture retreated to Amathus.

A violent earthquake finished off Mycenaean Enkomi-Alasia and Kition around 1050 BC; Palea Paphos continued to be inhabited, but effectively the Bronze Age was over. Not, however, before the Mycenaean-tutored island smelters had apparently mastered the working of **iron**, as borne out by large numbers of iron weapons appearing in excavated sites of the early eleventh century.

THE GEOMETRIC ERA

The beginning of the **Geometric Era** in Cyprus was an echo of the "Dark Ages" in surrounding realms: the Mycenaean homeland was now thoroughly overrun by the Dorians; the Hittite Empires of Anatolia; Egypt was stagnant. Cyprus was essentially **isolated** for around two centuries. Most Cypriots, now a mix of settlers and indigenous islanders, gravitated toward the Mycenaean-founded city-kingdoms, such as Salamis; nearby Enkomi-Alasia was gradually abandoned after an mid-eleventh-century earthquake, which along with the silting-up rendered its harbour unusable.

Despite the cultural doldrums, early Geometric **pottery** is quite startling; cups and shallow dishes were popular, painted boldly in black rings, very occasionally with human or animal figures. **Funerary customs** show Mycenaean habits, especial among the population descended from immigrants: chamber tombs were approached by long *dhromi* or passages, and slaves were occasionally sacrificed to serve their deceased master; cremations took place at Kourion, as did the use of ossuary urns for old bones when reusing a tomb – an increasingly common strategy. In one grave at Palea Paphos, **syllabic Greek script** was found for the first time on a meat skewer, spelling the name of the deceased in Arcadian dialect – partial confirmation of the foundation

myth of Palea Paphos by Agapinor, leader of the Arcadian contingent in the Trojan war.

Following stabilisation in the west Aegean around 800 BC, trade and other **contacts resumed** between Greece – particularly Euboia – and the indigenous or "Eteo-Cypriot" centre of Amathus, more extroverted than the Myceno-Cypriot centres. Further fresh input was provided by the peaceful **Phoenician** resettlement of Kition, whose temples had never been completely abandoned even after the natural disaster of the eleventh century. The Phoenicians, an up-and-coming mercantile empire of the Middle East, re-dedicated these shrines to Astarte, the oriental version of Aphrodite; the **multiple sanctuary**, rebuilt after a fire in 800, was the fulcrum of Phoenician culture on Cyprus, with worship continued until 312 BC. Not surprisingly, bichrome pottery of the eighth century BC throughout the island shows Phoenician characteristics of dress style and activities.

These exceptions aside, the Geometric culture of Cyprus was **deeply conservative** – Mycenaean observances, whether or not melded with Eteo-Cypriot expression, maintained static or even retrospective forms, a trend accentuated by the two-century gap in communication with most of the outside world. The seven city-states were ruled by despotic monarchies, unmindful of the recent experiments in constitutional government in Greece; the Arcadian dialect continued to be written in syllabic script, rather than a true alphabet, until the fourth century BC.

No better demonstration of this traditionalism can be found than the **royal tombs** at Salamis of just before 700 BC, where the details of several burials seem to have been taken from public readings of Homer. The grave artefacts themselves are manifestly oriental, in a blend of Phoenician and Egyptian styles, reflecting the royal taste of the time; but the numerous roasting spits – similar to the inscribed one at Palea Paphos – the skeletons of sacrificed chariot-horses at the entry to tombs, and great bronze cauldrons containing the ashes of cremated royalty can only be accounted for in light of the Homeric epics. Here was a perhaps politically motivated revival of the presumed funerary customs of Trojan-war character Tefkros, the reputed Mycenaean founder of Salamis.

ANCIENT ZENITH: THE ARCHAIC ERA

Some consider the start (750 BC) of the **Archaic Era** on Cyprus to overlap the end of Geometric by half a century, but the signal event was the island's domination by the **Assyrians** between 708 and 669 BC; but Cypriot kings were merely required to forward tribute regularly, and this episode left little trace on island life other than some suggestive beards and hairstyles in later sculpture. Upon the departure of the Assyrians, a century of **flourishing independence** followed, producing some of the finest ancient Cypriot art. Its genius was an innate inventiveness combined with a receptivity to surrounding influences and their skilful assimilation into styles that were more than the sum of their component elements.

ART

Archaic Cyprus excelled for the first time in large-scale **sculpture** in limestone, which exhibited strong similarity to the art of Ionia in Asia Minor. Figures were nearly always robed in the Ionian manner, rarely nude, with the great attention paid to facial expression contrasting with an often cursory rendering of body anatomy. Large almond-shaped eyes, prominent eyebrows and more than a trace of the celebrated "Archaic smile" were often surmounted by Asiatic hair and beard styles, bound by head bands or, later, elaborate headdresses. A famous example is the *statue of Zeus Keraunios* (Thunderbolt-Hurler) from Kition. Female statue-heads were adorned with suggestions of **jewellery** matching in all respects some exquisitely worked gold and precious-stone originals which have been found. **Pottery** advanced from the abstract to bichrome figurative ware, especially the so-called "free-field" style, where single, well-detailed animal or human figures are rampant on a bare background.

RELIGION

Religious observance in Archaic Cyprus varied considerably, a function of the increasing number of foreigners visiting or living on the island. In contrast to cosmopolitan ports where the Greek Olympian deities and other more exotic foreign gods like the Egyptian Bes or Phoenician Astarte competed for admirers, the important **rural shrines** of the seventh and sixth centuries were more conservative in their adoration of old chthonic gods, or localised variants of imported divinities. The Phoenicians had their own rural cult, in addition to the Kition temples: that of Baal Hamman at Méniko, in the middle of the island near the copper mines they controlled, though it displayed many elements – such as bull sacrifice – of native Cypriot religion. The other most important sanctuaries were that of Apollo Hylates near Kourion and the long-venerated one at Ayía Iríni, where 2000 terracotta figurines were discovered.

Such **figurines** were typically arranged as ex votos around the altar of the usually simple courtyard shrines; in accord with Cypriot belief that the deity often resided in the temple, these clay figures served as permanent worshippers, ready for the divine presence. Some of the terracottas were realistically modelled for individual detail, and so have been taken to be gifts of a particular worshipper, made to order at workshops adjacent to the shrines. Figurines of musicians and women in various attitudes (including childbirth) accumulated logically enough at Aphrodhite or mother-goddess shrines, while the preferred offerings to male deities were bulls, horse-drawn chariots or helmeted warriors such as formed the bulk of the finds at Ayía Iríni.

THE PERSIAN INFLUENCE

The sixth century BC saw a very brief interval of direct Egyptian rule which, while more stringent than the Assyrian era, left a similarly subtle legacy in the form of more outlandish beards or headresses on statues. Monumentally, this time is characterised by the strange subterranean "house" tombs at Tamassos, possibly built by itinerant Anatolian masons. The newest Asian power on the horizon – the **Persians** – assumed control over Egypt in 545 BC; with their existing ties to the Middle East through the Phoenicians, and relatively weak military resources, it was easy enough for the Cypriot kingdoms to reach a vassalage arrangement with King Cyrus in 545 BC. Yet for a while a measure of autonomy was preserved, and Evelthon, the late sixth-century king of Salamis, minted his own coinage.

In 499 BC, however, this modus vivendi dissolved as Persian rule under Darius became harsher and the non-Phoenician Cypriots joined the **revolt** of the Ionian cities. **Onesilos of Salamis** mutinied against his brother the Persian puppet-king and attempted to rally the other Mycenaeo-Cypriot city-kingdoms, but this hastily patched-together confederation, despite land and sea re-enforcements from the Ionians, was defeated in a major battle at Salamis, largely due to the treachery of the Kourion contingent. Onesilos' head was stuck on the city gate of pro-Persian Amathus as a warning, though after it filled with honeycomb an oracle advised the townspeople to bury it and revere his memory. After the battle, each of the remaining Cypriot city-kingdoms except Kition was **besieged** and reduced one by one, Soli and Palea Paphos being the last to capitulate in 498. Such prolonged resistance against the mighty Persian empire was made possible by vastly improved stone and mud-brick fortifications, which dwarfed the original designs of the Mycenaean settlers. The **pro-Persian Phoenicians** took the opportunity to extend their influence northward, placing their kings on the throne at Marion and Lapethos; in the aftermath of the revolt the hilltop palace of Vouni was also built by the king of Marion to intimidate nearby pro-Hellenic Soli. Never again, until this century, would Cyprus be both independent and united.

TURMOIL AND DECLINE: CLASSICAL CYPRUS

By the start of the fifth century, Cyprus had ten **city-kingdoms**: Kyrenia, Idalion, Amathus and Kition were added to the Mycenaeo-Cypriot seven, with Soli now subservient to Marion. The island now became thoroughly embroiled in the struggle between Greece and Persia; **Athens** repeatedly sent forces to "liberate" Cyprus, but the distance involved, plus pro-Persian factions on the island, made any victories transient. Athenian general **Kimon** led three of these expeditions to various parts of Cyprus, especially the pro-Persian strongholds of Marion, Salamis and Kition, dying at the hour of victory on his last attempt in 449 BC, outside the walls of Kition. Deprived of leadership, the Greeks sailed home, and the next year the Athenians signed a treaty with the Persians agreeing to drop the matter.

But if the political results of these campaigns were minuscule – the palace at Vouni was rebuilt to a nostalgic Mycenaean plan, though oligarchic, dynastic rule continued at most city-kingdoms whether pro-Greek or not – profound **cultural effects** attended the five decades of contact with Greece. A craze for Attic art swept the island in everything from pottery – imported via Marion and Salamis – to coinage, to the marked detriment of local creativity. Sarcophagi and Attic-style memorial *stelae* began to rival rock-cut tombs in popularity; the worship of Hercules and Athena as deities came into vogue, and many Phoenician divinities acquired a Hellenic veneer.

Before the truce, however, the Phoenician regime at Kition, perennial allies of the Persians, had again struck northwards, taking Idalion in 470 BC. The Persians took the peace itself as a cue to tighten their control yet again on island, and the stage was set for the emergence of a great Cypriot patriot and political genius, **Evagoras I of Salamis**. Born in 435, at the age of 24 he overthrew the Phoenician puppet king of the city, but skilful diplomatic spadework and judicious payment of tribute to the Persians ensured no repercussions then or for a long time after, giving him the necessary breathing space to build up his defences and elaborate his sophisticated intrigues. Though fiercely pro-Hellenic, he was able to act simultaneously as a mediator between the Athenians and the Persians, even convincing the latter to lend him a fleet for use against the Spartans on behalf of Athens which duly honoured him after the victory was accomplished. Evagoras' court became a haven for Attic artists or soldiers in exile voluntary or otherwise, and he vigorously promoted Greek culture throughout his expanding dominions, including the introduction of the **Greek alphabet**, which slowly replaced the Cypriot syllabic script over the next century.

His conduct of domestic statecraft, however, tended towards the megalomaniac; in attempting to forcibly **unite** all the Cypriot city-kingdoms into one state, Evagoras alienated Kition, Amathus and Soli sufficiently that they appealed for help to the Persians. Evagoras had finally overreached himself; despite some aid from the Athenians, he failed to depose the king of Kition, and another treaty in 386 between Greeks and Persians, acknowledging the latter's hegemony over the island, left him to effectively confront the eastern empire alone. But with some support from Anatolian Greek city-states he managed to carry the fight to the enemy's home court, causing confusion by landing on the Syrian coast. Though the Persians returned to Cyprus in force in 381, sacking Salamis, Evagoras battled them to a stalemate, and negotiated relatively favourable surrender terms, keeping his throne.

He and his eldest son were apparently murdered in a domestic plot at Salamis in 374 BC; he was a hard act to follow, and Evagoras' descendants were insignificant in comparison, not having his touch in handling the Persians – least of all in another abortive revolt of 351. Of his **successors** only Pytagoras salvaged a shred of dignity as a vassal king of the Persians, though pro-Hellenic in culture, ushering in the Hellenistic era.

RECOVERY: HELLENISTIC AND ROMAN CYPRUS

When **Alexander the Great** appeared on the scene in 333, the Cypriot city-kingdoms responded unequivocally, furnishing 120 ships for his successful siege of Persian Tyre. But following his general victory in the east Mediterranean it soon became clear that, while finally rid of the Persians, Cyprus was now a subordinated part of the Hellenistic empire, without even the minimal freedoms pertaining under their old masters.

When Alexander died in 323, the island became a battleground for his successors **Ptolemy** and **Antingonus**, with the city-kingdoms split in their support and **civil war** the result. Ptolemy's forces initially prevailed, and the losing cities – Kition, Marion, Lapithos and Kyrenia – razed or severely punished. **Nicocreon**, the pro-Hellenic king of Salamis, was promoted for his loyalty, but in 311 he was denounced for plotting with Antigonus, and Ptolemy sent an army under his deputy Menelaos to besiege Salamis. Rather than surrender, Nicocreon and his family set their palace alight and committed suicide, and the truth of the accusations remains uncertain; in any event the dynasty founded by Tefkros died with them.

Antigonus' adherents were still very much in the picture, though, and the dynastic war

continued in the person of his son **Demtrios Poliorketes**, who defeated both Ptolemy and Menelaos and single-handedly ruled the island from 306 to 294. The pendulum swung back one final time, however, for in an unguarded moment Ptolemy I Soter of Egypt – as he now styled himself – retook Cyprus, commencing two and a half centuries of relatively peaceful and prosperous **Ptolemaic, Egyptian-based rule**.

Cyprus became essentially a province of the Alexandria-based kingdom, exploited for its copper, timber, corn and wine, and administered by a military governor based first at Salamis, later at Nea Paphos. All city-kingdoms were now defunct, replaced by four **administrative districts** and uniform coinage for the whole island; its **cultural life** was now thoroughly Hellenised, with the usual range of athletic, dramatic and musical events. To existing religious life was added the cult of deified Ptolemaic royalty, and a fresh infusion of Egyptian gods. Art was largely derived from Alexandrine models, with little in the way of originality. Portraits in the soft local limestone or terracotta made up the majority of statuary, with the marble work common elsewhere in the Greek world relatively rare. The only idiosyncratic expressions were in funereal architecture, especially at Nea Paphos, where the subterranean "Tombs of the Kings" was a blend of Macedonian and Middle Eastern styles.

During the first century BC, the decline in the Ptolemys' fortunes was matched by the growing power of republican **Rome**, which annexed Cyprus in 58 BC; with the see-sawing of events the island reverted to Egyptian control twice, but Roman rule was consolidated in the Imperial period after 31 BC. The *Koinon Kyprion* or civic league of the Ptolemys continued under the Romans, charged with coordinating religious festivals, including emperor-worship. The four Ptolemaic districts were also retained but Cyprus as a whole was administered as a senatorial province, through a proconsul (one of the first was the orator Cicero), still based at Nea Paphos. Salamis, however, remained the most important town on the island, its commercial centre with a population of over a quarter million.

The Hellenistic pattern of **stability and prosperity** continued, permitting massive public works, some redone several times in the wake of earthquakes; Roman roads, bridges and aqueducts have long since vanished, but gymnasia, theatres and baths constitute most of the archaeological heritage visible on Cyprus today. Wealthier private citizens commissioned major projects as well, as borne out by the sophisticated villa-floor **mosaics** at Nea Paphos. Otherwise, however, there not much effort was expended to Latinise the island – Greek, for example, continued to be used as the official language – and as a largely self-sufficient backwater, Cyprus took little part in the larger affairs of the Roman Empire.

CHRISTIANITY

Christianity came early (45 AD) to Cyprus, which was evangelised by the apostles Paul and Barnabas, a native of Salamis. The pair ordained Iraklidhios of Tamassos as the island's first bishop, and supposedly converted Sergius Paulus, proconsul at Nea Paphos. Barnabas was subsequently martyred by the Jews of Salamis, who participated in the major **Jewish rebellion** which swept across all of the Middle East in 116 AD. Cyprus was particularly hard hit since, given its scant political and military importance, it was lightly garrisoned; some estimated that virtually the entire gentile population of Salamis was slaughtered by the rebels. The insurrection was finally put down by Hadrian, and a decree promulgated which expelled all Jews from Cyprus. Despite this removal of an obstacle to proselytizing, Christianity spread slowly on island, as suggested by the enthusiastically pagan Paphos mosaics executed on the eve of Emperor Constantine's designation of it in 323 as the official religion of the eastern empire.

The Roman Empire had been divided into **western and eastern portions** in 284, with capitals at Rome and Constantinople respectively, and local Cypriot administration transferred to Antioch in Syria – a situation which would last until the fifth century, when the opportune discovery of Barnabas' relics (see p.247) provided the justification for Cyprus' **ecclesiastic and civic autonomy**, answerable only to Constantinople. Cyprus' prestige in the Christian world was further enhanced by the 324 visit of Helena, Constantine's mother, who left fragments of the True Cross and that of the Penitent Thief.

THE BYZANTINE ERA

The break with antiquity was punctuated not only by a new faith and governmental order, but by two cataclysmic **earthquakes** – in 332 and 365 – which destroyed most Cypriot towns. Rebuilt Salamis was renamed Constantia, and designated again the capital of the island. As elsewhere in **Byzantium** – that portion of the empire centred on Constantinople – some of the more inhumane pagan-Roman laws were repealed, and mass conversion to Christianity proceeded apace, as evidenced by the huge fifth- and sixth-century basilica-type cathedrals erected in all cities. Foundations and **mosaic floors** for many of these are the most attractive early Byzantine remains on Cyprus; little else survives, however, owing to the repeated, devastating **raids of the Arab caliphate**, beginning in the seventh century AD. Their intent was not to conquer outright but to pillage, and to neutralise Cyprus as a Byzantine strongpoint; the Arabs' only significant legacy is the Hala Sultan *tekke* near Larnaca.

An immediate result of the raids was the **abandonment** of most coastal cities, far too vulnerable, and also plague- and drought-ridden at this time. By the terms of an **Arab-Byzantine treaty**, the island was to accept Muslim settlers, remain demilitarised except for naval bases of each side, and pay taxes equally to both the Caliphate and Byzantium. Except for occasional skirmishes, this strange agreement of condominium endured for three centuries, while Cyprus thrived on its silk trade and food exports, and served as a convenient place to exile dissidents from both Constantinople and the Caliphate.

Only in 963 did Byzantine Emperor **Nikiphoros Phokas** permanently end Arab co-rule on Cyprus, and the Muslim colonists left or converted to Christianity. For another two centuries Cyprus had a peaceful, if heavily taxed, respite as a fully-fledged province of Byzantium, during which most of its **existing towns** – Kyrenia, Famagusta, Nicosia, Limassol – were **founded** or grew suddenly, formidable **castles** raised against the threat of further attacks. At the same time, in the Troödhos mountains, the first **frescoed chapels** were endowed by wealthy private donors.

WESTERN RULE: THE LUSIGNANS AND VENETIANS

Trouble loomed again in the eleventh century, however; the **schism** between the Catholic and Orthodox churches in 1054 fostered political antagonism between the Byzantine Empire and most Latin principalities, and after their defeat of the Byzantines at the Battle of Manzikert in 1073, the **Seljuk Turks** were able to spread south and occupy the Holy Land. In response, the **First Crusade** was organised in western Europe during 1095, and Cyprus lay near or on the Latin knights' path towards the infidels. Although the first two crusades bypassed the island, the knights soon established mini-kingdoms in Palestine, and the Seljuks also occupied most of Anatolia, allowing a capricious, despotic Byzantine prince, **Isaac Comnenus**, to declare Cypriot independence from a fatally weakened Constantinople in 1184 and rule for seven years. Greedy, cruel and consequently unpopular, he was hardly an improvement on the succession of incompetent and unstable emperors in the capital; this collective misrule made Cyprus a ripe plum for the Crusaders.

In the spring of 1191 a small fleet bearing the sister and fiancée of **Richard the Lion-Heart of England** hove to off Limassol; Isaac, realising their value as hostages, tried to inveigle them ashore, but they wisely declined; he then refused them provisions. When the English king himself appeared, he landed in some force, considering his kinswomen to have been gravely insulted. After an unsuccessful attempt to secure Isaac's co-operation in the Third Crusade, Richard and his allies pursued the Byzantine forces across the island, defeating them at the battle of Tremetoushá on the Mesaoría; Isaac surrendered at the end of May, sent away in silver chains upon his insistence that he not be put in irons.

Richard had never intended to acquire Cyprus, and was still keen to resume crusading; having plundered the island, he quickly sold it to the **Knights Templar** to raise funds for his army. The Templars put forty percent of the purchase price down and had to raise the balance by confiscatory taxation; the Cypriots not unnaturally rebelled, with the knights quelling this viciously to save their skins.

Having received more than they bargained for, the Templars returned Cyprus to Richard, who quickly resold it to **Guy de Lusignan**, a minor French noble who had been the last crusader King of Jerusalem before having lost the city to Saladdin in 1187. Cyprus was essentially his consolation prize; Guy recreated the feudal system of his lost realm, parcelling out fiefs to more than five hundred supporters – principally landless allies without future prospects in what remained of Crusader Syria – and the Knights Hospitaller of Saint John, who soon displaced the Templars. Guy's brother and successor **Aimery** styled himself **king of Cyprus and Jerusalem**, the latter an honorific title used by all subsequent Lusignan rulers, though the Holy City went permanently back to Muslim control after 1244.

THE LUSIGNANS

Under the Lusignans, Cyprus acquired a **significance** far out of proportion to its size. European sovereigns, including **Holy Roman Emperor Frederick II Hohenstaufen**, stopped off obligatorily on their way to subsequent crusades, and the Lusignans – and their deputies the **Ibelins** – married into all the royal houses of Europe. **Regencies** for underage princes were common owing to the short life expectancy of crusader kings; an unusually long regency for Henry I in the early thirteenth century caused complications, obliging the Ibelin regents to defend Henry's title to the throne in a prolonged war against counterclaimant Frederick II Hohenstaufen.

Monumentally, the Byzantine **castles** of the Kyrenia range were refurbished, and new ones built around the capital Nicosia and the eastern port of Famagusta, which after the **1291 loss** of Acre, Sidon and Tyre, the last crusader toeholds in the Holy Land, saw an influx of Christian refugees from all over the Near East. For barely a century **Famagusta** served as the easternmost outpost of Christendom, and became one of the wealthiest cities on earth owing to a papal prohibition on direct European trade with the nearby infidel. No longer having to siphon off resources to defend their slender Syrian coastal strip also improved the military and financial health of the Cypriot kingdom. The Lusignan royalty were crowned in two massive, Gothic **cathedrals** at Nicosia and Famagusta: coronations for the Kingdom of Cyprus were conducted at Nicosia; at Famagusta, facing the Holy Land across the water, the honorary ceremony for Jerusalem took place. All major **monastic orders** were represented, though the sole surviving foundation is the abbey of Bellapais.

The **everyday life** of the nobility was notorious for its luxury and ostentation, a privilege definitely not shared by the common people. The Greek Orthodox population, which had initially welcomed the crusaders, soon discovered that they were effectively shut out from power or material security. Most of them lived as **serfs** of the Catholic overlords, and by a papal edict of 1260 the Orthodox archbishops were effectively **subordinated** to a Catholic metropolitan and furthermore exiled to rural sees. Orthodoxy was constrained to a rearguard holding action, awaiting a change in fortunes; yet during this time many of the fine so-called "Byzantine Revival" frescos were painted in rural chapels of the Troödhos Mountains.

In general, the Lusignan **kings** were a visibly overweight, mediocre bunch, probably resulting from a combination of hereditary thyroid problems and "riotous and unclean living", as one historian of the time put it. The most extravagant and activist sovereign was **Peter I** (1358–69), who in contrast to the live-and-let-live attitude of his lethargic predecessors canvassed Europe for support of his mini-Crusades along the neighbouring Muslim coasts, culminating in a thorough sacking of Alexandria in 1365. Also an inveterate womaniser, he was in the arms of one of his two mistresses when certain nobles, tired of his increasingly erratic behaviour and disregard for feudal law, burst into the bedchamber and murdered him.

Decline followed Peter's murder, though it was more the last straw than the root cause. If the Lusignans ran the Cypriot kingdom, the Venetians and Genoese were rivals for supremacy in its commercial life; at the 1373 Famagusta coronation of Peter II, a dispute between the two factions as to who would have the honour of leading the young king's horse escalated into destructive anti-Genoese riots. Incensed, **Genoa** sent a punitive expedition to ravage the island. For a year a virtual civil war raged, ending with the return of the throne to the Lusignans only upon payment of a huge indemnity – though the royal family was actually held prisoner in Genoa for 18 years –

and the retention of Famagusta by the Genoese. But the damage had been done; both Cyprus and the Lusignans were in disastrously weakened condition economically and politically.

A harbinger of worse "infidel" attacks to come took place in 1425–26, when the **Mamelukes** of Egypt, still smarting from Peter I's attack, landed on the south coast to plunder Limassol and Larnaca. **King Janus** met them near Stavrovoúni monastery, was roundly defeated and taken prisoner; the Mamelukes marched inland to sack Nicosia before returning with their treasure to Egypt. Janus was only released three years later after payment of a crippling ransom and a humiliating promise of a perpetual annual tribute to the Mamelukes.

With Janus' dissolute successor **John II**, the Lusignan saga entered its last chapters. He complicated matters by favouring his bastard son, **James II**, over his legitimate daughter **Charlotte**, and the two strong-willed offspring spent six years disputing the succession after John died in 1458. Securing Mameluke aid – which in effect meant an extension of the onerous tribute – James returned from Egypt and deposed his sister; he matched this success by finally evicting the Genoese from Famagusta, though it was far too late to restore that town to its former importance. A roistering, athletic man, James was relatively popular with his subjects for both his daring exploits and his fluency in **Greek**; indeed the language had recently begun to replace French in public use.

James did not run true to family form in his own choice of consort, contracting marriage with a Venetian noblewoman, **Caterina Cornaro**. Both the king and his infant son died mysteriously within a year of each other (1473 and 1474) – a Venetian poisoning plot has been suggested – leaving Caterina to reign precariously in her own right. Charlotte, in exile, intrigued ceaselessly against her until Charlotte died in 1485, and besides her foiled plot to assassinate Caterina, there was a Catalan-fomented rebellion in 1473. All this, and the growing **Ottoman threat**, convinced the Venetians that Caterina was better out of the way, and she was persuaded to **abdicate** in 1489, given as a sop the town and hinterland of Asolo in the Veneto, where she continued to keep a court of some splendour.

THE VENETIANS

Three centuries of Lusignan rule were over and the **Venetians** now governed the island directly through a *proveditore* or **military governor**. Their tenure was even more oppressive than the Lusignan one from the point of view of ordinary people; Cyprus was seen simply as a frontier fortress and money-spinner, with the island otherwise neglected and inefficiently administered. The Lusignan nobility retained their estates but were excluded from political power. The Venetians devoted most of their energy to overhauling the fortifications of Kyrenia, Nicosia and Famagusta in anticipation of the inevitable Ottoman attack. In the end, however, the undermanned Venetian forces were no match for the Turkish hordes, especially when relief failed to arrive from Venice: Nicosia fell after a seven-week **siege** in 1570, with almost half its population subsequently massacred, while Famagusta held out for ten months until July 1571 in one of the celebrated battles of the age (see p.236). The victor, **Lala Musta Paşa,** perhaps irked at having been so valiantly defied by the tiny garrison, went back on his promises of clemency, flaying commander **Marcantonio Bragadino** alive after butchered his lieutenants.

Surrounded on three sides by Ottoman territory, it was almost certain that Cyprus should eventually fall to them, but the specific impetus for the 1570–71 campaign is interesting. The incumbent sultan, **Selim the Sot**, had a particular fondness for Cypriot Commandaria wine; his chief advisor, **Joseph Nasi**, was a Spanish Jew whose family had suffered at the hands of the Venetians during their long exile after the 1492 expulsion, and who longed to take revenge on the Serene Republic – and perhaps secure a haven for Jewry. In fact the invasion plan was hatched over the objections of the Grand Vizier and others, who considered it unfeasible, and feared the wrath of the European powers. Selim died just three years later, fracturing his skull by slipping in his bath – while drunk on Commandaria.

STAGNATION: OTTOMAN RULE

Because the Lusignans had never made any attempt to bridge the gap between ruler and ruled, they remained an upper crust, all trace of which was swept away by the Turkish

conquest. By 1573 most of the monasteries and Latin churches had been destroyed, and most surviving **Catholics** had departed or converted to Islam; the tiny "Latin" minority on the island today is all that survives. Ancestors of the present **Turkish population**, on the other hand, date from the year of the conquest, when Ottoman soldiers and their families formed the nucleus, some 20,000 strong, of initial settlement, later supplemented by civilians from Anatolia. Their relations with the native Greek population were, if not always close, usually cordial.

The Greek Orthodox peasantry, perhaps surprisingly in the light of later events, actually **welcomed** the Ottomans at first; both were united in their hatred of the Franks, whose feudal system was abolished and lands distributed to the freed serfs. The Greeks also appreciated Ottoman **recognition of their church:** not only were certain Catholic ecclesiastical properties made over to Orthodoxy, but in 1660 the archbishop was officially acknowledged as the head of the Greek community in accord with prevailing Ottoman administrative practice, with the right of direct petition to the sultan. This was followed in 1754 by the revival of the role of **ethnarch**, with comprehensive civil powers, and in 1779 by the stipulation for a **dragoman**, a Greek appointed by the ethnarch to liaise with the island's Turkish governor. The most powerful and famous dragoman was **Hadjiyorgakis Kornesios**.

None of this, however, was done in a spirit of disinterested religious tolerance; the Ottomans used the ecclesiastical apparatus principally to collect **onerous taxes**, and the clerics, who eventually all but ran the island together with the dragoman, made themselves every bit as unpopular as the Turkish governors. In fairness the clergy often attempted to protect their flock from the more rapacious exactions of the various governors, who – minimally salaried and having paid huge bribes to secure their short-term appointments – were expected to recoup their expenses with extractions from the populace. People unable to meet assessments forfeited **land** in lieu of payment, the source of the Orthodox church's still-extensive real estate holdings.

If the Greeks had hoped for a definitive improvement in their lot with the end of Frankish rule, they were thoroughly disillusioned, as Cyprus became one of the **worst-governed and neglected** Ottoman provinces. Almost all tax revenues went to Istanbul, with next to nothing being spent to abate the drought, plagues and locusts which lashed the island, or on other local improvements; Turkish medieval monuments are rare on Cyprus, with most large mosques merely churches adapted for Muslim use. Between 1571 and the late 1700s the population dropped sharply, with many Greeks **emigrating** to Anatolia or the Balkans despite administrative reshuffles aimed at staunching the outflow.

Such conditions ensured that the three Ottoman centuries were punctuated by regular **rebellions** which often united the Muslim and Christian peasantry against their overlords. The first occurred in 1680; in 1764 the excesses of the worst governor, **Çil Osman**, precipitated a longer and bloodier revolt in which he was killed, the Turkish commander of Kyrenia mutinied, and the Greek bishops appealed to Istanbul for the restoration of order. With the rise of Balkan nationalism later that century, the *Filikí Etería* (Friendly Society), the Greek revolutionary fifth column, was active on Cyprus after 1810. To forestall any echo of the mainland Greek rebellion, Governor **Küçük Mehmet** got permission from the Sultan in 1821 to execute the unusually popular **Archbishop Kyprianos**, his three bishops and hundreds of leading Greek Orthodox islanders in Nicosia, not so coincidentally confiscating their considerable property and inaugurating another spell of unrest on the island, which ended in the revolt of 1833.

Such incidents were not repeated after European powers established more trading posts and watchful consulates at Larnaca, and the Church's power **waned** with the suspension of its right to collect taxes and the emergence of an educated, westernised class of Greek Cypriot. As the nineteenth century wore on, **Britain** found itself repeatedly guaranteeing the Ottoman Empire's territorial integrity in the path of Russian expansionism; in 1878, this relationship was formalised by the **Anglo-Turkish Convention**, whereby the Ottomans ceded occupation and administrative rights of Cyprus – though technically not sovereignty – to Britain in return for having halted the Russian advance outside Istanbul during the 1877–78 Russo-Turkish war, and for a contin-

ued undertaking to help defend what was left of Turkish domains. Curiously, retention of Cyprus was **linked** to Russia's occupation of Ardahan, Kars and Batumi, three strongpoints on Turkey's Caucasian frontier; Kars and Ardahan were returned to republican Turkey in 1921, but in the NATO era Turkey's and Britain's continued alliance against the Russian threat still served as justification for occupation of Cyprus.

BRITISH RULE

British forces landed peacefully at Larnaca in July 1878, assuming control of the island without incident; ironically, the British acquisition of Egypt and the Suez in 1882 made Cyprus of distinctly secondary importance as a **military base**, with civilian high commissioners soon replacing military ones.

The Greek Orthodox population, remembering Britain's cession of the Ionian islands to Greece in 1864, hoped for the same generosity here, and the Bishop of Kition (Larnaca)'s greeting speech to the landing party alluded directly to this. Free of the threat of Ottoman-style repression, the demand for **énosis** or union with Greece was to be reiterated regularly by the Greek Cypriots until 1960 – and beyond. From the very outset of the colonial period the Turkish Cypriots expressed their satisfaction with the status quo and their horror at the prospect of being Greek citizens.

What the Cypriots got instead, aside from separate Greek- and Turkish-language education, was a modicum of **better government** – re-afforestation, an end to banditry and extralegal extortion, and English legal system, water supplies, roads and a stamping out of disease and locusts – combined with a continuance of **crushing taxes**, which militated against any striking economic growth. An obscure clause of the Anglo-Turkish Convention mandated that the excess of tax revenues (appreciable) over local expenditures (almost nil) during the last five years of Ottoman rule was theoretically to be paid to the Turks, a rule which pressured colonial administrators to keep programmes modest so as to have some sum to forward – or to squeeze the Cypriots for more taxes. The practice was widely condemned by Cypriophiles and Turkophobes in England, including Churchill and Gladstone, but continued until 1927. Worse still, the monies went not to Istanbul, but to bond holders of an 1855 loan to Turkey on which the Ottoman rulers had defaulted. So while Cyprus recovered much of its population, the British-promised prosperity never appeared, the islanders in effect being required to **service an Ottoman debt**. The only apparatus of self-government was a very rudimentary **legislative council**, numerically weighted towards colonial civil servants and with limited powers in any case.

CYPRUS AS COLONY

Following Ottoman Turkey's 1914 entry into World War I as one of the Central Powers, Britain declared most provisions of the Anglo-Turkish Convention void, and formally **annexed** Cyprus. The next year she secretly offered the island to Greece as a territorial inducement to join the war on the Allied side, but Greece, then ruled by pro-German King Constantine I, declined, to the Greek Cypriots' infinite later regret. In the 1923 Treaty of Lausanne, republican Turkey renounced all claims to Cyprus, but the island did not officially become a British Crown Colony until 1925, by which time calls for *énosis* were again been heard; these increased in stridency, leading in **1931** to the first serious **civil disturbances**: the Greek Cypriot members of the legislative council resigned, and rioters burned down the Government House, a rambling bungalow diverted from use in Ceylon. The Cypriots' anger was not only sparked by the *énosis* issue, but derived from disappointment at the thus-far modest level of material progress under British rule, especially the woebegone state of agriculture.

ADVENT OF THE LEFT

The British **response** to the mini-rebellion was predictably harsh: reparations assessments for damages, bans on publications and flying the Greek flag, proscriptions of existing political parties (especially the KKK or Communists, who had organised strikes in 1929 at the asbestos mines), and imprisonment or deportation of activists – including two bishops. The legislative council was abolished, and Cyprus came under the nearest thing to martial law; only the **PEO** or Pancyprian Federation of Labour, though driven underground until 1936, remained as a pole of opposition to the colonial regime, and a haven for both left-wing Turks

and Greeks. **AKEL**, the new **communist party**, grew out of it in 1941, and has remained an important faction in the Greek-Cypriot community to this day. Municipal elections were finally held in 1943, and served as a barometer of public sentiment through the balance of the colonial period; the British could not very well profess to be fighting fascism while simultaneously withholding basic political freedoms.

During **World War II**, Cyprus belied its supposed strategic value by escaping much involvement other than as an important supply depot and staging post. The island suffered just a few stray Italian raids from Rhodes – after the German difficulties on Crete, Hitler had forbidden another paratroop action to seize Cyprus. Both Greek and Turkish Cypriots fought with British forces in Europe and North Africa, and the Greeks at least expected some political reward for this at war's end.

The extent of this was the 1947 offer by Governor Lord Winster of a **limited constitution** of self-rule, similar to that tendered in other colonies at the time. It was summarily rejected by the enosist elements, principally the Orthodox church, who proclaimed that anything less than *énosis* or at least provision for its implementation was unacceptable – a stance which probably guaranteed later bloodshed. AKEL was lukewarm on the idea; they were busy mounting the inconclusive but distinguished 1947–48 **strike** in the American-run copper mines of Soléa district.

<h2 style="background:black;color:white">THE POSTWAR YEARS</h2>

By 1950 demands for *énosis* had returned to the fore, in a **referendum** campaign organised by newly elected Archbishop and Ethnarch **Makarios III**, with results showing 96 percent support for *énosis* among Greek Cypriots. They seemed to ignore the fact that Greece, dominated by far-right-wing governments and still a stretcher case after the rigours of German occupation and a civil war, was a poor candidate as a partner for association; yet so great was the groundswell for union that even the PEO and AKEL subscribed to it after 1950, though they could both expect a fairly unpleasant fate in a rightist "Greater Greece". In general outsiders did, and still do, have trouble understanding the enormous emotional and historical appeal of *énosis*, whose advocates readily admitted that Cypriot living standards would drop sharply once the island was out of the sterling zone and yoked to chaotic, poor Greece.

Soon the at least theoretical possibility of *énosis* dawned on the island's **Turkish minority** – some 18 percent of the population – who began agitation in opposition, advocating either the status quo or some sort of affiliation with Turkey rather than becoming a truly insignificant minority in a greater Greece. As the Turkish Cypriots were scattered almost uniformly throughout the island, forming nowhere a majority, the option of a separate Turkish-Cypriot province did not seem available without painful population transfers.

Many Greek Cypriots retrospectively accused the British (and to a lesser extent the Americans) of **stirring up** Turkey and the Turkish Cypriots against them, and while there is some truth to this – divide and rule was very much a colonial strategy – mainland Turkey itself would probably have eventually become involved without cues from Britain, and the Turkish Cypriots were certainly not quiescent. Greek Cypriots saw the situation as a non-colonial problem of the island wishing to transfer its allegiance to the "mother country"; Britain, in their view, transformed matters into a general Greco-Turkish dispute under the guise of "harmony in the southeast flank of NATO", assuring that Turkey would forcefully block any move towards *énosis*.

After Egyptian independence in 1954, **British Mid-East Military HQ** was to be moved to Cyprus over a period of twenty months, making self-determination far less likely, and the British position increasingly inflexible – thanks to such intemperate Tory personalities as Anthony Eden, and murmurs of support for such policy by the Americans. In July of that year, the Minister of State for the Colonies declared that "certain Commonwealth territories, owing to their particular circumstances, can never expect to be fully independent" – and went on to express fears of AKEL dominating an independent Cyprus. To the Greek Cypriots this utterance seemed ludicrous in the light of independence being granted to far less developed parts of Asia and Africa. That "never" closed off all avenues of communication with more moderate Greek Cypriots, and came back repeatedly to haunt the British over the next five years.

In **Greece** the government encouraged a shrill, anti-British media barrage in support of *énosis*, accessible to any wireless on Cyprus. For the first time Greece also tried to internationalise the Cyprus issue at the **UN**, where it failed to get a full hearing though Turkey bared its teeth in the preliminary discussions, a promise of trouble in the future. Only the Greek ambassador to London had astutely seen that the mainland Turks were now an interested party and would have to be included in any solution.

THE EOKA REBELLION

In conjunction with **General George Grivas** (see also p.166), codenamed "Dhiyenis" after the hero of a Byzantine epic – but later nicknamed "Egregious" by an exasperated British public – Archbishop Makarios in 1954 secretly founded **EOKA**, *Ethnikí Orgánosis Kypríon Agonistón* or "National Organisation of Cypriot Fighters", as an IRA-type movement to throw off British rule. Late that year several clandestine shipments of arms and explosives were transferred from Rhodes to the deserted Páfos coast, though the Archbishop initially shrank back from advocating lethal force against persons, restricting Grivas to sabotage of property. EOKA's campaign of violence on Cyprus began spectacularly on 1 April 1955 with the destruction of the Government radio transmitter, among other targets.

Overseas, a hastily scheduled **trilateral conference** in July 1955, convening representatives of Greece, Turkey and Britain, flopped miserably; Makarios remarked that Greece's attendance at it had merely legitimised Turkish involvement in the Cyprus issue. Two months later, massive, Turkish government-inspired **rioting** in Istanbul caused staggering loss to Greek property and effectively dashed any hope for a reasonable future of the Greek Orthodox community there. Greek government recourse to the UN was again futile.

Newly appointed **High Commissioner John Harding**, a former Field Marshal, pursued a hard line against EOKA; ongoing negotiations with Makarios, who distanced himself at least publically from the armed struggle, were approaching a breakthrough when Grivas set off more strategically-timed bombs. Talks were broken off and the Archbishop and two associates **deported** in

March 1956 to comfortable house arrest in the Seychelles. Deprived of its ablest spokesman, EOKA now graduated to murderous **attacks** on Greeks disagreeing with them, as well as British soldiers and civilians. The island terrain was ideal for such an insurgency; despite massive searches, internments, collective punishments for aiding EOKA, and other now-familiar curtailments of civil liberties in such emergencies, the uprising couldn't be squelched. An estimated 300 guerrillas, based primarily in the Troödhos, tied up 20,000 regular British Army troops and 4500 special constables. The latter were overwhelmingly composed of Turkish-Cypriot auxiliaries – who often applied **torture** to captured EOKA suspects under the supervision of British officers, an assigned task which perceptibly increased intercommunal tensions. Spring and summer of 1956 also saw the **hangings** of nine convicted EOKA men, touching off violent protests in Greece and plunging British–Greek relations to an all-time low.

International pressure in **1957** – and Britain's realisation that no other Greek-Cypriot negotiating partner existed – brought about Makarios' release, just after Greece finally managed to get Cyprus on the UN agenda, resulting in a resolution accepting independence "in principle". Harding was replaced with the more conciliatory civilian **Governor Hugh Foot**, and a constitutional commissioner, Lord Radcliffe, was dispatched to make more generous proposals for limited self-government than in 1947. These were again rejected by the Greek Cypriots, because they didn't envision *énosis*, and by the Turkish Cypriots – represented by the **Turkish National Party**, headed by future vice-president **Fazil Küçük** – since it didn't specifically exclude that possibility.

TMT

After isolated intercommunal incidents since 1956, the **TMT** or *Turk Müdafaa Teskilati*, (Turkish Defence Organisation) was founded early in **1958** to counter EOKA's goals and work for *taksim* or partition of the island between Greece and Turkey. TMT's cell structure was modelled on EOKA, and it also duplicated EOKA's rabid **anti-communism**, killing various left-wing Turkish personalities, and pressurising Turkish Cypriots to leave PEO and AKEL,

virtually the last unsegregated institutions on the island. TMT also organised a boycott of Greek products, just as EOKA was presiding over a Greek-Cypriot boycott of British products.

INTERCOMMUNAL CLASHES

A June 1958 bomb explosion outside the Turkish press office in Nicosia – later shown to have been planted by TMT provocateurs – set off the first serious **intercommunal clashes** on the island. In Nicosia, Turkish gangs expelled Greeks from some mixed neighbourhoods, and induced some of their own to abandon villages in the south of the island in favour of the north – a forerunner of events in 1974. Shortly after, in what became known as the **Gönyeli incident**, seven EOKA suspects were released from British custody to walk home through a Turkish area, where they were duly stabbed to death – as was presumably the English intent. EOKA retaliated by targeting Turkish policemen, and also stepping up assaults on the British after a year's lull. The **death toll** for the whole insurrection climbed to nearly 600, of these almost half left-wing or pro-British Greek Cypriots killed by EOKA. **Truces** were declared in late summer by both TMT and EOKA, with many displaced Cypriots returning to their homes in mixed areas. The EOKA truce did not, however, extend to members of AKEL, which now favoured independence again – and continued to suffer fatal consequences.

One last mainland Greece-sponsored UN resolution for Cypriot "self-determination " (by now a code word for *énosis*) failed in 1958 to muster the necessary two-thirds majority in the General Assembly, so Makarios began to accept the wisdom of independence especially as both the British, in the person of Prime Minister Harold Macmillan, and the Turkish Cypriots were threatening to renew the option of partition and massive population movements.

Throughout the later 1950s, EOKA, Greece and most Greek Cypriots had failed to take seriously the **mainland Turkish position**: that Turkey would take steps to prevent strategically vital Cyprus becoming Greek territory, as Crete had after a 15-year period of supposed independence at the start of the century. Less genuine, perhaps, was Turkey's new-found concern for its "brothers" on the island – programmes broadcast regularly over Radio Ankara agitating feelings in its communal audience just as mainland Greek programmes did. The British, now faced with hostility from the Turkish Cypriots as well as from the Greeks, and contemplating the soaring costs of containing the rebellion, desperately sought a way out.

THE GRANTING OF INDEPENDENCE

In February 1959, the foreign ministers of Greece and Turkey met in **Zurich** to hammer out some compromise settlement, with a supplementary meeting including the British and Cypriots in **London** a few days later. The participants agreed on the establishment of an independent Cypriot republic, its **constitution** to be prepared by an impartial Swiss expert. Of its 199 clauses, 48 were unalterable, with *énosis* or *taksim* forbidden. The two ethnic communities were essentially to be co-founders, running the republic on a 70:30 Greek:Turk **proportional basis** that slightly favoured the Turkish minority. A single fifty-seat House of Representatives – with fifteen seats reserved for the Turks – two separate communal chambers funded partly by Greece and Turkey, and a Greek-Cypriot president plus a Turkish-Cypriot vice-president elected by their respective communities was also envisioned. With some misgivings Makarios gave his assent to the constitution.

The meetings also produced three interrelated **treaties**, which in turn were incorporated as articles of the constitution. Britain, Turkey and Greece simultaneously entered into a **Treaty of Guarantee**, by which they acted as guarantors to safeguard Cypriot independence. A **Treaty of Establishment** stipulated the existence of two military bases, their extent to be determined, and other training areas. The **Treaty of Alliance** provided for the stationing of Greek and Turkish military forces on the island and the training of a Cypriot army, presumably as an arm of NATO; this provision was roundly denounced by AKEL, and indeed in the long run this treaty was to prove the most destabilising element of the package.

Makarios, who had been in Greece since 1957, was finally permitted to **return to Cyprus**, where an amnesty was declared for most EOKA offenders. Grivas and the more hard-line enosists, excoriating Makarios for his supposed betrayal of the cause, flew off to self-imposed exile in Greece, while certain supporters stayed behind to punctuate most of 1959 with fulminations against the independence deal. More moderate individuals personally opposed to Makarios' personality cult, such as **Mayor Themistoklis Dhervis of Nicosia**, formed the first opposition party, the **Democratic Union**, to contest the presidential elections of December 1959 with the Archbishop's **Popular Front**. Makarios won handily with two-thirds of the vote, while Fazil Küçük ran unopposed for the vice-presidential seat.

Elections for the **House of Representatives** in February 1960 were poorly attended, with absenteeism and abstention rates of up to sixty percent in some districts reflecting popular disgust at the civic arrangements – and a poor omen for the future. The Popular Front took 30 seats, its coalition partners AKEL five, while Küçük's National Party got all 15 Turkish seats. Polling for the powerful **communal chambers**, charged with overseeing education, religion, culture, and consumer credit co-ops, showed a similar profile, though in the Greek chamber one seat each was reserved for the Armenian, Maronite and "Latin" communities.

Final independence, which had been set for no later than February 1960, was postponed until **16 August 1960**, as the Cypriots and the British haggled over the exact size of the two sovereign bases. By coincidence, Venetian and British rule lasted exactly the same time: 82 years.

THE UNITARY REPUBLIC: 1960–1964

The Republic of Cyprus seemed doomed from the start, with EOKA and TMT **ideologues** appointed to cabinet positions. Neither organisation completely disbanded, but maintained shadowy existences, waiting for the right moment to re-emerge. They and others made Makarios's life difficult: the enosists considered that he'd sold them out, the Turks were convinced that he was biding his time for an opportunity to impose it, and many of the communists felt he was too accommodating to the West.

On a **symbolic** level, communal iconography, street names, etc, all continued referring to persons and event in the "mother" countries; the respective national flags and national days were celebrated by each community, and while there was (and still is) a Cypriot flag, there never was a national anthem. Such institutionalised separatism was inimical to fostering a national consciousness. The **constitution**, an improbably intricate one for a population of just over half a million, proved unworkable in application. The Greek Cypriots chafed at it for having been imposed from outside, while the Turkish Cypriots took every opportunity to exploit its numerous clauses benefiting them. It was, as several outside observers remarked, the only democracy where majority rule was explicitly denied by its charter.

The **70:30 ratio**, running through all civil service institutions, could not be reached within the five months prescribed, and the **army**, supposed to be set up on a 60 : 40 ratio with ethnic mix at all levels, never materialised, since the Turks insisted on segregated companies; instead Makarios eventually authorised the establishment of an all-Greek **National Guard**. Both the president and the vice-president had **veto power** over foreign affairs, defence or internal matters, exercised frequently by Küçük. Laws had to clear the House of Representatives by a majority of votes from **both communal factions**: thus eight of the fifteen Turkish MPs could defeat any bill. When agreement could not be reached in the first two years of the republic's life, colonial rules were often extended as **stopgaps**.

For much of 1962 Cyprus had no uniform income tax or customs excise laws, the Turks having obstructed them in retaliation for Greek foot-dragging on implementation of separate municipalities for the five largest towns: another concession to the Turkish Cypriots was the maintenance of **separate municipalities**, first set up in the 1950s, for each community in the five largest towns an incredibly wasteful and time-consuming duplication from the Greek point of view. Yet they did not hesitate to pass **revenue** laws through their own communal chamber when frustrated in the parliament, thus perpetuating the apartheid by providing services only to the Greek-Cypriot community and those Turks choosing to acknowledge its jurisdiction.

Among the hardline elements, the TMT struck first, against its own community: on 23 April 1962 gunmen murdered **Ahmet Gurkan and Ayhan Hikmet**, leaders of the only Turkish-Cypriot political party to oppose Küçük's National Party, promoting closer co-operation between two communities. It was an echo of numerous such actions in 1958, and now as then no action was taken against TMT or its backers; **Rauf Denktaş**, protege of Küçük, even managed to get Emil Dirvana, Turkish Ambassador to Nicosia and one of many to condemn the murder, recalled. There would be no other significant Turkish opposition group until the 1970s.

In late November 1963, Makarios proposed to Küçük **thirteen amendments** to the constitution for make bicommunal public life possible. These included the abolition of both the presidential and vice-presidential right of veto, the introduction of simply majority rule in the legislature, the unification of the municipalities and justice system, and an adjustment of communal ratios in civil service and the still-theoretical army. Apparently, this proposal had been drafted with the advice of the British High Commissioner; the mainland Greeks subsequently deemed the bundle incredibly tactless, even if such reforms were worth introducing gradually. Turkey was sent the suggestions and denounced them, threatening military action if introduced unilaterally, even before Küçük had finished reading them, leaving him little room to manoeuvre.

FURTHER INTERCOMMUNAL FIGHTING

Reaction to the Turkish refusal was swift: on **21 December 1963** shots were exchanged between a Greek-Cypriot police patrol and a Turkish motorist, and within hours EOKA and TMT took to the field again. EOKA struck at Turkish neighbourhoods in Larnaca, and also in the mixed Nicosia district of Omórfita (Küçük Kaymakla), with an EOKA detachment under one **Nikos Sampson** rampaging through, seizing 700 hostages. In retaliation the Armenian community, accused of siding with the Greek Cypriots, was expelled by the Turks from north Nicosia on 23 December, and mainland Turkish troops left their barracks next day to take up positions along the Nicosia–Kyrenia road, with more forces concentrated on the Turkish mainland opposite; the mainland Greek force also deployed itself. Barriers, known as the **Green Line** after an English officer's crayon mark on a map, were set up to separate Greek and Turkish quarters in Nicosia after a UK-brokered cease fire was effected on Christmas Day.

Already, all Turkish Cypriots had **resigned** from the government and police forces, to begin setting up a parallel administration in North Nicosia and in the rapidly growing number of **enclaves**. Any Turkish Cypriot who might have thought to continue at his post in South Nicosia would have to run a gauntlet of both his own co-religionists, enforcing the sequestration, and Greeks who might shoot first and ask questions later. The enclaves in fact constituted a semi-deliberate policy of laying the physical basis for later partition, and the Turkish-Cypriot position from now on held that the 1960 constitution was **defunct**, and there were merely two provisional regimes on the island pending the establishment of a new arrangement. Makarios agreed that the 1960 constitution was hopeless – but differed in his conclusions: namely that majority rule would prevail as per his suggested amendments, with minority guarantees, whether the Turks liked it or not.

INTERNATIONAL REPERCUSSIONS

Because of the superpower interests involved, the Cyprus intercommunal dispute again took on **international** dimensions. The Greek Cypriots preferred, as they always had done, the UN as a forum; the US, UK, and both mainland Turkey and the Turkish Cypriots pressed for **NATO intervention**. Turkish opinion, expressed by Küçük and Denktaş's rightist Turkish National Party, helped plant the seeds of implacable American hostility to Makarios by successfully painting him with a pink (if not red) brush, calling attention to his forthright espousal of the **non-aligned movement**, and purchase of arms from the USSR and Czechoslovakia. In the event the Cypriot government, with the support of the Soviets and Greek Premier George Papandreou, had its way: in February 1964, a UN resolution dispatched **UNFICYP** (UN Forces in Cyprus) for an initial three-month peace-keeping assignment – extended later to six months and renewed since then without pause. A mediator was also sent. George Ball, US Under-secretary of State who had unsuccessfully tried to persuade Makarios to accept occupation by a NATO landing force, was later overheard to say "that son of a bitch [ie Makarios] will have to be killed before anything happens in Cyprus".

Little was accomplished immediately by UNFICYP; the death toll in the communal disturbances in the six months after December 1963 reached nearly 600, with the Turkish Cypriots suffering disproportionately. Unfortunately 10,000 **mainland Greek troops** also landed on the island, which gave EOKA and Greek Cypriots a false sense of being able to act with impunity. After TMT occupied Saint Hilarion castle and the Kyrenia-Nicosia as a core enclave, American President Lyndon Johnson sent Turkish Premier İnönü a letter, in his inimitably crude style, warning him off plans to invade. At the same time the US administration pressurised Greece to follow its prescription or possibly face Turkey alone on the battlefield; heads were to be knocked together, if necessary, to preserve NATO's southeast flank.

The UN mediator having reached a dead end (and himself soon dying anyway), the **Acheson Plan** – named after the US Secretary of State – was unveiled in mid-1964. It amounted to double *énosis*: the bulk of the island to Greece, the rest, plus the cession of the tiny but strategic Greek isle of Kastellórizo, to Turkey – effectively partition and the disappearance of Cyprus as an independent entity. After initial mulling over by both Greece and Turkey, the Greeks rejected the idea because of vociferous objections from Nicosia.

THE FIRST ENCLAVES

The **Kókkina incident** made world headlines in August 1964, when the newly-formed National Guard, commanded by a returned Grivas, attacked this coastal enclave in an effort to halt the landing of supplies and weapons from Turkey. Guarantors Greece and Turkey were again brought to the brink of war as Turkey extensively bombed and strafed the Pólis area, causing numerous casualties, and Makarios threatened to sanction attacks on Turkish Cypriots throughout the island unless Turkey ceased its air strikes. It was the first, but not the last, time that US-supplied NATO weapons were used in contravention of their ostensible purpose.

Any residual trust between the two island communities was destroyed by the end of 1964: the Turkish Cypriots were well **barricaded** in their enclaves, the central government retaliating by placing a ban on their acquisition of a wide range of essential materials deemed militarily strategic. The enclave inmates, numbers swelled by Turkish army personnel, retaliated by keeping all Greeks out, setting up a TMT-run state-within-a-state with its own police, radio station and other services, which provocation EOKA could not resist on numerous occasions.

Despite all this, Cypriot **economic progress** post-independence was considerable – though heavily weighted towards the Greek community, whose attitude towards the Turkish Cypriots at best resembled sending naughty children to bed without supper. The first of many **irrigation dams** to ease chronic water problems began to appear on the slopes of the Troödhos range and Kyrenia hills. Tourism became important for the first time, primarily on the sandy coast to either side of Famagusta and to a lesser extent around Kyrenia.

A TWILIGHT ZONE: 1965–1974

The new UN mediator **Galo Plaza** submitted his report in March 1965; it astutely diagnosed the shortcomings of the 1960 constitution and made forthright suggestions for a new one, principally that the Greek Cypriots must decisively renounce *énosis* and that the Turkish Cypriots must acquiesce to majority rule, with guarantees for certain rights. This did not go over well with them or the mainland Turks, who arranged to send him packing.

After April 1967 Greece had been taken over by a **military junta**, anxious – with American approval – to remove the "Cyprus problem" from the global agenda. However, secret summer meetings with Turkey, exploring variations of the Acheson Plan, came to nothing. In November, Grivas' National Guard attacked **Kofínou**, another enclave between Limassol and Larnaca, with considerable loss of Turkish life; Greece and Turkey both mobilised, Ankara again tendered an ultimatum to Athens, and American diplomats got little sleep as they shuttled between the two capitals. Despite its soldierly composition the Greek regime meekly complied with Turkish demands; **Grivas** and most of the 10,000 smuggled-in Greek mainland soldiers were shipped **back to Greece**. The National Guard, however, remained in place, an ideal Trojan horse for future plots.

In 1968 the UN sponsored direct **intercommunal negotiations**, which sputtered along until 1974, with **Glafkos Clerides**, President of the House of Representatives, and Rauf Denktaş as interlocutors. Substantial agreement on many points was actually reached, despite the Turks pressing for implementation of a high degree of local communal power in place of a spoiler role at the national level, and the Greek side holding out for more comprehensive central control. But Makarios never made the necessarily dramatic, generous concessions, and Clerides repeatedly offered to resign in the absence of what he saw was a lack of consistent support from Makarios.

GREEK CYPRIOT POLITICAL ORGANISATIONS

AKEL *Anorthotikón Kómma tou Ergazómenou Laoú* or "Regenerative Party of the Working People" – in plain English, the Communist Party of Cyprus; historically enemies of EOKA and conciliatory towards the Turkish Cypriots, though unreconstructed as opposed to Euro-communist.

ADISOK *Ananeótiko Dhimikratikó Sosialistikó Kómma* or "Renovating Democratic Socialist Party", a recent Euro-splinter off AKEL.

DIKO *Dhimikratikó Kómma* or "Democratic Party", headed by ex-President Spyros Kyprianou; pursues a relatively tough line in negotiations with the North.

DISY *Dhimokratikós Synayermós* or the "Democratic Rally", headed by three-time presidential candidate and former communal negotiator Glafkos Clerides; despite a right-wing domestic and foreign policy, advocates sweeping concessions to the North.

EDEK *Enoméni Dhimokratikí Énosis tou Kéndrou* or "United Democratic Union of the Centre" – despite the name this is a socialist party, perennial also-rans and coalition partners in national elections.

EOKA *Ethnikí Orgánosis Kypríon Agonistón* or "National Organisation of Cypriot Fighters"; rightwing, IRA-type group co-founded by Makarios and Grivas to effect *énosis* or union of Cyprus with Greece. Continued to exist after independence, metamorphosing into the virulently anti-Markarios, pro-fascist **EOKA-B**.

The Turkish enclaves were, though, finally **opened** to the extent of supplies going in and Turks coming out; with UN mediation, local arrangements – such as joint police patrols – were reached for a semblance of normal life in less tense areas of island. But in most details the leaders of the Turkish-Cypriot community still enforced a policy of **self-segregation** as a basis for a federal state. But whether they meant a federation as most outsiders understood it, or merely federation masquerading as partition, was highly moot. The Turkish Cypriots, biding their time in cramped and impoverished quarters, perhaps knew something that the Greek islanders didn't or wouldn't realise: that the mainland Turks were in earnest about **supporting** their cause materially and militarily as well as morally.

Both Makarios and Küçük were overwhelmingly re-elected early in 1968, though Makarios' three bishops had repudiated him for dropping *énosis* as a realistic strategy. This was just one aspect of his **deteriorating relations** with the Greek colonels, who – with the approval of the CIA – began **plotting** repeatedly to eliminate him, through the medium of the Greek regular army officers who by now controlled most of the National Guard.

A bizarre **counterplot** of the same year deserves mention: **Polycarpos Yiorgadjis**, a former EOKA operative and Minister of Interior, provided one Alekos Panagoulis in Greece with the explosives for an abortive attempt on the life of junta chief Papadopoulos. Exactly why Yiorgadhjis would do this – considering that EOKA and junta aims were now identical – remains a mystery; he was also implicated in a later attempt on Makarios' life, and was himself assassinated, either by junta operatives or forces loyal to the archbishop, in March 1970.

Grivas slipped back into Cyprus during 1971 and founded **EOKA-B** with the express intent of resuming the struggle for *énosis*; the old trouble-maker, now in his seventies, died in January 1974, still in hiding. EOKA-B and its allies set in motion various devices to destabilise the elected government of Cyprus, reserving – as had its predecessor – special venom for AKEL. Publically, the Greek junta demanded, and eventually got, the resignation of **Spyros Kyprianou**, long-time Foreign Minister and future president. The three dissident bishops of 1968, still acting as junta placemen, claimed at

one point to have defrocked Makarios, reducing him to lay status. Makarios retaliated by getting the **three bishops dismissed** with the help of other Middle Eastern prelates, and was re-elected in 1973 unopposed. By this time Küçük had died, replaced as nominal vice president by Rauf Denktaş.

1974: COUP AND INVASION

The junta, by early 1974 tottering and devoid of any popular support at home, now tried a Falklands-type diversion. Makarios, well aware of the intrigues of the junta's cadres in his National Guard, had proscribed EOKA-B in April 1974, and wrote to the Greek President on 2 July demanding that these officers be withdrawn. The junta's response was to give the go-ahead for the **archbishop's overthrow**, which despite advance knowledge, Markarios' primarily left-wing and poorly armed supporters proved powerless to prevent.

Early on **15 July**, National Guard troops attacked the Presidential Palace, gutted it and announced the archbishop's demise. But Makarios miraculously escaped to loyalist strongpoints in Páfos district and, with British help, left the island for Britain, which offered lukewarm support, and then the US, where he was refused recognition as head of state by Henry Kissinger, a man who had done as much as anyone to depose him. He got a warmer reception, as usual, at the UN.

Unfazed, the coup protagonists proclaimed as president **Nikos Sampson**, long-time EOKA activist and head of the (anything but) Progressive Party. A contemporary foreign correspondent characterised him as "an absolute idiot, though not quite illiterate – a playboy gunman. He spends every night in cabarets getting drunk, dancing on tables, pulling off his shirt to show his scars." Small wonder, then, that his term of office and EOKA-B's direct rule would last exactly one week.

On reflection, the EOKA-B people might have realised that their coup would give Turkey a **perfect pretext** to do what it had long contemplated: partition the island, claiming as guarantor to be acting as protectors of the threatened minority. Post-coup international opinion initially favoured Turkey, whose prime minister **Bülent Ecevit** went through the proper legalistic motions on 16–17 July of flying to Britain to propose joint action for protecting the Turkish minority, restoring Cypriot independence and demanding that Athens withdraw its officers. While Sampson was indeed quoted as saying "Now that we've finished with Makarios' people, let's start on the Turks," EOKA-B in the end **killed** more Greek opponents – estimates run to several hundred, including many wounded buried alive – than the 200–300 Turkish Cypriots killed at Tókhni and three villages around Famagusta.

"PHASE I"

At dawn on 20 July, Ecevit authorised the **Turkish invasion** of Cyprus, entailing amphibious armoured landings, napalm strikes, bombing raids of many towns and paratroop drops around Kyrenia. **"Phase I"** of the campaign lasted from **20 to 30 July**: despite the demoralising coup, and being outnumbered four to one, the Greek Cypriots managed to confine Turkish forces to a lozenge-shaped bridgehead straddling the Nicosia–Kyrenia road. In Greece, the junta chiefs ordered the Greek army to attack Turkey; its officers refused, precipitating the collapse of the junta on **23 July**, the same day Sampson fell from power.

Glafkos Clerides replaced him as acting head of state in Makarios' absence, as a civilian government took power in Athens. The first round of hastily convened **negotiations** between the Greek, Turkish and British foreign ministers convened in **Geneva**, resulting in the ceasefire of 30 July. On 8 August, talks resumed, with Clerides and Denktaş additionally present. On the night of 13–14 August, the Turkish foreign minister gave Clerides an effective **ultimatum** demanding approval of one or the other Turkish plans for "federation": either six dispersed cantons or a single amalgamated one under Turkish-Cypriot control, adding up to 34 percent of Cyprus. Clerides asked for 36 hours to consult his superiors, which was refused at 3am on 14 August; ninety minutes later, the Turkish army resumed its offensive.

"PHASE II"

"Phase II" was a two-day rout of the Greek Cypriots, who had no armour or air support to stop the Turkish juggernaut. The behaviour of the Turkish infantry in both phases of the war featured **gratuitous violence** against Greek-Cypriot civilians unlucky enough to lie in their path; word of the rapes, murders and looting which marked their advance was enough to convince approximately 165,000 Greek Cypriots to flee for their safety from the occupied areas, which at a second cease-fire on 16 August totalled 38 percent of the island's area – slightly more than had been demanded at Geneva – abutting a scalloped boundary, henceforth the **Attila Line**, extending from Káto Pýrgos in Soléa to Famagusta. The Greek Cypriot **death toll**, including combatants and civilians, rose to 3850; the **missing**, some apparently kidnapped by the Turkish army and none ever accounted for, totalled over 1600. **Turkish Cypriots** living in the South were put in an untenable position by the Turkish "peace action", as it was termed; EOKA-B units occupied or cleared out most of their enclaves, with reprisal killings at several points.

Since 15 July, a flurry of UN Security Council **resolutions**, calling on all concerned to desist from warlike actions and respect Cypriot independence, had been piling up, blithely disregarded then and in the years since. With the benefit of hindsight, UK parliamentary and US congressional committees duly **condemned** the timidity, lack of imagination, and simple shamefulness of their governments' respective past policies towards Cyprus, specifically the absence of any meaningful initiative to stop the Turkish war machine. The **British** claimed that with just over 5000 men on the sovereign bases, there was (despite their role as guarantor) little they could have done – other than ferry tourists to safety out of the North, and take in Turkish Cypriots fleeing EOKA-B gunmen in the South. In retrospect, though, it seems the UK had been content to follow American dictates rather than pursue an independent course.

On the part of the **US**, there was more of a failure of will than of ability to do something. President Nixon, on the point of resigning over Watergate, had deferred to the archpriest of *realpolitik*, **Henry Kissinger**, who made no secret of his "tilt" towards Turkey rather than Greece as the more valuable ally in the Aegean, or of his distaste for Makarios. Thus the integrity of Cyprus was sacrificed to NATO power politics; the only substantive American congressional action, over Kissinger's objections, was the temporary **suspension of military aid** to Turkey as a wrist-slap punishment.

TURKISH CYPRIOT POLITICAL ORGANISATIONS

DMP *Demokratik Mücadele Partisi* or "Democratic Struggle Party", an amalgam of three parties established to contest the 1990 elections – may split again into its components: Özker Özgür's **CTP** (*Cumhuriyetçi Türk Partisi*) or Republican Turkish Party, cast in the image of the namesake secularist Anatolian party; Mustafa Akancı's **TKP** (*Toplumcu Kurtulux Partisi*) or Communal Liberation Party, a centre-left grouping favouring rapprochement with the South; and the **YDP** (*Yeni Doğuş, Partisi*) or New Birth Party, representing Anatolian settlers.

TMT *Türk Müdafaa Teskilati* or "Turkish Defence Organisation", formed in 1958 to counter EOKA's activities; its ideology still guides the North's government to a great extent.

UBP *Ulusal Birlik Partisi* or "National Union Party", right-wing party established by Rauf Denktaş in 1974 and governing the North since; pro-Anatolian, nationalist and against significant accommodation with the South.

YKP *Yeni Kıbrıs Partisi* or "New Cyprus Party", centre-left faction headed by Alpay Durduran; anti-settler and anti-Turkish Army in platform.

During anti-American riots in Nicosia on **19 August**, the **US Ambassador Rodger Davies** and his administrative assistant were gunned down by EOKA-B hitmen; it was later revealed that Davies had probably been the CIA paymaster and handler for the EOKA-B coup, the deed being done to prevent him telling what he knew at subsequent inquests. Eleven days later **Vassos Lyssarides**, head of the socialist **EDEK** party supporting Makarios, narrowly escaped death at the hands of the same bunch. These lurid events demonstrated that clapping Sampson in jail – where he remained until 1992 – wouldn't cause his associates to simply disappear.

DE FACTO PARTITION: CYPRUS SINCE 1974

While still acting head of state, Clerides acknowledged that the Greeks and Greek Cypriots had been acting for years as if Turkey did not exist, and that some sort of **federal republic** was the best Cyprus could hope for. Makarios **returned** on 7 December 1974 to a diminished realm, and contradicted Clerides: the Greek Cypriots should embark on a "long-term struggle", using their favourite method of **internationalisation**, to induce the Turkish army to leave and get optimum terms from the Turkish Cypriots. This prefigured a final break between the two men the following year. In his homecoming speech in Nicosia, with half the South turned out to welcome him, Makarios also forgave his opponents – not that he had much choice, with EOKA-B operatives still swaggering about in full battle dress. But others, especially those who had lost relatives

at the hands of either the rebels or the Turks, were not in such a lenient mood; two decades on, assessing blame for the fiasco of 1974 still occupies a certain amount of the South's agenda.

Top priority was given to **re-housing the refugees** from both communities: the Turkish Cypriots simply occupied abundant abandoned Greek property in the North, but it took the South more than a decade to adequately house those who had fled the North. The international community, so disgracefully sluggish at the time the problem was created, was reasonably generous and prompt with **aid** to help reconstruct the island – aid which, however, went primarily to the South.

Strangely, intercommunal negotiations **resumed** almost immediately, though at first they centred almost entirely on the fate of Cypriots caught on the "wrong" side. Greeks in the South separated from relatives and homes in the North were at first allowed to rejoin them; the government initially attempted to prevent southern Turks from trekking north, but by late 1975 this had been allowed too. Once these Turks were safely on the "right" side of the Attila Line, most northern Greeks were expelled and the North pronounced, over the South's protests, that an equitable exchange of populations had been carried out.

The North declared itself the **Turkish Federated State of Cyprus** (TFSC) in February 1975, though as always what the Turkish Cypriots meant by federation, and with whom, was quite different from what the South had in mind. Clerides and Denktaş, brought together again by UN Secretary General **Kurt**

Waldheim, made hopeful noises of peace-making intent through much of 1975, but no substantive progress was registered. In 1977, Makarios and Denktaş met for the first time in fourteen years at the latter's request, agreeing on various **general guidelines** for a bicommunal, federal republic, the details of territorial jurisdiction to be determined later but envisioning a reduction in the amount of land held by the Turkish Cypriots.

After Makarios **died** in August 1977, **Spyros Kyprianou** replaced him as president and Greek-Cypriot representative at the on-again, off-again talks. As an initial good-will measure, it was first suggested in 1978 that the empty **ghost town of Varosha** be reset-tled by its former Greek-Cypriot inhabitants: the Greeks wanted this to precede any other steps, while the Turks would only countenance it under limited conditions and as part of an over-all settlement. The re-opening of Nicosia international airport has also been also mooted periodically. In 1981, Waldheim seized the initiative by presenting an "evaluation" of the talks thus far, and generating for the first time **detailed proposals** for the mechanics of a federal republic, which came to nothing.

In the international arena, the South increasingly **protested** Turkish and Turkish-Cypriot practices in the North – specifically the **expulsion** of most Greek Cypriots and denial of human rights to those remaining, the **settlement** of numerous Anatolian Turks to alter the demographic balance of the island, and vandalism against Greek religious property. Well-orchestrated boycotts of the North ensure – among other things – that **archaeological sites** are neglected, since no archaeologist would be permitted to work in a Greek-speaking country again if they were known to have visited the North, even just to inspect their old digs.

The North put a spanner in the works by unilaterally declaring full independence on 15 November 1983 as the **Turkish Republic of Northern Cyprus** (TRNC), generating the usual storm of pious UN resolutions of condemnation and widespread overseas support for the Greek Cypriot position. To date no other state besides Turkey has recognised the TRNC. Yet talks towards a peaceful island-wide solution continued: early 1984 saw more proposals by Kyprianou to the UN, not significantly different from those before or since. **Perez de Cuellar**, the new Secretary General, presented successively refined draft frameworks for a federal settlement between 1985 and 1986; first the South said yes, but the North no; then the Turks agreed, but Kyprianou wavered until the **opportunity was lost** – behaviour for which he was roundly pilloried, and which contributed to his loss of office in 1988.

POLITICS IN THE SOUTH

Coalitions have long been a fact of life among the Greek Cypriots, since no one party is strong enough to govern alone – though AKEL has historically mustered about a third of the votes in any contest, far more than in any western European country. And in such a small society, horse-trading and flexibility are essential, for if ideology is taken too seriously, public life becomes rapidly unliveable, as it did briefly in 1974: stances or declarations of one campaign are cheerfully eaten in the presence of new coalition partners in the next elections. Small parties such as EDEK often control swing votes, and are assiduously courted as partners in the ever-changing parliamentary constellations. The South has a **presidential** system, with no prime minister, and considerable power residing in the executive office. Both presidential and **parliamentary** elections occur every five years but are at present **out of sync**: the former in years ending in 8 and 3, the latter in years ending in 6 and 1.

Toh Kypriakó or the **"National Question"** – the most appropriate response to Cyprus' de facto partition – is the theoretically paramount electoral issue. In general, Kyprianou's centre-right party **DIKO** (*Dhimikratikó Kómma* or "Democratic Party") has stood for an idealistic solution over the long haul, relying on cumulative international pressures from any quarter to get the Turkish army to depart and the Turkish Cypriots to come to terms. Clerides' **DISY** (*Dhimokratikós Synayermós* or the "Democratic Rally) – eschewing excessive reliance on the UN, and preferring a pro-NATO/EC alignment, has stressed pragmatic deal-cutting directly with the Turkish Cypriots to get as many of the refugees home as quickly as possible. **AKEL** and **EDEK** can point to their track record of never having systematically harassed the Turkish minority as a valuable asset for bridge-building in a theoretical federal republic. Left unarticulated is the possibility of a partial solution necessitating massive concessions, with some politician allotted the unenviable task of indicating which refugee constituents can go home to the North, and which will have to stay.

After 1974, the leftist parties were in a position to exert additional pressure, with many **social-welfare measures** introduced for the first time by 1983 to alleviate some of the misery caused by the refugee influx – though despite US misgivings, a "dictatorship of the proletariat" was never in the cards; Cyprus is far too bourgeois for that, the unreconstructed Brezhnevism of AKEL notwithstanding.

In the House of Representative elections of **1976**, AKEL, EDEK, and Makarios' Popular Front combined to shut out Clerides' rightist DISY party, owing this sweep to a first-past-the-post system. After Makarios' death in 1977, his groomed successor Kyprianou was designated to serve out the remainder of the archbishop's presidential term, then re-elected unopposed in **1978** in his own right.

By **1981**, the parliamentary system had been changed to one of proportional representation; AKEL and DISY finished in a dead heat, with Kyrpianou's DIKO and EDEK holding the balance of power in the 35-seat House of Representatives; the **1983** presidential voting returned Kyprianou to office with AKEL backing, again shutting out Clerides.

In the **1988** presidential contest **George Vassiliou**, a professional businessman and political outsider, was elected, backed by the strange bedfellows of AKEL and DISY who, despite their wide differences on domestic issues, agreed that the timely resolution of the National Question was imperative and that Kyprianou had been repeatedly tried and found wanting.

The **1991** parliamentary polls showed a slight rightward swing in the House, now expanded to 56 seats: a DISY-Liberal coalition won 20, AKEL 18, DIKO 11 and EDEK 7.

On his fourth try for the presidency in February **1993**, DISY candidate **Clerides** upset AKEL-supported incumbent Vassiliou, by less than 2000 votes in run-off polling. The result is seen as a rejection of the UN-sponsored negotiations to date – Clerides intends to renegotiate "unacceptable" clauses of a proposed draft treaty – and an endorsement of his intent to pursue EC membership more strongly.

POLITICS IN THE NORTH

As borne out by the record of murderous suppression by TMT of its opponents, multiple parties were not actively encouraged in the Turkish-Cypriot community until after the founding of the Turkish Federated State of Cyprus in 1975; even since then Denktaş on a number of occasions has used questionable tactics to nip budding opposition – specifically against unsuccessful presidential candidate Ahmet Berberoqlu in 1975, and important opposition party chief Özker Özgür in 1988. Lately there has been **more genuine pluralism**, especially in the wake of Denktaş's announced impending retirement.

North Cyprus has a tiny electorate, with a high degree of **overlap** between government figures, business bigwigs, the ruling UBP party and President Denktaş's personal acquaintances. The description of the shifting coalition kaleidoscopes in the South applies doubly here, with politicking inevitably personalised in the prevailing village atmosphere: in 1990, 1 out of every 670 registered voters was a candidate. Though the North's system provides for both a **president and a prime minister**, Denktaş as president has always been the dominant figure. Presidential and parliamentary elections are held more or less together every five years, formerly in years ending in 6 and 1 but lately 5 and 0.

The first elections in the North were held in **1976**: Denktaş won easily, with 75 percent of the vote and the same percentage of seats for his **UBP** (National Unity Party) in the 40-seat legislative assembly. In **1981** the UBP margin of victory diminished: Denktaş squeaked by with just over half the votes, and while the UBP remained the largest party in the assembly, it no longer enjoyed an absolute majority, losing seats in a hung parliament to both Alpay Durduran's left-wing **TBP** (Communal Liberation Party), and Özker Özgür's **CTP** (Republican Turkish Party), with two minor parties holding the balance. Following an unstable period, and the 1983 UDI, the assembly was expanded to 50 seats, allowing Denktaş to pack the new ranks with compliant appointees and get on with the business of governing.

In the **1985** elections, only parties breaching the eight-percent barrier were awarded seats, which forced splinter factions to **disappear** or join with others. A previous constitutional clause prohibiting more than two consecutive presidential terms was eliminated, and Denktaş ran again as an **independent**. Although he stayed in office, the UBP's share of votes declined to just over a third of the electorate, reflecting disillusionment with its handling of affairs. Yet because of the various "reforms", its proportion of seats in the expanded assembly remained the same – about half.

Denktaş was re-elected yet again in the early **1990** presidential polls, and prior to the hard-fought May parliamentary elections, more **changes in the election laws** were introduced. These included a bonus-seat system for high-vote parties, a more-than-usually-enhanced system of proportional representation; prohibitions against voting across party lists and, most importantly, against coalition governments. The opposition's response to this last condition was to combine into a single unit, the **DMP** (Democratic Struggle Party). Composed of the CTP, TKP and YDP, it ran on a platform of anti-corruption, better economic management and liberalisation of the official electronic media – which not surprisingly gave little air time to opposition parties. But its lack of detailed proposals addressing the National Question and the economic doldrums, compared to the equally insubstantial but slick, nationalist-emotive campaign of the UBP, netted surprisingly disappointing results. With a bit under half the votes, the DMP received less than one-third of the available seats – mostly because of the bonus-seat rule. Alpay Durduran's new left-wing **YKP** (New Cyprus Party), running alone, gained no seats. Despite a disturbing number of polling irregularities – allegations of voters intimidated to vote UBP, the biased electronic media, etc – they were not decisive, and it appears that the UBP victory was genuine: DMP simply hadn't convinced enough voters that the UBP's shortcomings overrode its promises of continued national security in the face of the Greek Cypriot "threat".

1991–92 NEGOTIATIONS: LAST CHANCE?

Late in 1991, Cyprus returned to the global picture as it periodically does; then-President Bush, needing another foreign-policy feather in his cap prior to the 1992 US elections, called for a **new peace conference**, and visited both Turkey and Greece canvassing support for one – the first American presidential junket to either country in decades.

Intercommunal meetings did not actually materialise until mid-1992, with **Butros Butros-Ghali** now UN Secretary General. His "set of ideas" was similar in most respects to all proposals of preceding years: Varosha and some or all of the Mórfou plain would revert to Greek-Cypriot control, and Turkish-Cypriot-administered **territory** would shrink overall to 28 percent of the island's surface area. Left discussable was the degree of Greek refugees' return to the North; by juggling the boundaries of the Turkish-administered zone, a profile could be reached such that most Greek Cypriots could **go home** without complications – Varosha taking a big percentage of the total – and even if all Greeks formerly resident in the agreed Turkish zone decided to go back, they would still be in a minority there.

Politically, a joint foreign ministry and finance ministry was foreseen, with the Cyprus pound re-introduced throughout the island. Either a rotating or ethnically stipulated presidency was suggested, plus a supreme court equally weighted ethnically, and a bicameral legislature, with upper house biased towards the Turkish Cypriots in the sense that each federal unit would be represented equally rather than proportionately, as the states are in the US Senate.

July sessions between Vassiliou and Denktaş at the UN were inconclusive; Butros-Ghali had circulated to all interested parties a **tentative map** showing proposed adjustments of territory in a bizonal federation. When details of this were leaked, the North reacted strongly: "We Won't be Refugees a Third Time" was a typical newspaper headline, referring to the previous shifts in 1964 and 1974. Visits of high-level US envoys to Güzelyurt (Mórfou) in particular seemed to be testing the waters for just such an eventuality.

Before returning for the final October session, Denktaş caused further uproar by reviving his perennial threat to resettle Varosha ghost-town with more Turks. His position on Greek-Cypriot refugees maintains that, rather than be allowed to return to their old homes, they should be compensated financially for its lost value; in this he has the support of most

Northerners, who do not want Greek Cypriots to live among them again, and who prefer Turkey to have a right of unilateral intervention in any arrangement. There is less, but still appreciable, support for the persistence of a fully independent TRNC.

The October sessions in New York were again a washout; the Security Council passed yet another **resolution** late in November 1992, the most strongly worded in years, laying most of the blame for their failure on Denktaş for his intransigence in refusing to accept the Boutros-Ghali guidelines for a settlement. Denktaş's reaction was to threaten immediate resignation rather than sign any agreement under duress which he deemed unfavourable. As the years go by it is hard to avoid the lurking suspicion that he is content with the status quo, and has merely been humouring world opinion by his attendance at successive conferences.

Nearly two decades of UN-sponsored negotiations have repeatedly **foundered** on the same reefs: the Greek Cypriot vision of a well-integrated federal republic with relatively strong central powers, versus a Turkish-Cypriot ideal of vast devolution of power to local and communal entities and a token structure at the top. More concretely, the Greeks' insistence on Turkish withdrawal (including settlers), demilitarisation of the island, significant territorial adjustments, and the right of return of most if not all refugees remains incompatible with Turkish-Cypriot insistence on a mainland Turkish presence of all sorts, Turkey's perennial right of intervention, minimal territorial adjustments, and very restricted return of Greeks to the Turkish zone. In addition, if it is decided that certain people cannot go home, there is the matter of devising a just formula for

assessment of abandoned property – Greek and Turkish estimates differ wildly as to its extent and value – and who would foot the bill for **compensation**.

Given the late 1992 decision to greatly **scale down** the UNFICYP presence and leave the islanders more or less to themselves, it seems matters may be coming to a head. Alarmist scenarios of renewed fighting on Cyprus sound more plausible, fuelled by rumours that the Greek Cypriots are secretly **re-arming** with a view to pushing the Turkish army off the island. Although the South still commands international sympathy and has notched up an impressive number of UN resolutions in its favour, they would still probably come off worse in world opinion – not to mention militarily – if they tried to force matters.

It is difficult to overestimate the degree of **bitterness** that divides the two main island communities, and which persists unabated as the years pass. In the short run, perhaps the best that can be hoped for is a presidential victor in the North's 1995 elections whose personality and programme match Clerides' agenda closely enough to broker a peaceful settlement. But with memorials to those killed by whomever between 1954 and 1975 lovingly tended in every village of the island, and children on each side raised to believe that their counterparts come equipped with horns and a curly tail, it is likely to be another generation before any **significant rapprochement** takes place. All the islanders have their work cut out for them: bad examples (Bosnia, Lebanon, Georgia, etc) abound, with only Bulgaria's re-enfranchisement of its Turkish community as a recent hopeful note.

WILDLIFE

Cyprus' location has made it a "collecting basket" for wildlife from Asia Minor, Africa and the Mediterranean countries, and the island offers a rare chance to see plants and animals which could only be found by making separate journeys further afield.

Cyprus escaped the ravages of the Ice Ages which wiped out so many species in northern Europe, so within its territory there's a staggering diversity of rock types and natural habitats. The island supports a varied **flora** with some 1800 different species of flowering plants – comparable to the total number of wild species listed in Britain, but concentrated within an area about the size of Wales.

The current political division of Cyprus has parallels in the island's geological history. Until the Pleistocene period around one million years ago, the Troödhos to the south and Kyrenia mountains to the north stood as the hearts of separate islands. The primordial Athalas Sea in between. This became silted up to form the central plain (Mesaoría) at a time coinciding with the "dawn of man" and the most recent Ice Age in much of mainland Europe. Today, wherever winter streams cut through the plain, they expose fossil shells from that era which look like contemporary scallops, mussels and oysters.

Long-term isolation from neighbouring land masses such as Turkey has meant that some plants have had time to evolve into **distinct species**; there are currently over 120 endemic-

plants – species found only in Cyprus. To a lesser extent this is true for animals, and there are insects, birds and even races of shrews and mice that the island can claim as its own. Even the separation of the southern and northern mountain ranges has been long enough for plants in the Troödhos to have relatives in the Kyrenia hills which evolved separately from a common ancestor – for example, purple rock cress (*Arabis purpurea*) is abundant on volcanic rocks in the south, while the similar Cypriot rock cress (*Arabis cypria*) grows on the northern limestones.

Away from intensive cultivation and over-enthusiastic use of insecticides, the **insect fauna** is as diverse as the flora: butterflies, hawkmoths, beetles and mantids are abundant. The impact of human activity has changed Cyprus in the same way that much of the rest of the Mediterranean has been changed. Eratosthenes (275–195 BC) writes of a very different Cyprus, an island where innumerable streams flowed year round and even the Mesaoría was thickly forested. The Phoenicians and other traders up until the Venetians were attracted to the island by an abundance of timber suitable for ship-building: the destruction of the forests has contributed to drastic local climatic change since antiquity.

From the early days of British administration through to the present, forestry departments in Cyprus have been enlightened enough to manage and establish new forests throughout the island. Thus, about 18 percent of the island's territory is covered with "forest", although it's a much more open, park-like woodland than northern Europeans associate with the word. It is easy to remember only the negative side of human impact on the vegetation, but the commercial history of Cyprus has resulted in botanical benefits such as the palms, agaves, cacti, mimosas, eucalyptus and citrus trees which are a familiar part of today's landscape. Even the olive (*Olea europea*) originated in the Middle East and today its range is taken to broadly define the "limits" of Mediterranean vegetation and climate in Europe.

Bird life is diverse, especially in the mountains, and the island lies astride spring and autumn migration routes. Though having comparatively few mammals (sixteen species, including eight kinds of bats), Cyprus has a surprising range of reptiles and amphibians – in spite of the age-old association of snakes with evil, which seems to require that every snake crossing a road be crushed by car tyres.

WHEN TO COME

To sample the wildlife at its most varied, the **hot summer** months should be avoided: the ground is baked in the lowlands, sensible life-forms are hidden well away from the sun and there's no birdsong – crickets and cicadas loudly make up for the absence. However, many native flowers persist in the mountains through June and July and plants on the coast go on blooming throughout the year. In Cyprus bulbs start to flower with the first rains in October and November, anemones are in flower by Christmas, while orchids appear in abundance in the lowlands from February (even December in some years) through to early April. **Springtime** sees the real explosion of colour on the plains and lower hills.

In the winter months **weather** is unpredictable: until late March, days can change quickly from pleasantly warm to cloudy and windy in the space of a few hours. In recent years, a serious shortage of winter rains has left water levels in mountain reservoirs way below what is needed to cope with the summer tourist influx. By the end of April the plains are getting hot (summer temperatures in Nicosia reach 40°C and above with a more tolerable 35°C or so on the coast). In May, June and again in late September and October the mountains are a delight for the walker: warm, sunny and not another soul for miles.

HABITAT TYPES

Geographically, the island can be split into **three broad regions**: the **northern mountains**, which are mainly limestone; the **southern mountains** of igneous rocks from deep in the earth which have erupted volcanically through younger sedimentary rocks to leave volcanic mountain heights with flanks of chalks and limestone; and the **central plain** of comparatively recent deposits with schists forming conical hills at its edges. This geological diversity creates added interest in the **four main habitat types**: coastal, cultivated land, low hillsides less than 1000m, and mountains above 1000m.

COASTAL SCENERY

Coastal scenery is varied. Some **plains**, such as those in the north around Güzelyurt (Mórfou) which continue along the coast to Cape Koruçam (Kormakíti) and those in the south stretching westwards from Limassol, are kept moist much of the year. Water reaches them from the mountains in seasonal streams, or from deep wells. This enables them to support vast citrus orchards and, more recently, avocado groves. Reedy river mouths are rare nowadays, since reservoirs in the mountains hold back much of the winter rainfall, reducing some water courses to little more than a trickle. The wide, stone-strewn bed of the Xeropótamos between Páfos and Koúklia show that river's former extent.

Undeveloped **coastal wetlands** are found north of Famagusta, in pockets in the Mórfou and Pólis hinterland and in a limited area east of Xylofágou, near Ayía Nápa. Little of the once-extensive marshland at Asómatos, north of the Akrotíri saltlake, remains untouched and what is left can be hard to find because of drainage for vast fruit orchards.

Most resorts boast so-called "beaches", but some are just shingle or dirt-grey sand and hardly deserve the status. Naturalists and connoiseurs should try the west coast from Coral Bay to Lára and beyond to Cape Yerónisos, which takes in some interesting fossil-rich chalk (shark's teeth and sea urchins), which the sea has eroded into a stark lunar landscape. Further to the northwest, there are small **sandy beaches** on the Akámas peninsula. In the north, excellent beaches run from Famagusta to Tríkomo (İskele) on the east coast and on the north coast to the east of Kyrenia and on the Kárpas (Kırpaşa) peninsula.

Much of the coastline, however, consists of **low cliffs** of clay or limestone with rocks plummeting down to the sea; high cliffs occur between Episkopí and Pétra tou Romíou. Coastal plantations of eucalyptus date from attempts to control mosquitos by draining swamps: those of funeral cypress or Aleppo pine are more recent and form extensive **open woodlands** – near Hala Sultan Tekke and the Péyia Forest, for example. These plantations provide essential shelter and are rapidly colonised by all sorts of insects, birds and plants (orchids in particular).

CULTIVATED LAND

Large areas of **cultivated land** are maintained clinically free of weeds and insect pests by drastic measures such as deep ploughing, insecticides and fertilisers. But smaller areas on the Mesaoría – orchards near villages, olive groves (even in Nicosia) or carob orchards can be very colourful in the spring with numerous annuals. A direct consequence of the diverse plant life is that it supports rich populations of insects, lizards and occasional snakes – in the early morning orchards are good places to wander with binoculars and see small migrant birds.

Numerous species of flowering plants thrive in badly tended mountain vineyards and even at the edges of well-tended ones. One family of plants, always well represented, is the *Leguminosae* (vetches and peaflowers) – which also includes many commercially important crop plants such as peas, chickpeas, beans of all types and lentils. In Cyprus, these crops often play host to another family of plants, the parasitic broomrapes (*Orobanchaceae*) and when present in large numbers these are a crop pest.

LOW HILLSIDES

Low hillsides (slopes up to 1000m) occur over much of Cyprus away from the central and coastal plains. They take on a markedly different character according to whether the underlying soil is limestone (alkaline) or volcanic (neutral to slightly acidic). Over-grazing by **goats** is another factor affecting large areas of the island. These voracious animals leave pastures with few flowering plants other than tall spikes of white asphodels, one of the surprisingly few plants they find distasteful in a diet which can include woody and spiny shrubs. Government policy in the North has allowed settlers from the Turkish mainland to bring in their flocks, so that meadows which a few years ago were ablaze with flowers now have the goat-grazed look of their Southern counterparts.

In the Mediterranean region, low hills are extensively covered with a dense, low scrub composed of spiny, often aromatic shrubs. It forms a type of vegetation widely known as **garigue** – in the Greek-speaking world it's called **frígana** (sometimes written phrygana), literally "toasted". Left to grow it would become maquis, with bushes and low trees a few metres high. The final, or "climax", stage is the evergreen forest which once covered the island. In general, garigue and maquis often blend into one another on the same hillside.

On limestone or chalk, shrubby thymes, sages and a wickedly spined member of the rose family, *Sarcopoterium spinosum*, form an often impenetrable scrub. Numerous bulbous plants grow between and below the bushes, sheltered from the full glare of the sun and protected from all but the most determined goats. As you climb higher in the Troödhos foothills the soil changes quite dramatically in nature from white chalks to a range of browns due to the underlying serpentines and pillow lavas. A noticeable shift in vegetation accompanies the change in geology, with acres of **French lavender** (*Lavendula stoechas*), its flowers sticky to the touch, and various **rock roses** (genus *Cistus*) – a magnificent sight in late April and May when bushes are covered with large pink or white flowers .

Whatever the underlying rock types, garigue slowly evolves into a dense **maquis** – look over any hillside covered in dense bushes and the range of shades of green will show the sheer variety of species. In a limited area you can find **lentisk** (*Pistacia lentiscus*), **terebinth** (*Pistacia terebinthus*), **storax** (*Styrax officinalis*), **myrtle** (*Myrtus communis*), the red-barked **strawberry tree** (*Arbutus andrachne*) and several kinds of evergreen oaks, more like holly bushes than the stately oaks of Britain.

Many of the plants in the garigue and maquis are aromatic and, on a hot day, their oils vaporise to scent the air. In spring, after a few days outdoors, you may well find yourself almost absent-mindedly picking a leaf and gently crushing it before smelling it. Anyone venturing off paths and brushing shrubs will find their clothing has taken on the scent of the island where tiny amounts of fragrant essences – thyme, oregano or lavender – have rubbed off. Some of the plant oils are highly volatile and, on a really hot day, have been known to ignite spontaneously: the origin of Moses' burning bush, perhaps.

Aspect – the direction a slope faces – can make a great difference to the vegetation supported there because it determines how much sun and, on higher hills, how much rain the land will get. In Cyprus, there is an obvious change when you cross either mountain range and leave behind the rich, almost lush vegetation of the north-facing slopes to find the dry southern slopes, with their xerophytic (drought-adapted) species clinging to life in the "rain shadow".

Woodlands on the northern limestone hills are largely composed of **funeral cypress** and **Aleppo pine** grading into maquis, a pattern also repeated in the far west on the Akámas peninsula. In the Troödhos, woodlands in the low and middle regions are mainly extensive open pine forest, with less lofty specimens of **strawberry tree** (*Arbutus andrachne*): the wood has an attractive natural sheen and is used for making village chairs. Another characteristic small tree is the endemic evergreen **golden oak** (*Quercus alnifolia*) – the leaves have a leathery, dark-green upper surface and are golden-brown on the lower surface. Beneath the trees, a dense **understory** of assorted shrubs – cistus, lavender, thyme and honeysuckle – completes the picture.

THE HIGH TROÖDHOS

The high Troödhos – land over 1000m – is extensively forested and much reafforestation has been done using native species. Lower woods of **Calabrian pine** (*Pinus brutia)* yield to **black pine** (*Pinus nigra ssp pallasiana*) mixed with **stinking juniper** (*Juniper foetidissima*) and, near the summit of Khionístra, trees of both species appear gnarled as a consequence of their age, attained in a rigorous climate of long, hot summers and cold, snowy winters. On Khionístra you will also see trees where the trunk is violently twisted or split – the cause is lightning strikes which boiled the sap almost explosively to vapour. Under tremendous pressures the trunks split, but such incidents are seldom fatal to resilient trees and they continue to grow, albeit with an unexpected change of direction. In open areas there are low bushes of ankle-tearing **gorse** (*Genista sphacelata*), a spiny **vetch** (*Astragalus echinus*) and a **berberry** (*Berberis cretica*). The native **cedar** (*Cedrus libani ssp. brevifolia*) is being extensively propagated after becoming largely confined to the so-called "Cedar Valley" in the course of this century, especially after destructive fire-bombing of the forests by the Turkish airforce during the invasion of 1974.

Even though something, somewhere is in bloom throughout the year, things begin in earnest when the first rains of autumn relieve the summer drought and moisten the hard-baked soil. It only seems to take a few drops percolating into the parched soils of the plains to activate the bulbs of a tiny, light-blue **grape hyacinth** known locally as "Baby's Breath" (*Muscari parviflorum*) or the delicate, white **late-flowering narcissus** (*Narcissus serotinus*). In the mountains, under bushes of golden oak, you can find the **Cyprus cyclamen** (*Cyclamen cyprium*), with distinctive pink "teeth" to its otherwise white flowers. The flowering sequence continues with **friar's cowl** (*Arisarum vulgaris*), a curious candy-striped arum. The first of the **crown anemones** (*Anemone coronaria*) appears at Christmas time near the coast, followed by pink, then red varieties. Growing close by will be the highly scented **polyanthus narcissus** (*Narcissus tazetta*) and the royal purple stars of **Tempsky's sand crocus** (*Romulea tempskyana*).

Cyprus is justifiably famous among orchid enthusiasts for its unique assemblage of species: a good example of the "collecting basket" role mentioned earlier. The first **orchids** to appear are the robust, metre-high spikes of the **giant orchids** (*Barlia robertiana*). Look closely and you see flowers like tiny "Darth Vader" figures and perhaps catch a hint of its iris-like scent. Even by late December these orchids are blooming near the Hala Sultan Tekke, close to Larnaca airport, along with the fleshy-stemmed **fan-lipped orchid** (*Orchis saccata*). By late February to early March the season is in full swing, with an abundance of bee orchids including the remarkable endemic **Cyprus bee orchid** (*Ophrys kotschyi*), the pick of a fascinating bunch of insect mimics – this one has a fat black and white lip forming the insect "body". It occurs in scattered populations in the South near Larnaca, but is more common in the North.

In the **lowlands**, especially on the limestone soils of the northern slopes of the Kyrenia mountains, the Akámas peninsula and the southern Troödhos, the early **spring wildflower** display is staggering, with a profusion of **turban buttercups** (*Ranunculus asiaticus*) in white, yellow, various shades of pink, scarlet and even occasional bi-coloured forms. Less obvious to the eye, but equally diverse in colour, are the small pea and vetch family members with over 100 species listed in the island's flora, many of them indigenous to Cyprus. Two, in particular, stand out: the **veined vetch** (*Onobrychis venosa*), with white flowers and marbled leaves which spread over dry limestone, and the yellow-and-violet **crescent vetch** (*Vicia lunata*) which flourishes on volcanic soils – around Asínou church, for example.

Snow melting on the heights of Troödhos re-awakens one of the island's three native species of **crocus**, the **Cyprus crocus** (*Crocus cyprius*), followed by a pink **corydalis** (*Corydalis rutaefolia*), an endemic **golden drop** (*Onosma troodii*) and numerous other local flora from **dandelions** to **garlics** and **deadnettles**. Cyprus has two other species of crocus: the winter-flowering **late crocus** (*Crocus veneris*), especially frequent on the northern slopes of the Kyrenia range, and **Hartmann's crocus** (*Crocus hartmannianus*), usually encountered in early spring if you happen to be walking on peaks near Makherás.

By mid-March, many of the bulbous plants will already be dying back. The **annuals**, however, more than make up for the loss by providing sheets of colour, often created from surprisingly few species: scarlet **poppies**, the golden yellow of **crown marigolds** (*Chrysanthemum coronarium*), pink **Egyptian catchfly** (*Silene aegyptica*), perhaps tempered with white **chamomile** (*Anthemis chia*). In the days before intensive cultivation and deep ploughing, **field gladiolus** (*Gladiolus segetum*) made cornfields magenta with its stately spikes, and people still talk of looking down on a Mesaoría scarlet with tulips. Today, in the South, **wild tulips** (*Tulipa agenensis*) still survive under fruit trees near Stroumbí, north of Páfos, but to see the endemic **Cyprus tulip** (*Tulipa cypria*), with its dark red, almost purple flowers, you either have to visit bean fields and orchards around Çamlıbel (Mýrtou) or chance upon it in the wilder parts of the Akámas peninsula.

Two **coastal displays** of wildflowers are not to be missed. First appearing in late January and February, the **Persian cyclamen** (*Cyclamen persicum*) cascades over rocks on the north slopes of the Kyrenia mountains. You will also find them forcing their way through cracks and crevices around the Tombs of the Kings in Páfos, but the most spectacular display is on the natural rockery of the Akámas peninsula where they grow in white, pink and magenta shades waiting to be photographed with an azure blue sea below. A couple of months later, towards the beginning of April, there's another display: the **three-leaved gladiolus** (*Gladiolus triphyllus*) with scented pink and white flowers, growing in countless thousands, virtually all around the coast of the island.

In the **Troödhos mountains** things are slower off the mark. As you travel north from the coast, however, two new orchids – the yellow **Roman orchid** (*Dactylorhiza romana*) and the pink **Anatolian orchid** (*Orchis anatolica*) – become noticeable as soon as the soil changes from chalk to volcanic. From late May onwards, an unusual saprophytic orchid, the **violet limodore** (*Limodrum abortivum*), with purple stems and large purple flowers, is a common plant of the woodlands, inevitably growing beneath pines or close to them. It occurs in some abundance not far from Troödhos resort itself, with three other orchid companions: **Cyprus helleborine** (*Epipactis troodii*), **Holmboe's butterfly orchid** (*Platanthera holmboei*) and **red helleborine** (*Cephalanthera rubra*).

When the **plains** are burnt dry, **pink oleander** (*Nerium oleander*) brings a welcome touch of colour to dried stream beds. It has been widely planted as a flowering "hedge", and at the right season you can travel the Nicosia–Troödhos road flanked by these colourful flowering bushes. Few other species of plant, in flower now, relieve the grey and brown shades of a dessicated landscape. There are **thistles** – the **cardoon** (*Cyanurus cardunculus*), a wild artichoke growing several metres tall, is quite spectacular – and also a yellow dandelion relative forming sticky-leaved bushes, often covered in dust. This plant is one of those you see everywhere but rarely find in field guides: it's called **aromatic inula** (*Dittrichium viscosum*) and this is one of those cases where "aromatic" does not mean pleasant.

In the **middle heights** of the Troödhos massif, where the road climbs up to

Pródhromos, May is the time to see the white, lupin-like flowers of **Lusitanian milk vetch** (*Astragalus lusitanicus*), with **purple rock cress** (*Arabis purpurea*) in pink cushions hanging over rock faces above. Late in the day, shafts of sunlight on an open glade might illuminate scarlet **pæonies** (*Pæonia mascula*), almost making the flowers glow. This is the time of year when the **French lavender** (*Lavendula stoechas*) flowers on the pillow lavas, and whole hillsides can seem to be in bloom with a variety of **cistus**: white (*Cistus salviaefolius* and *C. monspessulanus*), pale pink (*C. parviflorus*) and deep pink (*C. creticus*).

In only a few places in the Troödhos does **water** run all the year round, but locate it and there, in early summer, you can find the rare (though you'd never think so here) **eastern marsh helleborine** (*Epipactis veratrifolia*), the **Crimean orchid** (*Dactylorhiza iberica*) and an indigenous **butterwort** (*Pinguicula crystallina*), a plant that traps insects on its sticky leaves. By July, even plants in the mountains find it too hot and only spiny things such as various gorses, brooms and berberry provide a bit of colour.

Surprisingly, it's only when the sand gets too hot to stand on in the day that delicate white **sea daffodils** (*Pancratium maritimum*) bloom: they were once so numerous on the east coast that they were called Famagusta lilies. Under these same "desert" conditions in coastal and other lowlands all over the island, you find tall spikes of starry-white flowers, growing leafless straight out of hard-baked ground. These are **sea squills** (*Urgineum maritimum*) and what becomes of the huge bulbs you might have wondered about, in spring, when you saw them half-pushed out of the ground, topped by long, strap-like, leathery leaves. The bulbs were once used as the source of a rat poison.

When little else is left in flower near the sea, you will find **carline thistles**, favourites of flower arrangers for their long-lasting flower heads. By now, it should come as no surprise that the tiny one with scarlet, daisy-like flowers you find near your beach in the South is yet another Cypriot native – the **dwarf carline thistle** (*Carlina pygmaea*).

Few who visit the island burnt dry at this time are aware of the changes that will take place when, in a few months, the first rains fall and the cycle begins again.

EXOTIC AND EDIBLE PLANTS

Introduced exotic plants, noted in the introductory section, now play an important part in the island's **food production**. The climate has favoured the introduction of sub-tropical species which are now widely cultivated: palms (from North Africa, Asia and the Americas), agave, avocado, prickly pear, tomatoes, potatoes, peppers and aubergine (the Americas), mimosa and eucalyptus (Australasia), citrus (originated in Asia) and pomegranate (Iran). The British administration introduced flowering trees from other colonies which, in maturity, have become a colourful feature of the parks and gardens in towns and cities: orchid tree (*Bauhinia variegata*), bougainvillea (*Bougainvillea spectabilis*) and silk oak (*Grevillea robusta*).

Cypriots north and south of the Attilla Line are essentially pragmatic people when it comes to natural resources, readily recognising **edible "weeds"** while remaining indifferent to or disparaging of less "useful" plants. Even town dwellers will head for the countryside in spring, perhaps to gather shoots of woody-stemmed **wild asparagus** (*Asparagus stipularis*) or of the **bladder campion** (*Silene inflata*), called *strouthkiá* – "little sparrows"). Both are fried with eggs to make a kind of omlette. In the Pólis region it's still possible to ask for *spatziá* (pronounced "spajá") or *faskómilo* – a tea made from the leaves of a bitter-tasting **wild sage** (*Salvia cypria*). In autumn, the slightest of bumps in in woodland leaf-litter can lead the sharp-eyed and knowledgeable villager to edible wild funghi. Outside private gatherings with Cypriot families, it is almost impossible to try most of these foods: only *káppari*, whole, spiney **caper stems** softened by pickling, are readily available.

Over the centuries, Cypriots have employed many plants as natural remedies for every imaginable ill; with increasing westernisation much of this lore has been forgotten. If you're interested in further study, some of the botanical field guides listed in the bibliography at the end of this article will be useful.

BIRDS

Cyprus no longer has the large numbers of birds of prey it once had – thanks to the mania, North and South, for the gun, along with the use of poisoned carcasses by misguided goat-herds, anxious to protect their flocks and their meagre income.

Fortunately **lammergeiers** still nest in colonies in the gorges of the Akámas peninsula as well as on the high cliffs to the west of Episkopí and in the Kyrenia hills. Although the days are long gone when up to 100 of these scavengers might gather round a suitably "ripe" carcass, the sight of a few, wheeling on thermal updraughts over the Akámas, is still a sight to quicken the heartbeat. **Kestrels** are still common but nesting **peregrine** only survive in remote strongholds in the Kyrenia range and offshore on the Klídhes islands at the tip of the Kárpas peninsula. **Bonelli's eagle** is far from common nowadays in either northern or southern mountain ranges, whereas in the past it was even known to have nested in the walls of Buffavénto castle.

Other raptors seen over the island are usually migrants, transient visitors on passage to nesting grounds in spring, returning in autumn. They tend to be seen as they hunt over reservoirs and at the salt lakes for prey to sustain them on their journey, or when flying over the peninsulas of Akámas and Kırpaşa (Kárpas). Species regularly observed include the **red-footed falcon** and the **hobby**, a small falcon which looks like a large swift in flight and which has the turn of speed and agility in the air to take swallows, martins and even swifts on the wing. There are also broad-winged raptors such as **marsh harrier**, **common buzzard** and **black kite**, for example, which can be seen soaring above scrub-covered hills or hunting low over reed beds.

Eleonora's falcons breed late in the year in colonies on the cliffs at Akrotíri, safely protected within the Episkopí Sovereign Base. They favour Cape Gáta at the tip of the peninsula and nest late, timing the hatching of their chicks to coincide with the autumn migration of exhausted hoopoes, orioles, swifts and sand-martins, exploiting the passerines' misfortunes. Once you have witnessed their mastery of flight, as they scythe through the air, they can be forgiven their opportunism.

In the Troödhos massif there are permanent nesting populations of familiar species such as **raven**, **jackdaw**, **rock dove** and **wood pigeon**. Less familiar to those used to watching birds in northern Europe will be **crag martin**, **Cretschmar's bunting** and the colourful **hoopoe** with pink body, black and white crest and a call which can be heard from afar. In the northern range, Kantára has always been a favourite place for birdwatchers in spring and, in the course of a couple of hours you might see **blue rock thrush**, **alpine swift**, **black-headed bunting** and **spectacled warbler**.

The **chukar**, an attractive rock partridge, manages to survive as a ground nester in dense scrub, in spite of it being the favourite target of hunters North and South: just enough seem to esape the hunters to maintain the population in a fragile equilibrium. The **black francolin**, exterminated in much of southern Europe by thoughtless hunting, just managed to recover from the brink of extinction in Cyprus when the British administration revoked gun licences during the EOKA troubles of the 1950s. Sadly, it's still hunted in one of its main strongholds in the Kárpas, to the east of Dipkarpaz (Rizokárpaso).

Rollers and **bee-eaters** are the most colourful of the spring migrants seen each year on passage through the island. Both species are known to breed locally, choosing suitable holes in sandy river banks or soft cliffs for the purpose. Being vividly coloured they attract the attention of hunters and have been regarded as articles of food. Cyprus suffered habitually in the past from depradation by **locusts** – government reports for the years 1878 and 1879 record how villagers were expected to catch locusts to be bagged up and weighed. Failure to comply with the directive or even to collect minimum weights brought fines and sometimes imprisonment. Ironically, locusts form part of a roller's diet – if these insects are around then they will eat nothing else.

Salt lakes provide both food (tiny brine shrimps siphoned up in their millions) and a resting place for the **greater flamingos** which winter at Akrotíri and Larnaca. Together with reservoirs, the salt lakes and marshes constitute the main areas of open water on the island and regular visitors have a chance to observe a changing variety of **water birds** in the course of a year. There are various species of **duck** (mallard, shoveler, teal and wigeon), **black-necked grebe** and larger birds such as several members of the heron family (**squacco heron**, **night heron**, **little bittern**, **little** and **cattle**

egrets). Shallow waters at the edges of reservoirs and salt lakes provide the mud in which waders probe incessantly for their food. Occasionally, one can be lucky and see **glossy ibis**, **black-winged stilt**, or **black-tailed godwit**. The migratory routes of storks do not pass over the island but, occasionally, individuals of both **black** or **white stork** and even **pelican** can be blown off course and spend a few days in the island, before resuming their journey.

Cyprus has several endemic bird species, distinct enough from their nearest relatives that they can be properly thought of as species; others are only regarded as distinct "races". The best known of the natives of is the **Cyprus warbler**, with a wide distribution in scrubby areas throughout the island. It closely resembles the Sardinian warbler but differs in having underparts marked with black — it also lacks the red ring around the eye and the red iris which are the trademarks of the Sardinian species. Only one other native is widespread and that is the **Cyprus scops owl**: the others — **pied wheatear**, **coal tit**, **jay**, **crossbill** and the **short-toed treecreeper** — are confined to the High Troödhos pine forest.

Both **Demoiselle** and **common cranes** spend the winter months in the Sudan but migrate via Cyprus — en route for the Demoiselle's breeding sites in Asia Minor and southern Russia in March and April, while the common crane flies in the opposite direction, leaving the Balkans, Turkestan, Asia Minor and northern Europe in August and September. They are often seen following the line of the Akámas peninsula in spring, but particularly evocative are hot, late-August nights over Nicosia: the birds are far out of sight, only the wing beats and trumpeting metallic calls identifying their passage.

MAMMALS – PAST & PRESENT

The Mediterranean Sea has had a chequered history, and geological evidence shows that it has even dried out on several occasions, enabling plants and animals to migrate to mountain peaks which have since become islands.

The basic shape of the **Mediterranean basin** was formed about 40 million years ago, but until around 20 million years ago it was open at either end to the Atlantic and Indian Oceans respectively. First the eastern channel closed up, isolating sea life but still allowing land animals to cross the between continents, and then the western outlet closed, effectively sealing it off.

Some six million years ago the land-locked sea **evaporated** almost completely; the Mediterranean became an arid, inhospitable basin with a few shallow salt lakes on its floor and some of today's islands standing as **forested oases**, in which animals congregated and developed. Drilling has revealed salt deposits which show that the Atlantic breached the debris dam at the present-day Straits of Gibraltar on several occasions over a 700,000-year period. Finally, the "dam" gave way and the basin was filled in about a century by a gigantic cascade of Atlantic water, isolating the forested hilltops and their inhabitants.

Excavations on the Mesaoría have revealed **fossil bones** showing that Cyprus, in Pleistocene times, was the home of mammals such as pygmy elephants, pygmy hippopotamus, ibex, genet and wild boar. Today the largest mammal on the island is the the **Cyprus mouflon** (*Ovis musimon*), possibly a survivor from those times. Although hunted almost to the point of extinction, it has been saved by a captive breeding programme in the forests of the southern mountains, and is widely used as a symbol of the island — visitors first meet it as the symbol of *Cyprus Airways*.

Although **foxes** are rarely seen in the open, they are not uncommon in the Akámas and Kárpas peninsulas. They have paler coats than north European races and blend easily with the browns and greys of the landscape. **Cyprian hares** (*Lepus cyprius*) can sometimes be seen as they break cover, but they are shy creatures — justifiably — barely able to sustain small populations between successive hunting seasons. Other small animals include the **Cyprian shrew**, a race of **spiny mouse** and **long-eared hedgehogs** — which look like the animal equivalent of an old Renault 4, with their long back legs keeping their rear end higher than the front. For years, hedgehogs were persecuted because of a reputation for climbing into chicken coops and trying to have their spiny way with the inhabitants. As laughable as it is physically impossible, the strongly-held superstition did the welfare of these creatures no good at all.

Of the eight species of bat recorded in Cyprus the **fruit-eating bat** (*Rousettus aegyptiacus*) is the most spectacular, with a powerful bird-like flight. They can sometimes be seen on the outskirts of Pólis and in villages along the northern coast, when they come in the evening to feed on ripe fruit. They live and breed in limestone caves and so are confined to the Akámas (where they were filmed for David Attenborough's series on the Mediterranean) and the Kyrenia mountains. Their visits to orchards have made them the target of hunters, but in the wild they have an important role to play because hard-coated fruit seeds pass undamaged through their digestive systems. Thus fruit-eating bats have played an unwitting but essential role in the propagation of trees by spreading seeds in their droppings.

REPTILES AND AMPHIBIANS

Saint Helena, mother of the Byzantine Emperor Constantine, apparently visited Cyprus on her return voyage from Jerusalem to Constantinople after a successful venture to discover the Holy Cross. She found an island gripped by the ravages of drought, but what really perturbed her was that it seemed to be infested with snakes and lizards. Her answer to the problem was to return with a shipload of cats to hunt them down, and these were landed at the tip of the Akrotíri peninsula, henceforth known as Cape Gáta (*gáta* = cat). Although feral cats in cities still take an enormous toll of lizards (and small birds), **reptiles and amphibians** still occur in numbers sufficient to interest those who want to see them.

Spring and autumn are the times to see the island's snakes: in winter they hibernate and in summer they are hidden, virtually comatose, from the unremitting heat. Looking like a glossy earthworm, the **worm snake** is the smallest: at a length which can reach two metres, the large **whip snake** just qualifies as the longest. The latter is easily recognised by its almost black back – it wriggles away when disturbed in vineyards or at field edges and will also climb trees. There are four other species of whip snake which, together with the **grass snake**, are all considered harmless. The **cat snake** and **Montpellier snake** feed on small lizards and produce venom which can paralyse or kill their prey in a matter of minutes. Humans fare better if bitten by either, since the inward-pointing fangs are set far back in the throat, but a large Montpellier snake can still inflict a wound which is slow to heal, with local swelling and headache as an accompaniment.

During the years of the British administration, problematically large numbers of rodents led to the idea of importing more Montpellier snakes from southern France as a biological control. Some were undoubtedly brought in to bolster the local population, but as to numbers involved, the period of time and the ultimate success of the venture, nobody seems certain. The **blunt-nosed viper** (called *koúfi* locally) has a distinctive yellow, horn-like tail and can inflict a bite which is highly **poisonous**: its fangs remain embedded in the tissue and the venom is pumped into the wound by movements of the jaws. In Cyprus all snakes have a bad press, based almost entirely upon superstition – none of the island's species is aggressive and individuals will only bite in a desperate move to defend themselves.

Small **lizards** seem to be everywhere. You will see tiny **geckos** coming out at night to feed on insects attracted to wall lights, or agile **sand lizards** racing over rocks or even suicidally dashing across roads. The largest lizard in Cyprus is the **starred agama** (*Agama stelio*) which grows up to 30cm long. It has a disproportionately large head, and if you see one at close quarters it's like looking back in time to the age of dinosaurs. They are shy creatures, often seen scuttling into cracks in walls or the trunks of ancient olive and carob trees. In Cyprus, the politest of the local names means "nosebiter", inspired by the oversized head.

In summer, **tree frogs** (*Hyla arborea*) are usually heard rather than seen when they call, often at night and far away from water, with a volume out of all proportion to their small size. In winter, they return to water to breed and lay eggs and can be found on bushes or reeds close to streams, ponds and rivers, where you might be lucky enough see their acrobatic climbing. **Marsh frogs** and **green toads** are considerably larger and, thus, correspondingly easier to find.

Caspian pond tortoises can still be found, even in surprisingly murky pools, although they have suffered badly from the effects of pollution – mainly from agricultural chemicals. A plop into a muddy pool as you approach will usually be a large frog – occasionally it might be a pond tortoise, which will surface several metres away to survey you, the intruder, with quiet confidence.

SEA TURTLES

Cyprus is one of the few places in the Mediterranean where **sea turtles** still come ashore to breed on the sandy beaches of the Kárpas and Akámas peninsulas. Tourism has driven them from the sands of the south coast, where they once nested on Governor's Beach to the east of Limassol. Since the early 1980s, the Fisheries Department has run a camp at Lára, near Páfos, with the express purpose of protecting nests and collecting hatchlings in order to transfer them to the water, safe from predation by crows and foxes. For years, a running battle has simultaneously been fought between conservationists and the developers who see the obvious tourist potential of this superb, sandy beach.

Both **loggerhead turtles** (*Caretta caretta*) and **green turtles** (*Chelonia mydas*) haul themselves ashore at night, landing from June onwards on beaches to the northwest of Páfos. In the north mainly loggerheads come ashore to lay eggs on sandy beaches east of Kyrenia and also on the Kárpas peninsula. Both species mate at sea.

The **green turtle** is the larger of the two species, with mature adults attaining a length of some 100–127cm, while the loggerhead grows from 75-100cm in length. They are smooth-shelled herbivores, feeding on sea grasses and seaweeds and, in the nesting season, a female can produce several clutches of eggs at two-week intervals – they tend to breed every two to three years. **Loggerheads** have a tapered shell or carapace, a short muscular neck and powerful jaws which can crush the shells of the molluscs which constitute a part of the varied diet along with jellyfish, crabs, sponges and aquatic plants. They breed every other year and will lay three or four clutches in a season

A popular local belief maintains that turtles will only lay on the two or three nights either side of the full moon. What is certainly true, however, is that turtles the world over prefer to emerge on bright, **moonlit nights**. The laborious journey up the beach, the digging of a nest, followed by egg-laying and then covering with sand, is an exhausting business which takes

several hours. Turtles disturbed as they come ashore will simply return to the sea, but when laying has started they carry on until virtually drained of energy – behaviour that has made them extremely vulnerable to hunters.

Temperature plays a very important part in the development of the embryo within the parchment-skinned turtle egg, as it not only controls the incubation rate, but also determines the sex of the offspring. Instinctively, the female selects a place on the beach and lays her eggs at such a depth (about 40cm) that the ambient temperature will stay fairly constant during the incubation period. Since sea turtles have evolved from land-based ancestors, their eggs will not develop in water; to survive, they need the air trapped between the grains of sand that surround them in the "nest".

Hatchlings appear some six to ten weeks after the white, ping-pong-ballish eggs are laid in batches of from 75 to 120; in Cyprus most nests are established in June, and hatchlings emerge throughout August into September. The lower in the sand an egg is placed, the cooler it is and hence the slower the development. Thus **hatchlings emerge** at different rates, a batch each day from the same nest. Immediately after biting and wriggling their way out from the egg, they still have part of the yolk-sac attached and will have to wait beneath the sand until that has been absorbed into the body. The young struggle the final few centimetres to the surface and make directly for the sea around dawn or in the evening when it's cool. Occasionally, their internal clocks can go wrong and they try to emerge in the hot sand with fatal consequences.

In some countries, hatchlings have to run a gauntlet of seabirds to reach the sea; in Cyprus, foxes have been the major **predators**. The hope is that the immediate danger of predation at Lára is removed by placing wire cages over nests, ensuring one less peril in the seven or eight years it will take them to reach maturity. It is very difficult to assess the success of conservation ventures with sea turtles because of other hazards they have to face: predation from other sea creatures when small, deliberate killing by fishermen, or being left to die, trapped in drift nets. The good news is that numbers have certainly not decreased in Cyprus in the fifteen years that a conservation programme has been operational.

INSECTS

As soon as the sun comes out, butterflies are in evidence as they fly over patches of open ground in scrub or hotel gardens where, often for the first time, visitors see the glorious **swallowtail butterfly** (*Papilio machaon*), rare in Britain yet common here, where its larvae thrive on wild carrots. Strawberry trees along the south and north coasts are the food-plant of the magnificent **two-tailed pasha** (*Charaxes jasius*), a powerful flyer which defends its territory against infiltrators by flying at them. When seen at close quarters a complex and beautiful striping of the under-wings is revealed.

Cyprus has several unique species of butterfly, including the **Paphos blue** (*Glaucopsyche paphia*) and **Cyprus festoon** (*Allancastria cerysi cypria*), a swallowtail rela-tive with scalloped margins to the wings. It has curiously spiked caterpillars which lives off a plant with a similarly bizarre appearance, the Dutchman's pipes (*Aristolochia* species), plants found thoughout the island's hills on chalk and volcanic soils. **Cleopatras** (*Gonepteryx cleopa-tra*) fly through sunny glades in the mountain woods, heralding the arrival of spring; the males are a deep sulphur yellow, with a splash of orange just visible on the forewings in flight.

In summer, numerous species usually referred to collectively as "browns" (*Satyrids*) and "blues" (*Lycaenids*) are found all over the island wherever weeds grow. In spite of heavy use of insecticides, enough weeds are left to enable caterpillars to thrive. Some larvae are very particular and restrict their diet to one species of plant, while others are virtually omnivorous, even resorting to cannibalism if there is nothing else to eat.

One of the things you notice in pine trees are the hanging nests of gossamer, spun by **caterpillars** after they hatch from their eggs. They feed on pine needles within the nest and then drop to the ground in a wriggling mass until one sets off and the others attach them-selves in a "follow my leader" arrangement. So successful are these processionary caterpillars of **pine beauty** and **gypsy moths** that they have become a forest pest, causing serious damage to trees.

Many moths can be grouped under the heading "small, brown and boring", but one family, the **hawkmoth**, rivals butterflies in terms of colour and are superbly equipped for fast, powerful flight with strong forewings and small hindwings. Their caterpillars are often more gaudily coloured than the parents and can assume a curious posture to frighten off preda-tors — a habit which has given them the common name of **sphinx moths**. In Cyprus, the most common member of the family is the **hummingbird hawk** (*Macroglossum stellat-urum*), which can be cheeky enough to approach on whirring wings and, with long, thin tongue, sample the liquid from the edges of your drink glass as you enjoy an evening meal outdoors. Less frequently seen are the beautiful **oleander hawks** (*Daphnis nerii*) with olive-shaded wings and the **death's-head hawk** (*Acherontia atropos*) whose large yellow- and-violet-striped caterpillars feed on potato plants and were quite common crop pests before the use of insecticides. **Praying mantids** are curious creatures and, in Cyprus, range from the small brown species to the larger **crested mantid** or *empúsa*, named after a Greek demi-goddess who visited men in their beds and made love with them until they expired: even the insect males have to be fast to avoid becoming the main item in the post-coital breakfast.

Not strictly insects, but coming into the general category of "crawlies", most Cypriot **spiders** are small except for the **European tarantula** which lives in burrows on open hill-sides venturing out to catch any suitable prey passing its way. **Scorpions** are not as common as they once were, primarily due to destruction of habitat and to the use of agricul-tural chemicals. By carefully turning up stones in chalky areas or looking in the cracks in old limestone walls you can still find them. They are shy, pale-coloured creatures, but in defence of their brood they will inflict a very painful sting. The large black **millipedes**, equipped with twin "hypodermics" at the tail end, can do the same: if camping in the wild shake out your sleeping bag carefully.

MARINE LIFE

The sea turtles mentioned above are the most spectacular of the marine creatures regularly seen in the waters around the island. Although **dolphins** are infrequently sighted off the north coast, their true haunts are much closer to Turkey's southern shore where there are more fish. The lack of tidal movement, coupled with very few streams providing nutrients to enrich the coastal water, keep plankton levels on the low side. Also, the building of Egypt's Aswan Dam drastically reduced the outflow of nutrient-rich Nile water into the southeastern end of the Mediterranean. Consequently, fish numbers around the coasts are not as high as might be expected, but there is still a surprising diversity of colourful species – scuba-diving is a very popular activity because the absence of plankton makes the waters very clear.

A visit to a quay when a fishing boat comes in is also a recommended experience. As the catch is unloaded you see a great mixture of fish, including **peacock** and **rainbow wrasse**, **parrot fish**, **red soldier fish** and **red** or **grey mullet**. Many of these are visible from the surface if you're lazily snorkelling, in addition to the ubiquitous **sea urchins**, **starfish**, **anemones** and an occasional **octopus**. Further out to sea are small, harmless **sharks** and several species of **ray** (including electric and thornback), making a total of around 200 species of fish recorded in the seas off the island. However, due to overfishing and high tourist levels in the south, the squid you dine on probably came in boxes from Taiwan, and nowadays boats have to sail almost to the Libyan coast in order to catch swordfish.

SITES

THE SALT LAKES: LARNACA AND AKROTÍRI

If you arrive in Cyprus in winter or spring and collect a hire car at Larnaca airport, the first taste of the island's wildlife is only a short drive away at the **Larnaca salt lake**, right next to Hala Sultan Tekke, burial place of Muhammad's aunt. From the tourist pavilion, you can see rafts of pink flamingos and from January onwards contemplate a walk under the pines to the west in pursuit of orchids. Luck might allow for flamingos, feeding on brine shrimp, to be near the road when you visit. They're here all winter in thousands, adults arriving first with juveniles following later from Turkey, Iran and even further afield. They start to leave by late March, with small flocks flying at low levels; the last stragglers quit in June for their nesting areas.

Near Limassol, **Akrotíri** is a reed-fringed lake which, with crossed fingers and a good map, you can try to approach on small roads from the north, but it's easier to take the road to the RAF base and turn left before reaching the gates. To prevent problems, check with military officials at the gate to avoid becoming the focus of an impromptu military exercise on the lake shore. On a good day in spring, it's possible to find scorpions, green toads, tree frogs and Cyprus bee orchids in the scrub around the lake. Throughout the year, it's a magnet for migrating birds and thus a favourite bird-watching site for off-duty military personnel, visiting ornithological tour parties and increasing numbers of local enthusiasts.

On maps, another salt lake is marked **near Paralímni**, but it only fills after heavy rains. It has always been a good area in which to observe migrant birds but, distressingly, has also long been a centre for the trade in tiny pickled birds caught on lime sticks (see "Conservation", p.300).

THE AKÁMAS PENINSULA

After a long controversy, the **Akámas peninsula** was the first area in Cyprus to have been designated a national park. The peninsula forms the northwestern tip of the island and its geology is varied, with outcrops, cliffs and deep gorges of limestone in addition to serpentine and other igneous rocks. This allows for a diversity of soil types and a rich plant life as a direct consequence – there is even a native alyssum (*Alyssum akamassicum*), for example.

Although once an inhabited area, as extensive remains of ancient settlements show, its separation from the contemporary concentrations of population, plus its long-time use as a practice range by the British Forces, means it has remained largely unspoiled. Scattered pine groves constitute the nearest thing to virgin forest the island can offer, but considerable tracts of land have suffered the depredations of feral goats. Where grazing has been controlled, the plant life is rich and, now under protected status, the whole peninsula should eventually be the same.

In February and March, coastal walks here take you over hillsides of cascading cyclamen, and you might see the first rollers and bee-eaters to have arrived on the spring migration.

Gorges hidden from view provide nesting sites for lammergeiers and cave roosts –especially near **Faslí** and **Andhrolíkou** – where you might discover some of the island's fruit bats. Green and loggerhead turtles use the beaches such as Lára for breeding, as discussed previously. And there are orchids too, although these have suffered as much as other plant species because of grazing. Encouragingly, numbers increase by the year and include the rare yellow flowered punctate orchid (*Orchis. punctulata*).

From Káthikas, at the more populated southern base of the Akámas, a road descends through Péyia to the coast and is worth travelling for the views alone. As a bonus, you pass through an area planted with pines – the **Péyia forest** – where orchids grow in both abundance and astonishing variety. High above the sea, it is a cool place which has also become something of a haven for small birds.

THE HIGH TROÖDHOS

High on the mountains, snow can remain in pockets until April – in fact the name of the summit **Khionístra** means "snow-pit". Thus, spring starts late but with a choice series of plants: crocus, corydalis, various vetches, an endemic buttercup (*Ranunculus cyprius var. cadmicus*) – no large-scale displays, more like a huge rock garden with many plants unique to the island. In colonial times the British established a network of paths, mostly on a contour, so that walks around Mt Olympus can be as long or as short as you like. Wherever the paths pass through the open forests of black pine you can look for the endemic coal tits, pied wheatear, jay, crossbill, and short-toed treecreeper.

Another nature trail follows the Krýos river past **Caldeonian Falls**, just southwest from and below Troödhos resort, and numbered posts indicate plants of interest; names are given in Greek and in Latin. In early summer there are various endemic plants – many of them with *troodii* as part of the Latin name. Groups of Crimean orchids (*Dactylorhiza iberica*), near the streams, and eastern marsh helleborines (*Epipactis veratrifolia*) around the Caledonian Falls near the end of the trail. Here, well out of reach on wet rocks behind the falls grows the rare Cyprus butterwort (*Pinguicula crystallina*).

The extensive forests to the northwest below Khionístra offer pæonies (*Pæonia mascula*) in May near Pródhromos; a curious red parasite, the Cyprus broomrape (*Orobanche cypria*) and a seemingly endless network of dirt roads, usually well maintained, which take you far from other visitors. Better roads run to Kýkko Monastery (the area has its very own buttercup – *Ranunculus kykkoensis*) and beyond leading to **Stavrós tis Psókhas**, a forestry station where it's possible to stay by prior arrangement, falling asleep to the sound of nightingales and waking to the scent of pines.

Several rather dejected-looking mouflon are kept penned here and, for most visitors to the island, they will be the only ones seen, even though the Páfos forest is their stronghold. The exact origins of this wild sheep are uncertain but remains have been found in Neolithic settlements, dating to around 8000 years ago. It could well have been a domesticated animal then, either brought to the island by settlers, or the direct descendant of creatures trapped when the Mediterranean filled for the last time. In Graeco-Roman times, mouflon were plentiful throughout the Troöhos and in the Kyrenia mountains, but hunting, especially during the Middle Ages, reduced the population drastically. In 1878, the first year of British rule, only twenty animals were counted, a situation which pertained until 1939 when game laws were strengthened and the Páfos forest became a game reserve. At the same time goat-grazing was banned in the reserve, removing competition for the available food; subsequently, numbers began to increase steadily, with counts of 100 animals in 1949; 200 in 1966; 800 in 1982....

The mouflon is a very agile animal, but shy and not readily seen – let alone approached. Its closest relatives are island races of wild sheep *Ovis musimon* in Sardinia and Corsica, which tend to live in open, rocky territory. The Cypriot race, however, has found its "niche" as a forest-dweller, although for fodder it prefers grasses to bush or tree shoots. When the uplands are snow-covered, it descends to lowland valleys, always relying on the cover provided by the forest. Mating takes place in November when competitive males become aggressive: the dominant male in a group sires the lambs and the gestation period is five months. In both males and females the summer coat is short and pale brown, becoming white on the underparts; in winter they grow a coat of dense brown hair.

The **"Cedar Valley"** is much advertised as a tourist attraction. It is certainly pleasant woodland with a rich flora and some attractive birds – Cyprus cyclamen (*Cyclamen cyprium*), various orchids and hoopoes for example – but not quite deserving its hype in tourist brochures. The particular attraction, for naturalists who like to wander, is the ease with which you can get off the beaten track – dirt roads from here to the coast are tortuous but negotiable. Allow time to linger as you travel from volcanic to limestone soils and pass interesting collections of roadside plants, see butterflies or notice birds. Cultivated fields in the area still sport collections of colourful cornfield weeds such as field gladiolus, corn marigold and a royal-purple poppy (*Roemeria hybrida*), so delicate that its petals seem to fall as soon as a camera is pointed its way.

Near Agrós looms **Mt Adhélfi**, at 1612m the second highest peak in the island. On its slopes and also on nearby hills grow some of the rare endemic bulbs of Cyprus, such as Hartman's crocus (*Crocus hartmannianus*) and Lady Lock's chionodoxia (*Chionodoxia lochiae*). From Agrós you can explore the Pitsiliá region which is known for its fruit and nut trees, but little explored by tourists. The roadsides and field edges are particularly interesting for a rich assortment of "weeds" – "candlesticks" of *Sedum lampusae*, various parasitic broomrapes and whole banks of purple vetch, for example.

Mt Adhélfi can also be approached from **Kakopetriá** where one of the few **permanent streams** in Cyprus is located. It runs close to the famous church of Aýios Nikólaos tís Steyís through a wild valley with abundant flowers (Cyprus broomrape, orchids, Cyprus butterwort). This wealth of flora inevitably attracts butterflies such as cleopatras and southern white admiral (*Limenitis reducta*) – as it sups nectar from tree honeysuckle you will see its open wings, and two rows of large white spots relieving the jet-black surface. Dutchman's pipe (*Aristolochia sempervirens*), food-plant of the larvae of the Cyprus festoon butterfly, straggles over ancient vines near here with its hanging rows of striking brown and yellow flowers – close by will be the butterflies themselves.

This little river is also the home of a curious, olive-green, freshwater crab (*Potamon fluviatilis*) which was once common around the island, especially in brackish streams near the coast. Sadly, numbers have dwindled as a direct consequence of pollution caused by agricultural chemicals running off into streams. In this, one of its last strongholds, it survives hiding under stones but will come out at night on to the bank to feed. Locals regret the disappearance since it was regarded as a good *mezé* or taverna snack.

THE TROÖDHOS FOOTHILLS

Although the core of the Troödhos range is igneous, overlying chalks were deposited much later than the volcanic rocks, when seas covered the land. Upheavals have pushed the underlying serpentines and pillow lavas through the chalk, and you can move confusingly between the two types of strata, noticing the dramatic changes in plant life. The road from Aýios Iraklídhios (southwest of Nicosia) to Makherás monastery epitomises these transitions. The route first takes in a cultivated area with great telegraph-pole spikes of flowering agave, then a dry chalk valley with orchids and grape hyacinths wherever the slightest humus builds up from fallen needles beneath the pines. Where the rocks change, the cistus and lavender bushes form a roadside scrub, with yellow Roman and pink Anatolian orchids protected beneath them.

Around Makherás itself, the woods are worth exploring since they are typical forest of the lower Troöhos with their eastern strawberry trees and golden oak. Early in the year, you find an occasional Hartman's crocus and in autumn the Cyprus cyclamen. Birdlife is varied, with scops owl frequently heard but seldom seen; Cyprus warblers and chukars prefer to run for cover through the bushes rather than fly.

From Limassol, journeys to Yermasóyia and its dam, to Léfkara and further west through Páhkna to Malliá and Vouní cut through country with dry, chalky soils which have proved good for viticulture. Even with abundant vines there are still pockets of scrub rich in the shrubby herbs that make up the *frígana*, giving protection to numerous plants such as yellow Star of Bethlehem, grape hyacinths, wavy-leaved monkey, and giant and dense-flowered orchids, as well as turban buttercups in whites, creams, yellows or even with a reddish tinge. You can see and hear stonechats and the Cyprus warbler standing sentinel on bushes, while dry chalk, with its high reflectance of light and heat, always seems particularly attractive to numerous small lizards and the occasional snake lazily sunning itself. If your eyesight is particularly acute you might spot a chameleon: they are fairly common but stay well hidden from view, camouflaged by their ability to match the varied browns and greens of their surroundings.

RIVERMOUTHS AND RESERVOIRS

Extensive natural **wetlands near Güzelyurt (Mórfou)** in the North and **near Limassol** in the South proved ideal for establishment of the extensive citrus groves that now occupy them, being fed by mountain waters and kept moist all year round. Death from malaria was common until early in the British period, when malarial swamps were drained by planting thirsty eucalyptus. In recent years, diversion of streams to fill the newly built and much-needed reservoirs is another factor which has cut down water flow. Thus reed beds – other than those planted as windbreaks – are a rarity in Cyprus.

In the South, try **east** and **west of Pólis** or **north of Akrotíri salt lake;** in the North, for the birdwatcher, there is **Glapsides** just to the north of Famagusta, where a popular beach is backed by a freshwater lake and wetland vegetation.

Also in the North are large **reservoirs** at **Köprülü** (Koúklia) and at **Gönyeli** on the northern perimeter of Nicosia which are important sites for over-wintering wildfowl (ducks, grebe and heron). They are also attractive to smaller lowland and mountain birds throughout the year, since insects always hover near water. Consequently, indigenous and migrating raptors patrol the reservoirs and their immediate environs, regarding these smaller birds as a readily available "in-flight meal". Areas of open water are attracting growing numbers of people, both visitors and locals, interested in the changing variety of birds throughout the year.

THE COAST AROUND CAPE KORUÇAM (KORMAKÍTI)

Although **Cape Koruçam** (Kormakíti) itself can be bleak in the winter months, being openly exposed to the prevailing winds, its spring wildflowers – anemones in particular – are delightful. Coastal rocks at first sight seem to provide an inhospitable environment, but fleshy-leaved stonecrops grow in the crevices with another succulent – *Mesembryanthemum crystallinum* – a relative of the colourful Livingstone daisies grown in gardens.

In Cyprus, dunes – however modest in size – will probably reveal flowering sea daffodils during the hotter months. They survive their arid environment by having a bulb buried so deeply that it would need an excavator to get to it. Even where the sand meets slow cliffs, and debris washed down by winter rains bakes dry to form a rock-like surface, these resilient plants are able to grow. Butterflies always seem to be abundant on Cape Koruçam and it's a good place to visit with binoculars and observe the arrival of spring migrants, which might include the occasional kingfisher providing an iridescent diversion as it darts over the rocks below you.

Between Güzelyurt (Mórfou) and Lapta (Lápithos), the road passes through cultivated fields, always tinted with splashes of colourful annuals, especially at their edges. However, the loveliest of the island's "weeds" of cultivation must be the native Cyprus tulip (*Tulipa cypria*). It has blackish-purple flowers and is abundant enough to colour cornfields on the road from Mýrtou to Nicosia; it also grows among the broad-bean plants in fields around the Maronite village of Koruçam (Kormakíti).

Sadly the best **beaches** along Mórfou Bay are now off-limits because of the Turkish military presence. You can get to Akdeniz (Ayía Iríni), where pygmy hippo fossils have been found, but no further; as a consolation prize, try exploring **near Yayla** (Syrianokhóri).

THE KYRENIA MOUNTAINS (BEŞ PARMAK OR PENDADHÁKTYLOS RANGE)

The sculpted limestone pinnacles of the **Kyrenia range**, whose Greek and Turkish names both mean "Five Fingers", have an appropriately "Gothic" look, mimicking the three medieval castles tucked among them. Their northern and southerly aspects are quite different: the northern slopes are much lusher, receiving more rain and less of a baking, so that in spring there are cyclamen, anemones and turban buttercups everywhere. Vegetation is mainly Aleppo pine with funeral cypress and dense maquis; the southern slopes have sparse, xerophytic (drought-tolerant) vegetation.

A mountain road built during the colonial period runs from **Saint Hilarion** westwards along the range for 18 miles (29km) via the highest peak Kyparrisóvouno – at 1023m, offering stupendous views right and left plus birds, butterflies, lizards and flowers in abundance. Avoid detours because of the heavy military presence on the south side of the route.

Only the eastern approach to **Buffavento** is open to the public; here you can see lammergeiers wheeling and a host of mountain birds mentioned earlier, such as the blue rock thrush. Around Saint Hilarion, Buffavento and Alevkaya, shaded limestone cliffs are the places to look for indigenous plants of the northern range, such as Cypriot rock cress (*Arabis cypria*), Cypriot sage (*Phlomis cypria*) and Saint Hilarion cabbage (*Brassica hilarionis*) an ancestor of the cultivated cauliflower.

At **Alevkaya** (Halévga), the old forest station is the site of the North Cyprus Herbarium, open since 1989 (open daily, 8am–4pm) and housing a collection of over 800 preserved plant species plus line drawings. This offers an opportunity to identify what you have seen and also to find out what more there is to spot. The area around Alevkaya has long been known for its orchids, especially the tiny insect-mimicking bee orchids (genus *Ophrys*) which have a lifestyle as bizarre as their appearance. They produce scents which are chemical cocktails with the power to fool tiny male solitary wasps into thinking they have found a female – each orchid produces a subtly different blend to delude a particular species of wasp. When they land they try to mate with the flower, eventually get frustrated and fly off in disgust, carrying pollen to the next orchid flower; fortunately memory is not an insect's strong point. The Cyprus bee orchid (*Ophrys kotschyi*) and Lapithos bee orchid (*Ophrys lapitheca*), both found growing here, are exclusive to the island.

THE KIRPAŞA (KÁRPAS) PENINSULA

Long, sparsely populated, but well cultivated in parts, the **Kırpaşa (Kárpas)** peninsula is a continuation of the limestone ridge of the Kyrenia range, which makes its final Cypriot appearance as the Klídhes islands before re-emerging as the Amanus range in southeast Turkey. Its spine is gently hilly, rising to 364m at Pámboulos. You can approach the peninsula from the northern side of the Kyrenia mountains by heading east from Kyrenia along the coast road, then turning south via Kantára, or by turning off further along, through Büyükkonuk (Komí Kebír). Alternatively, south of the hills, you can travel the coast road north from Famagusta with giant fennel lining your route. Whatever the choice, take your time – the roads are good but the wayside flowers in spring are superb and well worth lingering over.

In springtime, on reaching the peninsula itself, you will find multi-coloured displays of anemones, turban buttercups, poppies and gladiolus. Here, the "terra rossa" soil derived from limestone is often a rich red thanks to traces of iron compounds and, although it has long proved excellent for cultivating tomatoes, fruit trees and bananas, you can find numerous uncultivated pockets on the peninsula, where orchids and other lime-loving plants thrive on it. The long "panhandle" of the Kárpas provides a flight path into the island for numerous colourful migrants such as rollers, golden orioles and bee-eaters. Rollers are a familiar sight, perching on telegraph wires before taking off across country with a distinctive buoyant flight; they get their name from the way they somersault on the wing as part of their courtship displays.

Turtles – mainly loggerheads – come ashore to lay eggs on sandy beaches to the east of **Cape Yası Burnu (Plakotí)**, not far from the sixteenth-century monastery church of Panayia Eleoúsa. All along this coast, where rocks gently shelve to the sands, grow white sea daffodils in the height of the summer. At **Dipkarpaz (Rizokárpaso)** the land is well cultivated by the remaining Greek-Cypriot population, but a choice of roads beyond the village leads into wilder country, close to the shore. Along the north coast, the road leads to ancient Karpasia: by travelling across the fertile plains you reach Khelónes, (meaning "turtles" in Greek) and an amazingly **long beach**, stretching nearly to Zafer Burnu (Cape Apóstolos Andhréas), where loggerheads have been known to breed.

The **Klídhes islands** mark the last outpost of Cyprus to the east and are one of the few places where sea birds such as shag and Audoin's gull can nest undisturbed. The cliffs also provide one of the last strongholds for nesting peregrine falcons, which breed in March or April and are both fast and strong enough to make doves and pigeons a favourite prey for themselves and their ever-hungry nestlings.

CONSERVATION

People preoccupied with their own immediate survival feel that they cannot afford themselves the luxury of being Green. After the trauma of the 1974 invasion, when over 200,000 islanders lost homes and (often) family, the Cypriot sense of security was shattered, and many struggled to educate their children abroad – believing that training was one thing that could not be taken away. By dint of hard work, the South has grown prosperous again, with a highly educated and articulate population. Thanks to the joint efforts of comparatively few Cypriots and resident "foreigners", people are also becoming conscious of what has been lost environmentally by unbridled development since 1974 and, moreover, that remedial action has to be immediate and drastic.

Dedicated **conservationists** in the Cyprus Biological Society, Cyprus Wildlife Society, Friends of the Earth, and the Ornithological Society, as well as individuals in governmental departments such as education, fisheries and forestry, have all fought an at-times-difficult battle to alert people to what is in imminent danger of being lost for ever.

There have been have exhibitions, lectures, sets of stamps and avidly followed broadcasts of Attenborough's TV series, all part of the exercise to **increase public awareness**. Now, in a first for Cyprus, the Akámas has been declared a **national park** and granted the protection it so desperately needed from an unholy alliance of the Orthodox church and big business which foresaw its potential for development. Extensive coverage of the Akámas in the media awakened more and more people to the frightening rate at which other areas in the Cyprus countryside are being changed in the name of development.

One of the strongest cries from opponents to the Akámas conservation venture was that the Pafiot villagers, like their counterparts in Ayía Nápa, had an inalienable right to make unlimited pots of money. To try and ensure the prosperity of the area but simultaneously avoid the seemingly inevitable destruction of the last wilderness in the South, the Laona Project was set up to encourage **sustainable** or **"agro"-tourism** (see Chapter Three, p.108–109). Unscrupulous mega-operators think nothing of destroying in weeks what nature has fashioned over the ages, as long as there's a fast buck to be made. The Cyprus economy is at present largely tied to tourism, but many feel there can be more balanced development benefiting all, not just a few mandarins.

The impact of **hunting** on birds, particularly migrants, is devastating. In Cyprus North or South, hunting is a national pastime, the "kill" definitely secondary to the social aspect of getting out into the country with the boys. The right to have a hunting licence is passionately defended, and although the southern government ratified the Berne Treaty on endangered species, it subsequently bowed to pressure, allowing a more-or-less unrestricted spring shooting season. Another little-considered factor is that the weight of lead shot, falling annually on the land, presents a tangible pollution hazard.

Cypriots sometimes claim that it's the western Europeans, personified by Templars, who introduced **bird-liming** to the island. Cyprus is certainly not alone among Mediterranean countries as an offender, and has at least passed legislation to outlaw lime sticks and the use of mist nets (if not their import.). It is now far less socially acceptable than it was, but there is still a market in the Middle East, and during the 1980s conservative estimates claimed that millions of small passerines were taken annually in mist nets and on sticks coated with the sticky "lime". Exhausted migrants were trapped and their necks wrung, the pickled carcasses regarded as a delicacy in the Arab Middle East as well. At well over C£1 each, there's a ready cash incentive, and villages like Paralímni grew wealthy on the trade. Friends of the Earth* have mounted a valiant and tireless campaign to make people on and outside the island take note, by getting concerned organisations worldwide to besiege the government and tourist organisations with complaints.

Conservationists in Britain, particularly those concerned with ornithology, have often called upon naturalists to **boycott** the island. When tourism is as important to the economy as it is in Cyprus, considerable pressure can indeed be brought to bear by the threat of lost revenue. However, national pride over "outside intervention" – a justifiably touchy subject, given the history of Cyprus – will merely provoke a stubbornly defiant reaction. Perhaps the worst thing that armchair activists unwittingly manage to achieve is the effective isolation of those people on Cyprus working at the cutting edge. Local campaigns are considerably strengthened by support for their efforts from visiting outsiders – sabotage methods include ripping mist nets and urinating on lime sticks (a technique which renders them useless). If you see things you don't like while in Cyprus, complain in writing to the Cyprus Tourism Organisation and the government: it counts if enough people do it.

In the North there is now an active North Cyprus Society for the Protection of Birds (its initials KKKKD in Turkish) – and President Rauf Denktaş apparently has a keen interest in his country's wild flowers. **Hunting** is as much a problem in the North as in the South, with a large number of gun licences for the size of the population. Another pressing concern is the level of **grazing** permitted by the enormous herds of goats brought in by Anatolian settlers. Visiting botanists, especially Germans working on a detailed mapping of the orchid flora, have voiced great concern over changes seen over a two- or three-year period: once flower-filled hillsides now host little but grass, thistles and white asphodels. There is talk, but so far only that, of making the Kırpaşa (Kárpas) peninsula a protected area.

*Friends of the Earth (Cyprus), c/o Adrian Akers-Douglas, Maróni Village, Larnaca District, Cyprus.

BOOKS

Cyprus falls just outside the loose definition of Europe used in field guides other than those for birds. Thus, it's not easy to find good illustrations of its special plants or butterflies, and a well-nigh impossible task for many of the insects, snails and creatures which have a lower rating in the popularity stakes. Since a significant proportion of the Cypriot flora and fauna is found around much of the Mediterranean, you can make considerable headway with popular guides, but identifying endemic species is often difficult.

Perhaps the **best-value single purchase** specifically for the island is *Nature of Cyprus: Environment, Flora, Fauna* (South Nicosia, Cyprus) by Christos Georgiades. Widely available in bookshops in the south, this is a very useful introduction to local ecology by one of the island's top naturalists: it includes checklists of birds, butterflies, reptiles, indigenous plants, fish and mammals which are almost impossible to find anywhere else.

Some of the better natural history works are now **out of print**, but appear fairly regularly in catalogues of specialist secondhand and antiquarian book sellers dealing in natural history titles, who advertise in the natural history press.

FLOWERS AND PLANTS

K. P. Buttler *Fieldguide to the Orchids of Europe* (Crowood Press). Consultant editor Paul H. Davies. A wealth of colour pictures and modern nomenclature.

Paul H. Davies, Jenne Davies and Anthony J. Huxley *Wild Orchids of Britain and Europe* (Chatto & Windus/The Hogarth Press). Written while the authors lived in Cyprus, this includes all the island's orchids and where to find them.

Paul H. Davies and Bob Gibbons *Wild Flowers of Southern Europe* (Crowood Press). Useful for general Mediterranean flowers.

Christos Georgiades *Trees and Shrubs of Cyprus; Flowers of Cyprus; Plants of Medicine* (Nicosia, South Cyprus). Widely available in Cyprus; useful for indigenous plants.

Sonia Halliday and Laura Lushington *Flowers of Northern Cyprus* (Kemal Rüstem, Nicosia, North Cyprus). As much a close-up photo-essay as field guide.

Anthony J. Huxley *Flowers of Greece and the Aegean* (Chatto & Windus/The Hogarth Press). Helpful in conjunction with other general works – but does not specifically cover Cyprus. See also his **Flowers of the Mediterranean** (Chatto & Windus/The Hogarth Press) – a classic book on Mediterranean flowers; coverage general but surprisingly useful.

R. Desmond Meikle *Flora of Cyprus* (Bentham Trust; available from the Royal Botanic Gardens, Kew, Richmond, Surrey). Two-volume work for the serious plant freak who jettisons clothes from the luggage in favour of books. Whatever you'll find is in here: no colour pictures but plenty of line drawings. A model of clarity and erudition as far as this sort of work goes.

Oleg Polunin *Flowers of Greece and the Balkans* (Oxford University Press). Again, useful for plants generally distributed in the eastern Mediterranean.

I. and P. Schoenfelder *Wildflowers of the Mediterranean* (Collins). General but includes many of the ordinary Mediterranean species in Cyprus.

BIRDS

David and Mary Bannerman *Handbook of the Birds of Cyprus* (Kemal Rüstem, Nicosia, North Cyprus).

Peter Flint and Peter Stewart *The Birds of Cyprus* (British Ornithological Union). Available from the BOU, British Museum, Tring, Herts. A thorough checklist with details of good sites for birdwatching.

Heinzel, Fitter and Parslow *The Birds of Britain and Europe with North Africa and the Middle East* (Collins). Another useful item in your bags.

Hollom, Porter, Christensen and Willis *Birds of the Middle East and North Africa* (T. & A. D. Poyser). Very thorough, with good illustrations and distribution maps.

Lars Jonsson *Birds of Europe with North Africa and the Middle East* (Helm). Very good coverage, and excellent illustrations.

INSECTS

Michael Chinery *Collins Guide to the Insects of Britain and Western Europe* (Collins). A lovely book which excludes the Mediterranean but is still very useful for getting the genus, and also for things like hawkmoths and mantids.

Lionel Higgins and Norman Riley *A Field Guide to the Butterflies of Britain and Europe* (Collins). A very detailed classic which contains most of the Cyprus butterflies except the handful of indigenes.

Paul Whalley *The Mitchell Beazley Pocket Guide to Butterflies* (Mitchell Beazley). Marvellously illustrated guide which stops just short of Cyprus but has most species except the few natives.

REPTILES AND AMPHIBIANS

Arnold, Burton and Ovenden *A Field Guide to the Reptiles of Britain and Europe* (Collins) Most, but not all, species – again stops short of the Middle East.

Jiri Cihar *Amphibians and Reptiles* (Octopus). Selective in coverage, but has many species from Asia Minor and is useful for Cyprus.

MARINE LIFE

A. C. Campbell *The Hamlyn Guide to the Flora and Fauna of the Mediterranean* (Hamlyn/Country Life). Very useful but out of print, so buy secondhand if possible; also published as: *The Larousse Guide to the Flora and Fauna of the Mediterranean* (Larousse).

B. Luther and K. Fiedler *A Field Guide to the Mediterranean Seashore* (Collins). Very thorough, includes much of what occurs around the Cyprus coast.

Paul H. Davies

BOOKS

As befits a former Crown Colony, there are a fair amount of books on Cyprus in English. Many worthwhile classics have been re-issued recently, and others are often available in libraries. Publishers are detailed below in the format British/American, with "UK" or "US" specified when a volume is available in one country only. Occasionally a title is published, and most easily obtainable, in either south or north Nicosia, Cyprus.

Other abbreviations include O/P, for an out-of-print but still worthwhile book, and UP, for University Press.

ARCHAEOLOGY AND PRE-INDEPENDENCE HISTORY

There are a vast number of scholarly works on Cyprus, but most are expensive, hard to find, drily academic, or all three. The following titles are more accessible in every sense.

Vassos Karageorghis *Cyprus, from the Stone Age to the Romans* (Thames & Hudson, UK/US). Definitive, well-written introduction by one of the foremost Cypriot archaeologists, long director of the island's Antiquities Department. Three other titles by the same author and publisher, though long O/P, are *Salamis in Cyprus: Homeric, Hellenistic and Roman* and *Kition, Mycenaean and Phoenician Discoveries in Cyprus*; also, with F. G. Maier, *Paphos, History and Archaeology* (Nicosia, 1984) – all lavishly illustrated.

Porphyrios Dikaios *Khirokitia* (Oxford UP, UK, O/P). By the long-time excavator of the site. See also his *Enkomi Excavations 1948-1958* (Mainz, O/P) and *A Guide to the Cyprus Museum* (Nicosia, re-issued regularly).

Einar Gjerstad et al. *The Swedish Cyprus Expeditions, 1927–1931* (Stockholm, The Swedish Cyprus Expedition, 8 vols 1934–56). More anecdotal is his *Ages and Days in Cyprus* (Paul Åströms Förlag, Göteborg), a record of travels, personal encounters and life on the site digs.

Demetrios Michaelides and W. A. Daszewski *Mosaic Floors in Cyprus* (Ravenna, Edizioni del Girazole, 1988). More precisely, Part I covers the magnificent Roman mosaics of Paphos; Part II describes the mosaic floors of Christian basilicas across the island.

David Soren & Jamie James *Kourion, the Search for a Lost Roman City* (Anchor/Doubleday, US). Despite its American-pop style, a valuable account of the most recent finds at Kourion, particularly evidence of the mid-fourth-century earthquake.

Louis Palma di Cesnola *Cyprus: Its Cities, Tombs and Temples* (Star Graphics, South Cyprus). A reprinted classic – the diplomat and archaeologist/plunderer in his own shameless words, including fascinating vignettes of everyday life on the eve of British rule.

PRE-1955 HISTORY

Sir George Hill *A History of Cyprus* (Cambridge UP, UK, 4 vols, O/P). The standard, if sometimes flawed, pre-independence reference work – rare and pricey.

Doros Alastos *Cyprus in History* (Zeno, UK). Two massive tomes covering all periods to 1955; the author unfortunately died before finishing Volume III.

Sir David Hunt, ed *Footprints in Cyprus, an Illustrated History* (Trigraph, UK). Lavishly illustrated anthology covering all eras, more literate than the usual coffee-table book – available in paperback.

Peter W. Edbury *The Kingdom of Cyprus and the Crusades, 1191–1374* (Cambridge UP, UK/US). Plumbs the intricate power struggles of the relatively little-known Lusignan period, but frustratingly stops short of the Venetian tenure.

David and Iro Hunt *Caterina Cornaro, Queen of Cyprus* (Trigraph, UK). Picks up more or less where the preceding volume left off, but concentrates mostly on the life and times of the last sovereign of the island, a Venetian married into the Lusignan line.

Sir Harry Luke *Cyprus Under the Turks, 1571–1878* (Kemal Rüstem, Nicosia, North Cyprus). Extensive quotations from documents of the era, not as expository or interesting as it could be – but virtually the only source in English.

GUIDES, MONUMENTAL ART AND PHOTO PORTFOLIOS

George Jeffrey *A Description of the Historic Monuments of Cyprus* (Zeno, UK). Just that, by the founder of the eponymous museum. Exhaustive, and rather less dry than the Blue Guide.

Rupert Gunnis *Historic Cyprus, A Guide to its Towns and Villages, Monasteries and Castles* (Kemal Rüstem, Nicosia, North Cyprus). Gunnis visited every site on the island over a five-year period in the 1930s; this is the erudite result.

Andreas and Judith Stylianou *The Painted Churches of Cyprus* (Trigraph, UK). The last word on the Troödhos country churches especially.

Camille Enlart *Gothic Art and the Renaissance in Cyprus* (Trigraph, UK). Recently translated from the French, this highlights the magnificent architecture and exterior decoration left behind by the Lusignan rulers.

John Thomson *Through Cyprus with the Camera in the Autumn of 1878* (Trigraph, UK). First-ever photos of the island – showing how exotic it was just over a century ago.

Reno Wideson *Cyprus: Images of a Lifetime* (Demetra Publications, Limassol & UK) and *Portrait of Cyprus* (O/P). 42 years of stunning pictures by the top Cypriot photographer, the former a recently published colour study.

TRAVELOGUES & MEMOIRS

Claude Delaval Cobham *Excerpta Cypria, Materials for a History of Cyprus* (Kraus Reprint, Millwood, New York). An engaging, landmark endeavour: pithy snippets from travellers' and local protagonists' views of Cyprus from biblical times to the last century, diligently mined by all subsequent writers on Cyprus. But with the price-tag at well over £100, you'd have to be a rather dedicated researcher.

Leontios Makhairas *Recital Concerning the Sweet Land of Cyprus* (Clarendon, UK). Another rare and expensive medieval classic, translated by R. M. Dawkins.

Giovanni Mariti *Travels in the Island of Cyprus* (Zeno, UK). A wonderful eighteenth-century account, translated by Cobham; this edition includes Umberto Foglietta's seventeenth-century *The Sieges of Nicosia and Famagusta*.

Ludwig Salvator, Archduke of Austria *Levkosia, The Capital of Cyprus* (Trigraph, UK). Nicosia as it was in 1873, delightfully described by one of the Belle Epoque's great eccentrics – though his command of Greek and Turkish terminology was shaky at best, which can make identifying monuments difficult.

Anne Cavendish, ed *Cyprus 1878: The Journal of Sir Garnet Wolseley* (Academic & General, Larnaca). The memoirs of the first British High Commissioner, recently published at a modest price.

Sir Samuel Baker *Cyprus as I Saw it in 1879* (Macmillan, UK, O/P). By turns scathing and rapturous, with plenty of white-man's-burden stuff – including proposals to raze what remained of old Famagusta – from the first year of British administration.

Sir Ronald Storrs and B. J. O'Brien *The Handbook of Cyprus* (London, 1930, O/P). Detailed volume intended for colonial officials, co-written by one of the first high commissioners (Storrs); the last two chapters of his career memoirs *Orientations* (Nicholson and Watson, UK, O/P but easy to find) concern Cyprus.

Patrick Balfour *The Orphaned Realm* (Percival Marshall, UK, O/P; rare). Impressionistic and anecdote-laden account from the late 1940s.

Lawrence Durrell *Bitter Lemons* (Faber and Faber, UK/US). Durrell's lyrically told experiences as an English teacher, minor colonial official and bohemian resident of the Kyrenia hills in the EOKA-shadowed mid-1950s have worn remarkably well despite the intervening years.

Colin Thubron *Journey into Cyprus* (Penguin/Viking Penguin, UK/US). Account of a three-month trek round the island during 1972 – and in terms of history in context, and a finger on the pulse of contemporary Cyprus, arguably the single best book on the place ever written. Widely available in southern Cyprus.

Oliver Burch *The Infidel Sea* (Ashford, Buchanan and Enright, UK). North Cyprus as it was in the mid-1980s, before tourism had revived; heavily reliant on *Excerpta Cypria* for background filler, but excellent as a portrait of the northern community.

INDEPENDENCE AND AFTER

It is unfortunately very difficult to find anything more current than the mid-1980s – observers of the Cypriot scene, perhaps despairing of any substantive changes in the situation, seem reluctant to set down between hard covers the latest rumour or trend in intercommunal negotiations.

Nancy Cranshaw *The Cyprus Revolt: An Account of the Struggle for Union with Greece* (Allen and Unwin, UK, O/P). Factual but highly readable, this is the standard reference work on the rebellion.

Stavros Panteli *A New History of Cyprus, from the Earliest Times to the Present Day* (East-West Publications, UK, O/P). Choppy and partisan, this is nevertheless one of the best sources for the colonial period; coverage unfortunately stops at 1984. His slightly more recent *The Making of Modern Cyprus* (Interworld, UK) may also be of interest.

Michael Harbottle *The Impartial Soldier* (Oxford UP, UK, O/P). Worthwhile memoirs of the first (1964–68) UNFICYP commander.

Stanley Mayes *Makarios* (Macmillan, UK, O/P). The best biography of the man.

Polyvios Polyviou *Cyprus, Conflict and Negotiation 1960–80* (Duckworth, UK, O/P). Dry but detailed – and relatively objective.

Kyriakos Markides *The Rise and Fall of the Cyprus Republic* (Yale UP, UK/US, O/P but findable). The excellent standard history.

Michael Attalides *Cyprus: Nationalism and International Politics* (Q Press, UK, O/P). A wide-ranging and readable, if dated, discussion of all aspects of the problem.

Laurence Stern *The Wrong Horse* (Times Books, New York, O/P). Reveals America's involvement in the 1974 coup and the alleged "tilt" towards the Turks; back copies were supposedly bought up and destroyed by villain of the piece Henry Kissinger.

Peter Loizos *The Heart Grown Bitter: A Chronicle of Cypriot War Refugees* (Cambridge UP, UK). Describes Argáki (lately Akçay), a village on the Mórfou plain, and the fate of its inhabitants after the Turkish invasion; moreover an excellent introduction to the complexities of Cypriot communalism and politics, by a London professor with roots in Argáki.

P. N. Vanezis *Cyprus: The Unfinished Agony*, and *Makarios: Life and Leadership* (Abelard-Schuman, UK, O/P). These two relatively balanced works are preferable to Makarian hagiographies like *Faith and Power* or *Pragmatism versus Idealism*.

Keith Kyle *Cyprus, Minority Rights Group Report No. 30* (MRG, UK/Cultural Survival, US). One of the excellent series of pamphlets by this organisation, though the summary ceases in 1984 and has not been updated since.

THE TURKISH-CYPRIOT VIEWPOINT

As with most things in the international arena, the North's position gets less of a hearing – but try these.

Vamik Volkan *Cyprus – War and Adaptation; A Psychoanalytic History of Two Ethnic Groups in Conflict* (UP of Virginia, US, O/P). Heavy going through the Freudian jargon, but the Turkish-Cypriot/American author does outline the stresses and adaptive neuroses of the island's beleaguered Turks, pre- and post-1974.

Pierre Oberling *The Road to Bellapais: The Turkish Cypriot Exodus to Northern Cyprus* (Columbia UP, US). Objective and useful study, written just before the UDI.

Rauf Denktaş *The Cyprus Triangle* (Allen and Unwin, UK, O/P; Kemal Rüstem, Nicosia, North Cyprus). Point of view from one of the main protagonists.

Zaim Necatigil *The Cyprus Question and the Turkish Position in International Law* (Oxford UP, UK). Sets forth the official TRNC position, as of 1990 – and thus relatively current.

BOOKSTORES

The best **UK sources** for English-language books on Cyprus are *The Hellenic Bookservice* (91 Fortess Rd, London NW5, near Kentish Town tube; ☎071/267 9499), run by an Anglo-Greek-Cypriot family, or *Zeno's* (6 Denmark St, London W1, near Foyles; ☎071/836 2522), which also does many re-issues of old classics. Both are knowledgeable and well stocked with new, used and out-of-print titles. There is no shop in London dedicated specifically to Turkish Cyprus; the above two retailers make an effort to stock titles pertaining to the whole island.

Useful **bookstores in Cyprus** are detailed in the town listings for Larnaca, Limassol, Páfos and Nicosia south and north.

LANGUAGE

I asked in Greek and was answered in English. I asked again in Greek and was once again answered in English. It was a long moment before I recollected why. I was in the presence not, as I thought, of Turks who either knew no Greek, or would not condescend to speak it: no, I was in the presence of babus. To lapse into Greek with anyone who was not a peasant would involve a loss of face. It was rather sad.

Lawrence Durrell

Durrell's experience still applies, and to a great extent in the Turkish-Cypriot community as well. Speaking English in Cyprus is a badge of sophistication, the road to advancement and civil service employment. In touristed areas, your Greek or Turkish will have to be nearly perfect to get a reply in kind. Most tourists

can and will get by on the island without learning a word of either local language; leave the beaten track, however, especially in the North, and you'll be surrounded by a monolingual culture.

Both Cypriot **Greek** and Cypriot **Turkish** are strong dialects – some might say almost separate languages – from the standard phrasebook fare, and familiarity with the latter is not as much of an advantage as you'd think. You will be understood if you utter Athens or Istanbul pleasantries, but you may not catch the reply the first time round – and you won't be alone, since before the homogenising effect of continental Greek and Turkish television, islanders could carry on conversations virtually incomprehensible to visitors from the "mother" country. About 15 percent of the vocabulary of each community is still peculiar to Cyprus, and the distinctive island accent tends to make Cypriot Greek and Turkish sound almost identical to the untrained ear.

GREEK

So many Greek Cypriots have lived or worked abroad in Britain, and, to a lesser extent, North America and Australia, that you will find numbers of people speaking English in the remotest village. Add to this the fact that most adults grew up under British administration, that English is all but compulsory at school, and the overriding importance of the tourist industry, and it's easy to see how many British visitors never bother to learn a word of Greek.

GREEK LANGUAGE LEARNING MATERIALS

TEACH-YOURSELF GREEK COURSES

Breakthrough Greece (Pan Macmillan; book and two cassettes). Excellent, basic teach-yourself course – completely outclasses all the competition.

Greek Language and People (BBC Publications, UK; book and cassette available). More limited in scope but good for acquiring the essentials, and the confidence to try them.

Anne Farmakides *A Manual of Modern Greek* (Yale/McGill; 3 vols). If you have the discipline and motivation, this is one of the best for learning proper, grammatical Greek; indeed, mastery of just the first volume will get your a long way.

PHRASEBOOKS

Greek Travelmate (Drew, UK). The most functional of the pocket phrasebooks. Phrases are contemporary and laid out in dictionary form.

DICTIONARIES

The Oxford Dictionary of Modern Greek (Oxford University Press, UK/US). A bit bulky but generally considered the best Greek–English, English–Greek dictionary.

Collins Pocket Greek Dictionary (Harper Collins, UK/US). Very nearly as complete as the Oxford and probably better value for money. Also comes as conveniently miniature Collins Gem.

THE GREEK ALPHABET: TRANSLITERATION

Set out below is the Greek alphabet, the system of transliteration used in this book, and a brief aid to pronunciation.

Greek	Transliteration	Pronounced
Α, α	a	a as in father
Β, β	v	v as in vet
Γ, γ	y/g	y as in yes, except before consonants and a, o or long i, when it's a breathy, throaty version of the g in gap
Δ, δ	dh	th as in then
Ε, ε	e	e as in get
Ζ, ζ	z	z sound
Η, η	i	ee sound as in feet
Θ, θ	th	th as in theme
Ι, ι	i	i as in bit
Κ, κ	k	usually k sound, sometimes "tsch"
Λ, λ	l	l sound
Μ, μ	m	m sound
Ν, ν	n	n sound
Ξ, ξ	ks (initial; x medial)	ks sound
Ο, ο	o	o as in toad
Π, π	p	p sound
Ρ, ρ	r	r sound
Σ, σ, ς	s	s sound
Τ, τ	t	t sound
Υ, υ	i or y	long i, indistinguishable from η
Φ, φ	f	f sound
Χ, χ	kh (h if initial before vowel; often sh if medial)	harsh h sound, like the ch in loch
Ψ, ψ	ps	ps as in lips
Ω, ω	o	o as in toad, indistinguishable from o

Combinations and dipthongs

ΑΙ, αι	e	e as in get
ΑΥ, αυ	av/af	av or af depending on following consonant
ΕΙ, ει	i	long i, exactly like η
ΟΙ, οι	i	long i, identical again
ΕΥ, ευ	ev/ef	ev or ef, depending on following consonant
ΟΥ, ου	ou	ou as in tourist
ΓΓ, γγ	ng	ng as in angle
ΓΥ, γυ	g/ng	g as in goat at the beginning of a word; ng in the middle
ΜΠ, μπ	b	b as in bar, but rare in Cypriot Greek
ΝΤ, ντ	d/nd	d at the beginning of a word, nd in the middle
ΤΣ, τσ	ts	ts as in hits
ΣΙ, σι	sh	sh as in shame

You can certainly get by this way, but it isn't very satisfying, and the willingness and ability to say even a few words will transform your status from that of dumb *touristas* to the honourable one of *ksénos*, a word which can mean foreigner, traveller and guest all rolled into one.

LEARNING BASIC GREEK

Greek is not an easy language for English speakers but it is a very beautiful one and even a brief acquaintance will give you some idea of the debt owed to it by western European languages. On top of the usual difficulties of learning a new language, Greek presents the

GREEK WORDS AND PHRASES

Essentials

Yes	Néh	Yesterday	Khthés	Big	Megálo
Certainly	Málista	Now	Tóra	Small	Mikró
No	Ókhi	Later	Argótera	More	Perisótero
Please	Parakaló	Open	Aniktó	Less	Ligótero
Okay, agreed	Endáxi	Closed	Klistó	A little	Lígo
Thank you	Efkharistó (polí)	Day	Méra	A lot	Polí
(very much)		Night	Níkhta	Cheap	Ftinó
I (don't)	(dhen) Katalavéno	In the morning	To proí	Expensive	Akrivó
understand		In the afternoon	To apóyevma	Hot	Zestó
Excuse me, do	Parakaló, mípos	In the evening	To vrádhi	Cold	Krío
you speak	miláte angliká?	Here	Edhó	With	Mazí
English?		There	Ekí	Without	Khorís
Sorry/excuse	Signómi	This one	Aftó	Quickly	Grígora
me		That one	Ekíno	Slowly	Sigá
Today	Símera	Good	Kaló	Mr/Mrs	Kírios/Kiría
Tomorrow	Ávrio	Bad	Kakó	Miss	Dhespinís

Other Needs

To eat/drink	Trógo/Píno	Stamps	Gramatósima	Toilet	Toualéta
Bakery	Foúrnos, psomádhiko	Petrol station	Venzinádhiko	Police (force)	Astinomía
Pharmacy	Farmakío	Bank	Trápeza	Doctor	Iatrós
Post office	Takhidhromío	Money	Leftá/Khrímata	Hospital	Nosokomío

Requests and Questions

To ask a question, it's simplest to start with *parakaló*, then name the thing you want in an interrogative tone

Where is the bakery?	Parakaló, o foúrnos?	How many?	Pósi?
Can you show me the	Parakaló, o dhrómos	How much?	Póso?
road to . . . ?	ya . . ?	When?	Póte?
We'd like a room for two	Parakaló, éna dhomátio	Why?	Yatí?
	ya dhío átoma?	At what time . . . ?	Ti óra . . . ?
May I have a kilo of	Parakaló, éna kiló	What is/Which is . . . ?	Ti íneh/pió íneh..?
oranges?	portokália?	How much (does it cost)?	Póso káni?
Where?	Pou?	What time does it open?	Tí óra aníyi?
How?	Pos?	What time does it close?	Tí óra klíni?

Talking to People

Greek makes the distinction between the informal (*esí*) and formal (*esís*) second person, as French does with *tu* and *vous*. Young people, older people and country people nearly always use *esí* even with total strangers. In any event, no one will be too bothered if you get it wrong. By far the most common greeting, on meeting and parting, is *yá sou/yá sas* – literally "health to you".

Hello	Khérete	What's your name?	Pos se léne?
Good morning	Kalí méra	My name is . . .	Meh léne . . .
Good evening	Kalí spéra	Speak slower, please	Parakaló, miláte pió sigá
Good night	Kalí níkhta	How do you say it in	Pos léyete sta Eliniká?
Goodbye	Adío	Greek?	
How are you?	Ti kánis/Ti kánete?	I don't know	Dhen kséro
I'm fine	Kalá ímeh	See you soon	Kalí andamosí
(Common toast)	Ekhíva !	Let's go	Páme
Help yourself (to food)	Kopiáste !	Please help me	Parakaló, na me voithíste

Greek's Greek

There are numerous words and phrases which you will hear constantly, even if you rarely have the chance to use them. These are a few of the most common.

Éla	Come (literally) but also Speak to me! You don't say! etc.	*Po-po-po!*	Expression of dismay or concern, like French "O la la!"
Oríste	What can I do for you?	*Pedhí mou*	My boy/girl, sonny, friend, etc.
Embros!	Standard phone response	*Maláka(s)*	Literally "wanker", but not often heard in Cyprus.
Ti néa?	What's new?		
Ti yíneteh?	What's going on (here)?	*Sigá sigá*	Take your time, slow down
Étsi k'étsi	So-so	*Kaló taxídhi*	Bon voyage
Opá!	Whoops! Watch it!		

Accommodation

Hotel	*Ksenodhokhío*	Cold water	*krío neró*
A room . . .	*Éna dhomátio . . .*	Can I see it?	*Boró na to dho?*
for one/two/three people	*ya éna/dhío/tría átoma*	Can we camp here?	*Boróume na váloumeh ti skiní edhó?*
for one/two/three nights	*ya mía/dhío/trís vradhies*		
with a double bed	*meh megálo kreváti*	Campsite	*Kamping/Kataskínosi*
with a shower	*meh doús*	Tent	*Skiní*
hot water	*zestó neró*	Youth hostel	*Ksenodhokhío neótitos*

On the Move

Aeroplane	*Aeropláno*	Where are you going?	*Pou pas?*
Bus	*Leoforío*	I'm going to . . .	*Páo sto . . .*
Car	*Aftokínito, amáxi*	I want to get off at . . .	*Thélo na katévo sto . . .*
Taxi	*Taksí*	The road to . . .	*O dhrómos ya . . .*
Ship	*Plío/Vapóri/Karávi*	Near	*Kondá*
Bicycle	*Podhílato*	Far	*Makriá*
Hitching	*Otostóp*	Left	*Aristerá*
On foot	*Meh ta pódhia*	Right	*Dhexiá*
Trail	*Monopáti*	Straight ahead	*Katefthía*
Bus station	*Praktorío leoforíon*	A ticket to . . .	*Éna isistírio ya . . .*
Bus stop	*Stási*	Beach	*Paralía*
Harbour	*Limáni*	Cave	*Spiliá*
What time does it leave?	*Ti óra févyi?*	Centre (of town)	*Kéndro*
What time does it arrive?	*Ti óra ftháni?*	Church	*Eklisía*
How many kilometres?	*Pósa hiliómetra?*	Sea	*Thálassa*
How many hours?	*Póses óres?*	Village	*Khorió*

Numbers

1	*éna/mía*	12	*dhódheka*	90	*enenínda*
2	*dhío*	13	*dhekatrís*	100	*ekató*
3	*trís/tría*	14	*dhekatéseres*	150	*ekatón penínda*
4	*tésseres/téssera*	20	*íkosi*	200	*dhiakósies/ia*
5	*pénde*	21	*íkosi éna*	500	*pendakósies/ia*
6	*éksi*	30	*triánda*	1000	*khílies/ia*
7	*eftá*	40	*saránda*	2000	*dhío khiliádhes*
8	*okhtó*	50	*penínda*	1,000,000	*éna ekatomírio*
9	*enyá*	60	*eksínda*	first	*próto*
10	*dhéka*	70	*evdhomínda*	second	*dhéftero*
11	*éndheka*	80	*ogdhónda*	third	*tríto*

The time and days of the week

Sunday	*Kiriakí*	Saturday	*Sávato*	Five minutes past seven	*Eftá keh pénde*
Monday	*Dheftéra*	What time is it?	*Ti óra íneh?*	Half past eleven	*Éndheka keh misí*
Tuesday	*Tríti*	One/two/three o'clock	*Mía/dhío/trís óra/óres*	Half-hour	*misí óra*
Wednesday	*Tetárti*	Twenty minutes to four	*Tésseres pará íkosi*	Quarter-hour	*éna tétarto*
Thursday	*Pémpti*				
Friday	*Paraskeví*				

additional problem of an entirely separate **alphabet**. Despite initial appearances, this is in practice fairly easily mastered – a skill that will help enormously if you are going to get around independently (see the alphabet box on p.307). In addition, certain combinations of letters have unexpected results. This book's transliteration system should help you make intelligible noises but you have to remember that the correct **stress** (marked throughout the book with an acute accent) is crucial. With the right sounds but the wrong stress people will either fail to understand you, or else understand something quite different from what you intended.

Greek **grammar** is more complicated still: nouns are divided into three genders, all with different case endings in the singular and in the plural, and all adjectives and articles have to agree with these in gender, number and case. (All adjectives are arbitrarily cited in the neuter form in the lists on p.308.) Verbs are even worse. To begin with at least, the best thing is simply to say what you know the way you know it, and never mind the niceties. "Eat meat hungry" should get a result, however grammatically incorrect. If you worry about your mistakes, you'll never say anything.

IDIOSYNCRACIES OF CYPRIOT GREEK

The "b" sound of standard Greek is largely absent on Cyprus, with a simple "p" replacing it: thus *parpoúni* for the tasty reddish fish, not *barboúni*; *tapélla* for "sign, placard", not *tabélla*. Strong sibilants, lacking to most peninsular Greek-speakers, are also a feature of the dialect: the letter combination sigma-iota (s-i) is universally pronounced, and transliterated, as sh. The letter chi, when medial, is often pronounced the same way – *eshi*, not *ekhi*, for "there is" or "he/she/it/ has"; an initial kappa or "k" will sound like the "tsch" of Crete. Especially in Páfos district, Turkisms in the

vocabulary abound: examples include *chaki* instead of the standard *souyiás* for "pocket-knife", *chatália* (literally, "forks") for "pantaloons".

TURKISH

It's worth learning as much Turkish as you can while you're in North Cyprus; if you travel far from the tourist centres you may well need it, and Cypriots will always appreciate foreigners who show enough interest and courtesy to learn at least basic greetings. The main advantages of the language from the learner's point of view are that it's phonetically spelt, and grammatically regular. The disadvantages are that the vocabulary is completely unrelated to any language you're likely to have encountered at a European school, and the grammar, relying heavily on suffixes, gets more alien the further you delve into it. Concepts like vowel harmony, beyond the scope of this brief primer, further complicate matters. Trying to grasp at least the basics, though, is well worth the effort.

TURKISH PRONUNCIATION

Pronunciation in Turkish is worth mastering, since once you've got it the phonetic spelling and regularity helps you progress fast. The following letters differ significantly from English pronunciation.

Aa	short a similar to that in far.
Ââ	softly aspirated a, can sound as if preceded by a faint y or h.
Ee	as in bet.
İi	as in pit.
Iı	unstressed vowel similar to the a in probable.
Oo	as in mole.
Öö	like ur in burn.
Uu	as in blue.

Üü like ew in few.
Cc like j in jelly.
Çç like ch in chat.
Gg hard g as in get.
Uu generally silent, but lengthens the preceding vowel and between two vowels can be a y sound.
Hh as in hen, never silent.
Jj like the s in pleasure.
Ss as in six.
Mm like sh in shape.
Vv soft, between a v and a w.

DICTIONARIES AND PHRASE BOOKS

For a straightforward **phrasebook**, *Harrap's Turkish Phrasebook* (£1.95) is as good as any. If you want to **learn** more, Geoffrey L. Lewis's *Teach Yourself Turkish* (Hodder; £3.99) still probably has a slight edge over Yusuf Mardin's *Colloquial Turkish* (Routledge; £7.99); or buy both, since they complement each other well. Alternatively, there's Geoffrey Lewis's *Turkish Grammar* (OUP; £20), a one-volume solution.

Among widely available Turkish **dictionaries**, the best are probably those produced by Langenscheidt (Universal, £1.95; Pocket, £8.95) miniature or coat-pocket sizes, or the *Concise Oxford Turkish Dictionary* (£25), a hardback suitable for serious students. The Redhouse dictionaries produced in Turkey are the best value: the four-and-a-half-inch *Mini Sözlük* has the same number of entries as the seven-and-a-half-inch desk edition and is adequate for most demands; the definitive, two-tome version even gives Ottoman Turkish script and etymologies for each word, but it costs the earth and isn't exactly portable.

IDIOSYNCRACIES OF CYPRIOT TURKISH

Pafiot Turkish in particular, as long as it lasts as a separate sub-dialect, shows the effects of long cohabitation with Cypriot Greek. There is no indicative tense as in standard Turkish, the indefinite mood being used on most occasions; nor are there interrogative particles as in Turkey, a question being indicated by voice inflection as in Greek.

Moreover, refugees from *Páfos* (*Baf* in Turkish, incidentally) frequently use *etmek*, normally only an auxiliary verb in Anatolian Turkish, in place of *yapmak* for "to do, to make". Slurred pronoun constructions are common and confusing: *ba* for *bana* (to/for me), *sa* for *sana* (to/for you), *gen* for *kendin'e* (to/for oneself). *Na'pan*, the standard colloquial greeting, is an elision of *Ne yaparsın* (approximately, "Whaddya up to?" or "Whatcha doin'?")

That translation gives a fairly accurate idea of the casualness of Cypriot linguistic mores; the islanders derive some amusement from the painfully polite diction of İstanbul people, who in turn consider the island dialect just plain slovenly. However, Turkish television plus nearly two decades of army occupation and refugee status are steadily eroding these peculiarities, which will probably disappear over the next generation.

TURKISH WORDS AND PHRASES

Basics

Mr; follows first name	*Bey*	Good afternoon	*İyi Günler*
Miss; precedes first name	*Bayan*	Good evening	*İyi Akşamlar*
Mrs (literally lady) polite	*Hanım*	Good night	*İyi Geceler*
Ottoman title; follows first name		Hello	*Merhaba*
		Goodbye	*Allahaısmarladık*
Half-humorous honorific title bestowed on any tradesman; means "master craftsman"	*Usta*	Yes	*Evet*
		No	*Hayır*
		No (there isn't any)	*Yok*
		Please	*Lütfen*
Honorific of someone who has made the pilgrimage to Mecca	*Haci*	Thank you	*Teşekkür ederim/Mersi/ Sağol*
Good morning	*Günaydın*	You're welcome, that's OK	*Bir şey değil*

Basics (continued)

How are you?	*Nasılsınız? Nasılsın? Ne haber?*	Yesterday	*Dün*
		Now	*Şimdi*
I'm fine (thank you)	*(Sağol) İyiyim/İyilik Sağlık*	Later	*Sonra*
Do you speak English?	*İngilizce biliyormusunuz?*	Wait a minute!	*Bir dakika!*
		In the morning	*Sabahleyin*
I don't understand	*Anlamadım/Anlamıyorum*	In the afternoon	*Oğleden sonra*
I don't know	*Bilmiyorum*	In the evening	*Akşamleyin*
I beg your pardon, sorry	*Affedersiniz*	Here/there/over there	*Burda/Şurda/Orda*
		Good/bad	*İyi/Kötü, Fena*
Excuse me (in a crowd)	*Pardon*	Big/small	*Büyük/Küçük*
		Cheap/expensive	*Ucuz/Pahalı*
I'm sightseeing	*Geziyorum/Dolaşiyorum*	Early/late	*Erken/Geç*
I'm English/Scottish/ Irish/Australian	*İngilizim/İskoçyalım/ İrlandalıyım/Avustralyalım*	Hot/cold	*Sıcak/Soğuk*
		Near/far	*Yakın/Uzak*
I live in . . .	*. . .'de/da oturuyorum*	Vacant/occupied	*Boş/Dolu*
Today	*Bugün*	Quickly/slowly	*Hızlı/Yavaş*
Tomorrow	*Yarın*	With/without (milk) . . . (meat)	*(Sut)lu/(Sut)suz (Et)li/(Et)siz*
The day after tomorrow	*Öbür gün/Ertesi gün*	Enough	*Yeter*

Driving

Left	*Sol*	No entry	*Araç giremez*
Right	*Sağ*	No through road	*Çıkmaz sokak*
Straight ahead	*Doğru*	Slow down	*Yavaşla*
Turn left/right	*Sola dön/Sağa dön*	Road closed	*Yol kapalı*
Parking	*Park yapilir*	Crossroads	*Dörtyol*
No parking	*Park yapilmaz*	Pedestrian crossing	*Yaya geçidi*
One-way street	*Tek yön*		

Some Signs

Entrance/exit	*Giriş/Çıkış*	Beware	*Dikkat*
Free/paid entrance	*Giriş ücretsiz/Ücretlidir*	First aid	*İlk yardım*
Gentlemen	*Baylar*	No smoking	*Sigara İçilmez*
Ladies	*Bayanlar*	Don't tread on the grass	*Çimenlere basmayınız*
WC	*WC/Tuvalet/Umumî*		
Open/closed	*Açık/Kapalı*	Stop/halt	*Dur*
Arrivals/departures	*Varış/Kalkış*	Military Area	*Askeri bölge*
Pull/push	*Çekiniz/İtiniz*	Entry forbidden	*Girmek Yasaktir*
Out of order	*Arızalı*	Please take off your shoes	*Lütfen ayakkabılarınızı çıkartınız*
Drinking water	*İçilebilir su*		
To let/for hire	*Kiralık*	No entry on foot	*Yaya giremez*
Foreign exchange	*Kambiyo*		

Questions and Directions

Where is the . . . ?	*. . . Nerede?*	How far is it to . . . ?	*. . .'a/e ne kadar uzakta?*
When?	*Ne zaman?*	Can you give me a lift to . . . ?	*Beni . . . 'a/e götürebilirmisiniz?*
What (what is it?)	*Ne (ne dir?)*		
How much (does it cost?)	*Ne kadar/Kaça?*	What time does it open?	*Kaçta açılıcak?*
How many?	*Kaç tane?*		
Why?	*Niye?*	What time does it close?	*Kaçta kapanacak?*
What time is it?	*(polite) Saatınız var mı? (informal) Saat kaç?*	What's it called in	*Türkcesi ne dir? Turkçe nasıl söylersiniz?*
	. . .'a/e nasıl giderim?		

Accommodation

Hotel	*Hotel/Otel*	For one/two weeks	*Bir/İki haftalık*
Pension, Boarding house	*Pansiyon*	With an extra bed	*İlave yataklı*
Campsite	*Kamping*	With a double bed	*Çift kişilik yataklı*
Hostel	*Yurt*	With a shower	*Duşlu*
Tent	*Çadır*	Hot water	*Sicak su*
Is there a hotel nearby?	*Yakinda otel var mı?*	Cold water	*Soğuk su*
Do you have a room?	*Boş odanız var mı?*	Can I see it?	*Bakabilirmiyim?*
Single/double/triple	*Tek/Çift/Üç kişilik*	I have a booking.	*Reservasyonım var.*
Do you have a double room for one/two/three nights?	*Bir/İki/Üç gecelik çift yataklı odanız var mı?*	Can we camp here?	*Burda kamp edebilirmiyiz?*

Travelling

Aeroplane	*Uçak*	What time does it leave?	*Bir sonraki otobus/ vapur kaçta kalkıyor?*
Bus	*Otobus*	When is the next bus/ ferry?	*Nereden kalkıyor?*
Car	*Araba*		
Taxi	*Taksi*		
Bicycle	*Bisiklet*	Where does it leave from?	*Kaç mildir?*
Ferry	*Vapur/Feribot*		
Hitch-hiking	*Otostop*	How many miles is it?	*Ne kadar sürerbilir?*
On foot	*Yaya*	How long does it take?	*Hangi otobus . . . 'a*
Bus station	*Otogar*	Which bus goes to . . . ?	*gider?*
Ferry terminal/jetty	*İskele*	Which road leads to . . . ?	*A hangi yol . . . 'a çıkar?*
Harbour	*Liman*		
A ticket to . . .	*. . . 'a bir bilet Kaçta kalkıyor?*	Can I get out at a convenient place?	*Müsait bir yerde inebilirmiyim?*

Days of the week, Months and Seasons

Sunday	*Pazar*	January	*Ocak*	September	*Eylül*
Monday	*Pazartesi*	February	*Subat*	October	*Ekim*
Tuesday	*Salı*	March	*Mart*	November	*Kasım*
Wednesday	*Çarşamba*	April	*Nisan*	December	*Aralık*
Thursday	*Perşembe*	May	*Mais*	Spring	*İlkbahar*
Friday	*Cuma*	June	*Haziran*	Summer	*Yaz*
Saturday	*Cumartesi*	July	*Temmuz*	Autumn	*Sonbahar*
		August	*Ağustos*	Winter	*Kış*

Time Conventions

(At) 3 o'clock	*Saat üç(ta)*	It's 8.10	*Sekizi on geçiyor*
2 hours (duration)	*İki saat*	It's 10.45	*On bire çeyrek var*
Half hour (duration)	*Yarım saat*	At 8.10	*Sekizi on geçe*
Five-thirty	*Beş büçük*	At 10.45	*On bire çeyrek kala*

Numbers

1	*Bir*	7	*Yedi*	13	*On üç*	70	*Yetmiş*	200	*Yedi yüz*
2	*İki*	8	*Sekiz*	20	*Yirmi*	80	*Seksen*	700	*Bin*
3	*Üç*	9	*Dokuz*	30	*Otuz*	90	*Doksan*	1000	*Dokuz bin*
4	*Dört*	10	*On*	40	*Kırk*	100	*Yüz*	9000	*Bir*
5	*Beş*	11	*On bir*	50	*Elli*		*Yüz kırk*	1,000,000	*milyon*
6	*Altı*	12	*On iki*	60	*Altmış*	140	*İki yüz*		

Compounded numbers tend to be run together in spelling: 50,784 *Ellibinyediyüzseksendört*

GLOSSARY

For glossaries of acronyms of political parties, see p.276 and p.279.

ARCHAEOLOGICAL, ARTISTIC AND ARCHITECTURAL TERMS

ACROPOLIS Ancient, fortified hilltop.

AGORA Market and meeting place of an ancient Greek city.

AMPHORA Tall, narrow-necked jar for oil or wine.

APSE Polygonal or curved recess at the altar end of a church.

ARCHAIC PERIOD An era (750–475 BC) when Cypriot artistic expressiveness was most developed in its own right, though heavily influenced by the Middle East.

ASHLAR Dressed, squared masonry in an ancient structure, either free-standing or facing a rubble wall.

ATRIUM Open, inner courtyard of a house.

BASILICA Colonnaded, "hall-" or "barn-"type church, common in Cyprus

BETYL Bullet-shaped stone, sacred object of the Aphrodite cult and anointed like a Hindu Shiva *lingam*.

BRONZE AGE Spans a long period from Early (2500–1900 BC) to Late (1650–1050 BC), with the latter eras showing marked cultural influence of the Mycenaean migration from the Greek Peloponnese.

BYZANTINE EMPIRE Created by the division of the Roman Empire in 395 AD, this, the eastern half, was ruled from Constantinople (modern Istanbul). Byzantine rule ended in 1191 on Cyprus.

CAPITAL The top, often ornamented, of a column.

CHALKOLITHIC PERIOD Cultures (3900–2500 BC) distinguished by advanced ceramic and worked-stone artefacts, and by the first smelting of copper – from which Cyprus probably takes its name.

CLASSICAL ERA In Cyprus, from the start of the fifth century BC to the rule of the Macedonian kings late in the next century; a period of destruction at the hands of the Persians, and thus poor in home-grown artefacts.

CONCH Curved wall surface at the top of an apse.

DHROMOS Ramp leading to the subterranean entrance of a Mycenaean tomb.

FORUM Market and meeting place of a Roman-era city.

FRIGIDARIUM Cold plunge-pool room of a Roman or Byzantine bath.

GEOMETRIC Archaeological epoch (1050–750 BC) so named for the abstract designs of its pottery.

GROIN VAULTING Series of projecting curved stone ribs marking the junction of ceiling vaults; common feature of Lusignan monastic and military architecture.

HELLENISTIC ERA Extending from 325 to 50 BC, this meant for Cyprus rule by the Ptolemaic kings, based in Alexandria.

HYPOCAUST Hollow space, with round-brick struts, for hot-air circulation below the floor of an ancient bath.

ICONOCLASM Eight- and ninth-century Byzantine movement whereby the veneration of icons was forbidden as idolatrous; during this time many figurative frescos were destroyed as well.

IERÓN Literally, "sacred" – the space between the altar screen and the apse of a church, reserved for the priest.

KATHOLIKÓN Central chapel of a monastery.

KRATIR Large, usually two-handled ancient wine goblet.

LUSIGNAN DYNASTY Mostly French, Catholic nobility which ruled Cyprus from 1191 until 1489, a time typified by monumental Gothic architecture, the introduction of feudalism and the suppression of the Orthodox Church.

MACHICOLATIONS Openings at the edge of a castle's parapet or above its doorway, usually between corbels, for dumping noxious substances on invaders.

MITRÓPOLIS Cathedral of a large town.

NAOS The inner sanctum of an ancient temple; also, any Orthodox Christian shrine.

NARTHEX Vestibule or entrance hall of a church; also *exonarthex*, the outer vestibule when there is more than one.

NAVE Principal lengthwise aisle of a church.

NECROPOLIS Concentration of above-ground tombs, always outside the walls of an ancient city.

NEOLITHIC PERIOD Earliest era of settlement on Cyprus, divided into Neolithic I (7000–6000 BC, as at Khirokitía, and Neolithic II (4500–3800 BC).

PANDOKRÁTOR Literally "The Almighty", but generally refers to the stern portrayal of Christ in Majesty frescoed or in mosaic in the dome of many Byzantine churches.

PEDIMENT Triangular wall space between roof and wall of a chapel.

RHYTON Vessel, often horn-shaped, for libations or offerings.

STOA Colonnaded walkway in ancient marketplaces.

STELE Upright stone slab or column, usually inscribed; an ancient tombstone.

SYNTHRONON Semi-circular seating for clergy, usually in the apse of a Byzantine church.

TÉMBLON Wooden altar screen of an Orthodox church, usually ornately carved and painted and studded with icons.

TEMENOS Sacred precinct, often used to refer to the sanctuary itself.

TEPIDARIUM Warm anteroom of an ancient or Byzantine bath.

TESSERAE Cubes used to compose a mosaic, either naturally coloured rock or painted or gilded glass.

THOLOS Conical or beehive-shaped building, especially a Mycenaean tomb.

TRANSEPT The "arms" of a church, perpendicular to the nave.

TYMPANUM In Orthodox use, the semicircular space over a church side door reserved for dedicatory inscriptions, dates, frescos, etc.

XENON Hostel for pilgrims at an ancient shrine; the tradition continues at modern Cypriot Orthodox monasteries, though such inns are more accurately rendered *ksenónas* in modern Greek.

YINAIKONíTIS Women's gallery in an Orthodox church, almost always upstairs at the rear.

COMMON GREEK-CYPRIOT TERMS

ÁYIOS/AYÍA/ÁYII Saint or holy (m/f/pl). Common place name prefix (abbreviated Ag. or Ay.), often spelt AGIOS or AGHIOS.

ÁNO Upper; as in upper town or village.

EXOHIKÓ KÉNDRO Rural taverna, often functioning only at summer weekends.

KAFENÍO Coffee house or café; in a small village the centre of communal life and probably serving as the bus stop, too.

KÁTO Lower; as in lower town or village.

LOUKOÚMI Turkish delight – a sweet made primarily from powdered sugar, rosewater or citrus extract, and gelatin.

MESAORÍA The broad plain between the Troódhos and Kyrenia mountains; site of Nicosia.

MONÍ Monastery or convent.

MÚKHTAR Village headman.

NÉOS, NÉA, NÉO "New" – a common part of a town or village name.

PALEÓS, PALEÁ, PALEÓ "Old" – again common in town and village names.

PANAYÍA Virgin Mary.

PANIYÍRI Festival or feast – the local celebration of a holy day.

PLATÍA Square, plaza. KENTRIKÍ PLATÍA, central square.

COMMON TURKISH-CYPRIOT TERMS

AĞA A minor rank of nobility in the Ottoman Empire, and still a term of respect applied to a local worthy – follows the name (eg Ismail Ağa).

BAHÇE(Sİ) Garden.

BEDESTEN Covered market hall for textiles, often lockable.

BEKÇİ Caretaker at an archaeological site or monument.

BEY Another minor Ottoman title, like *Ağa*, still in use.

CAMİ(İ) Mosque.

ÇARŞI(SI) Bazaar, market.

DAĞI, DAĞLARI "Mount", and "mountains", respectively.

DOLMUŞ Literally "filled" – the shared taxi system operating in larger North Cyprus towns; some confusing overlap with "minibus", since not all of the latter are *dolmuşes*, and vice versa.

ESKİ "Old" – frequent modifier of place names.

EZAN The Muslim call to prayer.

HALK PLAJIPLAJLARI Free-of-charge public beach(es).

HAMAM(I) Turkish sauna-bath.

HASTANE(Sİ) Hospital.

HOCA Teacher in charge of religious instruction for children.

İMAM Usually just the prayer leader at a mosque, though it can mean a more important spiritual authority.

KALE(Sİ) Castle, fort.

KAPI(SI) Gate, door.

KİLİSE(Sİ) Church.

KONAK Large private residence, also the main government building of a province or city; genitive form *konağı*.

KULE(Sİ) Tower, turret.

MABET Temple, common signpost at ancient sites; genitive *mabedi*.

MAHALLE(Sİ) District or neighbourhood of a larger municipality.

MESARYA Turkish for the Mesaoría; officially renamed *İçova*

MEYDAN(I) Public square or plaza.

MEYHANE Tavern serving alcohol and food.

MEZAR(I) Grave, tomb; thus *mezarlık*, cemetery.

MİHRAB Niche in mosque indicating the direction of Mecca, and prayer.

MİMBER Pulpit in a mosque, from where the *imam* delivers homilies.

MİNARE Turkish for "minaret", the tower from which the call to prayer is delivered.

MUEZZIN Man who pronounces call to prayer from the minaret of a mosque; the call is often taped these days.

MUHTAR Village headman; *muhtarlık* is the office, both in the abstract and concrete sense.

NAMAZ The Muslim rite of prayer, performed five times daily.

PAŞA Ottoman honorific, approximately equivalent to "Lord"; follows the name.

SUFI Dervish – more properly an adherent of one of the heterodox mystical branches of Islam.

TABYA Bastion (on walls of north Nicosia or Famagusta).

TAPINAK Alternative term for "temple" at archaeological sites; genitive *tapınağı*.

TARIKAT Any one of the various Sufi orders.

TEKKE Gathering place of a Sufi order.

VAKIF Islamic religious trust, responsible for social welfare and religious buildings; holds extensive property, often donated by believers, in North Cyprus.

VIZIER The principal Ottoman minister of state, responsible for the day-to-day running of the empire.

YENİ "New" – common component of Turkish Cypriot place names.

INDEX

"Acapulco" beach 221
Accommodation 19
Aféndrika 255
Afxentiou, Grigorios 151
Agrós 148
Akámas Firing Range 116
Akámas peninsula 109–111, 114–118
Akapnoú 76
Akdeniz 216
AKEL 270, 280–281
Akhiropiítos monastery 212
Akrotíri (village) 81
Akrotíri peninsula 79–81
Aktí Kivernítou, see Governor's Beach
Alagadi beach 221
Alevkaya 225
Alsancak 212–213
Amathoúnda, see Amathus
Amathus 78–79
Ammokhostós, see Famagusta
Angelóktisti church 55
Antifonítis monastery 226
Aphrodite cult 104
Apóstolos Andhréas monastery 255
Apóstolos Varnávas monas-tery-museum 246–247
Arakapás 75
Arapköy 224
Archaeological Sites 32
Archbishop Makarios III 120–121, 273–280
Arkhángelos church, Galáta 142
Arkhángelos church, Pedhoulás 135
Aródhes, Páno/Káto 110
Asínou church 144
Attila Line, The 176, 278
Avgás gorge 108
Ayía Ekateríni church 110
Ayía Iríni, see Akdeniz
Ayía Mávra chapel 77
Ayía Moní monastery 122
Ayía Nápa 60–63
Ayía Nápa monastery 61

Ayía Paraskeví church 103
Ayía Triás basilica 253
Ayíou Nikoláou ton Gáton convent 80
Áyii Anáryiri Milioú 111
Áyios Ioánnis Lambadhistís monastery 138–139
Áyios Neófitos monastery 106–107
Áyios Nikólaos tis Steyís church 141–142
Áyios Yióryios 107
Áyios Amvrósios, see Esentepe
Áyios Epíktitos, see Çatalköy
Áyios Fílon basilicas 253
Áyios Fótios church 253
Áyios Mámas chapel, Louvarás 149
Áyios Sozómenos church143
Áyios Thýrsos 253
Áyios Yióryios (North), see Karaoğlanoğlu

Banks 14
Bargaining 36
Baths of Aphrodite, see Loutrá Afrodhítis
Béllapais abbey 218–219
Béllapais village, see Beylerbeyi
Beşinci Mil beach 210
Beşparmak summit 225
Beylerbeyi 218–220
Boğaz 249
Bogázi, see Boğaz
Boltaşlı 252
Books 303
British Sovereign Bases 61, 80–81
Buffavento castle 224–225
Buses 15

Caledonian falls 130
Çamlıbel 216
Cape Apostólou Andhréa, see Zafer Burnu
Cape Eléa, see Zeytin Burnu
Cape Gréko 64
Cape Lára 108
Car Hire 17
Çatalköy 220
Caterina Cornaro 237, 267
Cedar Valley, The 122

Cenotaph of Nicocreon 248
"Chapelle Royale", see Pýrga
Churches 32–33
Cinema 30
Clerides, Glafkos 276, 280–281
"Coral Bay" 107
Costs 13
Curium, see Kourion

Denktaş, Rauf 190–191, 281–283
Dháli 178
Dhavlós, see Kaplıca
Dherínia 63
Dhroúsha 110
DIKO 276, 280
Dipkarpaz 253
Dipkarpaz beaches 253, 255
DISY 276, 280
DMP 279, 282
Drinking 23, 26
Driving 16
Durrell, Lawrence 166, 218–221

Émba 105
Éngomi, see Enkomi-Alasia
Eating 21
EDEK 276, 279–281
Edremit 211
Electric Current 37
Enkomi-Alasia 248
EOKA 166-168, 271–272
EOKA-B 167, 277
Episkopí 86
Eptagónia 76
Esentepe 226
Evagoras of Salamis 241, 263
Evdhímou 87

FAMAGUSTA 230–241
  Accommodation 232–233
  Arrival 232
  Canbulat Bastion museum 233
  City walls 233, 236
  Eating and drinking 240
  Lala Mustafa Paşa Camii 237
  Listings 240
  Maraş 240
  Namik Kemal Meydanı 236
  Othello's Tower 238
  Saints Peter and Paul, church 236
Famagusta, Siege of 236–237
Farmakás 150

Ferries 4
Festivals 30
Fikárdhou 150
Fíni 134
Fíti 118
Flória beach 103
Fontána Amorósa 118
Four Mile Crossing 61, 81

Galáta 142
Galinóporni, see Kaleburnu
Gay Life 37
Gazimağusa, see Famagusta
Gemikonağı 199
Getting Around 15–18
Getting There from Britain 1–2
*Getting There from North
  America* 7–8
Girne, see Kyrenia
Glossary 314–316
Governor's Beach 79
Greeks of the Kárpas 254
Green Line, The 156, 171
Grivas, George "Dhiyenis"
  166–167, 271
Güzelyalı 214–215
Güzelyurt 198–199

Hadjiyorgakis Kornesios 165,
  268
Hala Sultan Tekke 54
Halévga, see Alevkaya
Handicrafts 57–58,
Harassment 34
Hazreti Ömer tomb 220
Health 9
*Hiking in the Akámas
  peninsula* 108, 116–118
Hiking in the Troödhos range
  123, 129–133, 147
Holidays 30–32

İnia 110
İskele 249
Icons 119, 139, 151
Iconoclast movement 61, 134
Idalion 178
Independence 273
Information 11
Insurance 10

Kakopetriá 140–141
Kaleburnu 252
Kalokhorió 149
Kalopanayiótis 138

Kambí 150
Kámbos 140
Kanakariá mosaics theft 168,
  252
Kantara castle 250–251
Kantára village 250
Kaplıca 251
Karákoumi, see Karakum
Karakum 220
Karaman 211
Karaoğlanoğlu 210
Karavás, see Alsancak
Karavostási, see Gemikonağı
Kármi, see Karaman
Kárpas peninsula 249–256
Karpásha, see Karpaşa village
Karpasia 254
Karşıyaka 214
Káthikas 110
Káto Léfkara 58
Káto Páfos 94–99
Káto Pýrgos 113
Kayalar 215
Kazáfani, see Ozanköy
Kelláki 75
Khionóstra peak, see Mount
  Olympus
Khirokitía 56
Khrysfíyeto tou Afxentíou 151
Khrysorroyiátissa monastery
  119
Kıbrıslı Şeyh Nazım, 200
Kırpaşa peninsula 249–256
Kırpaşa village 217
Kiláni 76
King James II 267
King Janus 59–60, 267
King Peter I 267
Kíti, see Angelóktisti church
Klepíni, see Arapköy
Klonári 76
*Knights Hospitaller of Saint
  John* 82, 266
Knights Templar 239, 266
Kofínou 58
Kókkina, enclave and incident
  113, 253
Kokkinokhoriá, The 63
Kolossi, castle and village 82
Kóma tou Yialoú, see Kumyalı
Kormakíti peninsula 215–
  217
Kormakíti village, see Koruçam

Kórnos 58
Koruçam 215–216
Koruçam Burnu, see Kormakíti
  peninsula
Koúklia (South) 103
Kourdhalí 147
Kourion 82–87
Kozan 217
Krítou Térra 110
Ktíma 99–101
Küçük, Dr Fazil 272– 274, 275
Kumyalı 251
Kýkko monastery 139–140
Kyperoúnda 147
KYRENIA 204–210

La Cavocle manor 104
Lady's Mile Beach 79
Lagoudherá 145
Lala Mustafa Paşa 236–237,
  268
Lambousa Treasure 170, 213
Language 306
Laona Project, The 109, 300
Lápithos, see Lapta
Lapta 214
Lara beach (North) 221
LARNACA 46–53
  Ancient Kition 51
  Arrival 47
  Áyios Lázaros 49
  Bazaar 50
  District Museum 51
  Eating and drinking 52
  Listings 53
  Nightlife 52
  Orientation 47
  Pierides Museum 50
  Staying 47
  Turkish quarter 49
Lárnaka tis Lapíthou, see
  Kozan
Látchi 113–114
Lazaniá 151
Léfka, see Lefke
Lefke 199–200
Lefkosía, see Nicosia, South
Lemesós, see Limassol
LIMASSOL 68–75
  Archaeological Museum 73
  Arrival 69
  Bazaar 72
  Castle 72
  Eating and drinking 74
  Folk Art Museum 73
  Listings 74

Nightlife 74
Orientation 69
Staying 69
Wineries 72
Limassol foothills, The 75
Liverás, see Sadrazamköy
Loutrá Afrodhiítis 116
Louvarás 149
Lusignans 266-267
Lythrangomí, see Boltaşlı

Máa, see "Coral Bay"
Madhári ridge 147
Magazines 29
Makherás monastery 151
Makriá Kondárka 133
Maps 12
Marathássa 135–140
Maróni 56
Maronites 216–217
Melíni 76
Mesaoría, The (South) 153, 175
Mesarya, The (North) 203, 229
Mesopótamos monastery 129
Metamórfosi tou Sotírou church 149
Mevlevi Sufi order 192
Money 14
Mórfou, see Güzelyurt
Mosques 33
Mount Adhélfi, see Madhári ridge
Mount Olympus 130–133
Moutoullás, see Panayía Moutoullá
Museums 32
Mýrtou, see Çamlıbel
Mycenaeans 260–261

Nadir, Asil 212–213
Neokhorío 114
Newspapers 29
Nicocreon of Salamis 241, 264
NICOSIA, NORTH 185–197
Arabahmet district 195
Arrival 186
Atatürk Meydanı 191
Bazaars 193
Bedesten 193
Derviş Paşa Konağı 195
Eating 196
Ethnography Museum 190
Mevlevî Tekke 190
Listings 197
Orientation 187

Ottoman baths and inns 192
Ramparts 187
Selimiye Camii 193–194
Sleeping 196
NICOSIA, SOUTH 153–174
Archbishop Makarios Cultural Centre 167
Archepiscopal palace area 165
Arrival 157
Commercial centre 163
Cyprus Museum 169
Eating and drinking 172
Entertainment 173
Famagusta gate 163, 173
Folk Art Museum 167
Hadjiyorgakis Kornesios mansion 165
Kaïmakli suburb 170
Khyrsaliniótissa district 168
Laïkí Yitoniá 164
Ledra Palace checkpoint 171
Leventis City Museum 164
Listings 173
National Struggle Museum 168
Nightlife 173
Ömeriye mosque 165
Orientation 158
Platía Faneroménis 163
Staying 158
Tahtakale district 168
Venetian walls 162
Nissí beach 62
North Cyprus Herbarium 225
Northern beaches 221

Odhoú 76
Ómodhos 77
Onüçüncü Mil beach 222
Órga, see Kayalar
Ottomans 268
Özker Özgür 191, 281

PÁFOS 92–102
Arrival 93
Ayía Kiriakí 97
Ayía Solomóni 98
Bazaar 99
Castle 94
Eating and drinking 101
Harbour 94
Listings 101
Museums 99
Orientation 93
Roman mosaics 94–97
Saranda Kolones 97
Staying 93
Tombs of the Kings 98
Package holidays 3

Pakhíamos 112
Palea Paphos 103–105
Palekhóri 149
Palma di Cesnola, Luigi 50, 83, 178
Panayía 119
Panayía Eleoússa church 253
Panayía Forviótissa, see Asínou church
Panayía Kanakariá church 252
Panayía Khryseléousa church 105
Panayía Moutoullá church 137
Panayía Pergamiótissa church 251
Panayía Podíthou church 143
Panayía Theotókou church, Galáta 143
Panayía tou Araká church 145–146
Páno Léfkara 57
Paphos, see Páfos
Paralímni 63
Pedhoulás 135–137
Peléndhria 148
Pendadháktylos, see Beşparmak
Perakhorió 178
Peristeróna 175
Perivólia 55
Pernéra 64
Pétra tou Romíou 87
Péyia 109
Phones 27
Pissoúri 87
Pitsiliá 145–151
Platanistása 146
Plátres 128–129
Police 34
Pólis 111–112
Pómos 112
Post 27
Potamós Liopetríou 60
Potamós tou Kámbou, see Yedidalga
Pródhromos 134
Pýrga 59

Radio 29
Red tape 9
Richard the Lionheart 68, 266

Rimbaud, Arthur 60, 130
Rizokárpaso, see Dipkarpaz
Royal Tombs 244–245

Sadrazamköy 215
Saint Barnabas 247
Saint Hilarion castle 222–224
Saint Lazarus 46, 49
Saint Mamas 149, 198–199
Salamis 241–244
Sampson, Nikos 274, 277
Sanctuary of Apollo Hylates 86–87
Seferis, George 80, 128
Shopping 35
Sipahi 253
Soléa 140–144
Soli 200–201
Sourp Magar monstery 225
Sports 35
Spyros Kyprianou 277, 280
Stavrós church 148
Stavrós tis Psókhas 123

Stavrós tou Ayiasmáti church 146–147
Stavrovoúni monastery 58

Tamassos 175
Taxis 16
Térra 110
Thróni hill 140
Tillyría 122–123
TMT 272–276, 279
Tríkomo, see İskele
Trimíthi, see Edremit
Troödhítissa monastery 134
Troödhos resort 130
Turkish-Cypriot enclaves 99, 275–277
"Turtle Bay" 222
Tuzla, see Cenotaph of Nicocreon
TV 29

UBP 279, 281–282
Umm Haram, see Hala Sultan Tekke

UN-sponsored negotiations 280, 282–283
UNFICYP 176–177, 275

Varósha ghost town 63, 239
Vasília, see Karşıyaka
Vassiliou, George 281
Vavilás, see Güzelyalı
Venetians 268
Víkla 76
Visas 9
Vouní 76
Vouni 201–202

Wish-trees 98, 140
Working 38

Yedidalga 199
Yenierenköy 253
Yeroskípos, see Yeroskípou
Yeroskípou 103
Yialoúsa, see Yenierenköy

Zafer Burnu 256
Zeytin Burnu beaches 251
Zíyi 56

■ HELP US UPDATE

We've gone to a lot of effort to ensure that this first edition of *Cyprus: The Rough Guide* is up-to-date and accurate. However, things do change – opening hours are notoriously fickle, new restaurants and hotels open all the time, and the situation in Cyprus could change suddenly permitting free travel between North and South – so any suggestions, comments or corrections would be much appreciated.

We'll credit all contributions, and send a copy of the next edition (or any other Rough Guide if you prefer) for the best letters. Please write to:

Marc Dubin, The Rough Guides, 1 Mercer Street, London WC2H 9QJ.

You are
A STUDENT

You travel
THE WORLD

You want
TO SAVE MONEY

Here's
how

The International Student Identity Card

Available at Student Travel Offices Worldwide.

Entitles you to discounts and special services worldwide.

BEFORE YOU TRAVEL THE WORLD, TALK TO AN EXPERIENCED STAMP COLLECTOR.

At STA Travel we're all seasoned travellers so we should know a thing or two about where you're headed. We can offer you the best deals on fares with the flexibility to change your mind as you go – without having to pay over the top for the privilege. We operate from 120 offices worldwide. So call in soon.

74 and 86 Old Brompton Road, SW7, 117 Euston Road, NW1. London.
Manchester. Leeds. Oxford. Cambridge. Bristol.
North America **071-937 9971.** Europe **071-937 9921.** Rest of World **071-937 9962**
(incl. Sundays 10am-2pm). **OR 061-834 0668 (Manchester)**

WHEREVER YOU'RE BOUND, WE'RE BOUND TO HAVE BEEN. STA

  Retail Agents for ATOL Holders

STA TRAVEL